P9-CMK-913

taste of home®
simple & delicious

REIMAN MEDIA GROUP, INC. • GREENDALE, WISCONSIN

A TASTE OF HOME/READER'S DIGEST BOOK

5400 S. 60th St., Greendale WI 53129

Editor in Chief: Catherine Cassidy
Vice President, Executive Editor/Books: Heidi Reuter Lloyd
Creative Director: Ardyth Cope
U.S. Chief Marketing Officer: Lisa Karpinski
Food Director: Diane Werner RD
Senior Editor/Books: Mark Hagen
Editor: Janet Briggs
Project Editor: Julie Schnittka
Art Directors: Edwin Robles, Jr., Gretchen Trautman
Content Production Supervisor: Julie Wagner
Design Layout Artists: Emma Acevedo, Catherine Fletcher
Proofreaders: Linne Bruskewitz, Amy Glander
Recipe Asset System Manager: Coleen Martin
Premedia Supervisor: Scott Berger
Recipe Testing & Editing: Taste of Home Test Kitchen
Food Photography: Taste of Home Photo Studio
Administrative Assistant: Barb Czysz

The Reader's Digest Association, Inc.
President and Chief Executive Officer: Mary G. Berner
President, U.S. Affinities: Suzanne M. Grimes
SVP, Chief Global Marketing Officer: Amy J. Radin
President/Publisher Trade Publishing: Harold Clarke
Associate Publisher: Rosanne McManus
Vice President, Sales and Marketing: Stacey Ashton

For other Taste of Home books and products, visit us at **tasteofhome.com.**

For more Reader's Digest products and information,
visit **rd.com** (in the United States)
or see **rd.ca** (in Canada).

International Standard Book Number (10): 0-89821-773-3
International Standard Book Number (13): 978-0-89821-773-5
Library of Congress Control Number: 2009935816

Pictured on front cover:
Turkey Mostaccioli Bake, p. 176; Glazed Snap Peas, p. 251;
Peanutty Cream-Filled Pastry Shells, p. 313; Ranch Chicken Salad, p. 179.

Pictured on the back cover:
Onion Soup with Sausage, p. 80; Easy Chocolate Clusters, p. 301; Ranch-Style Pork Burgers, p. 51.

Printed in China
1 3 5 7 9 10 8 6 4 2

table of contents

Simply Delicious...and Deliciously Simple!

Years ago, family cooks spent hours in the kitchen baking and cooking from-scratch meals, snacks and desserts. But in this day and age of working full-time, attending meetings and running the kids here and there, who has the time?

Everyone wants to provide wholesome, nutritious meals for their gang, but few have the time to do so. What's a busy cook to do? Turn to *Taste of Home Simple & Delicious*!

This timeless treasury offers **602 recipes** that are geared toward on-the-go families who want hearty foods that fit swamped schedules. Each in-a-dash dish tastes terrific but doesn't require a lot of fuss. With bright-eyed breakfast fare, speedy sandwiches and a host of enticing entrees, you can depend on *Taste of Home Simple & Delicious* around the clock.

602 Recipes for Dawn-to-Dusk Dining

Effortless Morning Eye-Openers

Make the most important meal of the day a memorable one for your family. Forego the cold cereal and serve Overnight Egg Casserole, Light 'n' Crispy Waffles, Simple Sticky Buns and Berry Smoothies.

Mmm...Mid-Day Meals!

Liven up ordinary lunches with a special selection of hearty sandwiches, including Southwest Panini, Baked Deli Sandwich and Crunchy Tuna Wraps. Have a hankering for a hamburger? Skip the fast food and fire up the grill for Ranch-Style Pork Burgers, Bacon-Wrapped Hamburgers or Garden Turkey Burgers.

Over 200 Entree Options

The main course is the part of the meal busy cooks fret about most. That's why *Taste of Home Simple & Delicious* is packed with hundreds of main dish options. Looking for new ideas for chicken and turkey? Check out South-of-the-Border Thighs, Pizza Chicken Roll-Ups, Turkey Tenderloin Supreme and Extra-Crispy Italian Chicken.

Beef up your weekday dinners and take your taste buds on a trip around the world with Asian Beef Noodle Toss, German Pizza, Mexican Beef and Dumplings, Casserole Italiano and, of course, All-American Chili!

If you prefer pork, Southwestern Sausage Skillet, Tender Glazed Pork Chops and Ham-Noodle Bake are for you.

Your family will fall hook, line and sinker for from-the-sea fare such as Oven Fish 'n' Chips, Garlic Lime Shrimp, Speedy Seafood Gumbo, Baked Tilapia and Pecan-Coated Roughy.

Swift Side Dishes and Salads

Round out any dinner with such speedy sides and salads as Glazed Carrot Coins, Vinaigrette Veggie Salad, Seasoned Oven Fries, Nutty Fruit Medley and Parmesan Vegetable Rice.

50 No-Fuss Snacks

The kids come home hungry after school. Unexpected guests drop in. Your gang just needs a little something to tide them over until supper. Reach for a quick snack like Cold Pizza Dip, Spicy Turkey Quesadillas, Apple Grape Drink, Savory Party Bread and Tart 'n' Tangy Citrus Cooler.

In-a-Dash Desserts

Kiddie Crunch Mix...Cookies 'n' Cream Pie...No-Bake Peanut Brownies...Blueberry Pear Crumble...Easy Tiramisu...Banana Upside-Down Cake. Whether you need an item for tomorrow's bake sale or want to surprise your family with a special treat, you'll find more than 100 confections to satisfy every sweet tooth.

Time Is on Your Side

Taste of Home Simple & Delicious keeps the time-crunched cook in mind by featuring recipes that fit the busiest of schedules.

369 Recipes Ready in 30 Minutes or Less!

That's right...more than half of the recipes in this book go from start to finish in under half an hour. (Check out the special time index on page 383. It indicates what recipes can be done in 30, 20 and even 10 minutes!)

Have only half an hour to spare? You can offer your family No-Bake Lasagna, Quick Chicken Cordon Bleu, Fruit-Glazed Pork Chops, Mustard Turkey Cutlets and so much more.

Country Barbecued Chicken...Quick Beef Stew...Sweet and Sour Pork...Shrimp-Stuffed Sole. Think those kinds of down-home dishes are only for when you have time on a weekend? Think again, because each is table-ready in 20 minutes.

Take 10 minutes to turn out Three-Step Stir-Fry, Basil Chicken Strips, Cajun Shrimp or Peppy Parmesan Pasta. It's true!

Slow Cookers Save Time

Hurried cooks can rely on the hands-off convenience of slow cookers to make mouthwatering meals like Hearty Jambalaya, Beef Burgundy, Chicken in Sour Cream Sauce and Cider-Glazed Ham.

The Magic of Microwaves and Grills

Using microwave ovens and grills is a great way to get dinner on the table fast. Rocky Ford Chili, Southwest Chicken and Rice, Herbed London Broil, Almond Sole Fillets and Moist Lemon Chicken may be short on time, but they're full of fantastic flavor!

150 Five-Ingredient Recipes

You don't need a long list of ingredients to create great-tasting dinners. Turn to five everyday items to make Apricot Ham Steak, Beef 'n' Tomato Mac, Chicken Spaghetti, Dilled Turkey Breast, Crumb-Coated Red Snapper, Easy Meat Loaf or Mexicali Pork Chops.

With time-saving techniques and few—yet flavorful—ingredients, *Taste of Home Simple & Delicious* provides busy home cooks with the tools they need to turn out satisfying, from-scratch meals for their families day after day...and year after year!

p. 25

effortless morning eye openers

p. 31
p. 29
p. 19

chocolate-pecan sticky buns

TAMMY LOGAN | CLINTON, TENNESSEE

You won't believe how delicious this easy, four-ingredient recipe is! These rolls have surprise chocolate kisses inside that guests will love.

PREP: 10 MIN. BAKE: 25 MIN.

- **1 can (15 ounces) coconut-pecan frosting**
- **1 cup pecan halves**
- **2 tubes (12 ounces *each*) refrigerated buttermilk biscuits**
- **20 milk chocolate kisses**

- Spread frosting over the bottom of a greased 9-in. square baking pan. Arrange pecans over frosting; set aside.
- Flatten each biscuit to 1/4-in. thickness. Place a chocolate kiss on one side of each biscuit. Fold edges of dough over kiss; pinch edges to seal. Arrange biscuits, flat side down, over pecans.
- Bake at 400° for 25-30 minutes or until golden brown. Cool on a wire rack for 5 minutes. Invert onto a serving plate; serve immediately. **Yield:** 20 servings.

cinnamon chip scones

BARBARA HUMISTON | TAMPA, FLORIDA

These scones will melt in your mouth. They taste terrific whether enjoyed hot, warm or even cold!

PREP: 25 MIN. BAKE: 10 MIN.

- **3-1/4 cups all-purpose flour**
- **1/3 cup plus 2 tablespoons sugar, *divided***
- **2-1/2 teaspoons baking powder**
- **1/2 teaspoon baking soda**
- **1/2 teaspoon salt**
- **3/4 cup cold butter, cubed**
- **1 cup buttermilk**
- **1 package (10 ounces) cinnamon baking chips**
- **2 tablespoons butter, melted**

- In a large bowl, combine the flour, 1/3 cup sugar, baking powder, baking soda and salt. Cut in butter until mixture resembles coarse crumbs. Stir in the buttermilk just until moistened. Fold in chips.
- Turn onto a lightly floured surface; knead gently 10-12 times or until dough is no longer sticky. Divide in half; gently pat or roll each portion into a 7-in. circle. Brush with butter and sprinkle with remaining sugar.
- Cut each circle into six wedges. Separate wedges and place on an ungreased baking sheet. Bake at 425° for 10-13 minutes or until lightly browned. Serve warm. **Yield:** 1 dozen.

Picking Bananas

Look for plump bananas that are evenly yellow-colored. Green bananas are under-ripe, while a flecking of brown flecks indicates ripeness. If bananas are too green, place in a paper bag until ripe.

apple turnovers

COLEEN CAVALLARO | OAK HILL, NEW YORK

I had a package of puff pastry in my freezer and mentioned to a friend that I'd like to make apple turnovers. She shared a recipe that I adapted for the puff pastry. These turnovers were a big hit on my first try!

PREP: 25 MIN. BAKE: 15 MIN.

- 1/3 cup sugar
- 1 tablespoon all-purpose flour
- 1/2 teaspoon ground cinnamon
- 4 cups chopped peeled apples
- 1 package (17.3 ounces) frozen puff pastry, thawed

TOPPING:

- 3 tablespoons butter, melted
- 2 tablespoons sugar
- 1/4 teaspoon ground cinnamon

Vanilla ice cream, optional

- In a large bowl, combine the sugar, flour and cinnamon; add apples and toss to coat. On a lightly floured surface, roll out each pastry sheet into a 12-in. square. Cut each into four squares.
- Spoon 1/2 cup apple mixture into the center of each square; fold diagonally in half and press edges to seal. Place on a parchment paper-lined baking sheet.
- In a small bowl, combine the butter, sugar and cinnamon; brush over pastry. Bake at 400° for 12-16 minutes or until golden brown. Serve warm with ice cream if desired. **Yield:** 8 servings.

honey fruit salad

TASTE OF HOME TEST KITCHEN

A light honey and lime dressing brings out the flavor of canned and fresh fruits. This is a colorful addition to any early-morning meal.

PREP/TOTAL TIME: 10 MIN.

- 1 can (11 ounces) mandarin oranges, drained
- 1 can (8 ounces) pineapple chunks, drained
- 1 cup green grapes
- 1 cup halved fresh strawberries
- 1 medium firm banana, sliced
- 3 tablespoons honey
- 2 teaspoons lime juice
- 1/4 teaspoon grated lime peel
- 1/4 teaspoon vanilla extract
- 1/4 teaspoon poppy seeds

Fresh mint, optional

- In a large bowl, combine fruit. In a small bowl, combine the honey, lime juice, peel and vanilla. Pour over fruit; gently toss to coat. Sprinkle with poppy seeds. Garnish with mint if desired. **Yield:** 4 servings.

cranberry cream cheese muffins

SHARON HARTMAN | TWIN FALLS, IDAHO

The sweet, creamy filling in these cranberry muffins makes them popular at my house. The tender treats also have a crispy sugar topping that is bound to be a hit.

PREP: 15 MIN. BAKE: 20 MIN.

- 1 package (3 ounces) cream cheese, softened
- 4 tablespoons sugar, *divided*
- 1 package (15.6 ounces) cranberry-orange quick bread mix
- 1 cup milk
- 1/3 cup canola oil
- 1 egg

■ In a small bowl, beat cream cheese and 2 tablespoons sugar until smooth; set aside. Place the bread mix in another bowl. Combine the milk, oil and egg; stir into bread mix just until moistened.

■ Fill paper-lined muffin cups one-fourth full with batter. Place 2 teaspoons of the cream cheese mixture in the center of each; top with the remaining batter. Sprinkle with the remaining sugar.

■ Bake at 400° for 18-20 minutes or until a toothpick inserted near the center comes out clean. Cool for 5 minutes before removing from pan to a wire rack. Serve warm. **Yield:** 1 dozen.

Avoid a Brunch Crunch

You don't have to crack under pressure when entertaining early in the day. The secret involves selecting a good assortment of foods and getting a lot done the night before.

When selecting recipes, look for some make-ahead choices (like Overnight Egg Casserole) and last-minute dishes.

If kids are part of the guest list, you may want to offer them the old standby of cereal and milk...they'll likely prefer it to some of your more "fancy" foods.

Get a head start on as many dishes as possible by chopping, slicing and dicing a day ahead.

The night before, measure the coffee. Then prepare it in the morning and transfer it to a thermal carafe for serving. Make and chill juice; put it in a pretty pitcher in the morning.

overnight egg casserole

JENNIFER HOWELL | FORT COLLINS, COLORADO

I love how easy it is to assemble this savory egg casserole. Putting it together the night before really frees up your time the next morning.

PREP: 10 MIN. + CHILLING
BAKE: 1 HOUR + STANDING

- 4 cups frozen shredded hash brown potatoes, thawed
- 1 cup cubed fully cooked ham
- 1 can (4 ounces) chopped green chilies
- 1/2 cup shredded Monterey Jack cheese
- 1/2 cup shredded cheddar cheese
- 6 eggs
- 1 can (12 ounces) evaporated milk
- 1/4 teaspoon pepper
- Salsa, optional

■ In a greased 8-in. square baking dish, layer the hash browns, ham, chilies and cheeses. In a large bowl, whisk the eggs, milk and pepper; pour over the casserole. Cover and refrigerate overnight.

■ Remove from the refrigerator 30 minutes before baking. Bake, uncovered, at 350° for 1 hour or until a knife inserted near the center comes out clean. Let stand for 5-10 minutes. Serve with salsa if desired. **Yield:** 9 servings.

overnight pecan french toast

LARRY LAATSCH | SAGINAW, MICHIGAN

Whenever our family gathers for Christmas brunch, this convenient, make-ahead dish is one crowd-pleaser I can count on. It's a mouthwatering cross between French toast and sticky pecan rolls—and really something to celebrate!

PREP: 15 MIN. + CHILLING BAKE: 30 MIN.

- 8 eggs, lightly beaten
- 1-1/2 cups half-and-half cream
- 2 tablespoons vanilla extract
- 8 to 10 slices French bread (3/4 inch thick)
- 1 cup packed brown sugar
- 1/2 cup butter, melted
- 1/2 cup maple syrup
- 1/2 cup chopped pecans

■ In an ungreased 13-in. x 9-in. baking dish, combine the eggs, cream and vanilla. Add bread slices; soak for 5 minutes. Turn bread over; cover and refrigerate overnight.

■ In a bowl, combine the brown sugar, butter, syrup and pecans. Pour into a greased 13-in. x 9-in. baking dish. Top with bread. Bake, uncovered, at 350° for 30-35 minutes or a knife inserted near the center comes out clean. **Yield:** 4 servings.

maple-glazed sausages

TRUDIE HAGEN | ROGGEN, COLORADO

I love to simmer up this cinnamony syrup that nicely coats a skillet full of breakfast sausages. They're my first choice when I want to round out a morning menu of French toast and fruit compote.

PREP/TOTAL TIME: 20 MIN.

- 2 packages (8 ounces *each*) brown-and-serve sausage links
- 1 cup maple syrup
- 1/2 cup packed brown sugar
- 1 teaspoon ground cinnamon

■ In a large skillet, cook sausage links until browned; drain. Combine syrup, brown sugar and cinnamon; stir into skillet. Bring to a boil; cook and stir until sausages are glazed. **Yield:** 6-8 servings.

Cream Substitution

No half-and-half on hand for Overnight Pecan French Toast? You can substitute 4-1/2 teaspoons melted butter plus enough whole milk to equal 1 cup. One cup of evaporated milk may also be substituted for each cup of cream.

garlic zucchini frittata

MICHELLE KRZMARZICK | REDONDO BEACH, CALIFORNIA

This flavorful egg dish can be made in minutes and is easily doubled. Sometimes I use leftover taco meat or chopped ham instead of bacon.

PREP/TOTAL TIME: 25 MIN.

- 1 tablespoon butter
- 1 tablespoon finely chopped onion
- 4 garlic cloves, minced
- 1 medium zucchini, shredded
- 6 eggs
- 1/4 teaspoon ground mustard
- 4 bacon strips, cooked and crumbled
- 1/4 teaspoon salt
- 1/8 teaspoon pepper
- 1/4 cup shredded Swiss cheese
- 1/4 cup sliced green onions

■ In a 10-in. ovenproof skillet, melt butter over medium-high heat. Add the onion and garlic; saute for 1 minute. Add the zucchini; cook for 3 minutes or until tender.

■ In a large bowl, beat eggs and mustard. Pour into skillet. Sprinkle with bacon, salt and pepper. As eggs set, lift edges, letting uncooked portion flow underneath. Cook until eggs are nearly set, about 7 minutes. Meanwhile, preheat broiler.

■ Place skillet under the broiler, 6 in. from the heat, for 30-60 seconds or until the eggs are completely set. Sprinkle with the cheese and green onions. Broil 30 seconds longer or until the cheese is melted. Cut into wedges. **Yield:** 4 servings.

fluffy hot chocolate

JO ANN SCHIMCEK | WEIMAR, TEXAS

Melted marshmallows provide the frothy texture that you'll savor in this sweet and speedy warm beverage. They're also what make this hot chocolate a step up from the instant, store-bought variety. Chocolaty and comforting, it's our daughter's favorite.

PREP/TOTAL TIME: 15 MIN.

- 8 teaspoons sugar
- 4 teaspoons baking cocoa
- 4 cups milk
- 1-1/2 cups miniature marshmallows
- 1 teaspoon vanilla extract

■ In a small saucepan, combine the first four ingredients. Cook and stir over medium heat until the marshmallows are melted, about 8 minutes. Remove from the heat; stir in vanilla. Ladle into mugs. **Yield:** 4 servings.

cappuccino smoothies

MICHELLE CLUNEY | LAKE MARY, FLORIDA

Topped with miniature marshmallows, this icy cappuccino beverage is a twist on traditional fruit smoothies. My mom and I created it when trying to fix an easy snack.

PREP/TOTAL TIME: 5 MIN.

- 1 cup (8 ounces) cappuccino *or* coffee yogurt
- 1/3 cup milk
- 3 tablespoons confectioners' sugar, optional
- 1 tablespoon chocolate syrup
- 1-1/2 cups ice cubes
- 1/2 cup miniature marshmallows, *divided*

■ In a blender, combine the yogurt, milk, sugar if desired and chocolate syrup. Add ice cubes and 1/4 cup marshmallows; cover and process until blended. Pour into chilled glasses; top with the remaining marshmallows. Serve immediately. **Yield:** 3 servings.

cinnamon raisin strata

BARBARA TRITCH | HOPE, IDAHO

This delightful dish, made with day-old raisin bread, is full of cinnamon flavor. I like to serve it for brunch with sliced bacon and a fruit compote.

PREP: 20 MIN. + CHILLING BAKE: 40 MIN.

- 1/4 cup butter, softened
- 3 tablespoons ground cinnamon
- 8 slices day-old raisin bread
- 4 tablespoons brown sugar, *divided*
- 6 eggs
- 1-1/2 cups milk
- 3 tablespoons maple syrup
- 1 teaspoon vanilla extract
- Additional maple syrup

■ In a small bowl, combine butter and cinnamon; spread over one side of each slice of bread. Place four slices, buttered side up, in a greased 8-in. square baking dish (trim to fit if necessary). Sprinkle with 2 tablespoons of brown sugar. Repeat with the remaining bread and brown sugar.

■ In a large bowl, whisk the eggs, milk, syrup and vanilla; pour over bread. Cover and refrigerate overnight.

■ Remove from the refrigerator 30 minutes before baking. Bake, uncovered, at 350° for 40-50 minutes or until golden and puffed. Serve with additional maple syrup. **Yield:** 4 servings.

eggs with feta and asparagus

CAROL HEINE | NEW PRAGUE, MINNESOTA

I whipped up this dish because I had an abundance of asparagus. Stuffed with bacon and feta cheese, this morning meal has become a staple in our house.

PREP/TOTAL TIME: 20 MIN.

- 1 cup cut fresh asparagus (2-inch pieces)
- 1 tablespoon butter
- 4 eggs
- 1/8 to 1/4 teaspoon seasoned salt
- 4 strips ready-to-serve fully cooked bacon, crumbled
- 1/4 cup crumbled feta cheese

■ Place 1 in. of water in a saucepan; add asparagus. Bring to a boil. Reduce heat; cover and simmer for 3-5 minutes or until crisp-tender.

■ Meanwhile, in a large skillet, heat butter until hot. Add eggs; reduce heat to low. Cook until whites are completely set and yolks begin to thicken but are not hard. Sprinkle with seasoned salt.

■ Transfer eggs to serving plates; top with asparagus, bacon and feta cheese. **Yield:** 2 servings.

french omelet

BERNICE MORRIS | MARSHFIELD, MISSOURI

This cheesy, chock-full-of-flavor omelet is modeled after one I tasted in a restaurant. My version is so hearty and rich-tasting that folks never guess it's low in fat.

PREP/TOTAL TIME: 20 MIN.

- 2 eggs, lightly beaten
- 1/2 cup egg substitute
- 1/4 cup fat-free milk
- 1/8 teaspoon salt
- 1/8 teaspoon pepper
- 1/4 cup cubed fully cooked lean ham
- 1 tablespoon chopped onion
- 1 tablespoon chopped green pepper
- 1/4 cup shredded reduced-fat cheddar cheese

■ In a small bowl, combine the eggs, egg substitute, milk, salt and pepper. Coat a 10-in. nonstick skillet with cooking spray and place over medium heat. Add the egg mixture. As eggs set, lift the edges, letting the uncooked portion flow underneath.

■ When eggs are set, sprinkle ham, onion, green pepper and cheese over one side; fold the omelet over filling. Cover and let stand for 1 minute or until the cheese is melted. **Yield:** 2 servings.

lazy doughnuts

ELOISE DEHOYOS | TRACY, CALIFORNIA

These doughnuts have a great taste without having to fry them. They come together so quickly on those busy mornings.

PREP: 15 MIN. BAKE: 20 MIN.

- 2 tablespoons plus 1-1/2 teaspoons shortening
- 1/2 cup sugar
- 2 eggs
- 2 cups all-purpose flour
- 2 teaspoons baking powder
- 1/2 teaspoon ground nutmeg
- 1/2 teaspoon salt
- 6 tablespoons milk

Butter, melted
Cinnamon-sugar

■ In a large bowl, cream shortening and sugar until light and fluffy. Add eggs, one at a time, beating well after each addition. Combine flour, baking powder, nutmeg and salt; gradually add to creamed mixture alternately with milk, beating well after each addition.

■ Fill greased muffin cups two-thirds full. Bake at 350° for 18 minutes or until a toothpick inserted near the center comes out clean. Cool for 5 minutes before removing from the pan to a wire rack. Dip the doughnuts in melted butter, then roll in the cinnamon-sugar. Serve warm. **Yield:** about 10 servings.

Preparing Mushrooms

Before using mushrooms in recipes, gently remove dirt by rubbing with a mushroom brush or wipe mushrooms with a damp paper towel. You can also quickly rinse under cold water, drain and pat dry with paper towels.

mini spinach frittatas

NANCY STATKEVICUS | TUCSON, ARIZONA

Packed with pepperoni, spinach and mushrooms, mini frittatas are a cinch to make and just delicious. The recipe doubles easily for a crowd.

PREP/TOTAL TIME: 30 MIN.

- 1 cup ricotta cheese
- 3/4 cup grated Parmesan cheese
- 2/3 cup chopped fresh mushrooms
- 1 package (10 ounces) frozen chopped spinach, thawed and squeezed dry
- 1 egg
- 1/2 teaspoon dried oregano
- 1/4 teaspoon salt
- 1/4 teaspoon pepper
- 24 slices pepperoni

■ In a small bowl, combine the first eight ingredients. Place a slice of pepperoni in each of 24 greased miniature muffin cups. Fill the muffin cups three-fourths full with the cheese mixture.

■ Bake at 375° for 20-25 minutes or until a toothpick inserted near the center comes out clean. Carefully run a knife around edges of muffin cups to loosen. Serve warm. **Yield:** 2 dozen.

brunch pizza squares

LACHELLE OLIVET | PACE, FLORIDA

I love using convenience items, like the crescent rolls in this recipe. When I serve it to guests, they always ask me for the recipe. To hurry along preparation, I frequently brown a few pounds of sausage ahead of time and keep it in the freezer.

PREP/TOTAL TIME: 30 MIN.

- 1 pound bulk pork sausage
- 1 tube (8 ounces) refrigerated crescent rolls
- 4 eggs
- 2 tablespoons milk
- 1/8 teaspoon pepper
- 3/4 cup shredded cheddar cheese

■ In a large skillet, crumble sausage and cook over medium heat until no longer pink; drain. Unroll crescent dough onto the bottom and 1/2 in. up the sides of a lightly greased 13-in. x 9-in. baking pan; seal the seams. Sprinkle with sausage.

■ In a large bowl, beat the eggs, milk and pepper; pour over sausage. Sprinkle with cheese.

■ Bake, uncovered, at 400° for 15 minutes or until a knife inserted in the center comes out clean. **Yield:** 8 servings.

Storing Eggs

Fresh eggs can be stored in their carton in the refrigerator for 4 to 5 weeks beyond the pack date. Some manufacturers stamp their cartons with a date 30 days beyond the pack date.

rippled coffee cake

JANE LEAR | PORTLAND, TENNESSEE

I add a fun layer of brown sugar and cinnamon to a yellow cake mix. The delicious glazed sweet is good for breakfast or dessert.

PREP: 10 MIN. BAKE: 30 MIN.

- 1 package (18-1/4 ounces) yellow cake mix
- 1 cup (8 ounces) sour cream
- 4 eggs
- 2/3 cup canola oil
- 1 cup packed brown sugar
- 1 tablespoon ground cinnamon

ICING:

- 2 cups confectioners' sugar
- 1/4 cup milk
- 2 teaspoons vanilla extract

■ In a large bowl, combine the dry cake mix, sour cream, eggs and oil; beat well. Spread half of the batter into a greased 13-in. x 9-in. baking pan. Combine brown sugar and cinnamon; sprinkle over batter. Carefully spread remaining batter on top.

■ Bake at 350° for 30-35 minutes or until a toothpick inserted near the center comes out clean. Combine icing ingredients; drizzle over warm cake. **Yield:** 16-20 servings.

ham & cheese egg bake

SUSAN MILLER | NORTH ANDOVER, MASSACHUSETTS

This make-ahead egg casserole is just the thing when entertaining in the morning. It's loaded with ham, cheese and mushrooms.

PREP: 25 MIN. + CHILLING BAKE: 35 MIN.

- 1-1/2 cups (6 ounces) shredded cheddar cheese
- 1-1/2 cups (6 ounces) shredded part-skim mozzarella cheese
- 1/2 pound fresh mushrooms, sliced
- 6 green onions, sliced
- 1 medium sweet red pepper, chopped
- 2 tablespoons butter
- 1-3/4 cups cubed fully cooked ham
- 1/4 cup all-purpose flour
- 8 eggs
- 1-3/4 cups milk

Salt and pepper to taste

■ In a large bowl, combine the cheeses; sprinkle into a greased 13-in. x 9-in. baking dish. In a large skillet, saute the mushrooms, onions and red pepper in butter; stir in ham. Spoon over the cheese.

■ In a large bowl, combine the flour, eggs, milk, salt and pepper. Pour over the ham mixture; cover and refrigerate overnight.

■ Remove from the refrigerator 30 minutes before baking. Bake, uncovered, at 350° for 35-45 minutes or until a knife inserted near the center comes out clean. Let stand for 5 minutes before serving. **Yield:** 8-10 servings.

lemon poppy seed muffins

DONNA GONDA | NORTH CANTON, OHIO

Bursting with poppy seeds, these luscious muffins are filled and drizzled with lots of lemony flavor. They're great with coffee or tea and couldn't be much easier to whip up.

PREP/TOTAL TIME: 30 MIN.

- 2 cups biscuit/baking mix
- 1 package (3.4 ounces) instant lemon pudding mix
- 1/4 cup poppy seeds
- 1/4 teaspoon grated lemon peel
- 2 eggs
- 1 cup milk
- 1/4 cup canola oil
- 3/4 cup confectioners' sugar
- 1 tablespoon lemon juice

■ In a large bowl, combine the baking mix, pudding mix, poppy seeds and lemon peel. In another bowl, combine the eggs, milk and oil; stir into dry ingredients just until moistened. Fill greased or paper-lined muffin cups two-thirds full.

■ Bake at 375° for 20-25 minutes or until a toothpick inserted near the center comes out clean. Cool for 5 minutes before removing from pan to a wire rack.

■ In a small bowl, combine confectioners' sugar and lemon juice; drizzle over muffins. **Yield:** 1 dozen.

tex-mex scramble

PAULA WHARTON | EL PASO, TEXAS

This homey mix of eggs, corn tortilla strips, roast beef and other savory ingredients is one of our favorite early morning meals.

PREP/TOTAL TIME: 25 MIN.

- 3 corn tortillas (6 inches), cut into thin strips
- 4 teaspoons olive oil, *divided*
- 2 tablespoons chopped onion
- 1 jalapeno pepper, seeded and chopped
- 4 eggs, lightly beaten
- 1 plum tomato, chopped
- 1/4 cup shredded cooked roast beef
- 1/8 teaspoon salt
- 1/8 teaspoon pepper
- 1/4 cup shredded Monterey Jack cheese

■ In a large nonstick skillet, cook the tortilla strips in 2 teaspoons oil for 5 minutes or until lightly golden brown but not crisp. Add the onion, jalapeno and remaining oil; cook 2 minutes longer.

■ Add the eggs, tomato, beef, salt and pepper; cook and stir until eggs are completely set. Sprinkle with cheese; cover and let stand for 2-3 minutes until cheese is melted. **Yield:** 2 servings.

Editor's Note: When cutting hot peppers, disposable gloves are recommended. Avoid touching your face.

baked oatmeal

FREIDA ROBERTSON | HARLOWTON, MONTANA

Give this oatmeal a try the next time you're looking for an easy breakfast on a busy morning. The brown sugar and cinnamon make it sweet, and I promise it will disappear fast.

PREP: 5 MIN. BAKE: 40 MIN.

- 3 cups quick-cooking oats
- 1 cup packed brown sugar
- 2 teaspoons baking powder
- 1 teaspoon salt
- 1 teaspoon ground cinnamon
- 1 cup milk
- 1/2 cup butter, melted
- 2 eggs, lightly beaten
- Additional milk

■ In a large bowl, combine the first eight ingredients. Spoon into a greased 9-in. square baking pan. Bake, uncovered, at 350° for 40-45 minutes. Serve warm with the milk. **Yield:** 8 servings.

breakfast parfaits

ADELL MEYER | MADISON, WISCONSIN

With pineapple, raspberries and banana, my yogurt treats are a bright and cheerful on-the-go breakfast.

PREP/TOTAL TIME: 10 MIN.

- 2 cups pineapple chunks
- 1 cup fresh *or* frozen raspberries
- 1 cup (8 ounces) vanilla yogurt
- 1 cup sliced ripe banana
- 1/2 cup chopped dates *or* raisins
- 1/4 cup sliced almonds

■ In four parfait glasses or serving dishes, layer the pineapple, raspberries, yogurt, banana and dates. Sprinkle with almonds. Serve immediately. **Yield:** 4 servings.

yogurt pancakes

CHERYLL BABER | HOMEDALE, IDAHO

Get your day off to a great start with delicious yogurt pancakes. Simply whip up a quick batch on the weekend—varying the fillings—and pop them in your freezer. Then, savor these flapjacks one morning at a time.

PREP: 15 MIN. COOK: 5 MIN./BATCH

- 2 cups all-purpose flour
- 2 tablespoons sugar
- 2 teaspoons baking powder
- 1 teaspoon baking soda
- 2 eggs
- 2 cups (16 ounces) plain yogurt
- 1/4 cup water

Semisweet chocolate chips, dried cranberries, sliced ripe bananas and coarsely chopped pecans, optional

- In a small bowl, combine the flour, sugar, baking powder and baking soda. In another bowl, whisk the eggs, yogurt and water. Stir into dry ingredients just until moistened.
- Pour batter by 1/4 cupfuls onto a hot griddle coated with cooking spray. Sprinkle with chocolate chips or dried cranberries if desired. Turn when bubbles form on top; cook until the second side is golden brown. Serve with bananas or pecans if desired.
- To freeze, arrange cooled pancakes in a single layer on baking sheet. Freeze overnight or until frozen. Transfer to a resealable plastic freezer bag. Pancakes may be frozen for up to 2 months. **Yield:** 12 pancakes.

Editor's Note: To use the frozen pancakes, place pancakes on a microwave-safe plate; microwave on high for 40-50 seconds or until heated through.

fluffy sausage omelet

JEAN TYNER | DARLINGTON, SOUTH CAROLINA

At Christmastime, we get family members together for a breakfast meal. I serve this hearty omelet with a fruit salad, hash brown casserole and hot biscuits.

PREP/TOTAL TIME: 30 MIN.

- 1/4 pound bulk pork sausage
- 2 tablespoons chopped onion
- 2 tablespoons chopped sweet red pepper
- 1/4 cup sour cream
- 3 eggs, *separated*
- 3 tablespoons milk
- 1/4 teaspoon salt
- 1/4 teaspoon baking powder
- 1/8 teaspoon pepper
- 1 tablespoon butter

■ Crumble the sausage into a small microwave-safe dish; add onion and red pepper. Cover and microwave on high for 2 minutes; drain. Stir in sour cream; set aside.

■ In a small bowl, whisk the egg yolks, milk, salt, baking powder and pepper. In a large bowl, beat egg whites until stiff peaks form. Gently fold into egg yolk mixture.

■ Place the butter in a greased 9-in. microwave-safe pie plate. Microwave on high for 30 seconds.

■ Pour egg mixture into plate. Microwave, uncovered, at 50% power for 3-5 minutes or until partially set. Lift edges, letting uncooked portion flow underneath. Cook at 50% power 2-3 minutes longer or until eggs are set. Spoon sausage mixture over one side; fold omelet over filling. **Yield:** 2 servings.

Editor's Note: This recipe was tested in a 1,100-watt microwave.

light 'n' crispy waffles

TASTE OF HOME TEST KITCHEN

Club soda gives these crisp waffles a fluffy texture. With only four ingredients, homemade waffles don't get much easier than this!

PREP/TOTAL TIME: 20 MIN.

- 2 cups biscuit/baking mix
- 2 eggs, lightly beaten
- 1/2 cup canola oil
- 1 cup club soda

■ In a large bowl, combine the biscuit mix, eggs and oil. Add club soda and stir until smooth.

■ Bake in a preheated waffle iron according to manufacturer's directions until golden brown. **Yield:** 12 waffles.

breakfast patties

JO ANN HONEY | LONGMONT, COLORADO

While looking for reduced-fat, high-protein breakfast options, I took an old sausage recipe and made it new again.

PREP/TOTAL TIME: 30 MIN.

- 2 pounds lean ground turkey
- 1-1/2 teaspoons salt
- 1 teaspoon dried sage leaves
- 1 teaspoon pepper
- 1/2 teaspoon ground ginger
- 1/2 teaspoon cayenne pepper

■ Crumble the turkey into a large bowl. Add the salt, sage, pepper, ginger and cayenne. Shape mixture into sixteen 2-1/2-in. patties.

■ In a large skillet, cook patties over medium heat for 4-6 minutes on each side or until a meat thermometer reads 165° and juices run clear. **Yield:** 16 patties.

frothy orange-pineapple cooler

DEIDRE FALLAVOLLITA | VIENNA, VIRGINIA

My kids think they've gone to heaven when I say "yes" to seconds of this smoothie. I never hesitate because it's a wholesome and nutritious recipe.

PREP/TOTAL TIME: 5 MIN.

- 2 cups unsweetened pineapple juice
- 1 cup (8 ounces) vanilla yogurt
- 1 can (6 ounces) frozen orange juice concentrate, thawed
- 2 small ripe bananas, cut into chunks
- 1/2 cup frozen unsweetened strawberries
- 1 drop coconut extract, optional

■ In a blender, combine all ingredients; cover and process on high until smooth. Pour into chilled glasses; serve immediately. **Yield:** 6 servings.

simple sticky buns

TYAN CADWELL | ST. JOHNS, MICHIGAN

I prepare these nutty rolls every Christmas Eve. Then I pop them in the oven while we're opening gifts on Christmas morning. They smell delicious while baking.

PREP: 15 MIN. + CHILLING BAKE: 35 MIN.

- 2 loaves (1 pound *each*) frozen bread dough, thawed, *divided*
- Ground cinnamon to taste
- 1/2 cup butter, cubed
- 1 cup packed brown sugar
- 1 package (4.6 ounces) cook-and-serve vanilla pudding mix
- 2 tablespoons milk
- 1 cup chopped pecans
- 1/2 cup raisins, optional

■ Cut each loaf of dough into 18 pieces. Arrange half in a greased 13-in. x 9-in. baking dish. Sprinkle with cinnamon.

■ In a large saucepan over low heat, melt butter. Remove from the heat; stir in the brown sugar, pudding mix and milk until smooth. Pour over dough. Sprinkle with pecans and raisins if desired. Arrange remaining pieces of dough over top. Cover and refrigerate overnight or let stand at room temperature for 3 hours.

■ Bake, uncovered, at 350° for 35 minutes or until center sounds hollow when tapped with fingers. Invert onto a serving platter or baking sheet. **Yield:** 12-15 servings.

Editor's Note: Frozen dinner roll dough (24 rolls) may be substituted for 2 loaves of bread dough.

Recipe Wording

Chopping an ingredient before or after measuring it can make a difference in the outcome of the recipe.

If the word "chopped" comes before the ingredient when listed in a recipe, then chop the ingredient before measuring.

If the word "chopped" comes after the ingredient, then chop after measuring.

For example, if a recipe states "1 cup nuts, chopped," you should measure 1 cup of nuts and then chop them.

broiled grapefruit

VICKI HOLLOWAY | JOELTON, TENNESSEE

This easy-to-prepare dish lends eye-catching appeal to a winter breakfast or brunch. Brown sugar sweetens the tart fruit, and the sugared grapes add a pretty accent.

PREP/TOTAL TIME: 25 MIN.

- 5 medium pink grapefruit
- 1/4 cup packed brown sugar
- 2 tablespoons plus 1/4 cup sugar, *divided*
- 2 tablespoons butter, melted
- Seedless red and green grape clusters

■ Cut each grapefruit in half horizontally. With a sharp knife, cut around each section to loosen fruit. Place grapefruit halves, cut side up, in a 15-in. x 10-in. x 1-in. baking pan.

■ Combine brown sugar and 2 tablespoons sugar; sprinkle over grapefruit. Drizzle with butter. Broil 4 in. from the heat until sugar is bubbly.

■ For garnish, rinse grape clusters and dip in remaining sugar. Place on grapefruit; serve warm. **Yield:** 10 servings.

toasted muesli

JENNIFER WILSON | VANCOUVER, BRITISH COLUMBIA

Try this mix for a healthful start to the day. The recipe can be made ahead so you can just grab and go on busy mornings.

PREP/TOTAL TIME: 20 MIN.

- 2 cups old-fashioned oats
- 1/4 cup sunflower kernels
- 1/4 cup sliced almonds
- 1/3 cup finely chopped dates
- 2 tablespoons oat bran
- 1 cup bran flakes
- 1/4 cup toasted wheat germ
- 1/4 cup raisins
- 1 tablespoon sugar
- 1-3/4 cups fat-free milk, optional

■ In a 15-in. x 10-in. x 1-in. baking pan, combine the oats, sunflower kernels and almonds. Bake at 350° for 10-15 minutes or until almonds are golden.

■ Place dates and oat bran in a large bowl; stir to coat dates with oat bran. Add the toasted oat mixture, bran flakes, wheat germ, raisins and sugar; stir gently to combine. Serve with milk if desired. Store in an airtight container. **Yield:** 7 servings.

breakfast crepes with berries

JENNIFER WEISBRODT | OCONOMOWOC, WISCONSIN

After a long day of blackberry picking, I whipped up a sauce to dress up some crepes I had on hand. This speedy dish really hit the spot and tied everything together beautifully! The crepes make an elegant addition to any brunch, and the sauce is delectable over warm waffles.

PREP/TOTAL TIME: 20 MIN.

1-1/2 cups fresh raspberries
1-1/2 cups fresh blackberries
1 cup (8 ounces) sour cream
1/2 cup confectioners' sugar
1 carton (6 ounces) orange creme yogurt
1 tablespoon lime juice
1-1/2 teaspoons grated lime peel
1/2 teaspoon vanilla extract
1/8 teaspoon salt
8 prepared crepes (9 inches)

■ In a large bowl, combine the raspberries and blackberries; set aside. In a small bowl, combine sour cream and confectioners' sugar until smooth. Stir in the yogurt, lime juice, lime peel, vanilla and salt.

■ Spread 2 tablespoons sour cream mixture over each crepe; top with about 1/3 cup berries. Roll up; drizzle with remaining sour cream mixture. Serve immediately. **Yield:** 8 servings.

dried fruit muesli

TASTE OF HOME TEST KITCHEN

Your day will start right when you prepare this comforting chilled cereal. Filled with wholesome ingredients, it sits in the fridge overnight for the perfect pick-me-up when the alarm clock rings.

PREP: 10 MIN. + CHILLING

1 cup quick-cooking oats
1 cup fat-free milk
1/4 cup orange juice
1/4 cup chopped dried apricots
1/4 cup dried cranberries
1/4 cup chopped dried apples
2 tablespoons chopped almonds
2 tablespoons honey
1/8 teaspoon salt
1/8 teaspoon ground cinnamon

■ In a large bowl, combine all of the ingredients. Cover and refrigerate for at least 8 hours or overnight. **Yield:** 4 servings.

berry smoothies

PATRICIA MAHONEY | PRESQUE ISLE, MAINE

Add a blush of color and a burst of frosty berry flavor to your meal with scrumptious, summery smoothies.

PREP/TOTAL TIME: 5 MIN.

2/3 cup 2% milk
3/4 cup frozen unsweetened strawberries
1/3 cup frozen unsweetened raspberries
2 tablespoons sugar
3/4 cup ice cubes

■ Place the milk, berries and sugar in a blender; cover and process until blended. Add ice cubes; cover and process until smooth. Pour into chilled glasses; serve immediately. **Yield:** 2 servings.

fruit smoothies

TERESA DUNLAP | LIMA, OHIO

These smoothies are great for breakfast, and they also make a delicious afternoon snack with cinnamon graham crackers. My family enjoys them anytime of day.

PREP/TOTAL TIME: 5 MIN.

- 1-1/4 cups milk
- 1 cup frozen unsweetened strawberries
- 1/2 cup frozen unsweetened sliced peaches
- 1 small ripe banana, halved
- 3 tablespoons sugar

■ Place all ingredients in a blender; cover and process until smooth. Pour into chilled glasses; serve immediately. **Yield:** 2-1/2 cups.

jam & cream french toast

B. MACKINNON | KODAK, TENNESSEE

My grandmother used to make this for me when I was a child. You can experiment with other flavors of jam and bread.

PREP/TOTAL TIME: 10 MIN.

- 2 tablespoons cream cheese, softened
- 2 thick slices cinnamon-raisin bread
- 2 tablespoons strawberry jam
- 1 egg
- 1 tablespoon butter

Maple syrup, optional

■ Spread cream cheese on one slice of bread. Spread jam on the other slice; place jam side down over the cream cheese. In a shallow bowl, beat egg. Dip both sides of bread into egg.

■ In a skillet, melt butter; cook bread for 3-4 minutes on each side or until golden brown. Serve with syrup if desired. **Yield:** 1 serving.

egg biscuit bake

ALICE LE DUC | CEDARBURG, WISCONSIN

Convenient refrigerated biscuits create a golden border around this all-in-one brunch dish. It's a variation of a simple egg-cheese combination my mother used to make. It's become our favorite comfort food.

PREP/TOTAL TIME: 30 MIN.

- 1 can (5 ounces) evaporated milk
- 8 ounces process cheese (Velveeta), cubed
- 1 teaspoon prepared mustard
- 3/4 cup cubed fully cooked ham
- 1/2 cup frozen peas
- 2 tablespoons butter
- 10 eggs, lightly beaten
- 1 tube (12 ounces) refrigerated buttermilk biscuits

■ In a large saucepan, combine milk, cheese and mustard; cook over low heat until smooth, stirring constantly. Stir in ham and peas.

■ Melt butter in a large skillet. Add eggs; cook and stir over medium heat until eggs are completely set. Add cheese sauce and stir gently.

■ Spoon into an ungreased shallow 2-qt. baking dish. Separate the biscuits and cut in half. Place with cut side down around outer edge of dish.

■ Bake, uncovered, at 375° for 15-20 minutes or until a knife inserted near the center comes out clean and biscuits are golden brown. **Yield:** 4-6 servings.

maple cream coffee

TASTE OF HOME TEST KITCHEN

On a crisp winter day, this creamy drink is perfect for after sledding or after dinner. Even non-coffee drinkers will enjoy the hint of maple and lighter coffee flavor.

PREP/TOTAL TIME: 10 MIN.

- 3/4 cup half-and-half cream
- 1/4 cup maple syrup
- 1-1/4 cups brewed coffee
- 1/4 cup whipped cream

■ In a small saucepan, cook and stir cream and syrup over medium heat until heated through. (Do not boil.) Divide evenly between two cups. Stir in coffee. Top with whipped cream. **Yield:** 2 servings.

Using Leftover Cream

Leftover whipped cream can be dolloped or piped onto waxed or parchment paper and frozen. Use to garnish the tops of cakes, cobblers, crisps or hot chocolate.

bacon & egg burritos

ROBYN LARABEE | LUCKNOW, ONTARIO

My husband and I discovered these delicious burritos when we drove truck as a team in the southwestern United States. He created this version that our guests enjoy as much as we do.

PREP/TOTAL TIME: 25 MIN.

- 6 bacon strips, diced
- 1 cup frozen cubed hash brown potatoes
- 2 tablespoons chopped onion
- 6 eggs
- 1/4 cup sour cream
- 3/4 cup shredded cheddar cheese, *divided*
- 2 tablespoons taco sauce
- 1/2 to 1 teaspoon hot pepper sauce
- 4 flour tortillas (10 inches), warmed
- Sour cream and chopped tomatoes, optional

■ In a large skillet, cook bacon over medium heat until crisp. Using a slotted spoon, remove to paper towels; drain, reserving 1 tablespoon drippings. Add potatoes and onion to drippings; cook and stir over medium heat until potatoes are golden brown.

■ In a large bowl, whisk eggs and sour cream. Stir in 1/4 cup cheese, taco sauce and hot pepper sauce. Pour over potato mixture; add bacon. Cook and stir over medium heat until eggs are completely set.

■ Spoon about 3/4 cup down the center of each tortilla; sprinkle with remaining cheese. Fold bottom and sides of tortilla over filling. Serve immediately with sour cream and tomatoes if desired. **Yield:** 4 servings.

apple spiced oatmeal

TASTE OF HOME TEST KITCHEN

This thick, satisfying oatmeal is wonderful to serve for breakfast when guests visit overnight, especially during the holidays. Set up an "oatmeal bar," offering a variety of fruits and nuts to top steaming bowlfuls.

PREP/TOTAL TIME: 10 MIN.

- 1 cup quick-cooking oats
- 1-3/4 cups apple cider
- 1 tablespoon butter
- 1 teaspoon ground cinnamon
- 1/8 teaspoon salt
- Sliced bananas and blueberries

■ In a microwave-safe bowl, combine the oats and cider. Microwave, uncovered on high for 2-3 minutes or until tender. Stir in the butter, cinnamon and salt. Serve with bananas and berries. **Yield:** 2 servings.

egg 'n' bacon sandwiches

SHARON PICKETT | AURORA, INDIANA

Try this healthful, homemade take on a fast-food favorite. My son-in-law created this recipe so my grandchildren could have a quick yet nutritious breakfast before school.

PREP/TOTAL TIME: 5 MIN.

- 2 eggs
- 1 teaspoon fat-free milk
- 1/4 teaspoon salt
- 1/8 teaspoon pepper
- 2 slices Canadian bacon (1/2 ounce *each*)
- 1 English muffin, split and toasted
- 2 tablespoons shredded reduced-fat cheddar cheese

■ In a small bowl, whisk the eggs, milk, salt and pepper. Divide between two 10-oz. microwave-safe custard cups coated with cooking spray. Microwave, uncovered, on high for 20 seconds. Stir; microwave 20-25 seconds longer or until center of egg is almost set.

■ Place a slice of bacon on each muffin half; top with egg and sprinkle with cheese. Microwave, uncovered, for 10-13 seconds or until cheese is melted. Let stand for 20-30 seconds before serving. **Yield:** 2 servings.

Editor's Note: This recipe was tested in a 1,100-watt microwave.

p. 51

speedy
sandwiches
p. 44
p. 47
p. 45

open-faced reubens

MARY ANN DELL | PHOENIXVILLE, PENNSYLVANIA

Anyone who likes the distinctive taste of reuben sandwiches is sure to love these. Using store-bought coleslaw mix speeds up the preparation.

PREP/TOTAL TIME: 20 MIN.

- 2-1/2 cups coleslaw mix
- 8 green onions, sliced
- 1/2 cup mayonnaise, *divided*
- 2 tablespoons cider vinegar
- 1/2 teaspoon salt
- 1/2 teaspoon pepper
- 1/4 cup Dijon mustard
- 8 slices rye bread, lightly toasted
- 16 slices Swiss cheese
- 1 pound thinly sliced deli corned beef

■ In a large bowl, combine the coleslaw mix, green onions, 1/4 cup mayonnaise, cider vinegar, salt and pepper. Cover; refrigerate until chilled.

■ Meanwhile, combine mustard and remaining mayonnaise. Spread over one side of each slice of toast; top with a cheese slice, corned beef and another cheese slice. Place on foil-lined baking sheets.

■ Bake at 450° for 5-6 minutes or until cheese is melted. Top each with 1/4 cup coleslaw. **Yield:** 8 servings.

broiled pizza burgers

ANN BAILES | ANDERSON, SOUTH CAROLINA

My mother made tasty burgers when I was growing up. Now I like to serve them to my family for Sunday supper. They're even faster to fix if you use pre-browned hamburgers from the freezer. We sometimes substitute slices of cheddar for the process cheese.

PREP/TOTAL TIME: 25 MIN.

- 1 pound ground beef
- 1 tablespoon chopped onion
- 2 teaspoons cornstarch
- 1 can (14-1/2 ounces) diced tomatoes, undrained
- 1 teaspoon dried oregano
- 1/4 teaspoon salt
- 1/4 teaspoon onion salt
- 10 slices process cheese (Velveeta), *divided*
- 4 hamburger buns, split

- In a large skillet, cook beef and onion over medium heat until the meat is no longer pink; drain. Sprinkle with the cornstarch; stir until blended. Stir in the tomatoes, oregano, salt and onion salt. Cook, uncovered, for 5 minutes or until slightly thickened. Add six cheese slices; cook and stir until cheese is melted and blended.
- Place hamburger buns cut side up on an ungreased baking sheet; spoon about 1/4 cup of the meat mixture onto each bun half. Cut the remaining cheese slices in half diagonally; place over the meat mixture. Broil 6-8 in. from the heat for 3-4 minutes or until the cheese is melted. **Yield:** 4 servings.

beef pitas with yogurt sauce

TASTE OF HOME TEST KITCHEN

Filled with tender, seasoned beef and sauteed onions, these gyros are sure to be a hit! Top them with a very easy-to-make yogurt sauce that doubles as a dip for warmed pita chips or a dressing for Greek salads.

PREP/TOTAL TIME: 25 MIN.

- 1 cup (8 ounces) fat-free plain yogurt
- 1/4 cup minced fresh parsley
- 1/2 teaspoon minced garlic
- 1/8 teaspoon salt

PITAS:

- 1 teaspoon dried oregano
- 1 teaspoon minced fresh rosemary
- 1/2 teaspoon salt
- 1/4 teaspoon pepper
- 1 pound beef top sirloin steak, cut into thin strips
- 1 large sweet onion, sliced
- 4 teaspoons olive oil, *divided*
- 4 whole gyro-style pitas (6 inches), warmed

- For sauce, in a small bowl, combine the yogurt, parsley, garlic and salt. Refrigerate until serving.
- In a large resealable plastic bag, combine the oregano, rosemary, salt and pepper; add the beef. Seal the bag and toss to coat.
- In a large nonstick skillet, saute onion in 2 teaspoons oil until golden brown. Remove and keep warm. Saute beef in remaining oil until no longer pink.
- Serve the beef and onion on the pitas with the yogurt sauce. **Yield:** 4 servings.

home run slugger sub

CATHY RUNYON | ALLENDALE, MICHIGAN

I trimmed long French bread to make these hearty hoagies look like baseball bats—only they're stuffed with cold cuts, veggies and cheese.

PREP/TOTAL TIME: 15 MIN.

- 1 French bread baguette (1 pound and 20 inches long)
- 1/4 pound thinly sliced fully cooked ham
- 1/4 pound thinly sliced bologna
- 1/4 pound thinly sliced hard salami
- 4 romaine leaves
- 6 slices Swiss cheese
- 6 slices Colby cheese
- 1 medium tomato, sliced

■ With a sharp knife, cut one end of the baguette in the shape of a baseball bat handle. Slice the loaf in half lengthwise.

■ On the bottom half, layer ham, bologna, salami, romaine, cheeses and tomato. Replace top. Secure with toothpicks if necessary. Cut into slices. **Yield:** 8 servings.

chicken cheddar wraps

RUTH ANDREWSON | LEAVENWORTH, WASHINGTON

By keeping cooked chicken in the freezer, these mildly spiced sandwiches are simple to assemble when you have to get a meal on the table in a hurry. Children love them and often eat more than one.

PREP/TOTAL TIME: 15 MIN.

- 1 cup (8 ounces) sour cream
- 1 cup chunky salsa
- 2 tablespoons mayonnaise
- 4 cups cubed cooked chicken
- 2 cups (8 ounces) shredded cheddar cheese
- 1 cup thinly sliced fresh mushrooms
- 2 cups shredded lettuce
- 1 cup guacamole, optional

- 12 flour tortillas (6 inches), room temperature

Tomato wedges and additional guacamole, optional

■ In a large bowl, combine the sour cream, salsa and mayonnaise. Stir in chicken, cheese and mushrooms.

■ Divide lettuce and guacamole if desired between tortillas. Place about 1/2 cup chicken mixture on each tortilla. Fold sides over the filling. Garnish with tomato and additional guacamole if desired. **Yield:** 12 wraps.

bacon-wrapped hamburgers

DANA MATTHIES | PARKER, SOUTH DAKOTA

We cook out a lot in summer, so I'm always on the lookout for new grilling recipes. My sister shared this one with me, and both of our families really enjoy it.

PREP/TOTAL TIME: 30 MIN.

- 1/2 cup shredded cheddar cheese
- 1 small onion, chopped
- 1 egg
- 2 tablespoons ketchup
- 1 tablespoon grated Parmesan cheese
- 1 tablespoon Worcestershire sauce
- 1/2 teaspoon salt
- 1/8 teaspoon pepper
- 1 pound ground beef
- 6 bacon strips
- 6 hamburger buns, split

■ In a large bowl, combine the first eight ingredients. Crumble beef over mixture and mix well. Shape into six patties. Wrap a bacon strip around each patty; secure with a toothpick.

■ Grill, covered, over medium-hot heat for 4-5 minutes on each side or until meat is no longer pink and a meat thermometer reads 160°. Discard toothpicks. Serve on buns. **Yield:** 6 servings.

Editor's Note: If you prefer, bake Bacon-Wrapped Hamburgers in a baking dish at 350° for 25 to 30 minutes or until the beef is no longer pink.

bacon avocado wraps

TASTE OF HOME TEST KITCHEN

A variety of flavored flour tortillas are now available in most grocery stores and would add nice variation to this recipe.

PREP/TOTAL TIME: 15 MIN.

- 1/3 cup mayonnaise
- 2 tablespoons chipotle sauce
- 1 tablespoon sour cream
- 1 package (2.1 ounces) ready-to-serve fully cooked bacon
- 4 flour tortillas (8 inches)
- 4 large lettuce leaves
- 1 large tomato, sliced
- 2 medium ripe avocados, peeled and sliced

■ In a small bowl, combine the mayonnaise, chipotle sauce and sour cream until smooth. Heat bacon according to package directions. Spread chipotle mayonnaise over tortillas; layer with lettuce, tomato, bacon and avocados. Roll up tightly. **Yield:** 4 servings.

Editor's Note: This recipe was tested with San Marcos brand chipotle sauce. It can be found in the Mexican section of your grocery store.

southwestern panini

JANET MILLER | MIDLAND, TEXAS

These hearty, quick-to-fix sandwiches are guaranteed to satisfy. Featuring a delicious southwestern flavor, they're a convenient way for me to serve a complete meal that tastes great.

PREP/TOTAL TIME: 20 MIN.

- 1 medium ripe avocado, peeled
- 1/2 teaspoon sugar
- 1/2 teaspoon garlic salt
- 1/2 teaspoon lemon juice
- 8 slices oat bread
- 1/2 pound thinly sliced deli ham
- 4 slices Swiss cheese
- 2 tablespoons butter

■ In a small bowl, mash the avocado with sugar, garlic salt and lemon juice. Spread over four slices of bread; layer with ham and cheese. Top with remaining bread.

■ Spread butter over both sides of sandwiches. Cook on an indoor grill for 2-3 minutes or until bread is browned and cheese is melted. **Yield:** 4 servings.

grilled pb&j

SANDI TUTTLE | HAYWARD, WISCONSIN

I enjoy peanut butter and jelly sandwiches so much, I turned them into a yummy breakfast treat reminiscent of stuffed French toast. I sometimes bake them in the oven, but cooking them in a skillet is quicker.

PREP/TOTAL TIME: 20 MIN.

- 1/2 cup egg substitute
- 1/2 teaspoon vanilla extract
- 1/8 teaspoon ground cinnamon
- 3 tablespoons reduced-fat peanut butter
- 4 teaspoons raspberry jam
- 4 slices light whole wheat bread

■ In a small bowl, combine the egg substitute, vanilla and cinnamon. Spread peanut butter and jam over two slices of bread; top with remaining bread. Brush sandwiches with egg substitute mixture.

■ In a large nonstick skillet coated with cooking spray, cook sandwiches over medium-high heat for 3-4 minutes on each side or until golden brown. **Yield:** 2 servings.

garden turkey burgers

SANDY KITZMILLER | UNITYVILLE, PENNSYLVANIA

These moist burgers get plenty of color and flavor from onion, zucchini and red pepper. I often make the mixture ahead of time and put it in the refrigerator. Later, after helping my husband with farm chores, I can put the burgers on the grill while whipping up a salad or side dish.

PREP/TOTAL TIME: 30 MIN.

- 1 cup old-fashioned oats
- 3/4 cup chopped onion
- 3/4 cup finely chopped sweet red *or* green pepper
- 1/2 cup shredded zucchini
- 1/4 cup ketchup
- 2 garlic cloves, minced
- 1/4 teaspoon salt, optional
- 1 pound ground turkey
- 6 whole wheat hamburger buns, split and toasted

■ Coat grill rack with cooking spray before starting the grill. In a bowl, combine the first seven ingredients. Crumble turkey over the mixture and mix well. Shape into six 1/2-in.-thick patties.

■ Grill, covered, over indirect medium heat for 6 minutes on each side or until a meat thermometer reads 165° and juices run clear. Serve on buns. **Yield:** 6 servings.

hawaiian ham salad pockets

MITZI SENTIFF | ANNAPOLIS, MARYLAND

Looking for a great way to use up leftover ham? Try some simple, low-fat sandwiches. Pineapple and mustard are traditional flavors with baked ham, and they work well in these sandwiches.

PREP/TOTAL TIME: 15 MIN.

1-1/4 cups cubed fully cooked lean ham
3/4 cup unsweetened pineapple tidbits
1 large carrot, chopped
1/4 cup fat-free mayonnaise
1 tablespoon honey mustard
2 pita breads (6 inches), halved
4 lettuce leaves

■ In a small bowl, combine the ham, pineapple and carrot. Stir in the mayonnaise and mustard until blended. Line each pita half with a lettuce leaf; fill with ham salad. **Yield:** 4 servings.

crab salad on croissants

KARI MOORE | WEST PALINS, MISSOURI

Seafood-filled croissants will leave you anything but crabby! We had used the filling as an appetizer, but found it makes a quick-and-easy sandwich, too.

PREP/TOTAL TIME: 20 MIN.

2 packages (8 ounces *each*) imitation crabmeat, flaked
2 celery ribs, chopped
1/4 cup chopped green onions
1/4 cup shredded cheddar cheese
3 tablespoons mayonnaise
3 tablespoons plain yogurt
8 croissants, split
Lettuce leaves and tomato slices

■ In a large bowl, combine the crab, celery, onions and cheese. In a small bowl, combine mayonnaise and yogurt until blended. Pour over crab mixture; toss to coat. Line croissants with lettuce; top with crab salad and tomato slices. **Yield:** 8 servings.

patty melts

LEAH ZIMMERMAN | EPHRATA, PENNSYLVANIA

My husband often orders patty melts when we go out to eat, so I started fixing them at home. I add horseradish to give them more zip, and now he loves my version better than any restaurant version.

PREP/TOTAL TIME: 30 MIN.

10 thin slices sweet onion
2 tablespoons butter, softened, *divided*
1/2 pound lean ground beef (90% lean)
1/4 teaspoon salt
1/4 teaspoon pepper
4 slices rye bread
2 tablespoons Thousand Island salad dressing
2 teaspoons prepared horseradish
2 slices process American cheese *or* Swiss cheese

■ In a large nonstick skillet, saute onion in 1 tablespoon butter until tender. Remove and keep warm.

■ Shape beef into two oval patties; sprinkle with salt and pepper. In the same skillet, cook patties over medium heat for 3-4 minutes on each side or until a meat thermometer reads 160 and meat juices run clear; drain. Remove and keep warm.

■ Spread remaining butter over one side of each slice of bread. Place in skillet, buttered side down, and toast until lightly browned.

■ Combine the salad dressing and horseradish. On two slices of toast, layer a slice of cheese, a beef patty, half of the onion and dressing mixture. Top with the remaining toast. **Yield:** 2 servings.

pepper steak quesadillas

BARBARA MOORE | FARMINGTON, NEW MEXICO

I came up with this savory snack when my family needed a quick lunch before running off in several directions. I threw together what I had in the fridge and it was a big hit!

PREP/TOTAL TIME: 30 MIN.

- 1/2 pound beef top sirloin steak
- 1/2 *each* medium green, sweet red and yellow pepper, julienned
- 1 tablespoon chopped red onion
- 1 garlic clove, minced
- 1 tablespoon minced fresh cilantro
- 1/4 teaspoon dried rosemary, crushed
- 4 flour tortillas (6 inches)
- 6 cherry tomatoes, halved
- 1/4 cup sliced fresh mushrooms
- 1 cup (4 ounces) shredded part-skim mozzarella cheese

- If grilling the steak, coat grill rack with cooking spray before starting the grill. Grill steak, covered, over medium heat or broil 4 in. from the heat for 4-6 minutes on each side or until the meat reaches desired doneness (for medium-rare, a meat thermometer should read 145°; medium, 160°; well-done, 170°). Let stand for 10 minutes.
- Meanwhile, in a large skillet coated with cooking spray, saute peppers and onion for 5-6 minutes or until tender. Add garlic; cook 1 minute longer. Sprinkle with cilantro and rosemary.
- Place two tortillas on a baking sheet coated with cooking spray. Cut steak into thin strips; place on tortillas. Using a slotted spoon, place pepper mixture over steak. Top with tomatoes, mushrooms, cheese and remaining tortillas; lightly spray top of tortillas with cooking spray.
- Bake at 425° for 5-10 minutes or until golden brown and cheese is melted. Cut each quesadilla into four wedges. **Yield:** 4 servings.

chicken caesar sandwiches

SARA SCHURTZ GONZALEZ | PHOENIX, ARIZONA

I adapted this easy sandwich recipe after eating something similar at a local restaurant. Mayonnaise keeps the chicken so moist, and Parmesan cheese gives it delightful tang. Serve it with your favorite crispy chips for a satisfying, yet not-too-heavy, weekend lunch.

PREP: 15 MIN. BAKE: 25 MIN.

- 4 boneless skinless chicken breast halves (4 ounces *each*)
- 1/3 cup mayonnaise
- 1/2 cup seasoned bread crumbs
- 1/2 cup grated Parmesan cheese
- 2 teaspoons minced fresh parsley
- 1/4 cup creamy Caesar salad dressing
- 4 hard rolls, split
- 4 romaine leaves
- 1 medium tomato, sliced

■ Flatten chicken to 1/4-in. thickness; spread mayonnaise over both sides. Combine the bread crumbs, cheese and parsley; sprinkle over chicken.

■ Place in a greased 11-in. x 7-in. baking dish. Bake, uncovered, at 375° for 25-30 minutes or until the meat is no longer pink.

■ Spread salad dressing over cut sides of rolls. Place romaine on roll bottoms; layer with chicken and tomato. Replace roll tops. **Yield:** 4 servings.

super pizza subs

KATHY BENNETT | HATTIESBURG, MISSISSIPPI

My husband loves this zippy sub sandwich. Italian sausage, pepperoni and salami provide the robust flavors in the family-pleasing fare. If you'd like, serve the crispy subs with extra pizza sauce for dipping.

PREP/TOTAL TIME: 30 MIN.

- 6 submarine sandwich buns (about 9 inches), split
- 1/2 pound bulk Italian sausage, cooked and drained
- 1 pound shaved deli ham
- 1 can (8 ounces) pizza sauce
- 18 slices part-skim mozzarella cheese (1 ounce *each*)
- 1 medium onion, halved and thinly sliced
- 36 mild banana pepper rings
- 2 packages (3-1/2 ounces *each*) sliced pepperoni
- 1/4 pound thinly sliced hard salami

■ On bottom half of sandwich buns, layer sausage, ham, pizza sauce, cheese, onion, banana peppers, pepperoni and salami. Replace tops. Wrap each sandwich in heavy-duty foil; place on baking sheets. Bake at 425° for 12-15 minutes or until cheese is melted. **Yield:** 6 servings.

roasted pepper 'n' egg salad sandwiches

RUBY WILLIAMS | BOGALUSA, LOUISIANA

Here's a fresh take on a classic sandwich. The egg salad gets an extra boost from red peppers and zesty seasonings.

PREP/TOTAL TIME: 15 MIN.

- 1/4 cup mayonnaise
- 2 tablespoons diced roasted sweet red pepper
- 1 tablespoon minced fresh parsley
- 1/2 teaspoon Dijon mustard
- 1/2 teaspoon dried oregano
- 1/8 teaspoon pepper
- 3 hard-cooked eggs, chopped
- 4 slices multigrain bread
- 2 romaine leaves

■ In a small bowl, combine the first six ingredients. Add the eggs; stir gently to combine. Spread mixture over two slices of bread. Top with the romaine and remaining bread. **Yield:** 2 servings.

Roasting Peppers

To roast your own red peppers, place whole peppers on aluminum foil; broil for about 10 minutes on each side or until blackened. Gather the foil around each pepper until cooled. Peel off the skin.

jerk chicken wraps

SALLY SIBTHORPE | SHELBY TOWNSHIP, MICHIGAN

Mango chutney sweetens these mouthwatering, jerk-seasoned wraps. Great picnic fare, they're scrumptious served warm or cold.

PREP/TOTAL TIME: 25 MIN.

- 1/2 pound boneless skinless chicken breast, cut into strips
- 3/4 teaspoon Caribbean jerk seasoning, *divided*
- 2 teaspoons olive oil
- 1/4 cup cream cheese, softened
- 2 flour tortillas (8 inches), warmed
- 1/4 cup mango chutney
- 2 lettuce leaves
- 1/4 cup julienned sweet red pepper
- 4 thin slices red onion

■ Sprinkle chicken with 1/2 teaspoon jerk seasoning. In a nonstick skillet over medium heat, cook chicken in oil for 5-6 minutes or until meat is no longer pink.

■ In a small bowl, combine cream cheese and remaining jerk seasoning; spread over tortillas. Spread chutney over cream cheese. Layer with the lettuce, chicken, red pepper and onion. Roll up tightly. **Yield:** 2 servings.

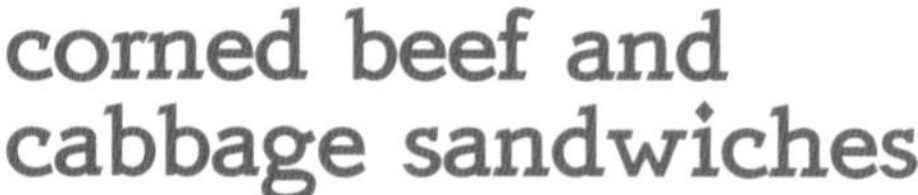

corned beef and cabbage sandwiches

TASTE OF HOME TEST KITCHEN

You don't have to wait for St. Patrick's Day to serve these festive sandwiches. Your family is sure to enjoy the cabbage and tender corned beef piled high on a hard roll any time of year.

PREP/TOTAL TIME: 10 MIN.

- 1/3 cup mayonnaise
- 1 tablespoon white vinegar
- 1/4 teaspoon ground mustard

- 1/4 teaspoon celery seed
- 1/4 teaspoon pepper
- 1-1/2 cups thinly shredded raw cabbage
- 4 kaiser *or* hard rolls, split
- 3/4 to 1 pound cooked corned beef, sliced

■ In a small bowl, combine the mayonnaise, vinegar, mustard, celery seed and pepper until blended. Stir in cabbage. Spoon onto the bottom halves of rolls. Cover with corned beef; replace roll tops. **Yield:** 4 servings.

creamy beef sandwiches

DORIS BYERLY | MONDOVI, WISCONSIN

This is a quick way to create a sandwich with a special taste. The creamy dressing and combination of beef and cheese make them ideal for lunches on the go.

PREP/TOTAL TIME: 20 MIN.

- 1/2 cup mayonnaise
- 2 to 3 tablespoons prepared ranch salad dressing
- 2 packages (2-1/2 ounces *each*) thinly sliced dried beef, chopped
- 1 cup (4 ounces) shredded cheddar cheese
- 12 slices white bread
- 1-1/2 cups shredded lettuce

■ In a small bowl, combine mayonnaise and ranch dressing. Stir in the beef and cheese. Spread about 1/3 cup on six slices of bread; top with lettuce and remaining bread. **Yield:** 6 servings.

hearty chicken club

DEBBIE JOHANESEN | MISSOULA, MONTANA

I discovered the recipe for this sizable sandwich awhile back and modified it to suit our tastes. We love it...the only problem is trying to open wide enough to take a bite!

PREP/TOTAL TIME: 15 MIN.

- 1/4 cup mayonnaise
- 2 tablespoons salsa
- 4 slices seven-grain sandwich bread
- 2 lettuce leaves
- 4 slices tomato
- 8 ounces sliced cooked chicken *or* turkey
- 4 bacon strips, cooked
- 4 slices cheddar cheese
- 1 ripe avocado, sliced

■ Combine mayonnaise and salsa; spread on two slices of bread. Layer with lettuce, tomato, chicken or turkey, bacon, cheese and avocado. Top with remaining bread. **Yield:** 2 servings.

monterey artichoke panini

JEAN ECOS | HARTLAND, WISCONSIN

Looking for a new sandwich idea? This wonderful combination of cheese, artichokes, spinach and tomatoes will have you smacking your lips.

PREP/TOTAL TIME: 25 MIN.

- 4 slices sourdough *or* multi-grain bread
- 4 slices Monterey Jack cheese (3/4 ounce *each*)
- 1/2 cup water-packed artichoke hearts, rinsed, drained and halved
- 1/2 cup fresh baby spinach
- 4 slices tomato
- 1 tablespoon butter, softened

■ On two slices of bread, layer a slice of cheese, artichokes, spinach, two slices of tomato and remaining cheese. Top with remaining bread. Spread the butter on outsides of the sandwiches.

■ Cook on a panini maker or indoor grill until bread is toasted and cheese is melted. **Yield:** 2 servings.

zesty salmon burgers

MELANIE DUNN | WILMORE, KANSAS

Burgers are quick and easy to make and are a regular summer main dish at our house. Horseradish adds a tasty zip to convenient canned salmon. Even people who do not care for salmon get "hooked" on its flavor.

PREP/TOTAL TIME: 20 MIN.

- 1 can (14-3/4 ounces) salmon, drained, skin and bones removed
- 2 eggs
- 1/2 cup dry bread crumbs
- 1/4 cup finely chopped onion
- 1/4 cup mayonnaise
- 1 to 2 tablespoons prepared horseradish
- 1 tablespoon pimientos
- 1/4 teaspoon salt
- 1/8 teaspoon pepper
- 2 tablespoons butter
- 4 kaiser rolls, split

Lettuce leaves

■ In a large bowl, combine the first nine ingredients. Shape into four patties.

■ In a large skillet, cook patties in butter over medium heat, for 5-6 minutes on each side or until browned. Serve on rolls with lettuce. **Yield:** 4 servings.

fish po'boys

TASTE OF HOME TEST KITCHEN

These tasty fish sandwiches are sure to hit the spot on a busy weeknight. Feel free to use your favorite brand of frozen breaded fish.

PREP/TOTAL TIME: 30 MIN.

- 2 packages (11.4 ounces *each*) frozen crunchy breaded fish fillets
- 1/2 cup mayonnaise
- 1 tablespoon minced fresh parsley
- 1 tablespoon ketchup
- 2 teaspoons stone-ground mustard
- 1 teaspoon horseradish sauce
- 2 to 4 drops hot pepper sauce
- 1-1/2 cups deli coleslaw
- 6 hamburger buns, split

■ Bake fish according to package directions. Meanwhile, in a small bowl, combine the mayonnaise, parsley, ketchup, mustard, horseradish sauce and hot pepper sauce until blended. Spoon 1/4 cup coleslaw onto the bottom of each bun; top with two pieces of fish. Spread with sauce; replace bun tops. **Yield:** 6 servings.

waldorf chicken salad sandwiches

KAREN SMALL | MAPLE SHADE, NEW JERSEY

Autumn is apple-picking time here in New Jersey. With such an abundance of that delicious fruit, it just seemed natural to toss a chopped apple into my chicken salad.

PREP/TOTAL TIME: 15 MIN.

- 3 cups cubed cooked chicken
- 1 medium tart apple, chopped
- 3/4 cup mayonnaise
- 1/4 cup raisins
- 1/4 cup chopped pecans, toasted
- 1 tablespoon apple juice
- 1/2 teaspoon salt
- 1/4 teaspoon ground nutmeg
- 8 slices pumpernickel bread
- Lettuce leaves, optional

■ In a large bowl, combine the first eight ingredients. Spread about 1 cup of the chicken salad over four slices of bread. Top with the lettuce if desired and the remaining bread. **Yield:** 4 servings.

roast beef roll-ups

CLARISSA JO SEEGER | COLUMBIANA, OHIO

So quick to prepare and a great party sandwich, these roll-ups get raves at tailgating parties! Serve in thin slices for appetizers or "reubenize" them by substituting corned beef, sauerkraut, caraway seeds and Thousand Island dressing.

PREP/TOTAL TIME: 15 MIN.

- 1 package (16 ounces) coleslaw mix
- 3/4 cup coleslaw salad dressing
- 1/2 cup mayonnaise
- 1/4 cup Dijon mustard

- 2 tablespoons cider vinegar
- 2 teaspoons sugar
- 1/2 teaspoon celery seed
- 1 pound thinly sliced deli roast beef
- 4 Italian herb flatbread wraps
- 1/2 pound Swiss cheese, thinly sliced

■ In a small bowl, combine the first seven ingredients. Divide roast beef among flatbread wraps. Top with cheese and coleslaw mixture; roll up tightly. **Yield:** 4 servings.

bacon-provolone chicken sandwiches

TASTE OF HOME TEST KITCHEN

Bacon and provolone take this hearty chicken sandwich over the top. Add a little Dijon mustard to spice things up a bit.

PREP/TOTAL TIME: 30 MIN.

- 4 boneless skinless chicken breast halves (6 ounces *each*)
- 1 teaspoon poultry seasoning
- 1 tablespoon olive oil
- 4 kaiser rolls, split
- 8 strips ready-to-serve fully cooked bacon
- 4 slices provolone cheese
- 8 romaine leaves
- 1 small onion, sliced
- 1/4 cup mayonnaise

■ Flatten chicken to 1/4-in. thickness; sprinkle with poultry seasoning. In a large skillet, cook chicken in oil over medium heat for 4-5 minutes on each side or until no longer pink; drain.

■ On roll bottoms, layer the bacon, chicken and cheese. Broil 4-6 in. from the heat for 1-2 minutes or until cheese is melted. Top with the romaine and onion. Spread mayonnaise over cut side of roll tops; replace tops. **Yield:** 4 servings.

pesto-mozzarella turkey burgers

JACQUELINE MARIE MORRIS | BENTONVILLE, ARKANSAS

Here's a great way to eat lighter without giving up flavor. These turkey burgers are stuffed with a tasty pesto sauce that spices up our barbecues.

PREP/TOTAL TIME: 30 MIN.

- 1 tablespoon steak sauce
- 2 garlic cloves, minced
- 3/4 teaspoon salt
- 1/2 teaspoon pepper
- 1-1/2 pounds ground turkey
- 1-1/2 cups (6 ounces) shredded part-skim mozzarella cheese
- 5 tablespoons prepared pesto sauce
- 8 slices marble rye bread *or* 4 Italian rolls, split

Lettuce leaves

- In a large bowl, combine the steak sauce, garlic, salt and pepper. Crumble turkey over mixture and mix well. Shape into eight thin oval patties.
- Combine cheese and pesto. Spoon about 1/4 cup in center of four patties. Top with remaining patties; press edges firmly to seal.
- Grill, covered, over medium heat for 5 minutes on each side or until a meat thermometer reads 165° and juices run clear. Serve on bread with lettuce. **Yield:** 4 servings.

ranch-style pork burgers

KATHLEEN BENNER | WILLIAMSVILLE, ILLINOIS

We use our grill all year, and this recipe is quick and easy enough for busy weeknights. My hefty burgers make a nice alternative to ground beef, and the ranch dressing punches up the flavor.

PREP/TOTAL TIME: 30 MIN.

- 1/2 pound ground pork
- 1 tablespoon ranch salad dressing mix
- 1 teaspoon dried minced onion
- 1/4 teaspoon pepper
- 2 slices Swiss cheese
- 2 hamburger buns, split

Lettuce leaves and tomato slices, optional

- In a small bowl, combine the pork, dressing mix, onion and pepper. Shape into two patties.
- Grill, uncovered, over medium heat for 7-8 minutes on each side or until a meat thermometer reads 160°. Top each patty with a cheese slice; cover and grill just until cheese begins to melt. Serve on buns with lettuce and tomato if desired. **Yield:** 2 servings.

turkey salad on wheat

MERRIJANE RICE | BOUNTIFUL, UTAH

Inspired by the turkey salad at a local deli, I developed this version to suit my family's tastes. You can serve it on whole grain bread for a filling meal or on croissants for an elegant luncheon. Precooked bacon and leftover turkey make it a snap to fix.

PREP/TOTAL TIME: 15 MIN.

- 2 cups chopped romaine
- 1-1/4 cups diced cooked turkey
- 1/2 cup shredded Swiss cheese
- 2 green onions, thinly sliced
- 6 bacon strips, cooked and crumbled
- 1/3 cup frozen peas, thawed
- 1/2 cup mayonnaise
- 1/4 teaspoon pepper
- 12 slices whole wheat bread

- In a large bowl, combine the first six ingredients. Add mayonnaise and pepper; toss to coat. Spread on six slices of bread; top with remaining bread. **Yield:** 6 servings.

triple-decker salmon club

JANE BONE | CAPE CORAL, FLORIDA

You're in for a tasty treat with these deliciously different triple-deckers. Even those who don't ordinarily like salmon or cottage cheese enjoy them.

PREP/TOTAL TIME: 15 MIN.

- 3/4 cup 4% cottage cheese
- 1/4 cup dill pickle relish
- 1 can (6 ounces) salmon, drained, bones and skin removed
- 1 celery rib, chopped
- 6 slices bread, toasted
- 2 lettuce leaves, optional

- In a small bowl, combine cottage cheese and pickle relish. In another bowl, combine salmon and celery. For each sandwich, top one piece of toast with lettuce if desired and half of the cottage cheese mixture. Top with a second piece of toast; spread with half of the salmon mixture. Top with a third piece of toast. **Yield:** 2 servings.

No Bones About It

Some people like to remove the bones from canned salmon...but they are edible. If you don't like the texture, mash the drained salmon; the bones will become undetectable in seconds.

roast beef blt

TASTE OF HOME TEST KITCHEN

A creamy horseradish spread adds zip to each satisfying wedge of this stacked sandwich. It tastes special yet is incredibly simple to prepare. Use any bread you like or change the sandwich fillings.

PREP/TOTAL TIME: 15 MIN.

- 1 loaf (12 ounces) focaccia bread
- 1/2 cup mayonnaise
- 1 teaspoon prepared horseradish
- 3 lettuce leaves
- 3/4 pound sliced deli roast beef
- 6 bacon strips, cooked
- 8 slices tomato

■ Cut the focaccia bread in half horizontally. Combine mayonnaise and horseradish; spread over cut sides of bread. Layer the lettuce, roast beef, bacon and tomato over bread bottom; replace bread top. Cut into wedges. **Yield:** 4 servings.

toasted pb & banana sandwiches

MARIAN PICKETT | ARGYLE, WISCONSIN

A sandwich worthy of Elvis himself, this grilled, finger-licking treat may surprise you, too, with its flavor. I saw the recipe and thought "no way"...but it's delicious!

PREP/TOTAL TIME: 20 MIN.

- 2 large ripe bananas
- 6 tablespoons reduced-fat peanut butter
- 8 slices whole wheat bread
- 2 tablespoons honey

Refrigerated butter-flavored spray

■ Cut each banana in half widthwise, then cut each half lengthwise into four pieces. Spread peanut butter on bread. Place banana slices on four slices of bread; drizzle with honey. Top with remaining bread.

■ Spritz outsides of sandwiches with butter-flavored spray. In a large nonstick skillet, toast sandwiches over medium heat until golden brown. **Yield:** 4 servings.

tortilla burgers

KATIE KOZIOLEK | HARTLAND, MINNESOTA

With pork instead of ground beef and tortillas in place of buns, these Southwestern-style burgers stand out from all others.

PREP/TOTAL TIME: 25 MIN.

- 1 teaspoon ground cumin
- 1/2 teaspoon dried oregano
- 1/2 teaspoon crushed red pepper flakes
- 1/4 teaspoon seasoned salt
- 1 pound ground pork
- 4 flour *or* corn tortillas (6 inches), warmed

Salsa, sour cream and shredded cheddar cheese, optional

■ In a small bowl, combine the first four ingredients. Crumble the pork over seasonings and mix well. Shape meat into four oval patties.

■ Grill, covered, over medium heat for 6-7 minutes on each side or until a meat thermometer reads 160° and juices run clear. Serve on tortillas with salsa, sour cream and cheese if desired. **Yield:** 4 servings.

firecracker burgers

KELLY WILLIAMS | MORGANVILLE, NEW JERSEY

Cheese-stuffed jalapenos add a little "pop" to tasty stuffed burgers. Topping the patties with guacamole and cheese dip is dynamite!

PREP: 20 MIN. GRILL: 15 MIN.

- 1 pound lean ground beef (90% lean)
- 1/4 cup chunky salsa
- 4 frozen breaded cheddar cheese jalapeno peppers, thawed
- 1/4 cup guacamole
- 4 hamburger buns, split and toasted
- 4 lettuce leaves
- 1/4 cup salsa con queso dip
- 1/4 cup sliced plum tomatoes
- 2 tablespoons sliced ripe olives
- 4 thin slices sweet onion

- In a large bowl, combine the beef and salsa. Shape into four patties. Place a jalapeno in the center of each; wrap beef around jalapeno, forming a ball. Reshape into patties, about 3-1/2 to 4 in. in diameter and 1 in. thick.
- Grill, covered, over medium-hot heat for 7-8 minutes on each side or until meat is no longer pink and a meat thermometer reads 160°.
- Spread guacamole over toasted side of bun tops. On each bun bottom, layer the lettuce, a burger, con queso dip, tomatoes, olives and onion; replace tops. **Yield:** 4 servings.

Festive Fourth

Firecracker Burgers will add some spark to July Fourth celebrations...and other occasions throughout the year! For an all-American meal, serve your favorite potato salad on the side.

barbecued pork sandwiches

MARY GOFF | ROWLESBURG, WEST VIRGINIA

A sweet yet tangy barbecue sauce flavors juicy, shredded pork to create savory sandwiches.

PREP/TOTAL TIME: 30 MIN.

- 3 tablespoons chopped onion
- 1 tablespoon butter
- 1 can (8 ounces) tomato sauce
- 2 tablespoons brown sugar
- 1-1/2 teaspoons Worcestershire sauce
- 1 teaspoon lemon juice
- 1 teaspoon prepared mustard
- 1 cup shredded *or* diced cooked pork
- 2 hamburger buns, split

■ In a small saucepan, saute onion in butter until tender. Stir in the tomato sauce, brown sugar, Worcestershire sauce, lemon juice and mustard. Bring to a boil. Reduce heat; simmer, uncovered, for 20 minutes.

■ Add pork; cook and stir until heated through. Serve on buns. **Yield:** 2 servings.

hot turkey sandwiches

ELAINE COOLEY | LOUISVILLE, KENTUCKY

My mom made turkey sandwiches as far back as I can remember...and I still make them often today. You'll love their fast-to-fix convenience.

PREP/TOTAL TIME: 20 MIN.

- 4 slices bread, toasted
- 4 teaspoons butter, softened
- 4 slices cooked turkey
- 1/2 cup shredded cheddar *or* process American cheese
- 8 bacon strips, cooked and drained
- 4 slices tomato, optional
- 1/4 cup grated Parmesan cheese

■ Spread each slice of toast with 1 teaspoon butter. Place toast in a shallow baking pan. Top with the turkey, cheddar cheese, two bacon strips and tomato if desired. Sprinkle with Parmesan cheese.

■ Broil 5 in. from the heat for 3-4 minutes or until cheddar cheese is melted. **Yield:** 4 servings.

crab melt loaf

LOUISE FAUTH | FOREMOST, ALBERTA

These decadent sandwiches are always a speedy supper solution. It's wonderful whether served hot on French bread or cold over fresh salad greens.

PREP/TOTAL TIME: 30 MIN.

- 1 pound imitation crabmeat, chopped
- 1/2 cup mayonnaise
- 1/4 cup thinly sliced green onions
- 1/4 cup diced celery
- 2 cups (8 ounces) shredded part-skim mozzarella cheese
- 1/8 teaspoon salt
- 1/8 teaspoon pepper
- 1 loaf (1 pound) unsliced French bread, halved lengthwise

■ In a large bowl, combine the crab, mayonnaise, green onions and celery. Stir in the cheese, salt and pepper. Spread over bottom of bread; replace top.

■ Wrap loaf in a large piece of heavy-duty aluminum foil. Place on an ungreased baking sheet. Bake at 400° for 20 minutes or until heated through. Cut into slices and serve. **Yield:** 8 servings.

crunchy tuna wraps

EDIE FARM | FARMINGTON, NEW MEXICO

Packed with protein-rich tuna and fresh crunchy veggies, these colorful wraps have sensational flavor...and they're good for you, too.

PREP/TOTAL TIME: 20 MIN.

- 2 tablespoons reduced-fat mayonnaise
- 2-1/4 teaspoons prepared mustard
- 1 pouch (7.06 ounces) light water-packed tuna, flaked
- 1/4 cup sliced water chestnuts, chopped
- 1/4 cup chopped green onions
- 1/4 cup finely chopped celery
- 3 tablespoons chopped sweet red pepper
- 2 spinach tortillas (8 inches), room temperature
- 1 cup shredded lettuce

■ In a small bowl, combine mayonnaise and mustard. Stir in the tuna, water chestnuts, onions, celery and red pepper. Spread over the tortillas; top with lettuce. Roll up tightly. **Yield:** 2 servings.

hoisin pork sandwiches

TASTE OF HOME TEST KITCHEN

Tuck warm pork slices, Chinese cabbage, red pepper and zesty hoisin sauce into toasty kaiser rolls for hefty sandwiches. They make a delicious, handheld meal in minutes!

PREP/TOTAL TIME: 15 MIN.

- 3/4 cup sliced sweet red pepper
- 2 green onions, cut into 2-inch pieces
- 2 teaspoons canola oil
- 1/2 cup shredded Chinese *or* napa cabbage
- 2 tablespoons mayonnaise

- 4 teaspoons hoisin sauce
- 2 kaiser rolls, split and toasted
- 1/2 pound cooked pork, sliced and warmed

■ In a small skillet, saute red pepper and onions in oil until tender. Add cabbage; saute 1 minute longer.

■ Combine mayonnaise and hoisin sauce; spread over roll bottoms. Top with pork and vegetable mixture; replace roll tops. **Yield:** 2 servings.

garbanzo bean pitas

SUSAN LEBRUN | SULPHUR, LOUISIANA

This wonderful, meatless recipe is great for informal dinners and quick lunches alike. I add a little horseradish to my pitas for extra flair.

PREP/TOTAL TIME: 20 MIN.

- 1 can (15 ounces) garbanzo beans *or* chickpeas, rinsed and drained
- 1/2 cup fat-free mayonnaise
- 1 tablespoon water
- 2 tablespoons minced fresh parsley
- 2 tablespoons chopped walnuts
- 1 tablespoon chopped onion
- 1 garlic clove, minced
- 1/8 teaspoon pepper
- 2 whole wheat pita breads (6 inches), halved
- 4 lettuce leaves
- 1/2 small cucumber, thinly sliced
- 1 small tomato, seeded and chopped
- 1/4 cup fat-free ranch salad dressing, optional

■ In a blender, combine the first eight ingredients; cover and process until blended. Spoon 1/3 cup bean mixture into each pita half. Top with lettuce, cucumber and tomato. Serve with ranch dressing if desired. **Yield:** 4 servings.

black bean rice burgers

LAURA WIMBROW | OCEAN CITY, MARYLAND

A simple, salsa-and-sour cream sauce helps dress up vegetarian burgers. My fiance, who's a confirmed meat-and-potatoes man, loves these sandwiches and asks for them often.

PREP/TOTAL TIME: 20 MIN.

- 1 can (15 ounces) black beans, rinsed and drained
- 1 cup cooked brown rice
- 1 small onion, finely chopped
- 1 egg, lightly beaten
- 2 tablespoons plus 1/4 cup salsa, *divided*
- 1/4 cup reduced-fat sour cream
- 4 lettuce leaves
- 4 slices reduced-fat cheddar cheese (1 ounce *each*)
- 4 hamburger buns, split

- In a large bowl, mash beans with a fork. Add the rice, onion, egg and 2 tablespoons salsa; mix well. Drop by 1/2 cupfuls into a large nonstick skillet coated with cooking spray. Flatten to 1/2-in. thickness. Cook over medium heat for 4-5 minutes on each side or until firm and browned.
- In a small bowl, combine sour cream and remaining salsa. Place a lettuce leaf, burger, sour cream mixture and slice of cheese on bun. **Yield:** 4 servings.

Rice at the Ready

Since rice freezes well, cooking it in advance is a good way to get ahead on meal preparation. Cook rice according to package directions. Let cool, then freeze in airtight bags. Reheat it as needed.

guacamole burgers

PATRICIA COLLINS | IMBLER, OREGON

Classic bacon cheeseburgers are taken to a whole new level with zippy green chilies and melted Monterey Jack. A dollop of guacamole adds a delicious twist.

PREP/TOTAL TIME: 30 MIN.

- 8 bacon strips
- 1/2 cup chopped onion
- 1 can (4 ounces) chopped green chilies
- 1 pound ground beef
- 4 slices Monterey Jack cheese
- 4 sandwich buns, split and toasted
- 1/4 cup guacamole

■ In a large skillet, cook bacon over medium heat until crisp. Remove to paper towels to drain. Meanwhile, in a small bowl, combine onion and green chilies; set aside. Shape beef into eight patties. Top half of the patties with onion mixture. Cover with remaining patties and firmly press edges to seal.

■ Grill, covered, over medium heat for 5-7 minutes on each side or until a meat thermometer reads 160° and juices run clear. Top each with bacon and cheese. Grill 1 minute longer or until cheese is melted. Serve on buns with guacamole. **Yield:** 4 servings.

sloppy joes

ANNA ADAMS | CHATSWORTH, CALIFORNIA

I adjusted three different recipes to come up with this one. Kids like the tangy taste and request the sandwiches for birthday parties.

PREP/TOTAL TIME: 20 MIN.

- 1 pound ground beef
- 1 cup finely chopped onion
- 3/4 cup finely chopped sweet red *or* green pepper
- 1/4 cup finely chopped celery
- 1/2 cup ketchup
- 1 tablespoon white vinegar
- 2 teaspoons chili powder
- 1-1/2 teaspoons Worcestershire sauce
- 1 teaspoon sugar
- 1 teaspoon salt
- 6 hamburger buns, split

■ In a large skillet, cook beef, onion, red pepper and celery over medium heat until meat is no longer pink and vegetables are crisp-tender; drain.

■ In a small bowl, combine the ketchup, vinegar, chili powder, Worcestershire sauce, sugar and salt; stir into beef mixture. Simmer, uncovered, for 10 minutes, stirring occasionally. Serve on buns. **Yield:** 6 servings.

apple-swiss turkey sandwiches

GLORIA UPDYKE | FRONT ROYAL, VIRGINIA

Honey mustard adds a sweet tang to this hearty concoction. Apple slices, Swiss cheese, cucumber and turkey are layered between slices of nutritious multi-grain bread. These delicious sandwiches pack well to take on-the-go.

PREP/TOTAL TIME: 15 MIN.

- 3 tablespoons honey mustard
- 8 slices multi-grain bread, toasted
- 2 medium unpeeled apples, thinly sliced
- 8 slices reduced-fat Swiss cheese
- 1/2 cup thinly sliced cucumber
- 8 ounces thinly sliced cooked turkey breast

■ Lightly spread mustard on each slice of toast; set aside. Place apples on a microwave-safe plate and microwave, uncovered, on high for 1 minute or until slightly softened.

■ Arrange half of the apple slices and cheese on 4 slices of toast. Top with cucumber and turkey. Add remaining apple and cheese slices. Top with remaining toast, mustard side down. **Yield:** 4 servings.

Editor's Note: This recipe was tested in a 1,100-watt microwave.

ham and mango wraps

BONNIE AUSTIN | GRENADA, MISSISSIPPI

The unusual pairing of savory ham and sweet, juicy mango in these luscious wraps makes a refreshing lunch. For extra flavor and pretty color, add some chopped watercress or parsley.

PREP/TOTAL TIME: 25 MIN.

- 1/3 cup sour cream
- 1/3 cup mayonnaise
- 2 tablespoons minced fresh basil
- 2 tablespoons minced chives
- 1 tablespoon lemon juice
- 1/8 teaspoon salt
- 1/8 teaspoon pepper
- 3 cups cubed fully cooked ham (about 1 pound)
- 2 to 3 medium mangoes, peeled, chopped and patted dry (about 2 cups)
- 6 flour tortillas (10 inches), room temperature

■ In a large bowl, combine the first seven ingredients. Stir in ham and mangoes. Spoon about 2/3 cup down the center of each tortilla; roll up tightly. **Yield:** 6 servings.

club sandwiches

JANET MILLER | MIDLAND, TEXAS

I'm a busy wife, mother, grandmother and great-grandmother, and I love to cook. One of my family's favorite layered sandwiches is what we call "hunka munka"...and it's a complete meal.

PREP/TOTAL TIME: 25 MIN.

- 1/2 cup mayonnaise
- 4 French rolls, split
- 1 cup shredded lettuce
- 8 slices tomato
- 1 medium ripe avocado, peeled and sliced
- 1/4 cup prepared Italian salad dressing

- 1/2 teaspoon coarsely ground pepper
- 12 cooked bacon strips
- 1/2 pound sliced deli turkey
- 1/2 pound sliced deli ham
- 4 slices Swiss cheese

■ Spread mayonnaise over cut sides of rolls. On roll bottoms, layer the lettuce, tomato and avocado. Drizzle with the dressing; sprinkle with pepper. Layer with bacon, turkey, ham and cheese. Replace roll tops. **Yield:** 4 servings.

basil-tomato grilled cheese

SYLVIA SCHMITT | SUN CITY, ARIZONA

The tastes of summer abound in this easy Italian-style grilled cheese sandwich. I am always busy, especially around lunchtime, so I need something that is quick and easy to prepare, but tasty and satisfying as well.

PREP/TOTAL TIME: 20 MIN.

- 8 slices Italian bread (3/4 inch thick)
- 8 slices part-skim mozzarella cheese
- 2 large plum tomatoes, sliced
- 2 tablespoons minced fresh basil
- 2 teaspoons balsamic vinegar
- Salt and pepper to taste
- 1/4 cup olive oil
- 3 tablespoons grated Parmesan cheese
- 1/4 teaspoon garlic powder

■ On four slices of bread, layer the cheese and tomatoes; sprinkle with the basil, vinegar, salt and pepper. Top with remaining bread.

■ In a small bowl, combine the oil, Parmesan cheese and garlic powder; brush over the outsides of each sandwich.

■ In a small skillet over medium heat, toast sandwiches until golden brown on both sides and cheese is melted. **Yield:** 4 servings.

chicken satay wraps

TASTE OF HOME TEST KITCHEN

Rotisserie chicken or refrigerated grilled chicken strips can be used to speed up the preparation of this recipe.

PREP/TOTAL TIME: 15 MIN.

- 2 tablespoons olive oil
- 2 tablespoons creamy peanut butter
- 2 green onions, chopped
- 1 teaspoon reduced-sodium soy sauce
- 1/4 teaspoon pepper
- 2 cups sliced cooked chicken
- 1 cup coleslaw mix
- 4 flour tortillas (8 inches), room temperature

■ In a large bowl, whisk the oil, peanut butter, onions, soy sauce and pepper until combined. Add the chicken and toss to coat. Sprinkle 1/4 cup of the coleslaw mix over each tortilla; top with the chicken mixture. Roll up tightly. **Yield:** 4 servings.

p. 71

soups & salads

rocky ford chili

KAREN GOLDEN | PHOENIX, ARIZONA

This hearty chili dish was served in the cafeteria when my brother and sister were in grade school. My siblings described it to my mother so she could duplicate it at home.

PREP/TOTAL TIME: 10 MIN.

- 2 cans (14.3 ounces *each*) chili with beans
- 1 package (10 ounces) frozen corn
- 4 cups corn chips
- 1 cup shredded lettuce
- 1 cup (4 ounces) shredded Mexican cheese blend
- 1 can (2-1/4 ounces) sliced ripe olives, drained
- 1/4 cup sour cream
- 1/4 cup salsa

■ In a large microwave-safe bowl, microwave chili and corn on high for 2-4 minutes or until heated through. Place corn chips in four large soup bowls; top with the chili mixture, lettuce, cheese, olives, sour cream and salsa. **Yield:** 4 servings.

Editor's Note: This recipe was tested in a 1,100-watt microwave.

fish chowder

PAT GONET | WENHAM, MASSACHUSETTS

The creamy, comforting flavor of my mom's chunky seafood chowder always receives compliments.

PREP/TOTAL TIME: 30 MIN.

- 1 bacon strip, diced
- 2 tablespoons chopped onion
- 1/2 cup water
- 1 medium potato, cubed
- 1/4 teaspoon seafood seasoning

Dash salt and pepper

- 1 haddock, halibut *or* cod fillet (6 ounces)
- 1 cup 2% milk
- 2 teaspoons butter

■ In a large saucepan, saute bacon and onion until tender. Add the water, potato, seafood seasoning, salt and pepper. Bring to a boil. Reduce heat; place fillet on top.

■ Cover and cook for 15-20 minutes or until fish flakes easily with a fork. Stir in milk and butter; heat through. Flake fish into pieces before serving. **Yield:** 2 servings.

potato bacon chowder

JACQUE MANNING | BURBANK, SOUTH DAKOTA

This chowder is like a bacon-topped baked potato in a bowl. On cold winter days, my family is thrilled to see this meal on the table.

PREP/TOTAL TIME: 30 MIN.

- 2 cups cubed peeled potatoes
- 1 cup water
- 8 bacon strips
- 1 cup chopped onion
- 1/2 cup chopped celery
- 1 can (10-3/4 ounces) condensed cream of chicken soup, undiluted
- 1-3/4 cups milk
- 1 cup (8 ounces) sour cream
- 1/2 teaspoon salt
- Dash pepper
- 1 tablespoon minced fresh parsley

■ Place potatoes in a small saucepan and cover with water. Bring to a boil. Reduce heat; cover and cook for 10-15 minutes or until tender.

■ Meanwhile, in a large skillet, cook the bacon until crisp; remove to paper towels to drain and set aside.

■ In the same skillet, saute onion and celery in drippings until tender; drain. Add to undrained potatoes. Stir in the soup, milk, sour cream, salt and pepper. Cook over low heat for 10 minutes or until heated through (do not boil).

■ Crumble bacon; set aside 1/4 cup. Add remaining bacon to soup along with parsley. Sprinkle with reserved bacon. **Yield:** 6 servings.

The Business of Bacon

Rarely does a recipe call for an entire package of bacon. But you may want to cook all of it anyway. Drain, cool and freeze the unused slices in a resealable plastic bag. As needed, remove any number of strips; reheat for a short time in the microwave. Enjoy the strips whole at breakfast and in sandwiches. Or cut up in recipes calling for diced cooked bacon.

vinaigrette veggie salad

CONNIE SMALL | SCHOOLCRAFT, MICHIGAN

All of my children love my salad. It's easy to make and attractive, too. Sometimes I cut up the vegetables ahead of time so dinner preparation goes faster.

PREP/TOTAL TIME: 15 MIN.

- 1 medium cucumber, sliced
- 1 medium green pepper, cut into 1-inch strips
- 1 cup halved cherry tomatoes
- 1/4 teaspoon salt
- 1/4 teaspoon celery seed
- 2 tablespoons canola oil
- 1 tablespoon white vinegar

■ In a serving bowl, combine the cucumber, green pepper and tomatoes. Sprinkle with salt and celery seed. In a small bowl, whisk oil and vinegar. Pour over salad; toss to coat. **Yield:** 6 servings.

white chili with chicken

CHRISTY CAMPOS | RICHMOND, VIRGINIA

Folks who enjoy a change from traditional tomato-based chili will enjoy this version. The flavorful blend has tender chunks of chicken, white beans and just enough zip.

PREP/TOTAL TIME: 30 MIN.

- 1 medium onion, chopped
- 1 jalapeno pepper, seeded and chopped, optional
- 1 tablespoon canola oil
- 2 garlic cloves, minced
- 4 cups chicken broth
- 2 cans (15-1/2 ounces *each*) great northern beans, rinsed and drained
- 2 tablespoons minced fresh parsley
- 1 tablespoon lime juice
- 1 to 1-1/4 teaspoons ground cumin
- 2 tablespoons cornstarch
- 1/4 cup cold water
- 2 cups cubed cooked chicken

■ In a large saucepan, cook onion and jalapeno if desired in oil until tender. Add garlic; cook 1 minute longer. Stir in the broth, beans, parsley, lime juice and ground cumin; bring to a boil. Reduce heat; cover and simmer for 10 minutes, stirring occasionally.

■ Combine cornstarch and water until smooth; gradually stir into chili. Add chicken. Bring to a boil; cook and stir for 2 minutes or until thickened. **Yield:** 6 servings.

Editor's Note: When cutting hot peppers, disposable gloves are recommended. Avoid touching your face.

chinese chicken soup

TASTE OF HOME TEST KITCHEN

This attractive simple soup begins with frozen stir-fry vegetables. Convenient refrigerated minced gingerroot adds to the Asian flavor.

PREP/TOTAL TIME: 25 MIN.

- 3 cans (14-1/2 ounces *each*) chicken broth
- 1 package (16 ounces) frozen stir-fry vegetable blend
- 2 cups cubed cooked chicken
- 1 teaspoon minced fresh gingerroot
- 1 teaspoon soy sauce
- 1/4 teaspoon sesame oil

■ In a large saucepan, combine all the ingredients. Bring to a boil. Reduce heat; cover and simmer for 15 minutes or until heated through. **Yield:** 6 servings.

sausage corn chili

RHEA LEASE | COLMAN, SOUTH DAKOTA

Nicely spiced Italian sausage and crunchy corn distinguish this thick chili from usual offerings. My daughter won a national contest with the recipe.

PREP/TOTAL TIME: 20 MIN.

- 1 pound bulk Italian sausage
- 1 tablespoon dried minced onion
- 1 can (16 ounces) kidney beans, rinsed and drained
- 1 can (15-1/4 ounces) whole kernel corn, drained
- 1 can (15 ounces) tomato sauce
- 2/3 cup picante sauce
- 1/3 to 1/2 cup water
- 1 teaspoon chili powder

■ In a large saucepan, cook sausage and onion over medium heat until meat is no longer pink; drain. Stir in the remaining ingredients. Simmer, uncovered, for 5-10 minutes or until heated through. **Yield:** 6 servings.

blt bread salad

TONYA VOWELS | VINE GROVE, KENTUCKY

Zesty and fun, this simple salad always draws raves. It tastes just like a BLT, has a light vinaigrette dressing and goes well with so many main dishes.

PREP/TOTAL TIME: 20 MIN.

- 3 cups cubed French bread
- 1 tablespoon water
- 1 tablespoon white wine vinegar
- 1 tablespoon reduced-fat mayonnaise
- 1-1/4 teaspoons sugar
- 1 teaspoon olive oil
- 1-1/2 cups torn leaf lettuce
- 1 large tomato, chopped
- 2 tablespoons crumbled cooked bacon
- 1 tablespoon chopped green onion

■ Place bread cubes on an ungreased baking sheet; coat lightly with cooking spray. Bake at 400° for 8-10 minutes or until golden brown.

■ For dressing, in a small bowl, whisk the water, vinegar, mayonnaise, sugar and oil until smooth. In a large salad bowl, combine the lettuce, tomato and bread cubes. Sprinkle with bacon and onion. Drizzle with dressing and toss to coat. Serve immediately. **Yield:** 4 servings.

macaroni bean soup

SUNDRA HAUCK | BOGALUSA, LOUISIANA

This chunky soup makes a great meatless main dish. Best of all, it's ready to serve in just 25 minutes. We like a lot of macaroni, so I often add more to the recipe.

PREP/TOTAL TIME: 25 MIN.

- 4 cups chicken broth
- 2 cups tomato juice
- 1 cup uncooked elbow macaroni
- 1 cup sliced fresh carrots
- 1 teaspoon minced garlic
- 2 medium yellow summer squash, sliced
- 1 can (16 ounces) kidney beans, rinsed and drained
- 1 teaspoon seasoned salt
- 1/8 teaspoon pepper
- 1/4 cup grated Parmesan cheese
- 1 tablespoon lemon juice

■ In a large saucepan, bring the broth, tomato juice, macaroni, carrots and garlic to a boil. Reduce heat; cover and simmer for 5 minutes or until carrots are tender.

■ Stir in the squash, beans, seasoned salt and pepper; simmer for 10 minutes or until macaroni and vegetables are tender. Remove from the heat; stir in cheese and lemon juice. **Yield:** 9 servings (about 2 quarts).

cheddar ham soup

MARTY MATTHEWS | CLARKSVILLE, TENNESSEE

I knew this recipe was a keeper when my mother-in-law asked for it! Chock-full of leftover ham, veggies and cheese, the hearty soup is creamy and comforting. Even though the recipe makes enough to feed a crowd, don't plan on having leftovers!

PREP/TOTAL TIME: 30 MIN.

- 2 cups diced peeled potatoes
- 2 cups water
- 1/2 cup sliced carrot
- 1/4 cup chopped onion
- 1/4 cup butter, cubed
- 1/4 cup all-purpose flour
- 2 cups milk
- 1/4 to 1/2 teaspoon salt
- 1/4 teaspoon pepper
- 2 cups (8 ounces) shredded cheddar cheese
- 1-1/2 cups cubed fully cooked ham
- 1 cup frozen peas, thawed

■ In a large saucepan, combine the potatoes, water, carrot and onion. Bring to a boil. Reduce heat; cover and cook for 10-15 minutes or until tender.

■ Meanwhile, in another saucepan, melt the butter. Stir in the flour until smooth. Gradually add the milk, salt and pepper. Bring to a boil; cook and stir for 2 minutes or until thickened. Stir in the cheese until melted. Stir into undrained potato mixture. Add the ham and peas; heat through. **Yield:** 7 servings.

italian tossed salad

MARY ELIZABETH COSTELLO | VENICE, FLORIDA

Artichoke hearts add plenty of flavor to this change-of-pace delight. Try it when you'd like to surprise your gang.

PREP/TOTAL TIME: 15 MIN.

- 4 cups torn iceberg lettuce
- 4 cups torn romaine
- 1 cup water-packed artichoke hearts, rinsed, drained and quartered
- 1 jar (2 ounces) sliced pimientos, drained
- 1 small red onion, thinly sliced
- 1/3 cup olive oil
- 2 tablespoons red wine vinegar
- 1/2 teaspoon salt
- 1/4 teaspoon pepper
- 1/3 cup grated Parmesan cheese

■ In a large salad bowl, combine the lettuce, romaine, artichokes, pimientos and onion. Cover and refrigerate until serving.

■ In a small bowl, whisk the oil, vinegar, salt and pepper. Just before serving, whisk the dressing. Pour over the salad; toss gently to coat. Sprinkle with the cheese; toss again. **Yield:** 6 servings.

blue cheese spinach salad

GRACE SANDVIGEN | ROCHESTER, NEW YORK

A simple dressing made of currant jelly and balsamic vinegar coats this colorful salad, sprinkled with crunchy pine nuts. If you like blue cheese, you'll love this refreshing toss.

PREP/TOTAL TIME: 15 MIN.

- 1/2 cup red currant jelly
- 3 tablespoons balsamic vinegar
- 6 cups fresh baby spinach
- 2 pints fresh strawberries, quartered
- 1 cup mandarin oranges, drained
- 1/2 medium red onion, thinly sliced
- 1/2 cup crumbled blue cheese
- 1/2 cup pine nuts, toasted

■ For dressing, heat jelly in a small saucepan over low heat; stir until smooth. Remove from heat; stir in vinegar.

■ In a large bowl, combine the spinach, strawberries, oranges, onion and blue cheese. Drizzle with dressing and toss to coat. Sprinkle with pine nuts. **Yield:** 12 servings.

Blue Cheese Choices

Blue cheese is a great addition to salads because it nicely balances the bitterness of the greens. Roquefort and Gorgonzola are two types of blue cheese that would work well in green salads.

Peeling Pointer

Ever peel a potato only to discover that it's bad inside when you slice it open? Here's a hint: cut potatoes in half before peeling. That way, you'll spend your time only prepping perfect potatoes.

veggie chowder

VICKI KERR | PORTLAND, MAINE

This brothy soup features potatoes, carrots and corn for a delightful entree. Since it's not too heavy, it would also be nice alongside sandwiches.

PREP/TOTAL TIME: 30 MIN.

- 2 cups reduced-sodium chicken broth
- 2 cups cubed peeled potatoes
- 1 cup chopped carrots
- 1/2 cup chopped onion
- 1 can (14-3/4 ounces) cream-style corn
- 1 can (12 ounces) fat-free evaporated milk
- 3/4 cup reduced-fat shredded cheddar cheese
- 1/2 cup sliced fresh mushrooms
- 1/4 teaspoon pepper
- 2 tablespoons real bacon bits

■ In a large saucepan, combine the broth, potatoes, carrots and onion. Bring to a boil. Reduce the heat; simmer, uncovered, for 10-15 minutes or until the vegetables are tender.

■ Add the corn, milk, cheese, mushrooms and pepper. Cook and stir 4-6 minutes longer or until heated through. Sprinkle with bacon. **Yield:** 7 servings.

greek garden salad

GLENDA PARSONAGE | MAPLE CREEK, SASKATCHEWAN

I like to dress up this salad by serving it in a lettuce-lined bowl. But it's gorgeous as well as tasty when served just by itself.

PREP/TOTAL TIME: 15 MIN.

- 2 large tomatoes, chopped
- 3/4 cup chopped cucumber
- 1/2 cup chopped green pepper
- 1/2 cup chopped sweet red pepper
- 1/2 cup crumbled feta cheese
- 1/4 cup thinly sliced green onions
- 1/4 cup sliced ripe olives
- 1/2 cup Italian salad dressing
- 1/8 teaspoon dried oregano
- Leaf lettuce, optional

■ In a bowl, combine the tomatoes, cucumber, peppers, cheese, green onions and olives. Cover and refrigerate until serving.

■ Just before serving, add the salad dressing and oregano; toss to coat. Serve salad in a lettuce-lined bowl if desired. **Yield:** 6 servings.

tortellini soup

DONNA MORGAN | HEND, TENNESSEE

Top bowls of this tasty soup with grated Parmesan cheese...and serve it with crusty bread to round out the meal.

PREP/TOTAL TIME: 20 MIN.

- 2 garlic cloves, minced
- 1 tablespoon butter
- 3 cans (14-1/2 ounces *each*) reduced-sodium chicken broth *or* vegetable broth
- 1 package (9 ounces) refrigerated cheese tortellini
- 1 can (14-1/2 ounces) diced tomatoes with green chilies, undrained
- 1 package (10 ounces) frozen chopped spinach, thawed

■ In a large saucepan, saute garlic in butter for 1 minute. Stir in the broth. Bring to a boil. Add tortellini; cook for 7-9 minutes or until tender. Stir in the tomatoes and spinach; heat through. **Yield:** 5 servings.

tomato olive salad

DONA HOFFMAN | ADDISON, ILLINOIS

With a little brown sugar in its dressing, my salad is amazingly simple and surprisingly sweet. Try topping it with either fresh mozzarella or feta cheese.

PREP/TOTAL TIME: 10 MIN.

- 4 cups torn leaf lettuce
- 1/2 cup cherry tomatoes
- 1/3 cup sliced red onion
- 1 can (2-1/4 ounces) sliced ripe olives, drained

DRESSING:

- 2 tablespoons canola oil
- 1 tablespoon red wine vinegar
- 1 tablespoon brown sugar

■ In a large bowl, combine the lettuce, tomatoes, onion and olives. In a small bowl, whisk the dressing ingredients. Drizzle over salad and toss to coat. **Yield:** 6 servings.

italian peasant soup

KIM KNIGHT | HAMBURG, PENNSYLVANIA

My father shared this recipe with me, and I use it when I need a hearty, healthful meal. It's my sons' favorite. Loaded with sausage, chicken, beans and spinach, the quick soup is nice for special occasions.

PREP/TOTAL TIME: 25 MIN.

- 1 pound Italian sausage links, casings removed and cut into 1-inch slices
- 2 medium onions, chopped
- 6 garlic cloves, chopped
- 1 pound boneless skinless chicken breasts, cut into 1-inch cubes
- 2 cans (15 ounces *each*) cannellini *or* white kidney beans, rinsed and drained
- 2 cans (14-1/2 ounces *each*) chicken broth
- 2 cans (14-1/2 ounces *each*) diced tomatoes
- 1 teaspoon dried basil
- 1 teaspoon dried oregano
- 6 cups fresh spinach leaves, chopped

Shredded Parmesan cheese, optional

- In a Dutch oven, cook sausage and onions over medium heat until no longer pink. Add garlic; cook 1 minute longer. Drain. Add chicken; cook and stir until no longer pink.
- Stir in the beans, broth, tomatoes, basil and oregano. Bring to a boil. Reduce heat; simmer, uncovered, for 10 minutes. Add the spinach and heat just until wilted. Serve with cheese if desired. **Yield:** 11 servings (2-3/4 quarts).

sausage bean soup

GAIL WILKERSON | HOUSE SPRINGS, MISSOURI

This soup is so simple to assemble with ingredients that are a breeze to keep on hand, and it's delicious to boot. The filling broth loaded with potato, sausage and vegetables always makes a satisfying dish in a hurry.

PREP/TOTAL TIME: 30 MIN.

- 4 cups water
- 1 medium potato, peeled and chopped
- 6 brown-and-serve turkey sausage links (1 ounce *each*)
- 2 cans (16 ounces *each*) kidney beans, rinsed and drained
- 1 can (28 ounces) diced tomatoes, undrained
- 1 cup chopped onion
- 1 medium green pepper, chopped
- 1 bay leaf
- 1/2 teaspoon garlic salt
- 1/2 teaspoon seasoned salt
- 1/2 teaspoon pepper
- 1/2 teaspoon dried thyme

- In a large saucepan, bring water and potato to a boil. Cover and cook for 10-15 minutes or until tender (do not drain). Meanwhile, crumble sausage into a skillet; cook over medium heat until browned. Drain if necessary. Add to saucepan.
- Stir in the remaining ingredients. Bring to a boil. Reduce the heat; simmer, uncovered, for 8-10 minutes or until heated through, stirring occasionally. Discard bay leaf. **Yield:** 10 servings.

raisin-walnut spinach salad

BOBBY TAYLOR | MICHIGAN CITY, INDIANA

With just a handful of ingredients, you can toss together this tasty, tangy salad. Not only is it fast, but it's light and refreshing, too.

PREP/TOTAL TIME: 5 MIN.

- 1 cup fresh baby spinach
- 1 tablespoon raisins
- 1 tablespoon chopped walnuts
- 1 tablespoon shredded part-skim mozzarella cheese
- 2 tablespoons sun-dried tomato salad dressing

- Place spinach on a salad plate; top with the raisins, walnuts and cheese. Drizzle with dressing. **Yield:** 1 serving.

shrimp 'n' black bean chili

ELIZABETH HUNT | KIRBYVILLE, TEXAS

It's not spicy, but this chili is sure to heat you up during those cold winter evenings. Since the recipe calls for precooked shrimp and canned goods, it is very quick to prepare.

PREP/TOTAL TIME: 25 MIN.

- 1/2 cup chopped onion
- 1/2 cup chopped green pepper
- 1 tablespoon canola oil
- 1 can (15 ounces) black beans, rinsed and drained
- 1 can (14-1/2 ounces) diced tomatoes, undrained
- 1 cup chicken broth
- 1/3 cup picante sauce
- 1 teaspoon ground cumin
- 1/2 teaspoon dried basil
- 1 pound cooked medium shrimp, peeled and deveined

Hot cooked rice, optional

- In a large saucepan, saute onion and green pepper in oil for 4-5 minutes or until crisp-tender. Stir in the beans, tomatoes, broth, picante sauce, cumin and basil. Reduce heat; simmer, uncovered, for 10-15 minutes or until heated through.
- Add shrimp; simmer 3-4 minutes longer or until heated through. Serve with rice if desired. **Yield:** 6 servings.

spicy chicken rice soup

MARY SHAVER | JONESBORO, ARKANSAS

Ready in less than half an hour, this no-fuss soup takes advantage of canned items for easy assembly.

PREP/TOTAL TIME: 25 MIN.

- 2 cans (14-1/2 ounces *each*) chicken broth
- 3 cups cooked rice
- 2 cups cubed cooked chicken
- 1 can (15-1/4 ounces) whole kernel corn, undrained

- 1 can (11-1/2 ounces) V8 juice
- 1 cup salsa
- 1 can (4 ounces) chopped green chilies, drained
- 1/2 cup chopped green onions
- 2 tablespoons minced fresh cilantro
- 1/2 cup shredded Monterey Jack cheese, optional

- In a large saucepan, combine the first nine ingredients. Bring to a boil. Reduce heat; cover and simmer for 15 minutes or until heated through. Sprinkle with cheese if desired. **Yield:** 8 servings.

black bean pineapple salad

JULIE MUCCILLO | CHICAGO, ILLINOIS

I created this change-of-pace item when I had leftovers in the fridge and needed something healthy and fast. The black beans and pineapple go well together.

PREP/TOTAL TIME: 10 MIN.

- 6 cups fresh baby spinach
- 1 can (15-1/2 ounces) unsweetened pineapple chunks, drained
- 1 can (15 ounces) black beans, rinsed and drained
- 1/2 cup *each* chopped sweet red and orange peppers
- 1/2 cup crumbled feta cheese
- 1/4 cup prepared balsamic vinaigrette

- In a large bowl, combine the spinach, pineapple, beans, peppers and cheese. Drizzle with vinaigrette; toss to coat. Serve with a slotted spoon. **Yield:** 6 servings.

chunky chicken noodle soup

SHARON SKILDUM | MAPLE GROVE, MINNESOTA

If winter holds me in its icy grip, I rely on this hearty, old-fashioned chicken soup to warm me right down to my toes.

PREP/TOTAL TIME: 25 MIN.

- 1/4 cup diced carrot
- 2 tablespoons diced celery
- 2 tablespoons chopped onion
- 1 teaspoon butter
- 2-1/2 cups chicken broth
- 2/3 cup diced cooked chicken
- 1/4 teaspoon salt
- 1/4 teaspoon dried marjoram
- 1/4 teaspoon dried thyme
- Dash pepper
- 1/2 cup uncooked medium egg noodles
- 1 teaspoon minced fresh parsley

■ In a large saucepan, saute the carrot, celery and onion in butter until tender. Stir in the broth, chicken and seasonings; bring to a boil. Reduce heat. Add noodles; cook for 10 minutes or until tender. Sprinkle with parsley. **Yield:** 2 servings.

peanut banana waldorf

BEV SPAIN | BELLVILLE, OHIO

This is a combination of two different salads that my children liked when they were growing up. It probably originated when I was making one or the other of the salads and didn't have enough apples or bananas to make the amount of salad I needed.

PREP/TOTAL TIME: 5 MIN.

- 1 small unpeeled red apple, cut into bite-size pieces
- 1 small firm banana, halved lengthwise and sliced
- 2 tablespoons peanuts
- 2 tablespoons mayonnaise
- 1 tablespoon peanut butter

■ In a small bowl, combine the apple, banana and peanuts. Combine mayonnaise and peanut butter. Pour over fruit mixture; toss to coat. **Yield:** 2 servings.

cheddar 'n' pea tossed salad

MANDY CMOC | YORKTON, SASKATCHEWAN

My family always says, "Yes!" when they see me preparing this easy, no-cook specialty. We live on a farm, so in summer our garden is a handy source for veggie salad ingredients.

PREP/TOTAL TIME: 10 MIN.

5 cups ready-to-serve salad greens
1 medium cucumber, sliced
1 medium tomato, chopped
1 cup cubed cheddar cheese
1/2 cup frozen peas, thawed
2 tablespoons canola oil
1 tablespoon white vinegar
1/4 teaspoon sugar
1/8 teaspoon onion powder
Dash salt and pepper

- In a large bowl, combine the salad greens, cucumber, tomato, cheese and peas.
- In a small bowl, whisk the oil, vinegar, sugar, onion powder, salt and pepper. Pour over salad; toss gently to coat. **Yield:** 8 servings.

ham and bean soup

TASTE OF HOME TEST KITCHEN

If you like ham and bean soup but don't want to spend hours in the kitchen, this tasty and timely version will leave you with a satisfied smile.

PREP/TOTAL TIME: 30 MIN.

2 medium carrots, sliced
2 celery ribs, chopped
1/2 cup chopped onion
2 tablespoons butter
4 cans (15-1/2 ounces *each*) great northern beans, rinsed and drained
4 cups chicken broth
2 cups cubed fully cooked ham
1 teaspoon chili powder
1/2 teaspoon minced garlic
1/4 teaspoon pepper
1 bay leaf

- In a large saucepan, saute the carrots, celery and onion in butter until tender. Stir in the remaining ingredients. Bring to a boil. Reduce heat; cook for 15 minutes or until heated through. Discard bay leaf. **Yield:** 7 servings.

creamy corn crab soup

CAROL ROPCHANI | WILLINGDON, ALBERTA

This creamy soup is fast and easy. Corn really stars in this delectable recipe, and crabmeat makes it a little more special. It will get high marks from both busy cooks and lovers of flavorful homemade food.

PREP/TOTAL TIME: 30 MIN.

1 medium onion, chopped
2 tablespoons butter
3 cups chicken broth
3 cups frozen corn
3 medium potatoes, peeled and diced
1 can (6 ounces) crabmeat, drained, flaked and cartilage removed *or* 1 cup flaked imitation crabmeat
1 cup milk
1/2 teaspoon salt
1/4 teaspoon pepper

- In a large saucepan, saute onion in butter until tender. Add the broth, corn and potatoes; bring to a boil. Reduce heat; cover and simmer for 15 minutes. Remove from the heat; cool slightly.
- In a blender, puree half of the corn mixture. Return to pan. Stir in the crab, milk, salt and pepper; cook over low heat until heated through (do not boil). **Yield:** 7 servings.

vegetable beef soup

MARIE CARLISLE | SUMRALL, MISSISSIPPI

Just brimming with veggies, this hearty soup will warm family and friends right to their toes! We think it's even better the second day.

PREP/TOTAL TIME: 30 MIN.

- 4 cups cubed peeled potatoes
- 6 cups water
- 1 pound ground beef
- 5 teaspoons beef bouillon granules
- 1 can (10-3/4 ounces) condensed tomato soup, undiluted
- 2 cups frozen corn, thawed
- 2 cups frozen sliced carrots, thawed
- 2 cups frozen cut green beans, thawed
- 2 cups frozen sliced okra, thawed
- 3 tablespoons dried minced onion

■ In a Dutch oven, bring potatoes and water to a boil. Cover and cook for 10-15 minutes or until tender. Meanwhile, in a large skillet, cook beef over medium heat until no longer pink; drain.

■ Add the bouillon, soup, vegetables, dried minced onion and beef to the undrained potatoes. Bring to a boil. Reduce heat; simmer, uncovered, for 8-10 minutes or until heated through, stirring occasionally. **Yield:** 14 servings (3-1/2 quarts).

beer cheese soup

SHARON LOCK | FORMAN, NORTH DAKOTA

Onion, parsley, paprika and beer flavor this smooth, rich soup. A family friend used to invite us for Sunday supper and served this several times. I just had to get the recipe!

PREP/TOTAL TIME: 20 MIN.

- 2 tablespoons finely chopped onion
- 1/2 teaspoon butter
- 2 cans (10-3/4 ounces *each*) condensed cream of celery soup, undiluted
- 1 cup beer *or* nonalcoholic beer
- 1 cup milk
- 1 teaspoon Worcestershire sauce
- 1/2 teaspoon dried parsley flakes
- 1/4 teaspoon paprika
- 3/4 pound process cheese (Velveeta), cubed

■ In a large saucepan, saute onion in butter. Stir in the soup, beer, milk, Worcestershire sauce, parsley and paprika. Reduce heat; stir in cheese until melted. Heat through (do not boil). **Yield:** 6 servings.

Cooking with Beer

Experiment with different kinds of beer when making Beer Cheese Soup. Darker beer (like an ale) will provide a more robust taste, while lighter beer (such as a pilsner) will lend a more mellow flavor.

pesto minestrone

NATALIE CATALDO | DES MOINES, IOWA

I turn to store-bought pesto to provide mild flavor to this chunky tortellini and vegetable soup. If you don't like zucchini, simply use another vegetable.

PREP/TOTAL TIME: 30 MIN.

- 1/2 cup chopped onion
- 2 teaspoons olive oil
- 1 teaspoon minced garlic
- 2-1/4 cups water
- 2 cups frozen mixed vegetables
- 1 can (14-1/2 ounces) vegetable broth
- 3/4 teaspoon dried oregano
- 1/2 teaspoon salt
- 1/2 teaspoon pepper
- 1 package (9 ounces) refrigerated cheese tortellini
- 2 cups diced zucchini
- 2 tablespoons prepared pesto

■ In a large saucepan, saute onion in oil until tender. Add garlic; cook 1 minute longer. Stir in the water, mixed vegetables, broth, oregano, salt and pepper. Bring to a boil. Reduce heat; cover and simmer for 3 minutes.

■ Add the tortellini, zucchini and pesto. Simmer, uncovered, 7-9 minutes longer or until pasta and vegetables are tender. **Yield:** 4 servings.

white turkey chili

LAURI POBANZ | LINCOLN, NEBRASKA

I combine white corn, great northern beans and leftover turkey to prepare this steaming chili. I appreciate how fast it is to make—and that my husband and our four children like it. I often bake a pan of corn bread to go with it.

PREP/TOTAL TIME: 30 MIN.

- 1/3 cup chopped onion
- 1 celery rib, chopped
- 1-1/2 teaspoons canola oil
- 1-3/4 cups chicken *or* turkey broth
- 2 cups cubed cooked turkey
- 1 can (15-1/2 ounces) great northern beans, rinsed and drained
- 1 can (11 ounces) white *or* shoepeg corn, drained
- 2 tablespoons chopped green chilies
- 1 teaspoon ground cumin
- 1/2 teaspoon salt

Shredded Monterey Jack cheese

■ In a large saucepan, saute onion and celery in oil until tender. Stir in the broth, turkey, beans, corn, chilies, cumin and salt. Bring to a boil. Reduce heat; cover and simmer for 15-20 minutes. Garnish with cheese. **Yield:** 5 servings.

onion soup with sausage

SUNDRA HAUCK | BOGALUSA, LOUISIANA

With a yummy slice of mozzarella cheese bread on top, this hearty broth makes an impressive luncheon or light supper. It looks great and tastes wonderful.

PREP/TOTAL TIME: 20 MIN.

- 1/2 pound pork sausage links, cut into 1/2-inch pieces
- 1 pound sliced fresh mushrooms
- 1 cup sliced onion
- 2 cans (14-1/2 ounces *each*) beef broth
- 4 slices Italian bread
- 1/2 cup shredded part-skim mozzarella cheese

- In a large saucepan, cook sausage over medium heat until no longer pink; drain. Add mushrooms and onion; cook for 4-6 minutes or until tender. Stir in the broth. Bring to a boil. Reduce heat; simmer, uncovered, for 4-6 minutes or until heated through.
- Ladle into four 2-cup ovenproof bowls. Top each with a slice of bread; sprinkle with cheese. Broil until cheese is melted. **Yield:** 4 servings.

greens with pears and blue cheese

LEANNE MOCKER | FALL RIVER, MASSACHUSETTS

Fresh greens, pear slices, crumbled Gorgonzola cheese, crunchy walnuts and a creamy citrus dressing make this healthful salad a refreshing delight! I first concocted it three years ago, and it was an instant sensation.

PREP/TOTAL TIME: 15 MIN.

- 3 tablespoons orange juice
- 2 tablespoons plus 1 teaspoon cider vinegar
- 4-1/2 teaspoons fat-free mayonnaise
- 1 tablespoon honey
- 2-1/4 teaspoons lemon juice
- 2-1/4 teaspoons olive oil
- 1/4 teaspoon salt
- 1/4 teaspoon coarsely ground pepper
- 12 cups spring mix salad greens
- 3 medium pears, thinly sliced
- 1/3 cup crumbled blue cheese
- 1/3 cup chopped walnuts, toasted

■ For the dressing, in a small bowl, whisk the first eight ingredients. On each salad plate, arrange 2 cups of greens, half of a pear and about 1 tablespoon each of blue cheese and walnuts. Drizzle each with 2 tablespoons dressing. **Yield:** 6 servings.

tangy caesar salad

PAULA STEWART | CRAWFORDVILLE, GEORGIA

When time is tight, I like to toss together this zippy salad. It's a breeze to make with bottled Caesar salad dressing and Caesar salad croutons.

PREP/TOTAL TIME: 15 MIN.

- 8 cups torn romaine
- 1/4 cup creamy Caesar salad dressing
- 1 tablespoon lemon juice
- 1/2 teaspoon pepper
- 1 cup Caesar salad croutons
- 1/3 cup grated Parmesan cheese

■ Place the romaine in a large salad bowl. Combine the salad dressing, lemon juice and pepper; drizzle over the romaine and toss to coat. Top with the croutons and cheese. **Yield:** 6-8 servings.

asian shrimp soup

DONNA HELLINGER | LORAIN, OHIO

A package of store-bought ramen noodles speeds up assembly of this colorful broth with shrimp and carrots. My mother passed the recipe on to me. It's delicious and so quick to fix.

PREP/TOTAL TIME: 15 MIN.

- 3-1/2 cups water
- 1 package (3 ounces) Oriental ramen noodles
- 1 cup frozen cooked small shrimp
- 1/2 cup chopped green onions
- 1 medium carrot, julienned
- 2 tablespoons soy sauce

■ In a large saucepan, bring the water to a boil. Set aside seasoning packet from noodles. Add the noodles to boiling water; cook and stir for 3 minutes.

■ Add the shrimp, onions, carrot, soy sauce and contents of seasoning packet. Cook 3-4 minutes longer or until heated through. **Yield:** 4 servings.

Use Leftover Veggies

Whenever you have leftover cooked veggies (especially beans, corn, carrots and peas), put them in a resealable plastic bag and freeze. Use them later to make Basil Turkey Soup...there's no need to thaw first!

nutty fruit medley

RUTH GLICK | APPLE CREEK, OHIO

I coat apples, grapes, banana and walnuts with a creamy dressing to make this Waldorf-like salad. I experimented with many different versions of this recipe until I got it just right.

PREP/TOTAL TIME: 10 MIN.

- 2 large red apples, chopped
- 1 cup green grapes
- 1 medium firm banana, sliced
- 1/2 cup chopped walnuts
- 1/4 cup mayonnaise
- 2 tablespoons sour cream
- 1/2 teaspoon sugar
- 1/2 teaspoon lemon juice
- Pinch salt

■ In a large bowl, combine the apples, grapes, banana and walnuts. Combine mayonnaise, sour cream, sugar, lemon juice and salt; pour over fruit mixture and toss gently to coat. **Yield:** 6-8 servings.

basil turkey soup

TASTE OF HOME TEST KITCHEN

After a busy day of Christmas shopping, it's easy to put together this soup with leftover turkey and frozen vegetables. It tastes like it simmered all day!

PREP/TOTAL TIME: 25 MIN.

- 2 cups beef broth
- 2-1/2 cups frozen mixed vegetables
- 1 can (14-1/2 ounces) diced tomatoes, undrained
- 3/4 cup uncooked small shell pasta
- 3/4 teaspoon dried basil
- 3/4 teaspoon pepper
- 2-1/2 cups cubed cooked turkey
- 2-1/2 teaspoons dried parsley flakes

■ In a large saucepan, combine the first six ingredients. Bring to a boil. Reduce heat; cover and simmer for 7-10 minutes or until the pasta and vegetables are tender. Stir in the turkey and parsley; heat through. **Yield:** 6 servings.

creamy lettuce salad

JACQUIE TROUTMAN | ZEPHYRHILLS, FLORIDA

Here's a family favorite I recall my mom serving often when I was growing up. She particularly liked it because it was so easy to make and called for things she usually had on hand. A sweet dressing tops packaged salad greens that are dressed up with hard-cooked eggs, tomato and onion.

PREP/TOTAL TIME: 15 MIN.

- 3 hard-cooked eggs
- 1 package (16 ounces) ready-to-serve salad greens
- 1 medium tomato, seeded and chopped
- 1/4 cup chopped onion

DRESSING:

- 3/4 cup mayonnaise
- 3 to 4 tablespoons milk
- 2 tablespoons sugar
- 2 tablespoons cider vinegar

■ Cut one egg into wedges for garnish; set aside. Chop the remaining eggs. In a salad bowl, combine the greens, tomato, onion and chopped eggs.

■ In a small bowl, whisk the dressing ingredients. Pour over salad; toss to coat. Garnish with reserved egg wedges. **Yield:** 10 servings.

cold day chili

LUCILE PROCTOR | PANGUITCH, UTAH

I like to make chili from beans I've soaked overnight, but this speedier version tastes just as good on a frosty winter day. The mildly sweet mixture of beef and beans is economical, too.

PREP/TOTAL TIME: 25 MIN.

- 1 pound ground beef
- 1 medium onion, halved and thinly sliced
- 2 cans (16 ounces *each*) kidney beans, rinsed and drained
- 1 can (14-1/2 ounces) diced tomatoes, undrained
- 1/2 to 3/4 cup water
- 1 to 2 tablespoons brown sugar
- 1 tablespoon chili powder
- 1 tablespoon white vinegar
- 2 teaspoons prepared mustard
- 1 teaspoon salt
- 1/8 teaspoon pepper

■ In a large saucepan, cook beef and onion over medium heat until the meat is no longer pink; drain. Add the remaining ingredients. Bring to a boil; reduce heat. Cover and simmer for 10 minutes or until heated through. **Yield:** 4 servings.

black bean corn chowder

SHELLY PLATTEN | AMHERST, WISCONSIN

I like to season my thick, Southwestern-style chowder with salsa, lime juice and cumin. I first made this for a special lunch with my daughter. We like it with gourmet-style tortilla chips.

PREP/TOTAL TIME: 25 MIN.

1/2 cup half-and-half cream
1 can (15 ounces) black beans, rinsed and drained, *divided*
1/2 cup chopped onion
1 teaspoon olive oil
2 garlic cloves, minced
1/2 cup salsa
1/3 cup fresh *or* frozen corn
1 tablespoon lime juice
3/4 teaspoon ground cumin
1/2 medium ripe avocado, peeled and chopped
Sour cream and shredded cheddar cheese, optional

- In a blender, combine cream and 3/4 cup black beans; cover and process until smooth. Set aside.
- In a small saucepan, saute onion in oil until tender. Add garlic; cook 1 minute longer. Stir in the salsa, corn, lime juice, cumin and remaining beans.
- Reduce heat; stir in cream mixture. Cook, uncovered, for 2-3 minutes or until heated through. Stir in avocado. Serve with sour cream and cheese if desired. **Yield:** 2 servings.

summer avocado salad

DEBORAH WILLIAMS | PEORIA, ARIZONA

Garden-fresh veggies, creamy avocado and a sprinkling of feta cheese make this chunky salad a healthful summer standout!

PREP/TOTAL TIME: 30 MIN.

1/2 cup chopped seeded peeled cucumber
1/3 cup chopped sweet yellow pepper
6 cherry tomatoes, seeded and quartered
2 tablespoons finely chopped sweet onion
1 tablespoon minced fresh basil *or* 1 teaspoon dried basil
1-1/2 teaspoons lemon juice
1-1/2 teaspoons olive oil
Dash garlic powder
1 medium ripe avocado, peeled and chopped
2 tablespoons crumbled feta cheese
Bibb lettuce leaves, optional

- In a small bowl, combine the first eight ingredients; cover and refrigerate for 15-20 minutes. Add avocado; toss gently. Sprinkle with feta cheese. Serve immediately on lettuce-lined plates if desired. **Yield:** 2 servings.

spicy tomato soup

JAIME HAMPTON | RICHMOND, VIRGINIA

When you'd rather be playing than cooking, you might want to give this tomato soup a try. Using canned corn and black beans, it goes together fast and is a great accompaniment to any kind of sandwich.

PREP/TOTAL TIME: 20 MIN.

- 8 ounces uncooked elbow macaroni
- 1 can (46 ounces) tomato juice
- 1 can (15-1/4 ounces) whole kernel corn, drained
- 1 can (15 ounces) black beans, rinsed and drained
- 1/4 cup salsa
- 3 teaspoons dried oregano
- 1-1/2 teaspoons garlic powder
- 1 teaspoon dried basil
- 1 teaspoon ground cumin
- 1/2 to 1 teaspoon crushed red pepper flakes, optional

Shredded cheddar *or* Monterey Jack cheese, optional

- Cook the macaroni according to package directions. Meanwhile, in a large saucepan, combine the tomato juice, corn, beans, salsa, oregano, garlic powder, basil, cumin and pepper flakes if desired; bring to a boil. Reduce heat; cover and simmer for 8-10 minutes.
- Drain macaroni; stir into the soup. Garnish with cheese if desired. **Yield:** 8-10 servings.

The Heat Is On!

You can adjust the heat of Spicy Tomato Soup by varying the type of salsa you use (mild, medium or hot) and by stirring in crushed red pepper flakes...or by not using any flakes at all.

chicken minestrone

TASTE OF HOME TEST KITCHEN

A packaged minestrone soup mix is jazzed up with cubed chicken, fresh zucchini, portobello mushrooms and crunchy croutons for this satisfying staple. It's easy to prepare, yet seems like you fussed.

PREP/TOTAL TIME: 30 MIN.

- 1 package (9.3 ounces) minestrone soup mix
- 1 medium zucchini, quartered lengthwise and sliced
- 1 cup chopped baby portobello mushrooms
- 1 pound boneless skinless chicken breasts, cubed
- 1 tablespoon olive oil
- 1/4 cup butter, melted
- 1 teaspoon dried parsley flakes
- 6 slices day-old French bread (1 inch thick), cubed
- 2 tablespoons grated Parmesan cheese

■ Prepare soup mix according to package directions, adding zucchini and mushrooms. Meanwhile, in a large skillet, cook chicken in oil for 10-12 minutes or until juices run clear. Stir into soup.

■ For croutons, in a large bowl, combine butter and parsley. Add bread cubes and toss to coat. Arrange in a single layer on an ungreased baking sheet.

■ Sprinkle with cheese. Bake at 400° for 7-8 minutes or until golden brown, stirring occasionally. Serve with soup. **Yield:** 5 servings.

mandarin pecan salad

JEAUNE HADL VAN METER | LEXINGTON, KENTUCKY

Crisp greens are mixed with nuts and citrus in this refreshing salad. Drizzled with a sweet-tart poppy seed dressing, it's an all-time favorite.

PREP/TOTAL TIME: 15 MIN.

- 2 cups torn romaine
- 1 snack-size cup (4 ounces) mandarin oranges, drained
- 10 pecan halves
- 1 tablespoon dried cranberries

POPPY SEED DRESSING:

- 3 tablespoons olive oil
- 4 teaspoons honey
- 1 tablespoon red wine vinegar
- 3/4 teaspoon Dijon mustard
- 1/8 teaspoon salt

Dash onion powder

- 1/2 teaspoon poppy seeds

■ Divide the romaine, oranges, pecans and cranberries between two salad plates. In a blender, combine the oil, honey, vinegar, mustard, salt and onion powder; cover and process until smooth. Stir in poppy seeds. Drizzle over salads. **Yield:** 2 servings.

About White Kidney Beans

Cannellini beans are large white kidney beans and are generally available dry and canned. If you can't find them at your local grocer, feel free to substitute navy beans or great northern beans.

zucchini tomato salad

ALPHA WILSON | ROSWELL, NEW MEXICO

I dice tomato and zucchini, then splash them with a fresh, flavorful dressing and serve it over salad greens for a party-pretty side dish that goes together in minutes.

PREP/TOTAL TIME: 30 MIN.

- 1/2 cup diced zucchini
- 1/2 cup seeded diced tomato, *divided*
- 2 tablespoons mayonnaise
- 1 tablespoon minced chives
- 1 teaspoon prepared mustard
- 1/8 teaspoon salt
- 1/8 teaspoon pepper
- 1 cup ready-to-serve salad greens

■ In a small bowl, combine the zucchini, 1/4 cup tomato, mayonnaise, chives, mustard, salt and pepper. Refrigerate for 20 minutes. Serve on salad greens; sprinkle with remaining tomato. **Yield:** 2 servings.

tuscan turkey soup

MARIE MCCONNELL | SHELBYVILLE, ILLINOIS

I like to ladle up this quick, creamy soup chock-full of leftover Thanksgiving turkey, pumpkin and beans to hungry family and friends. It's fabulous!

PREP/TOTAL TIME: 30 MIN.

- 1 cup chopped onion
- 1 cup chopped celery
- 2 tablespoons olive oil
- 1 teaspoon minced garlic
- 2 cans (14-1/2 ounces *each*) chicken broth
- 2 cups cubed cooked turkey
- 1 can (15 ounces) solid-pack pumpkin
- 1 can (15 ounces) white kidney *or* cannellini beans, rinsed and drained
- 1/2 teaspoon salt
- 1/2 teaspoon dried basil
- 1/4 teaspoon pepper

Shredded Parmesan cheese, optional

■ In a large saucepan, saute onion and celery in oil until tender. Add the garlic; cook 1 minute longer. Stir in the broth, turkey, pumpkin, beans, salt, basil and pepper. Bring to a boil.

■ Reduce heat; simmer, uncovered, for 10-15 minutes or until heated through, stirring occasionally. Serve with cheese if desired. **Yield:** 8 servings (2 quarts).

p. 95

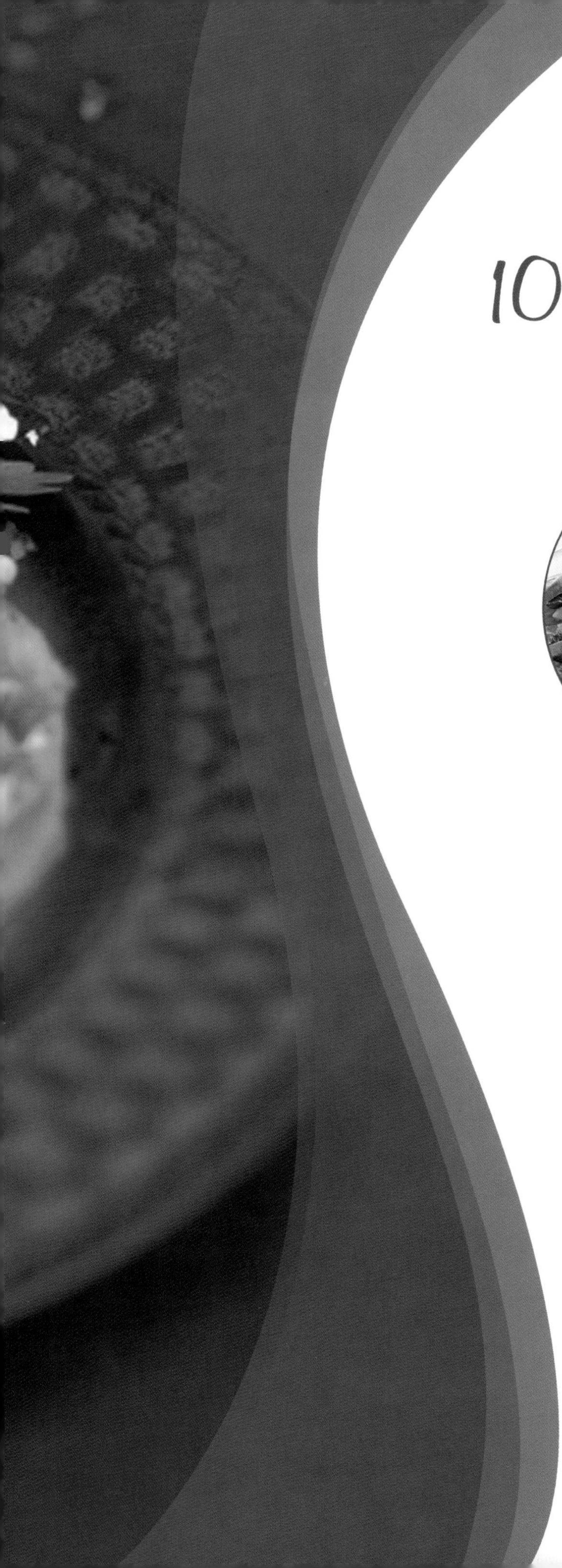

10 minutes to the table

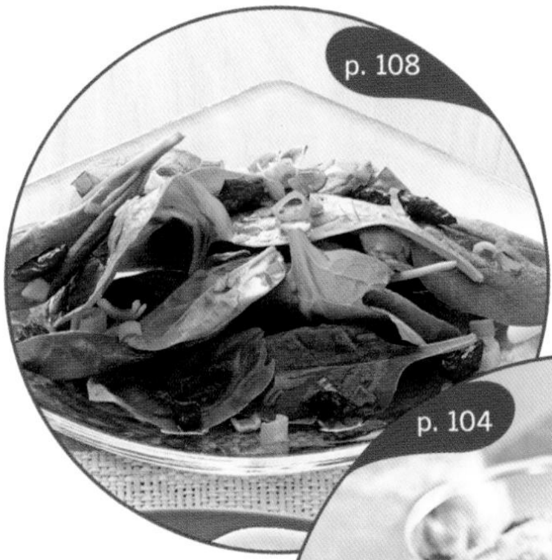

p. 108

p. 104

p. 90

tilapia with corn salsa

BRENDA COFFEY | SINGER ISLAND, FLORIDA

My family loves fish, and this super-fast and delicious entree is very popular at my house. Though it tastes like it takes a long time, it cooks in minutes under the broiler. We like it garnished with lemon wedges on the side.

PREP/TOTAL TIME: 10 MIN.

- 4 tilapia fillets (6 ounces *each*)
- 1 tablespoon olive oil
- 1/4 teaspoon salt
- 1/4 teaspoon pepper
- 1 can (15 ounces) black beans, rinsed and drained
- 1 can (11 ounces) whole kernel corn, drained
- 3/4 cup Italian salad dressing
- 2 tablespoons chopped green onion
- 2 tablespoons chopped sweet red pepper

■ Drizzle both sides of the fillets with oil; sprinkle with the salt and pepper.

■ Broil 4-6 in. from the heat for 5-7 minutes or until fish flakes easily with a fork. Meanwhile, in a small bowl, combine the remaining ingredients. Serve with the fish. **Yield:** 4 servings.

peppy parmesan pasta

DEBBIE HORST | PHOENIX, ARIZONA

My husband and I came up with this flavorful pasta dish when we needed to round out dinner in a hurry.

PREP/TOTAL TIME: 10 MIN.

- 8 ounces angel hair pasta
- 1 large tomato, chopped
- 1 package (3 ounces) sliced pepperoni
- 1 can (2-1/4 ounces) sliced ripe olives, drained
- 1/4 cup grated Parmesan cheese
- 3 tablespoons olive oil
- 1/2 teaspoon salt *or* salt-free seasoning blend, optional
- 1/4 teaspoon garlic powder

Cook pasta according to package directions. Meanwhile, in a serving bowl, combine the tomato, pepperoni, black olives, Parmesan cheese, oil, salt if desired and garlic powder. Drain the pasta; add to the tomato mixture and toss to coat. **Yield:** 4 servings.

tasty turkey soup

LAURIE TODD | COLUMBUS, MISSISSIPPI

Enjoy the comforting results in a snap by using leftover turkey and convenient ramen noodles. It's a quick-and-easy way to jazz up a can of soup.

PREP/TOTAL TIME: 10 MIN.

- 2 tablespoons chopped celery
- 2 tablespoons chopped onion
- 1 tablespoon butter
- 1 package (3 ounces) chicken-flavored ramen noodles
- 1-1/2 cups water
- 1 can (10-3/4 ounces) condensed turkey noodle soup, undiluted
- 1 cup chicken broth
- 1 cup cubed cooked turkey

Pepper to taste

- In a large saucepan, saute celery and onion in butter until tender. Discard seasoning packet from ramen noodles or save for another use.
- Stir the noodles, water, soup, broth, turkey and pepper into celery mixture. Cook for 3 minutes or until noodles are tender and heated through. **Yield:** 4 servings.

cheese 'n' dill peas

EVELYN KENNELL | ROANOKE, ILLINOIS

My family gladly eats their veggies when I combine peas with cheddar cheese and dill. It's colorful and flat-out fast!

PREP/TOTAL TIME: 10 MIN.

- 1 cup frozen peas
- 1 tablespoon water
- 1 tablespoon butter
- 1/2 teaspoon dill weed
- 2 tablespoons shredded cheddar cheese

- In a small microwave-safe bowl, combine peas and water. Cover and microwave on high for 3 minutes; drain. Stir in butter and dill. Sprinkle with cheese; let stand until cheese is melted. **Yield:** 2 servings.

Editor's Note: This recipe was tested in a 1,100-watt microwave.

sausage bean stew

BARB SCHUTZ | PANDORA, OHIO

I made this colorful, robust stew often when our three kids were living at home. Since it calls for lots of canned vegetables, it stirs up in a jiffy. It's versatile, too—you can use cubed turkey, chicken, ham or beef for the sausage.

PREP/TOTAL TIME: 10 MIN.

- 1 pound smoked sausage, halved and cut into 1/4-inch slices
- 2 cans (10 ounces *each*) diced tomatoes and green chilies, undrained
- 1 can (15-1/2 ounces) great northern beans, rinsed and drained
- 1 can (15-1/4 ounces) whole kernel corn, drained
- 1 can (15 ounces) lima beans, drained
- 1 can (15 ounces) black beans, rinsed and drained
- 1/2 teaspoon salt
- 1/8 teaspoon pepper

Hot cooked rice, optional

■ In a large saucepan, combine the first eight ingredients. Heat through. Serve with the rice if desired. **Yield:** 6-8 servings (2 quarts).

nutty broccoli

TASTE OF HOME TEST KITCHEN

Tender broccoli and crunchy pecans make this a side dish with lots of flavor in every bite. Try substituting the broccoli with different veggies such as frozen green beans or brussels sprouts. Just be sure to thaw them before cooking.

PREP/TOTAL TIME: 10 MIN.

- 1 package (16 ounces) frozen chopped broccoli, thawed
- 1/2 cup shredded Swiss cheese
- 1/2 cup chopped pecans
- 1/4 cup butter, melted
- 1/4 teaspoon garlic salt
- 1/4 teaspoon pepper

■ Place broccoli in a large microwave-safe bowl. Combine the remaining ingredients; pour over broccoli. Cover and microwave on high for 3-4 minutes or until tender. **Yield:** 4 servings.

Editor's Note: This recipe was tested in a 1,100-watt microwave.

black forest parfaits

BARBARA RUDOLPH | SEVIERVILLE, TENNESSEE

Pretty parfaits are guaranteed to sweeten up a meal, whether you're dining indoors or out. And with only five ingredients, they can be whipped up in no time!

PREP/TOTAL TIME: 10 MIN.

- 2 cups cold milk
- 1 package (3.9 ounces) instant chocolate pudding mix
- 1 can (21 ounces) cherry pie filling, *divided*
- 2 cups whipped topping, *divided*
- 6 maraschino cherries with stems, optional

- In a large bowl, whisk milk and pudding mix for 2 minutes. Let stand for 2 minutes or until soft-set. Stir in 1 cup pie filling; gently fold in 1 cup whipped topping.
- Spoon half of the pudding mixture into six tall glasses or cups. Top with remaining pie filling, pudding mixture and whipped topping. Garnish with cherries if desired. **Yield:** 6 servings.

in-a-snap bruschetta

TASTE OF HOME TEST KITCHEN

This simple yet elegant finger food looks like you fussed, but it's really easy to make!

PREP/TOTAL TIME: 10 MIN.

- 2 large garlic cloves
- 1/2 teaspoon salt
- 3 cups finely chopped Roma tomatoes, seeds removed *or* 1 can (28 ounces) petite diced tomatoes, well drained
- 1/4 cup prepared pesto
- 1/4 cup shredded Parmesan cheese
- 2 tablespoons olive oil
- 1/2 teaspoon sugar
- 1/4 teaspoon pepper
- 1 tub (8 ounces) cream cheese with herbs
- 1 baguette, sliced 1/4 inch thick, brushed with olive oil and toasted

Italian parsley leaves *or* minced fresh parsley

■ In a large bowl, mash the garlic and salt into a paste. Add the tomatoes, pesto, cheese, oil, sugar and pepper.

■ Spread the cream cheese on each baguette slice; top with the bruschetta mixture. Garnish with the parsley. **Yield:** 30-35 appetizers.

turkey quesadilla

EDIE FARM | FARMINGTON, NEW MEXICO

With only five ingredients, this recipe goes together in a flash yet tastes great.

PREP/TOTAL TIME: 10 MIN.

- 1 flour tortilla (10 inches)
- 1-1/2 teaspoons butter, softened
- 1/4 cup shredded Monterey Jack cheese
- 2 slices deli smoked turkey

Salsa, optional

■ Spread one side of tortilla with butter. Place tortilla greased side down on griddle. Sprinkle with cheese, then top with turkey.

■ Fold tortilla in half. Cook over low heat for 2-3 minutes on each side or until golden brown and cheese is melted. Serve with salsa if desired. **Yield:** 1 serving.

spiced ham steak

CONNIE MOORE | MEDWAY, OHIO

I quickly turn orange marmalade, mustard and a hint of ginger into a fast-to-fix glaze for ham. The mouthwatering entree may be short on time, but it's definitely long on flavor.

PREP/TOTAL TIME: 10 MIN.

- 1 bone-in fully cooked ham steak (about 1 pound)
- 1/4 cup orange marmalade
- 2 tablespoons water
- 1 tablespoon butter
- 1 tablespoon prepared mustard
- 1 teaspoon corn syrup
- 1/8 to 1/4 teaspoon ground ginger

■ In a large skillet coated with cooking spray, cook ham for 4 minutes on each side or until lightly browned; drain.

■ Combine the remaining ingredients in a saucepan; bring to a boil. Spoon over ham. Cover and cook for 1-2 minutes or until heated through. **Yield:** 4 servings.

A Lesson in Ham Steak

A ham steak is simply a piece of ham (1/2 to 2 inches thick) cut from the shank or leg. It's convenient when you crave ham but don't want to prepare a whole ham.

pizza dogs

RACHEL TOLLEFSON | SELBY, SOUTH DAKOTA

I'm asked to make these special hot dogs whenever I come home from college. Dressed up with pizza sauce, pepperoni and melted cheese, these sandwiches are sure to be a hit.

PREP/TOTAL TIME: 10 MIN.

- 1 jar (14 ounces) pizza sauce
- 15 slices slices pepperoni, chopped
- 1-1/2 cups (6 ounces) shredded part-skim mozzarella cheese
- 12 to 14 hot dog buns, split
- 12 to 14 hot dogs, cooked

■ In a large saucepan, combine pizza sauce and pepperoni; heat through. Stir in the cheese until melted. Spoon about 2 tablespoons into each bun; top with a hot dog. **Yield:** 12-14 servings.

maple baby carrots

KAREN WREN | FREEDOM, MAINE

I first tasted this three-ingredient side dish at my aunt's house. I thought they were the sweetest, most tender carrots I'd ever had. I make them all the time now.

PREP/TOTAL TIME: 10 MIN.

- 1 pound fresh baby carrots
- 1/4 cup butter, cubed
- 2 tablespoons maple syrup

■ Place carrots and a small amount of water in a 1-1/2-qt. microwave-safe dish. Cover and microwave on high for 4-6 minutes or until crisp-tender; drain. Add the butter; microwave for 30 seconds or until melted. Drizzle with syrup; toss to coat. **Yield:** 4 servings.

Editor's Note: This recipe was tested in a 1,100-watt microwave.

coconut creme brulee

GLORIA JABAUT | RED BLUFF, CALIFORNIA

There's always time for dessert, and this elegant, quick-to-fix treat is one I turn to regularly. After one bite, you may make it a favorite as well.

PREP/TOTAL TIME: 10 MIN.

- 2 refrigerated vanilla pudding snack cups (4 ounces *each*)
- 2 tablespoons brown sugar
- 2 tablespoons flaked coconut
- 2 teaspoons butter, melted

■ Spoon pudding into two 6-oz. ramekins or custard cups. Combine the brown sugar, coconut and butter; sprinkle over pudding. Broil 5-6 in. from the heat for 2-3 minutes or until topping is bubbly and golden brown. Serve warm. **Yield:** 2 servings.

taco turkey wraps

KATHY NEIDERMANN | HOLLAND, MICHIGAN

I get lots of compliments whenever I bring these roll-ups to potluck lunches. Sour cream, taco seasoning and shredded Mexican cheese bring south-of-the-border flair to deli turkey in the quick wraps.

PREP/TOTAL TIME: 10 MIN.

- 2/3 to 3/4 cup sour cream
- 2 tablespoons taco seasoning
- 6 flour tortillas (8 inches), warmed
- 1 cup (4 ounces) shredded Mexican cheese blend
- 1/2 pound thinly sliced deli turkey breast

Salsa, optional

■ In a small bowl, combine the sour cream and taco seasoning. Spread over the tortillas. Sprinkle with cheese. Top with the turkey; roll up. Serve with the salsa if desired. **Yield:** 6 servings.

pineapple-caramel sponge cakes

LYNN MAHLE | QUINCY, FLORIDA

Want the flavor of pineapple-upside-down cake without the hassle of baking? Then try this delicious no-bake dessert.

PREP/TOTAL TIME: 10 MIN.

1 can (8 ounces) unsweetened crushed pineapple, drained
1/2 cup caramel ice cream topping
4 individual round sponge cakes
1 pint vanilla ice cream

- In a small saucepan, combine pineapple and caramel topping. Cook over medium heat for 2-3 minutes or until heated through, stirring occasionally.
- Place sponge cakes on dessert plates. Top each with a scoop of ice cream and 1/4 cup pineapple sauce. Serve immediately. **Yield:** 4 servings.

beef 'n' cheese tortillas

MYRA INNES | AUBURN, KANSAS

I like to take these sandwiches along on our many outings. They can be made in advance and don't get soggy. You'll appreciate the convenience...your family and friends will love the great taste!

PREP: 10 MIN. + CHILLING

- 1/2 cup garlic-herb cheese spread
- 4 flour tortillas (10 inches)
- 3/4 pound thinly sliced cooked roast beef
- 20 to 25 whole spinach leaves
- 11 to 12 sweet banana peppers

■ Spread about 2 tablespoons cheese spread over each tortilla. Layer with roast beef and spinach. Remove seeds from peppers and slice into thin strips; arrange over spinach. Roll up each tortilla tightly; wrap in plastic wrap. Refrigerate until ready to serve. **Yield:** 4 servings.

Banana Pepper Pointers

Banana peppers get their name from their shape and color. Their flavor is generally mild, but you can find them in hotter varieties. The crisp texture makes banana peppers a favorite addition to sandwiches and salads.

southwest skillet corn

MARILYN SMUDZINSKI | PERU, ILLINOIS

This fast and colorful stir-fried side dish nicely complements any southwestern menu.

PREP/TOTAL TIME: 10 MIN.

- 1 medium sweet red pepper, chopped
- 1 tablespoon finely chopped seeded jalapeno pepper
- 1 tablespoon butter
- 1-1/2 teaspoons ground cumin
- 1 package (16 ounces) frozen corn, thawed
- 1/3 cup minced fresh cilantro

■ In a large nonstick skillet, saute red pepper and jalapeno in butter until tender. Add cumin; cook for 30 seconds. Add corn and cilantro; saute 2 minutes longer or until heated through. **Yield:** 4 servings.

Editor's Note: When cutting hot peppers, disposable gloves are recommended. Avoid touching your face.

mushroom rice pilaf

GENNY MONCHAMP | REDDING, CALIFORNIA

Fresh mushrooms and a hint of wine dress up instant rice. This speedy idea makes an effortless accompaniment to chicken, pork or beef.

PREP/TOTAL TIME: 10 MIN.

- 1 cup water
- 1 teaspoon chicken bouillon granules
- 1 cup uncooked instant rice
- 2 cups sliced fresh mushrooms
- 3 green onions, thinly sliced
- 1 tablespoon butter
- 1/4 cup white wine *or* chicken broth

■ In a large saucepan, bring the water and bouillon to a boil. Stir in rice. Remove from the heat; cover and let stand for 5 minutes.

■ Meanwhile, in a skillet, saute mushrooms and onions in butter and wine until mushrooms are tender and liquid is absorbed, about 6 minutes. Fluff rice with a fork; stir in mushroom mixture. **Yield:** 4 servings.

apricot ham steak

TASTE OF HOME TEST KITCHEN

Ham is a versatile main menu item that's a standby with all country cooks. One of the best and easiest ways to serve ham slices is topped off with a slightly sweet glaze, like this apricot version.

PREP/TOTAL TIME: 10 MIN.

- 4 boneless fully cooked ham steaks (5 ounces *each*)
- 2 tablespoons butter, *divided*
- 1/2 cup apricot preserves
- 1 tablespoon cider vinegar
- 1/4 teaspoon ground ginger
- Dash salt

■ In a large skillet, saute ham in 1 tablespoon butter until lightly browned on each side.

■ Meanwhile, in a small saucepan, combine the preserves, vinegar, ginger, salt and remaining butter. Cook over medium heat until heated through. Serve with ham. **Yield:** 4 servings.

artichoke-pepperoni tossed salad

ANGIE SMITH | CLARKSVILLE, TENNESSEE

I created this colorful and festive salad after my husband and I first tasted it in an Italian restaurant. It's fast, fresh and goes with almost any pasta meal I make. It takes only minutes to prepare, and I can vary the recipe by substituting different cheeses or Italian ham.

PREP/TOTAL TIME: 10 MIN.

- 1 package (10 ounces) ready-to-serve salad greens
- 1 can (14 ounces) water-packed artichoke hearts, rinsed, drained and chopped
- 1 cup (4 ounces) shredded Italian cheese blend, optional
- 1 package (3-1/2 ounces) sliced pepperoni
- 1/4 cup chopped red onion
- 1 jar (2 ounces) sliced pimientos, drained
- 1/3 to 1/2 cup Italian salad dressing

■ In a large salad bowl, combine the greens, artichokes, cheese if desired, pepperoni, onion and pimientos. Drizzle with dressing and toss to coat. Serve immediately. **Yield:** 6 servings.

almond sole fillets

ERNA FARNHAM | MARENGO, ILLINOIS

My husband is a real fish lover. This buttery treatment is his favorite way to prepare sole, perch or halibut. It cooks quickly in the microwave, so it's perfect for a busy weekday.

PREP/TOTAL TIME: 10 MIN.

- 1/3 cup butter, cubed
- 1/4 cup slivered almonds
- 1 pound sole fillets
- 2 tablespoons lemon juice
- 1/2 teaspoon dill weed
- 1/4 teaspoon salt
- 1/4 teaspoon pepper
- 1/4 teaspoon paprika

■ In a microwave-safe bowl, combine butter and almonds. Microwave, uncovered, on high for 1-1/2 minutes or until almonds are golden brown.

■ Place the fillets in a greased microwave-safe 11-in. x 7-in. dish. Top with almond mixture.

■ In a small bowl, combine the lemon juice, dill, salt and pepper; drizzle over fish. Sprinkle with paprika. Cover and microwave on high for 4-5 minutes or until fish flakes easily with a fork. **Yield:** 4 servings.

Editor's Note: This recipe was tested in a 1,100-watt microwave.

egg drop soup

MARY KELLEY | MINNEAPOLIS, MINNESOTA

This soup is a great way to start an Asian meal. If you want, you can add two minced water chestnuts to the broth along with the spinach and onions.

PREP/TOTAL TIME: 10 MIN.

- 5 cups chicken broth
- 1/2 teaspoon sugar
- 1 egg, lightly beaten
- 1/3 cup sliced fresh spinach
- 2 green onions, sliced

■ In a large saucepan, bring the broth and sugar to a boil over medium heat. Reduce heat to low. Drizzle beaten egg into hot broth. Remove from the heat; stir in spinach and onions. **Yield:** 4 servings.

peaches 'n' cream crisp

TASTE OF HOME TEST KITCHEN

This four-ingredient dessert can be ready in 10 minutes. When fresh peaches are not available, use frozen sliced peaches and adjust the microwave time.

PREP/TOTAL TIME: 10 MIN.

- 3 cups fresh *or* frozen sliced peaches
- 4 teaspoons butterscotch ice cream topping
- 4 tablespoons granola cereal without raisins
- 4 scoops vanilla ice cream

■ Place the peaches in four 8-oz. ramekins or custard cups. Top with butterscotch topping and granola. Microwave, uncovered, on high for 2-3 minutes or until bubbly. Top with ice cream. **Yield:** 4 servings.

Editor's Note: This recipe was tested in a 1,100-watt microwave.

basil chicken strips

BARBARA ROKOW | GENEVA, NEW YORK

I'm an attorney and my husband is an architect, so our careers keep our schedules busy. Seasoned with basil, this easy chicken entree is great for the weeknight rush. I serve it with broccoli and Parmesan noodles.

PREP/TOTAL TIME: 10 MIN.

- 1/2 pound boneless skinless chicken breasts, cut into strips
- 2 tablespoons all-purpose flour
- 3 tablespoons butter
- 2 tablespoons red wine vinegar
- 1/2 teaspoon dried basil

■ In a large resealable plastic bag, add chicken and flour. Seal bag; toss to coat.

■ In a large skillet over medium-high heat, melt the butter. Add the chicken; saute for 5 minutes. Stir in the red wine vinegar and basil; cook until the chicken is no longer pink. **Yield:** 2 servings.

blue cheese mashed potatoes

TASTE OF HOME TEST KITCHEN

Add your favorite cheese to homemade or prepared mashed potatoes for an easy side dish.

PREP/TOTAL TIME: 10 MIN.

- 1 package (2 pounds) refrigerated mashed potatoes
- 1/3 cup crumbled blue cheese

■ Heat potatoes according to package directions; stir in blue cheese. Serve immediately. **Yield:** 6 servings.

lemon chicken soup

JOAN FOTOPOULOS | TURAH, MONTANA

For years, I made Greek chicken soup from scratch. My daughter devised this super-simple version that she and her family can enjoy when time's short. Lemon juice makes the delicious difference.

PREP/TOTAL TIME: 10 MIN.

- 1 can (11-1/2 ounces) condensed chicken with rice soup, undiluted
- 1 can (10-3/4 ounces) condensed cream of chicken soup, undiluted
- 2-1/4 cups water
- 1 cup diced cooked chicken, optional
- 1 to 2 tablespoons lemon juice
- Pepper to taste
- Minced fresh parsley, optional

■ In a large saucepan, combine soups and water; cook until heated through. Add the chicken if desired. Stir in lemon juice and pepper. Garnish with parsley if desired. **Yield:** 4-5 servings.

1-2-3 snack mix

SUE SHERMAN | TOLEDO, OHIO

Salty and satisfying, this colorful, kid-friendly trail mix provides quick protein and energy by the handful on action-packed days. It's great for long car trips, too!

PREP/TOTAL TIME: 5 MIN.

- 1 package (6.6 ounces) miniature cheddar cheese fish-shaped crackers
- 1 package (6 ounces) dried cranberries
- 1-1/4 cups salted cashews

■ In a large bowl, combine the crackers, cranberries and cashews. Store in an airtight container. **Yield:** 6 cups.

berry cheesecake parfaits

JOYCE MART | WICHITA, KANSAS

I can serve up this easy dessert in no time. Impressive and delicious, it seems to be just the right touch after a full meal. We also recommend it as a midnight snack.

PREP/TOTAL TIME: 10 MIN.

- 1 package (8 ounces) cream cheese, softened
- 2 to 4 tablespoons sugar
- 1/2 cup vanilla yogurt
- 2 cups fresh raspberries *or* berries of your choice
- 1/2 cup graham cracker crumbs (8 squares)

■ In a large bowl, beat cream cheese and sugar until smooth. Stir in yogurt.

■ In four dessert glasses or bowls, alternate layers of raspberries, cream cheese mixture and cracker crumbs. Serve immediately or refrigerate for up to 8 hours. **Yield:** 4 servings.

special ladyfinger dessert

TASTE OF HOME TEST KITCHEN

Folks will swear you fussed over this pretty dessert, but it couldn't be much easier or quicker to whip up. Best of all, who'd believe such a sweet finish to a meal could be so light?

PREP/TOTAL TIME: 10 MIN.

- 2 ounces fat-free cream cheese
- 1 tablespoon Mascarpone cheese
- 1 tablespoon confectioners' sugar
- 6 ladyfingers, split
- 2 tablespoons reduced-sugar strawberry preserves
- 1/4 teaspoon baking cocoa
- 2 fresh strawberries

In a small bowl, combine the cheeses and confectioners' sugar. Split ladyfingers; spread cheese mixture over top halves and preserves over bottom halves. Sandwich halves together. Dust with cocoa. Garnish with strawberries. **Yield:** 2 servings.

antipasto platter

TERI LINDQUIST | GURNEE, ILLINOIS

We entertain often, and this is one of our favorite "party pleasers." It's such a refreshing change from the usual chips and dip.

PREP: 10 MIN. + CHILLING

- 1 jar (32 ounces) pepperoncinis, drained
- 1 can (15 ounces) garbanzo beans *or* chickpeas, rinsed and drained
- 2 cups halved fresh mushrooms
- 2 cups halved cherry tomatoes
- 1/2 pound provolone cheese, cubed
- 1 can (6 ounces) pitted ripe olives, drained
- 1 package (3-1/2 ounces) sliced pepperoni
- 1 bottle (8 ounces) Italian vinaigrette dressing
- Lettuce leaves

■ In a large bowl, combine the peppers, beans, mushrooms, tomatoes, cheese, olives and pepperoni. Pour vinaigrette over mixture; toss to coat. Refrigerate for at least 30 minutes or overnight. Arrange on a lettuce-lined platter. Serve with toothpicks. **Yield:** 14-16 servings.

cajun shrimp

DONNA THOMASON | EL PASO, TEXAS

I bring a little pizzazz to my table with a batch of zippy shrimp. Use as much or as little cayenne pepper as you like, depending on your family's tastes.

PREP/TOTAL TIME: 10 MIN.

- 2 teaspoons paprika
- 1 teaspoon dried thyme
- 1/2 teaspoon salt
- 1/4 teaspoon ground nutmeg
- 1/4 teaspoon garlic powder
- 1/8 to 1/4 teaspoon cayenne pepper
- 1 tablespoon olive oil
- 1 pound uncooked medium shrimp, peeled and deveined

■ In a large nonstick skillet, saute the paprika, thyme, salt, nutmeg, garlic powder and cayenne in oil for 30 seconds, stirring constantly. Add the shrimp; saute for 2-3 minutes or until the shrimp turn pink, stirring occasionally. **Yield:** 4 servings.

fruity cookie tarts

BEVERLY COYDE | GASPORT, NEW YORK

Sliced strawberries, kiwi and whipped topping dress up a soft chocolate chip cookie in this no-stress recipe. A little melted chocolate makes the delectable dessert fancy enough for even a special dinner.

PREP/TOTAL TIME: 10 MIN.

- 1/2 cup whipped topping
- 2 large soft chocolate chips cookies
- 1 kiwifruit, peeled and sliced
- 4 large strawberries, sliced
- 1/4 cup semisweet chocolate chips
- 1/2 teaspoon shortening

■ Spread whipped topping over cookies. Top with the kiwi and strawberries. In a microwave or heavy saucepan, melt chocolate chips and shortening; stir until smooth. Drizzle over fruit. Serve immediately. **Yield:** 2 servings.

creamed crab on toast

NINA DE WITT | AURORA, OHIO

This is a great, ready-in-a-jiffy luncheon dish or Sunday supper. Marjoram and lemon juice in the sauce complement the flavor of the crab quite nicely.

PREP/TOTAL TIME: 10 MIN.

- 1 can (10-3/4 ounces) condensed cream of mushroom soup, undiluted
- 1 can (6 ounces) crabmeat, rinsed, drained, and cartilage removed
- 1 tablespoon lemon juice
- 1/4 teaspoon dried marjoram
- Dash cayenne pepper
- Toast *or* biscuits

■ In a 1-qt. microwave-safe dish, combine the soup, crab, lemon juice, marjoram and cayenne. Cover and microwave on high for 3-4 minutes or until heated through, stirring once. Serve on toast or biscuits. **Yield:** 4 servings.

Editor's Note: This recipe was tested in a 1,100-watt microwave.

french green beans

TASTE OF HOME TEST KITCHEN

Frozen green beans get tasty herb flavor from rosemary and basil while toasted almonds add crunch.

PREP/TOTAL TIME: 10 MIN.

- 1 package (9 ounces) frozen French-style green beans
- 1 jar (4-1/2 ounces) sliced mushrooms, drained
- 3 tablespoons butter, melted
- 1/4 teaspoon dried rosemary, crushed
- 1/4 teaspoon dried basil
- Toasted slivered almonds

■ Cook green beans according to package directions; drain. Add mushrooms and keep warm. Combine the butter, rosemary and basil; drizzle over bean mixture and toss to coat. Sprinkle with almonds. **Yield:** 2 servings.

Crushing Dried Rosemary

Dried rosemary can be crushed with a spice grinder, a mortar and pestle or a knife on a cutting board. You can also coarsely crush the rosemary in the palm of your hand.

creamy chicken 'n' rice

RENEE LEETCH | CANTON, OHIO

This was my favorite dish when I was growing up. Now I appreciate it even more because it's fast and nutritious. Served with biscuits and a salad, it's a hearty meal.

PREP/TOTAL TIME: 10 MIN.

1 cup instant rice
1 cup water
1 can (15 ounces) mixed vegetables, drained
1 can (10-3/4 ounces) condensed cream of chicken soup, undiluted
1 can (5 ounces) chunk white chicken, drained
1/4 to 1/2 teaspoon dried basil
Pinch pepper

■ In a large saucepan, cook the rice in water according to package directions. Add the remaining ingredients; heat through. **Yield:** 4 servings.

pork with orange sauce

PENNY NIEDHAMER | FRESNO, CALIFORNIA

What a great way to use up leftover pork. No one guesses this fantastic dinner is ready in just a few moments.

PREP/TOTAL TIME: 10 MIN.

1 tablespoon cornstarch
1 cup orange juice
1 tablespoon jellied cranberry sauce
1-1/2 teaspoons soy sauce
Salt and pepper to taste
8 slices cooked pork (2 ounces *each*)

■ In a small saucepan, combine cornstarch and orange juice until smooth. Stir in the cranberry sauce, soy sauce, salt and pepper. Bring to a boil; cook and stir for 2 minutes or until thickened. Add pork; heat through. **Yield:** 4 servings.

Buying Zucchini

Select firm, plump zucchini with bright, smooth skin. Store it in the refrigerator for up to 4 days. Wash zucchini just before using. Because the skin is tender, there's no need to peel it first.

cheesy zucchini rounds

TASTE OF HOME TEST KITCHEN

Even kids will eat their veggies when you serve these rounds as a side dish or snack!

PREP/TOTAL TIME: 10 MIN.

1 medium zucchini, sliced
1/8 to 1/4 teaspoon dried basil
1/8 teaspoon onion powder
1/4 cup shredded reduced-fat cheddar cheese
1 bacon strip, cooked and crumbled
2 teaspoons grated Parmesan cheese

■ Place zucchini on a microwave-safe plate; sprinkle with basil and onion powder. Microwave, uncovered, on high for 45 seconds or until hot. Sprinkle with the cheddar cheese, bacon and Parmesan cheese; microwave on high for 20-45 seconds or until cheese is melted. **Yield:** 2 servings.

Editor's Note: This recipe was tested in a 1,100-watt microwave.

sweet-sour spinach salad

JUDITH PRIGLMEIER | AITKIN, MINNESOTA

The tang of this quick and easy salad rounds out any menu with a splash of color.

PREP/TOTAL TIME: 10 MIN.

1 package (9 ounces) fresh spinach, torn
1/4 cup dried cranberries
1/4 cup chopped green onions
1/2 cup canola oil
1/4 cup sugar
3 tablespoons cider vinegar
1/2 teaspoon ground mustard
1/8 to 1/4 teaspoon celery seed

■ In a large salad bowl, combine the spinach, cranberries and onions. In a small bowl, whisk the oil, sugar, vinegar, mustard and celery seed. Pour over salad; toss to coat. Serve immediately. **Yield:** 4 servings.

mexicali pork chops

LAURA COHEN | EAU CLAIRE, WISCONSIN

You'll need just 10 minutes to fix these tender skillet pork chops. They get their zippy flavor from a packet of taco seasoning and salsa.

PREP/TOTAL TIME: 10 MIN.

1 envelope taco seasoning
4 boneless pork loin chops (1/2 inch thick)
1 tablespoon canola oil
Salsa

■ Rub taco seasoning over pork chops. In a large skillet, cook chops over medium-high heat in oil until juices run clear, about 9 minutes. Serve with salsa. **Yield:** 4 servings.

ham 'n' corn chowder

DANNA CHAMBERS | TOPSHAM, MAINE

This soup comes together faster than you can believe! My family had a hard time finding a corn chowder we all liked, so I combined recipes we enjoyed and this was the result.

PREP/TOTAL TIME: 10 MIN.

1 can (14-1/2 ounces) diced new potatoes, drained
1-1/2 cups milk
1 can (10-3/4 ounces) condensed cheddar cheese soup, undiluted
1 can (8-3/4 ounces) cream-style corn
1 cup frozen corn, thawed
1 cup cubed deli ham

■ In a large microwave-safe bowl, combine all ingredients. Cover and microwave on high for 5-8 minutes or until heated through, stirring twice. **Yield:** 3 servings.

Editor's Note: This recipe was tested in a 1,100-watt microwave.

chocolate caramel fondue

CHERYL ARNOLD | LAKE ZURICH, ILLINOIS

It's easy to keep the ingredients for this wonderfully rich fondue on hand in case unexpected company drops by. I serve the thick sauce in punch cups, so guests can carry it on a dessert plate alongside their choice of fruit, pretzels and other dippers.

PREP/TOTAL TIME: 10 MIN.

- 1 can (14 ounces) sweetened condensed milk
- 1 jar (12 ounces) caramel ice cream topping
- 3 ounces unsweetened chocolate, chopped
- Assorted fresh fruit *and/or* pretzels

■ In a large saucepan, combine the milk, caramel topping and chocolate. Cook over low heat until chocolate is melted. Transfer to a fondue pot and keep warm. Serve with fruit and/or pretzels. **Yield:** 2-1/2 cups.

three-step stir-fry

AMY MASSON | CYPRESS, CALIFORNIA

I based this flavorful stir-fry on a fabulous dish I sampled in a San Francisco restaurant. It truly is a 10-minute main dish that looks and tastes like it took a lot longer.

PREP/TOTAL TIME: 10 MIN.

- 1 envelope stir-fry seasoning mix
- 1 package (16 ounces) broccoli coleslaw mix
- 2 tablespoons canola oil
- 8 ounces thinly sliced roast beef *or* other deli meat, cut into 1/2-inch strips
- 1 can (8 ounces) sliced water chestnuts, drained
- 3 plum tomatoes, quartered
- 2 teaspoons sesame seeds

■ Prepare the seasoning mix according to the package directions; set aside. In a large skillet, stir-fry the coleslaw mix in oil for 3 minutes or until crisp-tender. Add the beef, water chestnuts, tomatoes, sesame seeds and seasoning sauce. Cook 4 minutes longer or until heated through. **Yield:** 7 servings.

enchilada chicken soup

CRISTIN FISCHER | BELLEVUE, NEBRASKA

Canned soups, bottled enchilada sauce and a few other convenience items make this recipe one of my fast-to-fix favorites. Use mild green chilies if they suit your tastes, or try a spicier variety to give the soup more kick.

PREP/TOTAL TIME: 10 MIN.

- 1 can (11 ounces) condensed fiesta nacho cheese soup, undiluted
- 1 can (10-3/4 ounces) condensed cream of chicken soup, undiluted
- 2-2/3 cups milk
- 1 can (10 ounces) chunk white chicken, drained
- 1 can (10 ounces) enchilada sauce
- 1 can (4 ounces) chopped green chilies
- Sour cream

■ In a large saucepan, combine the soups, milk, chicken, enchilada sauce and chilies. Cook until heated through. Serve with sour cream. **Yield:** 7 servings.

rosemary chicken

LUKE ARMSTEAD | OREGON CITY, OREGON

This is a terrific recipe for anyone who cooks for one or two people. Plus, it can easily be doubled to feed more. It is perfect for fast-paced weekdays and makes a complete meal when served with buttered beans and rolls.

PREP/TOTAL TIME: 10 MIN.

- 2 boneless skinless chicken breast halves (4 ounces *each*)
- 2 teaspoons canola oil
- 1 tablespoon lemon juice
- 1 teaspoon dried rosemary, crushed
- 1/2 teaspoon dried oregano
- 1/4 teaspoon pepper

■ Flatten chicken to 1/4-in. thickness. In a nonstick skillet, cook chicken in oil over medium-high heat for 3-4 minutes on each side or until no longer pink. Sprinkle with lemon juice, rosemary, oregano and pepper. **Yield:** 2 servings.

chipped beef on toast

JANE FRY | LANCASTER, PENNSYLVANIA

Here's a fast-to-fix dish that makes a hearty breakfast or light lunch. A creamy sauce prepared in the microwave coats convenient packaged dried beef and is served over toast.

PREP/TOTAL TIME: 10 MIN.

- 1/4 cup butter, cubed
- 1/4 cup all-purpose flour
- 2 cups milk
- 2 packages (2-1/2 ounces *each*) thinly sliced dried beef
- 4 slices bread, toasted and halved

■ In a microwave-safe bowl, microwave butter on high for 35 seconds or until melted. Stir in the flour until smooth. Gradually stir in milk.

■ Microwave, uncovered, on high for 2-3 minutes or until thickened, stirring every minute. Stir in beef; cook on high for 1 minute or until heated through. Serve on toast. **Yield:** 4 servings.

Editor's Note: This recipe was tested in a 1,100-watt microwave.

crisp hash for two

FLO BURTNETT | GAGE, OKLAHOMA

This is a family favorite that provides a quick and nourishing meal. It is also a good way to use leftover roast beef. I remember Mother made this often when I was growing up. Other types of meat work well, too.

PREP/TOTAL TIME: 10 MIN.

- 2 tablespoons butter
- 1 cup diced cooked roast beef
- 1 cup diced cooked potato
- 1 medium onion, diced
- 1 tablespoon minced parsley
- 1/2 cup milk

Salt and pepper to taste

■ In a heavy skillet, melt butter over medium-high heat. In a large bowl, combine the remaining ingredients; add to the skillet. Cover; cook until crisp on the bottom. Turn and brown other side. **Yield:** 2 servings.

p. 145

beef entrees

p. 118

p. 122

p. 119

grilled cheeseburger pizza

TANYA GUTIERRO | BEACON FALLS, CONNECTICUT

I combined our daughter's two favorite foods—pizza and grilled cheeseburgers—to create this main dish. It's a fun change of pace for a backyard cookout.

PREP: 25 MIN. GRILL: 15 MIN.

- 3/4 pound ground beef
- 1 cup ketchup
- 2 tablespoons prepared mustard
- 1 prebaked 12-inch pizza crust
- 1 cup shredded lettuce
- 1 medium tomato, thinly sliced
- 1/8 teaspoon salt
- 1/8 teaspoon pepper
- 1 small sweet onion, thinly sliced
- 1/2 cup dill pickle slices
- 1 cup (4 ounces) shredded cheddar cheese
- 1 cup (4 ounces) shredded part-skim mozzarella cheese

■ Shape beef into three 1/2-in.-thick patties. Grill, covered, over medium-hot heat for 5 minutes on each side or until meat is no longer pink.

■ Meanwhile, combine ketchup and mustard; spread over the crust to within 1 in. of edge. Sprinkle with lettuce; top with tomato. Sprinkle with salt and pepper. When beef patties are cooked, cut into 1/2-in. pieces; arrange over tomato slices. Top with onion, pickles and cheeses.

■ Place pizza on a 16-in. square piece of heavy-duty foil. Prepare grill for indirect heat. Grill, covered, over medium indirect heat for 12-15 minutes or until cheese is melted and crust is lightly browned. Let stand for 5-10 minutes before slicing. **Yield:** 4-6 servings.

herbed london broil

SHARON PATNOE | ELKINS, ARKANSAS

I received this recipe from my stepfather. It's good whether you grill or broil the meat. I've never met a person who didn't enjoy the tender beef as much as we do. Serve with seasoned asparagus to round out the meal.

PREP: 10 MIN. + MARINATING GRILL: 15 MIN.

1/4 cup chopped onion
1/4 cup lemon juice
2 tablespoons canola oil
1 garlic clove, minced
1/4 teaspoon *each* celery seed, salt, dried thyme and oregano
1/4 teaspoon dried rosemary, crushed
Dash pepper
1 beef flank steak (1/2 to 3/4 pound)

- In a large resealable bag, combine the onion, lemon juice, oil, garlic and seasonings; add steak. Seal bag; turn to coat. Refrigerate for several hours or overnight, turning once.
- Drain and discard marinade. Grill steak, uncovered, over medium heat for 6-7 minutes on each side or until meat reaches desired doneness (for medium-rare, a meat thermometer should read 145°; medium, 160°; well-done, 170°). Slice thinly across the grain. **Yield:** 2 servings.

beef potpie

MARIAN CLIFTON | SELMA, CALIFORNIA

Ideal for a pair, this bubbly, golden-topped beef potpie is a tried-and-true meal pleaser. It makes a homey meal with plenty of comforting country flavor.

PREP: 20 MIN. BAKE: 25 MIN.

1 tablespoon butter
1 teaspoon dried minced onion
1 tablespoon all-purpose flour
1/8 teaspoon pepper
2/3 cup beef broth
1 cup frozen mixed vegetables, thawed
1/2 cup cubed cooked roast beef
CRUST:
1 egg
2 tablespoons milk
1/2 cup biscuit/baking mix

- In a small saucepan, melt butter. Add onion and cook for 1 minute. Stir in flour and pepper until blended. Gradually whisk in broth. Bring to a boil; cook and stir for 2 minutes or until thickened. Stir in the vegetables and beef; heat through. Transfer to two greased 10-oz. custard cups.
- In a small bowl, combine the egg and milk. Stir in the biscuit mix until smooth. Spoon evenly over the meat mixture. Place on an ungreased baking sheet. Bake at 400° for 25-30 minutes or until bubbly and the top is golden brown. **Yield:** 2 servings.

quick beef stew

VALERIE COOK | HUBBARD, IOWA

This recipe transforms leftover cooked roast beef into a hearty, home-style stew. Filled with vegetables, I feel good feeding this nutrient-packed meal to my family.

PREP/TOTAL TIME: 15 MIN.

2 cups cubed cooked roast beef
1 can (15 ounces) mixed vegetables, liquid drained and reserved
1 can (10-3/4 ounces) condensed cream of celery soup, undiluted
1 can (10-3/4 ounces) condensed cream of mushroom soup, undiluted
1/2 teaspoon dried thyme, optional
1/4 teaspoon dried rosemary, crushed, optional
Pepper to taste

- In a large saucepan, combine the beef, vegetables, soups and seasonings. Heat through. If desired, add reserved vegetable liquid to thin the stew. **Yield:** 4 servings.

pizza meatballs

KIM KANATZAR | BLUE SPRINGS, MISSOURI

With melted cheese inside, these tender meatballs have a popular pizza taste. Whether I make them for a church potluck or a family gathering, they're a hit with all ages.

PREP: 35 MIN. COOK: 25 MIN.

- 2 cups seasoned bread crumbs
- 1 cup milk
- 1/4 cup dried minced onion
- 2 teaspoons garlic salt
- 1/4 teaspoon pepper
- 2 pounds ground beef
- 8 ounces cubed part-skim mozzarella cheese (1/2-inch cubes)
- 1/3 cup all-purpose flour
- 1/4 cup canola oil
- 2 jars (28 ounces *each*) pizza sauce
- Hot cooked pasta *or* rice *or* sandwich buns, split

■ In a large bowl, combine the first five ingredients. Crumble beef over mixture and mix well. Shape into 48 meatballs. Stuff a cube of cheese into the center of each meatball; cover the cheese completely with meat. Roll lightly in flour.

■ In a large skillet, brown meatballs in oil; drain. Add pizza sauce; bring to a boil. Reduce heat; cover and simmer for 25-30 minutes or until meatballs are no longer pink. Serve with pasta, rice, in buns or as an appetizer. **Yield:** 4 dozen.

broccoli beef braids

PENNY LAPP | NORTH ROYALTON, OHIO

Each slice of this fast-to-fix, golden bread is like a hot sandwich packed with beef, broccoli and mozzarella.

PREP/TOTAL TIME: 30 MIN.

- 1 pound ground beef
- 1/2 cup chopped onion
- 3 cups frozen chopped broccoli
- 1 cup (4 ounces) shredded part-skim mozzarella cheese
- 1/2 cup sour cream
- 1/4 teaspoon salt
- 1/4 teaspoon pepper
- 2 tubes (8 ounces *each*) refrigerated crescent rolls

■ In a large skillet, cook beef and onion over medium heat until the meat is no longer pink; drain. Add the broccoli, cheese, sour cream, salt and pepper; heat through.

■ Unroll one tube of dough on a greased baking sheet; seal the seams and perforations, forming a 12-in. x 8-in. rectangle. Spread half of beef mixture lengthwise down the center. On each side, cut 1-in.-wide strips 3 in. into center.

■ Starting at one end, fold alternating strips at an angle across filling; seal ends. Repeat.

■ Bake at 350° for 15-20 minutes or until golden brown. **Yield:** 2 loaves (8 servings each).

fillets with mushroom sauce

CAROLYN BRINKMEYER | AURORA, COLORADO

Grilled tenderloin steaks get an extra-special treatment with onion, mushrooms and tomatoes. The savory sauce can be whipped up while the meat is on the grill. The main dish comes together quickly.

PREP/TOTAL TIME: 25 MIN.

- 4 beef tenderloin steaks (4 ounces *each*)
- 1 large onion, cut into 1/2-inch slices
- 1/2 pound fresh mushrooms, thickly sliced
- 2 tablespoons butter
- 1 can (14-1/2 ounces) diced tomatoes, undrained
- 1/4 cup water
- 1/2 teaspoon dried basil
- 1/2 teaspoon beef bouillon granules
- 1/8 teaspoon pepper

■ Grill steaks, covered, over medium heat for 6-9 minutes on each side or until meat reaches desired doneness (for medium-rare, a meat thermometer should read 145°; medium, 160°; well-done, 170°).

■ Meanwhile, in a large skillet, saute onion and mushrooms in butter until tender. Stir in the tomatoes, water, basil, bouillon and pepper. Bring to a boil; cook and stir over medium heat for 5 minutes or until thickened. Serve with beef. **Yield:** 4 servings.

au gratin taco bake

LINDA MUIR | BIG LAKE, MINNESOTA

This hearty hot dish relies on a package of au gratin potatoes for simple preparation. Chock-full of beef, potatoes, corn, tomatoes and cheese, this Southwestern supper is sure to be a hit with everyone!

PREP: 15 MIN. BAKE: 70 MIN.

- 1 pound ground beef
- 1 package (4.9 ounces) au gratin potatoes
- 1 can (15-1/4 ounces) whole kernel corn, undrained
- 1 can (14-1/2 ounces) no-salt-added stewed tomatoes, undrained
- 3/4 cup milk
- 1/2 cup water
- 2 tablespoons taco seasoning
- 1 cup (4 ounces) shredded cheddar cheese

■ In a large skillet, cook beef over medium heat until no longer pink; drain. Stir in the potatoes and contents of the sauce mix, corn, tomatoes, milk, water and taco seasoning. Transfer to a greased 2-qt. baking dish.

■ Cover and bake at 350° for 65-70 minutes or until potatoes are tender. Sprinkle with the cheese. Bake, uncovered, 5 minutes longer or until cheese is melted. **Yield:** 4-6 servings.

make-ahead meatballs

RUTH ANDREWSON | LEAVENWORTH, WASHINGTON

My husband and I have company often. Keeping a supply of these frozen meatballs on hand means I can easily prepare a quick, satisfying meal. I start with a versatile meatball mix that makes about 12 dozen meatballs, then freeze them in batches for future use.

PREP/TOTAL TIME: 25 MIN.

- 4 eggs
- 2 cups dry bread crumbs
- 1/2 cup finely chopped onion
- 1 tablespoon salt
- 2 teaspoons Worcestershire sauce
- 1/2 teaspoon white pepper
- 4 pounds lean ground beef (90% lean)

■ In a large bowl, beat eggs. Add the next five ingredients. Crumble beef over mixture and mix well. Shape into 1-in. balls, about 12 dozen.

■ Place meatballs on greased racks in shallow baking pans. Bake at 400° for 10-15 minutes or until no longer pink, turning often; drain. Cool.

■ Place about 30 meatballs into each freezer container. May be frozen for up to 3 months. **Yield:** 5 batches (about 30 meatballs per batch).

quick italian spaghetti

RUTH PETERSON | JENISON, MICHIGAN

This recipe has been one of my standbys for over 40 years now. I can make it in a jiffy, and there's no other spaghetti recipe my husband's even interested in trying!

PREP/TOTAL TIME: 25 MIN.

- 1/2 pound ground beef
- 3/4 cup thinly sliced green onions
- 3 cans (8 ounces *each*) tomato sauce
- 2 teaspoons sugar
- 1 teaspoon Worcestershire sauce
- 1/2 teaspoon salt
- 1/8 teaspoon pepper
- 1 can (2-1/4 ounces) sliced ripe olives, drained

Cooked spaghetti
Grated Parmesan *or* Romano cheese
Bacon bits, optional

■ In a large skillet, cook beef and onions over medium heat until meat is no longer pink; drain. Add the tomato sauce, sugar, Worcestershire sauce, salt and pepper. Bring to a boil. Reduce heat; cover and simmer for 10 minutes.

■ Add the olives; simmer 5 minutes longer. Spoon over spaghetti; sprinkle with cheese and bacon bits if desired. **Yield:** 4 servings.

baked ziti with fresh tomatoes

BARBARA JOHNSON | DECKER, INDIANA

We are a family of farmers and work up a big appetite after a long day outdoors. Not only does this hearty dish satisfy, it's a great time-saver because I can prepare the sauce in advance.

PREP: 70 MIN. BAKE: 30 MIN.

- 1 pound ground beef
- 1 cup chopped onion
- 3 pounds plum tomatoes, peeled, seeded and chopped (about 15 tomatoes)
- 1-1/2 teaspoons salt
- 1 teaspoon dried basil
- 1/4 teaspoon pepper
- 8 ounces uncooked ziti
- 2 cups (8 ounces) shredded part-skim mozzarella cheese, *divided*
- 2 tablespoons grated Parmesan cheese

■ In a Dutch oven, cook the beef and onion over medium heat until meat is no longer pink; drain. Stir in the tomatoes, salt, basil and pepper. Reduce heat to low; cover and cook for 45 minutes, stirring occasionally.

■ Cook ziti according to package directions; drain. Stir in the sauce and 1 cup mozzarella cheese. Transfer to a greased 3-qt. baking dish; sprinkle with the Parmesan and remaining mozzarella cheese.

■ Cover and bake at 350° for 15 minutes. Uncover; bake 15 minutes longer or until heated through. **Yield:** 6 servings.

pepper steak

NICKY HURT | APO, ENGLAND

This speedy steak recipe comes from my mom's files. The tender beef sirloin strips in a flavorful broth make it a favorite with our gang.

PREP/TOTAL TIME: 30 MIN.

- 1 pound beef top sirloin steak, cut into thin strips
- 1 tablespoon canola oil
- 2 garlic cloves, minced
- 2 cans (14-1/2 ounces *each*) beef broth
- 1 small sweet red pepper, sliced
- 1 small green pepper, sliced
- 4-1/2 teaspoons cornstarch
- 1/4 cup water
- 4 cups hot cooked rice

■ In a large skillet over medium-high heat, brown steak in oil. Add garlic; cook 1 minute longer. Drain. Add broth; bring to a boil. Reduce heat; simmer, uncovered, for 12-16 minutes or until broth is reduced by half.

■ Add peppers. Combine cornstarch and water until smooth; stir into broth. Bring to a boil; cook and stir for 2 minutes or until thickened. Serve with rice. **Yield:** 4 servings.

roast beef burritos

ANN NOLTE | ELMENDORF AFB, ALASKA

I rely on cumin, taco sauce and red pepper flakes to season these savory south-of-the-border sensations. The recipe is a great way to spice up leftover roast beef.

PREP: 10 MIN. COOK: 35 MIN.

- 1 medium onion, chopped
- 1 tablespoon canola oil
- 1 garlic clove, minced
- 4 medium tomatoes, chopped
- 2 cups chopped cooked roast beef
- 1 bottle (8 ounces) taco sauce
- 1 can (4 ounces) chopped green chilies
- 1/2 teaspoon ground cumin
- 1/8 teaspoon crushed red pepper flakes, optional
- 6 flour tortillas (7 inches), warmed

Shredded cheddar cheese and lettuce, optional

■ In a large skillet, saute onion in oil until tender. Add garlic; cook 1 minute longer. Stir in the tomatoes, roast beef, taco sauce, chilies, cumin and red pepper flakes if desired. Bring to a boil. Reduce heat; simmer, uncovered, for 25 minutes or until thickened.

■ Spoon about 2/3 cup down the center of each tortilla; fold over sides and ends. Serve with cheese and lettuce if desired. **Yield:** 6 servings.

meatballs with pepper sauce

JULIE NEAL | GREEN BAY, WISCONSIN

I've found these colorful meatballs keep well in a slow cooker for a no-fuss meal. We enjoy them served over pasta or rice.

PREP: 25 MIN. BAKE: 1-1/4 HOURS

- 1 cup evaporated milk
- 1 tablespoon Worcestershire sauce
- 1 envelope onion soup mix
- 2 pounds ground beef

SAUCE:

- 1/2 pound sliced fresh mushrooms
- 1-1/2 cups ketchup
- 3/4 cup packed brown sugar
- 3/4 cup water
- 1/2 cup chopped green pepper
- 1/2 cup chopped sweet red pepper
- 2 tablespoons chopped onion
- 1 tablespoon Worcestershire sauce

■ In a large bowl, combine the milk, Worcestershire sauce and soup mix. Crumble beef over mixture and mix well. Shape into 1-in. balls.

■ Place meatballs on a rack in a shallow baking pan. Broil 4-6 in. from the heat for 5-8 minutes or until browned. In a Dutch oven, combine all of the sauce ingredients. Bring to a boil. Reduce heat; add the meatballs. Simmer, uncovered, for 1 hour or until the meat is no longer pink. **Yield:** 60 meatballs.

Making Meatballs of Equal Size

A sure-fire way to make meatballs of the same size is to use a 1-1/2-inch-diameter cookie scoop. Simply scoop the meat mixture into equal-sized portions; gently roll into balls.

cheeseburger pie

SHARON SCHOLL | ARLINGTON, INDIANA

This is a meal my husband really enjoys, although it's a bit big for just the two of us. The good news is that it reheats nicely in the microwave.

PREP: 30 MIN. BAKE: 30 MIN.

- 1 cup plus 2 tablespoons biscuit/baking mix, *divided*
- 1/4 cup milk
- 1 pound ground beef
- 1 medium onion, chopped
- 1 tablespoon Worcestershire sauce
- 1/2 teaspoon salt
- 1/4 teaspoon pepper
- 1 can (14-1/2 ounces) diced tomatoes with garlic and onion, undrained
- 2 eggs, lightly beaten
- 2 cups (8 ounces) shredded cheddar cheese

Chili sauce, optional

- In a small bowl, combine 1 cup biscuit mix and milk; stir until a soft ball forms. Turn onto a floured surface; knead 5 times. Roll out dough to fit a 9-in. pie plate. Transfer to pie plate; trim and flute edges.
- In a large skillet, cook beef and onion over medium heat until the meat is no longer pink; drain. Stir in the Worcestershire sauce, salt, pepper and remaining biscuit mix. Pour into crust. Spoon tomatoes over top. Combine eggs and cheese; pour over tomatoes.
- Bake at 375° for 30-35 minutes or a thermometer reads 160°. Let stand for 5 minutes before cutting. Serve with chili sauce if desired. **Yield:** 6-8 servings.

easy meat loaf

PAT JENSEN | OAK HARBOR, OHIO

My mother-in-law invented this recipe by mistake. But it was so well received that it became the most popular way for her to make meat loaf. With just five ingredients, it couldn't be any easier.

PREP: 10 MIN. BAKE: 1-1/2 HOURS + STANDING

- 1 egg, lightly beaten
- 1 can (10-1/2 ounces) condensed French onion soup, undiluted
- 1-1/3 cups crushed butter-flavored crackers (about 33 crackers)
- 1 pound lean ground beef (90% lean)
- 1 can (10-3/4 ounces) condensed golden mushroom soup, undiluted

■ In a large bowl, combine the egg, onion soup and cracker crumbs. Crumble beef over mixture and mix well. Shape into a loaf. Place in a greased 11-in. x 7-in. baking dish. Bake, uncovered, at 350° for 30 minutes.

■ Pour mushroom soup over loaf. Bake 1 hour longer or until meat is no longer pink and a meat thermometer reads 160°; drain. Let stand for 10 minutes before slicing. **Yield:** 4 servings.

microwave classic chili

JOANNA JOHNSON | VESTAL, NEW YORK

For several years, I taught a microwave cooking class sponsored by a local department store. Class participants raved about this recipe the most and were amazed it takes less than 20 minutes to cook!

PREP/TOTAL TIME: 30 MIN.

- 1 pound ground beef
- 1 medium onion, finely chopped
- 2 cans (14-1/2 ounces *each*) stewed tomatoes
- 2 teaspoons chili powder
- 1-1/2 teaspoons prepared mustard
- 1 can (16 ounces) kidney beans, rinsed and drained

Salt and pepper to taste

■ Crumble the beef into a 2-qt. microwave-safe bowl. Add onion; mix well. Cover and microwave on high for 3 minutes or until meat is no longer pink; drain. Stir in the tomatoes, chili powder and mustard; mix well. Cover and microwave on high for 6-1/2 minutes. Add beans and mix well. Cover and microwave on high for 2 minutes longer. Add salt and pepper. **Yield:** 4-6 servings.

Editor's Note: This recipe was tested in a 1,100-watt microwave.

no-bake lasagna

NORMA MONTGOMERY | GROVELAND, CALIFORNIA

You don't need to turn on the oven for this lasagna, so it's perfect for summer. The noodles and sauce are simply layered on a plate...even my husband can make it! This is a satisfying vegetarian entree.

PREP/TOTAL TIME: 30 MIN.

- 1/2 cup sliced fresh mushrooms
- 1/4 cup chopped onion
- 1 teaspoon canola oil
- 3/4 cup spaghetti sauce
- 1/2 cup chopped fresh tomato
- 1/4 teaspoon dried basil
- 1/8 teaspoon pepper
- 4 lasagna noodles
- 1/2 cup shredded part-skim mozzarella cheese

Shredded Parmesan cheese

■ In a large skillet, saute mushrooms and onion in oil until tender. Add the spaghetti sauce, tomato, basil and pepper. Bring to a boil. Reduce heat; cover and simmer for 10 minutes, stirring occasionally. Meanwhile, cook lasagna noodles according to package directions.

■ Add mozzarella cheese to the sauce; cook on low until cheese is melted. Drain noodles; cut into thirds. For each serving, on a plate, layer 2 tablespoons of sauce and two noodle pieces. Repeat layers twice. Top with 2 tablespoons sauce. Sprinkle with Parmesan cheese. **Yield:** 2 servings.

beef and pasta salad

JO ANN SATSKY | BANDERA, TEXAS

My husband and I like zesty pasta salads and have tried many different types. This delightful dish can be eaten warm or cold, so it's a perfect meal anytime of year.

PREP: 30 MIN. + CHILLING

- 3 cups spiral pasta, cooked and drained
- 1 medium green pepper, julienned
- 1 cup halved cherry tomatoes
- 1/2 cup sliced ripe olives
- 1 pound beef top sirloin steak, cut into strips
- 2 tablespoons canola oil
- 1 bottle (8 ounces) Italian salad dressing
- 1-1/2 cups (6 ounces) shredded provolone *or* part-skim mozzarella cheese

■ In a large bowl, combine pasta, green pepper, tomatoes and olives. In a large skillet, stir-fry sirloin in oil until cooked as desired; drain.

■ If serving salad hot, add dressing to skillet and bring to a boil. Pour over pasta mixture; toss to coat. Add cheese; serve immediately.

■ If serving salad cold, let beef cool for 15 minutes. Add the beef, dressing and cheese to pasta mixture; toss to coat. Chill for at least 1 hour. **Yield:** 6 servings.

mexican beef and dumplings

SUE GRONHOLZ | BEAVER DAM, WISCONSIN

This spicy ground beef concoction is nicely seasoned with chili powder. The cornmeal dumplings are a fun variation and can be stirred up in no time.

PREP: 10 MIN. COOK: 30 MIN.

- 2 pounds ground beef
- 1 can (15-1/4 ounces) whole kernel corn, undrained
- 1 can (14-1/2 ounces) diced tomatoes, undrained
- 1 can (14-1/2 ounces) tomato sauce
- 1 small onion, chopped
- 1/2 cup chopped celery
- 1/4 cup chopped green pepper
- 1 tablespoon chili powder
- 1-1/2 teaspoons salt

DUMPLINGS:

- 1 cup all-purpose flour
- 1 cup cornmeal
- 2 teaspoons baking powder
- Pinch salt
- 1 cup milk

■ In a Dutch oven, brown beef over medium heat until no longer pink; drain. Stir in the next eight ingredients. Cover and simmer for 15 minutes.

■ For the dumplings, combine the flour, cornmeal, baking powder and salt; stir in the milk just until combined. Drop into eight mounds onto the boiling mixture. Reduce heat; cover and simmer for 12-15 minutes or until the dumplings test done. (Do not lift the cover while dumplings simmer.) **Yield:** 8 servings.

Freezing Cooked Browned Beef

On a day when you have a little time on your hands, crumble and brown several pounds of ground beef. Spread on a cookie sheet and freeze until solid.

Transfer to freezer bags in 1/2- or 1-pound amounts (whatever your favorite recipes call for). On busy days, pull out a bag and add to chili, tacos or any recipe that uses browned ground beef.

lasagna rolls

MARY LEE THOMAS | LOGANSPORT, INDIANA

Folks can't believe these flavor-filled rolls have just five ingredients. Using prepared spaghetti sauce saves me lots of cooking time. My family never complains when these appear on the table.

PREP: 25 MIN. BAKE: 10 MIN.

- 6 lasagna noodles
- 1 pound ground beef
- 1 jar (15-1/2 ounces) spaghetti sauce
- 1 teaspoon fennel seed, optional
- 2 cups (8 ounces) shredded part-skim mozzarella cheese, *divided*

■ Cook lasagna noodles according to package directions. Meanwhile, in a large skillet, cook beef over medium heat until no longer pink; drain. Stir in spaghetti sauce and fennel seed if desired; heat through.

■ Drain noodles. Spread 1/4 cup meat sauce over each noodle; sprinkle with 2 tablespoons cheese. Carefully roll up noodles and place seam side down in an 8-in. square baking dish. Top with remaining sauce and cheese.

■ Bake, uncovered, at 400° for 10-15 minutes or until heated through and cheese is melted. **Yield:** 6 servings.

beef and tomato pie

JUNE MULLINS | LIVONIA, MISSOURI

I bake this classic ground beef pie when my grandchildren come to visit. We all love its mouthwatering flavor. And you'll love that it's economical.

PREP: 20 MIN. BAKE: 25 MIN.

- 1 pound ground beef
- 1 large onion, chopped
- 2 tablespoons ketchup
- 1/2 teaspoon salt
- 2 cups biscuit/baking mix
- 2/3 cup milk
- 1 cup diced fresh tomato
- 1/2 cup shredded cheddar cheese

■ In a large skillet over medium heat, cook beef and onion until meat is no longer pink; drain. Remove from the heat. Stir in ketchup and salt; set aside.

■ Combine biscuit mix and milk just until moistened. Turn onto a lightly floured surface and knead 6-8 times. Roll into a 10-in. circle; transfer to a greased 9-in. pie plate. Flute edges.

■ Spoon the meat mixture into the crust. Sprinkle with the tomato. Bake at 425° for 20-25 minutes. Sprinkle with the cheese; bake 2 minutes longer or until the cheese is melted. **Yield:** 6 servings.

golden burger spirals

LISA SINYARD | LEXINGTON, ALABAMA

A co-worker gave me this recipe nearly 20 years ago, and it's still one I turn to when I'm in need of a fuss-free meal. It's also an excellent dish to serve at potlucks and church suppers, as everyone loves the classic hamburger flavor.

PREP: 15 MIN. BAKE: 30 MIN.

- 1 pound ground beef
- 1 medium onion, chopped
- 1 medium green pepper, chopped
- 1 can (10-3/4 ounces) condensed golden mushroom soup, undiluted
- 1 can (8 ounces) tomato sauce
- 1-1/2 cups (6 ounces) shredded cheddar cheese, *divided*
- 1/2 teaspoon salt
- 1 package (8 ounces) spiral pasta, cooked and drained

■ In a large skillet, cook the beef, onion and green pepper over medium heat until meat is no longer pink; drain. Add soup, tomato sauce, 1 cup cheese and salt. Stir in pasta.

■ Transfer to a greased 2-1/2-qt. baking dish. Sprinkle with remaining cheese. Bake, uncovered, at 350° for 30 minutes or until bubbly. **Yield:** 4-6 servings.

sesame beef

KIM CHAMPLIN | MIAMI, FLORIDA

Try this Asian-inspired recipe the next time you want a break from the usual. Delicious and quick to fix, it is sure to become a favorite with your family.

PREP/TOTAL TIME: 30 MIN.

- 1/4 cup sugar
- 6 tablespoons canola oil, *divided*
- 1/4 cup soy sauce
- 1/2 teaspoon pepper
- 6 green onions, thinly sliced
- 4 garlic cloves, minced
- 2 tablespoons sesame seeds
- 1 pound beef top sirloin steak, cut into 1/8-inch strips

Rice *or* chow mein noodles

■ In a large plastic resealable bag, combine the sugar, 4 tablespoons oil, soy sauce, pepper, onions, garlic and sesame seeds. Pour half into a small bowl; set aside. Add beef to remaining marinade; seal bag and toss to coat. Let stand 15 minutes.

■ Drain and discard marinade from beef. In a large skillet or wok, heat remaining oil over high heat; add beef and reserved marinade. Stir-fry until beef is brown and has reached desired doneness. Serve immediately with rice or noodles. **Yield:** 4 servings.

pizza english muffins

LEA DELUCA | ST. PAUL, MINNESOTA

My mother fixed these fun mini pizzas for me from the time I started elementary school until I went to college.

PREP: 35 MIN. BAKE: 15 MIN.

- 2 pounds ground beef
- 1-1/2 pounds bulk pork sausage
- 1 medium onion, chopped
- 1 can (6 ounces) tomato paste
- 1 teaspoon garlic salt
- 1 teaspoon dried oregano
- 1/2 teaspoon cayenne pepper
- 3 packages (12 ounces *each*) English muffins, split
- 3 cups (12 ounces) shredded part-skim mozzarella cheese
- 2 cups (8 ounces) shredded cheddar cheese
- 2 cups (8 ounces) shredded Swiss cheese

■ In a Dutch oven, cook the beef, sausage and onion over medium heat until meat is no longer pink; drain. Stir in the tomato paste, garlic salt, oregano and cayenne. Spread over the cut side of each English muffin. Place on baking sheets. Combine the cheeses; sprinkle over meat mixture.

■ Freeze for up to 3 months or bake at 350° for 15-20 minutes or until heated through. **Yield:** 6 dozen.

Editor's Note: To use frozen Pizza English Muffins, remove from freezer. Place on baking sheet; bake at 350° for 30 minutes.

baked spaghetti

BETTY RABE | MAHTOMEDI, MINNESOTA

This spaghetti bake pleases young and old, family and friends...anyone with a penchant for pasta! Add a tossed green salad and breadsticks to round out a memorable meal.

PREP: 20 MIN. BAKE: 30 MIN. + STANDING

- 8 ounces uncooked spaghetti, broken into thirds
- 1 egg
- 1/2 cup milk
- 1/2 teaspoon salt
- 1/2 pound ground beef
- 1/2 pound bulk Italian sausage
- 1 small onion, chopped
- 1/4 cup chopped green pepper
- 1 jar (14 ounces) meatless spaghetti sauce
- 1 can (8 ounces) tomato sauce
- 1 to 2 cups (4 to 8 ounces) shredded part-skim mozzarella cheese

■ Cook spaghetti according to package directions; drain. In a large bowl, beat egg, milk and salt. Add spaghetti; toss to coat. Transfer to a greased 13-in. x 9-in. baking dish.

■ In a large skillet, cook the beef, sausage, onion and green pepper over medium heat until meat is no longer pink; drain. Stir in spaghetti sauce and tomato sauce. Spoon over the spaghetti mixture.

■ Bake, uncovered, at 350° for 20 minutes. Sprinkle with the mozzarella cheese. Bake 10 minutes longer or until the cheese is melted. Let stand for 10 minutes before cutting. **Yield:** 6-8 servings.

creamy beef and mushroom skillet

TASTE OF HOME TEST KITCHEN

Enjoy the classic flavor of Stroganoff with this recipe. The saucy supper combines lean ground beef, sliced fresh mushrooms and onions in a delicious brown gravy.

PREP/TOTAL TIME: 25 MIN.

- 1 pound lean ground beef (90% lean)
- 2 cups sliced fresh mushrooms
- 2 medium onions, sliced
- 1 jar (12 ounces) fat-free beef gravy
- 1/3 cup reduced-fat sour cream
- 1/3 cup fat-free plain yogurt
- 1 tablespoon Worcestershire sauce
- 1/4 teaspoon dried thyme
- 1/4 teaspoon pepper
- 1/4 teaspoon browning sauce

Hot cooked noodles *or* rice

- 1/4 cup minced fresh parsley

■ In a large nonstick skillet, cook the beef, mushrooms and onions over medium heat until the meat is no longer pink; drain.

■ In a large bowl, combine the gravy, sour cream, yogurt, Worcestershire sauce, thyme, pepper and browning sauce. Stir into meat mixture; heat through. Serve with noodles or rice. Sprinkle with parsley. **Yield:** 5 servings.

herbed sirloin tip

JANICE CONNELLEY | SPRING CREEK, NEVADA

I turn to this recipe for big feasts as well as company suppers. It's simple to prepare and tasty every time.

PREP: 15 MIN. + MARINATING BAKE: 40 MIN.

- 2 teaspoons salt
- 1/2 teaspoon garlic salt
- 1/2 teaspoon celery salt
- 1/2 teaspoon dried rosemary, crushed
- 1/4 teaspoon onion powder
- 1/4 teaspoon paprika
- 1/4 teaspoon pepper
- 1/8 teaspoon dill weed
- 1/8 teaspoon rubbed sage
- 1 beef sirloin tip roast (2 pounds)

■ Combine seasonings; rub over entire roast. Cover and refrigerate for at least 2 hours.

■ Place roast on a rack in a large shallow roasting pan. Bake, uncovered, at 425° for 40-60 minutes or until meat reaches desired doneness (for medium-rare, a meat thermometer should read 145°; medium, 160°; well-done, 170°). Let roast stand for 10-15 minutes before slicing. **Yield:** 6-8 servings.

roast beef and gravy

ABBY METZGER | LARCHWOOD, IOWA

This is by far the simplest way to make roast beef and gravy. On busy days, I can put this main dish in the slow cooker and forget about it. My clan likes it with mashed potatoes and fruit salad.

PREP: 15 MIN. COOK: 8 HOURS

- 1 boneless beef chuck roast (3 pounds)
- 2 cans (10-3/4 ounces *each*) condensed cream of mushroom soup, undiluted
- 1/3 cup sherry *or* beef broth
- 1 envelope onion soup mix

■ Cut roast in half; place in a 3-qt. slow cooker. In a large bowl, combine the remaining ingredients; pour over roast. Cover and cook on low for 8-9 hours or until meat is tender. **Yield:** 8-10 servings.

quick 'n' easy lasagna

BRENDA RICHARDSON | RISON, ARIZONA

If you think lasagna has to be complicated, give this four-ingredient version a try. I often make it when my husband and I have friends over to play cards.

PREP: 25 MIN. BAKE: 35 MIN.

- 16 lasagna noodles
- 2 pounds ground beef
- 1 jar (28 ounces) spaghetti sauce
- 1 pound process cheese (Velveeta), cubed

■ Cook noodles according to package directions. Meanwhile, in a large skillet, cook beef over medium heat until no longer pink; drain. Add spaghetti sauce; heat through. Rinse and drain the noodles.

■ In a greased 13-in. x 9-in. baking dish, layer a third of the meat sauce and half of the noodles and cheese. Repeat layers. Top with remaining meat sauce.

■ Cover and bake at 350° for 35 minutes or until bubbly. **Yield:** 6-8 servings.

home-style meat loaf

ALLISON CRAIG | ORMSTOWN, QUEBEC

Down-home meat loaf is hard to resist, and with this recipe I can make sure that lots of friends and family get a chance to enjoy such a specialty. Guests seem to like the fact that this version uses both ground beef and ground pork.

PREP: 45 MIN. BAKE: 1-1/4 HOURS + STANDING

- 6 eggs, lightly beaten
- 4 cups milk
- 4 cups dry bread crumbs
- 2-1/2 cups shredded carrots
- 1-1/4 cups chopped onions
- 5 teaspoons salt
- 4 teaspoons pepper
- 10 pounds ground beef
- 5 pounds ground pork

- In two very large bowls, combine the first seven ingredients. Crumble meat over the top and mix well.
- Shape into five loaves; place each in an ungreased 13-in. x 9-in. baking pan. Bake, uncovered, at 350° for 75-85 minutes or until a meat thermometer reads 160° and meat juices run clear. Drain; let stand for 10 minutes before slicing. **Yield:** 5 meat loaves (12 servings each).

Making Meat Loaf

For a moist meat loaf, handle the meat as little as possible. Mix ingredients just until combined, then shape into a loaf.

corned beef stir-fry

ALESAH PADGETT | FRANKLIN, GEORGIA

The celery seed really comes through in this colorful combination of carrots, cabbage and corned beef. A woman at church shared the recipe with me. My husband and son love its slightly sweet taste.

PREP/TOTAL TIME: 30 MIN.

7 tablespoons canola oil, *divided*
3 tablespoons white vinegar
2 tablespoons sugar
1 teaspoon celery seed
1/4 teaspoon salt
6 cups coarsely chopped cabbage
1 cup shredded carrots
1/4 cup chopped green onions
1/2 pound thinly sliced deli corned beef

■ In a small bowl, whisk 4 tablespoons oil, vinegar, sugar, celery seed and salt until sugar is dissolved; set aside.

■ In a large skillet, saute the cabbage, carrots and green onions in the remaining oil for 15-16 minutes or until crisp-tender. Stir in the vinegar-oil mixture and the corned beef. Cover and simmer for 10 minutes or until heated through. **Yield:** 4-6 servings.

casserole italiano

NANCY SCHMIDT | DELHI, CALIFORNIA

I got this cherished recipe from my sister and now both of our families request it. Using prepared spaghetti sauce saves the time-consuming step of making your own.

PREP: 20 MIN. BAKE: 1 HOUR

1-1/2 pounds ground beef
1 medium onion, chopped
1 jar (14 ounces) spaghetti sauce
1/3 cup water
1-1/2 teaspoons salt
1 teaspoon sugar
1 teaspoon dried basil
1 teaspoon pepper
4 medium potatoes, peeled and thinly sliced
1/2 cup shredded mozzarella cheese

■ In a large skillet, cook beef and onion over medium heat until meat is no longer pink; drain. Add the spaghetti sauce, water and seasonings.

■ In a greased 13-in. x 9-in. baking dish, layer half of the potatoes and meat mixture; repeat the layers. Bake, uncovered, at 375° for 50 minutes. Sprinkle with cheese. Bake 10 minutes longer or until the potatoes are tender. **Yield:** 6 servings.

layered beef casserole

DOROTHY WIEDEMAN | EATON, COLORADO

With my busy days, I treasure meal-in-one recipes like this. Toss together a salad, and dinner is ready in no time.

PREP: 25 MIN. BAKE: 2 HOURS + STANDING

6 medium potatoes, peeled and thinly sliced
1 can (15-1/4 ounces) whole kernel corn, drained
1/2 cup chopped green pepper
1 cup chopped onion
2 cups sliced fresh carrots
1-1/2 pounds lean ground beef (90% lean)
1 can (8 ounces) tomato sauce
Salt and pepper to taste
1 cup (4 ounces) shredded process cheese (Velveeta)

■ In a greased 13-in. x 9-in. baking dish, layer the potatoes, corn, green pepper, onion and carrots. Crumble beef over vegetables. Pour tomato sauce over top. Sprinkle with salt and pepper.

■ Cover and bake at 350° for 2 hours or until meat is no longer pink and a meat thermometer reads 160°. Sprinkle with cheese. Let stand for 10 minutes before serving. **Yield:** 8 servings.

Editor's Note: Layered Beef Casserole can be divided between two 1-1/2 quart baking dishes. Bake one casserole to enjoy now and freeze the other for another meal. When ready to use, thaw in the refrigerator overnight. Bake as directed and sprinkle with cheese before serving.

saucy scalloped pie

JAN BREITKREUZ | ONOWAY, ALBERTA

This uncommon recipe features a ground beef shell and cheesy potato filling. I made this dish one day when I was short on time, and my family loved it!

PREP: 25 MIN. BAKE: 25 MIN.

- 1 package (5-1/4 ounces) cheesy scalloped potatoes
- 1 bottle (12 ounces) chili sauce
- 1 tablespoon Italian seasoning
- 1/2 cup dry bread crumbs
- 1/4 cup chopped onion
- 1 garlic clove, minced
- 1 pound ground beef
- 1 can (8 ounces) mushroom stems and pieces, drained
- 2 tablespoons grated Parmesan cheese

■ Prepare scalloped potatoes according to the package directions. Meanwhile, in a small bowl, combine chili sauce and Italian seasoning. In a large bowl, combine the bread crumbs, onion, garlic and 1 cup chili sauce mixture. Crumble beef over mixture and mix well.

■ Press onto the bottom and up the sides of an ungreased 9-in. pie plate. Bake at 350° for 15 minutes; drain. Add mushrooms and Parmesan cheese to scalloped potatoes. Spoon into meat shell.

■ Bake for 10 minutes or until potatoes are golden brown. Heat the remaining chili sauce mixture; serve with individual servings. **Yield:** 4 servings.

burrito bake

CINDEE NESS | HORACE, NORTH DAKOTA

Years ago when I was in college, my roommate would frequently make this economical casserole. It's so easy to put together, and one serving goes a long way.

PREP: 25 MIN. BAKE: 30 MIN.

- 1 pound ground beef
- 1 can (16 ounces) refried beans
- 1/4 cup chopped onion
- 1 envelope taco seasoning
- 1 tube (8 ounces) refrigerated crescent rolls
- 2 cups (8 ounces) shredded cheddar cheese
- 2 cups (8 ounces) shredded part-skim mozzarella cheese

Toppings: chopped green pepper, shredded lettuce, chopped tomatoes, sliced ripe olives

■ In a skillet, cook beef over medium heart until no longer pink; drain. Add beans, onion and taco seasoning.

■ Unroll crescent roll dough. Press onto the bottom and up the sides of a greased 13-in. x 9-in. baking dish; seal seams and perforations.

■ Spread the beef mixture over the crust; sprinkle with the cheeses. Bake, uncovered, at 350° for 30 minutes or until golden brown. Sprinkle with the toppings of your choice. **Yield:** 6 servings.

harvest stir-fry

KAY TOON | WORTHINGTON, INDIANA

I work full-time outside the home, so I'm always looking for fast-to-fix dishes. This colorful skillet supper appeals to young and old alike.

PREP/TOTAL TIME: 25 MIN.

- 1 pound ground beef
- 1 medium onion, chopped
- 6 small yellow summer squash, chopped
- 6 medium tomatoes, quartered
- 1-1/2 cups whole kernel corn
- 1 tablespoon minced fresh oregano *or* 1 teaspoon dried oregano
- 1 teaspoon salt
- 1/2 teaspoon coarsely ground pepper

■ In a large skillet, cook the beef and onion over medium heat until the meat is no longer pink; drain. Add the squash, tomatoes, corn, oregano, salt and pepper. Cook and stir for 5-10 minutes or until the vegetables are tender. **Yield:** 8-10 servings.

Easy Substitute

Ground turkey can replace ground beef in many recipes with equally tasty results.

german pizza

AUDREY NOLT | VERSAILLES, MISSOURI

Most of our family lives in Pennsylvania. They visit us often, and I like to serve this simple meal when they do. Even if it's just my husband, our son and me around the table, this pizza is a favorite.

PREP: 20 MIN. COOK: 35 MIN.

1 pound ground beef
1/2 medium onion, chopped
1/2 green pepper, diced
1-1/2 teaspoon salt, *divided*
1/2 teaspoon pepper
2 tablespoons butter
6 medium potatoes (about 2-1/4 pounds), peeled and finely shredded
3 eggs, lightly beaten
1/3 cup milk
2 cups (8 ounces) shredded cheddar cheese *or* shredded part-skim mozzarella cheese

- In a large skillet over medium heat, cook and stir the beef, onion, green pepper, 1/2 teaspoon salt and pepper until meat is no longer pink; drain. Remove and keep warm.
- Reduce heat to low; melt butter in pan. Spread potatoes over butter and sprinkle with remaining salt. Top with beef mixture. Combine eggs and milk; pour over all.
- Cover and cook about 30 minutes or until a meat thermometer reaches 160°. Sprinkle with cheese; cover and cook until cheese is melted, about 5 minutes. Cut into wedges. **Yield:** 4-6 servings.

cheesy beef stroganoff

GERRIE FERGUSON | TWINING, MICHIGAN

This easy-to-fix stroganoff has become a mainstay on our dinner table. The tender sirloin steak served over noodles or rice gets high marks from my hungry clan!

PREP: 15 MIN. COOK: 35 MIN.

1 beef top sirloin steak (1 pound), cubed
2 tablespoons canola oil
1 can (4 ounces) mushroom stems and pieces, drained
1/2 teaspoon salt
1/4 teaspoon pepper
1 can (10-3/4 ounces) condensed cream of mushroom soup, undiluted
1/2 cup milk
1 cup (8 ounces) sour cream
1/2 cup shredded part-skim mozzarella cheese
1/2 cup shredded Monterey Jack cheese
Hot cooked noodles *or* rice

- In a large skillet, cook beef over medium heat in oil until no longer pink. Add the mushrooms, salt and pepper. Combine soup and milk; add to skillet. Reduce heat; stir in sour cream. Cook 30 minutes longer (do not boil).
- Add cheeses; heat for 5 minutes or until melted. Serve with noodles or rice. **Yield:** 4 servings.

schoolhouse chili

MARY SELNER | GREEN BAY, WISCONSIN

When I was a school cook, the students loved my chili because they thought it didn't have beans in it. They didn't know I puree the beans, tomatoes, onions and green pepper to create a tasty, vitamin-packed chili!

PREP: 10 MIN. COOK: 65 MIN.

1 can (14-1/2 ounces) diced tomatoes, undrained
1 can (16 ounces) mild chili beans, undrained
1/2 cup chopped onion
1/4 cup chopped green pepper
1 pound ground beef
1-1/2 teaspoons salt
1 to 2 teaspoons chili powder
1 teaspoon ground cumin
1/2 teaspoon pepper
Hot cooked spaghetti, optional

- In a blender, combine the tomatoes, beans, onion and green pepper; cover and puree until smooth.
- In a large saucepan, cook beef over medium heat until no longer pink; drain. Add seasonings and pureed vegetables. Bring to a boil. Reduce heat; cover and simmer for 1 hour. Serve with spaghetti if desired. **Yield:** 6 servings.

On-Hand Onion

Instead of chopping an onion every time it's needed for a recipe, chop several at a time. Spread in a shallow pan and freeze. Transfer to a resealable plastic bag; return to freezer. Measure as much as needed.

hamburger mac skillet

BARBARA KEMMER | ROHNERT PARK, CALIFORNIA

This recipe makes just the right amount for my husband and me. I like the idea of cooking it all in one pan, and a touch of Worcestershire sauce adds a distinctive taste.

PREP/TOTAL TIME: 30 MIN.

- 1/2 pound ground beef
- 1/4 cup chopped onion
- 1/4 cup chopped green pepper
- 1 garlic clove, minced
- 1 can (11-1/2 ounces) tomato juice
- 1/2 cup uncooked elbow macaroni
- 1 teaspoon Worcestershire sauce
- 3/4 teaspoon salt
- 1/8 teaspoon pepper

- In a large skillet, cook the beef, onion and green pepper over medium heat until meat is no longer pink. Add garlic; cook 1 minute longer; drain.
- Add the tomato juice, macaroni, Worcestershire sauce, salt and pepper; bring to a boil. Reduce heat; cover and simmer for 20 minutes or until macaroni is tender. **Yield:** 2 servings.

asian beef noodle toss

SUE LIVANGOOD | WAUKESHA, WISCONSIN

Try this skillet supper the next time you're in the mood for "Far East" fare. It's a cinch to prepare and gives you a satisfying blend of Asian flavors.

PREP/TOTAL TIME: 30 MIN.

- 1 pound ground beef
- 2 packages (3 ounces *each*) Oriental-flavored ramen noodles
- 1 package (16 ounces) frozen stir-fry vegetable blend
- 2 cups water
- 4 to 5 tablespoons soy sauce
- 1/4 teaspoon ground ginger
- 3 tablespoons thinly sliced green onions

- In a large skillet, cook beef over medium heat until no longer pink; drain. Stir in contents of one noodle seasoning packet; set aside and keep warm.
- Break the noodles; place in a large saucepan. Add the contents of second seasoning packet, vegetables, water, soy sauce and ginger. Bring to a boil. Reduce heat; cover and simmer for 6-10 minutes or until vegetables and noodles are tender. Stir in the beef and onions. **Yield:** 4-6 servings.

beef pasties

TASTE OF HOME TEST KITCHEN

Looking to put leftover pot roast to good use? Just tuck the cooked beef, carrots, potatoes and onion into pie pastry...your family will be amazed at the tender and flaky results!

PREP: 20 MIN. BAKE: 20 MIN.

- 2 cups cubed cooked roast beef (1/4-inch pieces)
- 1-1/2 cup diced cooked potatoes
- 1 cup beef gravy
- 1/2 cup diced cooked carrots
- 1/2 cup diced cooked onion
- 1 tablespoon chopped fresh parsley
- 1/4 teaspoon dried thyme
- 1/2 teaspoon salt
- 1/8 to 1/4 teaspoon pepper
- Pastry for double-crust pie (9 inches)
- Half-and-half cream

- In a large bowl, combine the first nine ingredients; set aside. On a lightly floured surface, roll out a fourth of the pastry into an 8-in. circle. Mound 1 cup filling on half of circle. Moisten edges with water; fold dough over filling and press the edges with a fork to seal.
- Place on an ungreased baking sheet. Repeat with the remaining pastry and filling. Cut slits in top of each; brush with cream. Bake at 450° for 20-25 minutes or until golden brown. **Yield:** 4 servings.

Editor's Note: If using a purchased pre-rolled pastry, cut each circle in half. Mound filling on half of the pastry; fold over, forming a wedge.

blue cheese-topped steaks

TIFFANY VANCIL | SAN DIEGO, CALIFORNIA

These juicy tenderloin steaks, lightly crusted with blue cheese and bread crumbs, are special enough for holiday dining. When drizzled with wine sauce, the beef melts in your mouth.

PREP/TOTAL TIME: 30 MIN.

- 2 tablespoons crumbled blue cheese
- 4-1/2 teaspoons dry bread crumbs
- 4-1/2 teaspoons minced fresh parsley
- 4-1/2 teaspoons minced chives
- Dash pepper
- 4 beef tenderloin steaks (4 ounces *each*)
- 1-1/2 teaspoons butter
- 1 tablespoon all-purpose flour
- 1/2 cup reduced-sodium beef broth
- 1 tablespoon Madeira wine
- 1/8 teaspoon browning sauce, optional

■ In a small bowl, combine cheese, bread crumbs, parsley, chives and pepper. Press onto one side of each steak.

■ In a large nonstick skillet coated with cooking spray, cook steaks over medium-high heat for 2 minutes on each side. Transfer to a 15-in. x 10-in. x 1-in. baking pan coated with cooking spray.

■ Bake at 350° for 6-8 minutes or until meat reaches desired doneness (for medium-rare, a meat thermometer should read 145°; medium, 160°; well-done, 170°).

■ Meanwhile, in a small saucepan, melt butter. Whisk in flour until smooth. Gradually whisk in broth and wine. Bring to a boil; cook and stir for 2 minutes or until thickened. Stir in the browning sauce if desired. Serve with the steaks. **Yield:** 4 servings.

beef 'n' tomato mac

DARIA WICINSKI | ROUND LAKE, ILLINOIS

For a quick dinner, this one is tops. To turn up the heat, use two 10-ounce cans of diced tomatoes with green chilies instead of plain tomatoes.

PREP/TOTAL TIME: 25 MIN.

3 cups uncooked elbow macaroni
1 pound ground beef
1 medium onion, chopped
2 cans (14-1/2 ounces *each*) diced tomatoes, undrained
1 can (15-1/4 ounces) whole kernel corn, drained
Salt and pepper to taste

- Cook macaroni according to the package directions. Meanwhile, in a large skillet, cook beef and onion over medium heat until meat is no longer pink; drain. Stir in tomatoes and corn. Drain macaroni; stir into beef mixture.
- Cook, uncovered, for 12-15 minutes or until heated through; season with salt and pepper. **Yield:** 4-6 servings.

topsy-turvy pie

KARA KIMBERLINE | GALION, OHIO

I've enjoyed this upside-down potpie since I was a little girl, when my mother used to make it. It's both filling and flavorful.

PREP: 20 MIN. BAKE: 15 MIN.

1 pound ground beef
1/2 cup chopped onion
1/4 cup chopped green pepper
1 can (8 ounces) tomato sauce
1 can (4-1/4 ounces) chopped ripe olives
1 teaspoon chili powder
1/2 teaspoon salt

BISCUIT TOPPING:
1 cup biscuit/baking mix
1/4 cup milk
2 tablespoons butter, melted

- In a large skillet, cook the beef, onion and green pepper until meat is no longer pink; drain. Stir in the tomato sauce, olives, chili powder and salt. Pour into a 9-in. pie plate; set aside.
- For topping, in a small bowl, combine the baking mix, milk and butter just until combined.
- Turn onto a floured surface and knead 8-10 times. Roll into a 10-in. circle. Place over meat mixture; crimp edges to seal. Cut small slits in pastry.
- Bake at 425° for 15-20 minutes. Let stand for 5 minutes. **Yield:** 4-6 servings.

baked mostaccioli

ANDREA WARNEKE | ST. PAUL, MINNESOTA

I created this simple recipe when I had a large group to feed and only a few ingredients on hand. With cheddar cheese, salsa, pasta and spaghetti sauce, it's a sure-to-please dinner.

PREP: 10 MIN. BAKE: 50 MIN.

1 package (16 ounces) mostaccioli
1-1/2 pounds ground beef
1 jar (28 ounces) spaghetti sauce
1 jar (24 ounces) salsa
1-1/2 cups (6 ounces) shredded cheddar cheese

- Cook pasta according to package directions. Meanwhile, in a Dutch oven, cook beef over medium heat until no longer pink; drain. Stir in spaghetti sauce and salsa. Drain pasta; stir into meat mixture.
- Transfer to a greased 13-in. x 9-in. baking dish (dish will be full). Cover and bake at 350° for 40 minutes. Uncover; sprinkle with cheese. Bake 8-12 minutes longer or until heated through and cheese is melted. **Yield:** 6-8 servings.

ravioli skillet

TASTE OF HOME TEST KITCHEN

Dress up store-bought ravioli and make it really special—prosciutto and mozzarella help to do the trick.

PREP/TOTAL TIME: 30 MIN.

- 1 pound ground beef
- 3/4 cup chopped green pepper
- 1 ounce prosciutto *or* deli ham, chopped
- 3 cups spaghetti sauce
- 3/4 cup water
- 1 package (25 ounces) frozen cheese ravioli
- 1 cup (4 ounces) shredded part-skim mozzarella cheese

■ In a large skillet, cook beef, pepper and prosciutto over medium heat until meat is no longer pink; drain.

■ Stir in spaghetti sauce and water; bring to a boil. Add ravioli. Reduce heat; cover and simmer for 7-9 minutes or until ravioli is tender, stirring once. Sprinkle with cheese. Simmer, uncovered, 1-2 minutes longer or until cheese is melted. **Yield:** 4 servings.

crescent-topped casserole

TRANN FOLEY | COLUMBIA, MISSOURI

My husband is a very picky eater but requests this dish for dinner at least once a month. I keep the ingredients on hand for last-minute dinners.

PREP: 15 MIN. BAKE: 25 MIN.

- 2 pounds ground beef
- 1/4 cup chopped onion
- 2 cans (8 ounces *each*) tomato sauce
- 1 envelope spaghetti sauce mix
- 3/4 cup sour cream
- 2 cups (8 ounces) shredded part-skim mozzarella cheese
- 1 tube (8 ounces) refrigerated crescent rolls
- 2 tablespoons butter, melted
- 1/3 cup grated Parmesan cheese

■ In a large skillet, cook beef and onion over medium heat until meat is no longer pink; drain. Stir in tomato sauce and spaghetti sauce mix. Reduce heat; simmer, uncovered, for 5 minutes. Remove from the heat; stir in sour cream. Spoon into a greased 13-in. x 9-in. baking dish. Sprinkle with mozzarella cheese.

■ Unroll crescent dough into one rectangle; seal seams and perforations. Place over mozzarella cheese. Brush with butter and sprinkle with Parmesan cheese.

■ Bake, uncovered, at 375° for 25-30 minutes or until golden brown. **Yield:** 6-8 servings.

all-american chili

CHERYL GROENENBOOM | ROSE HILL, IOWA

Pork and beans make this chili an all-American meal everyone enjoys. It can be whipped up in less than a half hour, making it a perfect meal for busy weeknights.

PREP/TOTAL TIME: 25 MIN.

- 1 pound ground beef
- 1 medium onion, chopped
- 1/4 teaspoon pepper
- 1 can (15-3/4 ounces) pork and beans
- 1 can (10-3/4 ounces) condensed tomato soup, undiluted
- 1 can (10-1/2 ounces) condensed vegetable beef soup, undiluted

Shredded part-skim mozzarella cheese

■ In a large saucepan, brown the beef, onion and pepper until the beef is no longer pink; drain. Stir in beans and soups. Simmer, uncovered, for 15 minutes or until heated through. Garnish with the cheese. **Yield:** 4-6 servings (1-1/2 quarts).

cheeseburger biscuit bake

JOY FRASURE | LONGMONT, COLORADO

Popular cheeseburger ingredients create the tasty layers in this family-pleasing casserole. For the "bun," I use refrigerated biscuits to make a golden topping.

PREP: 15 MIN. BAKE: 20 MIN.

- 1 pound ground beef
- 1/4 cup chopped onion
- 1 can (8 ounces) tomato sauce
- 1/4 cup ketchup
- Dash pepper
- 2 cups (8 ounces) shredded cheddar cheese, *divided*
- 1 tube (12 ounces) refrigerated buttermilk biscuits, separated into 10 biscuits

■ In a large skillet, cook beef and onion over medium heat until meat is no longer pink; drain. Stir in the tomato sauce, ketchup and pepper. Spoon half into a greased 8-in. square baking dish; sprinkle with half of the cheese. Repeat layers.

■ Place biscuits around edges of dish. Bake, uncovered, at 400° for 18-22 minutes or until the meat mixture is bubbly and biscuits are golden brown. **Yield:** 5 servings.

beef crescent loaf

MABEL BILLINGTON | MAYVILLE, WISCONSIN

Served with a fresh green salad and a yummy dessert, this is a dinner that's guaranteed to please!

PREP: 15 MIN. BAKE: 25 MIN.

- 1-1/2 pounds ground beef
- 1/2 cup chopped onion
- 3/4 cup chopped green pepper
- 2 cans (11 ounces *each*) condensed cheddar cheese soup, undiluted
- 1 tablespoon Worcestershire sauce
- 1/2 teaspoon salt
- 1/4 teaspoon pepper
- 1 tube (8 ounces) refrigerated crescent rolls
- 1/2 cup shredded cheddar cheese

■ In a large skillet, brown ground beef and onion over medium heat until meat is no longer pink; drain. Stir in the green pepper, soup, Worcestershire sauce, salt and pepper; set aside.

■ On an ungreased baking sheet, separate crescent dough into two large rectangles. Join the longer sides together. Press edges and perforations together to form a 12-in. x 7-in. rectangle. Spread half of the meat mixture down the center of the rectangle to within 1 in. of edges. Set aside remaining meat mixture. Fold longer sides of dough over meat mixture to center; seal ends.

■ Bake at 375° for 15 minutes. Remove from oven and spoon remaining meat mixture down center of loaf. Sprinkle with cheddar cheese; bake 10 minutes longer or until loaf is golden brown and cheese is melted. **Yield:** 10-12 servings.

spaghetti and meatballs

DAVID STIERHEIM | PITTSBURGH, PENNSYLVANIA

When I was a teenager, I cooked dinner every night for our family of four. Through the years, I have modified this recipe to suit our tastes and to serve just two people. That's one of the great things about this dish...it's easy to adapt!

PREP: 15 MIN. COOK: 20 MIN.

- 1 egg
- 3 tablespoons Italian-seasoned bread crumbs
- 2 tablespoons chopped onion
- 1 tablespoon grated Parmesan cheese
- 1/8 teaspoon pepper
- 1/4 pound ground beef
- 1/4 pound bulk Italian sausage
- 1 jar (14 ounces) spaghetti sauce *or* 1-1/2 cups homemade spaghetti sauce
- Hot cooked spaghetti
- Additional Parmesan cheese, optional

■ In a large bowl, combine the first five ingredients. Crumble meat over mixture. Mix well. Shape into 2-in. meatballs.

■ In a large skillet, brown the meatballs over medium heat; drain. Stir in the spaghetti sauce. Simmer, uncovered, for 20-30 minutes or until the meatballs are no longer pink. Serve with the spaghetti; sprinkle with the cheese if desired. **Yield:** 2 servings.

busy day dinner

GLORIA HANDLEY | PHOENIX, ARIZONA

I originally found this recipe in our local newspaper. After a few additions and substitutions, it became my family's favorite weeknight main course. I prepare it at least twice a month.

PREP/TOTAL TIME: 30 MIN.

1 pound ground beef
1/4 cup chopped onion
3/4 teaspoon salt
1/4 teaspoon pepper
Dash garlic powder
1 can (19 ounces) ready-to-serve chunky beef vegetable soup
4 ounces spaghetti, cooked and drained
1 cup (4 ounces) shredded cheddar cheese
Minced fresh parsley, optional

- In a skillet, cook beef and onion over medium heat until meat is no longer pink; drain. Stir in salt, pepper and garlic powder. Transfer to a greased 2-qt. baking dish. Pour the soup over the meat mixture. Top with the spaghetti and cheese.
- Bake, uncovered, at 350° for 15-20 minutes or until heated through. Sprinkle with the parsley if desired. **Yield:** 4-6 servings.

no-fuss beef roast

LISE THOMSON | MAGRATH, ALBERTA

For Christmas dinner or other special occasions, this beef rib roast makes an elegant entree. I just coat the beef with a dry rub to spark the flavor, then stick it in the oven. It comes out perfect every time!

PREP: 5 MIN. BAKE: 1-3/4 HOURS + STANDING

1-1/2 teaspoons seasoned salt
1 teaspoon garlic powder
1/2 teaspoon onion powder
1/4 teaspoon cayenne pepper
1 bone-in beef rib roast (4 to 6 pounds)
1/2 cup butter

- Combine the first four ingredients; rub over roast. Place roast, fat side up, in a roasting pan. Dot with butter.
- Bake, uncovered, at 350° for 1-3/4 to 3 hours or until meat reaches desired doneness (for medium-rare, a meat thermometer should read 145°; medium, 160°; well-done, 170°). Let stand for 10-15 minutes before carving. Thicken pan drippings for gravy if desired. **Yield:** 6-8 servings.

Editor's Note: One envelope of meat marinade seasoning mix may be substituted for the seasoned salt, garlic powder, onion powder and cayenne pepper.

steak strips with spaghetti

IRIS POSEY | ALBANY, GEORGIA

I've been serving this super skillet supper for many years. The flavorful beef dish is equally appealing when you substitute pork or veal.

PREP: 10 MIN. COOK: 25 MIN. + STANDING

- 1 medium onion, chopped
- 1/4 cup finely chopped green pepper
- 1 tablespoon butter
- 1 pound beef top sirloin steak, cut into strips
- 1 can (8 ounces) tomato sauce
- 1 cup water
- 1/4 teaspoon salt-free seasoning blend
- 1/4 teaspoon dried thyme
- 1/8 teaspoon pepper
- 1/2 cup shredded part-skim mozzarella cheese
- 6 cups hot cooked spaghetti

■ In a nonstick skillet, saute onion and green pepper in butter until tender; remove and set aside. In the same skillet, brown beef over medium heat until no longer pink; drain. Add the tomato sauce, water, seasoning blend, thyme, pepper and vegetables. Cover and simmer for 20-30 minutes or until meat is tender.

■ Remove from the heat. Sprinkle with cheese; cover and let stand for 5 minutes or until cheese is melted. Serve with spaghetti. **Yield:** 6 servings.

Simple Side

Depend on convenience foods for speedy side dishes. Round out a dinner of Steak Strips with Spaghetti by relying on a packaged salad kit and frozen garlic bread.

p. 169

pork, ham &
sausage
p. 164
p. 159
p. 157

sausage and vegetable skillet

RUBY WILLIAMS | BOGALUSA, LOUISIANA

This hearty stovetop entree has been a family favorite for years. The variety of vegetables adds color, and the best part is the minimal cooking time.

PREP/TOTAL TIME: 20 MIN.

- 1 pound fresh Italian sausage links, cut into 1/2-inch slices
- 2 tablespoons canola oil
- 2 cups cubed yellow summer squash
- 1 cup chopped green onions
- 3 to 4 garlic cloves, minced
- 3 cups chopped tomatoes
- 4 teaspoons Worcestershire sauce
- 1/8 teaspoon cayenne pepper

■ In a large skillet over medium heat, cook sausage in oil until no longer pink; drain. Add squash and onions; cook for 3 minutes. Add garlic; cook 1 minute longer. Stir in the tomatoes, Worcestershire sauce and cayenne pepper; heat through. **Yield:** 4 servings.

meaty rigatoni bake

MARY JO GROSSMAN | CLOQUET, MINNESOTA

You'll fall for this super-easy Italian entree. I created this dish from ingredients I had on hand. My husband, Bob, and I are empty nesters, so I'm always on the lookout for delicious recipes that serve one or two.

PREP: 20 MIN. BAKE: 25 MIN.

- 1 cup uncooked rigatoni *or* large tube pasta
- 1/2 pound bulk Italian sausage
- 1-1/2 cups spaghetti sauce
- 1 can (4 ounces) mushroom stems and pieces, drained
- 1/2 cup shredded Italian cheese blend
- 8 slices pepperoni

■ Cook pasta according to package directions. Meanwhile, crumble sausage into a large skillet. Cook over medium heat until no longer pink; drain. Stir in the spaghetti sauce and mushrooms. Drain pasta; add to sausage mixture.

■ Transfer mixture to a 1-qt. baking dish coated with cooking spray. Top with the cheese and pepperoni. Cover and bake at 350° for 25-30 minutes or until heated through. **Yield:** 3 servings.

sunday pork chops

TRISHA KRUSE | EAGLE, IDAHO

I love this recipe because it tastes like a "real" Sunday supper, but I don't have to spend my whole Sunday making it. Instead, I can bike or work in my garden all day and still have this amazing dish on the table to end the weekend with a home-cooked, sit-down meal for my family.

PREP/TOTAL TIME: 25 MIN.

- 1 tablespoon brown sugar
- 1/4 teaspoon garlic powder
- 4 bone-in pork loin chops (1 inch thick and 6 ounces *each*)
- 1 tablespoon olive oil
- 1 can (11 ounces) Mexicorn, undrained
- 1-1/3 cups reduced-sodium chicken broth
- 1 package (6 ounces) corn bread stuffing mix
- 2 tablespoons butter

■ Combine brown sugar and garlic powder; rub over both sides of pork chops. In a large skillet, brown chops in oil over medium heat. Remove from the pan.

■ In the same skillet, combine the Mexicorn, broth, stuffing mix and butter; top with pork chops. Cover and cook for 10-12 minutes or until a meat thermometer reads 160°. **Yield:** 4 servings.

Fruity Flavor

To give the stuffing in Sunday Pork Chops a slightly sweet flavor, substitute apricot nectar for about half of the chicken broth.

roasted pork tenderloin and vegetables

DIANE MARTIN | BROWN DEER, WISCONSIN

There are no complicated steps to follow when preparing this roasted medley of tender pork and veggies. Just season with herbs, then pop it in the oven for less than an hour.

PREP: 10 MIN. BAKE: 30 MIN.

- 2 pork tenderloins (3/4 pound *each*)
- 2 pounds red potatoes, quartered
- 1 pound carrots, halved and cut into 2-inch pieces
- 1 medium onion, cut into wedges
- 1 tablespoon olive oil
- 2 teaspoons dried rosemary, crushed
- 1 teaspoon rubbed sage
- 1/2 teaspoon salt
- 1/4 teaspoon pepper

■ Place the pork in a shallow roasting pan coated with cooking spray; arrange the potatoes, carrots and onion around pork. Drizzle with oil. Combine the seasonings; sprinkle over meat and vegetables.

■ Bake, uncovered, at 450° for 30-40 minutes or until a meat thermometer reads 160°, stirring the vegetables occasionally. **Yield:** 6 servings.

jambalaya skillet

NORLENE RAZAK | KYLE, TEXAS

Quick, easy and delicious is how I describe my skillet supper. It remains a real standby recipe for me. I can always turn out a tasty batch of it in a hurry for unexpected company, yet it's a little more special than many spur-of-the-minute meals.

PREP/TOTAL TIME: 30 MIN.

- 1/2 pound boneless skinless chicken breast, cubed
- 2 tablespoons butter
- 1 pound smoked kielbasa *or* Polish sausage, halved lengthwise and cut into 1/4-inch slices
- 1 can (14-1/2 ounces) stewed tomatoes
- 1 cup chicken broth
- 1 medium green pepper, diced
- 1 medium onion, diced
- 1-1/2 cups uncooked instant rice
- 1/2 teaspoon salt, optional
- 1/2 teaspoon hot pepper sauce

■ In a large skillet, cook the chicken in butter over medium heat until no longer pink. Add the kielbasa, tomatoes, broth, green pepper and onion; bring to a boil. Stir in the rice, salt if desired and hot pepper sauce. Remove from the heat; cover and let stand for 5 minutes. **Yield:** 6 servings.

smoked sausage potato bake

JOANNE WERNER | LA PORTE, INDIANA

My mom passed this recipe along to me. I often fix it for company because it's pleasing to the eye as well as the appetite. I rarely have leftovers, since second helpings are a given.

PREP: 10 MIN. BAKE: 30 MIN.

- 1-3/4 cups water
- 2/3 cup milk
- 5 tablespoons butter, *divided*
- 1/2 teaspoon salt
- 2-2/3 cups mashed potato flakes
- 1 cup (8 ounces) sour cream
- 1 cup (4 ounces) shredded cheddar cheese
- 1 pound smoked sausage links, halved lengthwise and cut into 1/2-inch slices
- 1 cup (4 ounces) shredded Monterey Jack cheese
- 2 tablespoons dry bread crumbs

■ In a large saucepan, bring the water, milk, 4 tablespoons butter and salt to a boil. Remove from the heat; stir in potato flakes. Let stand for 30 seconds or until liquid is absorbed. Whip with a fork until fluffy. Stir in sour cream and cheddar cheese.

■ Spoon half into a greased 2-qt. baking dish. Top with sausage and remaining potatoes. Sprinkle with Monterey Jack cheese.

■ Melt remaining butter and toss with bread crumbs; sprinkle over the top. Bake, uncovered, at 350° for 30-35 minutes or until heated through and edges are golden brown. **Yield:** 4-6 servings.

microwave potato ham dinner

SHARON PRICE | CALDWELL, IDAHO

I've had this recipe for 15 years. From the first time I made it, my family couldn't get enough. Now that our three daughters are grown and married, they fix it for their families, too.

PREP/TOTAL TIME: 30 MIN.

- 2 cups cubed peeled potatoes
- 1 cup sliced carrots
- 1 cup chopped celery
- 1/2 cup water
- 2 tablespoons chopped green pepper
- 2 tablespoons chopped onion
- 2 tablespoons reduced-fat margarine
- 3 tablespoons all-purpose flour
- 1/4 teaspoon salt
- 1/8 teaspoon pepper
- 1-1/2 cups 2% milk
- 1/2 cup shredded reduced-fat cheddar cheese
- 2 cups cubed fully cooked lean ham

■ In a large microwave-safe bowl, combine the potatoes, carrots, celery and water. Cover and microwave on high for 5-1/2 minutes, stirring once. Add green pepper and onion; cover and microwave on high for 3-4 minutes or until crisp-tender, stirring once. Pour the mixture into a 2-qt. microwave-safe baking dish coated with cooking spray; set aside.

■ In a microwave-safe bowl, heat the margarine, covered, on high for 30-40 seconds or until melted. Stir in the flour, salt and pepper until smooth. Gradually add milk.

■ Cook, uncovered, on high for 1-1/2 to 2 minutes or until thickened and bubbly, stirring after each minute. Stir in the cheese until melted. Pour over the vegetables. Stir in ham. Cover and microwave on high for 3-4 minutes or until heated through. **Yield:** 4 servings.

Editor's Note: This recipe was tested in a 1,100-watt microwave.

ham and swiss casserole

JULIE JACKMAN | BOUNTIFUL, UTAH

Here's a delightfully rich and creamy, all-in-one meal. My family loves the easy-to-fix sauce, and it's a great way to use up leftover ham. For a delectable, creamy and comforting side dish, simply eliminate the ham.

PREP: 15 MIN. BAKE: 30 MIN.

- 8 ounces uncooked penne pasta
- 2 envelopes country gravy mix
- 1 package (10 ounces) frozen chopped spinach, thawed and squeezed dry
- 2 cups (8 ounces) shredded Swiss cheese
- 2 cups cubed fully cooked ham
- 4-1/2 teaspoons ground mustard

■ Cook pasta according to package directions. Meanwhile, in a large saucepan, cook gravy mix according to package directions. Stir in the spinach, cheese, ham and mustard. Drain the pasta; stir into ham mixture.

■ Transfer to a greased 13-in. x 9-in. baking dish. Cover and bake at 350° for 20 minutes. Uncover; bake 10-15 minutes longer or until heated through. **Yield:** 8 servings.

oven-barbecued pork tenderloins

RUBY WILLIAMS | BOGALUSA, LOUISIANA

Pork tenderloin is one of the leanest cuts of meat. That's why my family still savors and prepares this luscious heirloom recipe.

PREP: 5 MIN. BAKE: 35 MIN.

- 3 tablespoons ketchup
- 2 tablespoons cider vinegar
- 1 tablespoon maple syrup
- 2 teaspoons Dijon mustard
- 1 teaspoon Worcestershire sauce
- 1/8 teaspoon cayenne pepper
- 2 pork tenderloins (3/4 pound *each*)

■ In a small bowl, combine the first six ingredients. Place tenderloins on a rack in a shallow roasting pan; spoon some of the sauce over pork.

■ Bake, uncovered, at 425° for 35-40 minutes or until a meat thermometer reads 160°, basting occasionally with remaining sauce. Let stand for 5 minutes before slicing. **Yield:** 6 servings.

ham with mustard-cream sauce

LISA NELSON | BROKEN ARROW, OKLAHOMA

It's hard to believe that such common ingredients can turn a ham slice into something so uncommonly special. Microwave some potatoes and open a bag of salad mix for a fuss-free meal.

PREP/TOTAL TIME: 20 MIN.

- 4 boneless fully cooked ham steaks (about 5 ounces *each*)
- 1/4 cup water
- 1/4 cup honey mustard
- 1/2 cup sour cream
- 1/4 cup thinly sliced green onions

■ Place ham steaks in a large skillet. In a small bowl, combine water and mustard; pour over ham. Bring to a boil. Reduce heat; cover and simmer for 5 minutes on each side. Remove from the heat; stir in sour cream and onions. **Yield:** 4 servings.

Leftover Green Onions

If you chopped more green onions than you need in your recipe, store the leftovers in a covered clean glass jar in the refrigerator. They'll last a couple of weeks this way. Just shake them out as needed.

tender glazed pork chops

JUDITH WIEZOREK | GAINESVILLE, GEORGIA

Topped with a tangy apricot glaze, these moist pork chops are a breeze to put together. My mother and I both love this recipe. It's excellent with any veggie side dish and rolls.

PREP/TOTAL TIME: 30 MIN.

- 1/2 teaspoon onion powder
- 1/2 teaspoon garlic powder
- 1/2 teaspoon dried oregano
- 4 boneless pork loin chops (3/4 inch thick and 4 ounces *each*)
- 1 cup apricot preserves
- 1-1/2 teaspoons lime juice
- 1-1/2 teaspoons lemon juice
- 2 tablespoons olive oil

■ Combine the onion powder, garlic powder and oregano; sprinkle over pork chops. In a small saucepan, combine the apricot preserves, lime juice and lemon juice; cook and stir over low heat for 10 minutes or until the preserves are melted.

■ Meanwhile, in a large skillet, cook pork in oil over medium-low heat for 8-10 minutes or until lightly browned on one side. Turn chops; generously brush with apricot glaze. Cook 8-10 minutes longer or until a meat thermometer reads 160°. Serve with the remaining glaze. **Yield:** 4 servings.

polish sausage and veggies

RITA KODET | CHULA VISTA, CALIFORNIA

Looking for something different to prepare with Polish sausage, I created this entree one afternoon. My family liked it so well that I've made it time and again since.

PREP/TOTAL TIME: 30 MIN.

- 4 cups cubed peeled potatoes (about 2-1/2 pounds)
- 1 pound smoked Polish sausage *or* smoked kielbasa, cut into 1/4-inch slices
- 1/2 cup chopped onion
- 1/2 cup julienned sweet yellow pepper
- 1/2 cup julienned sweet red pepper
- 1-1/2 teaspoons Cajun seasoning
- 1 tablespoon canola oil
- 1 tablespoon butter

■ In a large skillet over medium heat, cook the potatoes, sausage, onion, peppers and Cajun seasoning in oil and butter for 15-20 minutes or until potatoes are tender, stirring occasionally. **Yield:** 6 servings.

linguine with garlic sauce

TASTE OF HOME TEST KITCHEN

On a chilly evening, this creamy pasta toss is sure to please. It's rich and flavorful with smoky bacon, fresh spinach and toasted pine nuts.

PREP/TOTAL TIME: 30 MIN.

- 12 ounces uncooked linguine
- 1/2 pound sliced bacon, diced
- 5 cups fresh baby spinach
- 1/2 cup chopped onion
- 1/2 teaspoon minced garlic
- 1-1/4 cups milk
- 1 package (8 ounces) cream cheese, cubed
- 2 tablespoons butter
- 1/2 teaspoon salt
- 1/4 teaspoon ground nutmeg
- 1/4 teaspoon pepper
- 1/2 cup pine nuts, toasted

■ Cook the linguine according to package directions. Meanwhile, in a large skillet, cook bacon over medium heat until crisp. Using a slotted spoon, remove to paper towels; drain, reserving 1 tablespoon drippings.

■ In the drippings, saute the spinach, onion and garlic until tender. Add the milk, cream cheese, butter, salt, nutmeg and pepper; stir until smooth. Stir in pine nuts and bacon; heat through. Drain the pasta; toss with the sauce. **Yield:** 4-6 servings.

pork chops with herbed cream sauce

EDITH RUTH MULDOON | BALDWIN, NEW YORK

This dish is perfect for a spur-of-the-moment lunch or no-fuss dinner. The meat cooks up moist and tender, and the bouillon lends instant flavor to the gravy.

PREP/TOTAL TIME: 20 MIN.

- 4 pork rib chops (1/2 inch thick and 7 ounces *each*)
- 2 tablespoons canola oil
- 1 tablespoon all-purpose flour
- 1/2 teaspoon beef bouillon granules
- 1 tablespoon minced fresh parsley
- 1/2 teaspoon dried basil, thyme *or* tarragon
- 2/3 cup whole milk *or* half-and-half cream
- 2 tablespoons water
- 1/8 to 1/4 teaspoon pepper

■ In a large skillet, cook pork chops in oil over medium heat for 5-7 minutes on each side or until a meat thermometer reads 160°. Remove and keep warm.

■ Drain drippings from skillet. Stir in flour, bouillon, parsley and basil. Gradually stir in milk, water and pepper until smooth. Bring to a boil; cook and stir for 2 minutes or until thickened. Serve with chops. **Yield:** 4 servings.

pork 'n' green chili tortillas

BOBBI JONES | CLAYPOOL, ARIZONA

Tortillas are a big hit with my family. I'm even asked to make them for special occasions.

PREP: 15 MIN. COOK: 30 MIN.

- 1/3 cup all-purpose flour
- 1 teaspoon salt
- 1/2 teaspoon pepper
- 2 pork tenderloins (1 pound *each*), cubed
- 1/4 cup canola oil
- 6 cans (4 ounces *each*) chopped green chilies
- 1/2 cup salsa
- 12 flour tortillas (8 inches), warmed
- Shredded cheddar cheese

■ In a large resealable plastic bag, combine the flour, salt and pepper; add the pork. Seal bag and toss to coat.

■ In a large skillet, cook pork over medium heat in oil until no longer pink. Add chilies and salsa. Bring to a boil. Reduce heat; cover and simmer for 30 minutes or until meat is tender.

■ Spoon 1/2 cup pork mixture down the center of each tortilla. Sprinkle with cheese; roll up. **Yield:** 6 servings.

italian sausage with bow ties

JANELLE MOORE | FEDERAL WAY, WASHINGTON

Here's a family favorite that's requested monthly in our house. The Italian sausage paired with creamy tomato sauce tastes out of this world. Not only is this dish simple to make, it tastes like you slaved over a hot stove for hours!

PREP/TOTAL TIME: 25 MIN.

- 1 package (16 ounces) bow tie pasta
- 1 pound bulk Italian sausage
- 1/2 cup chopped onion
- 1/2 teaspoon crushed red pepper flakes
- 1-1/2 teaspoons minced garlic
- 2 cans (14-1/2 ounces *each*) Italian stewed tomatoes, drained and chopped
- 1-1/2 cups heavy whipping cream
- 1/2 teaspoon salt
- 1/4 teaspoon dried basil
- Shredded Parmesan cheese

■ Cook pasta according to package directions. Meanwhile, in a Dutch oven, cook the sausage, onion and pepper flakes over medium heat for 4-5 minutes or until meat is no longer pink. Add garlic; cook 1 minute longer. Drain.

■ Stir in the tomatoes, cream, salt and basil. Bring to a boil over medium heat. Reduce heat; simmer, uncovered, for 6-8 minutes or until thickened, stirring occasionally. Drain pasta; toss with sausage mixture. Garnish with cheese. **Yield:** 5 servings.

Sweet Sausage

When a recipe calls for Italian sausage, it is referring to sweet Italian sausage. If you prefer your foods on the spicy side, you can substitute hot Italian sausage.

peanutty pork stir-fry

GINA BERRY | CHANHASSEN, MINNESOTA

The easy, colorful stir-fry with an Oriental flavor will become a popular mainstay at your house.

PREP/TOTAL TIME: 25 MIN.

- 1 can (8 ounces) pineapple chunks
- 1/2 pound pork tenderloin, cut into 1/2-inch strips
- 1 tablespoon sesame oil
- 3/4 cup julienned sweet red pepper
- 3/4 cup chopped carrot
- 2 green onions, chopped
- 3 tablespoons reduced-sodium soy sauce
- 3 tablespoons reduced-sodium teriyaki sauce
- 1 tablespoon creamy peanut butter
- 1/4 cup unsalted dry roasted peanuts, finely chopped
- Hot cooked rice, optional

■ Drain pineapple, reserving juice; set aside. In a large skillet, stir-fry pork in oil until no longer pink. Add the red pepper, carrot and onions; cook and stir for 2-3 minutes or until crisp-tender.

■ Stir in the soy sauce, teriyaki sauce, peanut butter and reserved pineapple juice. Bring to a boil; cook and stir for 1-2 minutes or until thickened. Stir in peanuts and pineapple. Serve with rice if desired. **Yield:** 2 servings.

spicy pork with noodles

ANN VAN TASSELL | MARYSVILLE, WASHINGTON

I've been making this quick pasta pork dish for years. It's convenient because the noodles don't need to be boiled separately.

PREP/TOTAL TIME: 30 MIN.

- 1/4 cup plus 2 tablespoons sliced green onions, *divided*
- 2 teaspoons minced fresh gingerroot
- 1 tablespoon canola oil
- 3 garlic cloves, minced
- 1/3 pound ground pork
- 1 can (8 ounces) sliced water chestnuts, drained
- 3 tablespoons reduced-sodium soy sauce
- 1 teaspoon sesame oil
- 1/4 teaspoon crushed red pepper flakes
- 2 cups uncooked egg noodles
- 1-1/2 cups water

■ In a large skillet, saute 1/4 cup onions and ginger in canola oil until tender. Add garlic; cook 1 minute longer. Add pork; cook until juices run clear. Drain.

■ Stir in the water chestnuts, soy sauce, sesame oil and pepper flakes. Add noodles and water. Bring to a boil. Reduce heat; cover and simmer for 5-7 minutes or until the noodles are tender. Sprinkle with the remaining onions. **Yield:** 3 cups.

franks and corn bread

MARILYN HOITEN | ROCKTON, ILLINOIS

We ate this corn bread-topped casserole often when our children were growing up. It's so easy to throw together after work that I still make it for my husband and me.

PREP: 10 MIN. BAKE: 40 MIN.

- 2 cans (16 ounces *each*) pork and beans
- 1 package (12 ounces) hot dogs, halved lengthwise and sliced
- 2 tablespoons brown sugar
- 2 tablespoons Worcestershire sauce
- 2 tablespoons prepared mustard
- 1 package (8-1/2 ounces) corn bread/muffin mix
- 1 cup (4 ounces) shredded cheddar cheese

■ In a large bowl, combine the pork and beans, hot dogs, brown sugar, Worcestershire and mustard. Transfer to a greased 9-in. square baking dish.

■ Prepare corn bread batter according to the package directions; stir in cheese. Drop by spoonfuls onto bean mixture. Bake, uncovered, at 350° for 40-45 minutes or until heated through. **Yield:** 6 servings.

ham with pineapple salsa

DAWN WILSON | BUENA VISTA, COLORADO

A dear friend shared this recipe with me when she moved from Hawaii to Colorado. Now it's one of my favorite ways to eat ham. I get lots of requests for the recipe when I make it for guests.

PREP/TOTAL TIME: 25 MIN.

- 1 can (8 ounces) crushed pineapple, drained
- 2 tablespoons orange marmalade
- 1 tablespoon minced fresh cilantro
- 2 teaspoons lime juice
- 2 teaspoons chopped jalapeno pepper
- 1/4 teaspoon salt
- 1 bone-in fully cooked ham steak (1-1/2 pounds)

■ For the salsa, in a small bowl, combine the first six ingredients; set aside.

■ Place the ham steak on an ungreased rack in a broiler pan. Broil 4-6 in. from the heat for 4-5 minutes on each side or until a meat thermometer reads 140°. Cut into serving-size pieces; serve with salsa. **Yield:** 4 servings.

Editor's Note: When cutting hot peppers, disposable gloves are recommended. Avoid touching your face.

mustard pork medallions

TASTE OF HOME TEST KITCHEN

Brushing these tasty pork medallions with mustard and coating them with seasoned dry bread crumbs before baking makes the meat tender and juicy.

PREP/TOTAL TIME: 25 MIN.

- 1/2 cup seasoned dry bread crumbs
- 1/2 teaspoon dried thyme
- 1/4 teaspoon garlic salt
- 1/4 teaspoon onion powder
- 1-1/4 pounds pork tenderloin
- 1/4 cup Dijon mustard
- 1 tablespoon butter, melted

■ In a shallow bowl, combine the crumbs, thyme, garlic salt and onion powder; set aside. Cut tenderloin widthwise into 12 pieces and pound each piece to 1/4-in. thickness. Combine mustard and butter; brush on each side of pork, then roll in reserved crumb mixture.

■ Place in a greased shallow baking pan. Bake, uncovered, at 425° for 10 minutes; turn and bake about 5 minutes more or until no longer pink. **Yield:** 4 servings.

pork and corn casserole

KAREN SESTO | SOUTH PORTLAND, MAINE

A satisfying supper includes this fresh-from-the-oven casserole, a garden salad and buttermilk biscuits. It's a winner every time!

PREP: 15 MIN. BAKE: 30 MIN.

- 7 cups uncooked egg noodles
- 1 pound ground pork
- 1 small green pepper, chopped
- 1 can (14-3/4 ounces) cream-style corn
- 1 can (11-1/2 ounces) condensed chicken with rice soup, undiluted
- 1 jar (2 ounces) diced pimientos, drained
- 8 ounces process cheese (Velveeta), cubed
- 1/2 cup dry bread crumbs
- 2 tablespoons butter, melted

- Cook noodles according to package directions; drain. Meanwhile in a large skillet, cook pork and green pepper over medium heat until meat is no longer pink; drain.
- In a large bowl, combine noodles, corn, soup, pimientos, cheese and pork mixture.
- Transfer to a greased shallow 2-1/2-qt. baking dish. Combine bread crumbs and butter; sprinkle over noodle mixture. Bake, uncovered, at 350° for 30-35 minutes or until bubbly and top is golden brown. **Yield:** 6-8 servings.

What is Process Cheese?

Process cheese is a blend of different cheeses that is similar in flavor to the natural cheese from which it's made. It stores at room temperature and stays smooth and creamy when heated.

glazed pork chops and apples

KATHY BARRY | LAKE FOREST, CALIFORNIA

This hearty dish was always a family favorite when I was growing up. Mom called the tender chops "fried monkey ears!" Now it's a favored meal with my own family.

PREP/TOTAL TIME: 30 MIN.

4 boneless pork loin chops (4 ounces *each*)
3/4 teaspoon rubbed sage
1/2 teaspoon salt
1 tablespoon canola oil
1 tablespoon all-purpose flour
1/2 cup reduced-sodium chicken broth
1 tablespoon cider vinegar
2 medium tart apples, thinly sliced
4 teaspoons brown sugar

- Sprinkle pork chops with sage and salt. In a large skillet, brown chops in oil on both sides. Transfer to an 11-in. x 7-in. baking dish coated with cooking spray.
- Stir flour into the pan drippings until blended. Gradually stir in broth and vinegar. Bring to a boil; cook and stir for 1-2 minutes or until thickened. Remove from the heat.
- Arrange apples over chops; sprinkle with brown sugar. Drizzle with broth mixture. Bake, uncovered, at 350° for 20-25 minutes or until a meat thermometer reads 160°. **Yield:** 4 servings.

pineapple ham casserole

MARSHA FLEMING | KULA, HAWAII

Living in Hawaii, I wanted to share this recipe, which features pineapple. It's our most important fruit crop.

PREP: 15 MIN. BAKE: 30 MIN.

- 2 cups uncooked wide egg noodles
- 1/2 cup chopped celery
- 2 tablespoons butter, *divided*
- 1 package (8 ounces) cream cheese, cubed
- 3/4 cup milk
- 2 cups cubed fully cooked ham
- 2 cans (8 ounces *each*) crushed pineapple, drained
- 2 teaspoons Worcestershire sauce
- 1/2 teaspoon salt
- Dash pepper
- 1/4 cup dry bread crumbs

■ Cook noodles according to package directions; drain. In a large skillet, saute celery in 1 tablespoon butter until tender. Stir in cream cheese and milk; cook and stir until cheese is melted. Add the noodles, ham, pineapple, Worcestershire sauce, salt and pepper.

■ Transfer to an ungreased 1-1/2-qt. baking dish. Melt remaining butter; toss with bread crumbs. Sprinkle over the top. Bake, uncovered, at 350° for 30-35 minutes or until heated through. **Yield:** 4 servings.

Fresh Lemon Juice

When you have excess lemons on hand, juice them and freeze the juice in ice cube trays. Measure 1 or 2 tablespoons of juice into each compartment in your ice cube tray. When frozen, remove the cubes and place them in resealable freezer bags.

lemon-pecan pork chops

KATIE SLOAN | CHARLOTTE, NORTH CAROLINA

I like to serve these quick-to-fry chops with garlic mashed potatoes and sweet peas.

PREP/TOTAL TIME: 30 MIN.

- 4 boneless pork loin chops (7 ounces *each*)
- 1 teaspoon lemon-pepper seasoning
- 1/2 teaspoon garlic salt
- 1 tablespoon butter
- 1 cup chopped pecans
- 1/4 cup lemon juice

■ Sprinkle pork chops with lemon-pepper and garlic salt. In a large skillet over medium heat, cook chops in butter for 8-10 minutes on each side or until a meat thermometer reads 160°. Remove and keep warm.

■ Add the pecans and lemon juice to the skillet; cook and stir for 1 minute or until heated through. Spoon over pork chops. **Yield:** 4 servings.

springtime penne

CHERYL NEWENDORP | PELLA, IOWA

With ham, asparagus, onion and pasta in a creamy sauce, this stovetop supper is tasty enough for even your pickiest guests. It's great with penne, but feel free to try it with mostaccioli or another type of pasta.

PREP/TOTAL TIME: 20 MIN.

- 3 cups uncooked penne pasta
- 1 pound fresh asparagus, trimmed and cut into 1-inch pieces
- 1 large onion, chopped
- 1/4 cup butter, cubed
- 1/2 pound cubed fully cooked ham
- 1/2 cup heavy whipping cream
- 1/4 teaspoon pepper
- 1/8 teaspoon salt

■ Cook pasta according to package directions. Meanwhile, in a large skillet, saute asparagus and onion in butter for 5-8 minutes or until asparagus is crisp-tender. Add the ham, cream, pepper and salt; bring to a boil. Reduce heat; cook over low heat for 1 minute. Drain pasta. Add to the asparagus mixture; toss to coat. **Yield:** 8 servings.

southwestern sausage skillet

VALERIE HERTEL | ST. LOUIS, MISSOURI

In 30 minutes flat and with only one pan, you can have a hearty and flavorful Mexican meal. This skillet dinner features tender pasta, mouthwatering pork sausage, diced veggies and lots of seasoning. It freezes nicely if made ahead.

PREP/TOTAL TIME: 30 MIN.

- 1/3 pound bulk pork sausage
- 1/3 cup chopped onion
- 1/3 cup chopped green pepper
- 3/4 cup canned diced tomatoes
- 3/4 cup buttermilk
- 3/4 cup uncooked small pasta shells
- 1 teaspoon sugar
- 1/2 teaspoon chili powder
- 1/4 teaspoon salt

■ In a large skillet, cook the sausage, onion and green pepper over medium heat until the meat is no longer pink; drain.

■ Stir in the remaining ingredients. Bring to a boil. Reduce heat; cover and simmer for 8-10 minutes or until pasta is tender. **Yield:** 2 servings.

pork and sweet potatoes

MARY RELYEA | CANASTOTA, NEW YORK

Sweet potatoes, sliced apple and moist pork tenderloin blend perfectly in this simple meal-in-one. Dried cranberries lend a burst of color, making the main course look just as good as it tastes!

PREP/TOTAL TIME: 30 MIN.

- 1 pork tenderloin (1 pound), cut into 12 slices
- 1/2 cup all-purpose flour
- 1/2 teaspoon salt
- 1/4 teaspoon pepper
- 1 tablespoon canola oil
- 1 can (14-1/2 ounces) reduced-sodium chicken broth
- 2 medium sweet potatoes, peeled and cubed
- 1/2 cup dried cranberries
- 1 tablespoon Dijon mustard
- 1 medium red apple, sliced
- 4 green onions, chopped

- Flatten pork to 1/4-in. thickness. In a large resealable plastic bag, combine the flour, salt and pepper; add pork, a few pieces at a time, and shake to coat.
- In a large nonstick skillet coated with cooking spray, brown pork in oil in batches. Remove and keep warm. Add the broth, sweet potatoes and cranberries to the skillet. Bring to a boil. Reduce heat; cover and simmer for 4-6 minutes or until the potatoes are almost tender. Stir in the mustard.
- Return pork to the pan; add apple and onions. Cover and simmer for 4-6 minutes or until meat juices run clear. **Yield:** 4 servings.

Slicing Pork Tenderloin

Keep pork tenderloin in the freezer for last-minute meals since it thaws and cooks quickly. To easily slice pork tenderloin, cut it while it's still partially frozen.

ham 'n' cheese pizzas

TASTE OF HOME TEST KITCHEN

With leftover ham, cheese and Alfredo sauce, these pizzas are sure to please. Best of all, they're very kid-friendly.

PREP/TOTAL TIME: 20 MIN.

- 1/4 cup refrigerated Alfredo sauce
- 4 pita breads (6 inches)
- 1 cup (4 ounces) shredded Swiss cheese
- 1-3/4 cups cubed fully cooked ham
- 1/2 cup shredded part-skim mozzarella cheese
- 1 tablespoon minced chives

■ Spread Alfredo sauce over pita breads. Top with the Swiss cheese, ham, mozzarella cheese and chives.

■ Place on an ungreased baking sheet. Bake at 350° for 10-15 minutes or until cheese is melted. **Yield:** 4 servings.

pork with pineapple salsa

NICOLE PICKETT | ORO VALLEY, ARIZONA

Not only does this easy entree taste awesome, but it's good for you, too. A little brown sugar, ground ginger and Dijon mustard help give the moist tenderloin its incredible flavor, and the tangy salsa can be made in no time.

PREP: 10 MIN. BAKE: 30 MIN.

- 1 can (20 ounces) unsweetened pineapple tidbits
- 1 pork tenderloin (1-1/4 pounds)
- 3 tablespoons brown sugar, *divided*
- 2 tablespoons Dijon mustard
- 1 teaspoon paprika
- 1/2 teaspoon ground ginger
- 1/3 cup finely chopped sweet red *or* green pepper
- 1/4 cup chopped green onions
- 1/8 teaspoon crushed red pepper flakes, optional

■ Drain pineapple, reserving 1/4 cup juice. Set aside 1 cup of pineapple (save remaining pineapple for another use). Place the pork on a rack in a shallow roasting pan. Combine 2 tablespoons brown sugar, mustard, paprika and ginger. Spread half over the pork.

■ Bake, uncovered at 450° for 15 minutes. Spread with remaining brown sugar mixture. Bake 15-20 minutes longer or until a meat thermometer reads 160°.

■ Meanwhile, for salsa, in a small bowl, combine the red pepper, onions, pepper flakes if desired, remaining brown sugar, reserved pineapple and juice. Let the pork stand for 5 minutes before slicing. Serve with the salsa. **Yield:** 4 servings.

pork and green chili casserole

DIANNE ESPOSITE | NEW MIDDLETOWN, OHIO

I work at a local hospital and also part-time for some area doctors, so I'm always on the lookout for good, quick recipes to fix for my family. Some of my co-workers and I exchange recipes. This zippy casserole is one that was brought to a picnic at my house. People raved over it.

PREP: 20 MIN. BAKE: 30 MIN.

- 1-1/2 pounds boneless pork, cut into 1/2-inch cubes
- 1 tablespoon canola oil
- 1 can (15 ounces) black beans, rinsed and drained
- 1 can (10-3/4 ounces) condensed cream of chicken soup, undiluted
- 1 can (14-1/2 ounces) diced tomatoes, undrained
- 2 cans (4 ounces *each*) chopped green chilies
- 1 cup quick-cooking brown rice
- 1/4 cup water
- 2 to 3 tablespoons salsa
- 1 teaspoon ground cumin
- 1/2 cup shredded cheddar cheese

■ In a large skillet, saute pork in oil until no pink remains; drain. Add the beans, soup, tomatoes, chilies, rice, water, salsa and cumin; cook and stir until bubbly.

■ Transfer to an ungreased 2-qt. baking dish. Bake, uncovered, at 350° for 30 minutes or until bubbly. Sprinkle with cheese; let stand a few minutes before serving. **Yield:** 6 servings.

creamed ham in toast cups

CATHERINE CRANDALL | AMITY, OREGON

My grandmother taught me many of her recipes in show-and-cook sessions. Usually, we had this dish on Mondays, following a Sunday lunch of ham, peas and corn. These buttery cups are one of my favorite ways to use leftover ingredients.

PREP/TOTAL TIME: 30 MIN.

- 8 slices bread
- 1/2 cup butter, softened, *divided*
- 1/4 cup all-purpose flour
- 1/8 teaspoon white pepper
- 1 cup milk
- 1 cup heavy whipping cream
- 2 cups chopped fully cooked ham
- 1 cup frozen green peas, thawed
- 1 cup whole kernel corn

Paprika

- Remove and discard crusts from bread; using a rolling pin, flatten to 1/8-in. thickness. Butter both sides of each slice, using 1/4 cup of butter.
- Press bread into eight greased muffin cups or 6-oz. custard cups. Bake at 350° for 15-18 minutes or until golden brown.
- Meanwhile, in a saucepan, melt the remaining butter. Stir in flour and pepper. Gradually stir in milk and cream. Bring to a boil; cook and stir for 2 minutes or until thickened. Reduce heat. Stir in the ham, peas and corn. Cook and stir for 5 minutes or until heated through. Pour mixture into warm toast cups; sprinkle with paprika. **Yield:** 4 servings.

Editor's Note: This recipe is best made with a soft-textured bread such as Wonderbread.

bacon-olive tomato pizza

CINDY CLEMENT | COLORADO SPRINGS, COLORADO

Bacon and tomatoes bring the taste of a BLT to this hearty and delicious pizza. I call this "championship pizza" because it's a winning recipe with my family.

PREP/TOTAL TIME: 30 MIN.

- 1 prebaked 12-inch pizza crust
- 1/3 cup ranch salad dressing
- 1 pound sliced bacon, cooked and crumbled
- 4 plum tomatoes, sliced
- 1 cup sliced fresh mushrooms
- 1 can (2-1/4 ounces) sliced ripe olives, drained
- 2 cups (8 ounces) shredded part-skim mozzarella cheese

- Place the crust on an ungreased 12-in. pizza pan. Top with the salad dressing, bacon, tomatoes, mushrooms, olives and cheese.
- Bake at 450° for 10-12 minutes or until cheese is melted. **Yield:** 8 slices.

ham-noodle bake

MARY RICHARDS | ELLENDALE, MINNESOTA

My husband and I build up an appetite after a long day doing chores on the farm. So I've come to rely on this creamy, comforting casserole. Horseradish and mustard add a little zip.

PREP: 10 MIN. BAKE: 30 MIN.

1/4 cup butter, cubed
1/4 cup all-purpose flour
1/2 teaspoon salt
1/8 teaspoon pepper
2-1/2 cups milk
3 to 4 teaspoons prepared horseradish
1 tablespoon prepared mustard
6 cups cooked wide egg noodles
2 cups cubed fully cooked ham
1 cup cubed cheddar cheese
1/2 cup soft bread crumbs, toasted

- In a large saucepan over medium heat, melt butter. Stir in the flour, salt and pepper until smooth. Gradually add milk. Bring to a boil. Cook and stir for 2 minutes or until thickened and bubbly. Add horseradish and mustard; mix well. Stir in the noodles, ham and cheese.
- Pour into a greased 2-1/2-qt. baking dish. Cover and bake at 350° for 20 minutes. Uncover; sprinkle with bread crumbs. Bake 10-15 minutes longer or until bubbly and heated through. **Yield:** 4-6 servings.

Soft Bread Crumbs

To make 1/2 cup soft bread crumbs, tear one slice of bread into 1-in. pieces. Place in a food processor or blender; cover and push pulse button several times to make coarse crumbs.

almond pork chops with honey mustard

LILLIAN JULOW | GAINESVILLE, FLORIDA

I love how crunchy almonds and sweet mustard sauce jazz up this tender pork dish. Usually, I double the recipe. One chop is never enough for my gang of grown children and grandkids.

PREP/TOTAL TIME: 25 MIN.

- 1/2 cup smoked almonds
- 1/2 cup dry bread crumbs
- 2 eggs
- 1/3 cup all-purpose flour
- 1/4 teaspoon salt
- 1/8 teaspoon pepper
- 4 boneless pork loin chops (1 inch thick and 6 ounces *each*)
- 2 tablespoons olive oil
- 2 tablespoons butter
- 1/2 cup reduced-fat mayonnaise
- 1/4 cup honey
- 2 tablespoons Dijon mustard

- In a food processor, process the almonds until finely chopped. Transfer to a shallow bowl; add bread crumbs. In another bowl, beat the eggs. In a large resealable plastic bag, combine flour, salt and pepper. Add pork chops, one at a time, and shake to coat. Dip in eggs, then coat with almond mixture.
- In a large skillet over medium heat, cook chops in oil and butter for 5 minutes on each side or until a meat thermometer reads 160°. Meanwhile, in a small bowl, combine the mayonnaise, honey and mustard. Serve with pork chops. **Yield:** 4 servings.

Clean Coating

To keep bread crumbs out of your egg mixture, use one hand to dip the chops in the egg and your other hand to dredge the chops in the bread crumbs.

sweet and sour pork

DORIS SOKOLOTOSKY | SMOKY LAKE, ALBERTA

My kids always asked for this tangy pork dish when they came home from college for the weekend. Today, they still appreciate the stir-fry's comforting flavor.

PREP/TOTAL TIME: 15 MIN.

- 1 can (20 ounces) pineapple chunks
- 2 tablespoons cornstarch
- 1/4 cup soy sauce
- 1 tablespoon honey
- 1/2 teaspoon chicken bouillon granules
- 1 garlic clove, minced
- 1/8 teaspoon pepper
- 2 tablespoons canola oil
- 3/4 pound pork tenderloin, cut into bite-size pieces
- 1 medium green pepper, thinly sliced

Hot cooked rice

- Drain pineapple, reserving the juice; set pineapple aside. Add enough water to juice to measure 3/4 cup. Combine the cornstarch, soy sauce, honey, bouillon, garlic, pepper and pineapple juice mixture until smooth; set aside.
- Heat oil in a large skillet; cook and stir pork and green pepper for 6-8 minutes or until pork is no longer pink and green pepper is crisp-tender.
- Stir the pineapple juice mixture; add to the skillet with the pineapple. Bring to a boil. Cook and stir for 1-2 minutes or until thickened and bubbly. Serve with the rice. **Yield:** 4 servings.

sausage and broccoli bake

ROBIN MOHERMAN | ASHLAND, OHIO

I make this easy meat and veggie bake often because it provides plenty of delicious leftovers for later. It would go over big as a featured entree for a brunch buffet.

PREP: 20 MIN. BAKE: 30 MIN.

- 3 cups frozen chopped broccoli
- 1 pound bulk Italian sausage
- 3 cups seasoned salad croutons
- 2 cups (8 ounces) shredded sharp cheddar cheese
- 4 eggs, lightly beaten
- 1 can (10-3/4 ounces) condensed cream of broccoli soup, undiluted
- 1-1/3 cups milk
- 1 can (2.8 ounces) french-fried onions

- Cook broccoli according to package directions; drain and set aside. In a large skillet, cook sausage over medium heat until the meat is no longer pink; drain. Add the broccoli, croutons and cheese.
- Transfer to a greased 2-qt. baking dish. In a large bowl, combine the eggs, soup and milk. Pour over sausage mixture. Bake, uncovered, at 375° for 25 minutes. Sprinkle with french-fried onions. Bake for 3-5 minutes longer or until a knife inserted near the center comes out clean. **Yield:** 6-8 servings.

p. 189

chicken & turkey

turkey mostaccioli bake

DONNA EBERT | RICHFIELD, WISCONSIN

I often serve this meal-in-one dish at casual dinner parties and always get compliments.

PREP: 35 MIN. BAKE: 30 MIN.

- 8 ounces uncooked mostaccioli
- 1/2 pound lean ground turkey
- 1 small onion, chopped
- 1 can (14-1/2 ounces) diced tomatoes, undrained
- 1 can (6 ounces) tomato paste
- 1/3 cup water
- 1 teaspoon dried oregano
- 1/2 teaspoon salt
- 1/8 teaspoon pepper
- 2 cups (16 ounces) fat-free cottage cheese
- 1 teaspoon dried marjoram
- 1-1/2 cups (6 ounces) shredded part-skim mozzarella cheese
- 1/4 cup grated Parmesan cheese

■ Cook the mostaccioli according to package directions. Meanwhile, in a large saucepan, cook the turkey and onion over medium heat until the meat is no longer pink; drain if necessary.

■ Stir in the tomatoes, tomato paste, water, oregano, salt and pepper. Bring to a boil. Reduce the heat; cover and simmer for 15 minutes.

■ In a small bowl, combine cottage cheese and marjoram; set aside. Drain mostaccioli.

■ Spread 1/2 cup meat sauce into an 11-in. x 7-in. baking dish coated with cooking spray. Layer with half of the mostaccioli, meat sauce and mozzarella cheese. Top with cottage cheese mixture. Layer with remaining mostaccioli, meat sauce and mozzarella cheese. Sprinkle with the Parmesan cheese (dish will be full).

■ Bake, uncovered, at 350° for 30-40 minutes or until bubbly and heated through. **Yield:** 6 servings.

Good-for-You Ground Turkey

If you're watching your fat intake, keep an eye on what kind of ground turkey you buy. Packages labeled "ground turkey" may contain skin and dark meat. For a leaner product, buy ground turkey breast.

turkey sausage stew

SHARON MOON | HARTSVILLE, SOUTH CAROLINA

My family loves traditional beef stew, so they were skeptical when I served my turkey sausage version. But they soon began asking for this time and again.

PREP: 10 MIN. COOK: 35 MIN.

- 1 package (16 ounces) frozen vegetables for stew
- 1 can (10-3/4 ounces) reduced-sodium condensed tomato soup, undiluted
- 2 cups water
- 1 pound low-fat smoked turkey sausage, sliced 1/4 inch thick
- 1/4 cup ketchup
- 2 garlic cloves, minced
- 1/2 teaspoon dried basil
- 1/4 teaspoon pepper

■ In a large saucepan, combine the vegetables, soup and water; bring to a boil. Reduce heat. Add remaining ingredients; simmer for 35-45 minutes or until the vegetables are tender. **Yield:** 8 servings.

tender turkey burgers

SHERRY HULSMAN | LOUISVILLE, KENTUCKY

These juicy, tender patties on whole wheat buns make wholesome, satisfying sandwiches. We especially like to grill them for get-togethers.

PREP/TOTAL TIME: 30 MIN.

- 2/3 cup soft whole wheat bread crumbs
- 1/2 cup finely chopped celery
- 1/4 cup finely chopped onion
- 1/4 cup egg substitute
- 1 tablespoon minced fresh parsley
- 1 teaspoon Worcestershire sauce
- 1 teaspoon dried oregano
- 1/2 teaspoon salt
- 1/4 teaspoon pepper
- 1-1/4 pounds lean ground turkey
- 6 whole wheat hamburger buns, split

■ In a large bowl, combine the first nine ingredients. Crumble turkey over mixture; mix well. Shape into six patties.

■ Pan-fry, grill or broil until a meat thermometer reads 165° and juices run clear. Serve on buns. **Yield:** 6 servings.

country barbecued chicken

TASTE OF HOME TEST KITCHEN

This moist chicken takes minutes to cook using the direct grilling method. The thick, zesty sauce is equally tasty over pork. If you'd like, make a double batch of sauce and reserve half of it to serve at the table.

PREP/TOTAL TIME: 15 MIN.

- 3/4 cup ketchup
- 1 tablespoon molasses
- 2 teaspoons brown sugar
- 1 teaspoon chili powder
- 1 teaspoon canola oil
- 1/2 teaspoon Worcestershire sauce
- 1 garlic clove, minced
- 1-1/2 to 2 pounds boneless skinless chicken breast halves
- 2 tablespoons butter, melted

■ In a small bowl, combine the first seven ingredients. Cover and refrigerate until ready to use.

■ Brush chicken with butter. Grill, uncovered, over medium heat for 3-4 minutes on each side or until browned. Baste with barbecue sauce. Grill 4-6 minutes longer or until a meat thermometer reads 170°, basting and turning often. **Yield:** 4-6 servings (3/4 cup barbecue sauce).

mushroom chicken italiano

BECKY KINNISON | CELINA, OHIO

My husband enjoys this easy chicken dish served with long grain and wild rice. Parsley potatoes would also be delicious with it.

PREP/TOTAL TIME: 30 MIN.

4 boneless skinless chicken breast halves (4 ounces *each*)
1 tablespoon canola oil
3/4 cup creamy Italian salad dressing
1/4 cup white wine *or* chicken broth
1-1/2 cups sliced fresh mushrooms
Hot cooked rice

■ In a large skillet, brown chicken in oil on all sides. In a small bowl, combine the salad dressing, wine and mushrooms; pour over chicken. Cover and simmer for 15-20 minutes or until a meat thermometer reads 170°. Serve with rice. **Yield:** 4 servings.

campfire chicken stew

FLORENCE KREIS | BEACH PARK, ILLINOIS

Chicken stew packets always appear on the menu during our family camping trips, but they're equally good on our backyard grill.

PREP: 30 MIN. GRILL: 40 MIN.

1 broiler/fryer chicken (3-1/2 to 4 pounds), cut up
3 to 4 medium potatoes, peeled and sliced
1 cup thinly sliced carrots
1 medium green pepper, sliced
1 can (10-3/4 ounces) condensed cream of mushroom soup, undiluted
1/4 cup water
1/2 teaspoon salt
1/4 teaspoon pepper

■ Grill chicken, covered, over medium heat for 3 minutes on each side. Place two pieces of chicken on each of four double thicknesses of heavy-duty foil (about 18 in. x 12 in.). Divide the potatoes, carrots and green pepper among the packets. Top each with soup, water, salt and pepper. Fold foil around mixture and seal tightly.

■ Grill, covered, over medium heat for 20-25 minutes on each side or until chicken juices run clear. Open foil carefully to allow steam to escape. **Yield:** 4 servings.

dilled turkey breast

NANCY BOHLEN | BROOKINGS, SOUTH DAKOTA

A handful of ingredients and a few moments are all I need to whip up this lovely stovetop specialty. It's perfect for busy weeknights.

PREP/TOTAL TIME: 15 MIN.

1 can (10-3/4 ounces) condensed cream of mushroom soup, undiluted
3/4 cup chicken broth
3/4 cup sour cream
1 tablespoon dill weed
Sliced cooked turkey, warmed

■ In a large saucepan, combine the soup, broth, sour cream and dill. Cook until heated through but do not boil. Arrange turkey slices on a platter; pour sauce over and serve immediately. **Yield:** 6-8 servings.

turkey florentine

EMILY CHANEY | BLUE HILL, MAINE

This creamy dish is one of my family's favorite ways to use up leftover turkey and gravy. With the spinach and noodles, it's a hearty meal-in-one.

PREP: 15 MIN. BAKE: 25 MIN.

1 package (10 ounces) frozen chopped spinach
2 tablespoons butter
2 cups cooked noodles
1-1/2 cups diced cooked turkey
1 cup turkey *or* chicken gravy
1 carton (8 ounces) sour cream onion dip
1/2 teaspoon onion salt
2 tablespoons grated Parmesan cheese

■ Cook spinach according to package directions; drain. Stir in butter. Place noodles in a greased 11-in. x 7-in. baking dish; top with spinach.

■ In a large bowl, combine the turkey, gravy, onion dip and onion salt; spoon over spinach. Sprinkle with cheese. Bake, uncovered, at 325° for 25 minutes or until bubbly. **Yield:** 6 servings.

ranch chicken salad

TASTE OF HOME TEST KITCHEN

Serving salad for dinner is anything but skimpy. There's chicken and cheese in every bite, and celery and apples give it a great crunch.

PREP/TOTAL TIME: 30 MIN.

- 2 tablespoons plus 1 teaspoon paprika
- 4 teaspoons brown sugar
- 3 teaspoons garlic powder
- 1 teaspoon seasoned salt
- 1/8 teaspoon cayenne pepper
- 4 boneless skinless chicken breast halves (4 ounces *each*)
- 2 packages (5 ounces *each*) spring mix salad greens
- 1 cup chopped celery
- 1 cup shredded carrots
- 1 medium apple, chopped
- 1/2 cup shredded cheddar cheese
- 1/2 cup reduced-fat ranch salad dressing

■ In a large resealable plastic bag, combine the first five ingredients. Add chicken, one piece at a time, and shake to coat. Place chicken on a greased broiler pan. Broil 6 in. from the heat for 6-8 minutes on each side or until chicken juices run clear.

■ Meanwhile, divide salad greens among four dinner plates. Top each with celery, carrots, apple and cheese. Cut chicken into strips; arrange over the salads. Drizzle with dressing. **Yield:** 4 servings.

Salad Substitutes

Make a salad to suit your tastes. Experiment with different salad greens, like romaine and a classic iceberg blend. Or toss in dried cranberries and juicy pomegranate seeds.

harvest vegetable bake

JANET WEISSER | SEATTLE, WASHINGTON

This delicious dish is packed with a large assortment of vegetables. Served with a green salad, it makes an excellent entree.

PREP: 10 MIN. BAKE: 1-1/2 HOURS

2-1/2 to 3 pounds boneless skinless chicken thighs
2 bay leaves
4 small red potatoes, cut into 1-inch pieces
4 small onions, quartered
4 small carrots, cut into 2-inch pieces
2 celery ribs, cut into 2-inch pieces
2 small turnips, peeled and cut into 1-inch peices
1 medium green pepper, cut into 1-inch pieces
12 small fresh mushrooms
2 teaspoons salt
1 teaspoon dried rosemary, crushed
1/2 teaspoon pepper
1 can (14-1/2 ounces) diced tomatoes, undrained

- Place chicken in a greased 13-in. x 9-in. baking dish; add bay leaves. Top with the potatoes, onions, carrots, celery, turnips, green pepper and mushrooms. Sprinkle with salt, rosemary and pepper. Pour tomatoes over all.
- Cover and bake at 375° for 1-1/2 hours or until chicken juices run clear and vegetables are tender. Discard bay leaves before serving. **Yield:** 6-8 servings.

sesame chicken

ELIZABETH LIMESTAHL | PORT CLINTON, OHIO

My mother passed down the recipe for this speedy and easy stir-fry. Served with wild rice and vegetables, it's a wholesome meal in minutes.

PREP/TOTAL TIME: 30 MIN.

1-1/4 pounds boneless skinless chicken breasts, cubed
2 tablespoons canola oil
1/4 cup soy sauce
1/4 cup sesame seeds
1 large onion, sliced
2 jars (4-1/2 ounces *each*) sliced mushrooms, drained *or* 2 cups sliced fresh mushrooms

- In a large skillet, cook chicken in oil until no longer pink. Stir in the soy sauce and sesame seeds. Cook and stir over medium heat for 5 minutes.
- Remove chicken with a slotted spoon; set aside and keep warm. In the same skillet, saute onion and mushrooms until onion is tender. Return chicken to pan; heat through. **Yield:** 5 servings.

chicken in a haystack

HELLE WATSON | THORNTON, COLORADO

This is probably one of the quickest meals in my recipe file and a wonderful way to please picky eaters. Youngsters will love "stacking" their favorite toppings over this creamy chicken and rice combo.

PREP/TOTAL TIME: 15 MIN.

1 can (10-3/4 ounces) condensed cream of chicken soup, undiluted
2 cups cubed cooked chicken
1/2 cup water
Hot cooked rice
TOPPINGS:
Cooked peas, raisins, pineapple tidbits, shredded cheddar cheese, sliced ripe olives, chow mein noodles *and/or* mandarin oranges

- In a microwave-safe bowl, combine the soup, chicken and water. Cover and microwave on high for 2-3 minutes or until heated through. Serve over rice. Top with toppings of your choice. **Yield:** 4 servings.

Editor's Note: This recipe was tested in a 1,100-watt microwave.

chicken spaghetti

REGINA CLACK | BONNEVILLE, ARKANSAS

My family loves this meal of tender chicken and noodles tossed with zippy tomatoes and a creamy cheese sauce. I like it because it doesn't heat up the kitchen on hot days.

PREP/TOTAL TIME: 30 MIN.

- 1 package (7 ounces) thin spaghetti
- 1 pound process American cheese (Velveeta), cubed
- 1 can (10 ounces) diced tomatoes and green chilies, undrained
- 4 cups cubed cooked chicken

■ Cook the spaghetti according to package directions. Meanwhile, in a large saucepan, combine cheese and tomatoes; cook and stir until cheese is melted. Add chicken; heat through. Drain spaghetti; toss with cheese sauce. **Yield:** 4-6 servings.

lattice chicken potpie

ANGIE COTTRELL | SUN PRAIRIE, WISCONSIN

My sister shared this great recipe with me. Because it features all four food groups, it's the only dish you have to prepare for dinner.

PREP: 10 MIN. BAKE: 35 MIN.

- 1 package (16 ounces) frozen California-blend vegetables
- 2 cups cubed cooked chicken
- 1 can (10-3/4 ounces) condensed cream of potato soup, undiluted
- 1 cup milk
- 1 cup (4 ounces) shredded cheddar cheese
- 1 can (2.8 ounces) french-fried onions
- 1/2 teaspoon seasoned salt
- 1 tube (8 ounces) refrigerated crescent rolls

■ In a large bowl, combine the vegetables, chicken, soup, milk, cheese, onions and seasoned salt. Transfer to a greased shallow 2-qt. baking dish.

■ Unroll the crescent roll dough and separate into two rectangles. Seal the perforations; cut each rectangle lengthwise into 1/2-in. strips. Form a lattice crust over the chicken mixture. Bake, uncovered, at 375° for 35-40 minutes or until golden brown. **Yield:** 4-6 servings.

easy italian chicken

JOAN ROSE | LANGLEY, BRITISH COLUMBIA

When we want a hearty Italian dish but I don't want to spend hours cooking, this is the recipe I choose. Boneless skinless chicken breasts are convenient to have in the freezer because they thaw and cook quickly. Plus, I always have the other ingredients in my pantry.

PREP/TOTAL TIME: 25 MIN.

- 4 boneless skinless chicken breast halves (4 ounces *each*)
- 1 can (14-1/2 ounces) Italian stewed tomatoes
- 1 can (4 ounces) mushroom stems and pieces, drained
- 1/2 teaspoon dried basil
- 1/4 teaspoon garlic powder
- 1 tablespoon cornstarch
- 1/3 cup cold water

Hot cooked spaghetti

■ In a large skillet coated with cooking spray, cook chicken for 5-6 minutes on each side or until a meat thermometer reads 170°.

■ Meanwhile, in a saucepan over medium heat, combine the tomatoes, mushrooms, basil and garlic powder; bring to a boil. Combine cornstarch and water; gradually add to tomato mixture. Cook and stir for 2 minutes or until thickened. Serve chicken with spaghetti; top with tomato sauce. **Yield:** 4 servings.

grilled turkey sandwiches

MARY DETWEILER | MIDDLEFIELD, OHIO

Moist grilled turkey sandwiches are a welcome change from the usual burger or grilled chicken sandwich. The flavorful marinade makes the meat so juicy and tender.

PREP: 20 MIN. + MARINATING GRILL: 10 MIN.

- 1/2 cup chicken broth
- 1/4 cup olive oil
- 4-1/2 teaspoons finely chopped onion
- 1 tablespoon white wine vinegar
- 2 teaspoons dried parsley flakes
- 1/2 teaspoon salt
- 1/2 teaspoon rubbed sage
- 1/8 teaspoon pepper
- 6 turkey breast cutlets (about 1 pound)
- 6 whole wheat hamburger buns, split
- 6 lettuce leaves
- 6 tomato slices

■ In a large resealable plastic bag, combine the first eight ingredients; add the turkey. Seal bag and turn to coat; refrigerate for 12 hours or overnight, turning once. If grilling the turkey, coat grill rack with cooking spray before starting the grill. Drain and discard marinade.

■ Grill turkey, covered, over indirect medium heat or broil 6 in. from the heat for 3-4 minutes on each side or until no longer pink. Serve on buns with lettuce and tomato. **Yield:** 6 servings.

Grilling Cutlets

Because turkey cutlets are very thin, they don't take too long to cook. To prevent the meat from becoming dry over the hot grill, be sure to time them carefully and not overcook them.

pizza chicken roll-ups

TANJA PENQUITE | OREGON, OHIO

I love the spinach-and-cream-cheese chicken roll-ups my mom made for special occasions. My own kids wouldn't eat those, so I came up with these pizza-flavored ones that the whole family enjoys.

PREP: 10 MIN. BAKE: 40 MIN.

- 4 boneless skinless chicken breast halves (4 ounces *each*)
- 12 pepperoni slices
- 8 slices slices part-skim mozzarella cheese
- 1 can (15 ounces) pizza sauce

■ Flatten chicken to 1/4-in. thickness. Place three slices of pepperoni and one slice of cheese on each. Roll up tightly; secure with toothpicks. Place in a greased 11-in. x 7-in. baking dish. Spoon pizza sauce over top.

■ Cover and bake at 350° for 35-40 minutes or until chicken is no longer pink. Uncover; top with the remaining cheese. Bake 5 minutes longer or until the cheese is melted. **Yield:** 4 servings.

tasty texas tenders

JOAN DINGER | FULSHEAR, TEXAS

When time gets away from you and your clan is hungry, prepare this fun, fast finger food. The chicken is crispy outside and tender inside. Kids of all ages will love it!

PREP: 10 MIN. BAKE: 30 MIN.

- 1 pound chicken tenders *or* boneless skinless chicken breasts
- 3 cups crisp rice cereal, crushed
- 1 teaspoon garlic salt
- 1 teaspoon dill weed
- 1/4 cup canola oil

Sour cream, optional

■ If using chicken breasts, cut into 4-in. strips; set aside. In a shallow bowl, combine the cereal, garlic salt and dill. Place oil in another shallow bowl. Dip chicken tenders in oil, then roll in cereal mixture.

■ Place on a foil-lined baking sheet. Bake, uncovered, at 350° for 30 minutes or until no longer pink. Serve with sour cream if desired. **Yield:** 4-6 servings.

italian chicken stew

JO CALIZZI | VANDERGRIFT, PENNSYLVANIA

My husband enjoys preparing this satisfying stew because it's so easy. With warm Italian bread, it's a winner on a cold day.

PREP/TOTAL TIME: 20 MIN.

1 pound boneless skinless chicken breasts, cubed
4 medium potatoes, peeled and cut into 1/4-inch cubes
1 medium sweet red pepper, chopped
2 garlic cloves, minced
1 to 2 tablespoons olive oil
1 jar (26 ounces) meatless spaghetti sauce
1-3/4 cups frozen cut green beans
1 teaspoon dried basil
1/4 to 1/2 teaspoon salt
1/4 teaspoon crushed red pepper flakes
Pepper to taste

■ In a large skillet, cook the chicken, potatoes, red pepper and garlic in oil until chicken is no longer pink and vegetables are tender. Stir in the remaining ingredients; cook and stir until heated through. **Yield:** 4 servings.

easy chicken chili

NANCY MAXEY | ROGUE RIVER, OREGON

We have lots of visitors on our farm, so I like to make down-home dishes. Whenever I serve this chili, I'm asked for the recipe, which I'm happy to share.

PREP/TOTAL TIME: 30 MIN.

1/2 cup chopped onion
1 tablespoon canola oil
2 cans (14-1/2 ounces *each*) chicken broth
2 cans (16 ounces *each*) great northern beans, rinsed and drained
1 can (4 ounces) chopped green chilies
2 cups cubed cooked chicken
2 garlic cloves, minced
2 tablespoons minced fresh cilantro
1 teaspoon salt
1 teaspoon dried oregano
1 teaspoon ground cumin
1/8 to 1/4 teaspoon cayenne pepper

■ In a large saucepan over medium heat, saute onion in oil until tender. Add remaining ingredients; bring to a boil. Reduce heat; cover and simmer for 10-15 minutes or until heated through. **Yield:** 6-8 servings.

parmesan chicken

MARGIE EDDY | ANN ARBOR, MICHIGAN

I like to make this yummy recipe when I have extra spaghetti sauce on hand. The herbed coating on the tender chicken gets nice and golden.

PREP/TOTAL TIME: 20 MIN.

1/2 cup seasoned bread crumbs
1/2 cup grated Parmesan cheese, *divided*
1-1/2 teaspoons dried oregano, *divided*
1/2 teaspoon dried basil
1/2 teaspoon salt
1/4 teaspoon pepper
1 egg
1 tablespoon water
4 boneless skinless chicken breast halves (4 ounces *each*)
2 tablespoons butter
2 cups meatless spaghetti sauce
1/2 teaspoon garlic salt
1 cup (4 ounces) shredded part-skim mozzarella cheese
Hot cooked fettuccine *or* pasta of your choice

■ In a shallow bowl, combine the bread crumbs, 1/4 cup Parmesan cheese, 1 teaspoon oregano, basil, salt and pepper. In another shallow bowl, combine the egg and water. Dip the chicken in the egg mixture, then coat with the crumb mixture.

■ In a large skillet, cook chicken in butter on both sides until a meat thermometer reads 170°.

■ Meanwhile, in a large saucepan, combine the spaghetti sauce, garlic salt and remaining oregano. Cook over medium heat until heated through. Spoon over chicken; sprinkle with mozzarella cheese and remaining Parmesan cheese. Serve with pasta. **Yield:** 4 servings.

mexican stir-fry

BECKY TAAFFE | SAN JOSE, CALIFORNIA

A blend of peppers makes this skillet meal a hit at my house. Not only have I prepared it for everyday meals, but also for church dinners, potlucks and family get-togethers. There are never any leftovers.

PREP/TOTAL TIME: 20 MIN.

1/2 cup chopped onion
2 teaspoons canola oil
2 garlic cloves, minced
1/2 cup finely chopped green pepper
1/2 cup finely chopped sweet red pepper
2 tablespoons minced jalapeno pepper
3/4 cup water
1/2 cup tomato puree
1/2 teaspoon chili powder
1/2 teaspoon chicken bouillon granules
1/4 teaspoon salt
Pinch cayenne pepper
1-1/3 cups diced cooked chicken
2/3 cup canned kidney beans, rinsed and drained
1 cup cooked rice
1/2 cup shredded cheddar cheese

- In a large skillet, saute onion in oil for 3 minutes or until crisp-tender. Add garlic; cook 1 minute longer. Add peppers; saute until crisp-tender, about 2 minutes.
- Stir in the water, tomato puree, chili powder, bouillon, salt and cayenne; bring to a boil. Reduce heat; simmer, uncovered, for 5 minutes. Add the chicken, beans and rice; heat through. Sprinkle with cheese. **Yield:** 2-4 servings.

Editor's Note: When cutting hot peppers, disposable gloves are recommended. Avoid touching your face.

wild rice mushroom chicken

JACQUELINE GRAVES | LAWRENCEVILLE, GEORGIA

I use a wild rice mix to put a tasty spin on a traditional chicken and rice dinner. It's simple and delicious with leftover chicken or turkey.

PREP: 15 MIN. COOK: 30 MIN.

2 packages (6 ounces *each*) long grain and wild rice mix
8 bone-in chicken breast halves (8 ounces *each*)
5 tablespoons butter, *divided*
1 large sweet red pepper, chopped
2 jars (4-1/2 ounces *each*) sliced mushrooms, drained

- Prepare rice according to package directions. Meanwhile, in a large skillet, cook chicken in 3 tablespoons butter for 10 minutes on each side or until browned and a meat thermometer reads 170°. Remove chicken and keep warm.
- Add remaining butter to pan drippings; saute red pepper until tender. Stir in mushrooms; heat through. Add to rice. Serve four chicken breasts with half of the rice mixture.
- Place remaining chicken in a greased 11-in. x 7-in. baking dish; top with remaining rice mixture. Cool. Cover and freeze for up to 3 months. **Yield:** 2 casseroles (4 servings each).

Editor's Note: To use frozen casserole, thaw it in the refrigerator. Cover and bake at 350° for 35-40 minutes or until heated through.

turkey ranch wraps

TASTE OF HOME TEST KITCHEN

Here's a cool idea that's ready to gobble up in no time. It's a terrific use for deli turkey. Just add lettuce, tomato, green pepper, shredded cheese and ranch dressing for a flavorful combination.

PREP/TOTAL TIME: 10 MIN.

8 thin slices cooked turkey
4 flour tortillas (6 inches), warmed
1 large tomato, thinly sliced
1 medium green pepper, cut into thin strips
1 cup shredded lettuce
1 cup (4 ounces) shredded cheddar cheese
1/3 cup prepared ranch salad dressing

- Place two slices of turkey on each tortilla. Layer with tomato, green pepper, lettuce and cheese. Drizzle with salad dressing. Roll up tightly. **Yield:** 4 servings.

country fried chicken

REBEKAH MILLER | ROCKY MOUNTAIN, VIRGINIA

This is one of our favorite recipes to take along on a picnic. We like to eat the chicken cold, along with a salad and watermelon. It's a real treat!

PREP: 20 MIN. COOK: 40 MIN.

1 cup all-purpose flour
2 teaspoons garlic salt
2 teaspoons pepper
1 teaspoon paprika
1/2 teaspoon poultry seasoning
1 egg
1/2 cup milk
1 broiler/fryer chicken (3 to 3-1/2 pounds), cut up
Oil for frying

- In a large resealable plastic bag, combine the flour and seasonings. In a shallow bowl, beat egg and milk. Dip chicken pieces into egg mixture, then add to bag, a few pieces at a time, and shake to coat.
- In a large skillet, heat 1/4 in. of oil; fry chicken in oil until browned on all sides. Cover and simmer for 35-40 minutes or until juices run clear and chicken is tender, turning occasionally. Uncover and cook 5 minutes longer. Drain on paper towels. **Yield:** 4 servings.

potato chicken delight

NICKI USSERY | MT. STERLING, ILLINOIS

French-fried onions, potato chips and cheddar cheese provide a pleasant golden color to this dish. It's a meat-and-potato lover's dream come true!

PREP: 10 MIN. BAKE: 1 HOUR

1 can (10-3/4 ounces) condensed cream of chicken soup, undiluted
3/4 cup sour cream
3/4 cup milk
1/2 teaspoon salt
2 cups cubed cooked chicken
2 cups (8 ounces) shredded cheddar cheese, *divided*
1 package (30 ounces) frozen shredded hash brown potatoes, thawed
1/2 cup crushed sour cream and onion potato chips
1/2 cup crushed french-fried onions

- In a large bowl, combine the soup, sour cream, milk and salt. Stir in chicken and 1-1/2 cups cheese. Stir in potatoes. Transfer to a greased 2-1/2-qt. baking dish. Cover and bake at 350° for 50 minutes.
- Uncover; sprinkle with remaining cheese. Top with potato chips and onions. Bake 10-15 minutes longer or until edges are bubbly and cheese is melted. Let stand for 5 minutes before serving. **Yield:** 8 servings.

mexican chicken soup

MARLENE KANE | LAINESBURG, MICHIGAN

This zesty dish is loaded with chicken, corn and black beans in a mildly spicy red broth. As a busy mom, I'm always looking for dinner recipes that can be prepared in the morning. The kids love the taco-like taste of this easy soup.

PREP: 10 MIN. COOK: 3 HOURS

1-1/2 pounds boneless skinless chicken breasts, cubed
2 teaspoons canola oil
1/2 cup water
1 envelope reduced-sodium taco seasoning
1 can (32 ounces) V8 juice
1 jar (16 ounces) salsa
1 can (15 ounces) black beans, rinsed and drained
1 package (10 ounces) frozen corn, thawed
6 tablespoons reduced-fat cheddar cheese
6 tablespoons reduced-fat sour cream
2 tablespoons minced fresh cilantro

- In a large nonstick skillet, saute chicken in oil until no longer pink. Add the water and taco seasoning; simmer, uncovered, until chicken is well coated.
- Transfer to a 5-qt. slow cooker. Stir in the V8 juice, salsa, beans and corn. Cover and cook on low for 3-4 hours or until heated through. Serve with the cheese, sour cream and cilantro. **Yield:** 6 servings.

turkey sausage and noodles

HELEN WANAMAKER VAIL | GLENSIDE, PENNSYLVANIA

During the winter months when our appetites are in full gear, my family practically licks this pan clean. I sometimes toss in a can of white kidney beans to make it even heartier.

PREP: 25 MIN. BAKE: 30 MIN.

- 2 cups uncooked egg noodles
- 2 pounds Italian turkey sausage, cut into 1-inch slices
- 1 large onion, chopped
- 2 medium carrots, sliced
- 1/2 cup chopped green pepper
- 1/2 cup all-purpose flour
- 2-1/2 cups milk
- 1/4 cup Worcestershire sauce
- 1/4 teaspoon rubbed sage

■ Cook the noodles according to package directions. Meanwhile, in a large skillet, cook the sausage, onion, carrots and green pepper over medium heat until meat is no longer pink. Stir in flour until blended. Gradually add the milk. Bring to a boil; cook and stir for 2 minutes or until thickened.

■ Drain noodles; add to the sausage mixture along with the Worcestershire sauce and sage. Toss to coat.

■ Transfer to a greased 2-1/2-qt. baking dish. Cover and bake at 350° for 20 minutes. Uncover; bake 10-15 minutes longer or until bubbly. **Yield:** 8 servings.

grilled chicken dinner

FLOYD HULET | APACHE JUNCTION, ARIZONA

This complete meal grilled in a foil packet is a palate-pleasing and mess-free dinner for one.

PREP: 10 MIN. GRILL: 50 MIN.

- 1 bone-in chicken breast half (8 ounces)
- 1 medium potato, peeled and quartered
- 1 large carrot, cut into 2-inch pieces
- 1/2 cup fresh vegetables (broccoli florets, peas *and/or* green beans)
- 1 tablespoon onion soup mix
- 2/3 cup condensed cream of chicken soup, undiluted

■ Place chicken in the center of a piece of double-layered heavy-duty foil (about 18 in. square). Place vegetables around chicken. Sprinkle with soup mix. Top with soup. Fold foil around vegetables and chicken; seal tightly.

■ Grill, uncovered, over medium-low heat for 50-60 minutes or until a meat thermometer reads 170°. Open the foil carefully to allow steam to escape. **Yield:** 1 serving.

extra-crispy italian chicken

FAYE WOLF | CAMDEN, INDIANA

A cousin shared this recipe with me several years ago. Since then, I've made it too many times to count! I especially like to serve the dish to guests because it's very attractive.

PREP: 30 MIN. BAKE: 30 MIN.

- 1-1/4 cups pancake mix
- 2 envelopes zesty Italian salad dressing mix
- 1 egg
- 1/3 cup club soda
- 1 broiler/fryer chicken (3-1/2 to 4 pounds), cut up
- Oil for deep-fat frying

■ In a shallow bowl, combine pancake mix and one envelope salad dressing mix. In another shallow bowl, combine the second envelope of salad dressing mix, egg and club soda. Dip the chicken pieces in the egg mixture, then coat with seasoned pancake mix. Place chicken pieces on a rack; let stand for 5 minutes.

■ In a deep-fat fryer, heat oil to 375°. Fry chicken, several pieces at a time, for 6 minutes or until golden brown. Place on an ungreased 15-in. x 10-in. x 1-in. baking pan.

■ Bake, uncovered, at 350° for 30 minutes or until juices run clear. **Yield:** 4 servings.

caribbean delight

LEIGH ANN GRADY | MURRAY, KENTUCKY

When hot summer nights drive me out of the kitchen, I head for the grill with this recipe. Along with a salad, my family loves the not-so-subtle spicy chicken.

PREP: 5 MIN. + MARINATING GRILL: 10 MIN.

- 2 tablespoons finely chopped onion
- 1/4 cup butter, cubed
- 2 garlic cloves, minced
- 1/3 cup white vinegar
- 1/3 cup lime juice
- 1/4 cup sugar
- 2 tablespoons curry powder
- 1 teaspoon salt
- 1/4 to 1/2 teaspoon cayenne pepper
- 6 boneless skinless chicken breast halves (4 ounces *each*)

■ In a small saucepan, saute onion in butter until tender. Add garlic; cook 1 minute longer. Stir in the vinegar, lime juice, sugar, curry, salt and cayenne. Place chicken in a large resealable plastic bag; add onion mixture. Seal bag and turn to coat. Refrigerate for at least 2 hours.

■ Drain and discard marinade. Grill chicken, uncovered, over medium heat, for 5-7 minutes on each side or until a meat thermometer reads 170°. **Yield:** 6 servings.

Evenly Cooked Chicken

To ensure that chicken breasts cook evenly, place them in a resealable plastic bag; seal bag. With the flat side of a meat mallet, pound them to 1/4-in. thickness. Cook as directed.

saucy turkey

MRS. JOHNYE MASTERES | RAYVILLE, LOUISIANA

Here's a speedy stovetop dish that takes advantage of leftover turkey. The spicy sauce is so quick to stir together because it uses convenience foods such as mustard, ketchup and hot pepper sauce.

PREP/TOTAL TIME: 30 MIN.

- 1/2 cup chopped green pepper
- 1/3 cup chopped onion
- 2 tablespoons butter
- 1-1/2 cups ketchup
- 1/2 cup chicken broth
- 1-1/2 teaspoons Worcestershire sauce
- 1 teaspoon prepared mustard
- 1/4 to 1/2 teaspoon hot pepper sauce
- 1/4 teaspoon pepper
- 3 cups cubed cooked turkey
- 4 sandwich buns, split, optional

■ In a large saucepan, saute the green pepper and onion in butter until tender. Stir in the ketchup, broth, Worcestershire sauce, mustard, hot pepper sauce and pepper. Add the turkey. Simmer, uncovered, for 20 minutes or until heated through. Serve on buns if desired. **Yield:** 4 servings.

No More Sticky Buns

Do you like to keep hamburger buns on hand in the freezer but find they stick together? Wrap them securely in plastic wrap, two per package, then place in a freezer bag.

comforting chicken

SALLY HOOK | MONTGOMERY, TEXAS

This combination of chicken and vegetables is simmered in a creamy sauce that's rich from whipping cream and butter. The hearty, meal-in-one-pot is an all-time family favorite.

PREP: 15 MIN. COOK: 45 MIN.

1 medium onion, sliced and separated into rings
1/2 cup butter, cubed
1 broiler/fryer chicken (3 to 4 pounds), cut up
4 medium potatoes, peeled and quartered
4 medium carrots, quartered widthwise
1 cup heavy whipping cream
1 tablespoon minced fresh parsley
1/2 teaspoon salt
1/4 teaspoon pepper

■ In a large skillet, saute onion in butter until tender. Remove with a slotted spoon and set aside. In the same pan, brown chicken pieces on all sides. Return onion to pan; add potatoes and carrots. Cover and cook over medium-low heat for 30 minutes or until chicken juices run clear and the vegetables are tender.

■ Stir in the cream, parsley, salt and pepper. Reduce heat. Simmer, uncovered, for 15 minutes or until slightly thickened. **Yield:** 4 servings.

moist lemon chicken

NANCY SCHICKLING | BEDFORD, VIRGINIA

I originally developed this marinade for seafood, but it's wonderful with chicken, too. It adds mild lemon zing and keeps the meat moist and tender.

PREP: 10 MIN. + MARINATING GRILL: 50 MIN.

3/4 cup water
1/4 cup lemon juice
2 tablespoons dried minced onion
1 tablespoon dried parsley flakes
1 tablespoon Worcestershire sauce
2 garlic cloves, minced
1 teaspoon dill seed
1/2 teaspoon salt, optional
1/2 teaspoon curry powder
1/2 teaspoon pepper
1 broiler/fryer chicken (3 to 3-1/2 pounds), cut up

■ In a large resealable plastic bag, combine the first 10 ingredients; add the chicken. Seal bag and turn to coat; refrigerate for 4-6 hours.

■ Drain and discard marinade. Grill chicken, covered, over low heat for 50-60 minutes or until juices run clear, turning several times. **Yield:** 4 servings.

chicken stir-fry

LORI SCHLECHT | WIMBLEDON, NORTH DAKOTA

This is a tasty, healthy meal that everyone in my house enjoys. Ginger complements the chicken and vegetables.

PREP: 15 MIN. + CHILLING COOK: 10 MIN.

4 boneless skinless chicken breast halves (4 ounces *each*)
3 tablespoons cornstarch
2 tablespoons soy sauce
1/2 teaspoon ground ginger
1/4 teaspoon garlic powder
3 tablespoons canola oil, *divided*
2 cups fresh broccoli florets
1 cup sliced celery (1/2-inch pieces)
1 cup thinly sliced carrots
1 small onion, cut into wedges
1 cup water
1 teaspoon chicken bouillon granules

■ Cut chicken into 1/2-in. strips; place in a resealable plastic bag. Add cornstarch and toss to coat. Combine the soy sauce, ginger and garlic powder; add to bag and shake well. Refrigerate for 30 minutes.

■ In a large skillet or wok, heat 2 tablespoons of oil; stir-fry chicken until no longer pink, about 3-5 minutes. Remove and keep warm.

■ Add remaining oil; stir-fry the broccoli, celery, carrots and onion for 4-5 minutes or until crisp-tender. Add water and bouillon. Return the chicken to pan. Cook and stir until thickened and bubbly. **Yield:** 4 servings.

15-minute marinated chicken

PAM SHINOGLE | ARLINGTON, TEXAS

Whenever I serve this to family and friends, which is quite often, I'm bound to be asked for the recipe. It's a fast and tasty meal that I'm happy to share with others.

PREP: 15 MIN. + MARINATING GRILL: 15 MIN.

1/4 cup Dijon mustard
2 tablespoons lemon juice
1-1/2 teaspoons Worcestershire sauce
1/2 teaspoon dried tarragon
1/4 teaspoon pepper
4 boneless skinless chicken breast halves (4 ounces *each*)

- In a large resealable plastic bag, combine the first five ingredients; add the chicken. Seal bag and turn to coat; marinate at room temperature for 15 minutes or refrigerate for several hours.
- Drain and discard the marinade. Grill, uncovered, over medium heat for about 8-12 minutes, turning once, or until a meat thermometer reads 170°. **Yield:** 4 servings.

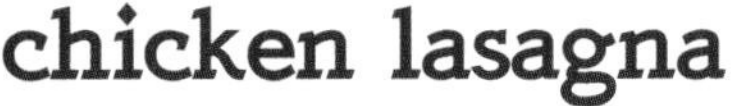

chicken lasagna

JANET LORTON | EFFINGHAM, ILLINOIS

When my nephews were younger, I would make their favorite meal for their birthdays...this is what they usually requested.

PREP: 20 MIN. BAKE: 35 MIN. + STANDING

9 uncooked lasagna noodles
2 cans (10-3/4 ounces *each*) condensed cream of chicken soup, undiluted
2/3 cup milk
2-1/2 cups frozen mixed vegetables
2 cups cubed cooked chicken
18 slices process American cheese

- Cook noodles according to package directions; drain. In a large saucepan, combine soup and milk. Cook and stir over low heat until blended. Remove from the heat; stir in vegetables and chicken.
- In a greased 13-in. x 9-in. baking dish, layer three noodles, a third of the soup mixture and six cheese slices. Repeat layers twice.
- Cover and bake at 350° for 30 minutes. Uncover; bake 5-10 minutes more or until bubbly. Let stand 15 minutes before cutting. **Yield:** 9-12 servings.

tender chicken nuggets

LYNNE HAHN | WINCHESTER, CALIFORNIA

Four ingredients are all it takes to create moist golden bites that are healthier than fast food. I serve them with ranch dressing and barbecue sauce for dipping.

PREP/TOTAL TIME: 25 MIN.

1/2 cup seasoned bread crumbs
2 tablespoons grated Parmesan cheese
1 egg white
1 pound boneless skinless chicken breasts, cut into 1-inch cubes

- In a large resealable plastic bag, combine bread crumbs and cheese. In a shallow bowl, beat the egg white. Dip chicken pieces in egg white, then place in bag and shake to coat.
- Place in a 15-in. x 10-in. x 1-in. baking pan coated with cooking spray. Bake, uncovered, at 400° for 12-15 minutes or until no longer pink, turning once. **Yield:** 4 servings.

potato chicken packets

PAM HALL | ELIZABETH CITY, NORTH CAROLINA

I season chicken breasts with a delightful combination of herbs before topping each with veggies. Servings are individually wrapped in foil, so I can enjoy nature's beauty in my backyard while the packets cook on the grill.

PREP: 15 MIN. GRILL: 30 MIN.

- 4 boneless skinless chicken breast halves (4 ounces *each*)
- 1/4 cup olive oil
- 3 teaspoons dried rosemary, crushed
- 1 teaspoon dried thyme
- 1/2 teaspoon dried basil
- 1 garlic clove, minced
- 8 to 10 small red potatoes, quartered
- 2 medium yellow summer squash, cut into 1/4-inch slices
- 1 large onion, chopped
- 2 tablespoons butter, cubed

Salt and pepper to taste

- Place each chicken breast on a double thickness of heavy-duty foil (about 12 in. square). Combine the oil, rosemary, thyme, basil and garlic; drizzle over chicken. Top with potatoes, squash, onion and butter. Sprinkle with salt and pepper. Fold foil over mixture and seal tightly.
- Grill, covered, over medium heat for 30 minutes or until a meat thermometer reads 170°. Open foil carefully to allow steam to escape. **Yield:** 4 servings.

garlic-lime chicken

DORIS CARNAHAN | LINCOLN, ARKANSAS

After tending the farm and growing our own produce, I don't have much time left for cooking. I've found this easy-to-prepare chicken is ideal for my many hectic days.

PREP: 5 MIN. + MARINATING GRILL: 10 MIN.

- 1/3 cup soy sauce
- 1/4 cup fresh lime juice
- 1 tablespoon Worcestershire sauce
- 1/2 teaspoon ground mustard
- 2 garlic cloves, minced
- 6 boneless skinless chicken breast halves (4 ounces *each*)
- 1/2 teaspoon pepper

■ In a large resealable plastic bag, combine the first five ingredients. Add the chicken; seal bag and turn to coat. Refrigerate for at least 30 minutes.

■ Drain and discard marinade. Sprinkle chicken with pepper. Grill, covered, over medium heat for 4-7 minutes on each side or a meat thermometer reads 170°. **Yield:** 6 servings.

chicken broccoli supper

HEATHER OBLINGER | GAHANNA, OHIO

Here's a meal for two that doesn't require you to cook the chicken or macaroni first. It's very easy to assemble.

PREP: 10 MIN. BAKE: 55 MIN.

- 1/2 pound boneless skinless chicken breasts, cubed
- 1-1/2 cups frozen broccoli florets
- 1/2 cup uncooked elbow macaroni
- 1/2 cup shredded cheddar cheese
- 1 can (10-3/4 ounces) condensed cream of chicken soup, undiluted
- 3/4 cup chicken broth
- 1/4 teaspoon garlic powder
- 1/4 teaspoon pepper

■ In a large bowl, combine the chicken, broccoli, macaroni and cheese. Whisk the soup, broth, garlic powder and pepper; stir into chicken mixture.

■ Transfer to a greased 1-1/2-qt. baking dish. Bake, uncovered, at 350° for 30 minutes. Stir; bake 25-30 minutes longer or until chicken is no longer pink and macaroni is tender. Let stand for 5 minutes before serving. **Yield:** 2 servings.

fiesta chicken

TERESA PETERSON | KASSON, MINNESOTA

Chili powder and picante sauce add just the right dash of zip to this hearty main dish. It's a snap to assemble since it uses convenience foods.

PREP: 15 MIN. BAKE: 40 MIN.

- 1 can (10-3/4 ounces) condensed cream of chicken soup, undiluted
- 1 can (10-3/4 ounces) condensed cream of mushroom soup, undiluted
- 2 small tomatoes, chopped
- 1/3 cup picante sauce
- 1 medium green pepper, chopped
- 1 small onion, chopped
- 2 to 3 teaspoons chili powder
- 12 corn tortillas (6 inches), cut into 1-inch strips
- 3 cups cubed cooked chicken
- 1 cup (4 ounces) shredded Colby cheese

■ In a large bowl, combine the soups, tomatoes, picante sauce, green pepper, onion and chili powder. In a greased 13-in. x 9-in. baking dish, layer half of the tortilla strips, chicken, soup mixture and cheese. Repeat layers.

■ Cover and bake at 350° for 40-50 minutes or until bubbly. **Yield:** 6-8 servings.

Quick Casseroles

When chicken pieces are on sale, buy several packages and bake all the chicken, skin side up, on foil-lined pans. When cool, remove the skin and bones, cube the meat and freeze in measured portions to use in casseroles and other quick suppers.

turkey tenderloin supreme

NANCY LEVIN | CHESTERFIELD, MISSOURI

Served over rice, this fast skillet supper makes a good home-cooked meal when there's little time.

PREP/TOTAL TIME: 25 MIN.

- 6 turkey breast tenderloin slices (3/4 inch thick and 4 ounces *each*)
- 1 tablespoon butter
- 3 green onions, thinly sliced
- 1 can (10-3/4 ounces) condensed cream of chicken soup, undiluted
- 1/4 cup water

■ In a large skillet, brown the turkey in butter. Add onions; cook for 1-2 minutes. Combine the soup and water; pour over turkey. Bring to a boil. Reduce heat; cover and simmer for 8-10 minutes or until a meat thermometer reads 170°. **Yield:** 4 servings.

easy chicken divan

VIOLET ENGLERT | LEICESTER, NEW YORK

I received this recipe from a co-worker and then made a few changes to it to suit my family's tastes. It's excellent with corn bread.

PREP: 15 MIN. BAKE: 20 MIN.

- 3 cups cubed cooked chicken
- 1/2 teaspoon salt
- 1/4 teaspoon pepper
- 6 cups frozen broccoli florets, thawed
- 2 cans (10-3/4 ounces *each*) condensed cream of chicken soup, undiluted
- 1/3 cup mayonnaise
- 1/4 cup milk
- 2 cups (8 ounces) shredded taco *or* Mexican cheese blend *or* cheddar cheese, *divided*

■ In a greased shallow 2-1/2-qt. baking dish, combine the chicken, salt and pepper. Top with broccoli. In a large bowl, combine the soup, mayonnaise, milk and 1-1/2 cups cheese; pour over the broccoli. Sprinkle with the remaining cheese.

■ Bake, uncovered, at 375° for 20-25 minutes or until heated through. **Yield:** 4-6 servings.

ranch chicken 'n' rice

ERLENE CRUSOE | LITCHFIELD, MINNESOTA

When I clipped this recipe from a neighborhood shopper a few years ago. I couldn't wait to try it. Just as I expected, it quickly became a family favorite.

PREP: 10 MIN. BAKE: 35 MIN.

- 2 cups uncooked instant rice
- 1-1/2 cups milk
- 1 cup water
- 1 envelope ranch salad dressing mix
- 1 pound boneless skinless chicken breasts, cut into 1/2-inch strips
- 1/4 cup butter, melted
- Paprika

■ Place rice in a greased shallow 2-qt. baking dish. In a bowl, combine the milk, water and salad dressing mix; set aside 1/4 cup. Pour remaining mixture over rice. Top with the chicken strips. Drizzle with the butter and the reserved milk mixture.

■ Cover and bake at 350° for 35-40 minutes or until rice is tender and chicken is no longer pink. Sprinkle with paprika. **Yield:** 4 servings.

herb 'n' spice turkey breast

TASTE OF HOME TEST KITCHEN

This nicely seasoned turkey breast is a great accompaniment to goose at Thanksgiving. Or prepare it throughout the year for a delicious dinner on its own.

PREP: 10 MIN. BAKE: 1-1/2 HOURS

- 3 tablespoons canola oil
- 1 tablespoon brown sugar
- 1 teaspoon salt
- 1/2 teaspoon rubbed sage
- 1/2 teaspoon dried thyme
- 1/2 teaspoon dried rosemary, crushed
- 1/4 teaspoon pepper
- 1/8 to 1/4 teaspoon ground allspice
- 1 bone-in turkey breast (4-1/4 to 6 pounds)

■ In a small bowl, combine the oil, brown sugar, salt, sage, thyme, rosemary, pepper and allspice. With fingers, carefully loosen the skin from both sides of turkey breast.

■ Spread half of the brown sugar mixture under the skin. Secure skin to underside of breast with toothpicks. Spread the remaining brown sugar mixture over the skin.

■ Line the bottom of a large shallow roasting pan with foil. Place turkey breast side up on a rack in prepared pan.

■ Bake, uncovered, at 325° for 2 to 2-1/2 hours or until a meat thermometer reads 170° (cover loosely with foil if turkey browns too quickly). Cover and let stand for 15 minutes before carving. **Yield:** 10-14 servings.

quick chicken cordon bleu

SHIRLEY JACKSON | ELKTON, VIRGINIA

Although I've since tried Cordon Bleu recipes that bake in the oven, this remains the quickest...and the best. The moist chicken and flavorful cheese sauce make this entree perfect for a special occasion.

PREP/TOTAL TIME: 30 MIN.

- 4 boneless skinless chicken breast halves (6 ounces *each*)
- 2 teaspoons Dijon mustard
- 1/2 teaspoon paprika
- 4 thin slices fully cooked ham
- 1 cup soft bread crumbs
- 1/4 cup grated Parmesan cheese
- 1/4 teaspoon pepper
- 3 to 4 tablespoons mayonnaise

SAUCE:

- 1 tablespoon butter
- 1 tablespoon all-purpose flour
- 1 cup milk
- 1/4 teaspoon salt
- 1/2 cup shredded Swiss cheese
- 2 tablespoons white wine

■ Flatten the chicken to 1/2-in. thickness. Spread mustard on one side; sprinkle with paprika. Top each with a ham slice. Roll up tightly; secure with toothpicks.

■ In a small bowl, combine the bread crumbs, Parmesan cheese and pepper. Brush chicken with mayonnaise; roll in crumb mixture.

■ Place chicken in a shallow 2-qt. microwave-safe dish; cover loosely. Microwave on high for 7 minutes; turn the chicken. Cook 5-1/2 minutes more or until meat is no longer pink; keep warm.

■ In a 1-qt. microwave-safe dish, heat butter on high for 20 seconds; stir in flour until smooth. Cook, uncovered, on high for 20 seconds. Add milk and salt. Cook 2-3 minutes longer or until thickened. Stir in cheese until smooth. Add wine. Discard toothpicks from chicken; serve with sauce. **Yield:** 4 servings.

Editor's Note: This recipe was tested in a 1,100-watt microwave.

swiss chicken bake

DORIS COHN | DENVILLE, NEW JERSEY

I try to keep the ingredients for this creamy casserole on hand for last-minute meals. Whenever I serve the dish at family dinners and potlucks, it's well-received.

PREP: 10 MIN. BAKE: 30 MIN.

- 1 package (7 ounces) thin spaghetti, cooked and drained
- 1 package (10 ounces) frozen chopped spinach, thawed and squeezed dry
- 1/2 cup half-and-half cream
- 1/3 cup shredded Parmesan cheese, *divided*
- 1/2 teaspoon salt
- 1/4 teaspoon pepper
- 1/8 to 1/4 teaspoon ground nutmeg
- 2 cups diced cooked chicken
- 1 cup (4 ounces) shredded Swiss cheese
- 1/2 cup sliced fresh mushrooms
- 2 bacon strips, cooked and crumbled
- 4 eggs, lightly beaten
- 1 cup ricotta cheese
- 1/4 cup chopped onion
- 1 garlic clove, minced

■ In a large bowl, combine the spaghetti, spinach, cream, 4 tablespoons Parmesan cheese, salt, pepper and nutmeg. Place in a greased 8-in. square baking dish. Top with the chicken, Swiss cheese, mushrooms and bacon.

■ In a small bowl, combine eggs, ricotta, onion and garlic; spread over the chicken. Sprinkle with the remaining Parmesan cheese.

■ Bake, uncovered, at 350° for 30-35 minutes or until bubbly. **Yield:** 4-6 servings.

chicken in sour cream sauce

JANE CARLOVSKY | SEBRING, FLORIDA

Tender chicken is deliciously dressed up in a flavorful cream sauce with fresh mushrooms. This is an excellent main course for your family or guests.

PREP: 15 MIN. COOK: 6 HOURS

- 1-1/2 teaspoons salt
- 1/4 teaspoon pepper
- 1/4 teaspoon paprika
- 1/4 teaspoon lemon-pepper seasoning
- 6 bone-in chicken breast halves, skin removed (7 ounces *each*)
- 1 can (10-3/4 ounces) condensed cream of mushroom soup, undiluted
- 1 cup (8 ounces) sour cream
- 1/2 cup dry white wine *or* chicken broth
- 1/2 pound fresh mushrooms, sliced

■ In a small bowl, combine the first four ingredients; rub over chicken. Place in a 3-qt. slow cooker. In a large bowl, combine the soup, sour cream and wine or broth; stir in mushrooms. Pour over chicken.

■ Cover and cook on low for 6-8 hours or until a meat thermometer reads 170°. Thicken the sauce if desired. **Yield:** 6 servings.

artichoke chicken

ROBERTA GREEN | HEMET, CALIFORNIA

This recipe has evolved through generations to satisfy my family's fondness for artichokes. I enjoy preparing it for casual suppers as well as special-occasion dinners.

PREP: 10 MIN. BAKE: 30 MIN.

- 2 cans (14 ounces *each*) water-packed artichoke hearts, rinsed, drained and quartered
- 2 tablespoons olive oil
- 3 garlic cloves, minced
- 2-2/3 cups cubed cooked chicken
- 2 cans (10-3/4 ounces *each*) condensed cream of chicken soup, undiluted
- 1 cup mayonnaise
- 1 teaspoon lemon juice
- 1/2 teaspoon curry powder
- 1-1/2 cups (6 ounces) shredded cheddar cheese
- 1 cup seasoned bread crumbs
- 1/4 cup grated Parmesan cheese
- 2 tablespoons butter, melted

■ In a small bowl, combine the artichokes, oil and garlic. Transfer to a greased 2-1/2-qt. baking dish. Top with chicken. Combine the soup, mayonnaise, lemon juice and curry; pour over the chicken. Sprinkle with cheddar cheese. Combine the bread crumbs, cheese and butter; sprinkle over top.

■ Bake, uncovered, at 350° for 30-35 minutes or until bubbly. **Yield:** 6-8 servings.

south-of-the-border thighs

PATRICIA COLLINS | IMBLER, OREGON

We may not live anywhere near the border, but we favor Mexican food! Served with warm tortillas and chili beans, this is a much-requested dish.

PREP: 5 MIN. GRILL: 20 MIN.

- 1 cup olive oil
- 4-1/2 teaspoons chili powder
- 1 tablespoon lime juice
- 2 teaspoons ground cumin
- 1 teaspoon ground coriander
- 1 teaspoon salt
- 1/2 teaspoon ground cloves
- 1/2 teaspoon cayenne pepper
- 1/2 teaspoon pepper
- 6 garlic cloves, minced
- 6 bone-in chicken thighs (about 2-1/4 pounds)

■ In a small bowl, combine the first 10 ingredients. Set aside half of marinade for basting; cover and refrigerate. Pour remaining marinade in a large resealable plastic bag; add chicken. Seal bag and turn to coat; refrigerate for at least 4 hours.

■ Drain and discard marinade. Grill chicken, uncovered, over medium-low heat, for 20-40 minutes or until a meat thermometer reads 180°, turning and basting frequently with reserved marinade. **Yield:** 4-6 servings.

Editor's Note: Watch closely; chicken may burn easily.

taste-of-summer chicken

BEVERLY SAUNDERS | LEXINGTON, VIRGINIA

I rely on bottled Italian salad dressing and pineapple juice for my made-in-minutes chicken marinade.

PREP: 5 MIN. + MARINATING GRILL: 15 MIN.

- 3/4 cup Italian salad dressing
- 3/4 cup unsweetened pineapple juice
- 3/4 cup white wine *or* white grape juice
- 6 boneless skinless chicken breast halves (4 ounces *each*)

■ In a large resealable plastic bag, combine the salad dressing, pineapple juice and wine or grape juice; add the chicken. Seal bag and turn to coat; refrigerate for 8 hours or overnight.

■ Drain and discard marinade. Grill chicken, covered, over medium heat for 6-7 minutes on each side or until a meat thermometer reads 170°. **Yield:** 6 servings.

basic chicken barbecue

SHERRY SCHMIDT | FRANKLIN, VIRGINIA

As far as I'm concerned, there's no better way to spend a summer night than sitting outdoors with the family and enjoying a hot-off-the-grill meal like this.

PREP: 10 MIN. + MARINATING GRILL: 35 MIN.

- 1 cup white vinegar
- 3 tablespoons sugar
- 2 tablespoons salt
- 1 cup water
- 1/2 cup canola oil
- 1 tablespoon poultry seasoning
- 1 tablespoon pepper
- 1 broiler/fryer chicken (3 to 3-1/2 pounds), cut up

- In a small bowl, whisk the vinegar, sugar and salt. Whisk in the water, oil, poultry seasoning and pepper. Reserve 1/2 cup of marinade for basting; cover and refrigerate. Pour the remaining marinade into a large resealable plastic bag; add the chicken. Seal bag and turn to coat. Refrigerate for 2-4 hours.
- Drain chicken and discard marinade. Grill, covered, over medium heat for 35-45 minutes or until juices run clear, turning and basting occasionally with reserved marinade. **Yield:** 4 servings.

garlic-herb roasted chicken

CINDY STEFFEN | CEDARBURG, WISCONSIN

Garlic and herbs roasting in and on the bird make this chicken so flavorful you can even eliminate the salt from the recipe if you like. The aroma from the oven while it's baking is tantalizing.

PREP: 10 MIN. BAKE: 1-1/2 HOURS

- 1 roasting chicken (4 to 5 pounds)
- 2 teaspoons *each* minced fresh parsley, rosemary, sage and thyme
- 3/4 teaspoon salt
- 1/4 teaspoon pepper
- 20 garlic cloves, peeled and sliced
- 1 medium lemon, halved
- 1 large whole garlic bulb
- 1 sprig *each* fresh parsley, rosemary, sage and thyme

■ With fingers, carefully loosen skin around the chicken breast, leg and thigh. Combine minced parsley, rosemary, sage, thyme, salt and pepper; rub half under skin. Place sliced garlic cloves under skin. Squeeze half of the lemon into the cavity and place the squeezed half in the cavity.

■ Remove papery outer skin from whole garlic bulb (do not peel or separate cloves). Cut top off garlic bulb. Place garlic bulb and herb sprigs in the cavity. Skewer chicken openings; tie drumsticks together with kitchen string.

■ Place chicken breast side up on a rack in a roasting pan. Squeeze the remaining lemon half over chicken; rub remaining herb mixture over chicken.

■ Bake, uncovered, at 350° for 1-1/2 to 1-3/4 hours or until chicken juices run clear and a meat thermometer reads 180° (cover loosely with foil if browning too quickly). Baste with pan drippings if desired.

■ Cover and let stand for 15 minutes. Remove and discard skin, garlic, lemon and herbs from cavity before carving. **Yield:** 8 servings.

Roasting Chickens

Before cooking a whole chicken, drain the juices and blot the cavity dry with paper towels. Rub the inside cavity and neck area with salt; bake as directed, allowing 23 to 25 minutes cooking time per pound.

chicken stuffing bake

NICOLE VOGL HARDING | SPOKANE, WASHINGTON

At my bridal shower a few years ago, each guest brought a recipe card for her best dish. We've tried everyone's recipe, but this is a favorite.

PREP: 5 MIN. BAKE: 45 MIN.

- 6 boneless skinless chicken breast halves (6 ounces *each*)
- 6 slices Swiss cheese
- 1 can (10-3/4 ounces) condensed cream of chicken soup, undiluted
- 1/3 cup white wine *or* chicken broth
- 3 cups seasoned stuffing cubes
- 1/2 cup butter, melted

■ Place chicken in a greased 13-in. x 9-in. baking dish; top with cheese. In a small bowl, combine soup and wine; spoon over cheese.

■ In a small bowl, combine croutons and butter; sprinkle over soup. Bake, uncovered, at 350° for 45-55 minutes or until a meat thermometer reads 170°. **Yield:** 6 servings.

barbecued turkey sandwiches

BARBARA SMITH | COLUMBUS, OHIO

These moist, shredded turkey sandwiches are a welcome break from beef barbecue or sloppy joes. The turkey cooks in a tangy sauce made with ketchup, vinegar, Worcestershire sauce and mustard.

PREP/TOTAL TIME: 25 MIN.

- 1/4 cup chopped onion
- 1 tablespoon butter
- 3 cups shredded cooked turkey
- 1/2 cup water
- 1/2 cup ketchup
- 1/4 cup red wine vinegar
- 1 tablespoon sugar
- 2 teaspoons Worcestershire sauce
- 1 teaspoon prepared mustard
- 1 teaspoon paprika
- 6 kaiser rolls, split

■ In a large nonstick skillet, saute onion in butter until tender. Add the turkey, water, ketchup, vinegar, sugar, Worcestershire sauce, mustard and paprika. Bring to a boil. Reduce heat; simmer, uncovered, for 15 minutes or until sauce is thickened. Serve on rolls. **Yield:** 6 servings.

creamy spinach chicken dinner

TASTE OF HOME TEST KITCHEN

Cleanup is a breeze with this all-in-one supper. To make things even easier, tear the spinach with your hands instead of cutting it.

PREP/TOTAL TIME: 30 MIN.

- 1-1/2 cups uncooked penne pasta
- 1 pound boneless skinless chicken breasts, cut into 1-inch cubes
- 1/2 cup chopped onion
- 2 teaspoons olive oil
- 1 can (10-3/4 ounces) condensed cream of mushroom soup, undiluted
- 1 cup heavy whipping cream
- 10 cups coarsely chopped fresh spinach
- 2 cups (8 ounces) shredded part-skim mozzarella cheese
- 1/8 teaspoon pepper

■ Cook pasta according to package directions. Meanwhile, in a Dutch oven over medium heat, cook and stir chicken and onion in oil for 5 minutes or until chicken is no longer pink.

■ Stir in soup and cream. Bring to a boil over medium heat. Reduce heat; simmer, uncovered, for 2 minutes. Stir in the spinach, cheese and pepper; cook for 1-2 minutes or until spinach is wilted and cheese is melted.

■ Drain pasta; add to chicken mixture and toss to coat. **Yield:** 4 servings.

Homemade Croutons

If you hate to waste the heel from a loaf of bread or a few leftover hot dog or hamburger buns, turn them into croutons! Cube the bread; place in a bowl. Spray with nonstick cooking spray; season with garlic powder, parsley and basil or oregano. Bake on a cookie sheet at 250° until crisp and brown.

cheddar chicken spirals

MIRIAM CHRISTOPHEL | BATTLE CREEK, MICHIGAN

My granddaughters just love this chicken dish. I try to make it every time they come to visit. Lucky for me, it goes together quick as a wink.

PREP/TOTAL TIME: 25 MIN.

1-1/2 cups uncooked spiral pasta
1/2 cup mayonnaise
1/3 cup milk
1/2 teaspoon salt
1/2 teaspoon dried basil
2 cups frozen mixed vegetables, thawed
1-1/2 cups cubed cooked chicken
1-1/2 cups (6 ounces) shredded cheddar cheese, *divided*

- Cook noodles according to package directions. Meanwhile, in a large bowl, combine the mayonnaise, milk, salt and basil. Stir in the vegetables, chicken and 1 cup cheese. Drain pasta; stir into vegetable mixture.
- Transfer to a greased 1-1/2-qt. microwave-safe dish. Sprinkle with remaining cheese. Cover and microwave on high for 4-5 minutes or until heated through and the cheese is melted. Let stand for 5 minutes before serving. **Yield:** 4 servings.

p. 213

swift seafood dishes
p. 211
p. 211
p. 215

tuna steaks with salsa

HARRIET STICHTER | MILFORD, INDIANA

Fish is often served with salsa in restaurants so I thought I'd try it at home. Mango and carrots make this salsa unlike any other.

PREP/TOTAL TIME: 25 MIN.

- 1 cup shredded carrots
- 3/4 cup chopped peeled mango
- 2 tablespoons lime juice
- 1 tablespoon minced chives
- 1/4 teaspoon salt, *divided*
- 1/4 teaspoon pepper, *divided*
- 1/8 teaspoon ground coriander
- 1/8 teaspoon ground cumin
- 4 tuna steaks (6 ounces *each*)

■ For salsa, in a bowl, combine the carrots, mango, lime juice, chives, 1/8 teaspoon salt, 1/8 teaspoon pepper, coriander and cumin; set aside. Sprinkle tuna steaks with remaining salt and pepper.

■ Coat grill rack with cooking spray before starting the grill. Grill tuna, covered, over medium heat for 5-7 minutes on each side or until fish flakes easily with a fork. Serve with salsa. **Yield:** 4 servings.

creamy seafood casserole

MARY BROWN | WHITMAN, MASSACHUSETTS

I love this recipe from my mother. It's easy and delicious and can be made the night before for added convenience, then popped in the oven the next day. Crushed potato chips or french-fried onions make other tasty topping options.

PREP: 15 MIN. BAKE: 25 MIN.

- 1 pound flounder fillets, cut into 1-1/2-inch pieces
- 1 pound uncooked medium shrimp, peeled and deveined
- 1 can (10-3/4 ounces) condensed cream of shrimp soup, undiluted
- 1/4 cup milk
- 1 cup crushed butter-flavored crackers (about 25 crackers)
- 1/4 cup grated Parmesan cheese
- 1 teaspoon paprika
- 2 tablespoons butter, melted

■ Arrange fish and shrimp in a greased 11-in. x 7-in. baking dish. Combine soup and milk; pour over seafood. Combine the cracker crumbs, Parmesan cheese, paprika and butter; sprinkle over top.

■ Bake, uncovered, at 350° for 25-30 minutes or until the fish flakes easily with a fork and the shrimp turn pink. **Yield:** 6-8 servings.

speedy seafood gumbo

LORI COSTO | THE WOODLANDS, TEXAS

I needed a quick meal one night when my husband was coming home late with the kids. I threw together this tasty gumbo with ingredients I had on hand. Everyone loved it! Using instant rice speeds along prep time.

PREP/TOTAL TIME: 15 MIN.

- 3 cups water, *divided*
- 1 tablespoon butter
- 1/4 teaspoon salt
- 1 cup uncooked instant rice
- 4 cans (10-3/4 ounces *each*) condensed chicken gumbo soup, undiluted
- 1 pound frozen cooked shrimp, peeled and deveined
- 1 package (10 ounces) frozen cut okra
- 1 package (8 ounces) imitation crabmeat, flaked
- 1 tablespoon dried minced onion
- 1 teaspoon Cajun seasoning
- 1/2 teaspoon garlic powder

■ In a small saucepan, bring 1 cup of water, butter and salt to a boil. Stir in rice; cover and remove from the heat. Let stand for 5 minutes.

■ Meanwhile, in a Dutch oven or soup kettle, combine the soup, shrimp, okra, crab, onion, Cajun seasoning, garlic powder and remaining water. Bring to a boil. Reduce heat; cover and cook over medium heat until heated through. Stir in cooked rice. **Yield:** 12 servings (3 quarts).

pecan-coated roughy

TASTE OF HOME TEST KITCHEN

Use your favorite whitefish fillets (like Alaskan pollack, red snapper or walleye) if orange roughy is not available.

PREP/TOTAL TIME: 30 MIN.

- 1 egg, lightly beaten
- 3/4 cup finely chopped pecans
- 4 orange roughy fillets (6 ounces *each*)
- 1 tablespoon chopped shallot
- 2 teaspoons butter
- 1/2 cup white wine
- 2 teaspoons cornstarch
- 1 cup orange juice
- 2 teaspoons Dijon mustard

■ Place the egg and pecans in separate shallow bowls. Dip fillets into egg, then coat with pecans. Place in a greased 15-in. x 10-in. x 1-in. baking pan. Bake, uncovered, at 400° for 20-25 minutes or until fish flakes easily with a fork.

■ Meanwhile, in a small saucepan, saute shallot in butter until tender. Add wine. Bring to a boil; cook for 1-2 minutes or until liquid is reduced by half.

■ In a small bowl, combine the cornstarch, orange juice and mustard until smooth; stir into wine mixture. Bring to a boil; cook and stir for 2 minutes or until thickened. Serve with orange roughy. **Yield:** 4 servings.

Seafood Substitute

Imitation crabmeat, most often made with Alaskan pollack, can be substituted for real crab in equal proportions in other recipes. Keep in mind that the flavor and texture will be different than the real thing.

easy crab cakes

CHARLENE SPELOCK | APOLLO, PENNSYLVANIA

Canned crabmeat makes these delicate patties simple enough for busy days. For a change of pace, try forming the crab mixture into four thick patties instead of eight cakes.

PREP/TOTAL TIME: 25 MIN.

- 2 cans (6 ounces *each*) crabmeat, drained, flaked and cartilage removed
- 1 cup seasoned bread crumbs, *divided*
- 1 egg, lightly beaten
- 1/4 cup finely chopped green onions
- 1/4 cup finely chopped sweet red pepper
- 1/4 cup reduced-fat mayonnaise
- 1 tablespoon lemon juice
- 1/2 teaspoon garlic powder
- 1/8 teaspoon cayenne pepper
- 1 tablespoon butter

- In a large bowl, combine the crab, 1/3 cup bread crumbs, egg, onions, red pepper, mayonnaise, lemon juice, garlic powder and cayenne.
- Divide the mixture into eight portions; shape into 2-in. balls. Roll in remaining bread crumbs. Flatten to 1/2-in. thickness. In a large nonstick skillet, cook crab cakes in butter for 3-4 minutes on each side or until golden brown. **Yield:** 4 servings.

skillet-grilled catfish

TRACI WYNNE | FALLS CHURCH, VIRGINIA

You can use this recipe with any thick fish fillet, but I suggest catfish or haddock. The Cajun flavor is great!

PREP/TOTAL TIME: 25 MIN.

- 1/4 cup all-purpose flour
- 1/4 cup cornmeal
- 1 teaspoon onion powder
- 1 teaspoon dried basil
- 1/2 teaspoon garlic salt
- 1/2 teaspoon dried thyme
- 1/4 to 1/2 teaspoon white pepper
- 1/4 to 1/2 teaspoon cayenne pepper
- 1/4 to 1/2 teaspoon pepper
- 4 catfish fillets (6 to 8 ounces *each*)
- 1/4 cup butter

- In a large resealable plastic bag, combine the first nine ingredients. Add the catfish, one fillet at a time, and shake to coat.
- Place a large cast-iron skillet on a grill rack over medium-hot heat. Melt butter in the skillet; add catfish. Grill, covered, for 6-8 minutes on each side or until fish flakes easily with a fork. **Yield:** 4 servings.

pesto shrimp pasta toss

FRAN SCOTT | BIRMINGHAM, MICHIGAN

I can whip up this elegant entree in just 30 minutes. Coated in pesto and topped with walnuts and Parmesan, the mix of pasta, shrimp and vegetables adds a dressy touch to any weeknight meal.

PREP/TOTAL TIME: 30 MIN.

- 9 ounces uncooked linguine
- 1 pound deveined peeled cooked medium shrimp
- 1 pound fresh asparagus, trimmed and cut into 2-inch pieces
- 1 medium yellow summer squash, sliced
- 1 cup fresh baby carrots, halved lengthwise
- 1 tablespoon butter, melted
- 1/2 teaspoon lemon-pepper seasoning
- 1/4 teaspoon salt
- 1/2 cup prepared pesto
- 1/2 cup shredded Parmesan cheese
- 1/2 cup chopped walnuts, toasted, optional

- Cook linguine according to package directions, adding shrimp during the last minute. Meanwhile, in a greased 15-in. x 10-in. x 1-in. baking pan, combine the asparagus, squash and carrots. Drizzle with butter; sprinkle with the lemon-pepper and salt.
- Bake, uncovered, at 450° for 15-20 minutes or until vegetables are tender, stirring once.
- Drain linguine and shrimp; transfer to a serving bowl. Add the vegetable mixture and pesto; toss gently. Sprinkle with cheese and walnuts if desired. **Yield:** 6 servings.

glazed salmon fillet

SHERRY WEST | NEW RIVER, ARIZONA

I love to cook and usually try a new recipe at least once a week. This salmon has a wonderful flavor. I've served it to company several times, and they always love it.

PREP/TOTAL TIME: 20 MIN.

- 1/4 cup reduced-sodium soy sauce
- 2 tablespoons brown sugar
- 1/4 teaspoon crushed red pepper flakes
- 1/4 teaspoon ground ginger
- 1/8 teaspoon sesame oil
- 1 salmon fillet (1-1/2 pounds)

■ In a bowl, combine the first five ingredients. If grilling the salmon, coat grill rack with cooking spray before starting the grill.

■ Grill salmon, covered, over medium heat or broil 4-6 in. from the heat for 5-6 minutes on each side or until salmon flakes easily with a fork, basting frequently with glaze. **Yield:** 6 servings.

stuffed mountain trout

LORETTA WALTERS | OGDEN, UTAH

You can substitute any whole fish in this recipe, but I like it best when it's made with fresh-caught trout from our local mountain streams.

PREP: 15 MIN. BAKE: 25 MIN.

- 2 trout (10 to 11 ounces *each*)
- 4 tablespoons plus 1-1/2 teaspoons lemon juice, *divided*
- 3 teaspoons dill weed, *divided*
- 2 teaspoons lemon-pepper seasoning, *divided*
- 1 small onion, chopped
- 1 tablespoon butter
- 1/2 cup minced fresh parsley
- 2 cups soft bread crumbs

■ Place trout in a 13-in. x 9-in. baking dish coated with cooking spray. Sprinkle 3 tablespoons lemon juice, 1-1/2 teaspoons dill and 1-1/2 teaspoons lemon-pepper in the fish cavities and over outside of fish; set aside.

■ In a nonstick skillet, saute onion in butter until tender. Add the parsley and remaining dill and lemon-pepper. Stir in bread crumbs; heat through. Sprinkle with remaining lemon juice; stir gently until moistened. Stuff into fish cavities.

■ Bake, uncovered, at 400° for 25-30 minutes or until fish flakes easily with a fork. **Yield:** 4 servings.

de-lightful tuna casserole

COLLEEN WILLEY | HAMBURG, NEW YORK

This mild, homemade tuna casserole will truly satisfy your family's craving for comfort food without all the fat!

PREP: 15 MIN. BAKE: 25 MIN.

- 1 package (7 ounces) elbow macaroni
- 1 can (10-3/4 ounces) reduced-fat reduced-sodium condensed cream of mushroom soup, undiluted
- 1 cup sliced fresh mushrooms
- 1 cup (4 ounces) shredded reduced-fat cheddar cheese
- 1 cup fat-free milk
- 1 can (6 ounces) light water-packed tuna, drained and flaked
- 2 tablespoons diced pimientos
- 3 teaspoons dried minced onion
- 1 teaspoon ground mustard
- 1/4 teaspoon salt
- 1/3 cup crushed cornflakes

■ Cook the elbow macaroni according to the package directions. Meanwhile, in a large bowl, combine the soup, mushrooms, cheese, milk, tuna, pimientos, onion, mustard and salt. Drain the macaroni; add to the tuna mixture and mix well.

■ Transfer to a 2-qt. baking dish coated with cooking spray. Sprinkle with cornflakes. Bake, uncovered, at 350° for 25-30 minutes or until bubbly. **Yield:** 5 servings.

Pistachio Tip

When buying unshelled pistachios, look for ones with the shell partially open so it's easier to retrieve the nut. Also, a closed shell indicates an immature nut.

pistachio-crusted fried fish

TASTE OF HOME TEST KITCHEN

This nut-crusted fish is so much better than ordinary breaded fish. Pistachios give it great color.

PREP/TOTAL TIME: 30 MIN.

- 1/2 cup dry bread crumbs
- 1/2 cup chopped pistachios
- 1/2 teaspoon seafood seasoning
- 1/4 teaspoon salt
- 1/4 teaspoon garlic powder
- 1/4 teaspoon pepper
- 1/2 cup all-purpose flour
- 1/2 cup milk
- 1-1/2 pounds whitefish *or* cod fillets
- 3 tablespoons canola oil

■ In a shallow bowl, combine the first six ingredients. Place flour and milk in separate shallow bowls. Dip fillets in flour, then in milk; coat with pistachio mixture.

■ In a large nonstick skillet, cook fillets in oil over medium heat for 4-5 minutes on each side or until fish flakes easily with a fork. **Yield:** 6 servings.

broiled greek fish fillets

JENNIFER MASLOWSKI | NEW YORK, NEW YORK

Olives, onion, dill and feta cheese combine in this tangy, Greek-inspired topping to boost the flavor of tilapia or your favorite whitefish. I usually serve it with a side of rice.

PREP/TOTAL TIME: 25 MIN.

- 8 tilapia fillets (4 ounces *each*)
- 1/4 teaspoon salt
- 1/4 teaspoon pepper
- 1/4 cup plain yogurt
- 2 tablespoons butter, softened
- 1 tablespoon lime juice
- 1 small red onion, finely chopped
- 1/2 cup pitted Greek olives
- 1 teaspoon dill weed
- 1/2 teaspoon paprika
- 1/4 teaspoon garlic powder
- 1/2 cup crumbled feta cheese

■ Sprinkle tilapia with salt and pepper. Place on a broiler pan coated with cooking spray.

■ In a small bowl, combine the yogurt, butter and lime juice. Stir in the onion, olives and seasonings. Spread down the middle of each fillet; sprinkle with feta cheese. Broil 3-4 in. from the heat for 6-9 minutes or until fish flakes easily with a fork. **Yield:** 8 servings.

split-second shrimp

JALAYNE LUCKETT | MARION, ILLINOIS

I use my microwave to hurry along preparation of this super-fast shrimp scampi that's buttery and full of garlic flavor. Serve it as an elegant entree or a special-occasion appetizer.

PREP/TOTAL TIME: 10 MIN.

- 2 tablespoons butter
- 1-1/2 teaspoons minced garlic
- 1/8 to 1/4 teaspoon cayenne pepper
- 2 tablespoons white wine *or* chicken broth
- 5 teaspoons lemon juice
- 1 tablespoon minced fresh parsley
- 1/2 teaspoon salt
- 1 pound uncooked large shrimp, peeled and deveined

■ In a 9-in. microwave-safe pie plate, combine the butter, garlic and cayenne. Cover and microwave on high for 1 minute or until butter is melted. Stir in the wine, lemon juice, parsley and salt. Add shrimp; toss to coat.

■ Cover and microwave on high for 2-1/2 to 3-1/2 minutes or until the shrimp turn pink. Stir before serving. **Yield:** 6 servings.

Editor's Note: This recipe was tested in a 1,100-watt microwave.

oven-fried fish nuggets

LADONNA REED | PONCA CITY, OKLAHOMA

My husband and I love fried fish, but we're both trying to cut back on fats. I made up the recipe for these light, buttery-tasting fish bites.

PREP/TOTAL TIME: 25 MIN.

- 1/3 cup seasoned bread crumbs
- 1/3 cup crushed cornflakes
- 3 tablespoons grated Parmesan cheese
- 1/2 teaspoon salt
- 1/4 teaspoon pepper
- 1-1/2 pounds cod fillets, cut into 1-inch cubes
- Butter-flavored cooking spray

■ In a shallow bowl, combine the bread crumbs, cornflakes, Parmesan cheese, salt and pepper. Coat the fish with butter-flavored spray, then roll in crumb mixture.

■ Place on a baking sheet coated with cooking spray. Bake at 375° for 15-20 minutes or until fish flakes easily with a fork. **Yield:** 4 servings.

baked tilapia

HOPE STEWART | RALEIGH, NORTH CAROLINA

I've decided to cook healthier for my family, and that includes having more fish at home. This is a great recipe, and it's fast, too!

PREP/TOTAL TIME: 20 MIN.

4 tilapia fillets (6 ounces *each*)
3 tablespoons butter, melted
3 tablespoons lemon juice
1-1/2 teaspoons garlic powder
1/8 teaspoon salt
2 tablespoons capers, drained
1/2 teaspoon dried oregano
1/8 teaspoon paprika

- Place tilapia in an ungreased 13-in. x 9-in. baking dish. In a small bowl, combine the butter, lemon juice, garlic powder and salt; pour over the fillets. Sprinkle with capers, oregano and paprika.
- Bake, uncovered, at 425° for 10-15 minutes or until fish flakes easily with a fork. **Yield:** 4 servings.

taco fish

EVELYN EYERMANN | CUBA, MISSOURI

Since I live on a lake and have a husband who's an avid angler, fish tops my list of mealtime ingredients. I use delicate fillets as the base for a tempting bake with a mild taco flavor. Kids and adults alike will go for the crunchy tortilla chip topping sprinkled with reduced-fat cheddar cheese.

PREP/TOTAL TIME: 30 MIN.

4 orange roughy *or* bass fillets (6 ounces *each*)
1/2 teaspoon salt
1/4 teaspoon chili powder
1/2 cup taco sauce
1/3 cup tortilla chips, crushed
1/3 cup shredded reduced-fat cheddar cheese

- Place fish in a 13-in. x 9-in. baking dish coated with cooking spray; sprinkle with salt and chili powder.
- Cover and bake at 350° for 20 minutes. Pour taco sauce over fish. Bake, uncovered, for 5-8 minutes longer or until heated through. Immediately sprinkle with tortilla chips and cheese. **Yield:** 4 servings.

clam stuffing bake

LILLIAN BUTLER | STRATFORD, CONNECTICUT

My mother came up with this delightful dish, and because I love stuffed clams, it's a favorite. I buy clams fresh in season and save the shells for times when I can't get fresh.

PREP/TOTAL TIME: 30 MIN.

- 2 tablespoons *each* chopped celery, green pepper and sweet red pepper
- 4-1/2 teaspoons chopped onion
- 2 tablespoons butter, *divided*
- 1/2 cup chicken broth
- 1/4 cup shredded carrot
- 1 cup seasoned stuffing mix
- 1 can (6-1/2 ounces) minced clams, drained
- 1/4 teaspoon lemon juice

■ In a small saucepan, saute the celery, peppers and onion in 1 tablespoon butter until almost tender. Stir in broth and carrot. Bring to a boil. Stir in stuffing mix. Remove from the heat; cover and let stand for 5 minutes. Stir in clams.

■ Transfer to two 6-oz. ramekins or custard cups coated with cooking spray. Melt remaining butter; stir in lemon juice. Drizzle over the stuffing mix. Bake, uncovered, at 350° for 15-20 minutes or until heated through and golden brown. **Yield:** 2 servings.

Freeze Extra Broth

Whenever you have extra chicken, beef or vegetable broth, pour the leftovers into an ice cube tray and freeze for future use. Generally, one compartment in an ice cube tray holds 2 tablespoons liquid.

scallops florentine

TASTE OF HOME TEST KITCHEN

This elegant, spinach-and-scallops dish makes a special entree for two. A pleasant Parmesan-garlic sauce complements the scallops in a scrumptious way.

PREP/TOTAL TIME: 25 MIN.

- 5 tablespoons water, *divided*
- 2 tablespoons white wine *or* chicken broth
- 1 garlic clove, minced
- 1/4 teaspoon salt
- 1/4 teaspoon dried tarragon, crushed
- Dash pepper
- 1/2 pound fresh *or* frozen sea scallops, thawed and halved
- 4 teaspoons all-purpose flour
- 1/3 cup fat-free evaporated milk
- 2 tablespoons grated Parmesan cheese
- 1 package (10 ounces) fresh spinach, torn

■ In a nonstick skillet, combine 4 tablespoons water, wine or broth, garlic, salt, tarragon and pepper. Bring to a boil; add scallops. Reduce heat; cover and simmer for 2-3 minutes or until scallops are opaque. Remove with a slotted spoon and set aside.

■ In a small bowl, combine flour and milk until smooth; stir into pan juices. Bring to a boil; cook and stir for 1-2 minutes or until thickened. Reduce heat; stir in cheese.

■ Return scallops to the pan; cook for 1-2 minutes or until heated through. Meanwhile, place the spinach and remaining water in a microwave-safe dish; cook on high for 1-1/2 to 2 minutes or until slightly wilted. Drain well. Serve scallop mixture over warm spinach. **Yield:** 2 servings.

Editor's Note: This recipe was tested in a 1,100-watt microwave.

Better Coating

To help the potato flakes adhere to the fillets in Crunchy-Coated Walleye, the recipe instructs you to first dredge the fish in flour. Then dip in the egg before coating with potato flakes.

crunchy-coated walleye

SONDRA OSTHEIMER | BOSCOBEL, WISCONSIN

Potato flakes make a golden coating for subtly seasoned fish fillets that are a breeze to fry on the stovetop.

PREP/TOTAL TIME: 20 MIN.

1/3 cup all-purpose flour
1 teaspoon paprika
1/2 teaspoon salt
1/4 teaspoon pepper
1/4 teaspoon onion powder
1/4 teaspoon garlic powder
2 eggs
2-1/4 pounds walleye, perch *or* pike fillets
1-1/2 cups mashed potato flakes
1/3 cup canola oil
Tartar sauce and lemon wedges, optional

- In a shallow bowl, combine flour, paprika, salt, pepper, onion powder and garlic powder. In another bowl, beat the eggs. Dip fillets in flour mixture and eggs, then in eggs; coat with potato flakes.
- In a large skillet, fry fillets in oil for 5 minutes on each side or until fish flakes easily with a fork. Serve with tartar sauce and lemon if desired. **Yield:** 4 servings.

breaded flounder fillets

MICHELLE SMITH | SYKESVILLE, MARYLAND

I use flounder in this recipe, but any fish fillets can be prepared with this tasty coating. It's quick and easy when time is short.

PREP/TOTAL TIME: 20 MIN.

1/4 cup all-purpose flour
1/4 cup cornmeal
1 teaspoon salt
1/2 teaspoon paprika
1/2 teaspoon pepper
2 egg whites
1/4 cup fat-free milk
4 flounder fillets (6 ounces *each*)
1 tablespoon grated Parmesan cheese

- In a shallow bowl, combine the flour, cornmeal, salt, paprika and pepper. In another shallow bowl, beat egg whites and milk. Coat the fish with cornmeal mixture, then dip into the egg white mixture. Coat the fish again in the cornmeal mixture.
- In a 15-in. x 10-in. x 1-in. baking pan coated with cooking spray, arrange fish in a single layer. Sprinkle with cheese.
- Bake, uncovered, at 425° for 8-10 minutes or until fish flakes easily with a fork. **Yield:** 4 servings.

sauteed spiced salmon

KATHY GARRISON | FORT WORTH, TEXAS

My husband and friends love this crusty salmon. We think you will love that it's so rich in heart-healthy omega-3 fatty acids—and so delicious!

PREP/TOTAL TIME: 15 MIN.

2 teaspoons dill weed
2 teaspoons chili powder
1 teaspoon salt-free lemon-pepper seasoning
1/2 teaspoon ground cumin
4 salmon fillets (4 ounces *each*), skin removed
1 tablespoon canola oil
Lemon wedges, optional

- Combine the dill, chili powder, lemon-pepper and cumin; rub over fillets.
- In a large nonstick skillet coated with cooking spray, cook salmon in oil over medium-high heat for 5-6 minutes on each side or until fish flakes easily with a fork. Serve with lemon if desired. **Yield:** 4 servings.

vegetable shrimp toss

SHARYN CRAIG | EL CAJON, CALIFORNIA

Whenever I cook too much spaghetti, I just pop it in the refrigerator. The next time I have leftover veggies, I combine them with the pasta, some sauteed shrimp and a little Parmesan cheese.

PREP/TOTAL TIME: 15 MIN.

- 1/2 pound uncooked medium shrimp, peeled and deveined
- 1/4 cup butter, cubed
- 1/2 teaspoon minced garlic
- 2 cups cooked mixed vegetables
- 2 cups cooked spaghetti
- 2 tablespoons shredded Parmesan cheese

■ In a large skillet, saute the shrimp in butter until the shrimp turn pink. Add the garlic; cook 1 minute longer. Remove and keep warm.

■ In the same skillet, saute vegetables until heated through. Add the spaghetti and shrimp; heat through. Sprinkle with cheese. **Yield:** 2-3 servings.

salmon supper

DEBRA KNIPPEL | MEDFORD, WISCONSIN

With a husband and four children to cook for, I'm always in search of quick recipes. This recipe was given to me many years ago by my mother-in-law.

PREP/TOTAL TIME: 30 MIN.

- 1/3 cup chopped green pepper
- 3 tablespoons chopped onion
- 2 tablespoons canola oil
- 1/4 cup all-purpose flour
- 1/2 teaspoon salt
- 1-1/2 cups milk
- 1 can (10-3/4 ounces) condensed cream of celery soup, undiluted
- 2 pouches (3 ounces *each*) boneless skinless pink salmon
- 1 cup frozen peas
- 2 teaspoons lemon juice
- 1 tube (8 ounces) refrigerated crescent rolls

■ In a large skillet, saute green pepper and onion in oil for 3-4 minutes or until crisp-tender.

■ In a small bowl, combine flour, salt, milk and soup until blended. Add to the skillet. Bring to a boil. Reduce heat; cook and stir for 2 minutes or until smooth. Stir in the salmon, peas and lemon juice.

■ Pour into an ungreased 11-in. x 7-in. baking dish. Do not unroll crescent dough; cut into eight equal slices. Arrange over salmon mixture. Bake, uncovered, at 375° for 10-12 minutes or until golden brown. **Yield:** 4 servings.

easy haddock bake

DOROTHY BATEMAN | CARVER, MASSACHUSETTS

We call this recipe "Mock Lobster Casserole" because it turns haddock into something fancy. The canned soup lends a creamy touch, making the dinner seem indulgent even though it's actually quite light.

PREP: 15 MIN. BAKE: 25 MIN.

- 2 pounds haddock fillets
- 1 can (10-3/4 ounces) condensed cream of shrimp soup, undiluted
- 2 tablespoons lemon juice
- 2 tablespoons sherry *or* reduced-sodium chicken broth
- 2 tablespoons finely chopped onion
- 2 garlic cloves, minced
- 4-1/2 teaspoons butter
- 1/4 cup dry bread crumbs
- 1/4 teaspoon Worcestershire sauce

■ Place the fillets in a 13-in. x 9-in. baking dish coated with cooking spray. In a small bowl, combine the soup, lemon juice and sherry or broth. Pour over fillets. Bake, uncovered, at 350° for 20 minutes.

■ In a small nonstick skillet, saute onion and garlic in butter for 2 minutes. Stir in bread crumbs and Worcestershire sauce. Sprinkle over fillets. Bake 5-10 minutes longer or until fish flakes easily with a fork. **Yield:** 6 servings.

Try Tilapia

If you're looking for a mild-tasting white fish, give tilapia a try. Not only does it cook quickly, it's a relatively inexpensive, low-fat and low-calorie source of protein.

sea bass with shrimp and tomatoes

SUSAN ORR SCHWARZ | SHERMAN OAKS, CALIFORNIA

This is one of my husband's favorite simple and delicious recipes. The ingredients make it into a sort of Greek stew. Besides making it for my husband and myself, I like serving this impressive dish to company.

PREP: 5 MIN. BAKE: 45 MIN.

- 2 sea bass *or* halibut steaks (8 to 10 ounces *each*)
- 6 to 8 large uncooked shrimp, peeled and deveined
- 1/2 small red *or* sweet onion, thinly sliced
- 1 can (14-1/2 ounces) Italian-style stewed tomatoes
- 1 package (4 ounces) crumbled feta cheese

■ Place the fish in a greased 8-in. square baking dish. Top with shrimp, onion, tomatoes and feta cheese. Bake, uncovered, at 325° for 45-50 minutes or until fish flakes easily with a fork. **Yield:** 2 servings.

dilled fish and vegetable packet

SHIRLEY GEVER | TOMS RIVER, NEW JERSEY

Ideal for anyone counting calories, this convenient foil-packet meal is so tasty and couldn't be much quicker or easier. I recommend serving it with baked potatoes.

PREP: 15 MIN. BAKE: 20 MIN.

- 4 tilapia fillets (4 ounces *each*)
- Refrigerated butter-flavored spray
- 1/2 teaspoon salt, *divided*
- 1/4 teaspoon pepper, *divided*
- 2 cups fresh snow peas
- 2 cups fresh baby carrots, halved lengthwise
- 1 green onion, thinly sliced
- 2 tablespoons minced fresh dill
- 2 garlic cloves, minced
- 1/2 cup white wine *or* reduced-sodium chicken broth

■ Place an 18-in. x 12-in. piece of heavy-duty foil on a large baking sheet. Arrange fillets in a single layer on foil; spritz with butter-flavored spray. Sprinkle with 1/4 teaspoon salt and 1/8 teaspoon pepper.

■ Combine the snow peas, carrots, green onion, dill, garlic and remaining salt and pepper; spoon over the fish. Drizzle with wine or broth. Top with a second large piece of foil. Bring edges of foil pieces together; crimp to seal, forming a large packet.

■ Bake at 400° for 20-25 minutes or until fish flakes easily with a fork and vegetables are crisp-tender. Open foil carefully to allow steam to escape. **Yield:** 4 servings.

grilled halibut with mustard dill sauce

LAURA PERRY | CHESTER SPRINGS, PENNSYLVANIA

Moist fish steaks are draped in a thick and creamy sauce in this flavorful dish. The topping makes a nice alternative to traditional tartar sauce and is just as good on swordfish.

PREP/TOTAL TIME: 20 MIN.

- 1/3 cup fat-free plain yogurt
- 2 tablespoons reduced-fat mayonnaise
- 2 tablespoons snipped fresh dill *or* 2 teaspoons dill weed
- 2 teaspoons Dijon mustard
- 4 halibut steaks (6 ounces *each*)
- 1/4 teaspoon salt
- 1/8 teaspoon pepper

■ In a small bowl, combine the yogurt, mayonnaise, dill and mustard; cover and refrigerate.

■ Sprinkle halibut with salt and pepper. Coat grill rack with cooking spray before starting the grill. Grill halibut, covered, over medium heat for 4-6 minutes on each side or until fish flakes easily with a fork. Serve sauce with halibut. **Yield:** 4 servings.

salsa catfish

TERESA HUBBARD | RUSSELLVILLE, ALABAMA

Give your fish a Southwestern "kick" with this change-of-pace preparation. My sister doesn't like seafood, so I figured I'd disguise it with a mix of interesting tastes and textures. Everyone was surprised by the slightly crunchy tortilla chip coating.

PREP/TOTAL TIME: 20 MIN.

- 1 cup finely crushed baked tortilla chip scoops
- 1/2 to 1 teaspoon chili powder
- 3 tablespoons lemon juice
- 1 tablespoon canola oil
- 4 catfish fillets (4 ounces *each*)
- 1 cup salsa, warmed

■ In a shallow bowl, combine tortilla chip crumbs and chili powder. In another bowl, combine lemon juice and oil. Dip fish in lemon mixture, then coat with crumb mixture.

■ Place in a 13-in. x 9-in. baking dish coasted with cooking spray. Sprinkle with any remaining crumbs.

■ Bake at 450° for 8-10 minutes or until fish easily flakes with a fork. Serve with salsa. **Yield:** 4 servings.

snapper with spicy pineapple glaze

TASTE OF HOME TEST KITCHEN

Ginger and cayenne bring spice to this tangy treatment for red snapper fillets. Sweet pineapple preserves round out the delectable combination of flavors.

PREP/TOTAL TIME: 30 MIN.

- 1/2 cup pineapple preserves
- 2 tablespoons rice vinegar
- 2 teaspoons minced fresh gingerroot
- 2 garlic cloves, minced
- 3/4 teaspoon salt, *divided*
- 1/4 teaspoon cayenne pepper
- 4 red snapper fillets (6 ounces *each*)
- 3 teaspoons olive oil

■ In a small bowl, combine the preserves, vinegar, ginger, garlic, 1/2 teaspoon salt and cayenne; set aside. Place fillets on a broiler pan coated with cooking spray. Spoon oil over both sides of fillets; sprinkle with remaining salt.

■ Broil 4-6 in. from the heat for 5 minutes. Baste with half of the glaze. Broil 5-7 minutes longer or until the fish flakes easily with a fork. Baste with the remaining glaze. **Yield:** 4 servings.

sea scallops 'n' mushrooms

LYNNAE NEUBERGER | MARSHFIELD, WISCONSIN

This is a foolproof yet elegant way to make sea scallops. Microwave preparation makes it simple.

PREP/TOTAL TIME: 15 MIN.

- 1 pound fresh *or* frozen sea scallops, thawed and rinsed
- 12 small fresh mushrooms, halved
- 1 tablespoon white wine *or* chicken broth
- 1-1/2 teaspoons lemon juice
- 1/2 teaspoon lemon-pepper seasoning
- 1/4 teaspoon dried thyme
- 1/8 teaspoon garlic powder
- 1/8 teaspoon seasoned salt
- 2 teaspoons butter, melted

■ Place the scallops and mushrooms in a 9-in. glass pie plate or dish. Combine the wine, lemon juice and seasonings; pour over scallop mixture.

■ Cover and microwave at 50% power for 2 minutes; stir. Cover and microwave at 50% power 4 to 4-1/2 minutes longer or until scallops turn opaque. Stir in melted butter. **Yield:** 3 servings.

Editor's Note: This recipe was tested in a 1,100-watt microwave.

Buying Shrimp

Shrimp in the shell (fresh or frozen) are available in different varieties and sizes (medium, large, extra large, jumbo). Fresh shrimp should have a firm texture with a mild odor.

oven fish 'n' chips

JANICE MITCHELL | AURORA, COLORADO

Crunchy fillets with cayenne and crispy potatoes are a quick and tasty light meal for two.

PREP: 20 MIN. BAKE: 25 MIN.

- 1 tablespoon olive oil
- 1/4 teaspoon pepper, *divided*
- 2 medium potatoes, peeled
- 3 tablespoons all-purpose flour
- 1 egg
- 1 tablespoon water
- 1/3 cup crushed cornflakes
- 1-1/2 teaspoons grated Parmesan cheese
- Dash cayenne pepper
- 1/2 pound haddock fillets
- Tartar sauce, optional

■ In a large bowl, combine oil and 1/8 teaspoon pepper. Cut potatoes lengthwise into 1/2-in. strips. Add to oil mixture and toss to coat. Place on a baking sheet coated with cooking spray. Bake at 425° for 25-30 minutes or until golden brown and crisp.

■ Meanwhile, in a shallow bowl, combine the flour and remaining pepper. In another shallow bowl, beat egg and water. In a third bowl, combine the cornflakes, Parmesan cheese and cayenne. Dredge fillets in flour, then dip in egg mixture and coat with crumbs.

■ Place on a baking sheet coated with cooking spray. Bake at 425° for 10-15 minutes or until fish flakes easily with a fork. Serve with chips and tartar sauce if desired. **Yield:** 2 servings.

barbecue shrimp over pasta

MICHELE FIELD | SYKESVILLE, MARYLAND

Diced bacon and barbecue sauce really give this shrimp dish a fun kick.

PREP/TOTAL TIME: 25 MIN.

- 1 package (16 ounces) linguine
- 12 bacon strips, diced
- 1 medium onion, chopped
- 1-1/4 pounds uncooked large shrimp, peeled and deveined
- 1-1/4 cups barbecue sauce
- 1/3 cup grated Parmesan cheese

■ Cook linguine according to package directions. Meanwhile, in a large skillet, cook bacon over medium heat until crisp. Remove with a slotted spoon to paper towels; drain, reserving 1 tablespoon drippings. Saute onion in the drippings until tender. Add shrimp; cook and stir until no longer pink.

■ Return bacon to the skillet. Add barbecue sauce; cook and stir over medium heat until heated through. Drain linguine; top with the shrimp mixture. Sprinkle with the cheese. **Yield:** 6 servings.

Storing Fresh Parsley

To keep fresh parsley in the refrigerator for several weeks, wash the entire bunch in warm water, shake off all excess moisture, wrap in paper towel and seal in a plastic bag. Then simply snip off and mince the amount needed.

garlic lime shrimp

GERTRAUD CASBARRO | SUMMERVILLE, SOUTH CAROLINA

Our son showed me how to make this fast shrimp and noodle dish zipped up with garlic and cayenne.

PREP/TOTAL TIME: 20 MIN.

1 pound uncooked large shrimp, peeled and deveined
5 garlic cloves, minced
1/2 teaspoon salt
1/4 to 1/2 teaspoon cayenne pepper
1/2 cup butter
3 tablespoons lime juice
1 tablespoon minced fresh parsley
Hot cooked pasta

- In a large skillet, saute the shrimp, garlic, salt and cayenne in butter until the shrimp turn pink, about 5 minutes. Stir in the lime juice and parsley. Serve with the pasta. **Yield:** 4 servings.

fried bluegill fillets

DOUG WRIGHT | MAIZE, KANSAS

The secret to this recipe is double-dipping the fillets in a perfectly seasoned bread-crumb coating. The fish turns out flaky and flavorful every time!

PREP/TOTAL TIME: 20 MIN.

1 cup seasoned bread crumbs
1 cup grated Parmesan cheese
1/2 teaspoon salt
1/2 teaspoon lemon-pepper seasoning
1/4 teaspoon pepper
6 eggs
1-1/2 pounds bluegill *or* crappie fillets
1/2 cup canola oil, *divided*

- In a shallow bowl, combine the first five ingredients. In another bowl, whisk the eggs. Dip fillets in eggs, then coat with crumb mixture. Dip again in eggs and crumb mixture.
- In a large skillet over medium-high heat, cook fillets in batches in 2 tablespoons oil for 2-3 minutes on each side or until fish flakes easily with a fork, adding oil as needed. **Yield:** 6 servings.

crumb-coated red snapper

CHARLOTTE ELLIOTT | NEENAH, WISCONSIN

You'll reel in compliments with these moist, crispy-coated fillets whenever you serve them. Heart-healthy omega-3 oils are an added bonus with this simple but delicious entree that's done in mere minutes. I pair this fish with instant rice and microwaved frozen beans or broccoli to keep things quick!

PREP/TOTAL TIME: 30 MIN.

- 1/2 cup dry bread crumbs
- 2 tablespoons grated Parmesan cheese
- 1 teaspoon lemon-pepper seasoning
- 1/4 teaspoon salt
- 4 red snapper fillets (6 ounces *each*)
- 2 tablespoons olive oil

■ In a shallow bowl, combine the bread crumbs, cheese, lemon-pepper and salt; add fillets, one at a time, and turn to coat.

■ In a heavy skillet over medium heat, cook fillets in oil in batches for 4-5 minutes on each side or until fish flakes easily with a fork. **Yield:** 4 servings.

peanut shrimp kabobs

HELEN GILDEN | MIDDLETOWN, DELAWARE

Soy sauce and peanut butter combine in a glaze that gives plain shrimp an Asian flair. I like to serve the kabobs as an appetizer when I'm entertaining.

PREP/TOTAL TIME: 15 MIN.

- 1/4 cup sugar
- 1/4 cup reduced-sodium soy sauce
- 1/4 cup reduced-fat creamy peanut butter
- 1 tablespoon water
- 1 tablespoon canola oil
- 3 garlic cloves, minced
- 1-1/2 pounds uncooked medium shrimp, peeled and deveined

■ In a small saucepan, combine the first six ingredients until smooth. Cook and stir over medium-low heat until blended and sugar is dissolved. Set aside 6 tablespoons of the sauce.

■ If grilling the kabobs, coat the grill rack with cooking spray before starting the grill. On eight metal or soaked wooden skewers, thread the shrimp. Brush with remaining sauce.

■ Grill kabobs, uncovered, over medium heat or broil 4 in. from the heat for 2-3 minutes on each side or until shrimp turn pink, turning once. Brush with reserved sauce before serving. **Yield:** 8 servings.

shrimp-stuffed sole

ROBERT BISHOP | LEXINGTON, KENTUCKY

If you like stuffed fish, this recipe is the way to go. It's so easy to assemble and cooks in just a few minutes in the microwave. Try it with chicken instead of sole, if you prefer, for a meal that's equally good.

PREP/TOTAL TIME: 15 MIN.

- 4 sole fillets, halved lengthwise
- 1 tablespoon lemon juice
- 1/8 teaspoon onion salt *or* onion powder
- 1/4 cup butter, melted, *divided*
- 1 can (6 ounces) small shrimp, rinsed and drained
- 1/3 cup milk
- 1/4 cup finely chopped celery
- 2 teaspoons minced fresh parsley
- 1 cup cubed bread, toasted

Dash paprika

- Sprinkle fillets with lemon juice and onion salt; set aside. Pour 2 tablespoons of the butter into an 8-in. square microwave-safe dish. Add the shrimp, milk, celery and parsley. Cover and microwave on high for 1 to 1-1/2 minutes or until celery is tender. Stir in bread cubes.
- Spoon shrimp mixture onto fillets. Starting with a short side, roll up each and secure with toothpicks. Place in a greased shallow microwave-safe dish. Brush with remaining butter; sprinkle with paprika.
- Cover and microwave on high for 4-6 minutes or until fish flakes easily with a fork. Let stand for 5 minutes before serving. Discard toothpicks. **Yield:** 4 servings.

Editor's Note: This recipe was tested in a 1,100-watt microwave.

Buying and Storing Fish

Purchase fish that smells and looks good, whether it's refrigerated or frozen. High-quality refrigerated fish does not have a heavy fishy odor. Store fish in the coolest part of your refrigerator for no more than 2 days. Frozen fish should be thawed in its original package in the refrigerator. Do not refreeze fish that has thawed.

cod delight

NANCY DAUGHERTY | CORTLAND, OHIO

Though I used to whip up this delightful seasoned cod with tomatoes and onion in the oven, the microwave lets me enjoy it even faster. I like to serve the pretty main course to company. Everyone likes it and requests the recipe.

PREP/TOTAL TIME: 10 MIN.

- 1 pound cod fillets
- 1/2 cup chopped tomatoes
- 1/3 cup finely chopped onion
- 2 tablespoons water
- 2 tablespoons canola oil
- 4-1/2 teaspoons lemon juice
- 1 teaspoon dried parsley flakes
- 1/2 teaspoon minced garlic
- 1/2 teaspoon minced fresh basil
- 1/8 teaspoon salt
- 1 teaspoon seafood seasoning

- Place the cod fillets in a shallow microwave-safe dish. In a small bowl, combine the tomatoes, onion, water, oil, lemon juice, parsley, garlic, basil and salt; spoon over cod. Sprinkle with seafood seasoning.
- Cover and microwave on high for 6 minutes or until fish flakes easily with a fork. **Yield:** 4 servings.

Editor's Note: This recipe was tested in a 1,100-watt microwave.

Testing Fish Fillets for Doneness

To check fish fillets for doneness, insert a fork at an angle into the thickest portion of the fish and gently part the meat. When it is opaque and flakes into sections, it is cooked completely.

cajun-style catfish

DOLORES BARNAS | BLASDELL, NEW YORK

These nicely spiced fillets are sure to win you a boatload of compliments! I got the original recipe from a chef in the culinary arts department of a college where I used to work.

PREP/TOTAL TIME: 20 MIN.

4-1/2 teaspoons paprika
1 teaspoon onion powder
1 teaspoon dried oregano
1 teaspoon pepper
1/2 teaspoon white pepper
1/2 teaspoon dried thyme
1/4 teaspoon cayenne pepper
4 catfish fillets (6 ounces *each*)
Refrigerated butter-flavored spray

- In a shallow bowl, combine the first seven ingredients. Spritz both sides of fish with butter-flavored spray. Dip one side of each fillet in spice mixture.
- Place spice side down in a large skillet coated with butter-flavored spray. Cook over medium-high heat for 4-5 minutes on each side or until fish flakes easily with a fork. **Yield:** 4 servings.

baked shrimp and asparagus

JANE RHODES | SILVERDALE, WASHINGTON

I invented this casserole when I needed to serve 30 co-workers at a holiday party. I knew it was a hit when people asked for the recipe. Now I make it frequently for guests because it tastes delicious and is fast to fix.

PREP/TOTAL TIME: 30 MIN.

1 package (12 ounces) frozen cut asparagus
1 pound uncooked medium shrimp, peeled and deveined
1 can (10-3/4 ounces) condensed cream of shrimp soup, undiluted
1 tablespoon butter, melted
1 teaspoon soy sauce
1/2 cup salad croutons, optional
Hot cooked rice

- In a large bowl, combine the first five ingredients. Spoon into a greased 8-in. square baking dish.
- Bake, uncovered, at 425° for 20 minutes or until shrimp turn pink. Top with croutons if desired; bake 5 minutes longer. Serve with rice. **Yield:** 4-6 servings.

flavorful fish fillets

NELLA PARKER | HERSEY, MICHIGAN

I like to make this entree whenever there's a special occasion in my large family. The fish has an impressive taste without the time-consuming preparation of other dishes, and people always ask for the recipe.

PREP/TOTAL TIME: 20 MIN.

1 package (18.7 ounces) frozen breaded fish fillets
3 tablespoons olive oil
1 jar (26 ounces) spaghetti sauce
3 tablespoons prepared horseradish
1 cup (4 ounces) shredded part-skim mozzarella cheese

- In a large skillet, cook fish in oil for 4 minutes on each side or until crisp and golden brown. Meanwhile, in a large saucepan, combine the spaghetti sauce and horseradish; cook until heated through.
- Spoon over fish; sprinkle with cheese. Cover and remove from the hat. Let stand for 5 minutes or until cheese is melted. **Yield:** 4-5 servings.

crab lo mein

LAURA MRYYAN | TOPEKA, KANSAS

I came up with this one night when I had some leftover spaghetti I needed to use up. When stirring up the sauce, I like to use half soy sauce and half oyster sauce for a richer, more developed flavor.

PREP/TOTAL TIME: 25 MIN.

- 4 ounces uncooked angel hair pasta *or* thin spaghetti
- 1 medium onion, thinly sliced
- 1 medium green pepper, cut into 1-inch strips
- 1 package (9 ounces) frozen broccoli cuts, thawed
- 1/4 cup sliced fresh mushrooms
- 2 tablespoons canola oil
- 1 tablespoon cornstarch
- 1-1/4 cups chicken broth
- 1/4 cup water
- 1/4 cup soy sauce
- 12 ounces imitation crabmeat, cut into 1-inch pieces

■ Cook pasta according to package directions. Meanwhile, in a large skillet or wok, stir-fry the onion, green pepper, broccoli and mushrooms in oil for 3-4 minutes or until crisp-tender.

■ In a small bowl, combine the cornstarch, broth, water and soy sauce until smooth. Gradually stir into skillet. Bring to a boil; cook and stir for 2 minutes or until thickened. Stir in crab; cook 2-3 minutes longer or until heated through. Drain pasta; toss with crab mixture. **Yield:** 6 servings.

baked walleye with vegetables

SONDRA OSTHEIMER | BOSCOBEL, WISCONSIN

We love fish, so I'm always looking for new recipes to try. This fast-to-fix dish is a family favorite, and a great way to load up on veggies, too.

PREP: 15 MIN. BAKE: 20 MIN.

- 1 small onion, thinly sliced
- 1 tablespoon olive oil
- 2 small zucchini, julienned
- 1 cup sliced fresh mushrooms
- 1/4 teaspoon pepper
- 1/8 teaspoon garlic powder
- 2 tablespoons lemon juice
- 2 tablespoons grated Parmesan cheese, *divided*
- 4 walleye fillets (about 6 ounces *each*)
- 1 tablespoon butter, melted

■ In a nonstick skillet, cook onion in oil over medium heat for about 2 minutes. Stir in zucchini and mushrooms; cook and stir 2 minutes longer. Sprinkle with pepper and garlic powder; stir in the lemon juice. Cook and stir 30 seconds longer. Remove from the heat and stir in 1 teaspoon Parmesan cheese.

■ Place fillets in a 13-in. x 9-in. baking dish coated with cooking spray. Top each fillet with about 1/4 cup onion mixture. Drizzle with butter and sprinkle with remaining Parmesan cheese.

■ Bake, uncovered, at 375° for 18-22 minutes or until fish flakes easily with a fork. **Yield:** 4 servings.

shrimp pizza

SUSAN LEBRUN | SULPHUR, LOUISIANA

Topped with fresh shrimp and melted cheese, this delicious main dish makes a timely supper with a special touch.

PREP/TOTAL TIME: 30 MIN.

- 1 tablespoon butter
- 4-1/2 teaspoons all-purpose flour
- 1/4 to 1/2 teaspoon ground mustard
- 1/8 to 1/4 teaspoon cayenne pepper
- 1/8 teaspoon salt
- 1 cup 2% milk
- 1 small onion, chopped
- 1 pound uncooked medium shrimp, peeled and deveined
- 1 prebaked 12-inch pizza crust
- 3/4 cup shredded part-skim mozzarella cheese

■ In a small nonstick saucepan, melt butter. Stir in the flour, mustard, cayenne and salt until smooth; gradually add milk. Bring to a boil; cook and stir for 2 minutes or until thickened. Remove from the heat; set aside.

■ In a large nonstick skillet coated with cooking spray, cook onion over medium heat for 2 minutes. Add shrimp; cook and stir 2-3 minutes longer. Drain.

■ Place crust on a pizza pan or baking sheet; spread with white sauce. Top with shrimp mixture and cheese. Bake at 425° for 8-12 minutes or until shrimp turn pink and cheese is melted. **Yield:** 6 slices.

p. 254

simple side dishes
p. 251
p. 245
p. 238

italian broccoli with peppers

MAUREEN MCCLANAHAN | ST. LOUIS, MISSOURI

This healthy side dish goes with just about anything. And for a satisfying meal, we like it over pasta and grilled chicken or turkey breasts.

PREP/TOTAL TIME: 20 MIN.

- 6 cups water
- 4 cups fresh broccoli florets
- 1 medium sweet red pepper, julienned
- 1 medium sweet yellow pepper, julienned
- 1 tablespoon olive oil
- 1 garlic clove, minced
- 1 teaspoon dried oregano
- 1/2 teaspoon salt
- 1/4 teaspoon pepper
- 1 medium ripe tomato, cut into wedges and seeded
- 1 tablespoon grated Parmesan cheese

■ In a large saucepan, bring water to a boil. Add broccoli; cover and boil for 3 minutes. Drain and immediately place broccoli in ice water. Drain and pat dry.

■ In a large nonstick skillet, saute the peppers in oil for 3 minutes or until crisp-tender. Add the broccoli, garlic, oregano, salt and pepper; saute 2 minutes longer. Add the tomato; heat through. Sprinkle with Parmesan cheese. **Yield:** 6 servings.

Broccoli Basics

Select firm yet tender stalks of broccoli with compact, dark green or slightly purplish florets. Refrigerate unwashed in an open plastic bag up to 4 days. One pound yields about 3-1/2 cups florets.

garlic-almond green beans

GENNY MONCHAMP | REDDING, CALIFORNIA

This is my family's favorite way to eat a popular vegetable. Boiling beans keeps them so bright and crisp. To speed things up even more, you could use frozen green beans instead of fresh.

PREP/TOTAL TIME: 20 MIN.

- 1 pound fresh green beans
- 2 garlic cloves, minced
- 1 tablespoon olive oil
- 1/4 cup slivered almonds, toasted
- Pepper to taste

- Place the beans in a large saucepan and cover with water. Bring to a boil; cook, uncovered, for 8-10 minutes or until crisp-tender.
- Meanwhile, in a large skillet, cook garlic in oil for 1 minute. Drain beans; add to the skillet along with almonds and pepper. Toss to coat. **Yield:** 4 servings.

twice-baked deviled potatoes

KAROL CHANDLER-EZELL | NACOGDOCHES, TEXAS

These potatoes are flavored with bacon, cheddar and a hint of Dijon mustard. And since they take under 30 minutes, they're perfect for a quick weeknight dinner.

PREP/TOTAL TIME: 30 MIN.

- 4 small baking potatoes
- 1/4 cup butter, softened
- 1/4 cup milk
- 1 cup (4 ounces) shredded cheddar cheese
- 1/3 cup real bacon bits
- 2 green onions, chopped
- 1 teaspoon Dijon mustard
- Dash paprika

- Scrub and pierce potatoes; place on a microwave-safe plate. Microwave, uncovered, on high for 7-10 minutes or until tender, turning once. Let stand for 5 minutes. Cut a thin slice off the top of each potato and discard. Scoop out pulp, leaving a thin shell.
- In a large bowl, mash the pulp with butter and milk. Stir in the cheese, bacon, onions, mustard and paprika. Spoon into potato shells. Return to the microwave-safe plate. Microwave, uncovered, on high for 1-2 minutes or until cheese is melted. **Yield:** 4 servings.

Editor's Note: This recipe was tested in a 1,100-watt microwave.

Fettuccine Facts

Fettuccine means "little ribbons" in Italian. You can find these flat, wide pasta strands in egg, egg-free and spinach varieties. Its hearty shape holds up well to heavy sauces, like Alfredo.

basil walnut fettuccine

TASTE OF HOME TEST KITCHEN

Buttery fettuccine is studded with toasted nuts and lightly flavored with garlic and fresh basil. It goes well with a variety of entrees.

PREP/TOTAL TIME: 20 MIN.

- 1 package (12 ounces) fettuccine
- 1 teaspoon minced garlic
- 6 tablespoons butter, *divided*
- 1/4 cup finely chopped walnuts, toasted
- 1 tablespoon minced fresh basil *or* 1 teaspoon dried basil
- 1/4 teaspoon salt
- 1/8 teaspoon pepper

■ Cook fettuccine according to package directions. In a large skillet, saute garlic in 1 tablespoon butter for 1 minute or until crisp-tender. Add the walnuts, basil, salt, pepper and remaining butter; cook and stir for 2 minutes or until heated through. Drain fettuccine; add to skillet and toss to coat. **Yield:** 6 servings.

swiss creamed peas

LIN CARR | WEST SENECA, NEW YORK

A creamy cheese sauce turns ordinary peas into a succulent side dish. I make this quite often for family gatherings, and it's always well received.

PREP/TOTAL TIME: 20 MIN.

- 1 cup chopped green onions
- 4-1/2 teaspoons butter
- 1 tablespoon all-purpose flour
- 1/2 teaspoon salt
- 1 cup heavy whipping cream
- 3/4 cup shredded Swiss Cheese
- 3 cups cooked peas

■ In a large saucepan, saute onions in butter until tender. Stir in flour and salt until blended; gradually add the cream. Bring to a boil; cook and stir for 2 minutes or until thickened. Reduce heat; stir in cheese until melted. Add peas; cook and stir until heated through. **Yield:** 4 servings.

spiced acorn squash

GEORGE MANKIN | HORSHAM, PENNSYLVANIA

When fall arrives, I like to prepare my wonderful cinnamon-and-maple-flavored squash recipe. It's so quick and easy in the microwave, and it's a good source of vitamins A and C, potassium and fiber.

PREP/TOTAL TIME: 25 MIN.

- 1 medium acorn squash
- 1 tablespoon butter, melted
- 2 teaspoons maple syrup
- 1/2 teaspoon cider vinegar
- 1/8 teaspoon *each* ground ginger, cinnamon and mace

■ Pierce squash several times with a fork. Place on microwave-safe paper towels; microwave on high for 10 minutes. Let stand for 5-10 minutes.

■ In a small bowl, combine the butter, syrup and vinegar. Combine the ginger, cinnamon and mace. Cut squash in half; discard seeds. Brush cut sides with butter mixture; sprinkle with spice mixture.

■ Place on a large microwave-safe plate; cover with microwave-safe paper towels. Cook on high for 5-10 minutes or until squash is tender. **Yield:** 2 servings.

Editor's Note: This recipe was tested in a 1,100-watt microwave.

cheese fries

MELISSA TATUM | GREENSBORO, NORTH CAROLINA

I came up with this recipe after my daughter had cheese fries at a restaurant and couldn't stop talking about them. She loves that I can fix them so quickly at home.

PREP/TOTAL TIME: 20 MIN.

- 1 package (28 ounces) frozen steak fries
- 1 can (10-3/4 ounces) condensed cheddar cheese soup, undiluted
- 1/4 cup milk
- 1/2 teaspoon garlic powder
- 1/4 teaspoon onion powder
- Paprika

■ Arrange the steak fries in a single layer in two greased 15-in. x 10-in. x 1-in. baking pans. Bake at 450° for 15-18 minutes or until tender and golden brown.

■ Meanwhile, in a small saucepan, combine the soup, milk, garlic powder and onion powder; heat through. Drizzle over fries; sprinkle with paprika. **Yield:** 8-10 servings.

basil baked tomatoes

MARY DETZI | WIND GAP, PENNSYLVANIA

This recipe has been in our family for many years. My mother brought it with her when she came to the United States from Italy. When fresh tomatoes are plentiful, this is a great way to serve them.

PREP/TOTAL TIME: 25 MIN.

- 1 garlic clove, minced
- 1 tablespoon olive oil
- 1/2 cup soft bread crumbs
- 2 large tomatoes
- 4 fresh basil leaves, chopped
- 1/8 teaspoon coarsely ground pepper

■ In a small skillet, saute garlic in oil for 1 minute. Add bread crumbs; cook and stir until lightly browned. Remove from the heat.

■ Cut tomatoes in half widthwise. Place cut side up in an 8-in. square baking dish. Sprinkle with basil and pepper; top with the bread crumb mixture. Bake at 325° for 15-20 minutes or until the tomatoes are slightly softened. **Yield:** 4 servings.

mediterranean couscous

BETH TOMLINSON | STREETSBORO, OHIO

With garlic, tomatoes and Parmesan cheese, it's a great side dish for just about any entree. It relies on a boxed item to get started, then it's just a matter of adding a few ingredients.

PREP/TOTAL TIME: 15 MIN.

- 2 tablespoons chopped onion
- 2 tablespoons olive oil, *divided*
- 3 teaspoons minced garlic
- 1-1/4 cups water
- 1 package (5.6 ounces) couscous with toasted pine nuts
- 1-1/2 teaspoons chicken bouillon granules
- 1/2 cup cherry tomatoes, halved
- 2 tablespoons grated Parmesan cheese

■ In a small skillet, saute onion in 1 tablespoon oil for 3-4 minutes or until tender. Add garlic; cook 1 minute longer.

■ In a large saucepan, combine the water, contents of seasoning packet from couscous mix, bouillon and remaining oil. Bring to a boil.

■ Stir in onion mixture and couscous. Cover and remove from the heat; let stand for 5 minutes. Fluff with a fork. Stir in tomatoes and cheese. **Yield:** 4 servings.

swirled dill rolls

TASTE OF HOME TEST KITCHEN

You'll need just four ingredients to bake a pan of these golden-brown rolls. With their fresh-from-the-oven aroma and mild dill flavor, they complement most any entree.

PREP/TOTAL TIME: 20 MIN.

- 1 tube (8 ounces) refrigerated crescent rolls
- 2 tablespoons butter, softened
- 1/4 teaspoon onion powder
- 1/4 teaspoon snipped fresh dill

■ Do not unroll crescent dough; cut into eight equal slices. Place cut side down on an ungreased baking sheet. Bake at 375° for 11-13 minutes or until golden brown. Meanwhile, in a small bowl, combine the butter, onion powder and dill. Spread over warm rolls. **Yield:** 8 rolls.

Freeze Fresh Dill

You can freeze fresh dill sprigs for up to 2 months. Although the color will darken a bit, the flavor is not affected. There's no need to thaw it first...simply snip what's needed for your recipe.

Veggie Topper

To give steamed, broiled or sauteed veggies a little crunch, sprinkle them with sauteed almonds, sesame seeds or sunflower kernels.

herbed corn

EDNA HOFFMAN | HEBRON, INDIANA

A pleasant blend of herbs dresses up this buttery, fresh-flavored corn dish that I often take to carry-in dinners. It's a must for my family's Thanksgiving meals.

PREP/TOTAL TIME: 20 MIN.

- 12 cups frozen corn
- 1 cup water
- 1/2 cup butter, cubed
- 2 tablespoons minced fresh parsley
- 2 teaspoons salt
- 1 teaspoon dill weed
- 1/2 teaspoon garlic powder
- 1/2 teaspoon Italian seasoning
- 1/4 teaspoon dried thyme

■ In a large saucepan, combine corn and water. Bring to a boil. Reduce heat; cover and simmer for 4-6 minutes or until the corn is tender. Drain; stir in the remaining ingredients. **Yield:** 10-12 servings.

seasoned green beans

TASTE OF HOME TEST KITCHEN

The mild flavor of the crisp-tender green beans and mushrooms in this side is sure to appeal to everyone in your family.

PREP/TOTAL TIME: 20 MIN.

- 1 tablespoon canola oil
- 1 tablespoon lemon juice
- 1 tablespoon cider vinegar
- 2 teaspoons dried basil
- 3/4 teaspoon brown sugar
- 1/4 teaspoon salt
- 1/8 teaspoon pepper
- 1 pound fresh green beans, trimmed
- 1 cup sliced fresh mushrooms
- 2 tablespoons butter

■ In a small bowl, combine the first seven ingredients; set aside. In a large skillet, saute green beans and mushrooms in butter until crisp-tender.

■ Add lemon juice mixture; bring to a boil. Reduce heat; cover and simmer for 5 minutes or until vegetables are tender. **Yield:** 4 servings.

italian-style peas

KATHLEEN VALLE | PHILADELPHIA, PENNSYLVANIA

This side dish is a big hit on any occasion. I've been making it for at least 35 years, and it was made by my mother before me.

PREP/TOTAL TIME: 15 MIN.

- 1 small onion, diced
- 4 ounces diced fully cooked lean ham
- 4 teaspoons olive oil
- 1 package (16 ounces) frozen peas
- 1/2 teaspoon salt
- 1/4 teaspoon dried oregano
- 1/4 teaspoon pepper

■ In a nonstick skillet, saute onion and ham in oil until onion is tender. Add the remaining ingredients. Reduce heat; cover and cook until peas are tender. **Yield:** 4 servings.

herbed sour cream biscuits

AUDREY HURD | FOUNTAIN HILLS, ARIZONA

Being a student can make cooking impossible, so I took an easy biscuit recipe and added an herb mixture of my own...and voila! These tender rolls make my quick home meals a real treat.

PREP/TOTAL TIME: 25 MIN.

1 cup biscuit/baking mix
1/2 teaspoon sugar
1 garlic clove, minced
Dash dried rosemary, crushed
1/4 teaspoon dried basil
1/4 cup club soda
2 tablespoons sour cream

- In a small bowl, combine the biscuit mix, sugar, garlic, rosemary and basil. Combine club soda and sour cream; stir into dry ingredients just until moistened.
- Drop by heaping tablespoonfuls 2 in. apart onto a baking sheet coated with cooking spray. Bake at 400° for 10-12 minutes or until golden. Serve warm. **Yield:** 6 biscuits.

speedy spanish rice

ANGIE RORICK | FORT WAYNE, INDIANA

Mexican food is big with our family. In fact, one of my nephews loves this dish so much that he always requests it for his special birthday dinner!

PREP/TOTAL TIME: 25 MIN.

- 1-1/2 cups uncooked instant brown rice
- 1 medium onion, chopped
- 1 small green pepper, chopped
- 1 tablespoon butter
- 1 garlic clove, minced
- 1-1/2 cups water
- 1 tablespoon minced fresh cilantro
- 2 teaspoons ground cumin
- 1-1/2 teaspoons chicken bouillon granules
- 1/4 teaspoon pepper
- 1 cup picante sauce

■ In a large nonstick skillet, saute the rice, onion and green pepper in butter until rice is lightly browned and vegetables are crisp-tender. Add garlic; cook 1 minute longer. Stir in the water, cilantro, cumin, bouillon and pepper; bring to a boil. Reduce heat; cover and simmer for 5 minutes.

■ Remove from the heat; let stand for 5 minutes. Fluff with a fork. Stir in picante sauce. **Yield:** 4 servings.

Swap Out Cilantro

If you find the flavor of cilantro to be too strong for your liking, simply use fresh parsley instead.

stewed tomatoes with dumplings

VIOLA STUTZ | GREENWOOD, DELAWARE

When I was young and did not feel well, my mother would always make this because it was one of my favorite dishes. Just smelling it cook made me feel better, along with her tender, loving care.

PREP/TOTAL TIME: 20 MIN.

- 1 can (14-1/2 ounces) diced tomatoes, undrained
- 1 tablespoon sugar
- 1/4 teaspoon salt
- 1/4 teaspoon pepper
- 2 tablespoons butter
- 1/2 cup biscuit/baking mix
- 3 tablespoons milk

■ In a large saucepan, combine the tomatoes, sugar, salt, pepper and butter. Bring to a boil over medium heat, stirring occasionally.

■ In a small bowl, combine biscuit mix and milk. Drop batter in four mounds onto the tomatoes. Reduce heat; cover and simmer for 10 minutes or until a toothpick inserted in a dumpling comes out clean (do not lift the cover while simmering). **Yield:** 2 servings.

orange-glazed sweet potatoes

TASTE OF HOME TEST KITCHEN

These delicious potatoes bring a great flavor and color to your plate. The delicate sweetness of the potato is fresh tasting, and a nice contrast from the more usual sticky-sweet, candied yams.

PREP/TOTAL TIME: 25 MIN.

- 1 pound sweet potatoes, peeled and cut into 1/2-inch slices
- 1/2 cup orange juice
- 1 tablespoon butter
- 1/2 teaspoon grated orange peel
- 1/4 teaspoon pumpkin pie spice

■ Place sweet potatoes in a small saucepan and cover with water. Bring to a boil. Reduce heat; cover and simmer for 4-6 minutes or just until tender.

■ Meanwhile, in a small skillet, bring the orange juice, butter, orange peel and pumpkin pie spice to a boil. Reduce heat; simmer, uncovered, for 3-4 minutes or until thickened. Drain sweet potatoes; return to pan. Pour glaze over potatoes and stir gently to coat. **Yield:** 3 servings.

sweet herbed carrots

BEVERLY CHRISTOFFERSON | SIOUX CITY, IOWA

The original recipe, which my mother acquired over 45 years ago, called for two bunches of small carrots so I had to guess how much to use. I eventually got the recipe amounts worked out to my liking.

PREP/TOTAL TIME: 25 MIN.

- 2 tablespoons butter
- 1/4 teaspoon sugar
- 2 cups sliced fresh carrots
- 3 to 4 lettuce leaves
- 2 tablespoons water
- 2 tablespoons minced fresh parsley
- 2 tablespoons heavy whipping cream
- 1 tablespoon minced fresh tarragon *or* 1 teaspoon dried tarragon
- 1/4 teaspoon salt
- 1/8 teaspoon pepper

■ In a large skillet, cook and stir the butter and sugar over medium heat until butter is melted and sugar is dissolved. Stir in carrots; cover with lettuce leaves. Sprinkle with water. Cover and simmer for 15-20 minutes or until carrots are crisp-tender.

■ Discard the lettuce. Stir in the parsley, cream, tarragon, salt and pepper. Bring to a boil. Reduce heat; simmer, uncovered, for 1-2 minutes or until heated through. Serve with a slotted spoon. **Yield:** 2 servings.

sunny snow peas

KATHLEEN BAILEY | CHESTER SPRINGS, PENNSYLVANIA

Turn crispy snow peas into something unique by tossing them with this lovely honey-orange sauce. I enjoy serving fresh vegetables, especially when I can prepare a sauce that seems to add the bright warmth of the sun.

PREP/TOTAL TIME: 25 MIN.

- 1/2 cup orange juice
- 2 tablespoons honey
- 1 tablespoon butter

- 1 to 2 teaspoons grated orange peel
- 1/2 teaspoon salt
- 1/8 teaspoon ground cardamom
- 1 pound fresh snow peas *or* sugar snap peas

■ In a small saucepan, combine the orange juice, honey, butter, orange peel, salt and cardamom; bring to a boil. Reduce heat; simmer, uncovered, until mixture is reduced by half, about 15 minutes.

■ Meanwhile, in another saucepan, bring 1 in. of water to a boil. Add peas. Reduce heat; cover and simmer for 3-4 minutes or until crisp-tender. Drain and transfer to a serving bowl. Add orange juice mixture and toss to coat. **Yield:** 6 servings.

chili cheese corn

NADENE MELTON | SAN JUAN CAPISTRANO, CALIFORNIA

I received this yummy corn recipe from a co-worker years ago. It's so easy and tasty that it's become a tradition in our family, usually for holidays or special meals. I've had many requests for the recipe.

PREP/TOTAL TIME: 15 MIN.

- 1 package (8 ounces) cream cheese, cubed
- 2 tablespoons butter
- 4 cups fresh *or* frozen corn, thawed
- 1 can (4 ounces) chopped green chilies
- 1/4 cup milk
- 1/4 teaspoon garlic salt
- 1/8 teaspoon salt
- 1/8 teaspoon cayenne pepper

■ In a large saucepan, combine cream cheese and butter. Cook and stir over medium heat for 4-5 minutes or until smooth. Stir in all of the remaining ingredients. Cook for 5 minutes or until heated through. Serve with a slotted spoon. **Yield:** 6 servings.

herbed potatoes and veggies

JENELLE PARKS | HAYFIELD, MINNESOTA

I came up with this family favorite when I needed to use up leftover baked potatoes and extra produce from our garden. It's a great-tasting side dish. My husband requests it all the time and brags about it to company.

PREP/TOTAL TIME: 25 MIN.

- 4 medium baking potatoes
- 1-1/2 cups diced zucchini
- 3 tablespoons olive oil
- 2 tablespoons plus 1 teaspoon savory herb with garlic soup mix
- 1/4 teaspoon pepper
- 10 cherry tomatoes, halved

■ Scrub and pierce potatoes; place on a microwave-safe plate. Cover and microwave on high for 5-6 minutes on each side or until tender. When potatoes are cool enough to handle, cut into cubes.

■ In a large skillet, saute the potatoes and zucchini in oil for 5 minutes or until tender. Sprinkle with soup mix and pepper. Cook until heated through, stirring occasionally. Add tomatoes; cook 1 minute longer. **Yield:** 6 servings.

Editor's Note: This recipe was tested in a 1,100-watt microwave.

cauliflower with buttered crumbs

TASTE OF HOME TEST KITCHEN

This recipe is a home-style way to add flavor and interest to steamed cauliflower. Serve this simple side dish with a variety of entrees.

PREP/TOTAL TIME: 20 MIN.

- 1 large head cauliflower, broken into florets
- 1/3 cup butter
- 1 tablespoon lemon juice
- 1/4 cup dry bread crumbs
- 1/4 cup grated Parmesan cheese
- 2 tablespoons minced fresh parsley
- 1/8 teaspoon salt
- 1/8 teaspoon pepper

■ Place 1 in. of water in a large saucepan; add cauliflower. Bring to a boil. Reduce the heat; cover and simmer for 10-12 minutes or until crisp-tender.

■ Meanwhile, in a small heavy saucepan, cook butter over medium heat for 5 minutes or until golden brown, stirring frequently. Remove from the heat; stir in lemon juice. In a small bowl, combine the bread crumbs, cheese, parsley, salt and pepper; stir in 3 tablespoons browned butter.

■ Drain cauliflower and place in a serving dish. Drizzle with the remaining browned butter; sprinkle with bread crumb mixture. **Yield:** 6 servings.

glazed snap peas

IDA TUEY | KOKOMO, INDIANA

I serve veggies with every meal, and this recipe is perfect for busy days. I love the natural sweet taste from snap peas.

PREP/TOTAL TIME: 20 MIN.

- 2 packages (24 ounces *each*) frozen sugar snap peas
- 1/4 cup honey
- 2 tablespoons butter
- 1 teaspoon salt
- 1/4 teaspoon crushed red pepper flakes
- 1/4 cup real bacon bits

■ Cook peas according to package directions; drain. Stir in the honey, butter, salt and pepper flakes. Sprinkle with bacon. **Yield:** 10 servings.

maple syrup corn bread

ROGER HICKUM | PLYMOUTH, NEW HAMPSHIRE

Here's a good-old New England recipe. Enhanced with a hint of maple syrup, the corn bread makes a perfect companion to spicy chili or stew.

PREP/TOTAL TIME: 30 MIN.

- 1-1/4 cups all-purpose flour
- 1 cup cornmeal
- 2 teaspoons baking powder
- 1 teaspoon salt
- 1 egg
- 3/4 cup fat-free milk
- 1/2 cup maple syrup
- 3 tablespoons butter, melted

■ In a large bowl, combine the flour, cornmeal, baking powder and salt. In a small bowl, whisk together the egg, milk, syrup and butter; stir into the dry ingredients just until moistened.

■ Pour into a 9-in. square baking pan coated with cooking spray. Bake at 400° for 15-20 minutes or until a toothpick inserted near the center comes out clean. Serve warm. **Yield:** 12 servings.

Easy Asparagus Prep

Before using asparagus, rinse the spears well in cold water to clean. Snap off the stalk ends as far down as they will easily break when gently bent, or cut off the tough white portion.

skillet sausage stuffing

JENNIFER LYNN CULLEN | TAYLOR, MICHIGAN

I dressed up a package of stuffing mix with pork sausage, mushrooms, celery and onion to make this. It impressed my in-laws at a family gathering and has since become a popular side dish with my husband and children.

PREP/TOTAL TIME: 25 MIN.

- 1 pound bulk pork sausage
- 1-1/4 cups chopped celery
- 1/2 cup chopped onion
- 1/2 cup sliced fresh mushrooms
- 1-1/2 teaspoons minced garlic
- 1-1/2 cups reduced-sodium chicken broth
- 1 teaspoon rubbed sage
- 1 package (6 ounces) stuffing mix

■ In a large skillet, cook the sausage, celery, onion and mushrooms over medium heat until meat is no longer pink. Add garlic; cook 1 minute longer; drain. Stir in broth and sage.

■ Bring to a boil. Stir in stuffing mix. Cover and remove from the heat; let stand for 5 minutes. Fluff with a fork. **Yield:** 8 servings.

mexican veggies

PATRICIA MICKELSON | SAN JOSE, CALIFORNIA

I came up with this oh-so-easy, colorful combination while looking for a veggie side to complement my Mexican dinners. Corn, zucchini, salsa and fresh, crunchy flavor make this recipe a keeper!

PREP/TOTAL TIME: 15 MIN.

- 1 medium zucchini, diced
- 1/2 cup fresh *or* frozen corn
- 1/2 cup salsa *or* picante sauce

■ Place 1 in. of water in a small saucepan; add zucchini and corn. Bring to a boil. Reduce heat; cover and simmer for 3-4 minutes or until zucchini is almost tender. Drain. Stir in salsa; heat through. **Yield:** 2 servings.

savory asparagus

TASTE OF HOME TEST KITCHEN

Fresh asparagus dresses up a weeknight meal with aromatic tarragon. Try substituting the asparagus spears with broccoli for a twist.

PREP/TOTAL TIME: 15 MIN.

- 1 pound fresh asparagus, trimmed
- 2 tablespoons olive oil
- 1/4 to 1/2 teaspoon dried tarragon
- 1/4 teaspoon onion powder
- 1/8 teaspoon pepper

■ In a large skillet, bring 1/2 in. of water to a boil. Add asparagus; cover and cook for 3-4 minutes or until crisp-tender.

■ Meanwhile, in a small bowl, combine the oil, tarragon, onion powder and pepper until blended. Drain asparagus; drizzle with oil mixture and toss to coat. **Yield:** 4 servings.

glazed carrot coins

HELEN BETHEL | MAYSVILLE, NORTH CAROLINA

Flavored with orange juice, cinnamon and ginger, these glossy carrots are pretty enough for a special meal. To save time, you could also use two 15-ounce cans of carrots for the fresh ones.

PREP/TOTAL TIME: 25 MIN.

- 2 tablespoons butter
- 2 tablespoons brown sugar
- 2 tablespoons orange juice
- 1/4 teaspoon salt
- 1/4 teaspoon ground ginger
- 1/8 teaspoon ground cinnamon
- 6 medium carrots, cut into 1/2-inch slices

■ In a small saucepan, melt butter over medium heat. Stir in the brown sugar, orange juice, salt, ginger and cinnamon. Add the carrots; cover and cook for 20-25 minutes or until tender, stirring occasionally. **Yield:** 4 servings.

seasoned oven fries

PAT FREDERICKS | OAK CREEK, WISCONSIN

For a speedy, health-conscious side dish or snack, I whip up these fun wedges. They're just as tasty as the deep-fried version, but with less mess.

PREP/TOTAL TIME: 25 MIN.

- 2 medium baking potatoes
- 2 teaspoons butter, melted
- 2 teaspoons canola oil
- 1/4 teaspoon seasoned salt

■ Cut each potato lengthwise in half; cut each piece into four wedges. In a large resealable plastic bag, combine the butter, oil and seasoned salt. Add potatoes; shake to coat.

■ Place potatoes in a single layer on a baking sheet coated with cooking spray. Bake at 450° for 20-25 minutes or until tender, turning once. **Yield:** 2 servings.

corn with a kick

NANCY MCDONALD | BURNS, WYOMING

Here's a zesty summer side that's great with canned, frozen or leftover corn. Tomato and green pepper add bright color and taste. It's terrific at barbecues and potlucks.

PREP/TOTAL TIME: 20 MIN.

- 1/4 cup chopped onion
- 1/4 cup chopped green pepper
- 1 tablespoon butter
- 2 cups whole kernel corn
- 1/4 cup diced tomato
- 1 teaspoon salt
- 1/8 teaspoon pepper
- Cayenne pepper to taste

■ In a large saucepan, saute onion and green pepper in butter until tender. Stir in the corn, tomato, salt, pepper and cayenne. Cover and simmer for 5-10 minutes or until heated through, stirring occasionally. **Yield:** 4 servings.

Corn Cues

To give this corn an even bigger kick, saute some chopped jalapeno pepper along with the onion and green pepper.

herb roasted squash

TASTE OF HOME TEST KITCHEN

Roasting vegetables in simple seasonings gives them great flavor.

PREP/TOTAL TIME: 20 MIN.

- 1 medium zucchini, cut into 1/4-inch slices
- 1 yellow summer squash, cut into 1/4-inch slices
- 1 medium tomato, seeded and chopped
- 1/2 cup chopped onion
- 1 teaspoon dried parsley flakes
- 1/2 teaspoon dried rosemary, crushed
- 1/4 teaspoon salt
- 1/4 teaspoon pepper
- 1 tablespoon olive oil

■ In a large bowl, combine the first eight ingredients. Drizzle with oil and toss to coat.

■ Place vegetables in a single layer in a greased 15-in. x 10-in. x 1-in. baking pan. Bake, uncovered, at 450° for 10-15 minutes or until lightly browned and tender, stirring once. **Yield:** 4 servings.

creamed spinach

ANN VAN DYK | WRIGHTSTOWN, WISCONSIN

Using fresh spinach instead of frozen really enhances the flavor of this classic recipe. The hint of nutmeg makes this dish even more appealing.

PREP/TOTAL TIME: 25 MIN.

- 3/4 pound fresh spinach, torn
- 2 tablespoons olive oil
- 6 tablespoons butter, cubed
- 1/4 cup chopped onion
- 1/4 cup all-purpose flour
- 1/2 teaspoon salt
- 1/8 teaspoon ground nutmeg
- 1-1/2 cups milk

■ In a Dutch oven, cook spinach in oil for 3 minutes or until wilted. Transfer to a cutting board; chop. Melt butter in the Dutch oven. Add onion; saute for 2 minutes or until crisp-tender.

■ Stir in flour, salt and nutmeg until combined. Gradually whisk in milk until blended. Bring to a boil; cook and stir for 2 minutes or until thickened. Add chopped spinach. Reduce heat to low; cook, uncovered, for 5 minutes or until heated through. **Yield:** 4 servings.

Simple Snack

You can also serve Garlic Cheese Bread as an appetizer at parties. Cut the bread into thin slices and serve alongside heated marinara sauce.

buttered poppy seed noodles

SHIRLEY JOAN HELFENBEIN | LAPEER, MICHIGAN

Mom's delicious fried noodles are absolute comfort food. She would roll out the dough, and we kids got to cut the long noodles and hang them up to dry.

PREP/TOTAL TIME: 25 MIN.

1 package (16 ounces) egg noodles
1 medium onion, chopped
3 tablespoons butter
2 green onions, chopped
2 tablespoons poppy seeds
Salt and pepper to taste
1 tablespoon minced fresh parsley

- Cook noodles according to package directions. Meanwhile, in a large heavy skillet, saute onion in butter until it begins to brown. Drain noodles; add to skillet. Cook and stir until noodles begin to brown.
- Add the green onions, poppy seeds, salt and pepper; cook and stir 1 minute longer. Sprinkle with the parsley. **Yield:** 8 servings.

garlic cheese bread

JANET RODAKOWSKI | WENTZVILLE, MISSOURI

Crunchy slices of this buttery and perfectly seasoned loaf make a finger-lickin' feast of any Italian dinner!

PREP/TOTAL TIME: 15 MIN.

1 cup butter, softened
1 cup (4 ounces) shredded Parmesan cheese
1/2 cup finely chopped onion
1 tablespoon garlic powder
2 teaspoons minced chives
2 teaspoons minced fresh parsley
1 loaf (1 pound) French bread, halved lengthwise
1 cup (4 ounces) shredded part-skim mozzarella cheese
1/2 cup shredded cheddar cheese

- In a small bowl, combine the first six ingredients; spread over cut sides of bread. Sprinkle with mozzarella and cheddar cheeses.
- Place on an ungreased baking sheet. Broil 4-6 in. from the heat for 2-3 minutes or until lightly browned. Cut into slices. **Yield:** 8 servings.

broccoli with mustard sauce

BECKY RUFF | MONONA, IOWA

Stir up this smooth, delectable sauce in a jiffy in the microwave, and you'll be delighted with how it complements steamed vegetables. Start with fresh veggies or make things even easier by using a frozen blend.

PREP/TOTAL TIME: 25 MIN.

- 2 pounds fresh broccoli florets, cauliflowerets *or* sliced carrots
- 1/2 cup mayonnaise
- 1/3 cup milk
- 1/4 cup grated Parmesan cheese
- 1/4 cup shredded Swiss cheese
- 2 teaspoons lemon juice
- 2 teaspoons prepared mustard

Salt and pepper to taste

■ Place broccoli in a steamer basket; place in a large saucepan over 1 in. of water. Bring to a boil; cover and steam for 5-8 minutes or until crisp-tender.

■ Meanwhile, in a small microwave-safe bowl, combine the remaining ingredients. Cover and microwave at 50% power for 2 minutes or until heated through, stirring every 30 seconds. Drain the broccoli. Serve with the sauce. **Yield:** 4 servings.

Editor's Note: This recipe was tested in a 1,100-watt microwave.

bacon mashed potatoes

PAT MATHISON | MEADOWLANDS, MINNESOTA

Featuring cheddar cheese, bacon and chives, these rich and hearty potatoes go well with anything. For a slightly different twist, add some chopped parsley.

PREP/TOTAL TIME: 25 MIN.

2-1/2 cups cubed peeled potatoes (3/4 pound)
1/4 cup milk
1/4 cup mayonnaise
4-1/2 teaspoons minced chives
1/8 teaspoon garlic powder
1/8 teaspoon pepper
1/2 cup shredded cheddar cheese
3 bacon strips, cooked and crumbled

- Place potatoes in a large saucepan and cover with water. Bring to a boil. Reduce heat; cover and cook for 10-15 minutes or until tender. Drain.
- Transfer to a large bowl. Add the milk, mayonnaise, chives, garlic powder and pepper; mash potatoes. Stir in cheese and bacon. **Yield:** 3 servings.

sesame breadsticks

TASTE OF HOME TEST KITCHEN

Try these not-too-spicy sticks when you want a mild herb bread that goes great with pasta. The family will love them, and you'll love the quick preparation.

PREP/TOTAL TIME: 20 MIN.

1 tube (11 ounces) refrigerated breadsticks
1 tablespoon butter, melted
1 tablespoon sesame seeds, toasted
1 to 2 teaspoons dried basil
1/4 to 1/2 teaspoon cayenne pepper

- Unroll and separate breadsticks. Twist each breadstick two to three times and place on an ungreased baking sheet; brush with the butter. Combine the sesame seeds, basil and cayenne; sprinkle over the breadsticks. Bake at 375° for 10-12 minutes or until golden brown. Serve warm. **Yield:** 1 dozen.

Editor's Note: This recipe was tested with Pillsbury refrigerated breadsticks.

Toasting Sesame Seeds

Toast sesame seeds in a dry skillet over medium heat for 10-15 minutes until lightly browned, stirring occasionally.

lemony brussels sprouts

TRISHA KRUSE | EAGLE, IDAHO

The tangy lemon glaze and toasted almonds make this easy vegetable dish popular at my table. It even pleases those who say they don't care for brussels sprouts.

PREP/TOTAL TIME: 15 MIN.

1 pound fresh brussels sprouts, trimmed and halved
2 tablespoons water
2 tablespoons butter, melted
2 tablespoons lemon juice
2 teaspoons grated lemon peel
1/4 teaspoon salt
1/4 teaspoon lemon-pepper seasoning
1/4 cup sliced almonds, toasted

- Place brussels sprouts in a microwave-safe dish; add water. Cover and cook on high for 7-9 minutes or until tender, stirring twice; drain.
- Stir in the butter, lemon juice, peel, salt and lemon-pepper. Sprinkle with almonds. **Yield:** 4 servings.

Editor's Note: This recipe was tested in a 1,100-watt microwave.

Frozen Peppers

Wash, seed and chop green peppers. Place in freezer bags; freeze for 3 to 6 months. When a cooked dish calls for diced peppers, you can use them directly from the freezer.

baby carrots with almonds

JANE KITTLE | COLUMBIA CROSS ROADS, PENNSYLVANIA

These not-so-candied carrots are a treat for my diabetic husband, but they are actually something we all enjoy.

PREP/TOTAL TIME: 10 MIN.

- 1 pound fresh baby carrots
- 2 tablespoons water
- 2 tablespoons slivered almonds, toasted
- 1 tablespoon sugar
- 1 tablespoon butter
- 1/8 teaspoon salt

■ Place carrots and water in a microwave-safe bowl. Cover and microwave on high for 4-6 minutes or until tender; drain. Stir in the remaining ingredients. **Yield:** 4 servings.

Editor's Note: This recipe was tested in a 1,100-watt microwave.

parmesan vegetable rice

NOLA NIELSEN | DARIEN, ILLINOIS

With its red tomatoes and green pepper, this healthful rice dish is colorful enough to serve guests during the holidays. But I love it so much I make it whenever I have a craving for a special rice dish.

PREP/TOTAL TIME: 20 MIN.

- 1/2 cup uncooked instant rice
- 1/2 cup chopped green pepper
- 2 teaspoons butter
- 1 garlic clove, minced
- 1 plum tomato, seeded and chopped
- 1/4 teaspoon salt
- 1/4 teaspoon celery salt
- 1/4 teaspoon pepper
- 2 tablespoons shredded Parmesan cheese, *divided*

■ Cook rice according to package directions. Meanwhile, in a small nonstick skillet coated with cooking spray, saute green pepper in butter for 2 minutes. Add garlic; cook 1 minute longer. Stir in the tomato, salt, celery salt and pepper and cook 2 minutes.

■ Add the rice and 1 tablespoon cheese; heat through. Sprinkle with remaining cheese. **Yield:** 2 servings.

scalloped potatoes and veggies

LINDA RENBERGER | DERBY, KANSAS

If you're like me, you're always searching for easy side dishes. This vegetable medley in a creamy cheese sauce couldn't be simpler to put together.

PREP/TOTAL TIME: 30 MIN.

- 2 large potatoes, peeled and sliced
- 1 cup sliced carrots
- 1 small onion, sliced
- 1/4 cup water
- 1 cup frozen peas
- 2 tablespoons all-purpose flour
- 1-1/2 teaspoons seasoned salt
- 1/4 teaspoon ground mustard
- 1/8 teaspoon pepper
- 1 cup milk
- 1/2 cup process cheese (Velveeta)

■ In a 2-qt. microwave-safe dish, combine the potatoes, carrots, onion and water. Cover and microwave on high for 5-1/2 minutes. Add peas; cook 3 minutes longer or until vegetables are tender.

■ In a 1-qt. microwave-safe dish, combine the flour, seasoned salt, mustard, pepper and milk until smooth.

■ Microwave, uncovered, on high for 3-4 minutes or until thickened and bubbly, stirring occasionally. Stir in cheese until melted. Drain vegetables; add cheese sauce and toss. **Yield:** 7 servings.

Editor's Note: This recipe was tested in a 1,100-watt microwave.

p. 269

speedy snacks & **appetizers**

sesame salmon spread

SANDY SANFORD | ANCHORAGE, ALASKA

Alaska is known for its salmon, and this is one of our favorite appetizers. I pack the spread and crackers in our picnic lunch when my husband and I head out to harvest wood, which we do several times a year. We look forward to the task just to have this special treat!

PREP: 10 MIN. + CHILLING

- 1 package (8 ounces) cream cheese, softened
- 2 tablespoons lemon juice
- 1 can (14-3/4 ounces) salmon, drained, bones and skin removed
- 1/4 cup sour cream
- 1 garlic clove, minced
- 2 tablespoons sesame seeds
- 2 teaspoons Liquid Smoke, optional
- 1 teaspoon minced fresh cilantro
- 1 teaspoon minced fresh parsley
- 1/4 teaspoon dill weed
- 1/4 teaspoon salt
- 1/8 teaspoon pepper

Assorted crackers

■ In a small bowl, beat cream cheese and lemon juice until fluffy. Add the salmon, sour cream, garlic, sesame seeds, Liquid Smoke if desired, cilantro, parsley, dill, salt and pepper; beat until combined. Cover and refrigerate for at least 2 hours. Serve with crackers. Refrigerate leftovers. **Yield:** 2-1/2 cups.

easy meatballs

CHRISTINE SMOOT | CHILDRESS, TEXAS

Only three ingredients are needed for this speedy appetizer. The meatballs are so different from all the others...you will never bring home any leftovers.

PREP/TOTAL TIME: 15 MIN.

- 1 package (12 ounces) frozen fully cooked Italian meatballs, thawed
- 1 cup barbecue sauce
- 1/2 cup sweet-and-sour sauce

■ Place the meatballs in a 3-qt. microwave-safe dish; cover and microwave on high for 3-4 minutes or until heated through. In a small microwave-safe bowl, combine the sauces; cover and heat on high for 2-3 minutes or until heated through. Pour over meatballs; cover and microwave on high for 1-2 minutes, stirring occasionally. **Yield:** 2 dozen.

Editor's Note: This recipe was tested in a 1,100-watt microwave.

apple cranberry cider

TASTE OF HOME TEST KITCHEN

Spiced with cinnamon sticks and cloves, this warm-you-up sipper is sure to chase away winter's chill.

PREP/TOTAL TIME: 30 MIN.

- 1 quart apple cider *or* juice
- 2 cups cranberry juice
- 1/3 cup packed brown sugar
- 4 whole cloves
- 2 cinnamon sticks (3 inches)

■ In a large saucepan, combine the cider, cranberry juice and brown sugar. Place cloves and cinnamon sticks on a double thickness of cheesecloth; bring up corners of cloth and tie with kitchen string to form a bag. Add to pan.

■ Bring to a boil over medium heat. Reduce the heat; simmer, uncovered, for 15-20 minutes. Discard the spice bag. **Yield:** 6 servings.

shrimp tartlets

GINA HUTCHISON | SMITHVILLE, MISSOURI

Mini tart shells are filled with a cream cheese mixture, then topped with seafood sauce and shrimp for a picture-perfect look and delightful taste. This recipe makes a great appetizer, but you can also serve several for a fast, light meal.

PREP/TOTAL TIME: 15 MIN.

1 package (8 ounces) cream cheese, softened
1-1/2 teaspoons Worcestershire sauce
1 to 2 teaspoons grated onion
1 teaspoon garlic salt
1/8 teaspoon lemon juice
2 packages (1.9 ounces *each*) frozen miniature phyllo tart shells
1/2 cup seafood cocktail sauce
30 deveined peeled cooked medium shrimp

■ In a small bowl, combine the first five ingredients. Spoon into tart shells. Top with seafood sauce and shrimp. Refrigerate until serving. **Yield:** 2-1/2 dozen.

orange chocolate fondue

MARY JEAN DEVRIES | GRANDVILLE, MICHIGAN

Invite your family and friends to dip cubes of cake and pieces of fruit into this rich, luscious fondue for a special treat during the holiday season.

PREP/TOTAL TIME: 15 MIN.

1/2 cup milk chocolate chips
3 ounces bittersweet chocolate
1/2 cup heavy whipping cream
3 tablespoons thawed orange juice concentrate
1 frozen pound cake (16 ounces), thawed and cut into 1-inch cubes
Sliced bananas and star fruit, orange segments, sweet cherries *or* strawberries *or* fruit of your choice

■ In a heavy saucepan over low heat, cook and stir the chocolate chips, bittersweet chocolate and cream until smooth. Stir in the orange juice concentrate. Keep warm. Serve with cake and fruit. **Yield:** 1-1/3 cups.

apple snack wedges

JACQUIE BERG | ST. CLOUD, WISCONSIN

Kids of all ages will love these easy apple wedges. With protein from peanut butter and a hint of sweetness, the quick-to-fix bites make a fun and healthful treat.

PREP/TOTAL TIME: 10 MIN.

- 2 medium apples
- 1 cup Rice Chex, crushed
- 1-1/2 teaspoons packed brown sugar
- 2 tablespoons reduced-fat creamy peanut butter

- Core the apples and cut each into six wedges. Pat dry with paper towels.
- In a small shallow bowl, combine the cereal and brown sugar. Spread cut sides of apples with peanut butter; roll in cereal mixture. Serve immediately. **Yield:** 4 servings.

mini bagelizzas

STEPHANIE KLOS-KOHR | MOLINE, ILLINOIS

Garlic powder gives these speedy mini pizzas extra pizzazz. Not only are they a snap to put together, but best of all, the ingredient list is easy on your pocketbook. My family loves them as an after-work or after-school snack.

PREP/TOTAL TIME: 25 MIN.

- 8 miniature bagels, split
- 1 cup spaghetti sauce with miniature meatballs
- 32 slices pepperoni
- 3/4 teaspoon garlic powder
- 2 cups (8 ounces) shredded part-skim mozzarella cheese

- Spread the cut sides of bagels with spaghetti sauce. Top each with two slices of pepperoni; sprinkle with garlic powder and cheese.
- Place on ungreased baking sheets. Bake at 350° for 15-20 minutes or until the cheese is melted and bubbly. **Yield:** 8 servings.

lemon quencher

CLARA COULSTON | WASHINGTON COURT HOUSE, OHIO

Tart and refreshing, this minty-lemon drink is sweetened with just a touch of honey. It makes a lovely summer cooler any time of day.

PREP: 15 MIN. + CHILLING

- 5 cups water, *divided*
- 10 fresh mint leaves
- 1 cup lemon juice
- 2/3 cup honey
- 2 teaspoons grated lemon peel

Ice cubes

Mint sprigs and lemon peel strips, optional

- In a blender, combine 1 cup water and mint leaves; cover and process for 1 minute. Strain mixture into a pitcher, discarding mint. Add the lemon juice, honey, lemon peel and remaining water; stir until blended. Cover and refrigerate for at least 2 hours.
- Serve in chilled glasses over ice. Garnish with mint sprigs and lemon peel if desired. **Yield:** 8 servings.

mushroom cheese bread

DOLLY MCDONALD | EDMONTON, ALBERTA

This savory grilled bread is delightful with barbecued steak, baked potatoes and corn on the cob. My clan prefers it to rolls at Sunday dinners. For variation, we sometimes use half cheddar cheese and half mozzarella.

PREP/TOTAL TIME: 15 MIN.

- 1 cup (4 ounces) shredded part-skim mozzarella cheese
- 1 can (4 ounces) mushroom stems and pieces, drained
- 1/3 cup mayonnaise
- 2 tablespoons shredded Parmesan cheese
- 2 tablespoons chopped green onion
- 1 loaf (1 pound) unsliced French bread

■ In a small bowl, combine mozzarella cheese, mushrooms, mayonnaise, Parmesan cheese and onion. Cut bread in half lengthwise; spread cheese mixture over cut sides.

■ Grill, covered, over indirect heat or broil 4 in. from the heat for 5-10 minutes or until lightly browned. Slice and serve warm. **Yield:** 10-12 servings.

bacon nachos

RUTH ANN BOTT | LAKE WALES, FLORIDA

These crispy nachos have always been a big hit in our house. Topped with kid-friendly ingredients like ground beef and cheddar cheese, they're sure to be requested by your children. And older kids will appreciate that they can microwave the nachos themselves.

PREP/TOTAL TIME: 20 MIN.

- 1/2 pound ground beef
- 4 cups tortilla chips
- 1/4 cup real bacon bits
- 2 cups (8 ounces) shredded cheddar cheese
- 1/2 cup guacamole dip
- 1/2 cup sour cream

Chopped tomatoes and green onions, optional

■ In a small skillet, cook beef over medium heat until no longer pink; drain. Place tortilla chips on a microwave-safe serving plate. Layer with the beef, bacon and cheese.

■ Microwave, uncovered, on high for 1-2 minutes or until cheese is melted. Top with guacamole and sour cream. Sprinkle with the tomatoes and onions if desired. **Yield:** 4-6 servings.

Editor's Note: This recipe was tested in a 1,100-watt microwave.

crab bruschetta

MARY PETRARA | LANCASTER, PENNSYLVANIA

I usually use only vegetables in my bruschetta, but I wondered how crab would taste. My family loves crab cakes, and now we love this appetizer, too.

PREP/TOTAL TIME: 20 MIN.

- 1/2 cup finely chopped shallots
- 2 tablespoons plus 1/4 cup olive oil, *divided*
- 2 garlic cloves, minced
- 2 cans (6 ounces *each*) lump crabmeat, drained
- 1 cup chopped seeded plum tomatoes
- 1-1/2 teaspoons minced fresh basil *or* 1/2 teaspoon dried basil
- 3/4 teaspoon minced fresh oregano *or* 1/4 teaspoon dried oregano
- 8 slices Italian bread (1/2 inch thick)

■ In a large skillet, saute shallots in 2 tablespoons oil until tender. Add garlic; cook 1 minute longer. Add the crab, tomatoes, basil and oregano; cook and stir for 5-6 minutes or until heated through. Remove from the heat.

■ Brush both sides of each slice of bread with remaining oil. In another large skillet, toast bread for 1-2 minutes on each side. Cut each slice in half; top with crab mixture. **Yield:** 16 appetizers.

summertime strawberry punch

MARY MACQUEEN | WOODSTOCK, ONTARIO

This thirst-quenching drink is perfect for a summer picnic or family get-together. When I serve it in a punch bowl, I'll often make an ice ring of ginger ale with a few berries in it to float on top rather than use ice cubes.

PREP/TOTAL TIME: 10 MIN.

- 1 can (12 ounces) frozen pink lemonade concentrate, thawed, undiluted
- 1 package (20 ounces) frozen unsweetened strawberries, partially thawed
- 1/4 cup sugar
- 2 cups cold brewed strong tea
- 2 liters ginger ale, chilled
- Ice cubes

■ In a food processor, combine lemonade concentrate, strawberries and sugar. Cover and process until smooth. Transfer to a large pitcher or punch bowl; stir in tea. Add the ginger ale and ice cubes. Serve immediately. **Yield:** 3-1/2 quarts.

garlic bean dip

KALLEE MCCREERY | ESCONDIDO, CALIFORNIA

I've contributed this thick dip to many get-togethers, and there's never any left to bring home. Try serving the starter with pita chips or fresh veggies.

PREP: 10 MIN. + CHILLING

- 1 can (15 ounces) garbanzo beans *or* chickpeas, rinsed and drained
- 1/3 cup reduced-fat mayonnaise
- 2 tablespoons minced fresh parsley
- 4-1/2 teaspoons lemon juice
- 1 garlic clove, peeled
- 1/4 teaspoon salt
- Pita bread wedges

■ In a food processor, combine the beans, mayonnaise, parsley, lemon juice, garlic and salt; cover and process until smooth.

■ Transfer to a serving dish. Cover and refrigerate for 1 hour. Serve with pita bread. **Yield:** 6 servings.

orange-glazed smokies

JUDY WILSON | SUN CITY WEST, ARIZONA

I always get rave reviews when I bring these tasty sausages to a party. They can be whipped up in a matter of minutes, and the tangy-citrus sauce is an instant conversation starter.

PREP/TOTAL TIME: 15 MIN.

- 1 cup packed brown sugar
- 1 tablespoon all-purpose flour
- 1/4 cup thawed orange juice concentrate
- 2 tablespoons prepared mustard
- 1 tablespoon cider vinegar
- 1 package (16 ounces) miniature smoked sausages

■ In a large microwave-safe bowl, combine the first five ingredients. Add the sausages; stir to coat. Cover and microwave on high for 3-4 minutes or until bubbly, stirring three times. **Yield:** about 4 dozen.

Editor's Note: This recipe was tested in a 1,100-watt microwave.

sausage-stuffed mushrooms

KATHY DEEZIK | HARTSTOWN, PENNSYLVANIA

A few years back, I was looking for a snack that would suit my family's tastes. I combined three different recipes and came up with this one. They love the rich Parmesan flavor.

PREP/TOTAL TIME: 30 MIN.

- 20 to 24 large fresh mushrooms
- 2 tablespoons finely chopped onion
- 1 tablespoon butter
- 2 to 3 garlic cloves, minced
- 1/4 pound bulk pork sausage, cooked, crumbled and drained
- 3 tablespoons seasoned bread crumbs
- 3 tablespoons grated Parmesan cheese
- 1 tablespoon dried parsley flakes
- 1 egg white

■ Remove mushroom stems from caps. Set caps aside (discard stems or save for another use). In a small skillet, saute onion in butter until tender. Add the garlic; cook 1 minute longer.

■ In a large bowl, combine the sausage, bread crumbs, cheese, parsley and egg white. Stir in onion mixture. Fill the mushroom caps; place in a lightly greased 15-in. x 10-in. x 1-in. baking pan.

■ Bake at 350° for 10-15 minutes or until mushrooms are tender and tops are browned. **Yield:** about 2 dozen.

frosted ruby punch

SANDRA PICHON | SLIDELL, LOUISIANA

With its crimson ice ring and dollops of sherbet, this punch is pretty for parties.

PREP: 5 MIN. + FREEZING

- 4 cups cranberry juice
- 1-1/2 cups sugar
- 1-1/2 cups lemon juice
- 1 cup orange juice
- 4 cups ginger ale, chilled
- 1 quart raspberry sherbet

■ Pour the cranberry juice into a 5-cup ring mold. Freeze overnight.

■ In a punch bowl, combine the sugar, lemon juice and orange juice until sugar is dissolved; stir in the ginger ale. Remove ice ring from mold; float in punch. Place scoops of sherbet around ring. **Yield:** 8 servings.

Unmolding an Ice Ring

To remove an ice ring from a mold, wrap the bottom of the mold with a hot, damp dish towel. Invert onto a baking sheet; place in a punch bowl.

chicken turnovers

SANDRA LEE HERR | STEVENS, PENNSYLVANIA

These hot and filling appetizers are a great way to use up leftover chicken. Sometimes, I serve it with fruit salad for a delicious, light meal for up to four people.

PREP/TOTAL TIME: 30 MIN.

- 1 cup diced cooked chicken breast
- 1 cup (4 ounces) shredded reduced-fat cheddar cheese
- 1/4 cup chopped celery
- 1 tablespoon finely chopped onion
- 1/4 teaspoon salt
- 1/4 teaspoon pepper
- 1 tube (8 ounces) refrigerated reduced-fat crescent rolls

■ In a small bowl, combine the chicken, cheese, celery, onion, salt and pepper. Separate crescent dough into eight triangles; top each with chicken mixture. Fold dough over and seal edges.

■ Place turnovers on an ungreased baking sheet. Bake at 375° for 13-17 minutes or until golden brown. Serve warm. **Yield:** 8 servings.

marinated mushrooms and cheese

KIM MARIE VAN RHEENEN | MENDOTA, ILLINOIS

I like to serve these savory mushrooms alongside sliced baguettes and crackers. They're colorful and so versatile. You might like to vary the cheese or add olives, artichokes or a little basil.

PREP: 10 MIN. + MARINATING

- 1/2 cup sun-dried tomatoes (not packed in oil), julienned
- 1 cup boiling water
- 1/2 cup olive oil
- 1/2 cup white wine vinegar
- 2 garlic cloves, minced
- 1/2 teaspoon salt
- 1/2 pound sliced fresh mushrooms
- 8 ounces Monterey Jack cheese, cubed

■ In a small bowl, combine the tomatoes and water. Let stand for 5 minutes; drain. In a large resealable plastic bag, combine the oil, vinegar, garlic and salt; add the tomatoes, mushrooms and cheese. Seal bag and toss to coat. Refrigerate for at least 4 hours before serving. Drain and discard marinade. **Yield:** 12-14 servings.

hot crab pinwheels

KITTI BOESEL | WOODBRIDGE, VIRGINIA

I got the recipe for these crabmeat bites from a friend. What amazed me most is that my husband, who hates seafood, couldn't stop eating them.

PREP: 15 MIN. + CHILLING BAKE: 10 MIN.

- 1 package (8 ounces) reduced-fat cream cheese
- 1 can (6 ounces) crabmeat, drained, flaked and cartilage removed
- 3/4 cup finely chopped sweet red pepper
- 1/2 cup shredded reduced-fat cheddar cheese
- 2 green onions, finely chopped
- 3 tablespoons minced fresh parsley
- 1/4 to 1/2 teaspoon cayenne pepper
- 6 flour tortillas (6 inches)

■ In a small bowl, beat cream cheese until smooth. Stir in the crab, red pepper, cheese, onions, parsley and cayenne. Spread 1/3 cupful over one side of each tortilla; roll up tightly. Wrap the tortillas in plastic wrap and refrigerate for at least 2 hours.

■ Cut and discard ends of roll-ups. Cut each roll-up into six slices. Place on baking sheets coated with cooking spray. Bake at 350° for 10 minutes or until bubbly. Serve warm. **Yield:** 3 dozen.

Slicing Tortillas

Be sure to cut the rolled tortillas with a sharp knife so that the individual slices keep their shape.

apple grape drink

DEBORAH BUTTS | UNION BRIDGE, MARYLAND

Why settle for plain juice at brunch when you can sip this fizzy morning beverage by stirring together just four ingredients? Everyone loves the taste of this refreshing punch.

PREP/TOTAL TIME: 15 MIN.

- 6 cups apple juice, chilled
- 3 cups white grape juice, chilled
- 1 can (12 ounces) frozen lemonade concentrate, thawed
- 1 liter club soda, chilled

■ In a large container, combine the juices and lemonade concentrate. Stir in club soda. Pour into chilled glasses. Serve immediately. **Yield:** 3-3/4 quarts.

slumber party pizza

TASTE OF HOME TEST KITCHEN

You only need a handful of ingredients for this palate-pleaser. A prebaked crust, bottled barbecue sauce, shredded chicken and lots of cheese make it one of the tastiest pizzas you'll ever try.

PREP/TOTAL TIME: 15 MIN.

- 1 prebaked 12-inch pizza crust
- 3 cups shredded cooked chicken
- 1 cup barbecue sauce
- 1 cup (4 ounces) shredded part-skim mozzarella cheese
- 1/2 cup shredded cheddar cheese
- Minced fresh parsley

■ Place crust on a 14-in. pizza pan. Combine chicken and barbecue sauce; spread over crust. Sprinkle with cheeses.

■ Bake at 450° for 8-10 minutes or until cheese is melted. Sprinkle with parsley. **Yield:** 8 slices.

baked deli sandwich

SANDRA MCKENZIE | BRAHAM, MINNESOTA

Frozen bread dough, easy assembly and quick baking time make this stuffed sandwich an appetizer I rely on often. This is one of my most-requested recipes. It's easy to double for a crowd or to experiment with different meats and cheeses.

PREP/TOTAL TIME: 30 MIN.

- 1 loaf (1 pound) frozen bread dough, thawed
- 2 tablespoons butter, melted
- 1/4 teaspoon garlic salt
- 1/4 teaspoon dried basil
- 1/4 teaspoon dried oregano
- 1/4 teaspoon pizza seasoning *or* Italian seasoning
- 1/4 pound sliced deli ham
- 6 thin slices part-skim mozzarella cheese
- 1/4 pound sliced deli smoked turkey breast
- 6 thin slices cheddar cheese
- Pizza sauce, warmed, optional

■ On a baking sheet coated with cooking spray, roll dough into a small rectangle. Let rest for 5-10 minutes.

■ In a small bowl, combine the butter and seasonings. Roll out dough into a 14-in. x 10-in. rectangle. Brush with half of the butter mixture. Layer ham, mozzarella cheese, turkey and cheddar cheese lengthwise over half of the dough to within 1/2 in. of edges. Fold dough over and pinch firmly to seal. Brush with remaining butter mixture.

■ Bake at 400° for 10-12 minutes or until golden brown. Cut into 1-in. slices. Serve immediately with pizza sauce if desired. **Yield:** 4-6 servings.

raspberry fondue dip

EDNA HOFFMAN | HEBRON, INDIANA

I delight guests with this fun, non-traditional fondue. Creamy apple butter and cinnamon red-hot candies add tangy flair!

PREP/TOTAL TIME: 25 MIN.

1 package (10 ounces) frozen sweetened raspberries
1 cup apple butter
1 tablespoon red-hot candies
2 teaspoons cornstarch
Assorted fresh fruit

- Place raspberries in a small bowl; set aside to thaw. Strain raspberries, reserving 1 tablespoon juice; discard seeds.
- In a small saucepan, combine the strained berries, apple butter and red-hots; cook over medium heat until candies are dissolved, stirring occasionally.
- In a small bowl, combine the cornstarch and reserved juice until smooth; stir into the berry mixture. Bring to a boil; cook and stir over medium heat for 1-2 minutes or until mixture thickens.
- Transfer to a serving dish, fondue pot or 1-1/2-qt. slow cooker. Serve warm or cold with fruit. **Yield:** 1 cup.

hearty rye melts

MELANIE SCHLAF | EDGEWOOD, KENTUCKY

When we moved from the Midwest to Kentucky, we were invited to a neighborhood gathering where this appetizer was served. "Hanky panky"—as it's often called around here—is traditionally served at Derby Day parties, but at our home it's a year-round favorite.

PREP/TOTAL TIME: 30 MIN.

1/2 pound lean ground beef (90% lean)
1/2 pound bulk pork sausage
1-1/2 teaspoons chili powder
8 ounces process cheese (Velveeta), shredded
24 slices snack rye bread
Fresh parsley sprigs, stems removed

- In a large skillet, cook the beef and sausage over medium heat until no longer pink; drain. Add chili powder and cheese; cook and stir until cheese is melted. Spread a heaping tablespoonful onto each slice of bread. Place on a baking sheet.
- Bake at 350° for 12-15 minutes or until edges of bread begin to crisp. Garnish with parsley. Serve warm. **Yield:** 2 dozen.

smoky sesame cheese log

KATIE SLOAN | CHARLOTTE, NORTH CAROLINA

We love the bacon flavor in this cheesy mixture. It's yummy served with wheat or sesame crackers.

PREP: 15 MIN. + CHILLING

2 packages (8 ounces *each*) cream cheese, softened
1 cup (4 ounces) shredded Monterey Jack cheese
1/2 cup crumbled cooked bacon
2 tablespoons sesame seeds, toasted
2 tablespoons Worcestershire sauce
1 teaspoon Liquid Smoke, optional
TOPPING:
1/2 cup crumbled cooked bacon
1/2 cup sesame seeds, toasted
1 tablespoon minced chives
Assorted fresh vegetables *or* crackers

- In a large bowl, beat the first five ingredients until blended. Add Liquid Smoke if desired. Shape mixture into a log. Cover and refrigerate for 8 hours or overnight.
- For topping, combine the bacon, sesame seeds and chives; roll cheese log in topping. Serve with vegetables or crackers. **Yield:** 1 cheese log.

grilled shrimp with cilantro sauce

TASTE OF HOME TEST KITCHEN

You just have to try this zippy, change-of-pace recipe for a lip-smacking cilantro sauce. It really dresses up grilled shrimp.

PREP/TOTAL TIME: 25 MIN.

1-1/2 cups fresh cilantro leaves
4 teaspoons minced fresh gingerroot
2 garlic cloves, peeled
3 tablespoons plus 1-1/2 teaspoons canola oil
1-1/2 teaspoons lemon juice
6 uncooked jumbo shrimp (about 1/3 pound), peeled and deveined
1 teaspoon lemon-pepper seasoning

- In a small food processor, combine the cilantro, ginger and garlic; cover and process until cilantro and garlic are chopped. While processing, gradually add oil and lemon juice in a steady stream until smooth. Transfer to a small serving bowl; set aside.
- Coat grill rack with cooking spray before starting the grill. Thread shrimp onto two metal or soaked wooden skewers. Sprinkle with lemon-pepper. Grill, uncovered, over medium heat for 5-8 minutes on each side or until shrimp turn pink. Serve with cilantro sauce. **Yield:** 2 servings.

cold pizza dip

JACKIE BASS | CLINTON, ILLINOIS

My sisters and I each have our specialty recipes, and this is mine. Make the recipe your own by adding your favorite pizza toppings to the cream cheese "crust."

PREP: 20 MIN. + CHILLING

2 packages (8 ounces *each*) cream cheese, softened
1 can (8 ounces) pizza sauce
1 jar (4-1/2 ounces) sliced mushrooms, drained
1/4 pound shaved deli ham, chopped
1 can (2-1/4 ounces) sliced ripe olives, drained
25 slices pepperoni, quartered
3 green onions, chopped
1/3 cup chopped green pepper
2 cups (8 ounces) finely shredded part-skim mozzarella cheese
Tortilla chips

- Spread cream cheese onto a 14-in. pizza pan. Spread pizza sauce to within 1/2 in. of edges. Sprinkle with the mushrooms, ham, olives, pepperoni, onions, green pepper and cheese. Cover and refrigerate for 1 hour or until chilled. Serve with tortilla chips. **Yield:** 4 cups.

bacon pinwheels

JANNE ROWE | WICHITA, KANSAS

I whip up these savory rolls with a rich cream cheese, mushroom and bacon filling. The yummy pinwheels will make a scrumptious addition to any buffet table.

PREP/TOTAL TIME: 30 MIN.

6 bacon strips, diced
6 ounces cream cheese, softened
1/2 cup mayonnaise
1 can (4 ounces) mushroom stems and pieces, drained
1/2 teaspoon garlic powder
1 tube (8 ounces) refrigerated crescent rolls

- In a large skillet, cook bacon over medium heat until crisp. Using a slotted spoon, remove to paper towels to drain. In a small bowl, beat cream cheese and mayonnaise until smooth. Add the mushrooms, garlic powder and bacon.
- Separate the crescent dough into four rectangles; seal perforations. Spread cream cheese mixture over each rectangle to within 1/4 in. of edges. Roll up jelly-roll style, starting with a short side; pinch seams to seal. Cut each into six slices.
- Place slices cut side down on greased baking sheets. Bake at 375° for 10-12 minutes or until golden brown. Serve warm. Refrigerate leftovers. **Yield:** 2 dozen.

Editor's Note: Reduced-fat or fat-free mayonnaise is not recommended for this recipe.

spicy turkey quesadillas

TASTE OF HOME TEST KITCHEN

A bit of spice livens up cranberries and turkey while cream cheese rounds out the bold flavors in this easy appetizer. You'll love this recipe!

PREP/TOTAL TIME: 25 MIN.

- 3 ounces fat-free cream cheese
- 1/4 cup chopped fresh *or* frozen cranberries, thawed
- 1 tablespoon chopped green chilies
- 1-1/2 teaspoons honey
- 1 teaspoon Louisiana-style hot sauce
- 4 flour tortillas (6 inches)
- 1 cup diced cooked turkey breast

■ In a small bowl, beat cream cheese until smooth. Stir in the cranberries, chilies, honey and hot sauce until blended. Spread over one side of each tortilla. Place turkey on two tortillas; top with remaining tortillas.

■ Cook in a large nonstick skillet over medium heat for 2-3 minutes on each side or until lightly browned. Cut into wedges. **Yield:** 2 servings.

tart 'n' tangy citrus cooler

JOYLYN TRICKEL | HELENDALE, CALIFORNIA

This is a sweet and refreshing beverage that's perfect when cooling off in the shade. In summer, I make the sugar syrup in advance, so I can mix up a quick batch after we've been out in the sun. The syrup can keep for up to a week.

PREP: 20 MIN. + CHILLING

- 6 cups water, *divided*
- 3 cups sugar
- 3 cups fresh lime juice *or* key lime juice
- 3 cups orange juice
- Crushed ice

■ In a large saucepan, bring 3 cups water and sugar to a boil; stir until the sugar is dissolved. Cook and stir for 3 minutes. Remove from heat; transfer to a bowl. Cover and refrigerate for at least 3 hours.

■ In a large pitcher, combine the sugar mixture, lime juice, orange juice and remaining water; stir well. Refrigerate until chilled. Serve over ice. **Yield:** 3-1/4 quarts.

A Lesson in Limes

Store fresh limes at room temperature for about 3 days. For longer storage, place in your refrigerator's crisper drawer for 2 to 3 weeks. One lime yields roughly 2 tablespoons of juice.

garlic-onion cheese spread

MICHELLE DEFRIEZ | GRAND BLANC, MICHIGAN

Whenever there's an event at church, my friends always remind me to bring this cheese spread. Once you add it to crackers, it's impossible to resist.

PREP/TOTAL TIME: 10 MIN.

- 2 packages (8 ounces *each*) cream cheese, softened
- 2 to 3 tablespoons apricot preserves
- 3 green onions (green portion only), chopped
- 3 tablespoons crumbled cooked bacon
- 1/2 to 1 teaspoon minced garlic
- Dash pepper
- Assorted crackers

■ In a small bowl, beat cream cheese and preserves until blended. Stir in the onions, bacon, garlic and pepper. Refrigerate until serving. Serve with the crackers. **Yield:** 2-1/4 cups.

creamy parsley veggie dip

JOYCE OCHSENWALD | VIRGINIA BEACH, VIRGINIA

You can choose to use either fat-free or reduced-fat ingredients in this creamy dip for fresh vegetables, as it makes no difference in taste. I've found it tastes best after being chilled in the fridge overnight.

PREP: 5 MIN. + CHILLING

- 1 cup fat-free mayonnaise
- 1 cup (8 ounces) reduced-fat sour cream
- 1/3 cup minced fresh parsley
- 2 tablespoons finely chopped onion
- 1 tablespoon Dijon mustard
- 1 garlic clove, minced
- 1/2 teaspoon salt
- 1/4 teaspoon pepper
- Assorted fresh vegetables

■ In a large bowl, combine the first eight ingredients. Cover and refrigerate for at least 2 hours. Serve with vegetables. **Yield:** 9 servings.

ranch pizza pinwheels

JENNIFER DIETZ | FARGO, NORTH DAKOTA

I developed this appetizer to mimic a dish at one of my favorite restaurants. I often need to double the recipe because one batch disappears quickly!

PREP/TOTAL TIME: 25 MIN.

- 1 tube (13.8 ounces) refrigerated pizza crust
- 1/4 cup prepared ranch salad dressing
- 1/2 cup shredded Colby-Monterey Jack cheese
- 1/2 cup diced pepperoni
- 1/4 cup chopped green onions
- Pizza sauce, warmed *or* additional ranch salad dressing, optional

■ On a lightly floured surface, roll pizza dough into a 12-in. x 10-in. rectangle. Spread ranch dressing evenly to within 1/4 in. of edges. Sprinkle with cheese, pepperoni and onions. Roll up jelly-roll style, starting with a long side.

■ Cut into 1-in. slices. Place cut side down on a greased baking sheet. Bake at 425° for 10-13 minutes or until lightly browned. Serve warm with pizza sauce or additional ranch dressing if desired. Refrigerate leftovers. **Yield:** 1 dozen.

hot cheddar-mushroom spread

BECKY RUFF | MCGREGOR, IOWA

One of my high school friends brought this fuss-free spread to a get-together, and the rest of us couldn't get enough of it. I've since made it for family parties and potlucks, where it's always a hit.

PREP/TOTAL TIME: 25 MIN.

- 2 cups mayonnaise
- 2 cups (8 ounces) shredded cheddar cheese
- 2/3 cup grated Parmesan cheese
- 4 cans (4-1/2 ounces *each*) sliced mushrooms, drained
- 1 envelope ranch salad dressing mix
- Minced fresh parsley
- Assorted crackers

■ In a large bowl, combine the mayonnaise, cheddar and Parmesan cheeses, mushrooms and dressing mix. Spread into a greased 9-in. pie plate.

■ Bake, uncovered, at 350° for 20-25 minutes or until the cheese is melted. Sprinkle with the parsley. Serve with crackers. **Yield:** 3 cups.

Editor's Note: Reduced-fat or fat-free mayonnaise is not recommended for this recipe.

speedy homemade salsa

SARAH ELIZABETH BERGER | MINNEAPOLIS, MINNESOTA

I love Mexican food and this refreshing salsa is easy to prepare. You won't have lots of leftovers to deal with! I think it tastes even better than the store-bought variety.

PREP/TOTAL TIME: 20 MIN.

- 1 can (14-1/2 ounces) whole tomatoes, drained
- 1/4 cup chopped red onion
- 1/4 cup chopped onion
- 1 jalapeno pepper, seeded
- 1 tablespoon cider vinegar
- 1 tablespoon minced fresh cilantro
- 1 garlic clove, peeled
- 1 teaspoon ground cumin
- 1/4 teaspoon salt

■ In a food processor, combine all of the ingredients; cover and process until chunky. Transfer to a small bowl. **Yield:** 1-1/3 cups.

Editor's Note: When cutting hot peppers, disposable gloves are recommended. Avoid touching your face.

blt dip

EMALEE PAYNE | EAU CLAIRE, WISCONSIN

Fans of bacon, lettuce and tomato sandwiches will fall for this creamy dip. It's easy to transport to different functions and always draws recipe requests.

PREP/TOTAL TIME: 10 MIN.

2 cups (16 ounces) sour cream
2 cups mayonnaise
2 pounds sliced bacon, cooked and crumbled
6 plum tomatoes, chopped
3 green onions, chopped
Assorted crackers *or* chips

- In a large bowl, combine the sour cream, mayonnaise, bacon, tomatoes and onions. Refrigerate until serving. Serve with crackers or chips. **Yield:** 6 cups.

savory party bread

KAY DALY | RALEIGH, NORTH CAROLINA

It's impossible to stop nibbling on warm pieces of this savory onion bread. The sliced loaf fans out for a fun presentation.

PREP/TOTAL TIME: 30 MIN.

1 unsliced round loaf (1 pound) sourdough bread
1 pound Monterey Jack cheese, sliced
1/2 cup butter, melted
1/2 cup chopped green onions
2 to 3 teaspoons poppy seeds

- Cut the bread lengthwise and widthwise without cutting through the bottom crust. Insert cheese between cuts. Combine butter, onions and poppy seeds; drizzle over the bread. Wrap in foil; place on a baking sheet. Bake at 350° for 15 minutes. Unwrap; bake 10 minutes longer or until the cheese is melted. **Yield:** 6-8 servings.

sugar 'n' spice nuts

JOAN KLINEFELTER | UTICA, ILLINOIS

My daughters, grandkids...everyone looks forward to this mouthwatering mix of crunchy nuts, spices and fruit when they're home for the holidays. Tuck it in tins to make a handy last-minute gift for a busy hostess or drop-in visitors.

PREP/TOTAL TIME: 30 MIN.

1/4 cup packed brown sugar
1/2 teaspoon ground cinnamon
1/4 teaspoon cayenne pepper
1 egg white
1 cup salted cashews
1 cup pecan halves
1 cup dry roasted peanuts
1/2 cup dried cranberries

- In a small bowl, combine the brown sugar, cinnamon and cayenne pepper; set aside. In a large bowl, whisk the egg white; add the nuts and cranberries. Sprinkle with the sugar mixture and toss to coat. Spread in a single layer on a greased baking sheet.
- Bake at 300° for 18-20 minutes or until golden brown, stirring once. Cool. Store in an airtight container. **Yield:** 3-1/2 cups.

christmas cheese balls

MARGIE CADWELL | EASTMAN, GEORGIA

Christmas at our house just wouldn't be complete without these rich cheese balls. Friends and family ask for them every year—and I can make three gifts from just one recipe.

PREP: 20 MIN. + CHILLING

4 packages (8 ounces *each*) cream cheese, softened
4 cups (1 pound) shredded cheddar cheese
1 cup chopped pecans
1/4 cup evaporated milk
1 can (4-1/4 ounces) chopped ripe olives, drained
2 garlic cloves, minced
1/2 teaspoon salt
Minced fresh parsley, chopped pecans and paprika
Assorted crackers

- In a small bowl, beat cream cheese and cheddar cheese. Stir in the pecans, milk, olives, garlic and salt. Divide into thirds; roll each into a ball.
- Roll one ball in the parsley and one in the nuts. Sprinkle one with the paprika. Cover and refrigerate. Remove from the refrigerator 15 minutes before serving. Serve with crackers. **Yield:** 3 cheese balls.

parmesan pretzel rods

CINDY WINTER-HARLEY | CARY, NORTH CAROLINA

For the snack fans on your gift list, these cheesy pretzels are terrific. The coated rods get fantastic flavor from garlic powder, oregano and cayenne.

PREP: 10 MIN. BAKE: 20 MIN. + COOLING

- 1 cup grated Parmesan cheese
- 1 teaspoon garlic powder
- 1 teaspoon dried oregano
- 1/2 teaspoon cayenne pepper
- 6 tablespoons butter, cubed
- 1/4 cup olive oil
- 1 package (10 ounces) pretzel rods

■ In a small bowl, combine the Parmesan cheese, garlic powder, oregano and cayenne; set aside. In a small saucepan, heat butter and oil until butter is melted. Coat two-thirds of each pretzel rod with butter mixture, then roll in cheese mixture. Reheat butter mixture if needed.

■ Place in an ungreased 15-in. x 10-in. x 1-in. baking pan. Bake at 275° for 20-25 minutes or until golden brown, turning once. Cool. Store in an airtight container. **Yield:** about 2-1/2 dozen.

Storing Garlic Powder

Garlic powder tends to absorb moisture from the air, especially during warm weather months. Store it in an airtight spice jar to keep it as free from moisture and humidity as possible.

buffalo chicken dip

PEGGY FOSTER | FLORENCE, KENTUCKY

This is a great dip my family loves for holiday and football parties. Everywhere I take it, people ask for the recipe.

PREP/TOTAL TIME: 30 MIN.

- 1 package (8 ounces) cream cheese, softened
- 1 can (10 ounces) chunk white chicken, drained
- 1/2 cup buffalo wing sauce
- 1/2 cup ranch salad dressing
- 2 cups (8 ounces) shredded Colby-Monterey Jack cheese

Tortilla chips

- Spread cream cheese into an ungreased shallow 1-qt. baking dish. Layer with chicken, buffalo wing sauce and ranch dressing. Sprinkle with cheese.
- Bake, uncovered, at 350° for 20-25 minutes or until the cheese is melted. Serve warm with tortilla chips. **Yield:** about 2 cups.

chili con queso

MARIE STOUT | APO, AP

I make this Southwestern staple for parties because it is so easy, and I usually have all the ingredients on hand. I double the recipe and warm it in my slow cooker so it will not scorch. This makes preparation completely worry-free.

PREP/TOTAL TIME: 15 MIN.

- 1 pound process cheese (Velveeta), cubed
- 1/2 cup chunky-style salsa
- 1 can (4 ounces) chopped green chilies
- 1 jar (4 ounces) diced pimientos, drained
- 1/2 teaspoon garlic powder
- 1/4 teaspoon cayenne pepper
- 1/8 teaspoon ground cumin
- 1/8 teaspoon crushed red pepper flakes

Tortilla chips

- In a microwave-safe bowl, combine the first eight ingredients. Cover and microwave on high for 6-7 minutes or until cheese is melted, stirring occasionally. Serve with tortilla chips. **Yield:** 2-3/4 cups.

Editor's Note: This recipe was tested in a 1,100-watt microwave.

basil cream cheese bruschetta

MICHELLE WENTZ | FORT POLK, LOUISIANA

This appealing appetizer takes classic bruschetta to new heights. Instead of olive oil, these savory treats are spread with reduced-fat cream cheese, then topped with tomato, green onion and ripe olives.

PREP/TOTAL TIME: 20 MIN.

- 12 slices French bread (1/2 inch thick)
- 1/2 cup chopped seeded tomato
- 2 tablespoons chopped green onion
- 1 tablespoon chopped ripe olives
- 4 ounces reduced-fat cream cheese
- 1 tablespoon minced fresh basil

- Place bread on an ungreased baking sheet. Broil 6-8 in. from the heat for 3-4 minutes or until golden brown. Meanwhile, in a small bowl, combine the tomato, onion and olives; set aside.
- Combine cream cheese and basil; spread over the untoasted side of bread. Broil 3 minutes longer or until cheese is melted and edges are golden brown. Top with tomato mixture. Serve warm. **Yield:** 1 dozen.

popcorn delight

CHERYL BULL | BLUE GRASS, IOWA

Whenever I take this sweet mix somewhere, I bring copies of the recipe because people always ask for it.

PREP: 15 MIN. + CHILLING

- 14 cups popped popcorn
- 2 cups salted peanuts
- 2 cups crisp rice cereal
- 2 cups miniature marshmallows
- 1 pound white candy coating, coarsely chopped
- 3 tablespoons creamy peanut butter

■ In a large bowl, combine the popcorn, peanuts, cereal and marshmallows. In a microwave, melt candy coating and peanut butter; stir until smooth. Pour over the popcorn mixture; toss to coat.

■ Spread onto waxed paper-lined baking sheets; refrigerate for 15 minutes or until set. Break into pieces. Store in an airtight container in the refrigerator. **Yield:** about 6 quarts.

warm crab dip

COLLEEN TALIAFERRO | WOODBINE, MARYLAND

Maryland's Chesapeake Bay is known for crabs, and they're a big favorite of ours. When fresh crabmeat is available, we'll use it in this dip, but canned works just as well. This appetizer is nice for any holiday or gathering.

PREP/TOTAL TIME: 15 MIN.

- 1 package (8 ounces) cream cheese, cubed
- 1/2 cup mayonnaise
- 1 tablespoon lemon juice
- 2 teaspoons Worcestershire sauce
- 1/2 teaspoon sherry, optional
- 2 cans (6 ounces *each*) lump crabmeat, drained
- 1 tablespoon chopped green onion

Assorted crackers *or* baked pita chips

■ In a large heavy saucepan, heat the cream cheese, mayonnaise, lemon juice, Worcestershire sauce and sherry if desired over low heat, stirring often. Stir in crab and onion; heat through. Serve warm with crackers. **Yield:** 2-1/4 cups.

grilled jerk chicken wings

CAREN ADAMS | FONTANA, CALIFORNIA

This recipe is one of my standbys every time I host a party. It's so simple to fix, doesn't take a lot of ingredients and is always a favorite with my guests.

PREP/TOTAL TIME: 30 MIN.

- 1/2 cup Caribbean jerk seasoning
- 18 fresh chicken wingettes (2 to 3 pounds)
- 2 cups honey barbecue sauce
- 1/3 cup packed brown sugar
- 2 teaspoons prepared mustard
- 1 teaspoon ground ginger

■ Coat grill rack with cooking spray before starting the grill. Place jerk seasoning in a large resealable plastic bag; add chicken wings, a few at a time, and shake to coat. In a small bowl, combine the barbecue sauce, brown sugar, mustard and ginger; set aside.

■ Grill chicken wings, covered, over medium heat for 12-16 minutes, turning occasionally. Brush with sauce. Grill, uncovered, 8-10 minutes longer or until juices run clear, basting and turning several times. **Yield:** 6 servings.

Editor's Note: Caribbean jerk seasoning may be found in the spice aisle of your grocery store.

pastrami asparagus roll-ups

SHARON WALLER | AROMAS, CALIFORNIA

When folks first see these roll-ups, they're often skeptical about the combination. But once they take that first bite, they're hooked! The addictive treat is enhanced with a flavorful pesto sauce.

PREP/TOTAL TIME: 25 MIN.

- 24 fresh asparagus spears (about 1 pound), trimmed
- 1/2 cup prepared pesto
- 24 thin slices (1 pound) provolone cheese
- 24 thin slices deli pastrami (3/4 pound)

■ In a large skillet, bring 1/2 in. of water to a boil. Add asparagus; cover and boil for 3 minutes. Drain and immediately place asparagus in ice water. Drain and pat dry.

■ Spread 1 teaspoon of pesto over each slice of cheese. Top each with an asparagus spear; roll up tightly. Place each on a slice of pastrami; roll up tightly. Refrigerate until serving. **Yield:** 2 dozen.

southwest corn spread

REBECCA SUE DICKSON | IREDELL, TEXAS

My Aunt Christine shared this recipe with me at a family reunion a few years ago. The thick spread's Southwestern flavor has mass appeal.

PREP: 10 MIN. + CHILLING

- 2 packages (8 ounces *each*) cream cheese, softened
- 1/4 cup lime juice
- 1 can (4 ounces) chopped green chilies
- 3 green onions, thinly sliced
- 1 tablespoon ground cumin
- 1 teaspoon cayenne pepper
- 1 teaspoon pepper
- 1/2 to 1 teaspoon salt
- 1 can (8-3/4 ounces) whole kernel corn, drained
- 1 cup chopped walnuts, optional

Tortilla chips *or* crackers

■ In a large bowl, combine cream cheese and lime juice until smooth. Add the chilies, onions, cumin, cayenne pepper and salt; beat until combined. Stir in corn and walnuts if desired. Cover and refrigerate for at least 4 hours. Serve with crackers or chips. **Yield:** about 3 cups.

hook, line 'n' sinker mix

TASTE OF HOME TEST KITCHEN

As the name implies, your guests will fall hook, line and sinker for this munchable mixture that features pretzel-stick "fishing rods" and cheddar cheese goldfish crackers. It takes mere minutes to toss the ingredients together and zap the mix in the microwave.

PREP/TOTAL TIME: 10 MIN.

- 3 tablespoons butter, melted
- 1 tablespoon dried parsley flakes
- 3/4 teaspoon dried tarragon
- 1/2 teaspoon onion powder
- 1/4 to 1/2 teaspoon celery salt
- 1 cup goldfish crackers
- 1 cup pretzel sticks
- 1/2 cup Cheerios
- 1/2 cup dry roasted peanuts

■ In a 2-qt. microwave-safe bowl, combine the first five ingredients. Add the crackers, pretzels, Cheerios and peanuts; toss to coat.

■ Microwave, uncovered, on high for 1 minute, stirring once. Let cool completely. Store in an airtight container. **Yield:** 3 cups.

Editor's Note: This recipe was tested in a 1,100-watt microwave.

turkey egg rolls

LUCILLE GENDRON | PELHAM, NEW HAMPSHIRE

Coleslaw mix hurries along the preparation of these deep-fried egg rolls served with sweet-and-sour sauce. The elegant appetizers are as easy to make as they are to eat.

PREP/TOTAL TIME: 30 MIN.

- 1/2 pound ground turkey
- 2 cups coleslaw mix
- 1 tablespoon soy sauce
- 1/2 teaspoon ground ginger
- 1/4 teaspoon onion salt
- 1/4 teaspoon garlic powder
- 10 egg roll wrappers

Oil for deep-fat frying
Sweet-and-sour sauce

■ In a large skillet, cook turkey over medium heat until no longer pink; drain. Stir in the coleslaw mix, soy sauce, ginger, onion salt and garlic powder. Place 1/4 cup in the center of each egg roll wrapper. Fold bottom corner over filling; fold sides toward center. Moisten remaining corner of wrapper with water; roll up tightly to seal. Repeat.

■ In an electric skillet or deep-fat fryer, heat oil to 375°. Fry egg rolls, a few at a time, for 3-4 minutes or until golden brown, turning often. Drain on paper towels. Serve with sweet-and-sour sauce. **Yield:** 10 egg rolls.

p. 318

in-a-dash desserts

p. 321

p. 314

p. 313

Homemade Pie Crust

To make a graham cracker crust, combine 1-1/2 cups crumbs (about 24 squares), 1/4 cup sugar and 1/3 cup butter, melted; blend well. Press into the bottom and up the sides of an ungreased 9-in. pie plate. Chill 30 minutes before filling.

chocolate mousse pie

LOIS MULKEY | CARLSBAD, CALIFORNIA

Sky-high and scrumptious, this fluffy chocolate delight is super to serve to company. You can put the pie together in a wink—and it'll disappear just as fast!

PREP: 20 MIN. + CHILLING

- 1 milk chocolate candy bar with almonds (7 ounces)
- 16 large marshmallows *or* 1-1/2 cups miniature marshmallows
- 1/2 cup 2% milk
- 2 cups heavy whipping cream, whipped
- 1 graham cracker crust *or* chocolate crumb crust *or* pastry shell, baked (9 inches)

■ In a heavy saucepan, heat the candy bar, marshmallows and milk over low heat until chocolate is melted and mixture is smooth, stirring constantly. Cool. Fold in whipped cream; pour into crust.

■ Refrigerate for at least 3 hours. Refrigerate leftovers. **Yield:** 8 servings.

triple peanut pizza

TRACY HOUDESHELL | MARION, IOWA

The tasty combination of chocolate and peanut butter has been a longtime favorite of mine, and now our son, Blake, enjoys it too. Since most kids love pizza, I created this fun fuss-free dessert for his birthday.

PREP: 20 MIN. BAKE: 15 MIN. + CHILLING

- 1 tube (16-1/2 ounces) refrigerated peanut butter cookie dough
- 1 cup (6 ounces) semisweet chocolate chips
- 1 package (8 ounces) cream cheese, softened
- 1/3 cup creamy peanut butter
- 1/4 cup packed brown sugar
- 1 teaspoon vanilla extract
- 2 cups chopped peanut butter cups (about 15 large)

■ Press cookie dough onto a greased 14-in. pizza pan. Bake at 350° for 15-18 minutes or until deep golden brown. Sprinkle with chocolate chips; let stand for 4-5 minutes. Spread melted chips over crust. Freeze for 10 minutes or until set.

■ Meanwhile, in a small bowl, beat cream cheese, peanut butter, sugar and vanilla until creamy. Spread over chocolate. Sprinkle with the peanut butter cups. Chill until serving. Refrigerate leftovers. **Yield:** 12-14 slices.

crunchy candy clusters

FAYE O'BRYAN | OWENSBORO, KENTUCKY

Before retiring, I enjoyed taking these clusters to work. They're so simple, however, that I still make them for holidays because my family looks forward to them.

PREP: 15 MIN. COOK: 1 HOUR

- 2 pounds white candy coating, coarsely chopped
- 1-1/2 cups peanut butter
- 1/2 teaspoon almond extract, optional
- 4 cups Cap'n Crunch cereal
- 4 cups crisp rice cereal
- 4 cups miniature marshmallows

■ Place the candy coating in a 5-qt. slow cooker. Cover and cook on high for 1 hour. Add the peanut butter. Stir in the almond extract if desired.

■ In a large bowl, combine the cereals and marshmallows. Stir in the peanut butter mixture until well coated. Drop by tablespoonfuls onto waxed paper. Let stand until set. Store at room temperature. **Yield:** 6-1/2 dozen.

five-minute blueberry pie

MILDA ANDERSON | OSCEOLA, WISCONSIN

If you like the taste of fresh blueberries, you'll adore this pie! Since it's a breeze to whip up, I make it often, especially on hot summer days.

PREP: 15 MIN. + CHILLING

- 1/2 cup sugar
- 2 tablespoons cornstarch
- 3/4 cup water
- 4 cups fresh *or* frozen blueberries, thawed
- 1 graham cracker crust (9 inches)

Whipped cream, optional

■ In a large saucepan, combine sugar and cornstarch. Stir in water until smooth. Bring to a boil over medium heat; cook and stir for 2 minutes. Add blueberries. Cook for 3 minutes, stirring occasionally. Pour into crust. Chill. Garnish with the whipped cream if desired. **Yield:** 6-8 servings.

frozen raspberry pie

DOROTHY LATTA-MCCARTY | LAKEWOOD, COLORADO

Guests' eyes will light up at the sight of this appealing make-ahead pie. The light raspberry flavor is accented by the pleasant crunch of almonds. It's especially refreshing after a heavy meal or in summer.

PREP: 10 MIN. + COOLING

1 jar (7 ounces) marshmallow creme
1 cup (8 ounces) raspberry yogurt
1 cup raspberry sherbet, softened
2 cups whipped topping
1/2 cup chopped toasted slivered almonds
1 graham cracker crust (9 inches)
Additional whipped topping and almonds, optional

- Place marshmallow creme in a deep microwave-safe bowl. Microwave, uncovered, on high for 1 minute or until it puffs and becomes smooth when stirred.
- Cool to room temperature, stirring occasionally. Stir in yogurt and sherbet. Fold in whipped topping and almonds.
- Pour into crust. Cover and freeze for 6 hours or overnight. Remove from the freezer 10-15 minutes before serving. Garnish with whipped topping and almonds if desired. **Yield:** 6-8 servings.

quick little devils

DENISE SMITH | LUSK, WYOMING

Enjoy the classic combination of peanut butter and chocolate in these speedy squares. A short list of ingredients, including devil's food cake mix, yields chocolaty results that are sure to satisfy any sweet tooth.

PREP/TOTAL TIME: 30 MIN.

1 package (18-1/4 ounces) devil's food cake mix
3/4 cup butter, melted
1/3 cup evaporated milk
1 jar (7 ounces) marshmallow creme
3/4 cup peanut butter

- In a large bowl, combine the cake mix, butter and milk. Spread half the mixture into a greased 13-in. x 9-in. baking pan. In a small bowl, combine marshmallow creme and peanut butter; carefully spread over cake mixture to within 1 in. of edge.
- Drop remaining cake mixture by teaspoonfuls over marshmallow mixture. Bake at 350° for 20-22 minutes or until edges are golden brown. Cool completely on a wire rack. Cut into squares. **Yield:** about 2-1/2 dozen.

chocolate mousse

JUDY SPENCER | SAN DIEGO, CALIFORNIA

I adore this recipe for rich mousse that I received from a friend. I love to cook and have many recipes, but this one is a favorite and always draws raves. Best of all, it's easy to make.

PREP: 20 MIN. + CHILLING

1/4 cup semisweet chocolate chips
1 tablespoon water
1 egg yolk, lightly beaten
1-1/2 teaspoons vanilla extract
1/2 cup heavy whipping cream
1 tablespoon sugar
Whipped cream, optional

- In a small saucepan, melt the chocolate chips with the water; stir until smooth. Stir a small amount of the hot chocolate mixture into the egg yolk; return all to the pan, stirring constantly. Cook and stir for 2 minutes or until slightly thickened. Remove from the heat; stir in the vanilla. Cool, stirring several times.
- In a small bowl, beat the whipping cream until it begins to thicken. Add the sugar; beat until soft peaks form. Fold in the cooled chocolate mixture. Cover and refrigerate for at least 2 hours. Garnish with the whipped cream if desired. **Yield:** 2 servings.

strawberry raspberry trifle

PATRICIA SCHROEDL | JEFFERSON, WISCONSIN

A fantastic finale to any meal, this tantalizing trifle helped me finish first in a local competition. It took top prize in the low-fat category in the Wisconsin Strawberry Festival recipe contest.

PREP/TOTAL TIME: 20 MIN.

- 3 cups cold fat-free milk
- 2 packages (1 ounce *each*) sugar-free instant white chocolate pudding mix
- 1 prepared angel food cake (14 ounces), cut into 1-inch cubes
- 3 cups sliced fresh strawberries
- 3 cups fresh raspberries
- 1 carton (8 ounces) frozen reduced-fat whipped topping, thawed
- 3 whole strawberries, quartered

■ In a large bowl, whisk milk and pudding mix for 2 minutes. Let stand for 2 minutes or until soft-set.

■ Place a third of the cake cubes in a trifle bowl or 3-1/2-qt. glass serving bowl. Top with a third of the pudding, 1 cup sliced strawberries, 1-1/2 cups raspberries and a third of the whipped topping. Layer with a third of the cake cubes and pudding, 1 cup of strawberries and a third of the whipped topping.

■ Top with the remaining cake, pudding, strawberries, raspberries and whipped topping. Garnish with quartered strawberries. Serve immediately or cover and chill until serving. **Yield:** 14 servings.

caramel top hats

NOVA MACISSAC | SOURIS, PRINCE EDWARD ISLAND

A plain purchased pound cake's at the heart of this elegant-looking dessert. I've used angel food cake, cupcakes, doughnuts and even a stack of cookies as the base in place of the pound cake. Top it off with a fun selection of sundae makings—nuts, orange rinds or cherries.

PREP/TOTAL TIME: 10 MIN.

- 1 cup packed brown sugar
- 1/4 cup evaporated milk
- 2 tablespoons butter
- 2 tablespoons corn syrup
- 4 slices pound cake

Butter pecan ice cream

■ In a small saucepan, combine brown sugar, milk, butter and corn syrup; mix well. Cook and stir over medium-low heat until heated through (do not boil).

■ Top each slice of cake with a scoop of ice cream; drizzle with warm caramel sauce. Serve immediately. Refrigerate any leftover sauce. **Yield:** 4 servings.

quick graham cracker cake

MARY LOU MCCULLOUGH | NEW GALILEE, PENNSYLVANIA

Imagine two food favorites—graham crackers and whipped cream—in one wonderful cake. The results are heavenly!

PREP: 20 MIN. BAKE: 25 MIN. + COOLING

- 1-1/4 cups graham cracker crumbs, *divided*
- 1 package (18-1/4 ounces) white cake mix
- 2 tablespoons sugar
- 1-1/2 cups water
- 2 egg whites
- 4 tablespoons canola oil
- 1 pint heavy whipping cream *or* 1 carton (12 ounces) frozen whipped topping, thawed

■ Set aside 2 tablespoons graham cracker crumbs. In a large bowl, beat the remaining crumbs, cake mix, sugar, water, egg whites and oil for 2 minutes.

■ Pour into two greased and floured 9-in. layer pans. Bake at 350° for 25-30 minutes or until a toothpick inserted near center comes out clean. Let stand a few minutes; remove from pans to wire racks to cool completely.

■ Cut each cake horizontally into two layers. Place bottom layer on a serving plate. Spread whipped cream between layers and frost entire cake. Sprinkle reserved graham cracker crumbs on top. Refrigerate until serving time. **Yield:** 16-20 servings.

berry special pie

EVE GAUGER VARGAS | PRAIRIE VILLAGE, KANSAS

I developed this refreshing dessert after tasting something similar at a restaurant. Thanks to a prepared crumb crust, it goes together quickly. We love it with raspberries, but you can use any fresh berries.

PREP/TOTAL TIME: 10 MIN.

- 1/2 cup semisweet chocolate chips
- 1-1/2 teaspoons shortening
- 1 chocolate crumb crust (8 inches)
- 2 cups fresh raspberries
- 1 carton (8 ounces) frozen whipped topping, thawed

■ In a microwave, melt chocolate chips and shortening; stir until smooth. Spread over the bottom of pie crust. Top with raspberries and whipped topping. Refrigerate until serving. **Yield:** 6-8 servings.

pudding pound cake dessert

TAMMY LOGAN | CLINTON, TENNESSEE

Here's a layered treat that relies on convenient instant pudding and store-bought pound cake. It's so irresistible that everyone will want seconds.

PREP/TOTAL TIME: 30 MIN.

- 1 frozen pound cake (10-3/4 ounces), thawed
- 3 cups cold milk
- 2 packages (3.9 ounces *each*) instant chocolate pudding mix
- 3 cups whipped topping
- 1/2 cup chopped walnuts
- 3/4 cup chopped cream-filled chocolate sandwich cookies

■ Cut cake horizontally into fourths; place two pieces side by side in an 8-in. square dish. In a large bowl, whisk milk and pudding mixes for 2 minutes. Let stand for 2 minutes or until soft-set; fold in whipped topping.

■ Spoon half over cake; sprinkle with walnuts and 1/2 cup cookies. Layer with remaining cake, pudding mixture and cookies (dish will be full). Refrigerate until serving. **Yield:** 9 servings.

cool strawberry cream

JOYCE COOPER | MOUNT FOREST, ONTARIO

This fruity, luscious dessert makes a wonderful ending to a special dinner. When fresh strawberries are not available, I substitute two packages of the frozen unsweetened kind, thawed and drained.

PREP: 30 MIN. + FREEZING

- 2 packages (8 ounces *each*) cream cheese, softened
- 3/4 cup sugar
- 1/2 cup sour cream
- 3 cups fresh strawberries, mashed
- 1 cup whipped topping

BLUEBERRY SAUCE:

- 1 package (12 ounces) frozen unsweetened blueberries
- 1/3 cup sugar
- 1/4 cup water

■ Line a 9-in. x 5-in. loaf pan with a double thickness of foil; set aside. In a large bowl, beat the cream cheese, sugar and sour cream until smooth. Fold in strawberries and the whipped topping. Pour into prepared pan. Cover and freeze for several hours or overnight.

■ In a small saucepan, bring the blueberries, sugar and water to a boil; cook and stir for 3 minutes. Cool slightly. Transfer to a blender; cover and process until pureed. Refrigerate until chilled.

■ Remove dessert from the freezer 15-20 minutes before serving. Use foil to lift out of pan; remove foil. Cut into slices with a serrated knife. Serve with blueberry sauce. **Yield:** 10-12 servings.

lemonade pie

PEGGY FINE | HELENA, MONTANA

The tangy taste of this pie makes it a hit in the summertime. We especially like it after a spicy meal.

PREP: 10 MIN. + CHILLING

- 1 can (14 ounces) sweetened condensed milk
- 1 can (12 ounces) frozen pink lemonade, thawed and undiluted
- 1 carton (6 ounces) frozen whipped topping, thawed
- 1 graham cracker crust (9 inches)

Graham cracker crumbs

■ In a large bowl, combine the milk, lemonade and whipped topping. Pour into the crust. Refrigerate for at least 12 hours. Garnish with crumbs. **Yield:** 8 servings.

easy chocolate clusters

DORIS REYNOLDS | MUNDS PARK, ARIZONA

You can use this simple recipe to make a big batch of chocolate candy without a lot of fuss. I've sent these clusters to my husband's office a number of times...and passed the recipe along as well.

PREP: 10 MIN. + STANDING COOK: 2 HOURS

- 2 pounds white candy coating, broken into small pieces
- 2 cups (12 ounces) semisweet chocolate chips
- 4 ounces German sweet chocolate, chopped
- 1 jar (24 ounces) dry roasted peanuts

■ In a 3-qt. slow cooker, combine the candy coating, chocolate chips and German chocolate. Cover and cook on high for 1 hour. Reduce heat to low; cover and cook 1 hour longer or until melted, stirring every 15 minutes.

■ Stir in peanuts. Drop by teaspoonfuls onto waxed paper. Let stand until set. Store at room temperature. **Yield:** 3-1/2 dozen.

chocolate swirl cheesecake

AIDA BABBEL | COQUITLAM, BRITISH COLUMBIA

The wonderful flavors of orange and chocolate combine in this creamy cheesecake.

PREP: 25 MIN. BAKE: 1-1/4 HOURS + CHILLING

1/3 cup graham cracker crumbs
4 packages (8 ounces *each*) cream cheese, softened
1-1/3 cups sugar
4 eggs, lightly beaten
2 tablespoons orange juice
2 teaspoons grated orange peel
3 ounces semisweet chocolate, melted
Whipped cream, optional

- Place a lightly greased 9-in. springform pan on a double thickness of heavy-duty foil (about 18 in. square). Securely wrap foil around pan. Sprinkle crumbs over bottom and sides of the pan; set aside.
- In a large bowl, beat the cream cheese and sugar until smooth. Add eggs; beat on low speed just until combined. Stir in orange juice and peel. Set aside 3/4 cup; pour remaining filling into pan.
- Stir chocolate into reserved filling. Drop by spoonfuls over filling; cut through batter with a knife to swirl.
- Place springform pan in a large baking pan; add 1 in. of hot water to larger pan. Bake at 350° for 75-80 minutes or until center is just set and top appears dull.
- Remove springform pan from water bath. Cool on a wire rack for 10 minutes. Carefully run a knife around edge of pan to loosen; cool 1 hour longer. Refrigerate overnight. Serve with the whipped cream if desired. **Yield:** 12-16 servings.

butter pecan crunch

JULIE STERCHI | FLORA, ILLINOIS

"Elegant but easy" is how I describe this frozen treat. It's based on a recipe from my mother.

PREP: 15 MIN. + FREEZING

2 cups graham cracker crumbs
1/2 cup butter, melted
2 cups milk
2 packages (3.4 ounces *each*) instant vanilla pudding mix
1 quart butter pecan ice cream, softened
1 carton (8 ounces) frozen whipped topping, thawed
2 Heath candy bars (1.4 ounces *each*), crushed

- Combine cracker crumbs and butter; press into a 13-in. x 9-in. dish. Chill.
- In a large bowl, whisk the milk and pudding mixes for 2 minutes. Let stand for 2 minutes or until soft-set. Fold in ice cream and whipped topping. Spoon over crust. Sprinkle with candy.
- Freeze for at least 2 hours. Remove from the refrigerator 20 minutes before serving. **Yield:** 12-16 servings.

pumpkin chiffon pie

MARIJEAN ACKERS | RIVERSIDE, CALIFORNIA

Even those on restricted diets should be able to enjoy a good piece of pie once in a while. This wonderful dessert is a treat for the whole family. Folks are shocked to discover it's sugar-free and low in fat.

PREP: 10 MIN. + CHILLING

2-1/2 cups cold fat-free milk
2 packages (1.5 ounces *each*) sugar-free instant vanilla pudding mix
1 can (15 ounces) solid-pack pumpkin
1 teaspoon ground cinnamon
1/2 teaspoon ground ginger
1/4 teaspoon ground cloves
1 reduced-fat graham cracker crust (9 inches)
Reduced-fat whipped topping and additional cinnamon, optional

- In a large bowl, combine the milk and pudding mix. Beat for 1 minute (mixture will be thick). Add pumpkin and spices; beat 1 minute longer. Pour into pie crust.
- Cover and refrigerate for 2 hours or until firm. If desired, garnish with whipped topping and sprinkle with cinnamon. **Yield:** 8 servings.

fluffy lemon-lime pie

MRS. C.G. ROWLAND | CHATTANOOGA, TENNESSEE

You can't go wrong with this refreshing treat. I just mix together three ingredients, put the combination into a prepared crust and pop it in the refrigerator.

PREP: 15 MIN. + CHILLING

- 1 envelope (.13 ounce) unsweetened lemon-lime soft drink mix
- 1 can (14 ounces) sweetened condensed milk
- 1 carton (8 ounces) frozen whipped topping, thawed
- 1 graham cracker crust (9 inches)

■ In a large bowl, dissolve soft drink mix in milk; fold in whipped topping. Spoon into crust. Cover and refrigerate for 3 hours or until set. **Yield:** 6-8 servings.

cran-raspberry pie

VERONA KOEHLMOOS | PILGER, NEBRASKA

Jewel-toned fruits team up to pack this lattice-topped pie. It's a lovely addition to holiday meals.

PREP: 15 MIN. BAKE: 50 MIN. + COOLING

- 2 cups chopped fresh *or* frozen cranberries
- 5 cups fresh *or* frozen unsweetened raspberries, thawed
- 1/2 teaspoon almond extract
- 1 to 1-1/4 cups sugar
- 1/4 cup quick-cooking tapioca
- 1/4 teaspoon salt

Pastry for double-crust pie (9 inches)

■ In a large bowl, combine the cranberries, raspberries and extract. Combine the sugar, tapioca and salt. Add to fruit mixture; toss gently to coat. Let stand for 15-20 minutes.

■ Line pie plate with bottom pastry; trim to 1 in. beyond edge of plate. Add filling. Roll out remaining pastry; make a lattice crust. Trim, seal and flute edges. Cover edges loosely with foil.

■ Bake at 375° for 40-45 minutes or until the crust is golden brown and the filling is bubbly. Cool on a wire rack. **Yield:** 6-8 servings.

Chocolate Curls

To make chocolate curls, set out a 4-ounce chocolate bar in a warm place (80° to 85°) until thoroughly warm but not melted. With a vegetable peeler, draw along the flat side of the chocolate bar, making a curl.

almond mocha pie

EDNA JOHNSON | ST. CROIX FALLS, WISCONSIN

I received this recipe from an aunt years ago. The creamy chocolate pie—with a hint of coffee—is nice to have in the freezer for a quick reward on a hectic day.

PREP: 15 MIN. + FREEZING

1 teaspoon instant coffee granules
2 tablespoons boiling water
1 milk chocolate candy bar with almonds (7 ounces)
1 carton (8 ounces) frozen whipped topping, thawed
1 pastry shell (9 inches), baked
Chocolate curls and additional whipped topping, optional

- In a small bowl, dissolve coffee in boiling water; set aside. In a microwave, melt candy bar; stir until smooth. Cool slightly. Fold in half of the whipped topping. Fold in coffee and remaining whipped topping. Pour into the pastry shell; freeze.
- Remove from the freezer 15 minutes before serving. Garnish with chocolate curls and additional whipped topping if desired. **Yield:** 6-8 servings.

rapid raspberry torte

RUTH PETERSON | JENISON, MICHIGAN

This tasty layered dessert is simple to assemble because it calls for a frozen pound cake, raspberry jam and little cups of prepared lemon pudding.

PREP/TOTAL TIME: 15 MIN.

3/4 cup heavy whipping cream
1 tablespoon confectioners' sugar
2 snack-size cups (3-1/2 ounces *each*) lemon pudding
1 loaf (10-3/4 ounces) frozen pound cake, thawed
1/3 cup raspberry jam, *divided*

- In a small bowl, beat cream until soft peaks form. Add confectioners' sugar; beat until stiff peaks form. Place pudding in a bowl; fold in whipped cream.
- Cut cake horizontally into three layers. Place bottom layer on a serving plate; top with half the jam. Repeat layers. Top with third cake layer. Cut into slices; dollop with pudding mixture. **Yield:** 7-10 servings.

Editor's Note: This recipe was tested with Hunt's Snack Pack lemon pudding.

five-minute trifle

JULIA TRACHSEL | VICTORIA, BRITISH COLUMBIA

Frozen pound cake, pudding mix and whipped topping make this trifle true to its name. Any type of cake can be used. Then add your favorite berries or fruit and any flavor of pudding.

PREP/TOTAL TIME: 10 MIN.

2 cups cold milk
1 package (3.4 ounces) instant vanilla pudding mix
1 loaf (10-3/4 ounces) frozen pound cake, thawed
3 cups fresh *or* frozen raspberries, thawed
Whipped topping and additional raspberries

- In a small bowl, whisk the milk and pudding mix for 2 minutes. Let stand for 2 minutes or until soft-set.
- Cut the cake into 1-in. cubes; place in a 2-qt. glass bowl. Top with raspberries and pudding. Cover and refrigerate until serving. Garnish with the whipped topping and additional raspberries. **Yield:** 6 servings.

cherry-lemon icebox pie

MARY WELLER | TWIN LAKE, MICHIGAN

This recipe makes a nice and refreshing finish to a heavy meal. Lemon and cherries are perfect partners.

PREP: 25 MIN. + CHILLING

Pastry for single-crust pie (9 inches)
1 can (14 ounces) sweetened condensed milk
1/2 cup lemon juice
1/2 teaspoon vanilla extract
1/2 teaspoon almond extract
1-1/2 cups heavy whipping cream
1 can (21 ounces) cherry pie filling

- Line a 9-in. deep-dish pie plate with pastry; trim and flute edges. Line pastry shell with a double thickness of heavy-duty foil. Bake at 450° for 8 minutes. Remove foil; bake 5-7 minutes longer or until lightly browned. Cool on a wire rack.
- In a large bowl, whisk the milk, lemon juice and extracts until thickened, about 2 minutes. Beat cream until stiff peaks form; fold into milk mixture. Pour into crust.
- Refrigerate for 30 minutes; spoon pie filling over the top. Chill at least 2 hours before serving. **Yield:** 8 servings.

apple spice snack cake

REBA SAVOIE | ROSWELL, NEW MEXICO

Nothing could be simpler or more delicious than this moist apple cake. It's easy to create the four-ingredient treat with a spice cake mix.

PREP: 10 MIN. BAKE: 30 MIN.

1 package (18-1/4 ounces) spice cake mix
1 can (21 ounces) apple pie filling
2 eggs
2 tablespoons canola oil

- In a large bowl, combine all the ingredients; beat on low speed for 30 seconds. Beat on medium for 2 minutes.
- Pour into a greased 13-in. x 9-in. baking dish. Bake at 350° for 30-35 minutes or until a toothpick comes out clean. Cool on a wire rack. **Yield:** 15 servings.

raspberry-cherry pie

FERN BUFFINGTON | TRAER, IOWA

My family prefers this pie with a lattice crust, but feel free to save time by topping it any way you like.

PREP: 10 MIN. + STANDING
BAKE: 40 MIN. + COOLING

2 cups fresh *or* frozen unsweetened raspberries
1 cup pitted fresh, frozen *or* canned tart cherries
1-1/2 cups sugar
3 tablespoons quick-cooking tapioca
1 teaspoon lemon juice
Pastry for double-crust pie (9 inches)
1 to 2 tablespoons butter

- In a large bowl, combine raspberries and cherries. Stir in the sugar, tapioca and lemon juice. Let stand for 1 hour.
- Line pie plate with bottom crust; add the filling. Dot with butter. Top with a lattice crust.
- Bake at 450° for 10 minutes; reduce heat to 350°. Bake 30 minutes longer or until crust is golden brown and filling is bubbly. Cool on a wire rack. **Yield:** 6-8 servings.

cookies 'n' cream pie

JULIE STERCHI | FLORA, ILLINOIS

Convenience items—including instant pudding, frozen whipped topping, cookies and prepared crumb crust—make this make-ahead dessert a treat for the cook.

PREP: 10 MIN. + FREEZING

1-1/2 cups half-and-half cream
1 package (3.4 ounces) instant vanilla pudding mix
1 carton (8 ounces) frozen whipped topping, thawed
1 cup crushed cream-filled chocolate sandwich cookies (about 11 cookies)
1 chocolate crumb crust (9 inches)

- In a large bowl, whisk the cream and pudding mix for 2 minutes. Let stand for 2 minutes or until soft-set. Fold in whipped topping and cookies.
- Spoon into crust. Freeze until firm, about 6 hours or overnight. May be frozen for up to 3 months. Remove from the freezer 10 minutes before serving. **Yield:** 6-8 servings.

root beer float cake

GAIL TOEPFER | IRON RIDGE, WISCONSIN

When I came across this fun and festive recipe, I knew I had to give it a try. I hope you try it, too!

PREP: 15 MIN. + CHILLING BAKE: 35 MIN. + COOLING

1 package (18-1/4 ounces) white cake mix
1-1/4 cups root beer
2 eggs
1/4 cup canola oil

FROSTING:
1 envelope whipped topping mix (Dream Whip)
1/2 cup chilled root beer

- In a large bowl, combine the first four ingredients. Beat on low speed for 30 seconds; beat on high for 2 minutes. Pour into a greased 13-in. x 9-in. baking pan.
- Bake at 350° for 35-40 minutes or until a toothpick inserted near the center comes out clean. Cool completely on a wire rack.
- In a small bowl, beat frosting ingredients until stiff peaks form. Frost cake. Chill. **Yield:** 12-15 servings.

strawberry cheesecake pie

JANIS PLOURDE | SMOOTH ROCK FALLS, ONTARIO

A creamy concoction is so refreshing on a hot day. With the dessert's appealing look, company will never know how simple it is to assemble.

PREP: 10 MIN. + CHILLING

2 cups sliced fresh strawberries
1/4 cup chopped almonds, toasted
1 tablespoon sugar
1 graham cracker crust (9 inches)
1 package (8 ounces) cream cheese, softened
2 cups cold milk, *divided*
1 package (3.4 ounces) instant vanilla pudding mix

- In a small bowl, combine the strawberries, almonds and sugar. Pour into crust; set aside. In a large bowl, beat cream cheese until smooth; gradually add 1/2 cup of milk. Add pudding mix and remaining milk. Beat for 1 minute or until blended; pour over strawberries. Cover and refrigerate for 2 hours or until set. **Yield:** 8 servings.

Try a Tray

If you don't have a Popsicle mold for the Orange Cream Pops, an ice cube tray can be used instead. The recipe will yield more because the pops won't be as big.

orange cream pops

TASTE OF HOME TEST KITCHEN

For a low-fat alternative to ice cream-filled pops, try slurping this citrus novelty. The tangy orange flavor will make your taste buds tingle...while the silky smooth texture offers cool comfort, no matter how high the temperatures soar.

PREP: 10 MIN. + FREEZING

- 1 package (3 ounces) orange gelatin
- 1 cup boiling water
- 1 cup (8 ounces) vanilla yogurt
- 1/2 cup 2% milk
- 1/2 teaspoon vanilla extract
- 10 plastic cups *or* Popsicle molds (3 ounces *each*)
- 10 Popsicle sticks

■ In a large bowl, dissolve gelatin in boiling water. Cool to room temperature. Stir in the yogurt, milk and vanilla. Pour 1/4 cup into each cup or mold; insert Popsicle sticks. Freeze until firm. **Yield:** 10 ice pops.

ice cream sandwich dessert

JODY KOERBER | CALEDONIA, WISCONSIN

No one will believe this dessert is just dressed-up ice cream sandwiches. For my son's birthday party, I decorated it with race cars and checkered flags because he's a big racing fan. It was a huge success!

PREP: 15 MIN. + FREEZING

- 19 ice cream sandwiches
- 1 carton (12 ounces) frozen whipped topping, thawed
- 1 jar (11-3/4 ounces) hot fudge ice cream topping
- 1 cup salted peanuts

■ Cut one ice cream sandwich in half. Place one whole and one half sandwich along a short side of an ungreased 13-in. x 9-in. pan. Arrange eight sandwiches in opposite direction in the pan. Spread with half of the whipped topping. Spoon fudge topping by teaspoonfuls onto whipped topping. Sprinkle with 1/2 cup peanuts. Repeat layers with remaining ice cream sandwiches, whipped topping and peanuts (pan will be full).

■ Cover and freeze for up to 2 months. Remove from the freezer 20 minutes before serving. Cut into squares. **Yield:** 15 servings.

ice cream supreme

KATHLEEN CLAPP | BLUE HILL, MAINE

Summers here in Maine are too short to spend a lot of time in the kitchen, so we're always looking for simple, quick recipes to make. This fast dessert fits our family of ice cream lovers just fine!

PREP: 15 MIN. + FREEZING

- 1 cup (6 ounces) chocolate chips
- 1/3 cup creamy peanut butter
- 3 cups crispy rice cereal
- 1/2 gallon vanilla ice cream, softened

- In a small saucepan over low heat, melt chocolate and peanut butter. Add cereal; stir until coated. Spread on waxed paper to cool. Set aside 3/4 cup for topping.
- Combine remaining mixture with ice cream. Spread into a 10-in. springform pan; sprinkle with reserved topping. Freeze for 4 hours or overnight. **Yield:** 10 servings.

raspberry crisp

PATRICIA STAUDT | MARBLE ROCK, IOWA

Our raspberry patch keeps my family well supplied with luscious treats. We enjoy these beautiful sweet berries in many desserts, including this one.

PREP: 10 MIN. BAKE: 30 MIN.

- 4 cups fresh *or* frozen raspberries
- 1/3 cup sugar
- 1/3 cup plus 3 tablespoons all-purpose flour, *divided*
- 3/4 cup quick-cooking oats
- 1/3 cup packed brown sugar
- 1/4 cup cold butter, cubed

- In a large bowl, gently toss raspberries with sugar and 3 tablespoons flour. Transfer to a greased 9-in. square baking dish.
- In another large bowl, combine the oats, brown sugar and remaining flour; cut in butter until the mixture resembles coarse crumbs. Sprinkle over berries.
- Bake at 350° for 30 minutes or until golden brown. **Yield:** 6 servings.

chocolate malt shoppe pie

BETH WANEK | LITTLE CHUTE, WISCONSIN

I especially like serving this pie at a cookout or at any event where there are children—it's always a big hit!

PREP: 20 MIN. + FREEZING

1-1/2 cups chocolate wafer crumbs
1/4 cup butter, melted
1 pint vanilla ice cream, softened
1/2 cup crushed malted milk balls
2 tablespoons milk, *divided*
3 tablespoons chocolate malted milk powder
3 tablespoons marshmallow creme
1 cup heavy whipping cream
Additional heavy whipping cream, whipped, optional
Additional malted milk balls, optional

- Combine wafer crumbs and butter; press into an ungreased 9-in. pie pan. Freeze until set. Combine the ice cream, crushed malted milk balls and 1 tablespoon milk; spoon into crust. Freeze for 1 hour.
- In a large bowl, combine the malted milk powder, marshmallow creme and remaining milk. Add cream; whip until soft peaks form. Spread over ice cream layer. Freeze for several hours or overnight.
- Just before serving, garnish each serving with whipped cream and malted milk balls if desired. **Yield:** 6-8 servings.

banana upside-down cake

LOIS SCHLICKAU | HAVEN, KANSAS

Because this starts with a cake mix, it's a fast and easy cake to make. Plus, it uses up your ripe bananas and tastes great!

PREP: 15 MIN. BAKE: 30 MIN. + STANDING

1/4 cup butter
1/2 cup packed brown sugar
3 medium firm bananas, cut into 1/2-inch slices
1 package (9 ounces) yellow cake mix
Whipped cream

- Place butter in a 9-in. square baking pan. Heat at 350° for 4-5 minutes or until melted; sprinkle with brown sugar. Arrange bananas in pan; set aside. Prepare cake mix according to package directions; pour over bananas.
- Bake at 350° for 30-35 minutes or until a toothpick inserted near the center comes out clean. Immediately invert the cake onto a serving platter. Let stand for 5 minutes; remove the pan. Serve warm with the whipped cream. **Yield:** 9 servings.

Editor's Note: This recipe was tested with Jiffy cake mix.

peanutty cream-filled pastry shells

TERI RASEY-BOLF | CADILLAC, MICHIGAN

These delicious desserts say indulgent and decadent, but couldn't be any easier to make. Make them ahead for that weekend party coming up; they're perfect for guests.

PREP: 15 MIN. + FREEZING BAKE: 20 MIN.

2 packages (10 ounces *each*) frozen puff pastry shells
1 package (8 ounces) cream cheese, softened
1 cup creamy peanut butter
1 can (14 ounces) sweetened condensed milk
1 teaspoon lemon juice
1-1/2 cups whipped topping
Chocolate hard-shell ice cream topping
1/4 cup chopped unsalted peanuts

- Bake puff pastry shells according to package directions. Cool completely. Meanwhile, in a large bowl, beat cream cheese until light and fluffy. Add the peanut butter, milk and lemon juice. Fold in whipped topping.
- Place shells on a waxed paper-lined baking sheet. Remove tops; save for another use. Pour 1 teaspoon hard-shell topping into each pastry shell. Mound 1/3 cup cream cheese mixture over topping. Drizzle with an additional 1 teaspoon topping; sprinkle with peanuts. Freeze for 30 minutes or until firm.
- Let stand at room temperature for 5 minutes before serving. **Yield:** 12 servings.

chilly coconut pie

JEANNETTE MACK | RUSHVILLE, NEW YORK

Everyone loves this creamy coconut pie. It's so easy to make that I keep several in the freezer for those occasions when I need a quick ending to a meal.

PREP: 10 MIN. + FREEZING

- 1 package (3 ounces) cream cheese, softened
- 2 tablespoons sugar
- 1/2 cup milk
- 1/4 teaspoon almond extract
- 1 cup flaked coconut
- 1 carton (8 ounces) frozen whipped topping, thawed
- 1 graham cracker crust (9 inches)

■ In a large bowl, beat the cream cheese and sugar until smooth. Gradually beat in milk and extract. Fold in coconut and whipped topping. Spoon into crust. Cover and freeze for at least 4 hours.

■ Remove from the freezer 30 minutes before serving. **Yield:** 6-8 servings.

strawberry lover's pie

LAURETHA ROWE | SCRANTON, KANSAS

The second question people ask when I serve them this pie is, "What's your recipe?" It comes right after their first question—"May I have another slice?"

PREP: 25 MIN. + CHILLING

- 3 ounces semisweet chocolate
- 1 tablespoon butter
- 1 pastry shell (9 inches), baked
- 2 packages (3 ounces *each*) cream cheese, softened
- 1/2 cup sour cream
- 3 tablespoons sugar

- 1/2 teaspoon vanilla extract
- 3 to 4 cups fresh strawberries, hulled
- 1/3 cup strawberry jam, melted

■ In a large saucepan, melt 2 oz. chocolate and butter over low heat, stirring constantly; spread or brush over the bottom and up the sides of pastry shell. Chill.

■ Meanwhile, in a large bowl, beat the cream cheese, sour cream, sugar and vanilla until smooth. Spread over chocolate layer; cover and chill for 2 hours.

■ Arrange strawberries over the filling; brush with jam. Melt the remaining chocolate and drizzle over the top. **Yield:** 6-8 servings.

orange whip

SUE THOMAS | CASA GRANDE, ARIZONA

It takes me mere minutes to blend together this cool, silky smooth dessert. Yogurt adds tang to the light orange flavor. It's so pretty and refreshing on warm summer days.

PREP: 10 MIN. + FREEZING

- 1 can (11 ounces) mandarin oranges, drained and patted dry
- 1 cup (8 ounces) vanilla yogurt
- 2 tablespoons orange juice concentrate
- 2 cups whipped topping

■ In a large bowl, combine the oranges, yogurt and orange juice concentrate. Fold in whipped topping. Spoon into serving dishes. Cover and freeze until firm. Remove from the freezer 10 minutes before serving. **Yield:** 4 servings.

blueberry pear cobbler

SUSAN PUMPHREY | HOT SPRINGS, ARIZONA

Mom used her home-canned pears in this warm cobbler, but the store-bought variety works just as well. People are always amazed something that comes together in a cinch tastes this wonderful.

PREP/TOTAL TIME: 25 MIN.

- 2 cans (15-1/4 ounces *each*) sliced pears
- 1 package (7 ounces) blueberry muffin mix
- 3 tablespoons butter

■ Drain pears, reserving 3/4 cup juice (discard remaining juice or save for another use). Pour pears and reserved juice into a greased 2-qt. baking dish. Sprinkle with muffin mix; dot with butter.

■ Bake, uncovered, at 400° for 20-25 minutes or until bubbly and top is lightly browned. **Yield:** 8 servings.

white chocolate berry pie

CONNIE LAUX | ENGLEWOOD, OHIO

When strawberries are in season, I love to make this elegant pie featuring a smooth cream cheese filling.

PREP: 20 MIN. + CHILLING

- 5 ounces white baking chocolate, chopped, *divided*
- 2 tablespoons milk
- 1 package (3 ounces) cream cheese, softened
- 1/3 cup confectioners' sugar
- 1 teaspoon grated orange peel
- 1 cup heavy whipping cream, whipped
- 1 graham cracker crust (9 inches)
- 2 cups sliced fresh strawberries

■ In a microwave, melt four ounces of white chocolate with milk at 70% power for 1 minute; stir. Microwave at additional 10- to 20-second intervals, stirring until smooth. Cool to room temperature.

■ Meanwhile, in a large bowl, beat cream cheese and sugar until smooth. Beat in orange peel and melted chocolate. Fold in whipped cream.

■ Spread into crust. Arrange strawberries on top. Melt remaining white chocolate; drizzle over the berries. Refrigerate for at least 1 hour. Store in the refrigerator. **Yield:** 8 servings.

easy tiramisu

NANCY BROWN | DAHINDA, ILLINOIS

Tiramisu in less than half an hour? It's true! The secret is to start with a frozen pound cake and a few kitchen staples.

PREP/TOTAL TIME: 20 MIN.

- 1 package (10-3/4 ounces) frozen pound cake, thawed
- 3/4 cup strong brewed coffee
- 1 package (8 ounces) cream cheese, softened
- 1 cup sugar
- 1/2 cup chocolate syrup
- 1 cup heavy whipping cream, whipped
- 2 Heath candy bars (1.4 ounces *each*), crushed

■ Cut cake into nine slices. Arrange in an ungreased 11-in. x 7-in. dish, cutting to fit if needed. Drizzle with coffee.

■ In a small bowl, beat cream cheese and sugar until smooth. Add chocolate syrup. Fold in whipped cream. Spread over cake. Sprinkle with crushed candy bars. Refrigerate until serving. **Yield:** 8 servings.

Whipping Cream

Choose a deep metal bowl for whipping cream. Place the bowl and beaters in the freezer for at least 15 minutes before using. Beat quickly, scraping the bowl occasionally. Do not overbeat.

creamy lime sherbet

MARY BETH DELL SPIESS | INDUSTRY, TEXAS

The lime flavor in this cool, creamy treat is perfect for hot summer days. The pastel color makes it so pretty whether served in a dish or a cone.

PREP: 15 MIN. PROCESS: 20 MIN./BATCH + FREEZING

- 1 package (3 ounces) lime gelatin
- 1 cup boiling water
- 1-1/4 cups sugar
- 1 can (6 ounces) frozen limeade concentrate, thawed
- Dash salt
- 4 cups milk
- 2 cups half-and-half cream
- 8 drops green food coloring, optional

■ In a large bowl, dissolve gelatin in water. Stir in the sugar, limeade and salt until the sugar is dissolved. Add the remaining ingredients.

■ Fill cylinder of ice cream freezer two-thirds full; freeze according to the manufacturer's directions. Refrigerate remaining mixture until ready to freeze. When ice cream is frozen, transfer to a freezer container; freeze for 2-4 hours before serving. **Yield:** about 2 quarts.

Blueberry Basics

Before refrigerating blueberries in a tightly covered container, discard any that are crushed or moldy. Store for up to 1 week. Wash berries when ready to use. One pint yields 1-1/2 to 2 cups.

blueberry lemon trifle

ELLEN PEDEN | HOUSTON, TEXAS

A refreshing lemon filling and fresh blueberries give this sunny dessert sensation plenty of color. Don't worry about heating up the oven. This recipe doesn't require baking.

PREP: 15 MIN. + CHILLING

- 3 cups fresh blueberries, *divided*
- 2 cans (15-3/4 ounces *each*) lemon pie filling
- 2 cups (8 ounces) lemon yogurt
- 1 prepared angel food cake (8 inches), cut into 1-inch cubes
- 1 carton (8 ounces) frozen whipped topping, thawed

Lemon slices and fresh mint, optional

- Set aside 1/4 cup blueberries for garnish. In a large bowl, combine pie filling and yogurt.
- In a 3-1/2-qt. serving or trifle bowl, layer a third of the cake cubes, lemon mixture and blueberries. Repeat layers twice. Top with whipped topping. Cover and refrigerate for at least 2 hours. Garnish with reserved blueberries, and lemon and mint if desired. **Yield:** 12-14 servings.

pound cake with sherbet

JUDY BERNACKI | LAS VEGAS, NEVADA

Here's a treat that's lusciously light and refreshing. I like to vary the fruit depending on what's in season.

PREP/TOTAL TIME: 10 MIN.

- 4 slices pound cake (3/4 inch thick)
- 1 pint raspberry sherbet *or* flavor of your choice
- 1 cup fresh raspberries *or* fruit of your choice

- Place pound cake on dessert plates. Top each slice with a scoop of sherbet and raspberries. **Yield:** 4 servings.

peanut butter cup pie

TAMMY CASALETTO | GOSHEN, INDIANA

I can put this pie together in 10 minutes and just pull it out of the freezer when we're ready for a scrumptious dessert. Feel free to substitute different flavors of pudding mix and candy bars, such as butterscotch pudding and Butterfinger candy bars.

PREP: 25 MIN. + FREEZING

- 1-1/2 cups cold milk
- 1 package (3.9 ounces) instant chocolate pudding mix
- 1 cup plus 2 tablespoons coarsely chopped peanut butter cups, *divided*
- 1 carton (8 ounces) frozen whipped topping, thawed
- 1 chocolate crumb crust (8 or 9 inches)

- In a large bowl, whisk milk and pudding mix for 2 minutes. Let stand for 2 minutes or until soft-set. Fold in 1 cup chopped peanut butter cups. Fold in whipped topping. Spoon into the crust. Cover and freeze for 6 hours or overnight.
- Remove from the freezer 15-20 minutes before serving. Garnish pie with the remaining peanut butter cups. **Yield:** 6-8 servings.

granola apple crisp

BARBARA SCHINDLER | NAPOLEON, OHIO

Tender apple slices are tucked beneath a sweet crunchy topping in this comforting crisp. For variety, replace the apples with your favorite fruit.

PREP: 20 MIN. COOK: 5 HOURS

- 8 medium tart apples, peeled and sliced
- 1/4 cup lemon juice
- 1-1/2 teaspoons grated lemon peel
- 2-1/2 cups granola with fruit and nuts
- 1 cup sugar
- 1 teaspoon ground cinnamon
- 1/2 cup butter, melted

■ In a large bowl, toss the apples, lemon juice and peel. Transfer to a greased 3-qt. slow cooker. Combine cereal, sugar and cinnamon; sprinkle over apples. Drizzle with the butter.

■ Cover and cook on low for 5-6 hours or until the apples are tender. Serve warm. **Yield:** 6-8 servings.

fresh blueberry tarts

PAT HABIGER | SPEARVILLE, KANSAS

These attractive individual tarts deliver a burst of blueberry flavor in every bite!

PREP: 10 MIN. + CHILLING

- 1 package (8 ounces) cream cheese, softened
- 1/4 cup packed light brown sugar
- 1 package (6 count) individual graham cracker tart shells
- 2 cups fresh blueberries, *divided*
- 3 tablespoons sugar
- 1 teaspoon lemon juice
- 1 teaspoon grated lemon peel

■ In large bowl, beat cream cheese and brown sugar until smooth. Spread in tart shells.

■ In a small bowl, mash 3 tablespoons blueberries with sugar, lemon juice and peel. Add remaining berries and toss. Spoon into tarts. Chill for 1 hour. **Yield:** 6 servings.

Any kind of tart apple can be used to make Granola Apple Crisp (and other apple desserts). Varieties include Braeburn, Empire, Granny Smith, Jonathan, McIntosh and Rome Beauty.

mocha mousse pie

BEVERLY GOTTFRIED | CANDLER, NORTH CAROLINA

Coffee and chocolate are perfectly paired in this lovely layered treat. A convenient chocolate crumb crust holds the fluffy filling.

PREP: 15 MIN. + CHILLING

- 1-1/2 cups semisweet chocolate chips
- 2 cups heavy whipping cream
- 2 tablespoons instant coffee granules
- 2 tablespoons sugar
- 1 teaspoon vanilla extract
- 1 chocolate crumb *or* graham cracker crust (9 inches)

Chocolate shavings, optional

■ In a large microwave-safe bowl, melt chocolate chips; stir until smooth. Set aside to cool.

■ In a large bowl, beat the cream, coffee granules, sugar and vanilla on low until coffee and sugar are dissolved. Beat on high just until stiff peaks form. Set aside 1-1/2 cups for the topping.

■ Gradually fold remaining cream mixture into cooled chocolate until well blended. Pour into pie crust. Spread with reserved cream mixture. Refrigerate for 3 hours.

■ Garnish with chocolate shavings if desired. Store in the refrigerator. **Yield:** 6-8 servings.

raspberry cheesecake trifle

WENDY BLOCK | ABBOTSFORD, BRITISH COLUMBIA

Fresh raspberries add lovely layers of color to this easy-to-assemble dessert. A rich mixture of sweetened cream cheese and whipped cream is a nice change from the pudding found in many trifles.

PREP: 20 MIN. + CHILLING
BAKE: 20 MIN. + COOLING

- 1 package (9 ounces) white cake mix
- 1 package (8 ounces) cream cheese, softened
- 1/4 cup confectioners' sugar
- 1-1/2 cups heavy whipping cream, whipped
- 4 cups fresh raspberries
- 2 ounces semisweet chocolate, coarsely grated *or* shaved
- Grated chocolate *or* chocolate curls, optional

■ Prepare and bake cake according to package directions. Cool; cut into 3/4-in. cubes. In a small bowl, beat cream cheese and confectioners' sugar until smooth. Fold in whipped cream.

■ In a trifle bowl or individual dessert glasses, layer half of cake cubes, 1-1/2 cups raspberries, half of cream cheese mixture and half of chocolate. Repeat layers.

■ Top with the remaining raspberries. Refrigerate for 4 hours or overnight. Garnish with chocolate if desired. **Yield:** 12-14 servings.

creamy peanut butter pie

RHONDA MCDANIEL | ROSSVILLE, GEORGIA

Quartered peanut butter cups top this rich smooth pie that's always a hit at gatherings. It saves time, too, because it can be made in advance and frozen until needed.

PREP: 15 MIN. + CHILLING

- 2 packages (8 ounces *each*) cream cheese, softened
- 1 cup sugar
- 2/3 cup creamy peanut butter
- 2/3 cup whipped topping
- 14 peanut butter cups, *divided*
- 1 chocolate crumb crust (9 inches)

■ In a small bowl, beat the cream cheese, sugar and peanut butter until light and fluffy. Fold in whipped topping. Coarsely chop half of the peanut butter cups; stir into cream cheese mixture.

■ Spoon into crust. Quarter remaining peanut butter cups; arrange over the top. Refrigerate for at least 4 hours before serving. **Yield:** 6-8 servings.

cranberry crumble

KAREN RIORDAN | LOUISVILLE, KENTUCKY

My family enjoys this crumble so much I make it year-round. But I especially like to serve it fresh from the oven with whipped cream on cool winter evenings.

PREP: 10 MIN. BAKE: 35 MIN.

- 1-1/2 cups quick-cooking oats
- 1 cup packed brown sugar
- 1/2 cup all-purpose flour
- 1/3 cup cold butter, cubed
- 1 can (14 ounces) whole-berry cranberry sauce
- Whipped cream *or* ice cream, optional

■ In a large bowl, combine oats, brown sugar and flour. Cut in butter until crumbly. Press half into a greased 8-in. square baking dish.

■ Spread the cranberry sauce evenly over crust. Sprinkle with remaining oat mixture.

■ Bake at 350° for 35-40 minutes or until golden brown and filling is hot. Serve warm with whipped cream or ice cream if desired. **Yield:** 9 servings.

freezer peanut butter pie

NINA RUFENER | ZAPATA, TEXAS

You just can't beat the combination of peanut butter and chocolate. And when those flavors combine in a frosty treat, everyone lines up for a slice!

PREP: 15 MIN. + FREEZING

- 1 quart vanilla ice cream, softened
- 1 graham cracker crust (9 inches)
- 1/2 cup peanut butter
- 1/3 cup light corn syrup
- Chocolate syrup
- Chopped walnuts

■ Spread half of the ice cream into crust. Combine peanut butter and corn syrup; spread over ice cream. Top with remaining ice cream. Drizzle with chocolate syrup and sprinkle with nuts.

■ Cover and freeze for 3-4 hours. Remove from the freezer 15 minutes before serving. **Yield:** 6-8 servings.

easy apple betty

SHARON KNELSEN | COALDALE, ALBERTA

I've been cooking since I was a young girl and am always on the lookout for easy yet delicious dishes. This recipe fits the bill.

PREP: 15 MIN. BAKE: 40 MIN.

- 10 cups sliced peeled tart apples (about 3 pounds)
- 1/4 cup unsweetened apple juice
- 1-3/4 cups crushed oatmeal cookies (about 18)
- 1/4 cup butter, melted
- 1/2 teaspoon ground cinnamon

■ Toss apples and apple juice; arrange half in a 13-in. x 9-in. baking dish coated with cooking spray. Combine cookie crumbs, butter and cinnamon; sprinkle half over apples. Repeat layers.

■ Bake at 375° for 40-45 minutes or until apples are tender and topping is golden brown. **Yield:** 12 servings.

rocky road pizza

TASTE OF HOME TEST KITCHEN

Looking for a new, interesting sensation to offer your hungry clan? Chocolate lovers will relish this palate-pleasing pizza that cleverly captures the flavor of rocky road ice cream. Folks will have a hard time eating just one slice!

PREP/TOTAL TIME: 20 MIN.

Pastry for single-crust pie (9 inches)
3/4 cup semisweet chocolate chips
1/2 cup miniature marshmallows
1/4 cup salted peanuts

- On a lightly floured surface, roll pastry into a 9-in. circle; place on a lightly greased baking sheet. Prick with a fork. Bake at 450° for 8-10 minutes or until lightly browned. Sprinkle with chocolate chips. Bake 1-2 minutes longer or until chocolate is softened.
- Spread chocolate over crust to within 1/2 in. of edges. Sprinkle with marshmallows. Bake for 1-2 minutes or until marshmallows puff slightly and are lightly browned. Sprinkle with peanuts. Remove to a wire rack to cool. **Yield:** 6-8 slices.

strawberry jelly roll

JEANETTE FUEHRING | CONCORDIA, MISSOURI

This pretty jelly roll makes a wonderful dessert any time of year. It gets a head start with a convenient angel food cake mix.

PREP: 15 MIN. + CHILLING BAKE: 15 MIN. + COOLING

1 package (16 ounces) angel food cake mix
1 quart fresh strawberries, sliced
1/4 cup sugar
4 cups fat-free whipped topping

- Mix cake according to package directions. Spread batter into a greased and waxed paper-lined 15-in. x 10-in. x 1-in. baking pan. Bake at 375° for 15-17 minutes or until cake springs back when lightly touched. Cool for 5 minutes.
- Invert onto a kitchen towel dusted with confectioners' sugar. Gently peel off waxed paper. Roll up cake in the towel jelly-roll style, starting with a short side. Cool completely on a wire rack.
- Combine the strawberries and sugar; set aside. To serve, drain the strawberries. Unroll the cake; spread with half of the topping. Cover with the berries. Roll up again. Place on a serving plate, seam side down. Spread with the remaining topping. Refrigerate for 30 minutes before serving. **Yield:** 10 servings.

sweetheart trifle

LORIE COOPER | CHATHAM, ONTARIO

If you're a peanut butter and chocolate lover, this fantastic trifle is for you. It's a hit every time I serve it. I always have requests for the recipe.

PREP: 20 MIN. BAKE: 30 MIN. + CHILLING

1 package (18-1/4 ounces) chocolate cake mix
1 package (10 ounces) peanut butter chips
4-1/4 cups cold milk, *divided*
1/2 cup heavy whipping cream
1/4 teaspoon vanilla extract
2 packages (5.9 ounces *each*) instant chocolate pudding mix
1 carton (12 ounces) frozen whipped topping, thawed
4 Nestlé Crunch candy bars (1.55 ounces *each*), crumbled

- Prepare cake mix according to package directions. Pour the batter into a greased 13-in. x 9-in. baking pan.
- Bake at 350° for 30-35 minutes or until a toothpick inserted near center comes out clean. Cool on a wire rack.
- In a heavy saucepan, combine chips, 1/4 cup milk and cream. Cook and stir over low heat until chips are melted. Remove from the heat; stir in vanilla. Cool to room temperature. In a large bowl, whisk the milk and pudding mixes for 2 minutes. Let stand for 2 minutes or until soft-set.
- To assemble, crumble half of the cake into a 4-qt. trifle bowl or large bowl. Layer half of the peanut butter sauce, pudding, whipped topping and candy bars; repeat layers. Cover and refrigerate for at least 3 hours before serving. **Yield:** 12-15 servings.

p. 330

time-saving **treats**

brownies in a cone

MITZI SENTIFF | ANNAPOLIS, MARYLAND

Brownie-filled ice cream cones are a fun addition to any summer get-together. They appeal to the child in everyone.

PREP: 10 MIN. BAKE: 25 MIN. + COOLING

- 1 package fudge brownie mix (13-inch x 9-inch pan size)
- 17 ice cream cake cones (about 2-3/4 inches tall)
- 1 cup (6 ounces) semisweet chocolate chips
- 1 tablespoon shortening
- Colored sprinkles

■ Prepare brownie batter according to package directions, using 3 eggs. Place the ice cream cones in muffin cups; spoon about 3 tablespoons batter into each cone.

■ Bake at 350° for 25-30 minutes or until a toothpick inserted in the center comes out clean and the top is dry (do not overbake). Cool completely.

■ In a microwave, melt the chocolate chips and shortening; stir until smooth. Dip the tops of the brownies in melted chocolate; allow excess to drip off. Decorate with the sprinkles. **Yield:** 17 servings.

Editor's Note: This recipe was tested with Keebler ice cream cups. These brownies cones are best served the day they're prepared.

chewy oatmeal cookies

RUTH O'DONNELL | ROMEO, MICHIGAN

When our family gathered at my aunt's summer home on Mackinac Island a few years back, she pulled out her tried-and-true recipe and made these wholesome cookies. I think of her and that memorable vacation every time I bake these for my own family.

PREP: 15 MIN. BAKE: 10 MIN./BATCH

- 1 cup butter, softened
- 1 cup sugar
- 1 cup packed brown sugar
- 2 eggs
- 1 teaspoon vanilla extract
- 1-1/2 cups all-purpose flour
- 1 teaspoon baking soda
- 1 teaspoon baking powder
- 1 teaspoon salt
- 2 cups quick-cooking oats
- 2 cups cornflakes
- 1 cup flaked coconut
- 1 cup salted peanuts

■ In a large bowl, cream butter and sugars until light and fluffy. Add the eggs, one at a time, beating well after each addition. Beat in vanilla. Combine flour, baking soda, baking powder and salt; gradually add to the creamed mixture and mix well. Stir in remaining ingredients.

■ Drop by level tablespoonfuls 2 in. apart onto ungreased baking sheets. Bake at 350° for 10-12 minutes or until lightly browned. Remove to wire racks to cool. **Yield:** about 6-1/2 dozen.

lemon nut balls

PAT TUBACH | MANHATTAN, KANSAS

I roll these soft lemon bites in a crunchy coating of chopped pecans. They are easy for young children to help prepare.

PREP: 15 MIN. + CHILLING

- 1/2 cup butter, melted
- 1/4 cup lemon juice
- 5 cups confectioners' sugar
- 3/4 cup nonfat dry milk powder
- 1 cup finely chopped pecans

■ In a large bowl, beat the butter and lemon juice until smooth. Combine confectioners' sugar and milk powder; gradually add to butter the mixture; beat until smooth. Refrigerate for 1 hour.

■ Shape into 1-in. balls; roll in nuts. Store in the refrigerator. **Yield:** 6-1/2 dozen.

double chocolate cookies

CHANTAL CORNWALL | PRINCE RUPERT, BRITISH COLUMBIA

When I make these yummy treats with my young grandson, Ben, I use an extra-big mixing bowl to prevent the flour and other ingredients from flying all over. He seems to enjoy making the cookies almost as much as eating them!

PREP: 15 MIN. BAKE: 10 MIN./BATCH

1-1/4 cups butter, softened
2 cups sugar
2 eggs
2 teaspoons vanilla extract
2 cups all-purpose flour
3/4 cup baking cocoa
1 teaspoon baking soda
1/2 teaspoon salt
2 cups (12 ounces) semisweet chocolate chips

- In a large bowl, cream butter and sugar until light and fluffy. Beat in eggs and vanilla. Combine the flour, cocoa, baking soda and salt; gradually add to creamed mixture and mix well. Stir in chocolate chips.
- Drop by rounded teaspoonfuls 2 in. apart onto greased baking sheets. Bake at 350° for 8-10 minutes or until set. Cool for 2 minutes before removing from pans to wire racks. **Yield:** about 9 dozen.

Choose Other Chips

Vary the flavor of Double Chocolate Cookies by replacing the semisweet chocolate chips with raspberry or mint chocolate chips or peanut butter, butterscotch or white baking chips.

peanut butter cupcakes

ALYCE WYMAN | PEMBINA, NORTH DAKOTA

My family just loves these cupcakes, especially the subtle taste of peanut butter in the frosting. Chocolate frosting is equally delicious on top.

PREP: 15 MIN. BAKE: 20 MIN. + COOLING

- 1 package (18-1/4 ounces) white cake mix
- 18 miniature peanut butter cups
- 1-1/3 cups prepared vanilla frosting
- 2 tablespoons creamy peanut butter

■ Prepare cake mix according to package directions. Spoon about 2 tablespoons of batter into each paper-lined muffin cup. Place a peanut butter cup in each; fill two-thirds full with remaining batter.

■ Bake at 350° for 20-25 minutes or until lightly browned and a toothpick inserted into a cupcake comes out clean. Cool for 10 minutes before removing to wire racks to cool completely.

■ In a small bowl, combine frosting and peanut butter until smooth. Frost cupcakes. **Yield:** 1-1/2 dozen.

after-school treats

ANDREA NEILSON | EAST DUNDEE, ILLINOIS

These no-bake bars satisfy my craving for chocolate and are easier to whip up than brownies or cookies from scratch. Requiring just five ingredients, they're especially handy for a bake sale or after-school treat.

PREP: 10 MIN. + COOLING

- 2 cups (12 ounces) semisweet chocolate chips
- 1/4 cup butter-flavored shortening
- 5 cups crisp rice cereal
- 1 package (10 ounces) Milk Duds
- 1 tablespoon water

■ In a large microwave-safe bowl, combine chocolate chips and shortening. Cover and microwave on high until chocolate is melted; stir until smooth. Stir in cereal until well coated.

■ In another microwave-safe bowl, combine Milk Duds and water. Cover and microwave on high for 30-40 seconds or until mixture is pourable; mix well. Stir into cereal mixture. Spread into a buttered 13-in. x 9-in. pan. Cover and refrigerate for 30 minutes or until firm. Cut into bars. **Yield:** 2 dozen.

Editor's Note: This recipe was tested in a 1,100-watt microwave.

lemon coconut squares

DONNA BIDDLE | ELMIRA, NEW YORK

The tangy lemon flavor of this no-fuss bar dessert is especially delicious on a warm day. It reminds me of selling lemonade on the sidewalk as a little girl.

PREP: 15 MIN. BAKE: 35 MIN.

- 1-1/2 cups all-purpose flour
- 1/2 cup confectioners' sugar
- 3/4 cup cold butter
- 4 eggs
- 1-1/2 cups sugar
- 1/2 cup lemon juice
- 1 teaspoon baking powder
- 3/4 cup flaked coconut

■ In a small bowl, combine flour and confectioners' sugar; cut in the butter until crumbly. Press into a lightly greased 13-in. x 9-in. baking dish. Bake at 350° for 15 minutes.

■ Meanwhile, in another small bowl, beat the eggs, sugar, lemon juice and baking powder until combined. Pour over crust; sprinkle with coconut.

■ Bake at 350° for 20-25 minutes or until golden brown. Cool on a wire rack. Cut into squares. **Yield:** 4 dozen.

Cutting Fudge

It's easier to cut Butterscotch Peanut Fudge when it's out of the pan. So line the greased pan with foil, allowing 2 inches to hang over each short side. Coat the foil with cooking spray. When fudge is firm; lift the foil out of the pan. Cut into squares.

kiddie crunch mix

KARA DE LA VEGA | SOMERSET, CALIFORNIA

This no-bake snack mix is a real treat for kids, and you can easily increase the amount to fit your needs. Place it in individual plastic bags or pour some into colored ice cream cones and cover with plastic wrap for a fun presentation.

PREP/TOTAL TIME: 10 MIN.

- 1 cup animal crackers
- 1 cup chocolate bear-shaped crackers
- 1 cup miniature pretzels
- 1 cup salted peanuts
- 1 cup M&M's
- 1 cup chocolate- *or* yogurt-covered raisins

■ In a bowl, combine all ingredients. Store in an airtight container. **Yield:** 6 cups.

butterscotch peanut fudge

PEGGY KEY | GRANT, ALABAMA

I am a substitute teacher and found this fudge recipe in a very old book in our school library. It was written long before microwaves, so I modified it to make a quick treat. The faculty and staff gave it rave reviews.

PREP: 15 MIN. + CHILLING

- 1 can (14 ounces) sweetened condensed milk
- 1 package (12 ounces) butterscotch chips
- 1-1/2 cups miniature marshmallows
- 2/3 cup peanut butter
- 1 teaspoon vanilla extract
- 1 cup chopped salted peanuts

■ In a microwave-safe bowl, combine the milk, chips and marshmallows. Microwave, uncovered, at 80% power for 3 minutes or until the chips and marshmallows are melted, stirring frequently. Stir in the peanut butter and vanilla until combined. Fold in the peanuts.

■ Pour the mixture into an 11-in. x 7-in. pan coated with cooking spray. Cover and refrigerate for 2 hours or until firm. Cut into squares. Store in the refrigerator. **Yield:** about 6-1/2 dozen.

Editor's Note: This recipe was tested in a 1,100-watt microwave.

almond butter cookies

LYNNE ROMYN | FAYETTEVILLE, NORTH CAROLINA

I came up with this cookie recipe as a way to capture a butter cake popular in my husband's native Netherlands. Almond paste and butter make each melt-in-your-mouth morsel simply irresistible.

PREP: 15 MIN. BAKE: 10 MIN./BATCH

- 1/2 cup butter, softened
- 1/2 cup shortening
- 6 ounces almond paste
- 1-1/3 cups sugar
- 1 egg
- 2 cups all-purpose flour
- 1 teaspoon baking soda

■ In a large bowl, cream the butter, shortening, almond paste and sugar until light and fluffy. Beat in egg. Combine flour and baking soda; gradually add to the creamed mixture.

■ Roll into 1-in. balls. Place 2 in. apart on ungreased baking sheets. Bake at 400° for 8-10 minutes or until lightly browned. Remove to wire racks. **Yield:** 6-1/2 dozen.

poppin' cereal bars

EDNA HOFFMAN | HEBRON, INDIANA

A melted marshmallow coating holds together all sorts of goodies in these yummy bars. The addition of colorful M&M's makes them especially appealing to kids of all ages.

PREP/TOTAL TIME: 15 MIN.

- 2 cups popped popcorn
- 2 cups Life cereal
- 1 cup miniature pretzels
- 1 cup M&M's, *divided*
- 1 package (10-1/2 ounces) miniature marshmallows
- 1/4 cup butter, cubed

■ In a large bowl, combine the popcorn, cereal, pretzels and 1/2 cup M&M's. In a microwave, melt marshmallows and butter; stir until smooth. Fold into cereal mixture.

■ Spread batter into a greased 11-in. x 7-in. dish. Sprinkle with the remaining M&M's; press lightly. Cut into bars. **Yield:** 1-1/2 dozen.

fudgy brownies

EVIE GLOISTEIN | SUSANVILLE, CALIFORNIA

I can stir up these moist and chocolaty brownies in a snap. They're oh-so-easy to make and oh-so-scrumptious to eat.

PREP: 15 MIN. BAKE: 35 MIN.

1/2 cup butter
4 ounces unsweetened chocolate, chopped
2 cups sugar
4 eggs, lightly beaten
1 teaspoon vanilla extract
1/2 cup all-purpose flour
1/2 teaspoon salt
2 cups chopped pecans, optional
Confectioners' sugar, optional

- In a microwave, melt butter and chocolate; stir until smooth. Cool slightly. In a large bowl, beat sugar and eggs. Stir in vanilla and chocolate mixture. Combine flour and salt; gradually add to chocolate mixture. Stir in pecans if desired.
- Spread into two greased 8-in. square baking pans. Bake at 325° for 35-40 minutes or until a toothpick inserted near the center comes out clean. Cool on a wire rack. Dust with confectioners' sugar if desired. Cut into bars. **Yield:** 32 brownies.

berry surprise cupcakes

SUSAN LUCAS | BRAMPTON, ONTARIO

Tasty fruit rolls and chewy fruit snacks add a burst of flavor to these simple white cupcakes. Add them to kids' lunches for an afternoon treat.

PREP: 20 MIN. BAKE: 15 MIN. + COOLING

1 package (18-1/4 ounces) white cake mix
1-1/3 cups water
3 egg whites
2 tablespoons canola oil
3 strawberry Fruit Roll-Ups, unrolled
1 can (16 ounces) vanilla frosting
6 pouches strawberry Fruit Snacks

- In a large bowl, combine the cake mix, water, egg whites and oil. Beat on low speed for 30 seconds. Beat on medium for 2 minutes.
- Fill paper-lined muffin cups half full. Cut each fruit roll into eight pieces; place one piece over batter in each cup. Fill two-thirds full with remaining batter.
- Bake at 350° for 15-20 minutes or until a toothpick inserted near the center comes out clean. Cool for 10 minutes before removing from pans to wire racks to cool completely. Frost with vanilla frosting; decorate with fruit snacks. **Yield:** 2 dozen.

Editor's Note: This recipe was tested with Betty Crocker Fruit Roll-Ups and Nabisco Fruit Snacks.

pretzel-topped sugar cookies

MICHELLE BRENNEMAN | ORRVILLE, OHIO

It's tough to beat a three-ingredient sweet...especially one that's so easy! I rely on refrigerated cookie dough to make these munchable morsels, then dress up each cookie with a white fudge-covered pretzel and melted white chocolate.

PREP/TOTAL TIME: 30 MIN.

2 tubes (18 ounces *each*) refrigerated sugar cookie dough
2-1/2 cups vanilla *or* white chips, *divided*
1 package (7-1/2 ounces) white fudge-covered pretzels

- Crumble cookie dough into a large bowl; stir in 1-1/2 cups chips. Drop by tablespoonfuls 2 in. apart onto ungreased baking sheets.
- Bake at 325° for 15-18 minutes or until lightly browned. Immediately press a pretzel into the center of each cookie. Remove to wire racks to cool.
- In a microwave, heat remaining chips at 70% power for 30-40 seconds or until melted; stir until smooth. Drizzle over cookies. **Yield:** about 4-1/2 dozen.

Editor's Note: This recipe was tested with Nestle Flipz. This recipe was tested in a 1,100-watt microwave.

chocolate chip cheese bars

TERI LINDQUIST | GURNEE, ILLINOIS

This is my most requested dessert recipe. Everyone loves these yummy bars with their soft cream cheese filling...and the recipe couldn't be easier.

PREP: 15 MIN. BAKE: 35 MIN.

- 1 tube (18 ounces) refrigerated chocolate chip cookie dough
- 1 package (8 ounces) cream cheese, softened
- 1/2 cup sugar
- 1 egg

- Cut cookie dough in half. For crust, press half of the dough onto the bottom of a greased 8-in. square baking pan.
- In a large bowl, beat the cream cheese, sugar and egg until smooth. Spread over the crust. Crumble remaining dough over top.
- Bake at 350° for 35-40 minutes or until a toothpick inserted near the center comes out clean. Cool on a wire rack. Refrigerate leftovers. **Yield:** 12-16 servings.

Editor's Note: 2 cups of your favorite chocolate chip cookie dough can be substituted for the refrigerated dough.

peanut butter chocolate cups

ALJENE WENDLING | SEATTLE, WASHINGTON

Featuring the classic combination of chocolate and peanut butter, kids of all ages will love these rich, creamy candies.

PREP: 20 MIN. + CHILLING

- 1 milk chocolate candy bar (7 ounces)
- 1/4 cup butter
- 1 tablespoon shortening
- 1/4 cup creamy peanut butter

- In a microwave, melt the chocolate, butter and shortening; stir until smooth. Place foil or paper miniature baking cups in a miniature muffin tin. Place 1 tablespoon of chocolate mixture in each cup.
- In a microwave, melt peanut butter; stir until smooth. Spoon into cups. Top with remaining chocolate mixture. Refrigerate for 30 minutes or until firm. **Yield:** 1 dozen.

Editor's Note: This recipe was tested in a 1,100-watt microwave.

2 a.m. feeding snack bars

AME ANDREWS | LITTLE ROCK, ARKANSAS

I assured my friend that she didn't have to wait to try one of these scrumptious brownies until she got up in the middle of the night to feed the baby! But the chocolaty treats are a perfect pick-me-up (anytime) for new parents short on sleep and energy.

PREP: 10 MIN. BAKE: 25 MIN. + COOLING

- 1-1/3 cups all-purpose flour
- 1-1/4 cups sugar
- 1/2 cup baking cocoa
- 1 teaspoon baking powder
- 1/2 teaspoon salt
- 4 eggs, lightly beaten
- 3/4 cup butter, melted
- 1/2 cup *each* milk chocolate chips, semisweet chocolate chips and vanilla *or* white chips
- 3 Snickers candy bars (2.07 ounces *each*), cut into 1/4-inch pieces

- In a large bowl, combine the flour, sugar, cocoa, baking powder and salt. In a small bowl, combine the eggs and butter; add to the dry ingredients and mix well. Stir in the chips.
- Transfer to a greased 13-in. x 9-in. baking pan. Bake at 350° for 25-30 minutes or until a toothpick inserted near the center comes out clean. Immediately sprinkle with candy bar pieces. Cool on a wire rack. Cut into bars. **Yield:** 2 dozen.

snack bars

CAROLYN FISHER | KINZER, PENNSYLVANIA

If your family likes granola bars, they're sure to love these tempting treats. Full of hearty ingredients, they're a perfect snack for taking along on picnics and bike trips or for packing in brown bag lunches.

PREP: 20 MIN. + COOLING

- 9 cups Rice Chex, crushed
- 6 cups quick-cooking oats
- 1 cup graham cracker crumbs
- 1 cup flaked coconut
- 1/2 cup toasted wheat germ
- 2 packages (one 16 ounces, one 10-1/2 ounces) large marshmallows
- 1 cup butter, cubed
- 1/2 cup honey
- 1-1/2 cups raisins, M&M's miniature baking bits *or* miniature semisweet chocolate chips, optional

■ In a very large bowl, combine the first five ingredients. In a Dutch oven over low heat, cook and stir marshmallows and butter until the marshmallows are melted. Add honey and mix well.

■ Pour over the cereal mixture; stir until blended. Add the raisins, M&M's or chocolate chips if desired. Pat two-thirds into a greased 15-in. x 10-in. x 1-in. pan and the remaining third into a 9-in. square pan. Cool before cutting into bars. **Yield:** 5 dozen.

simple sugar cookies

MAXINE GUIN | BARNHART, MISSOURI

Powdered sugar takes the place of granulated sugar in this sweet standby. I received the recipe for this tasty cookie from a cook I worked with at our local school.

PREP: 15 MIN. + CHILLING BAKE: 10 MIN./BATCH

- 1 cup butter, softened
- 1-1/4 cups confectioners' sugar
- 1 egg
- 1 teaspoon vanilla extract
- 2 cups all-purpose flour
- 1 teaspoon baking soda
- 1 teaspoon cream of tartar
- 1/8 teaspoon salt

■ In a large bowl, cream butter and sugar until light and fluffy. Beat in egg and vanilla. Combine the flour, baking soda, cream of tartar and salt; gradually add to the creamed mixture. Shape into two 5-in. rolls; wrap in plastic wrap. Refrigerate for 1 hour or until firm.

■ Unwrap dough; cut into 1/4-in. slices. Place 2 in. apart on ungreased baking sheets. Bake at 350° for 8-10 minutes. Remove to wire racks to cool. **Yield:** 3-1/2 dozen.

black walnut brownies

CATHERINE BERRA BLEEM | WALSH, ILLINOIS

These brownies, studded with big chunks of black walnuts, are crisp on top and chewy on the inside. Our friends have given this treat rave reviews, especially those who live in areas where black walnuts are hard to come by.

PREP: 10 MIN. BAKE: 30 MIN. + COOLING

- 1 cup sugar
- 1/4 cup canola oil
- 2 eggs
- 1 teaspoon vanilla extract
- 1/2 cup all-purpose flour
- 2 tablespoons baking cocoa
- 1/2 teaspoon salt
- 1/2 cup chopped black walnuts

■ In a small bowl, beat sugar and oil until blended. Beat in eggs and vanilla. Combine the flour, cocoa and salt; gradually add to the sugar mixture and mix well. Stir in the walnuts.

■ Pour into a greased 8-in. square baking pan. Bake at 350° for 30-35 minutes or until a toothpick comes out clean. Cool on a wire rack. **Yield:** 16 servings.

cupcakes with whipped cream frosting

TASTE OF HOME TEST KITCHEN

While not as sweet as buttercream, this frosting made with whipping cream is smooth, creamy and a pleasure to pipe onto cupcakes.

PREP: 25 MIN. BAKE: 15 MIN.

- 1 package (18-1/4 ounces) white cake mix
- 1-1/4 teaspoons unflavored gelatin
- 5 teaspoons cold water
- 1-1/4 cups heavy whipping cream
- 5 tablespoons confectioners' sugar
- 1/4 teaspoon vanilla extract
- Red and yellow food coloring

- Prepare and bake cake mix according to package directions for cupcakes. Cool on wire racks.
- In a small saucepan, sprinkle gelatin over water; let stand for 1 minute to soften. Heat over low heat, stirring until gelatin is completely dissolved. Remove from the heat; cool.
- In a large bowl, beat cream until it begins to thicken. Add sugar, vanilla and gelatin mixture; beat until soft peaks form. Set aside 1 cup for decorating.
- Spread remaining frosting over tops of cupcakes. Divide reserved frosting in half; tint one portion pink and the other yellow.
- Use a toothpick to outline shape of heart, flower or sunburst on tops of cupcakes. Use medium star tip to pipe pink or yellow stars along outline. Fill in shape with piped stars as desired. **Yield:** 2 dozen.

angel macaroons

RENEE SCHWEBACH | DUMONT, MINNESOTA

These chewy coconut cookies start with a boxed angel food cake mix so it's a cinch to whip them up on a moment's notice.

PREP: 5 MIN. BAKE: 10 MIN./BATCH + COOLING

- 1 package (16 ounces) angel food cake mix
- 1/2 cup water
- 1-1/2 teaspoons almond extract
- 2 cups flaked coconut

- In a large bowl, beat the cake mix, water and extract on low speed for 30 seconds. Scrape bowl; beat on medium speed for 1 minute. Fold in the coconut.
- Drop by rounded teaspoonfuls 2 in. apart onto a parchment paper-lined baking sheet. Bake at 350° for 10-12 minutes or until lightly browned. Remove paper with cookies to wire racks to cool. **Yield:** 5 dozen.

Parchment Paper

There is no right or wrong side to parchment paper, so either side can be used. For the best baking results, use a fresh sheet of parchment paper for each pan of cookies.

mini brownie treats

PAM KOKES | NORTH LOUP, NEBRASKA

I like to take these quick-and-easy treats to potlucks and family gatherings. They disappear quickly!

PREP: 15 MIN. BAKE: 20 MIN. + COOLING

- 1 package fudge brownie mix (13-inch x 9-inch pan size)
- 48 striped chocolate kisses

■ Prepare brownie mix according to package directions for fudge-like brownies. Fill paper-lined miniature muffin cups two-thirds full.

■ Bake at 350° for 18-21 minutes or until a toothpick inserted near the center comes out clean.

■ Immediately top each with a chocolate kiss. Cool for 10 minutes before removing from pans to wire racks to cool completely. **Yield:** 4 dozen.

strawberry cookies

NANCY SHELTON | BOAZ, KENTUCKY

My family finds these fruity cookies to be a light treat in summer. I sometimes use lemon cake mix in place of the strawberry.

PREP/TOTAL TIME: 30 MIN.

- 1 package (18-1/4 ounces) strawberry cake mix
- 1 egg, lightly beaten
- 1 carton (8 ounces) frozen whipped topping, thawed
- 2 cups confectioners' sugar

■ In a large bowl, combine the cake mix, egg and whipped topping until well combined. Place confectioners' sugar in a shallow dish.

■ Drop dough by tablespoonfuls into sugar; turn to coat. Place 2 in. apart on greased baking sheets.

■ Bake at 350° for 10-12 minutes or until lightly browned around the edges. Remove to wire racks to cool. **Yield:** about 5 dozen.

salted peanut chews

IRENE YODER | MILLERSBURG, OHIO

I took these great treats to an evening reunion. They disappeared fast, and soon people were asking for the recipe.

PREP: 25 MIN. BAKE: 15 MIN.

1-1/2 cups all-purpose flour
1/2 cup packed brown sugar
3/4 cup butter, softened, *divided*
3 cups miniature marshmallows
2 cups peanut butter chips
2/3 cup corn syrup
2 teaspoons vanilla extract
2 cups crisp rice cereal
2 cups salted peanuts

- In a large bowl, combine the flour, brown sugar and 1/2 cup of the butter. Press into an ungreased 13-in. x 9-in. baking pan. Bake at 350° for 12-15 minutes or until lightly browned.
- Sprinkle with marshmallows and return to the oven for 3-5 minutes or until marshmallows begin to melt; set aside.
- In a large saucepan, cook and stir the peanut butter chips, corn syrup, vanilla and remaining butter until smooth. Remove from the heat; stir in cereal and peanuts. Pour over prepared crust, spreading to cover. Cool on a wire rack before cutting into bars. **Yield:** 2 dozen.

no-fuss peanut butter cookies

MARY BROWNING | NORTH OGDEN, UTAH

This recipe is easy to make and yields a big batch of yummy, golden cookies. It's hard to resist that sweet peanut butter flavor. Kids of all ages find these cookies a favorite.

PREP/TOTAL TIME: 30 MIN.

1 cup peanut butter
1/4 cup butter-flavored shortening
1/2 cup sugar
1/2 cup packed brown sugar
1/3 cup boiling water
2 cups biscuit/baking mix
Additional sugar

- In a large bowl, cream peanut butter, shortening and sugars. Beat in water. Gradually add dry biscuit mix.
- Roll dough into 1-in. balls. Place 2 in. apart on greased baking sheets. Flatten with a fork dipped in sugar, forming a criss-cross pattern. Bake at 400° for 9-11 minutes or until edges are golden brown. **Yield:** 4-1/2 dozen.

Editor's Note: Reduced-fat or generic brands of peanut butter are not recommended for this recipe.

layered mint candies

RHONDA VAUBLE | SAC CITY, IOWA

These incredible, melt-in-your-mouth candies have the perfect amount of mint nestled between layers of mild chocolate. Even when I make a double batch for everyone to enjoy, the supply never lasts long!

PREP: 15 MIN. + CHILLING

1 tablespoon butter
1-1/2 pounds white candy coating, coarsely chopped, *divided*
1 cup (6 ounces) semisweet chocolate chips
1 teaspoon peppermint extract
4 drops green food coloring, optional
3 tablespoons heavy whipping cream

- Line a 13-in. x 9-in. pan with foil. Grease the foil with 1 tablespoon butter; set aside.
- In a microwave, melt 1 pound candy coating and chocolate chips; stir until smooth. Spread half into prepared pan; set remaining mixture aside.
- Melt remaining candy coating; stir in extract and food coloring if desired. Stir in cream until smooth (mixture will be stiff). Spread over first layer; refrigerate for 10 minutes or until firm.
- Warm reserved chocolate mixture if necessary; spread over mint layer. Refrigerate for 1 hour or until firm.
- Lift out of the pan with foil and remove the foil. Cut into 1-in. squares. Store in an airtight container in the refrigerator. **Yield:** about 2 pounds (about 9-1/2 dozen).

macaroon bars

CAROLYN KYZER | ALEXANDER, ARKANSAS

Guests will never recognize the refrigerated crescent roll dough that goes into these almond-flavored bars. You can assemble these chewy coconut treats in no time.

PREP: 10 MIN. BAKE: 30 MIN.

- 3-1/4 cups flaked coconut, *divided*
- 1 can (14 ounces) sweetened condensed milk
- 1 teaspoon almond extract
- 1 tube (8 ounces) refrigerated crescent rolls

■ Sprinkle 1-1/2 cups coconut into a well-greased 13-in. x 9-in. baking pan. Combine milk and extract; drizzle half over the coconut. Unroll crescent dough; arrange in a single layer over coconut. Drizzle with remaining milk mixture; sprinkle with remaining coconut.

■ Bake at 350° for 30-35 minutes or until golden brown. Cool completely on a wire rack before cutting. Store in the refrigerator. **Yield:** 3 dozen.

cream cheese brownies

CAROLYN REED | NORTH ROBINSON, OHIO

A friend from church shared this recipe with me. Cream cheese lends itself to a moist and chewy bar that's finger-lickin' good!

PREP: 20 MIN. BAKE: 35 MIN. + COOLING

- 2 packages (8 ounces *each*) cream cheese, softened
- 2 cups sugar, *divided*
- 3 tablespoons milk
- 1 cup butter, softened
- 2/3 cup instant hot cocoa mix
- 4 eggs
- 2 teaspoons vanilla extract
- 1-1/2 cups all-purpose flour
- 1 cup chopped nuts

■ In a small bowl, beat the cream cheese, 1/2 cup sugar and milk until fluffy; set aside. In a large bowl, cream the butter, cocoa mix and remaining sugar until light and fluffy. Beat in eggs and vanilla. Stir in the flour and nuts; mix well.

■ Pour half into a greased 13-in. x 9-in. baking pan. Spread with the cream cheese mixture. Top with remaining batter. Cut through batter with a knife to swirl the cream cheese.

■ Bake at 350° for 35-40 minutes or until a toothpick inserted near the center comes out clean. Cool on a wire rack. Cut into bars. **Yield:** 2-1/2 dozen.

Editor's Note: This recipe was tested with Swiss Miss instant cocoa.

no-bake peanut brownies

CONNIE WARD | MT. PLEASANT, IOWA

Chopped peanuts add a delightful flavor to these no-fuss brownies. I like the fact that you can prepare the treats without heating up the oven.

PREP: 25 MIN. + CHILLING

- 4 cups graham cracker crumbs
- 1 cup chopped peanuts
- 1/2 cup confectioners' sugar
- 1/4 cup peanut butter
- 2 cups (12 ounces) semisweet chocolate chips
- 1 cup evaporated milk
- 1 teaspoon vanilla extract

■ In a large bowl, combine the crumbs, peanuts, sugar and peanut butter until crumbly. In a small saucepan, melt the chocolate chips and milk over low heat, stirring constantly until smooth. Remove from the heat; add vanilla. Set aside 1/2 cup.

■ Pour remaining chocolate mixture over crumb mixture and stir until well blended. Spread evenly in a greased 9-in. square dish. Frost with the reserved chocolate mixture. Cover and refrigerate for 1 hour. **Yield:** 2-1/2 dozen.

chocolate chip blondies

RHONDA KNIGHT | HECKER, ILLINOIS

Folks who love chocolate chip cookies will enjoy that same great flavor in these golden bars that can be mixed up in a jiffy and taste wonderful. They're perfect for occasions when company drops by unexpectedly or you need a treat in a hurry.

PREP: 10 MIN. BAKE: 20 MIN. + COOLING

- 1-1/2 cups packed brown sugar
- 1/2 cup butter, melted
- 2 eggs, lightly beaten
- 1 teaspoon vanilla extract
- 1-1/2 cups all-purpose flour
- 1/2 teaspoon baking powder
- 1/2 teaspoon salt
- 1 cup (6 ounces) semisweet chocolate chips

- In a large bowl, combine the brown sugar, butter, eggs and vanilla just until blended. Combine the flour, baking powder and salt; add to brown sugar mixture. Stir in chocolate chips.
- Spread into a greased 13-in. x 9-in. baking pan. Bake at 350° for 18-20 minutes or until a toothpick inserted near the center comes out clean. Cool on a wire rack. Cut into bars. **Yield:** 3 dozen.

Freezing Bars

Chocolate Chip Blondies freeze well for fast, anytime snacks. Bake and cool as directed; cut into bars. Wrap individually in waxed paper; then freeze in a heavy-duty resealable plastic bag.

quick chocolate sandwich cookies

MARY REMPEL | ALTONA, MANITOBA

These cookies freeze well, so it's easy to keep some on hand for last-minute munching. In summer, I often make them larger to use for ice cream sandwiches.

PREP: 15 MIN. BAKE: 10 MIN./BATCH + COOLING

- 2 packages (18-1/4 ounces *each*) devil's food cake mix
- 1 cup canola oil
- 4 eggs

FILLING:

- 1 package (8 ounces) cream cheese, softened
- 1/4 cup butter, softened
- 2-1/2 cups confectioners' sugar
- 1 teaspoon vanilla extract

■ In a large bowl, combine the cake mixes, oil and eggs until well blended. Roll into 1-in. balls. Place 2 in. apart on ungreased baking sheets. Do not flatten.

■ Bake at 350° for 8-10 minutes or until set. Cool for 5 minutes before removing to wire racks (cookies will flatten as they cool).

■ In a small bowl, beat cream cheese and butter until fluffy. Beat in sugar and vanilla until smooth. Spread on the bottom of half of the cookies; top with remaining cookies. Store in the refrigerator. **Yield:** about 6 dozen.

couldn't be simpler bars

KERRY BOUCHARD | AUGUSTA, MONTANA

Every time I take these sweet bars to a gathering or serve them to guests, I get lots of compliments. They're easy to make, too—just sprinkle a few ingredients in a pan and bake.

PREP: 10 MIN. BAKE: 25 MIN. + COOLING

- 1/2 cup butter, melted
- 1 cup graham cracker crumbs (about 16 squares)
- 1 cup flaked coconut
- 1 cup (6 ounces) semisweet chocolate chips
- 1 cup butterscotch chips
- 1 can (14 ounces) sweetened condensed milk
- 1 cup chopped walnuts

■ Pour butter into a greased 13-in. x 9-in. baking pan. Sprinkle with crumbs and coconut. Top with chips. Pour milk over all. Sprinkle with walnuts.

■ Bake at 350° for 23-28 minutes or until browned and bubbly. Cool completely on a wire rack before cutting. **Yield:** about 3-1/2 dozen.

no-bake bars

SUSIE WINGERT | PANAMA, IOWA

These chewy treats are big on taste but need only a little effort. They are handy to make when the weather is hot, since the oven never has to be turned on.

PREP/TOTAL TIME: 20 MIN.

- 4 cups Cheerios
- 2 cups crisp rice cereal
- 2 cups dry roasted peanuts
- 2 cups M&M's
- 1 cup light corn syrup
- 1 cup sugar
- 1-1/2 cups creamy peanut butter
- 1 teaspoon vanilla extract

■ In a large bowl, combine the first four ingredients; set aside. In a large saucepan, bring corn syrup and sugar to a boil. Cook and stir just until sugar is dissolved.

■ Remove from the heat; stir in peanut butter and vanilla. Pour over cereal mixture; toss to coat evenly. Spread into a greased 15-in. x 10-in. x 1-in. pan. Cool. Cut into 3-in. squares. **Yield:** 15 bars.

beary good snack mix

DORIS WEDIGE | ELKHORN, WISCONSIN

My family loves to hike and be outdoors so we take this snack mix along to munch on whenever we need a boost of energy.

PREP/TOTAL TIME: 10 MIN.

- 1 package (10 ounces) honey bear-shaped crackers (about 4 cups)
- 1 package (7 ounces) dried banana chips (about 2 cups)
- 2 cups M&M's
- 1 cup salted peanuts
- 1 cup dried cranberries

■ In a large bowl, combine all the ingredients. Store in an airtight container. **Yield:** 10 cups.

Sticky Situation

When measuring a sticky substance like corn syrup and honey, first spray the measuring cup. The corn syrup and honey will pour right out with little left in the cup.

double chocolate bars

NANCY CLARK | ZEIGLER, ILLINOIS

A friend brought these fudgy bars a few years ago to tempt me with yet another chocolate treat. They are simple to make...and cleanup is a breeze! They're very rich, though, so be sure to cut them into bite-size pieces.

PREP/TOTAL TIME: 20 MIN.

- 1 package (16 ounces) cream-filled chocolate sandwich cookies, crushed
- 3/4 cup butter, melted
- 1 can (14 ounces) sweetened condensed milk
- 2 cups (12 ounces) miniature semisweet chocolate chips, *divided*

■ Combine cookie crumbs and butter; pat onto the bottom of an ungreased 13-in. x 9-in. baking pan.

■ In a microwave, melt milk and 1 cup chocolate chips; stir until smooth. Pour over the crust. Sprinkle with the remaining chips.

■ Bake at 350° for 10-12 minutes or until chips begin to melt but do not lose their shape. Cool on a wire rack. **Yield:** about 4 dozen.

chocolate oat scotchies

STEPHANIE HELMKE | DEFIANCE, OHIO

My mom found this recipe a long time ago, and it was a hit with our family. Each bite is packed with chocolate, butterscotch and peanut flavors.

PREP: 20 MIN. BAKE: 15 MIN.

- 2/3 cup butter, cubed
- 1 cup packed brown sugar
- 1/4 cup corn syrup
- 1/4 cup plus 2/3 cup chunky peanut butter, *divided*
- 1 teaspoon vanilla extract
- 4 cups quick-cooking oats
- 1 package (11-1/2 ounces) milk chocolate chips
- 1/2 cup butterscotch chips
- 1 cup salted peanuts

■ In a large saucepan over low heat, melt the butter; stir in brown sugar and corn syrup until the sugar is dissolved. Stir in 1/4 cup peanut butter and vanilla until blended. Add the oats.

■ Press into a greased 13-in. x 9-in. baking pan. Bake at 375° for 12-15 minutes. Meanwhile, in a microwave oven, melt chips and remaining peanut butter; stir until smooth. Stir in peanuts. Spread over crust. Refrigerate until cool; cut into bars. **Yield:** 6-1/2 dozen.

Editor's Note: Reduced-fat or generic brands of peanut butter are not recommended for this recipe.

raspberry swirl cupcakes

CHRISTINE SOHM | NEWTON, ONTARIO

I grew up on a farm and have always enjoyed baking up sweet treats of every kind. These cupcakes are a favorite of mine.

PREP: 20 MIN. BAKE: 20 MIN.

1 package (18-1/4 ounces) white cake mix
1/4 cup raspberry pie filling
1/2 cup shortening
1/3 cup milk
1 teaspoon vanilla extract
1/4 teaspoon salt
3 cups confectioners' sugar
Fresh raspberries and mint, optional

- Prepare and bake the cake mix according to package directions. Fill paper-lined muffin cups two-thirds full. Drop 1/2 teaspoon of pie filling in the center of each; cut through batter with a knife to swirl.
- Bake at 350° for 20-25 minutes or until a toothpick inserted near the center comes out clean. Cool for 10 minutes before removing from pans to wire racks to cool completely.
- In a large bowl, beat shortening until fluffy. Add the milk, vanilla, salt and confectioners' sugar; beat until smooth. Frost cupcakes. Garnish with raspberries and mint if desired. **Yield:** about 1-1/2 dozen.

chocolate chip butter cookies

JANIS GRUCA | MOKENA, ILLINOIS

At the downtown Chicago law firm where I work, we often bring in goodies for special occasions. When co-workers hear I've baked these melt-in-your-mouth cookies, they make a special trip to my floor to sample them. Best of all, these crisp, buttery treats can be made in no time.

PREP/TOTAL TIME: 30 MIN.

1 cup butter, cubed
1/2 teaspoon vanilla extract
2 cups all-purpose flour
1 cup confectioners' sugar
1 cup (6 ounces) miniature semisweet chocolate chips

- Melt butter in a microwave or double boiler; stir in vanilla. Cool completely. In a large bowl, combine flour and sugar; stir in the butter mixture and chocolate chips (the mixture will be crumbly).
- Shape into 1-in. balls. Place 2 in. apart on ungreased baking sheets; flatten slightly. Bake at 375° for 12 minutes or until edges begin to brown. Cool on wire racks. **Yield:** about 4 dozen.

popcorn snacks

VICKI THEIS | SHAKOPPE, MINNESOTA

We always had popcorn balls at Christmastime when I was growing up. A couple years ago, my mother gave me this recipe for an updated version.

PREP: 20 MIN. + STANDING

1 package (16 ounces) miniature marshmallows
1/2 cup butter, cubed
1/2 cup canola oil
1 teaspoon vanilla extract
1/2 teaspoon salt
6 quarts popped popcorn
1 package (16 ounces) milk chocolate M&M's
1 jar (16 ounces) dry roasted peanuts

- In a large saucepan over medium heat, cook and stir the marshmallows, butter and oil until the marshmallows are melted. Remove from the heat; stir in vanilla and salt.
- In a very large bowl, combine the popcorn, M&M's and peanuts. Pour marshmallow mixture over popcorn and mix well. Press into two greased 13-in. x 9-in. pans. Let stand for 2 hours or until set. Cut into bars and remove from pans. Store in an airtight container. **Yield:** 9 dozen.

Creative Kisses

You can find chocolate kisses in a variety of flavors, such as dark chocolate and nut, caramel or chocolate filled. Use an assortment when making Chocolate Pretzel Rings.

chocolate pretzel rings

KIM SCURIO | CAROL STREAM, ILLINOIS

These salty-sweet treats will be an instant hit with kids and adults alike. You'll find it hard to eat just one, so make plenty of extras!

PREP/TOTAL TIME: 30 MIN.

- 48 to 50 pretzel rings *or* miniature pretzels
- 48 to 50 milk chocolate *or* striped chocolate kisses
- 1/4 cup milk chocolate M&M's

- Place the pretzels on greased baking sheets; place a chocolate kiss in the center of each ring. Bake at 275° for 2-3 minutes or until chocolate is softened. Remove from the oven.
- Place an M&M's candy on each, pressing down slightly so chocolate fills the ring. Refrigerate for 5-10 minutes or until chocolate is firm. Store in an airtight container at room temperature. **Yield:** about 4 dozen.

snickers cookies

KARI PEASE | CONCONULLY, WASHINGTON

A sweet surprise is inside these two-ingredient cookies. It's a great way to dress up refrigerated cookie dough.

PREP/TOTAL TIME: 30 MIN.

- 1 tube (18 ounces) refrigerated chocolate chip cookie dough
- 24 to 30 miniature Snickers candy bars

- Cut dough into 1/4-in.-thick slices. Place a candy bar on each slice and wrap dough around it. Place 2 in. apart on ungreased baking sheets. Bake at 350° for 8-10 minutes or until lightly browned. Remove to wire racks to cool. **Yield:** 2 to 2-1/2 dozen.

Editor's Note: 2 cups of any chocolate chip cookie dough can be substituted for the refrigerated dough. Use 1 tablespoon of dough for each cookie.

chocolaty popcorn

DIANE HALFERTY | CORPUS CHRISTI, TEXAS

Bagged in individual servings, this is a great treat for a bake sale.

PREP: 15 MIN. + CHILLING

- 12 cups butter-flavored microwave popcorn
- 1 package (12 ounces) semisweet chocolate chips
- 2 teaspoons shortening, *divided*
- 1 package (10 to 12 ounces) vanilla *or* white chips
- 2 cups coarsely chopped pecans, toasted

■ Place the popcorn in a greased 15-in. x 10-in. x 1-in. pan; set aside. Melt chocolate chips and 1 teaspoon shortening; stir until smooth. Drizzle over popcorn.

■ Place vanilla chips and remaining shortening in a microwave-safe bowl. Microwave, uncovered, at 70% power for 1 minute; stir. Microwave at additional 10- to 20-second intervals, stirring until smooth. Drizzle over popcorn; toss gently to coat. Sprinkle with pecans. Chill until firm before breaking into pieces. **Yield:** 16 cups.

Editor's Note: This recipe was tested in a 1,100-watt microwave.

quick brownies

MRS. ED FITCH | CLIFTON, ARIZONA

These moist brownies get a head start from a convenient chocolate cake mix. Peanut butter chips add fun flavor.

PREP: 10 MIN. BAKE: 35 MIN.

- 1 package (18-1/4 ounces) chocolate cake mix
- 1/2 cup butter, melted
- 1/2 cup vegetable oil
- 2 eggs
- 1 cup peanut butter chips

■ In a large bowl, beat the first four ingredients until blended. Stir in chips.

■ Pour into a greased 11-in. x 7-in. baking pan. Bake at 350° for 35-40 minutes or until a toothpick comes out clean. Cool on a wire rack. **Yield:** 18 servings.

p. 366

slow cookers, microwaves & grills

fruit-glazed pork chops

EDIE DESPAIN | LOGAN, UTAH

Here's a fast and simple way to grill chops. Your meal can be ready in half an hour, and other fruit preserves can be easily substituted. They're also nice broiled in the oven.

PREP/TOTAL TIME: 30 MIN.

- 1/3 cup hickory smoke-flavored barbecue sauce
- 1/2 cup apricot *or* peach preserves
- 1 tablespoon corn syrup
- 1 teaspoon prepared mustard
- 1/4 teaspoon ground cloves
- 6 bone-in pork loin chops (3/4 inch thick and 8 ounces *each*)
- 1/2 teaspoon salt
- 1/2 teaspoon pepper

- In a small bowl, combine the barbecue sauce, preserves, corn syrup, mustard and cloves; set aside.
- Coat grill rack with cooking spray before starting the grill. Sprinkle pork chops with salt and pepper. Grill, covered, over medium heat for 6-8 minutes on each side or until a meat thermometer reads 160°, basting frequently with sauce mixture. **Yield:** 6 servings.

Great Grilling Tips

To ensure grilled foods are evenly cooked, bring foods to a cool room temperature before putting on the grill. Don't crowd the foods on the grill...allow some space around each piece.

creamy ham & potatoes

WENDY ROWLEY | GREEN RIVER, WYOMING

If you love scalloped potatoes, this cozy, comforting version with tender chunks of ham is just for you.

PREP: 20 MIN. COOK: 5 HOURS

- 2 large red potatoes, cubed
- 1/3 cup cubed process cheese (Velveeta)
- 3/4 cup cubed fully cooked ham
- 1 tablespoon dried minced onion
- 2/3 cup condensed cream of celery soup, undiluted
- 2/3 cup 2% milk
- 1 tablespoon all-purpose flour
- 1/4 teaspoon pepper

■ In a 1-1/2-qt. slow cooker coated with cooking spray, layer the potatoes, cheese, ham and onion. In a small bowl, combine soup and milk; whisk in flour and pepper. Pour over potatoes. Cover and cook on low for 5-6 hours or until potatoes are tender. Stir before serving. **Yield:** 2 servings.

cheese and chicken enchiladas

CHRISTINE TAYLOR | GREENFIELD, WISCONSIN

This Southwestern favorite relies on the microwave to make quick work out of dinner. Easy and mild, they're perfect for the whole family.

PREP/TOTAL TIME: 20 MIN.

- 1/2 cup chopped onion
- 1/2 teaspoon minced garlic
- 1 package (9 ounces) frozen diced cooked chicken breast, thawed and chopped
- 4 ounces cream cheese, cubed
- 1 can (4 ounces) chopped green chilies
- 1/4 cup chicken broth
- 2 teaspoons chili powder
- 1/2 teaspoon ground cumin
- 6 flour tortillas (8 inches), warmed
- 4 ounces process cheese (Velveeta), cubed
- 1/2 cup diced fresh tomato, *divided*
- 2 tablespoons milk

■ In a large microwave-safe bowl, combine onion and garlic. Cover and microwave on high for 30-60 seconds or until onion is tender, stirring twice. Stir in the chicken, cream cheese, green chilies, broth, chili powder and cumin. Cover and microwave on high for 45-90 seconds or until cream cheese is melted, stirring twice.

■ Spoon about 1/3 cup down the center of each tortilla. Roll up and place seam side down in an ungreased microwave-safe 8-in. square dish.

■ In a microwave-safe bowl, combine the process cheese, 1/4 cup tomato and milk. Microwave, uncovered, on high for 30-60 seconds or until cheese is melted, stirring twice; drizzle over enchiladas. Top with remaining tomato. Microwave enchiladas, uncovered, on high for 45-90 seconds or until heated through. **Yield:** 3 servings.

Editor's Note: This recipe was tested in a 1,100-watt microwave.

mustard turkey cutlets

DEBORAH WILLIAMS | PEORIA, ARIZONA

Grilled turkey cutlets are treated with a slightly sweet sauce that mustard-lovers will thoroughly enjoy. This recipe feels fancy, but it's ideal for a weeknight.

PREP/TOTAL TIME: 25 MIN.

- 2 teaspoons cornstarch
- 1/2 teaspoon salt, *divided*
- 1/8 teaspoon plus 1/4 teaspoon pepper, *divided*
- 1/2 cup thawed apple juice concentrate
- 1/4 cup Dijon mustard
- 1-1/2 tablespoons minced fresh rosemary *or* 1-1/2 teaspoons dried rosemary, crushed
- 1 package (17.6 ounces) turkey breast cutlets
- 1 teaspoon olive oil

■ In a small saucepan, combine the cornstarch, 1/4 teaspoon salt and 1/8 teaspoon pepper. Gradually whisk in the concentrate, mustard and rosemary until blended. Cook and stir over medium-high heat until thickened and bubbly. Reduce heat; cook and stir 2 minutes longer. Set aside 1/4 cup sauce.

■ Coat grill rack with cooking spray before starting the grill. Brush turkey with oil; sprinkle with remaining salt and pepper. Grill, covered, over medium heat for 2-3 minutes on each side or until no longer pink, basting occasionally with remaining sauce. Brush with reserved sauce before serving. **Yield:** 4 servings.

cider-glazed ham

JENNIFER FOOS-FURER | MARYSVILLE, OHIO

We raise our own pork so I'm always looking for new ways to serve it that'll warm up everyone at the end of a long day. This dinner wins the hearts of all.

PREP: 15 MIN. COOK: 4 HOURS

- 1 boneless fully cooked ham (3 pounds)
- 1-3/4 cups apple cider *or* juice
- 1/4 cup packed brown sugar
- 1/4 cup Dijon mustard
- 1/4 cup honey
- 2 tablespoons cornstarch
- 2 tablespoons cold water

■ Place ham in a 5-qt. slow cooker. In a small bowl, combine the cider, brown sugar, mustard and honey; pour over ham. Cover and cook on low for 4-5 hours or until a meat thermometer reads 140°. Remove ham and keep warm.

■ Pour cooking juices into a small saucepan. Combine cornstarch and water until smooth; stir into cooking juices. Bring to a boil; cook and stir for 2 minutes or until thickened. Serve with ham. **Yield:** 8 servings.

pork chops & acorn squash

MARY JOHNSON | COLOMA, WISCONSIN

My husband and I can never get enough fresh buttery squash from our garden. These chops cook up sweet and tender in the slow cooker, and the classic, comfort-food flavor doesn't take up my whole day to prepare.

PREP: 15 MIN. COOK: 4 HOURS

- 6 boneless pork loin chops (4 ounces *each*)
- 2 medium acorn squash, peeled and cubed
- 1/2 cup packed brown sugar
- 2 tablespoons butter, melted
- 1 tablespoon orange juice
- 3/4 teaspoon salt
- 1/2 teaspoon grated orange peel
- 3/4 teaspoon browning sauce, optional

■ Place pork chops in a 5-qt. slow cooker; add the squash. Combine the brown sugar, butter, orange juice, salt, orange peel and browning sauce if desired; pour over squash.

■ Cover and cook on low for 4 hours or until meat and squash are tender. **Yield:** 6 servings.

slow-cooked southwest chicken

BRANDI CASTILLO | SANTA MARIA, CALIFORNIA

With just 15 minutes of prep, you'll be out of the kitchen in no time. This deliciously low-fat dish gets even better served with reduced-fat sour cream and chopped cilantro.

PREP: 15 MIN. COOK: 6 HOURS

- 2 cans (15 ounces *each*) black beans, rinsed and drained
- 1 can (14-1/2 ounces) reduced-sodium chicken broth
- 1 can (14-1/2 ounces) diced tomatoes with mild green chilies, undrained
- 1/2 pound boneless skinless chicken breasts
- 1 jar (8 ounces) chunky salsa
- 1 cup frozen corn
- 1 tablespoon dried parsley flakes
- 1 teaspoon ground cumin
- 1/4 teaspoon pepper
- 3 cups hot cooked rice

■ In a 2- or 3-qt. slow cooker, combine the beans, broth, tomatoes, chicken, salsa, corn and seasonings. Cover and cook on low for 6-8 hours or until chicken shreds easily with two forks.

■ Shred chicken and return to the slow cooker; heat through. Serve with rice. **Yield:** 6 servings.

pacific rim salmon

AMY SAUSER | OMAHA, NEBRASKA

I came across this recipe in a local fundraiser cookbook. I made some slight adjustments to it since then, but it is a great recipe to use when grilling. It's a favorite summer meal.

PREP: 15 MIN. + MARINATING GRILL: 15 MIN.

- 1/2 cup unsweetened pineapple juice
- 1/4 cup soy sauce
- 2 tablespoons prepared horseradish
- 2 tablespoons minced fresh parsley
- 5 teaspoons sesame oil, *divided*
- 2 teaspoons honey
- 1/2 teaspoon coarsely ground pepper
- 8 salmon fillets (6 ounces *each*)
- 5 green onions, coarsely chopped

■ In a small bowl, combine the pineapple juice, soy sauce, horseradish, parsley, 3 teaspoons sesame oil, honey and pepper. Pour 2/3 cup marinade into a large resealable plastic bag; add the salmon and green onions. Seal bag and turn to coat; refrigerate for 1 to 1-1/2 hours, turning occasionally. Add remaining sesame oil to remaining marinade. Cover and refrigerate for basting.

■ Coat grill rack with cooking spray before starting the grill. Drain and discard marinade. Grill salmon, covered, over medium heat or broil 4-6 in. from the heat for 8-12 minutes or until fish flakes easily with a fork, basting frequently with reserved marinade. **Yield:** 8 servings.

pot roast with gravy

DEBORAH DAILEY | VANCOUVER, WASHINGTON

My family loves this tangy, slow-cooked beef roast with gravy. We always hope to have some leftovers that I can turn into hearty sandwiches.

PREP: 30 MIN. COOK: 7-1/2 HOURS

- 1 beef rump roast *or* bottom round roast (5 pounds)
- 6 tablespoons balsamic vinegar, *divided*
- 1 teaspoon salt
- 1/2 teaspoon garlic powder
- 1/4 teaspoon pepper
- 2 tablespoons canola oil
- 3 garlic cloves, minced
- 4 bay leaves
- 1 large onion, thinly sliced
- 3 teaspoons beef bouillon granules
- 1/2 cup boiling water
- 1 can (10-3/4 ounces) condensed cream of mushroom soup, undiluted
- 4 to 5 tablespoons cornstarch
- 1/4 cup cold water

■ Cut roast in half; rub with 2 tablespoons vinegar. Combine the salt, garlic powder and pepper; rub over meat. In a

large skillet, brown roast in oil on all sides. Transfer to a 5-qt. slow cooker.

■ Place the garlic, bay leaves and onion on roast. In a small bowl, dissolve bouillon in boiling water; stir in soup and remaining vinegar. Slowly pour over roast. Cover and cook on low for 7-8 hours or until meat is tender.

■ Remove roast; keep warm. Discard bay leaves. Whisk cornstarch and cold water until smooth; stir into cooking juices. Cover and cook on high for 30 minutes or until gravy is thickened. Slice roast; return to slow cooker and heat through. **Yield:** 10 servings.

chicken athena

RADELLE KNAPPENBERGER | OVIEDO, FLORIDA

Greek flavors abound in this tasty and tender chicken dish that's made in the slow cooker. Olives, sun-dried tomatoes, lemon juice and balsamic vinegar combine with chicken for a special treat any night of the week.

PREP: 15 MIN. COOK: 4 HOURS

- 6 boneless skinless chicken breast halves (6 ounces *each*)
- 2 medium onions, chopped
- 1/3 cup sun-dried tomatoes (not packed in oil), chopped
- 1/3 cup pitted Greek olives, chopped
- 2 tablespoons lemon juice
- 1 tablespoon balsamic vinegar
- 3 garlic cloves, minced
- 1/2 teaspoon salt

■ Place chicken in a 3-qt. slow cooker. Add the remaining ingredients. Cover and cook on low for 4 hours or until a meat thermometer reads 170°. **Yield:** 6 servings.

Microwave Wattage

If your microwave is higher than 1,100 watts, adjust the cooking time to about two-thirds of what's called for and follow the recipe's doneness test.

southwest chicken and rice

PENNY HAWKINS | MEBANE, NORTH CAROLINA

With brown rice, whole grains, tomatoes and corn, this meal is a tasty way to get your family to eat more fiber.

PREP/TOTAL TIME: 10 MIN.

- 2 packages (8-1/2 ounces *each*) ready-to-serve Santa Fe whole grain rice medley
- 2 packages (6 ounces *each*) ready-to-use Southwestern chicken strips, cut into chunks
- 1 can (10 ounces) diced tomatoes and green chilies, drained
- 1/2 cup shredded Monterey Jack cheese

■ Heat rice according to the package directions. In a 2-qt. microwave-safe dish, combine chicken and tomatoes; stir in rice. Cover and microwave on high for 2-3 minutes. Sprinkle with cheese; cook 1 minute longer or until cheese is melted. **Yield:** 4 servings.

Editor's Note: This recipe was tested in a 1,100-watt microwave.

all-american loaded burgers

MARSHA URSO | PITTSBURGH, PENNSYLVANIA

I found this recipe almost 8 years ago and tried it for my daughter's first birthday party. I got so many compliments, I don't make burgers any other way now!

PREP/TOTAL TIME: 25 MIN.

- 1 cup dry bread crumbs
- 1/2 cup finely chopped onion
- 1/2 cup Italian salad dressing
- 2 eggs, lightly beaten
- 2 pounds ground beef
- 6 kaiser rolls, split

Leaf lettuce, Colby cheese slices, tomato slices, ketchup, prepared mustard *and/or* french-fried onions, optional

■ In a large bowl, combine the bread crumbs, onion, salad dressing and eggs. Crumble beef over mixture and mix well. Shape into six patties.

■ Grill burgers, covered, over medium heat or broil 4 in. from heat for 5-7 minutes on each side or until a meat thermometer reads 160° and juices run clear. Serve on rolls with lettuce, cheese, tomato, ketchup, mustard and french-fried onions if desired. **Yield:** 6 servings.

slow-cooked pork roast dinner

JANE MONTGOMERY | PIQUA, OHIO

This easy and delicious recipe will give you the moistest pork you have ever tasted! You can cut it with a fork, and any leftovers are just as tender.

PREP: 25 MIN. COOK: 6 HOURS

- 1 large onion, halved and sliced
- 1 boneless pork loin roast (2-1/2 pounds)
- 4 medium potatoes, peeled and cubed
- 1 package (16 ounces) frozen sliced carrots
- 1 cup hot water
- 1/4 cup sugar
- 3 tablespoons cider vinegar
- 2 tablespoons reduced-sodium soy sauce
- 1 tablespoon ketchup
- 1/2 teaspoon salt
- 1/2 teaspoon pepper
- 1/4 teaspoon garlic powder
- 1/4 teaspoon chili powder
- 2 tablespoons cornstarch
- 2 tablespoons cold water

■ Place onion in the bottom of a 5-qt. slow cooker. Add the pork, potatoes and carrots. Whisk the hot water, sugar, vinegar, soy sauce, ketchup, salt, pepper, garlic powder and chili powder; pour over pork and vegetables.

■ Cover and cook on low for 6-8 hours or until a meat thermometer reads 160° and the pork and potatoes are tender.

■ Remove pork and vegetables; keep warm. Pour cooking juices into a small saucepan and skim fat. Combine the cornstarch and cold water until smooth; stir into the cooking juices. Bring to a boil; cook and stir for 1-2 minutes or until thickened. Serve with the pork and vegetables. **Yield:** 8 servings.

summer sausage hobo packets

TONIA ANNE CARRIER | ELIZABETHTON, TENNESSEE

We love to grill, especially when we go camping in our RV. This is a favorite of our family and the foil packet makes for fast cleanup.

PREP: 25 MIN. GRILL: 20 MIN.

- 1 pound summer sausage, cut into 1-inch pieces
- 4 medium potatoes, peeled and cut into 1/2-inch cubes
- 3 cups shredded cabbage
- 1 large sweet onion, halved and sliced
- 1 medium green pepper, cut into strips
- 1 medium sweet red pepper, cut into strips
- 1 small zucchini, sliced
- 1 small yellow summer squash, sliced
- 1 pound chicken tenderloins, cut into 1-inch pieces
- 2 medium tomatoes, cut into wedges
- 1/2 cup butter, cut into eight cubes
- 1/4 cup prepared Italian salad dressing

■ In a large bowl, combine the first eight ingredients. Gently stir in the chicken and tomatoes. Divide mixture among eight double thicknesses of heavy-duty foil (about 12 in. square). Top each with a butter cube.

■ Fold foil around mixture and seal tightly. Grill, covered, over medium heat for 20-25 minutes or until chicken is no longer pink and vegetables are tender. Carefully open foil to allow steam to escape; drizzle with the dressing. **Yield:** 8 servings.

loaded vegetable beef stew

KARI CAVEN | POST FALLS, IDAHO

I first had this dish during a trip to Argentina a few years ago. It inspired me to re-create it at home. It turned out so well, I wrote "Yum!" on the recipe card!

PREP: 40 MIN. COOK: 8-1/2 HOURS

- 8 bacon strips, diced
- 3 pounds beef stew meat, cut into 1-inch cubes
- 6 medium carrots, cut into 1-inch pieces
- 6 medium tomatoes, peeled and cut into wedges
- 4 medium potatoes, peeled and cubed
- 3 cups cubed peeled butternut squash
- 2 medium green peppers, chopped
- 2 teaspoons dried thyme
- 2 garlic cloves, minced
- 2 cans (14-1/2 ounces *each*) beef broth
- 6 cups chopped cabbage
- 1/2 teaspoon pepper

■ In a large skillet, cook bacon over medium heat until crisp. Using a slotted spoon, remove to paper towels to drain. In the drippings, brown the beef in batches. Refrigerate the bacon until serving.

■ In a 6-qt. slow cooker, combine the carrots, tomatoes, potatoes, squash, green peppers, thyme and garlic. Top with beef. Pour broth over the top. Cover and cook on low for 8 hours.

■ Stir in cabbage and pepper. Cover and cook on high for 30 minutes or until cabbage is tender. Sprinkle each serving with bacon. **Yield:** 12 servings (1-1/3 cups each).

hearty jambalaya

JENNIFER FULK | MORENO VALLEY, CALIFORNIA

I enjoy anything with Cajun spices, so I came up with this slowcooker jambalaya that's just as good as that served in restaurants. If you can't find andouille sausage, hot links, smoked sausage or chorizo will also work. I often serve it with warm corn bread.

PREP: 15 MIN. COOK: 6-1/4 HOURS

- 1 can (28 ounces) diced tomatoes, undrained
- 1 pound fully cooked andouille sausage links, cubed
- 1/2 pound boneless skinless chicken breasts, cut into 1-inch cubes
- 1 can (8 ounces) tomato sauce
- 1 cup diced onion
- 1 small sweet red pepper, diced
- 1 small green pepper, diced
- 1 cup chicken broth
- 1 celery rib with leaves, chopped
- 2 tablespoons tomato paste
- 2 teaspoons dried oregano
- 2 teaspoons Cajun seasoning
- 1-1/2 teaspoons minced garlic
- 2 bay leaves
- 1 teaspoon Louisiana-style hot sauce
- 1/2 teaspoon dried thyme
- 1 pound cooked medium shrimp, peeled and deveined
- Hot cooked rice

■ In a 5-qt. slow cooker, combine the first 16 ingredients. Cover and cook on low for 6-7 hours or until chicken juices run clear. Stir in shrimp. Cover and cook 15 minutes longer or until heated through. Discard bay leaves. Serve with rice. **Yield:** 8 servings.

beef burgundy

MARY JO NIKOLAUS | MANSFIELD, OHIO

I trim the meat, cut up the vegetables and store them in separate containers the night before. The next day, I can toss all of the ingredients into the slow cooker in minutes. Shortly before dinnertime, I cook the noodles and bake some cheesy garlic toast to complete the meal.

PREP: 10 MIN. COOK: 5-1/2 HOURS

1-1/2 pounds beef stew meat, cut into 1-inch cubes
1/2 pound whole fresh mushrooms, halved
4 medium carrots, chopped
1 can (10-3/4 ounces) condensed golden mushroom soup, undiluted
1 large onion, cut into thin wedges
1/2 cup Burgundy wine *or* beef broth
1/4 cup quick-cooking tapioca
1/2 teaspoon salt
1/4 teaspoon dried thyme
1/4 teaspoon pepper
Hot cooked egg noodles

■ In a 5-qt. slow cooker, combine the first 10 ingredients. Cover and cook on low for 5-1/2 to 6-1/2 hours or until meat is tender. Serve with noodles. **Yield:** 6 servings.

chicken pesto clubs

TERRI CRANDALL | GARDNERVILLE, NEVADA

This colorful sandwich has a crisp, golden-brown outside and fresh-tasting, full-flavored filling the whole family will love. It's supper in 10 minutes flat!

PREP/TOTAL TIME: 10 MIN.

4 slices ready-to-serve fully cooked bacon
4 slices sourdough bread
2 tablespoons prepared pesto
1 cup ready-to-use grilled chicken breast strips
2 slices cheddar cheese
1 medium tomato, sliced
1 cup fresh arugula *or* baby spinach
1 tablespoon olive oil

■ Heat bacon according to package directions. Meanwhile, spread bread slices with pesto. Layer two slices with chicken, cheese, tomato, arugula and bacon; top with remaining bread slice. Brush outsides of sandwiches with oil. Cook on an indoor grill for 3-4 minutes or until bread is browned and cheese is melted. **Yield:** 2 servings.

sweet potato spinach bake

TASTE OF HOME TEST KITCHEN

This wonderful meal-in-one is loaded with layers of flavor. Gouda cheese and bacon lend a rich, savory taste to the sweet potato and spinach combination.

PREP: 25 MIN. BAKE: 10 MIN.

4 medium sweet potatoes, peeled and thinly sliced
1/2 cup water
3 tablespoons finely chopped onion
1/4 cup butter, cubed
1 package (10 ounces) frozen chopped spinach, thawed and squeezed dry
1/4 cup all-purpose flour
1/4 teaspoon salt
1/4 teaspoon ground nutmeg
1/4 teaspoon pepper
2 cups milk
2 cups (8 ounces) shredded Gouda cheese
3 tablespoons crumbled cooked bacon

■ Place sweet potatoes in a 1-1/2-qt. microwave-safe dish; add water. Cover and microwave on high for 8-10 minutes or until tender.

■ Meanwhile, in a large saucepan, saute the onion in butter until tender. Add the spinach. Stir in flour and seasonings until blended. Gradually stir in the milk. Bring to a boil; cook and stir for 2 minutes or until thickened. Remove from the heat.

■ Drain sweet potatoes. Spread half of the spinach mixture into a greased 11-in. x 7-in. baking dish. Top with half of the potatoes and cheese. Repeat layers. Sprinkle with bacon. Cover and bake at 375° for 10-15 minutes or until bubbly. **Yield:** 4 servings.

Editor's Note: This recipe was tested in a 1,100-watt microwave.

glazed corned beef dinner

SHANNON STRATE | SALT LAKE CITY, UTAH

This recipe is so good that it's the only way my family will eat corned beef. The glaze is the kicker!

PREP: 20 MIN. COOK: 8 HOURS 20 MIN.

- 8 medium red potatoes, quartered
- 2 medium carrots, sliced
- 1 medium onion, sliced
- 1 corned beef brisket with spice packet (3 pounds)
- 1-1/2 cups water
- 4 orange peel strips (3 inches)
- 3 tablespoons orange juice concentrate
- 3 tablespoons honey
- 1 tablespoon Dijon mustard

- Place the potatoes, carrots and onion in a 5-qt. slow cooker. Cut brisket in half; place over vegetables. Add the water, orange peel and contents of spice packet. Cover and cook on low for 8-9 hours or until the meat and vegetables are tender.
- Using a slotted spoon, transfer the corned beef and vegetables to a 13-in. x 9-in. baking dish. Discard the orange peel.
- Combine the orange juice concentrate, honey and mustard; pour over meat. Bake, uncovered, at 375° for 20 minutes, basting occasionally. **Yield:** 8 servings.

Index

Alphabetical Index

This handy index lists every recipe in alphabetical order so you can easily find your favorite dish.

D

E

F

G

H

S

T

V

W

Y

Z

General Recipe Index

This handy index lists every recipe by food category and/or major ingredient so you can easily locate dishes that suit your needs.

FISH & SEAFOOD

Main Dishes *(continued)*

Sandwiches

Snacks

Soups

FREEZER RECIPES

Desserts *(also see pies)*

Main Dishes

Pies

FRENCH TOAST

FRUIT *(also see specific kinds)*

GARLIC

GRILLED & BROILED RECIPES

Breads

Breakfast

Main Dishes

Sandwiches and Burgers

Snacks

GROUND BEEF

Main Dishes

Time Index

This index calls out the more than 300 recipes that go from start to finish in 10, 20, and 30 minutes!

10-MINUTE RECIPES

20-MINUTE RECIPES

30-MINUTE RECIPES

7th Edition

SELLING
THE PROFESSION

FOCUSING ON BUILDING RELATIONSHIPS

DAVID J. LILL & JENNIFER K. LILL-BROWN

Project Manager: Martha Lill

Cover Design/Book Layout: Justin Oefelein

Contributing Consultants: Don and Barb Evans, Jimmie and Linda Carter

Case Studies and Role Plays: Dr. William Barnett

Contact the authors if you would like information on how to access all aspects of the curriculum developed exclusively to assist you in the preparation of lecture material, tests, case studies, and other classroom or lecture activities.

Website:
sellingtheprofession.com

This book may be purchased for educational, business, or sales promotional use. For information or to place an order, please contact:

Dr. David J. Lill
DM Bass Publications
6635 Broken Bow Drive
Cane Ridge, TN 37013
615.941.2747 (business)
615.476.5035 (personal)
615.941.2458 (fax)

ISBN-13: 978-0-9652201-1-8

SEVENTH EDITION

The Library of Congress Cataloging-in-Publication data

Lill, David and Jennifer Lill Brown

Selling the Profession / Focusing on Building Relationships /

Dr. David Lill and Jennifer Lill Brown

7th ed. ISBN 978-0-9652201-1-8 (paper)

1. Business 2. Sales Training. 3. Career Development 4. Self-Help

Printed in the United States of America

DEDICATION

To Martha - We love you so much.

You are the best Mother, Grandma, and Wife anyone could ever hope for.

BRIEF CONTENTS

TABLE OF CONTENTS

Preface

Approach and Purpose

The ideas, concepts, and style of this text are the result of years spent teaching professional selling to college and university students, conducting seminars for sales professionals, and professional business consulting, combined with over thirty five years of personal experience in various phases of the business of selling. As professionals and seasoned salespeople who love the sales environment and desire to see an improvement in the ethical business climate, we wanted a text that would:

1. Give new and experienced salespeople ***tangible skills*** that are instantly transferable to the field, no matter the industry.
2. Convince motivated, creative students that selling is a phenomenal career to consider—not just something you do until something better comes along.
3. Demonstrate how a sales career will be a ***source of tremendous financial and personal satisfaction.***

Selling: The Profession focuses on building relationships. It is this relationship-building style that spells success for salespeople operating in a highly competitive business environment and dealing with today's sophisticated buyers who demand correct answers to complex problems. The book's style and organization makes it fun to read, easy to comprehend, and highly practical as a training tool for anyone really interested in developing their skills as a salesperson. The sales process is broken down into its most basic components, in an attempt to simplify the complex buyer-seller interaction that takes place in an actual selling situation, with the result being an ***eight-step sales cycle model*** that we explore in depth in over one-half of the book.

Because attitude is so important for achieving success in selling, communication and social style chapters are included as foundation stones. An understanding of these concepts allows you to more readily appreciate the complex, dynamic behavioral relationships that take place in selling. You will be introduced to the availability and usefulness of social media and its countless applications in the world of selling. Global competition has enlarged the playing field. As global competition brings new challenges, technology brings new tools that help sales professionals sell more effectively and efficiently.

You will see the "real world" of selling through review of current sales studies and surveys, personal experience, and insight from other successful active sales professionals who put the theory contained in the book into everyday practice. As one top salesperson said, *"Practice without theory is blind and theory without practice is sterile."*

Your ability to develop and maintain long-term relationships is the key to your success as a person, a student, and a business professional. For customers, a buying decision means a decision to enter into a relationship with a salesperson and their company. It is very much like a "business marriage." *Selling: The Profession* shows you how to bring about that union.

Relationships can be more important than the actual product being sold. Customers don't always know the components of a product, how a company functions, or how they will be treated after money changes hands, but they can make an assessment about a salesperson and about the relationship that has occurred over the course of the selling process.

Ultimately, customers' decisions are based on the fact that they trust and believe in what a salesperson says.

Therefore, the quality of the relationship with a customer is the competitive advantage that enables salespeople to succeed over rivals who may have similar products and services. Just as optometrists help improve their patients' vision, this textbook serves as a "prescription" for the study of professional selling. You wouldn't expect to enhance your eyesight without the right corrective lenses. So why would you expect your understanding of relationship selling to improve without having the right tools for success?

Read the following five part descriptions so that you can see the logic of the chapter sequence and how you can get the most out of the organization of the book. Remember, this is *your* textbook, your personal prescription for sharpened focus and success in relationship selling.

PART 1
Relationship Building and the Sales Cycle Framework

Chapter 1 discusses the consultative nature and problem-solving approach to professional selling and details the characteristics that successful salespeople possess. Relationship selling is interactive, involves two-way communication, encourages prospect participation, employs empathy, and promotes mutually beneficial environment. Today's style of selling favors building close and trusting long-term relationships. Positioning yourself as a consultant creates a partnership with customers. You are peers working to solve problems together.

You gain a better understanding of the complete selling situation and the problems it generates by breaking the sale into its basic tasks. There are several steps to achieving a successful sale. An eight-step sales cycle is introduced in **Chapter 2** and explained in detail in chapters 7 to 14. It just makes sense that if you understand what the steps are in the *Sales Cycle Framework for Relationship Selling*, and what is required to make each step a successful endeavor, you will become a professional in selling much quicker than those who are simply stumbling through the process trying to figure it out.

PART 2
Cultivating an Ethical Climate and Developing Communication Skills

Few professions give you more opportunities for rejection on a daily basis than does the field of sales. **Chapter 3** discusses the need for a strong ethical and moral character to sustain a sales

career. Honest and caring service brings customers back and assures success. Success in professional selling also depends upon your ability to have a productive exchange of information with prospects and customers. As detailed in **Chapter 4**, the more you understand about prospects and their decision-making process, the more readily you can discover what they need and want. Because success in relationship selling depends on accurately getting your message across to prospects, chapter 4 also describes how to break through communication barriers.

An especially useful tool for gaining insight into how the prospect is thinking is knowledge of the social styles model, presented in **Chapter 5**. A social style is the way a person sends and receives information. It is a method for finding the best way to approach a prospect and to set up a working relationship with that person.

PART 3
Gaining Knowledge, Preparing, and Planning for the Presentation

The information in **Chapter 6** prepares you for success in a sales career by focusing on gaining product knowledge, developing a plan for self-motivation and goal setting, and introducing the use of sales force technology. Chapters 7 and 8 discuss the procedures for locating and qualifying prospects and identifying the information needed to prepare for an effective presentation. **Chapter 7** is a thorough look at prospecting. As the saying goes, "I'd rather be a master prospector than a wizard of speech and have no one to tell my story to." **Chapter 8** discusses the process of gathering preapproach information and presents a *six-step telephone track* for making appointments for that all-important personal interview.

PART 4
The Face-to-Face Relationship Model of Selling

Chapters 9 to 13 are the very heart of professional selling. This is considered the "how to" portion of the textbook. This is referred to as the face-to-face portion of the sales cycle. It is the valuable time spent in the actual sales interview—the time when a commitment is obtained and kept.

What happens in the opening minutes is crucial to the overall success of the sales interview, so **Chapter 9** focuses on the approach. **Chapter 10** is devoted to the art of asking questions and listening effectively. Questioning and listening guidelines are presented to carry you through the entire sales interview. **Chapter 11** details the techniques to use in the actual presentation. Units of conviction are the building blocks for creating and making a meaningful sales presentation. The five elements that comprise a complete unit of conviction are explained and illustrated.

Chapters 12 and 13 present the psychology behind handling objections and closing the sale. A plan to handle objections is introduced, and a separate section in **Chapter 12** explains several ways of dealing with the difficult price objection. **Chapter 13** stresses that closing the sale is the natural conclusion to a successful sales interview.

PART 5
Management Aspect: Personal and Organizational

The service you give the customer after the sale has been completed can be as important, or even more important, than the sale itself because that is what builds true loyalty and fosters relationships. Keeping current customers happy is the focus of **Chapter 14**. The customer absolutely defines quality in every transaction. Great salespeople don't talk customer service—*they live perfect service*.

Chapter 15 shows you how to get better control of your time and your activities. The chapter really is all about personal organization and self-management. You cannot manage time, but you can manage yourself and your personal activities. Administrative ability on the part of the salesperson is fundamental to success. Statistics indicate that only about 20 percent of a salesperson's time during a typical day is spent in face-to-face interviews with prospects. **Chapter 16** details the job responsibilities of the sales manager, and provides a useful introduction for classes in sales management.

Chapter Structure

This seven-part structure is a guide for you to follow as you study and learn the material in the various chapters:

1. **Learning Objectives.** The bullet points and overview at the beginning of each chapter acquaint you with the important concepts. They appear on the first page and serve as guidelines to follow as you read through the chapter.
2. **Main Chapter Body.** Chapters are organized with an easy-to-understand structure and complemented by examples of actual sales situations that take the theory and put it into practice. The material in all 16 chapters is well documented with examples and exhibits taken from actual sales experience.
3. **The Social Media Connection.** These brand new sections that can be found in every chapter are designed to give you real-world application on how to utilize all that social media has to offer to get the most out of your efforts.
4. **Summary.** This section outlines the main points of the chapter to reinforce learning. Reading the various summaries in bullet point format gives you a feel for the content of the chapter and the key points to remember.
5. **Review Questions.** Each chapter ends with a series of questions to challenge the student's understanding of the material. These questions are useful when studying for quizzes or exams.
6. **In-Class Exercises.** These practical exercises are designed to have you do things inside and outside the classroom. They get you involved in active learning, since the best way to learn new skills is through action. Research shows that students who just sit and listen to a teacher retain only 20 percent of what they hear. However, participants involved in active learning and doing retain a much higher percentage of the information they receive.
7. **Case Studies.** The case studies require you to apply the critical skills discussed in each chapter and give you training through practical learning situations.

About the Authors

David Lill has a combined forty years of professional sales, sales training, and teaching experience. He taught selling and marketing classes at Baylor University, Belmont University and New Mexico State University. He earned his Ph.D. degree in Marketing from the University of Alabama. Dr. Lill is also a business consultant specializing in sales, advertising, and communications skills development. He currently conducts seminars and training courses on sales and marketing related topics. His relationship selling model is being successfully used by companies throughout the country in a wide variety of industries including insurance, telecommunications, real estate, publishing, banking, hospitality, chemical, and automotive.

Dr. Lill is the founder and president of DM Bass Publications through which he wrote, published, marketed, and sells *Selling: The Profession*, now in its 7th edition. He owned and operated an advertising firm in Louisiana where he developed and implemented advertising and marketing campaigns for a number of companies, including a local bank and department store.

Dr. Lill is the co-author of *Cause Selling: The Sanford Way*, *The Handbook for Relationship Selling: Acquire Your Selling Focus*, and *The Official Handbook for Health Club Sales*. In addition, Dr. Lill has published over eighty-five articles in various academic, trade, and professional publications. These include: *Selling Power*, *Journal of Advertising*, *Journal of the Academy of Marketing Science*, *Sales & Marketing Management*, *Business Topics*, *Nashville Business Journal*, and the *Journal of Pharmaceutical Marketing & Management*.

Dr. Lill has sold successfully for two large telecommunications companies, specializing in marketing information technology. He also worked for the *Milwaukee Journal* in their Advertising Laboratory Division. While there, he brought in prestigious clients such as General Mills, General Foods, and Nabisco and conducted marketing studies using Milwaukee as a test market for new product launches.

David lives in Nashville, TN with his wife, Martha. A housewife turned commercial real estate agent, she was the company's top producer. They are blessed to have two exceptional children, David, Jr. and Jennifer, and four grandchildren. David is an engineer with TVA in Chattanooga, TN where he lives with his wife Amber, and their daughter, Madelyn. Jennifer is a published author, ghostwriter, and entrepreneur.

Jennifer Lill-Brown comes from a background of sales, authorship, and entrepreneurship. She is a renowned ghostwriter who has assisted more than thirty prominent professionals and public figures put their passions into words. Some of her more notable clients include NFL Hall of Fame quarterback Joe Theismann, Dr. Josh Axe, James Malinchak, and Dr. Asa Andrew, to name a few. She has a unique talent for researching and writing from the perspective of virtually anyone from any background.

Jennifer has also co-authored four books of her own. She and her father's most recent endeavor is *Cause Selling: The Sanford Way*, which is based on the vision of billionaire philanthropist T. Denny Sanford. She was also the co-founder, along with business partner Tom Black, of the *Tom Black Center for Selling Inc*. While working with Tom, she edited and produced his widely acclaimed sales book, ***The Boxcar Millionaire***. Jennifer marketed and promoted Tom as a keynote speaker and sales trainer through a personal branding strategy that she formulated.

While obtaining her degree in finance from the University of Alabama, Jennifer had the opportunity to sell for one of the most respected sales organizations in the country, ***The Southwestern Company***. She sold educational products door-to-door by relocating and fully running the business from concept to sales, delivery, and customer service. She was the awarded "Top First Year Dealer Award" and facilitated the recruitment and sales training of new recruits, as well as formulating and developing a system of lead finding and a unique delivery method.

Today Jennifer lives in Nashville, TN with her husband Will, their sons, Porter, Wyatt, and Jesse. Her parents, Martha (Grandma) and David (Papa), live just a mile away and are proud, devoted grandparents to her handsome boys.

Acknowledgments

Since one of our primary goals was to produce a text with real-world concepts and applications, we could not have been successful without the assistance of all those in sales who took time to share their thoughts, as well as a team of supportive friends and family. The insightful comments made by the sales professionals highlighted throughout the book add an important dimension to student learning. The success they have achieved in all areas of their lives through hard work and dedication, while upholding high standards of business ethics, should serve as a model for young, aspiring business professionals.

David's Acknowledgements

Special thanks goes to five friends and business colleagues who have been true blessings to me: Deryl Bass, Jimmie Carter, Don Evans, Tom Hoek, and Dan McGinley—friends and sales professionals, who each in their own way have had a profound effect on the way I think and the actions I take.

I want to thank Donald Silberstein, former Director of Business Development for the Bureau of Business Practice, Inc., for his efforts in providing the 150 cases that he made available for my use. Twenty-four of those cases were used as end-of-chapter cases in the 4th and 5th editions of this text. The 32 new cases in this 7th edition are the work of Dr. William Barnett. I cannot thank him enough for the exceptional case studies he has provided us.

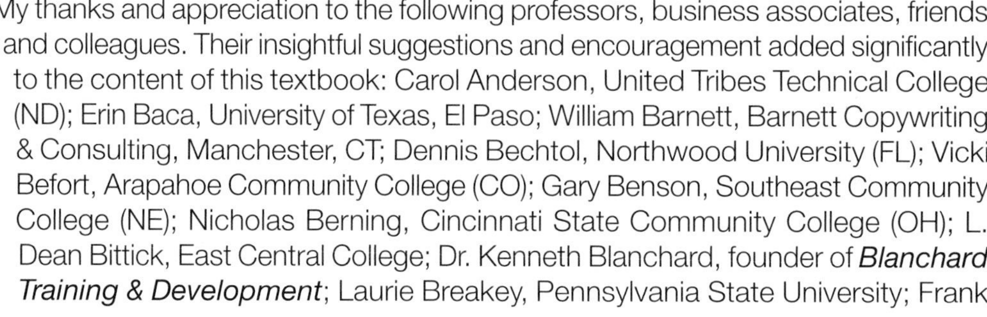

My thanks and appreciation to the following professors, business associates, friends and colleagues. Their insightful suggestions and encouragement added significantly to the content of this textbook: Carol Anderson, United Tribes Technical College (ND); Erin Baca, University of Texas, El Paso; William Barnett, Barnett Copywriting & Consulting, Manchester, CT; Dennis Bechtol, Northwood University (FL); Vicki Befort, Arapahoe Community College (CO); Gary Benson, Southeast Community College (NE); Nicholas Berning, Cincinnati State Community College (OH); L. Dean Bittick, East Central College; Dr. Kenneth Blanchard, founder of ***Blanchard Training & Development***; Laurie Breakey, Pennsylvania State University; Frank

Bingham, Bryant University; Bob Bricker, Pikes Peak Community College (CO); David Braun, L.A. Pierce College (CA); Miriam Burgos, Azusa Pacific University (CA); Laura Cailloux, Skagit Valley College; Glen Carwell, Kendall College (IL); Cindy Claycomb, Wichita State University; Dave Colby, Mid-State Technical College (WI); Kristi Cranwell, NCTA (NE); Dale Davis, Eastern New Mexico University; Patricia DeCorte, Delta College (MI); Bruce Dickinson, Southeast Technical Institute; Claude Dotson, Northwest College; Kenneth DuVall, LDS Business College (UT); Terri Dwyer, Montana State University; Cinda Echard and Carol Goodrich, Glenville State College (WV); Pat Ellsburg, Lower Columbia College (WA); Richard English, San Diego State University; Ken Erby, Northeastern Technical College (SC); David Fee, Utah Valley State College; Sandra Fields, University of Delaware; Bert Fisher, COO, Our Community Credit Union (WA); Olene Fuller, San Jacinto College (Pasadena, TX); Wil Goodheer, president of International University (Vienna, Austria); Shawn Green, Aurora University (IL); Carl Grunander, Weber State University (UT); Donna Gutschmidt, Lake Region State College; Dan Hall, East Central College; Michael Harstine, Grace College & Seminary (IN); Dan Heck, Kendall College (IL); Tom Hoek, former president of Insurance Systems of Tennessee; Norm Humble, Kirkwood Community College; Denise Hunt, Allegany College of Maryland; Marie Johnson, Skagit Valley College; Pam Jodway, Michigan State University; George Johnson, Marshalltown Community College; Carolyn Keck, San Jacinto College; David Kimball, Elms College (MA); Gary Kritz, Coastal Carolina University; Harold Krul, Baker College (MI); Nancy Krumland, Southeast Community College (NE); Carsha Lapp, Northwest Technical College (MN); Desiree Cooper Larsen, Weber State University (UT); John Lavin, WCTC (WI); James Lollar, Radford University (VA); Chuck Loomis, Edmonds Community College (WA); Ruth Lumb, Concordia College at Moorhead; Shawna MaHaffey, Delta College (MI); Cyndy Mascola, Trumbull Business College (OH); Luis Martinez, Manager, Five Star Program, Chrysler Corporation; Dr. Morris L. Mayer, University of Alabama; Claudine McIntyre, Mt. San Antonio College (CA) Linda Myers, Baker College (MI); Dan McGinley, Director, Sanford Institute of Philanthropy (National University, CA); Becky Miles, Delaware Tech; Phillip Millage, Indiana Wesleyan University; Linda Mohr, Northwood University (FL); David Miller, Panhandle State University (TX); Dan Moore, President, The Southwestern Company; Gary Mucica, University of Massachusetts, Lowell; Kathleen Naasz, Centenary College (NJ); Judith Nickel, WCTC (WI); Philip Nitse, Idaho State University; Darren Olson, Bemidji State University (MN); Barbara Ollhoff, WCTC (WI); Steven Osinski, San Diego State University; Dr. Norman Vincent Peale, author of *The Power of Positive Thinking*; Nenita Perez, Guam Community College: Phillip M. Pfeffer, former president of Random House Inc.; Robin Peterson, New Mexico State University; Chris Plouffe, Florida State University; Bob Quade, Centenary College (NJ); Lyn Richardson, Ball State University; John Robbins, Winthrop University; Michael Powell, North Georgia College & State University; Tim Reese, Eastern Idaho Technical College; Les Rubenstein, St. Mary College; Luis Salas, Delta College (MI); Allen Schemmel,WSM-AM/FM Radio (Nashville); Gary Schirr, Radford University (VA); Bonnie Schultz, Northeast Community College; Holly Schrank, Purdue University; Denny Sheehan, Phoenix College (AZ); Kent Sickmeyer, Kaskaskia College (IL); Judy Signaw, Cornell University; Mary Lee Short, Santa Fe Community College; Robert Skalla, Blackhawk Technical College; Pat Swarthout, Central Lakes College (MN); Bob Tangsrud, University of North Dakota; Sandra Taylor, Athens Area Technical Institute (GA); Harry Taute, Utah Valley State College; Ray Thomas, Edith Cowan University, Perth, Australia; Chet Trybus, Ferris State University (MI); William Youngs, SUNY College at Cobleskill (NY); Kevin Ward, Augusta Tech College (GA); Patricia Watson, Mid-State Technical College (WI); Carolyn Waits, Cincinnati State Community College;

Emma Watson, Arizona State University; Sandy Weaver, Athens Technical College (GA); Brian Williams, Southeast Tech Institute (SD); Amy Wojciechowski, West Shore Community College; Curtis Youngman, Salt Lake Community College (UT).

These individuals warrant a special thank you:

Gladys Hudson, former vice-president of Success Motivation in Waco, TX. She was my original mentor, editor and creative inspiration for many ideas in this textbook.

My family: To my wonderful and precious wife, Martha – the love of my life! And my two remarkable children: David Jr., you have made me so proud—what a phenomenal son, father and husband you are. And Jennifer— what a fantastic daughter and fantastic mother to our grandsons, Porter, Wyatt, and Jesse! She is my co-author and editor-in-chief for the 5th, 6th, and 7th editions! There is no way this book could have been completed without all of their love and support!

Jennifer's Acknowledgements

To my father, Dr. Lill – Dad, thanks for giving me the opportunity to work on the various book projects with you to watch the “master” at work! And my deepest gratitude for your love and belief in me.

To my mother, Martha – Mom, you are my best friend and sounding board for all things big and small. I love you more than words can express.

To my husband, Will – I love you! Thanks for being my buddy and for giving me your unconditional support and being my biggest fan.

To my sons, Porter, Wyatt, and Jesse, you guys are the little lights of my life! You've made my life so full of joy. Every day is an adventure with my boys.

To my brother and sister-in-law, Dave and Amber, and my beautiful niece, Madelyn—I love you guys so much!

"THERE IS ONLY ONE BOSS. **THE CUSTOMER.** And he can fire everybody in the company from the chairman on down, simply by spending his money somewhere else."

– Sam Walton

PART I

RELATIONSHIP BUILDING AND THE SALES CYCLE FRAMEWORK

CHAPTER 1 discusses the consultative nature and problem-solving approach to professional selling and details the characteristics that successful salespeople possess. Relationship selling is interactive, involves two-way communication, encourages prospect participation, employs empathy, and promotes a mutually beneficial environment. Today's style of selling favors building close and trusting long-term relationships. Positioning yourself as a consultant creates a partnership with customers. *You are peers working to solve problems together.*

You gain a better understanding of the complete selling situation and the problems it generates by breaking the sale into its basic tasks. There are several steps to achieving a successful sale. An eight-step sales cycle is introduced in ***CHAPTER 2*** and explained in detail in chapters 7 to 14. It makes sense that if you understand what the steps are in the *Sales Cycle Framework for Relationship Selling*, and what is required to make each step a successful endeavor, then you will become a professional in selling much quicker than those who are simply stumbling through the process trying to figure it out.

CHAPTER 1

A CAREER IN PROFESSIONAL SELLING

OVERVIEW

Chapter 1 discusses the consultative nature and problem-solving approach to professional selling and details the characteristics that the most successful salespeople possess. Relationship selling is interactive, involves two-way communication, encourages prospect participation, employs empathy, and promotes a winning environment for everyone involved. Today's style of selling favors building close and trusting long-term relationships. Positioning yourself as a consultant creates a partnership with customers. You are peers working to solve problems together.

OBJECTIVES

- Appreciate the role of selling in our economy.
- Understand the purpose of personal selling.
- Examine professional selling as a viable career opportunity.
- Recognize the different types of sales jobs and the requirements for success in each.
- Identify the personal characteristics that are needed for success in a selling career.

YOU ARE ALREADY SELLING

Countless daily interactions between people involve the act of selling. Some of them are universally recognized as selling: Retail salespeople sell you clothes, furniture, or smartphones; an auto dealer sells you a car; and your insurance agent sells you a policy. ***In fact, a company is not in business until somebody makes a sale.***

However, many other common transactions not typically recognized as selling involve the same skills, goals, and behavior patterns that professional salespeople use: Waiters may sell you on trying a new entrée or getting dessert; politicians try to convince constituents to vote for them or persuade other politicians to join them in promoting certain projects; celebrities sell themselves and their ideas of what is beautiful and hip through reality television and social media; and family members influence decisions such as where to live, who will use the family car on Friday night, whether to borrow money for a vacation, and even what to fix for dinner.

In other words, you are already selling. You are selling yourself, your ideas, and your desire for cooperation and companionship to almost everyone you engage in anything more than the most casual conversation.

Partnerships, maintaining customer relationships, strategic alliances, social networking, and global strategies are more than mere phrases to sales organizations. They are the tools with which winning strategies are fashioned. Competitiveness among the world's major corporations will only continue to grow, and using yesterday's sales strategies is dangerous and increasingly ineffective as global competitors battle each other.

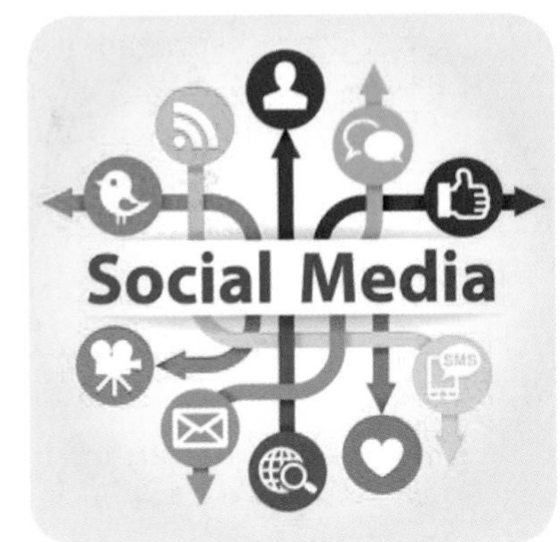

The latest and best marketing and sales practices are essential in gaining new customers and keeping those you currently serve, whether that means checking in with customers and prospects through Facebook or launching an entire social media sales campaign through a combination of the many social networking options that exist today.

A true sales professional does not succeed on the merits of basic personality traits or skills alone, but on the ability to handle change, to harness technology, and to respond to customers' evolving needs. The sales profession must rise to the challenge because, as hotel magnate Conrad Hilton said, "Success seems to be connected with action. Successful people keep moving."[1]

Successful salespeople must keep growing and moving forward.

It is crucial to understand the business world today and know what challenges customers face, so you can truly become a *solutions provider*. Sales professionals demonstrate their value to customers by providing productive information and helping solve problems.

THE VALUE OF SALESPEOPLE

New and innovative products and services are never accepted automatically. Neither individual nor business consumers can keep up with all the innovations that become available. So how do businesses expect to keep up with significant developments just in their own fields? They rely on salespeople!

A salesperson's job is to identify customer needs, determine ways those needs could be met by the products or services they offer, and then provide that information to the customer. They also work in the other direction, by identifying customer needs that cannot be satisfied by their current product line and communicating those needs to their company for consideration in the development of new products. Salespeople who consistently bring a sincere sales approach to their work build trust and loyalty with customers and become an invaluable resource to their company.[2] Therefore, they are facilitators of information that keeps them and their customers competitive. Sales is the most important job in any organization.

Compensation Potential

Because of their vital role in business, salespeople are among the best-paid employees of a company. More salespeople earn above $100,000 annually than people in any other profession.[3] According to an annual survey of telesales representatives, the average salary is around $65,000.[4] And according to other studies on pay for sales and marketing positions, product managers in sales positions have an average base salary of more than $98,000.[5]

These are just averages—some salespeople make less, while some make considerably more. Salespeople are the catalysts of the economy. They are responsible for keeping goods, services, and ideas flowing.

Importance of Sales Training

In today's exceedingly competitive environment, all kinds of companies provide continuing sales training on a regular basis, and many of these companies spend considerable amounts of money for training. Corporate training—including sales training—is increasing at more rapid rates than ever before. The reason? Mounting research points to the fact that more and more organizations suffer from a "skills supply chain" challenge. Not only do more than 70 percent of organizations cite "capability gaps" as one of their top five challenges, but many companies also say that it takes three to five years to take a sales professional and make him or her fully productive.[6] That makes the right sales training even more important if you want to shorten the amount of time it takes to get up and running in a sales career.

Sales training as preparation for the future isn't an option—it is an imperative. According to

Simon Bartley, CEO of UK Skills, neglecting to train today will lead to a decline in economic growth tomorrow. This means companies must see the importance of building up each individual salesperson, for the good of the entire organization. "On the ground is where skills allow an individual to achieve their goals of having a better quality of life and a real sense of personal achievement," says Bartley. In today's competitive market, companies cannot cut corners and expect to have the same results as their better-trained competitors. Training is not just a good way to stay competitive; it can serve a bigger purpose by boosting your company's bottom line.[7]

Today's corporations view sales training as an *investment*, and adequate training generates a desired return in the form of increased gross and net profits as well as improved cash flow.[8] Companies know that it is essential to spend money on training productive salespeople who will be long-term assets to the organization. In a study by the *Society for HR Management*, the hiring of unsuccessful salespersons is estimated to cost companies $20,000 for intermediate positions, $100,000 for senior management, and $300,000 for sales representatives, figures that include both the hard and soft costs of recruitment, training, and lost-opportunity costs.[9] A well-trained salesperson is indispensable!

"Our study concludes that this is the percentage of our customers who will buy from us without any effort whatsoever on our part."

After spending large amounts of money and devoting months to training, companies have made a significant investment in each salesperson. Productive salespeople are eager to receive this training because they know that learning never stops, and their companies are equally interested in their continued growth. By providing intensive hands-on training programs, companies build confidence in their sales force, enabling them to make superior product presentations. This ability also shows customers that they are dealing with a product expert who knows how to solve their problems by providing educated solutions.[10]

THE POSITIVE NATURE OF SELLING

Any seasoned sales manager will tell you—it's hard to find (and keep) talented salespeople. This seems to be especially true among young people, due in part to the fact that many college students have historically held less than positive perceptions and attitudes toward selling as a career. Employers say many young workers are uninterested in sales—a field they perceive as risky and defined by fierce competition.[11]

Why do negative perceptions about the profession exist? It may be due to the fact that many people have had little opportunity to observe career salespeople at work. Our primary contact with salespeople has been with retail salespeople (many of whom have been put on the floor with little to no sales training), and the telemarketing reps that call you during dinner. Unfortunately, these are the models we see when we think of sales, and consequently many tend to view sales as a job to accept if nothing better is available rather than an exciting career option.

An understanding of the personal characteristics that a career in professional selling actually requires should dispel any outdated myths an individual may possess. Four areas of your personality are involved:

PERSONAL INTEGRITY. Continued success in sales requires the highest possible ethical standards for dealing with prospects, customers, and your own company. A salesperson who lies or deceives customers to complete a sale is soon out of a job because customers do not place repeat orders and prospects soon get the word that this person is not to be trusted. An outstanding salesperson has high values and always operates in the most ethical manner.

PERSONALITY STRUCTURE. Sales is a demanding career, which is why you must have a positive self-image, and a persevering spirit. A person who is unable to accept the reality that not every prospect becomes a client will be devastated by failures and feel an overwhelming sense of personal rejection. The persistent myth that salespeople are arrogant, overbearing, and excessively aggressive contradicts reality. Successful salespeople are, instead, highly interested in other people and their needs and eager to be of real service to prospects and clients.

PERSONAL RELATIONSHIPS. Salespeople are recognized as productive, capable professionals. You are not required to pretend, to conceal your own personality or needs, or to become a doormat for customers. Success in professional selling does not call for assuming an inferior position socially, psychologically, or financially. Companies may spend millions on customer relationship management systems to monitor customer retention and defection, but a vigilant salesperson can just as effectively use the personal touch to solve a problem and keep customers from leaving.[12]

PERSONAL ABILITIES. Success in sales requires high levels of intellect and developed skills. You must be able to understand—sometimes quickly and almost intuitively—a customer's business needs and problems. Salespeople must interpret those needs and suggest viable solutions even if customers themselves do not have a clear picture of their own needs or cannot verbalize those needs clearly. The development of these skills requires not only intelligence but also continuous training, the willingness to be flexible and adapt to change, and the ability to grow beyond preconceived beliefs in an ever-changing sales world.[13]

More accurate information and education today is helping to improve attitudes toward sales as a career. Students responding to recent surveys now support the view that selling is more challenging and prestigious, requires creativity, offers career opportunities, fosters increasing integrity, and provides better financial incentives than did students in earlier studies.[14]

THE BASICS OF PERSONAL SELLING

How do you define the type of personal selling which forms the basis of this book? A comprehensive definition follows:

Personal Selling is the process of *seeking* out people who have a particular need, *assisting* them to recognize and define that need, *demonstrating* to them how a particular service or product fills that need, and *persuading* them to make a decision to use that service or product.

This definition is broad enough to include any type of selling in which you may engage. It describes the commercial aspect of selling a product or service, as well as the process used to solicit funds for charitable organizations or enlist leaders for youth organizations. It also includes the activities of athletic coaches, political parties, clergy, and personnel officers in all kinds of organizations.

Because every sales situation is unique, your career in sales is an exciting and demanding one in which every day brings opportunities to develop new skills and sales strategies and ways to refine existing ones. The potential for personal and professional growth never ends. Because different prospects have varying needs, interests, ability to pay, and authority to make decisions, selling is different in every situation—and this constant change creates new possibilities and increased income potential.

Salespeople are Made, not Born

Too many people involved in selling have not attempted to learn the basic skills needed for success in the profession. They are quick to throw in the towel, claiming that they weren't born to be salespeople. They can be called "90-day wonders" because after 90 days they wonder why they ever got into the sales business. On the other hand, professional salespeople read books, take courses, ask questions, study the techniques of successful salespeople, work hard for their customers, and continually strive to outperform themselves.

Don't be a "90-Day Wonder." Instead, do your job so well that it makes people *wonder* how they can get hired too!

Selling requires a working knowledge of psychology, sociology, communication, and persuasion. It is not a natural process to close a sale. It is a skill to be learned, just like anything else. Even experienced salespeople can fail if they get to the point where they think they know it all. Success in selling is a constant learning process. You must always be a student of your profession.

Successful salespeople are made, not born, and they are made with concentrated attention, repeated practice, sincere desire and goal-directed action.[15]

Exhibit 1.1 illustrates the ongoing debate—*Can selling be taught?* We are all like computers in that we are only as good as we have philosophically, emotionally, and intellectually programmed ourselves to be. Becoming a master salesperson takes time and effort. Even the best salespeople continually adapt and refine their skills throughout their careers.

EXHIBIT 1.1 CAN SELLING BE TAUGHT?

Absolutely! In Daniel Pink's book, *To Sell is Human*, he points out that it's impossible for human beings to avoid influencing, and being influenced by, other people's words and deeds. People are going to be moved — the trick is to make sure that the ideas and products with genuine merit do the moving.[16]

Selling is definitely an art for many successful salespeople, but it is also a skill that must be honed and practiced. If you want to become good at influencing others, then you simply need to learn how. It's not magic, and it's certainly not innate. It may sometimes feel innate, but that's because people are often able to pick up on effective strategies implicitly—without conscious awareness—through experience and observation. Not realizing you are learning makes your abilities feel innate, even when they aren't.

Learn from the seasoned salespeople around you and get the most out of your training. Then, armed with the knowledge of what works, practice it. Everything gets easier, more automatic, and more natural with practice. You have what it takes; you just need to learn to use it.[17]

ADVANTAGES OF A SALES CAREER

The once-popular *Wide World of Sports* television program promised the viewer "the thrill of victory, the agony of defeat." This thrill of victory makes sales an exciting and satisfying career, but the thrill comes not just from earning the monetary rewards or beating out the competition. Those are actually minor parts of the satisfaction of successful selling. What truly makes a career in professional selling so rewarding is a combination of the following three things—all combined with the personal satisfaction you receive from doing your job well:

1. A Sense of Independence and Variety

A sales career frees you from a mundane daily routine. Salespeople are likely to work in a variety of places and deal with prospects who have widely different personalities. What works with one prospect may antagonize another. Consequently, they must always be aware of every element of the environment and adjust quickly. Selling is never boring.

Salespeople can exercise a greater measure of control over their time and activities than many other professionals. Sales is not a nine-to-five job. The hours are quite flexible, long one day and short another. Because their day-to-day sales activities are not usually structured for them, they must also be self-starters and stay motivated.

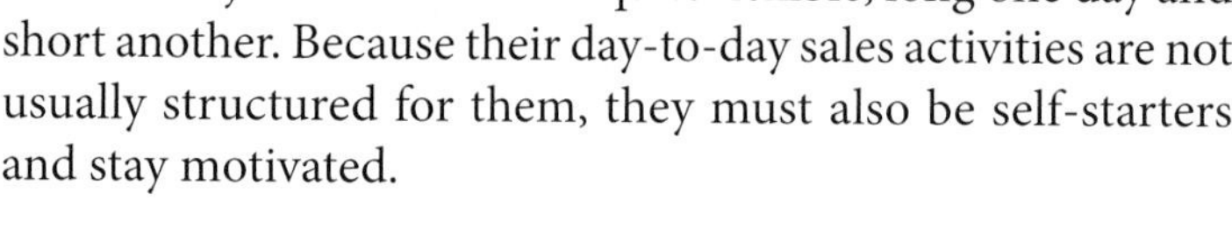

2. Opportunities for Advancement

Effective salespeople are not forced into one career path. Almost any option for career advancement is open to those who are motivated to be successful and seek advancement.

Exhibit 1.2 illustrates a potential career path for a highly motivated salesperson. As you move up the corporate hierarchy, the various options require a different blending of personal skills and characteristics. As a result, there is no guarantee that a successful salesperson will also make a successful manager. In fact, many talented salespeople actually refuse promotion to higher managerial positions. They simply love what they do and can often earn more money selling than they could by moving into a middle-management position.

ENTREPRENEURSHIP. Sales is an ideal career for those who plan to one day own and run their own businesses. No business can survive without a viable marketing organization. An owner or chief executive who has been involved in sales truly understands this part of the business and is in an excellent position to launch and manage a new enterprise successfully. An entrepreneur can find people who understand manufacturing and finance, but the sales and marketing staff must share the founder's dream if the concept is to become a reality.

PROMOTION TO SALES MANAGEMENT. A sales manager may have either limited or extremely broad duties. The first step into sales management often consists of supervising two or three other salespeople—monitoring their activities, providing field training through joint sales calls, and recruiting additional sales representatives while continuing personal sales activities. More comprehensive sales management positions involve managing an entire local, regional, or nationwide sales division. Such a position might include budgeting, planning for sales training, sales promotion, and recruiting, in addition to executive duties and status in the company.

TOP MANAGEMENT POSITIONS. Sales experience makes an executive a valuable member of the management team. Although chief executive officers (CEOs) have traditionally come from the financial and legal ranks, companies are increasingly tapping into the sales and marketing departments to find their leaders. Organizations are looking for CEOs who are not only good leaders of people and have good strategic minds, but also have good interpersonal skills and the ability to carry out an initiative.[18] Many skills used in selling closely resemble those needed in top management. Both jobs require great people skills. It is important in both positions to maintain control under stress, to recognize opportunities and threats, and to locate, and analyze vast amounts of information.[19]

3. Security

Companies will always need salespeople. In fact, though jobs in other sectors are still hard to come by for many, sales jobs appear to be among the first to have recovered from the poor performing years of 2008 and 2009.[20] Ambitious salespeople are eagerly sought, and most organizations provide excellent rewards for their top sales performers. They know that quality salespeople who become dissatisfied can easily go to work for a competitor and possibly take their established customers with them.

Because salespeople are usually paid according to performance, you can directly affect your own income by deciding how much time and effort to invest in the job. Thus, your security comes from your own personal decisions about how hard and how efficiently you want to work. Work, in many ways, is like money; *if you are willing to expend enough of it, you can have almost anything you want.*[21]

DISADVANTAGES OF A SALES CAREER

Like any other profession, selling has some drawbacks and reasons why it is not right for everybody. The same qualities that some may see as advantages to a career in selling are in fact distinct disadvantages to others. Some people view a fixed salary as more secure than a commission-based income dependent entirely upon their direct performance in a given time period. Some see the fluctuation in the economy as a deterrent to venturing into sales and would rather their own financial well being not be based on the stability of the global economic climate. Others dislike the irregular hours or the travel often required. Still others prefer a line of work that doesn't require as much initiative or creative energy in order to get the job done.

Probably the greatest problem faced by every salesperson is handling rejection. Not every sales presentation produces a sale. Not every prospect needs the service or product, and an ethical salesperson never presses for an order from a prospect whose needs will not be met by that product. No salesperson can ever be 100 percent successful in closing sales, even when the prospect truly needs the product or service. The best salespeople learn quickly that rejection is not directed toward them personally.

Prospects who do not buy are rejecting the product or service —not the salesperson.

The decision seldom has anything to do with the salesperson's worth as a human being. Even the occasional prospect who reacts negatively to a salesperson does so as a result of the prospect's personal opinion—an opinion that may be colored by prejudice or completely unfounded. Rejection is not proof that the salesperson is in some way unworthy or inadequate. Salespeople who cannot separate their own personal worth from the product they sell may become too paralyzed by fear to approach another prospect because they face a renewal of rejection.

CLASSIFICATION OF SALES JOBS

Sales jobs are so diverse that they fit a wide variety of personal needs and interests. Variety exists from industry to industry. The responsibilities of a salesperson who calls on large manufacturing companies to create awareness of computer systems for production-control are vastly different from those of the real estate salesperson who sells homes to families. Sales careers vary within industries as well. For example, the residential real estate salesperson is in a different world from that of the real estate developer who puts together multimillion-dollar projects office complexes or shopping centers. As different as sales jobs may be, they all share some basic similarities:

- The need to understand the prospect's problem.
- The need for appropriate technical and/or product knowledge.
- The need for self-discipline to relentlessly execute a sales plan.
- The ability to translate product features into benefits that resolve the prospect's problem.

There are many ways to classify different types of sales jobs: Business-to-business (B2B), business-to-consumer (B2C), direct selling, indirect selling, or personal selling, to name a few. No matter how you label the different types of selling, they can be broken down into the same basic categories. Newer tools for selling may be introduced over time, but the categories remain fundamental. The classification format developed by Derek Newton is a standard model because of his empirical research with over 1,000 sales executives from manufacturing, wholesaling, retail, and service firms. Newton's model is presented here as our basis for the four types of selling found across this variety of industries:[22]

1. Trade Selling

The trade seller's primary responsibility is to increase business from present and potential customers through merchandising and promotional assistance. They usually deal with buyers

who are resellers (wholesalers and retailers). Long-term relationships are important for success. In addition to delivering orders and replenishing inventory, this salesperson's tasks involve persuading the customer to provide additional shelf space, setting up product displays in the store, rotating stock as inventory is replenished, and perhaps conducting in-store demonstrations or distributing samples to customers. Companies usually do not encourage their trade sellers to conduct vigorous sales efforts. They are expected to generate increased sales by assisting the customer move a larger volume of inventory.

2. Missionary Selling

The missionary salesperson's task is largely one of educating those who ultimately decide what product the consumer will use. The most familiar example of the missionary salesperson is the drug detail salesperson who calls on physicians to introduce and describe the pharmaceutical company's products and persuade them to prescribe their medications for patients who could benefit from them. In addition to pharmaceutical firms, food and beverage manufacturers, transportation firms, and public utility companies employ missionary salespeople.

3. Technical Selling

A fast-growing class of salespeople is the technical specialist group, the engineers, scientists, and others with the technical expertise to explain the advantages of the company's product. These salespeople sell directly to the firms that use their products.

They are very important in such industries as chemicals and machinery. They act like management consultants in that they identify, analyze, and solve their customers' problems. In the past, technical specialists have been more concerned with explaining the product than with securing the order, but many decision-makers are now more knowledgeable about technology and more likely to respond favorably to the technical specialist. Consequently, many companies are teaching these salespeople basic selling skills to help them be persuasive in making presentations and closing sales.

4. New Business Selling

This type of salesperson seeks out and persuades new customers to buy for the very first time. They are extremely vital to firms putting their focus on sales growth. New business selling includes selling new products to existing customers or existing products to new customers. The characteristics discussed later in this chapter—perseverance, empathy, ability to ask questions, initiative, and resourcefulness—are vital to sales success for this category of salesperson.

ORDER TAKERS VS. ORDER GETTERS. The *order taker* simply responds to requests and the order getter is a creative problem solver. The salesperson whose work is described as order taking reacts to customers' expressed desires. Responsive selling jobs may be either inside or outside. Inside sales jobs include retail clerks in department stores and other retail establishments. By being helpful and pleasant, retail clerks may create a few sales, but they generally just assist customers in completing the purchase of goods they have already chosen. Outside order takers are route salespeople who mainly service retail clients to deliver orders or replenish inventory.

The order taker may engage in *suggestive selling*—that is, ask you to purchase an additional item. The next time you stop at a Chick-fil-A drive-thru and the person asks, "Would you like a chocolate cookie or lemonade to go with your Spicy Chicken Sandwich?" You are observing suggestive selling in action. And it works!

Order getting, or creative selling, requires ingenuity and the ability to generate demand for a product or service among potential buyers. The product may be tangible such as automobiles or real estate, or the product may be intangible such as investment services or advertising. Creative personal selling generally offers the greatest opportunity for high income because it demands the highest level of personal skill, dedication, and effort.

If you are interested in a profession filled with creative order getting—instead of just order taking—then social networking may be able to assist you in finding the right company and career for you, as you will read about in this chapter's *Social Media Connection* box below.

THE SOCIAL MEDIA CONNECTION

Using Social Media to Land Your Dream Sales Career

Is it possible to tweet your way to a new career? It may not be quite that easy, but career and online experts recommend leveraging social media sites such as Facebook, Twitter, and especially LinkedIn as a part of your job search.

Carisa Miklusak, principal of *Ingenium Consulting Group* and co-founder of *SoMedios*, an emerging media solutions organization, suggests job seekers use social media every step of the way. Starting out, social media is a useful way to research the culture of companies that interest you. While a corporate website can provide extensive information about an organization, its social-media presence can often offer more insight into a company's culture and the way it interacts with employees and customers.

"On Facebook, for example, a job seeker may be able to read about the organization on the Information tab, see pictures of a recent team outing to get a feel for the culture and follow recent conversations between customers and the company—all critical factors in making a decision," Miklusak said. "Candidates should use these tools to pre-interview companies and determine if they are a true fit."

Once you get an interview, use social-media sources to learn about the decision makers you will be meeting. "By conducting a LinkedIn or Google search, it is likely that a candidate will be able to gather a great deal of information about the background of their interviewer," Miklusak said. "This is becoming a very common practice and prepares the candidates to customize their talk track and interview presentation to what they've learned about their interviewer. This also empowers candidates to come prepared with better questions."

At the offer stage, use social media to reach out to current or past employees. "This is a common practice in the social-media space, and a very quick dialog can provide productive company insights," such as standard salary ranges, work assignments and conditions, she said.

The reach and influence of social networking is only getting higher and stronger. So, go ahead and see what social media can do for you during your career search.[23]

ATTRIBUTES OF SUCCESSFUL SALESPEOPLE

There is not one list of traits that accurately describes every successful salesperson. They are as diverse as members of any other profession. They include both extroverts and introverts—and all the degrees in between: Shy and outspoken, talkative and quiet. However, certain core characteristics seem to be present to some degree in most successful salespeople, despite the numerous ways individuals express those characteristics and adapt them to their own styles and purposes.[24]

Enthusiasm

Ralph Waldo Emerson said, "Nothing great was ever achieved without enthusiasm." One of the most important characteristics in new salespeople is *enthusiasm*—but a distinction must be made between people who are enthusiastic about their product and those who are merely eager to take the prospect's money. Enthusiasm in salespeople is based on a genuine belief in the product and a conviction that it will serve the needs of the prospect.[25] Such enthusiasm is communicated both verbally and nonverbally to the prospect in terms of your own personality. Enthusiasm may be expressed as calm, quiet confidence or as excited activity. However it is demonstrated, real enthusiasm is highly attractive and reassuring to prospects.

Empathy

Empathy, the ability to understand another person's concerns, opinions, and needs, whether sharing them or not, provides salespeople with the sales edge of being able to think and understand "with" the prospect during a sales call. Empathy is the ability to pick up on the subtle clues and cues provided by others in order to accurately assess what they are feeling.

Empathy is most useful in the sales process for handling objections and midcourse changes by the prospect. Empathetic salespeople can sense changes in prospects and adjust their presentations accordingly. By careful listening, effective salespeople absorb prospects' reactions, generate an upbeat environment, and sell themselves to prospects. The combination of sincerity and compassion enables them to tailor the presentation to mesh precisely with the prospect's stated needs.

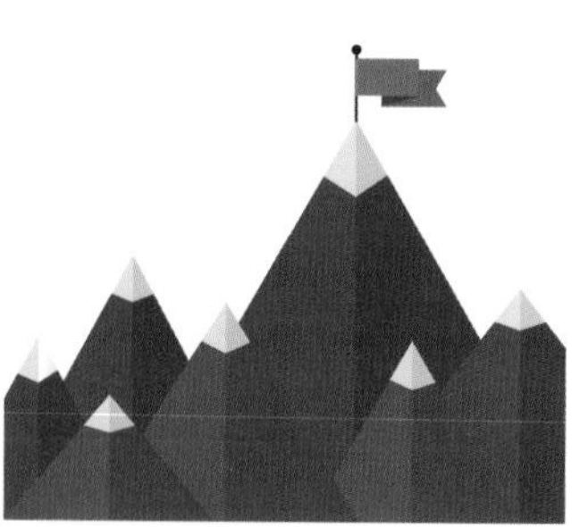

Goal Direction

The best salespeople stay focused on their goals through the course of their daily activities. They have an understanding of how personal sales goals and organizational goals are interrelated, and they work to make both objectives happen.[26] Goal-directed salespeople often respond positively to incentives such as money, prestige, recognition, and pride of accomplishment, which they see as tools they can use to reach their overall goals. When these incentives fit into their overall plan for achieving the goals that represent self-actualization for them, salespeople go all-out to win them.

Ability to Ask Questions

Good salespeople ask questions; poor ones just keep talking. You need to remain in control of the sales interview, and the person who is asking questions is the one in control. When you learn to ask the right kinds of questions, you will gain new prospects, discover valuable qualifying information, uncover the prospects' buying motives, and be able to anticipate most objections. Questioning is your best tool for keeping the interview on track and moving toward a successful close, while also giving the prospect the feeling of remaining in control of the situation.

Resourcefulness

Top salespeople are the ones who are most resourceful. On the spur of the moment, they can think of new ways to make an old point, new applications and creative uses for products, and unique reasons for a particular prospect to make a buying decision. They can think on their feet under pressure. For these people, resourcefulness is an automatic response, like a reflex. Resourcefulness comes from an agile and analytical mind and allows you to stay on the right side of the fine line between being just right and very wrong.

In a sales situation, the right word or phrase clears away the fog and reveals the solutions. The wrong word or phrase is like putting a drop of ink into a glass full of water: It obscures everything!

Administrative Ability

Efficient self-management, especially the management of time, is essential to success in selling. Your most productive time is spent face-to-face with prospects. But you are also required to attend meetings, travel, wait, prepare for interviews, read, study, attend to paperwork, and conduct after-sale follow-up and service.

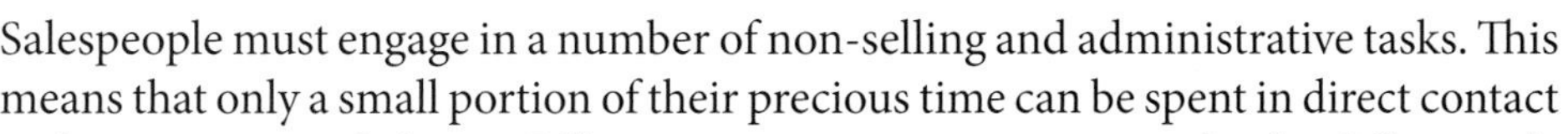

Salespeople must engage in a number of non-selling and administrative tasks. This means that only a small portion of their precious time can be spent in direct contact with prospects and clients. Efficient time management can make the difference between success and failure. Time and territory management is one of the most critical issues for salespeople today. According to a survey of more than 840 salespeople among companies with large sales forces, high-performing salespeople find ways to increase time with customers and maximize the effectiveness of their time spent on administrative duties. In a comparison of high-performing companies and low-performing companies, salespeople for the high-performers spent 40 percent more time with their best potential customers and 30 percent less time on administrative duties.[27]

Initiative

The best salespeople have a powerful, unrelenting, internal drive to excel. This intrinsic motivation can be shaped and molded, but it cannot be taught. This type of motivation is what keeps great salespeople with their head above water when others are sinking during tough economic times.[28] Successful salespeople are self-motivated. They are self-starters who exercise initiative. They do not wait to be told to prospect, to be assigned calls to make, or to be urged to end the presentation with a close. They see the work that needs to be done and take personal responsibility for doing it.

Perseverance

Setbacks often outnumber triumphs, and when this happens, salespeople must have reserves of strength and resilience to fall back on. Depending upon the type of sales activity and the product or service being marketed, the number of sales closed compared to the number of presentations made usually ranges from 5 percent to 50 percent or more. Salespeople need perseverance in several areas:

- The ability to keep going to another prospect no matter how many have said no.
- The ability to make repeated presentations to the same prospect.
- The ability to continue asking for an appointment until one is finally granted.

Pleasant Personality

"You don't close a sale; you open a relationship if you want to build a long-term, successful enterprise."

Patricia Fripp

The way to make a friend is to be one. The salesperson with a pleasant, outgoing disposition is remembered and favored. A key to forming a pleasant personality is to like people and genuinely enjoy knowing as many different kinds of people as possible. People respond to those who like them.

Department store entrepreneur J.C. Penney said, "All great business is built on friendship." How do you build friendships in today's tough competitive sales climate? Find out what the buyer needs, then make every effort to deliver it. Ask yourself: "What would I do if I really wanted to be friends with this person?" The answer will tell you how to build a long-term relationship.

SUMMARY

- Selling is a basic component of all human interaction. It involves discovering needs and providing products or services that satisfy those needs.
- Salespeople are among the highest-paid professionals and make the greatest impact on profitability and success for an organization.
- Partnerships, customer relationships, strategic alliances, empowerment, and global alliances are more than mere words to sales organizations today. They are the tools with which winning strategies are fashioned.
- Professional selling offers opportunities that involve a number of different skill levels and a wide diversity of activities.

- All the personality types can be successful in sales, but certain characteristics enhance the likelihood of success: Enthusiasm, empathy, goal direction, ability to ask questions, resourcefulness, administrative ability, initiative, perseverance, and a pleasant personality.
- Selling is a demanding career that offers substantial rewards and outstanding opportunities for personal achievement.

REVIEW QUESTIONS

1. In the sense that all persuasion is a form of "selling," name the types of situations in which you most frequently "sell." In which of these are you most often successful? If persuasion is an important part of selling, is selling also a form of leadership? Explain your answer.
2. What career limits are imposed on one who chooses sales? Illustrate.
3. Are salespeople born or made? Justify your answer.
4. Why is a feeling of rejection a problem for salespeople? Is this feeling an inevitable part of a sales career?
5. Describe the four broad classes of sales jobs and give examples of each.
6. In addition to securing orders for products, in what ways do companies depend upon salespeople?
7. What responsibilities belong to the salesperson after the order is signed? How does the discharge of these responsibilities affect the entire sales process?
8. Salespeople are interdependent with other individuals in their company. Why is this true in respect to the following factors: product changes, pricing, shipping, and competition?
9. Name some qualities that seem to be shared by most successful salespeople. How do these traits contribute to success? Can they be developed, or are they innate? Does this mean that a single type of personality style is required for success in sales?

IN-CLASS EXERCISES

The following in class exercises help build teams, improve communication, and emphasize the real-world side of selling. They are meant to be challenging, to help you learn how to deal with problems that have no single right answer, and to use a variety of skills beyond those employed in a typical review question. Read and complete each activity. Then in the next class, discuss and compare answers with other classmates.

EXERCISE 1.1 – WHAT DO SALESPEOPLE THINK?

Pair up with another student whom you do not already know. Contact a salesperson who does NOT work in retail sales (that is, AVOID department stores, electronics stores, auto dealerships, etc.; consult the types of sales positions in Chapter 1) and arrange an interview.

During the interview, ask the salesperson what sort of knowledge, skills, and personal characteristics contribute most to that person's success. How is success measured or determined? Ask, further, what are the greatest challenges or obstacles to success in that person's current position. How does the person try to deal with these challenges or obstacles? Feel free to follow up with additional questions.

In class, be prepared to role-play the results of your interview; at the very least, be prepared to discuss what you learned in relation to Chapter 1.

EXERCISE 1.2 – WHO ARE YOU, REALLY?

You will work individually on this role-play. Copy the brief survey below onto a separate sheet of paper. Rate yourself on each of the personal characteristics, and put the results aside.

Enlist the help of 5 friends outside of this class who know you reasonably well. On a separate sheet of paper for each, copy the brief survey below and ask each person to complete the survey about you. Assure them that you want an honest appraisal of your personal characteristics because you are trying to determine whether you are suited for a particular profession; do not mention sales or selling.

After all 5 persons have completed and returned the survey, compare the results to your own self-rating. Are there any discrepancies between your friends' ratings and your own? If so, how do you account for or explain them? Do the results confirm or weaken your confidence in pursuing a career in sales? Which personal characteristics do you think you need to work on to become more successful? Be prepared to discuss such questions in class or online.

Please rate the person who gave you this survey according to the following personal characteristics by circling the appropriate response. Since your friend will use the results to help determine whether he/ she is suited for a particular profession, it is important that you be candid. When you are finished, return the completed survey to your friend.

1. Enthusiastic

Always Usually Seldom Never

2. Empathetic, Able to Understand Others

Always Usually Seldom Never

3. Goal-Directed

Always Usually Seldom Never

4. Able to Ask Good Questions

Always Usually Seldom Never

5. Resourceful, Creative

Always	Usually	Seldom	Never

6. Well Organized, Efficient

Always	Usually	Seldom	Never

7. Self-Motivated, Responsible

Always	Usually	Seldom	Never

8. Persevering, Determined, Tenacious

Always	Usually	Seldom	Never

9. Pleasant, Personable, Outgoing

Always	Usually	Seldom	Never

CASE STUDIES

The following case studies present you with selling scenarios that require you to apply the critical skills discussed in the chapter and give you training through practical learning situations. They are meant to be both engaging and challenging, and like the exercises, don't have one right answer.

CASE 1.1 – WHOM WOULD YOU RECOMMEND?

Imagine that you work for a professional recruiting firm that has been retained by a large electrical equipment-manufacturing corporation to recommend a new salesperson for the corporation's regional sales force. Your job as a recruiter is to select and pass along the résumé of the single applicant whom you judge most likely to succeed. You conduct your search under conflicting pressures: on the one hand, you have time to interview only three candidates; on the other hand, the one you recommend must be retained by the corporation for at least three months, or your firm will be required to return its fee.

1. **Greg** strikes you immediately as a go-getter. Upon entering your office, he strides confidently across the room, arm outstretched to shake your hand, while he looks you in the eye and announces how pleased he is to meet you. Before you can invite him to sit, he perches on the edge of the chair in front of your desk and launches into a list of reasons about why he is qualified for this job. As he talks, you become aware that he is pleasant, well dressed, outgoing, and very enthusiastic about working for your client. He has researched the company and has marshaled all of the factors in his background that make him a good match for the position. Although you haven't said much, you really didn't need to, since Greg has done a good job of anticipating your questions and concerns. After about 20 minutes, he asks if you need anything else and stands, thanking you for such a pleasant interview.

2. **Martha** presents a somewhat reserved demeanor. Although pleasant and friendly, she is obviously nervous despite her impressive résumé. As you ask about her prior experience, she reveals that her last employer terminated her because she didn't meet her sales quota. Compelled to take a direct sales job in an office supply store because of her family's relocation to New Jersey, Martha claims that she never received significant product training or positive support from management when she couldn't produce. Nevertheless, because of her previous success as a B2B (business-to-business) representative for a hardwood importing company, she feels that she would thrive in a similar B2B environment. She exhibits pride in telling you how she cultivated potential customers for as long as two years and how she always followed up with her repeat clients to make sure that their needs were being met. Before she leaves, she briefly summarizes her selling success in a B2B situation and hopes that her lack of technical knowledge won't hamper her being considered for this position.

3. **Cynthia** is an older applicant who wants to change careers. There is a direct, no-nonsense air about her as she explains why. For 17 years, she worked as a mechanical engineer for a major tool and die manufacturer, rising to the level of design supervisor. When her position was outsourced to a plant overseas, she found herself at a crossroads. Frankly, she was tired of working in a design lab with the same dozen people all day, and similar jobs in her field were becoming rare. Although she admits that she has no sales training whatever, she is hoping that her technical background will gain the attention of the company's sales manager. At the conclusion of her interview, she points out that working for the same company for 17 years testifies to her perseverance, dedication, and ability to work with others. You assure her that her application will receive every consideration.

With your own firm's fee on the line, which applicant will you recommend, and why?

Which applicant most closely approximates your personality and style, and why?

CASE 1.2 – THE DEJECTED COLLEAGUE

Mike was on a rampage. Having knocked over the water cooler in the copy room, he proceeded to kick in the front of one of the copiers. Hearing the commotion, Frank, his friend and colleague, burst through the closed door, finding Mike slumped over and in tears.

"Hey, buddy, what's the matter? What's wrong?" Frank asked, putting his arm around Mike's shoulder.

"I just can't take it anymore," Mike managed to choke out between sobs. "I'm a failure. I'm going to quit. I've failed my family and myself."

"Has anything in particular happened?" Frank knew that Mike had been in a sales slump, but he didn't know exactly what Mike was coping with.

"I've lost 2 big accounts. I can't take the rejection anymore," Mike sobbed. "And the long hours and travel are killing my family life."

"I understand," said Frank softly as Mike's sobbing subsided. "Here, let me help you clean up this mess. Then, let's go get a cup of coffee somewhere so we can talk about all this."

What should Frank say to Mike in the coffee shop? Mike is clearly having some problems with aspects of the sales profession in general. Are these problems the sort of thing that salespersons can reasonably expect to encounter? What should Frank help Mike call to mind that would get Mike back on the right track? How can Frank be empathetic without allowing Mike's dejection to continue to be overwhelming?

Chapter 1 Footnotes

1. Conrad Hilton in *Sales Success: 62 Quotes, Special Report*, accessed April 20, 2011, www.eyeonsales.com.
2. Dean M Brenner, "Task-oriented selling," *Advisor Today*. Vol. 98, Is. 12, (December 2003), 62.
3. Susan Hodges," Recommissioning your sales," *ELT*, Vol.15, Is. 2 (February 2003), 22-28.
4. Anonymous, "Surveys Reveal Compensation for Call-Center Sales Professionals," *IOMA's Report on Salary Surveys*. New York: (Sep 2009), Vol 09, Is 9, 2.
5. Anonymous, "Two Surveys Examine Pay for Sales and Marketing Positions," *IOMA's Report on Salary Surveys*. New York: (Jun 2010), Vol 10, Is 6, 9.
6. Simon Bartley, "Seeing is believing!" *Training Journal*. Ely: (Feb 2008), 16.
7. Bersin, Josh. "Spending on Corporate Training Soars: Employee Capabilities Now A Priority." *Forbes*. Forbes, Feb 4, 2014. Web.
8. Bob O'Connor, "Business Sense: Training Yourself and Your Staff to Win," *Motor*; (Feb 2007).
9. Dave Hagel, "Why You Need to Hire the Best," *The Canadian Manager*. Toronto: (Spring 2007), Vol. 32, Is. 1, 12.
10. Charles W. Stephens, "Why is Training so Important?" *Industrial Distribution*, Vol. 89, No. 2 (February 2000), 4.
11. Weber, Lauren. "Why It's So Hard to Fill Sales Jobs." *The Wall Street Journal*, February 6, 2015. Web.
12. Laura Mazur, "UK banks must refocus on the personal touch," *Marketing*, (March 4, 2004), 16.
13. Jack Foster, "A Novel Approach To the Market," *Agency Sales*. Irvine: (Dec 2009), Vol. 39, Is. 11, 10.
14. See the following sources: D.L. Thompson, "Stereotype of the Salesperson," *Harvard Business Review*, Vol. 50, No. 1, (January/February 1972), 20-29; Robert W. Cook and Timothy Hartman, "Female College Student Interest in a Sales Career: A Comparison," *Journal of Personal Selling & Sales Management*, Vol. 6, (May 1986), 29-34; Michael Swenson, William Swinyard, Frederick Langrehr, and Scott Smith, "The Appeal of Personal Selling as a Career: A Decade Later," *The Journal of Personal Selling & Sales Management*, Vol. 13, No. 1 (Winter 1993), 51; "Sales Strikes Out on Campus," *Sales & Marketing Management* (November 1997), 13; "Selling Sales to Students," *Sales & Marketing Management* (January 1998), 15; Harry Harmon, "An Examination of Students' Perceptions

of a Situationally Described Career in Personal Selling," *Journal of Professional Services Marketing*, Vol. 19, No. 1 (Fall 1999), 119-136; Susan DelVecchio, "An Investigation of African-American Perceptions of Sales Careers," *The Journal of Personal Selling & Sales Management*, Vol. 29, No. 1 (Winter 2000), 43-52.

15. Anonymous, "Power of self-image psychology," *The American Salesman*, Vol. 48, Is. 5, (May 2003), 21.

16. Pink, Daniel. *To Sell is Human: The Surprising Truth About Moving Others.* Riverhead: New York, 2013. Print.

17. Halvorson, Heidi Grant. "Yes, You Can Learn to Sell." *Harvard Business Review*, Feb 19, 2013. Web.

18. Steven N. Kaplan, Mark M. Klebanov, and Morten Sorensen, "Which CEO Characteristics and Abilities Matter?" *University of Chicago Graduate School of Business*, August 2008.

19. Chitwood, Roy. "Best salesperson in the company should be the CEO." *Puget Sound Business Journal*. July 30, 2013.

20. "Sales Departments Are Ready to Spend Money and Hire People in 2011," *PR Newswire*. New York: (Jan 7, 2011), and David J. Cicelli, "Smart Management: Selling Into 2010: A Cause for Optimism?" *Sales&Marketing.com*, posted July 31, 2010, accessed Mar 20, 2015. Web.

21. Sherry Siegel, "Selling Your Way to the Top," *Success*, (January/February 2014), Vol. 34, No. 1, 44.

22. Derek Newton, *Sales Force Performance and Turnover* (Cambridge, MA: Marketing Science Institute, 1973), 3; Derek Newton, "Get the Most Out of Your Sales Force," *Harvard Business Review* (September/ October 1969), 130-143.

23. Donston-Miller, Debra. "How to Leverage Social Networking to Get Your Next Job." *The Ladders.com*. The Ladders, August 31, 2015. Web.

24. David McClelland, "Hiring Top Performers,"*Success* (May 1994), Vol. 41, No. 4, 34; Brian Azar, "Are You a Master Salesperson," *Personal Selling Power* (April 1992), Vol. 12, No. 3, 27; and "Qualities to Look for When You're Hiring," *Sales and Marketing Management*, (August 13, 1995), 84-87.

25. Howard Feiertag, "Listening skills, enthusiasm top list of salespeople's best traits," *Hotel and Motel Management*, Vol. 217, Is. 13, (July 15, 2002), 20.

26. Tom Cunningham, Dorman Woodall, Willard Scott, and Paul Wheaton, "Training New Hires for Competitive Advantage," *Salesandmarketing.com*, posted Nov 16, 2010, accessed June 20, 2015, Web.

27. "Time Management Key to Successful Sales Results, Watson Wyatt Survey Finds," *PR Newswire*. New York: (Oct. 5, 2006).

28. Jim John, "Tough Times Reveal True Sales Professionals," *Salesandmarketing.com*, posted July 31, 2010, accessed April 20, 2015, Web.

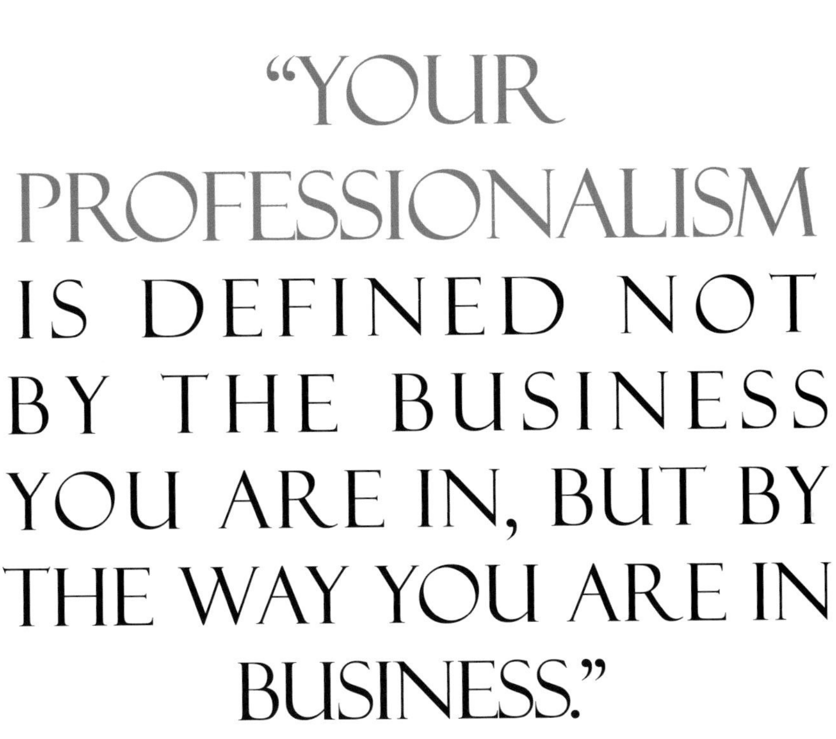
"YOUR PROFESSIONALISM IS DEFINED NOT BY THE BUSINESS YOU ARE IN, BUT BY THE WAY YOU ARE IN BUSINESS."
–DR. TONY ALESSANDRA

CHAPTER 2 RELATIONSHIP SELLING

OVERVIEW

You gain a better understanding of the complete selling situation and the problems it generates by breaking the sale into its basic tasks. There are several steps to achieving a successful sale. An eight-step sales cycle is introduced in chapter 2 and explained in detail in chapters 7 to 14. If you understand what the steps are in the Sales Cycle Framework for Relationship Selling and what is required to make each step a successful endeavor, then you will become a professional in selling much quicker than those who are simply stumbling through the process trying to figure it out.

OBJECTIVES

- Understand the role of relationship selling in today's market and how it differs from past stereotypes of selling.
- Learn the steps in relationship selling and the purpose of each step.
- Compare and contrast relationship selling and the traditional sales model.
- Introduce the Sales Cycle Framework for Relationship Selling.
- Examine the usefulness of continuous quality improvement in a sales organization.
- Understand the importance of relationships in today's multicultural world.

THE HEART OF SELLING

The profound effects of the Internet and technology on professional selling are impossible to deny. According to a new report by *Forrester Research Inc.*, 60 percent of U.S. retail sales will involve the Internet by 2017, either as a direct e-commerce transaction or as part of a shopper's research on a laptop or mobile device.[1] With all the changes that have taken place in selling over the past decade, it's easy to see why some industry observers speculate that advances in technology have made the traditional salesperson obsolete. But it's not the salesperson that's become obsolete. It's the old sales techniques themselves that have become obsolete because of trends that are reshaping the sales process.[2]

As a salesperson, are you really at risk of being replaced by a website? The truth is that unless you are truly helping your customers achieve results they otherwise would not be able to achieve without you, what you do is at risk. That doesn't mean that the sales profession is going away. In fact, it will only continue to grow once more salespeople realize that their job descriptions have changed. They can no longer simply be order takers. Instead, they must see their role as being the ones to help customers find and develop new opportunities. Today's sales force must assume a far greater role in the success of their customers and clients—and relationship selling is the way to achieve that.[3]

View yourself not as the conveyor of information, but as the developer of opportunities.

The role of the salesperson has never been more important. In the relationship process, the buyer requires advice and advanced expertise, and it is here that face-to-face selling has been and will continue to be the most effective channel to the customer. Even Internet sales companies such as Charles Schwab and Dell Computer have created face-to-face sales forces to reach the segments of their markets requiring complex customized products and services. This new selling is all about value creation: ***How the selling process itself can be used to create value for the customer.***

Relationship selling, in which sales professionals demonstrate not just a product's technical features, but also how it can solve a business or consumer problem and save money isn't a novel idea. The concept has been alive in marketing circles for a long time, and with the decrease in consumer confidence during tough economic times and the rise of Internet sales, it is hard to imagine companies still not adopting this style of selling.[4] Positioning yourself as consultant and partner creates a more equal relationship with prospects and customers. The willingness and ability to meet each client's needs is the cornerstone of building partnerships.

Build or Break a Relationship

Partnership is a positive word that makes customers feel that you are looking out for their best interests. The partnership formed between the buyer and seller is not a legal partnership; it is a part of the continuous quality improvement process companies are implementing. Today's sales forces take time to get to know the customer's business situation, needs, cash flow issues, decision-making process, and the competitive environment. For customers, a buying decision usually means a decision to enter into a long-term relationship with salespeople and their companies. It is much like a "business marriage." They have a variety of options and choices open to them, including not buying anything at all. When customers make a decision to buy from a salesperson, they become dependent on that sales rep. And since they have likely had unpleasant buying experiences in the past, they are often uneasy and uncertain about getting into this kind of dependency relationship.[5]

Exhibit 2.1 illustrates the key elements that can build or break this trust-bond relationship between buyer and seller. Relationship selling allows you to grasp a company's needs by putting yourself on the customer's side of the desk. *You are first a diagnostician.*

EXHIBIT 2.1 HOW TO BUILD OR BREAK A RELATIONSHIP

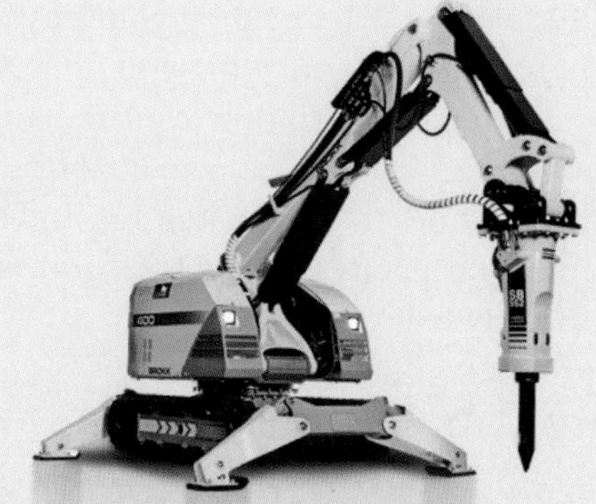

RELATIONSHIP BUILDERS

1. Treat customers like lifelong partners.
2. Become a solutions provider.
3. Deliver more service than you promise.
4. Schedule regular service calls.
5. Develop open and honest communication.
6. Use the "we can" approach.
7. Take responsibility for mistakes made.
8. Be an ally for the customer's business.

RELATIONSHIP BREAKERS

1. Focus only on making the sale.
2. Simply wait for a problem to develop.
3. Over-promise and under-deliver.
4. Wait for customers to call you.
5. Lie or make exaggerated claims.
6. Use the "us versus them" approach.
7. Blame somebody else. Knock a competitor.
8. Focus on your own personal gain.

Relationship salespeople create an information transfer, a support for client goals, and enthusiasm for their success. The top salespeople have escaped the "selling" mentality and let the customer tell them their needs. In the face of increased competition and the plethora of options that exist in the software space, *Huddle*—a provider of secure cloud-based collaboration software for large enterprises and government agencies—knows that the customers' needs absolutely come first. They know that with 80 percent of a company's future revenue coming from just 20 percent of its existing customers, it's essential that customers are always front-of-mind when you're developing the strategy for your organization and executing your business. In essence, this means thinking about how the customer would react in everything they do and putting themselves in the customer's shoes.[6]

That is the precise mentality that will insure a company's survival. It isn't always about who has the better product or best price, but who can best provide solutions to the customer on a consistent basis, and on their terms.

To be a consultant rather than just a salesperson you have to be a creative resource, a value provider, and a friend to clients. The relationship salesperson works hard helping others succeed—not just helping them purchase. Unless you are willing to commit to excellence, consultation will not occur. Here are some key characteristics of relationship selling:

- Discover and understand the customers' problems and needs.
- Partner with your customers and become a valuable resource for information.
- Demonstrate to customers how they can achieve their goals with your product or service.
- Have a true conviction that your company, your product, and your services are the best for your customers.
- Believe in yourself because a positive attitude makes it all work.

RELATIONSHIP SELLING VS. TRADITIONAL SELLING

If you understand what the steps are in the *Relationship Cycle of Selling*, and what it takes to make each step a successful endeavor, then you will become a professional in selling much more quickly than those individuals who are simply stumbling through the process trying to figure it out. The sales cycle model in the actual face-to-face meeting between the salesperson and the prospect includes these four steps:

- The Approach
- Identifying Needs
- Making the Presentation
- Handling Objections and Gaining Commitment

Exhibit 2.2 contrasts the amount of time the relationship salesperson and the traditional salesperson spend in each step. You can see from the figure that the old pyramid model of selling has been turned upside down. The 40 percent of the equation for the traditional model that used to be closing is now building trust in the relationship model. Meanwhile reassuring the customer and closing has shrunk to just 10 percent in the new model.

The relationship salesperson spends the vast majority of time in the first two steps—building trust, asking questions and listening—whereas the traditional salesperson exerts most of the effort and the majority of time on presenting features and trying to close. The goal is to learn how to communicate with your business partners and establish an alliance that is extensive in scope and relevant to the customer's own vision.[7]

EXHIBIT 2.2 RELATIONSHIP SELLING VERSUS TRADITIONAL SELLING

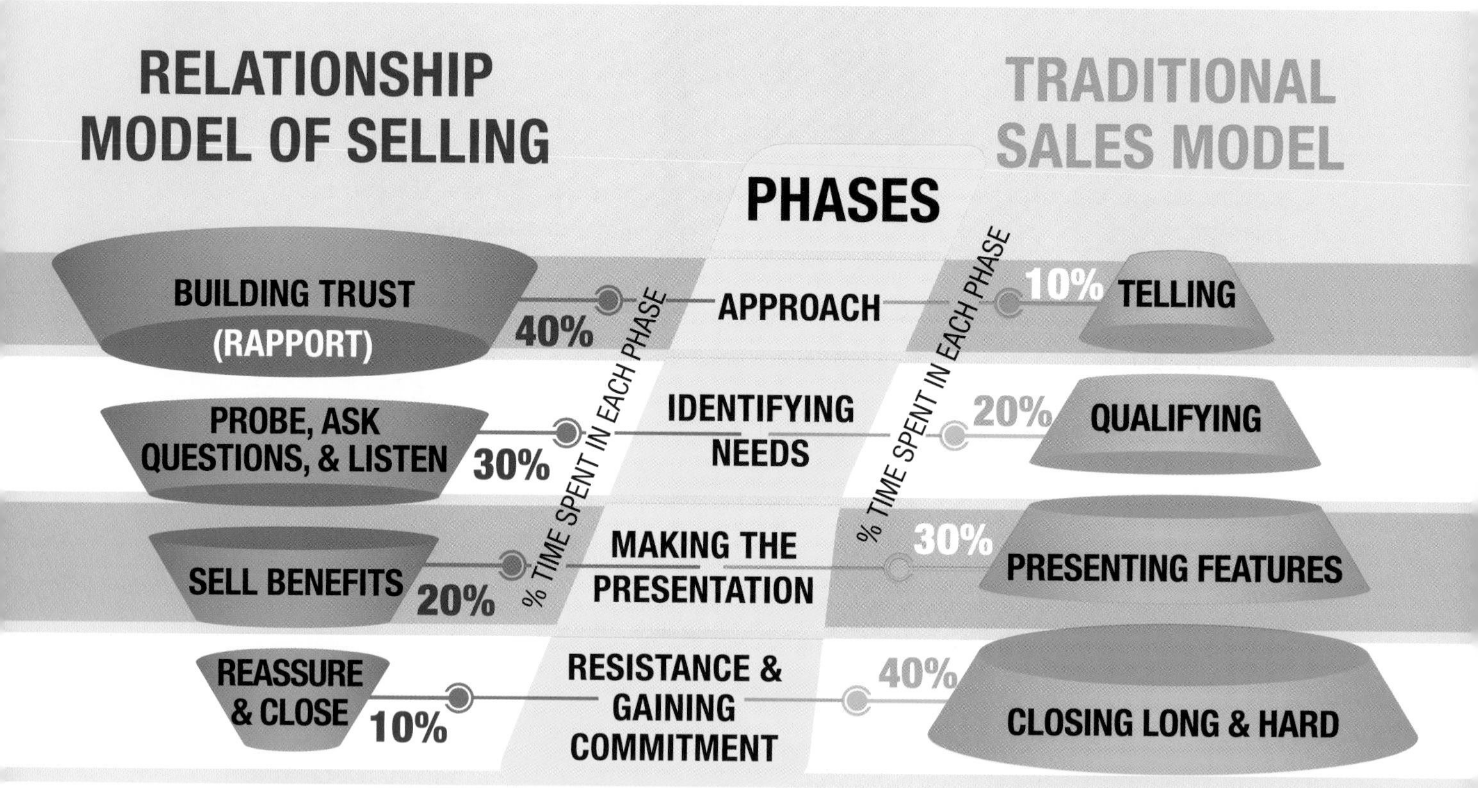

RELATIONSHIP MODEL OF SELLING	% TIME SPENT IN EACH PHASE	PHASES	% TIME SPENT IN EACH PHASE	TRADITIONAL SALES MODEL
BUILDING TRUST (RAPPORT)	40%	APPROACH	10%	TELLING
PROBE, ASK QUESTIONS, & LISTEN	30%	IDENTIFYING NEEDS	20%	QUALIFYING
SELL BENEFITS	20%	MAKING THE PRESENTATION	30%	PRESENTING FEATURES
REASSURE & CLOSE	10%	RESISTANCE & GAINING COMMITMENT	40%	CLOSING LONG & HARD

Customers Buy Solutions

Technology helps open new markets, speeds communications between sellers and their prospects and customers, and frankly, creates a whole new set of problems that you can help clients solve. Customers can now conduct many of their transactions online and have little need for a salesperson that doesn't add value to the transaction. This requires a much more sophisticated and complex set of skills than those possessed by the traditional salesperson.

Low-end selling—which is essentially transaction processing and order taking—continues to shift away from traditional sales forces into the more efficient, cost-effective, and faster setting provided by online sales. But this doesn't mean that the Internet will replace the professional salesperson; selling is simply becoming more strategic. It's moving up the food chain, and the need for relationship selling is increasing. Your company may sell accounting services, office equipment, or design websites. However, that's really not what customers are buying—customers are trying to increase sales and improve efficiency. By demonstrating how you can help customers achieve the goals of their organization, you distinguish yourself from competitors. Selling is still about relationships, and people buy from people they like.[8]

Order-takers will vanish, but creative salespeople who know that selling is about building long-term partnerships will flourish.

THE RELATIONSHIP SELLING CYCLE

A better understanding of the complete selling situation and the problems it generates may be gained by breaking the sale into its basic tasks. These steps are presented in a logical sequence, but they are not necessarily chronological and the order of the steps will vary. The ebb and flow of a sales interview defies attempts to package it into nice, neat compartments.

Regardless of account size or potential, certain predictable tasks must be performed. These tasks, such as identifying prospects and determining needs, may be called the steps in a sale or the selling cycle. When organized into a prescribed sequence they comprise an overall structure rather than a lock-step approach to selling. The eight basics of successful selling described in Exhibit 2.3 are the focus of chapters 7 through 14, and they represent your guide to a successful sales career.

EXHIBIT 2.3

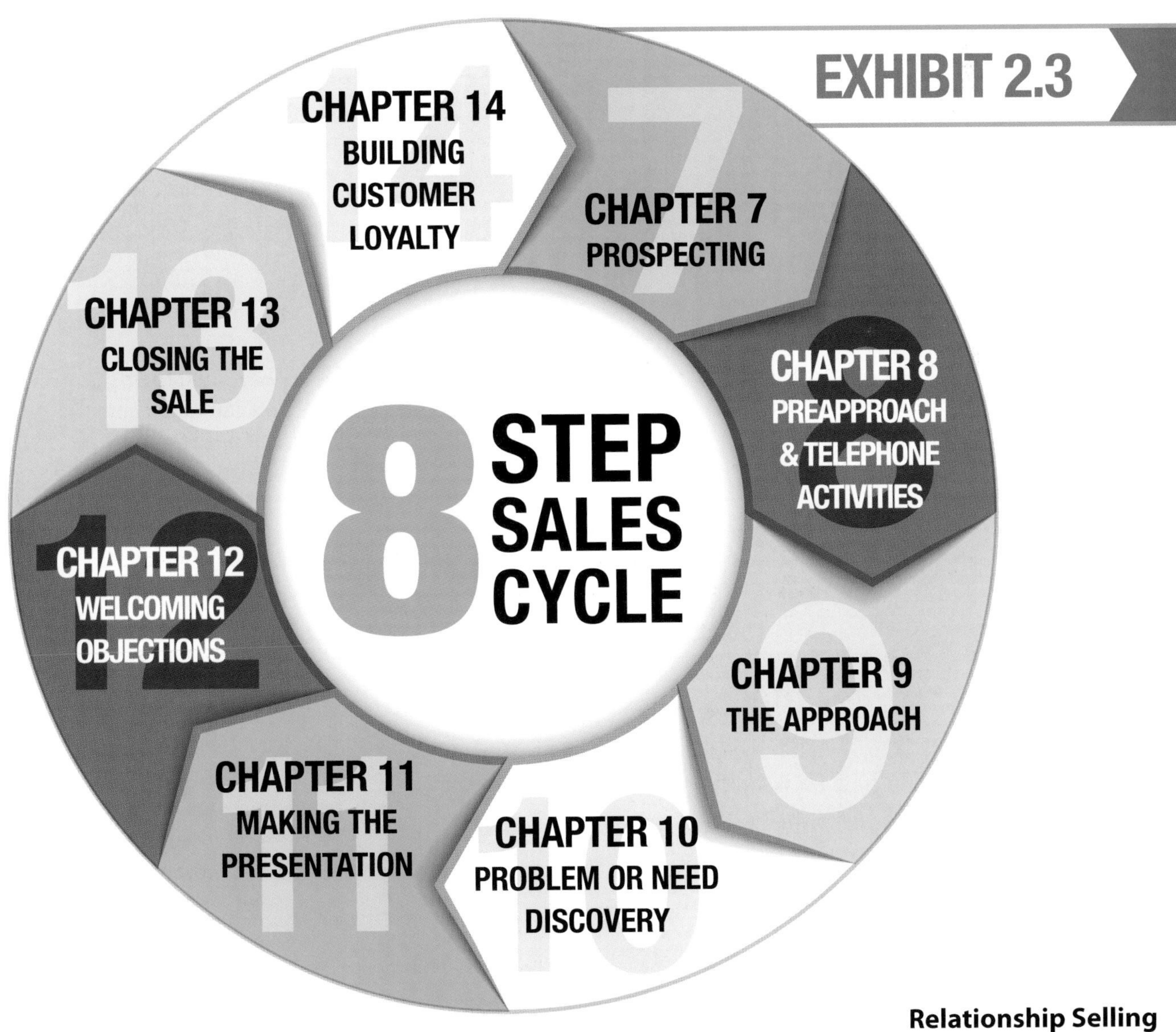

Phase One

IDENTIFYING A QUALIFIED PROSPECT. *Prospecting* is the process of searching for someone with a need for the product or service, the ability to pay for it, and the authority to make a buying decision. One of the first steps in the process of finding these qualified prospects is to review your current accounts to see who needs service, who might want to increase the quantity purchased, or who may buy new products or services for the first time. At the same time, survey your territory to identify new leads and find out information on the businesses in your area that might be interested in your product. The reason for this step is simple: Sales professionals must study the people they want to approach.[9]

PLANNING PREAPPROACH ACTIVITIES. After you identify qualified prospects, establish a definite purpose for each sales call. To accomplish this, you must make an evaluation of your potential customers' needs and determine also who the decision-makers are in the companies you have studied. These activities equip you to interact with the customer and then develop an action plan and call schedule to set appointments.

THE SOCIAL MEDIA CONNECTION

How Social Media Can Make Cold Calling a Little Easier

If you have ever been to the chiropractor, you know that they like to take x-rays and observe your posture before they ever make their first adjustment. Such "pre-checks" make the entire adjustment a more helpful and relevant experience. Like a chiropractor, if you jump and try to 'fix' a prospect's problems too soon without the proper preapproach, you will simply not get through to as many people as you should.

The good news is that by using effective social media "touches" before your next sales call, you will have a greater likelihood to make a genuine connection with prospects—and hopefully secure that first appointment with them. And the best part is you will seem more professional and less intrusive. Here are some great ways to use social media to get on your prospects' radar to turn a cold call into a warm call:

- If they have a blog, comment on a relevant post.
- Follow that prospect on Twitter.
- Send a LinkedIn request prior to your first call so that your name is familiar.
- Retweet or mention your prospect in a tweet.
- Join the same LinkedIn group and contribute to a conversation within that group.
- Like a comment made by the prospect.
- Endorse them for a skill on LinkedIn.

Phase Two

APPROACHING THE PROSPECT. What happens during the opening minutes of the face-to-face encounter affects the success of the whole presentation. Some people simply do not thaw out immediately, and you must find icebreakers that help the prospect feel at ease with you. This is why you should spend time finding the prospect's comfort level.[10] Most first-time meetings between salesperson and prospect produce an *egocentric predicament* arising from your fear of being rejected and the prospect's fear of being sold something that is not really wanted or needed. By redesigning your approach to selling, you can calm the prospect's fear of buying and reduce your own fear of selling.

TREAT PROSPECTS AS INDIVIDUALS AND NOT AS CARBON COPIES OF EVERYONE ELSE.

DISCOVERING NEEDS. During this step of the sales encounter, you and your client discover together whether the client needs or wants something that you can provide. Because the success of the whole process rests on this basic discovery, the relationship salesperson spends whatever time is necessary and asks questions to get to know the prospect's needs and problems. For this reason, one of your primary goals in every sales situation should be to *create an atmosphere within which an act of trust can occur*—to make a friend rather than a sale, a customer who has confidence in the integrity and ability of the salesperson, and confidence in the company and its product or service. You don't talk prospects into a sale; you listen them into a sale.

MAKING THE PRESENTATION. Your evaluation of the prospect's situation should lead you naturally into the presentation of product benefits that fit the needs your client expressed. Every product or service has both features and benefits. A *feature* is any fact about the product or service, tangible or intangible. For example, a feature of a particular automobile is front-wheel drive. However, prospects want to know about *benefits* rather than features. The front-wheel drive feature is meaningless unless it satisfies some need, solves some problem, or provides some benefit to the prospective customer. The benefits of front-wheel drive might be explained in terms of ease of handling, safety, or some other performance quality that promises to satisfy the prospect's need.

"In professional selling, as in medicine, prescription before diagnosis is malpractice."
Tony Alessandra

A prospect does not buy without being certain that what you are saying is true. That is why you do not create sales; rather, people buy based on their own expectations. No one likes to be sold. They like to see the value of what is being presented, and then they make their own buying decisions based on their own assessment of whether or not your product satisfies their needs. The salesperson who holds confident, positive expectations closes far more sales than the one who expects rejection.

HANDLING OBJECTIONS AND GAINING COMMITMENT. Now is the time to verbally clarify and confirm what both you and the client will do to make the solution work. This part of the overall process helps to avoid misunderstandings by bringing any that exist out into the open so they can be handled. Each clarification and confirmation adds weight to the case in favor of a

positive decision. As shown in Exhibit 2.4, when the scale of decision tips far enough toward the positive side, the prospect can, and does, say yes. When that happens, everyone wins—the client, you, and your company. Relationship selling is a matter of presenting positive benefits that respond to a need, use, and value. Selling in this manner reduces your need to deal with resistance, answer objections, or haggle over price. Since the client has been an active participant throughout, the commitment and close should be the natural conclusion to a successful sales interview.

EXHIBIT 2.4 THE SCALE OF DECISION

SELLING POSITIVE BENEFITS TIPS THE SCALE OF DECISION...

OBJECTIONS
EXCUSES
RESISTANCE

NEED
USE
VALUE

Phase Three

SERVICE AFTER THE SALE. The final phase of relationship selling is service after the sale. "Whether you call it customer retention, account management, relationship management, or just staying in touch, developing a strategy so that you don't lose the customers or clients you have is vital to the success of any business—especially now," says Rhonda Abrams, president of *The Planning Shop*, publisher of books for entrepreneurs.[11] Service, service, and more service is what counts and gives you a competitive edge. Plenty of satisfied customers do not come back unless you create some kind of trust-bond relationship.

Ultimately, you should look at customer satisfaction as an economic asset just like any other asset of the company. Service after the sale must be viewed as another essential step within the sales cycle.[12] Creating customer satisfaction is an income-producing endeavor. Clients must sense that you truly care about them. Service after the sale is your way of expressing appreciation for their business. Service makes the difference—and is as important as the quality of the product.

CONTINUOUS QUALITY IMPROVEMENT

There has been so much written on the concept of Total Quality Management that some have dismissed it as merely a theory that is discussed because it sounds good. But to ignore the underlying principles of TQM would not be sensible. The scope of a typical TQM program covers three main areas: 1) The quality system, 2) The process of continuous improvement, and 3) The development of the staff involved.[13] TQM is an essential building block for relationship selling, and the principles have practical implications for salespeople.

How does TQM fit into relationship selling? Most organizations have a strong strategic plan in place to achieve excellence and make sales. Where they struggle is in the execution. Organizations get the outcomes they seek only when they successfully hardwire excellence across all operational areas, and one way to achieve this is through implementation of Total Quality Management.[14] TQM has a customer orientation, and it is an outside-in approach to business. The center of all discussions is the customer; every one inside and outside the company is a customer. Continuous quality improvement is a philosophy, an overall style of management that focuses on customer satisfaction.

Federal Express CEO Fred Smith states that, "We aim for 100 percent customer satisfaction and all FedEx employees must have an 'above and beyond' attitude when doing their jobs. The attitude of doing whatever it takes to serve the customers is reflected from top to bottom in the organization's structure; this kind of spirit is integral to the FedEx work culture."[15] But even before the customers can be serviced, Smith states that, "Employee satisfaction is a prerequisite to customer satisfaction."[16] Therefore, TQM not only focuses on fostering healthy relationships with customers, but also on building connections within organizations.

The list below highlights the main points of TQM that deal directly with fostering relationships and building lasting associations. While there are variations in the language and scope of TQM programs, it is possible to target these five principles that are especially relevant in the practice of relationship selling:

1. Listen and learn from your customers and your employees.
2. Continuously improve the partnership.
3. Build teamwork by establishing trust and mutual respect.
4. Do it right the first time to ensure customer satisfaction.
5. Improve communication in your own company to broaden the utilization of your company's resources. Everybody is involved in the relationship.

Service Quality

The concept of *service quality* has two dimensions: 1.The process of delivering the service, and 2. The actual outcome. What does an organization have to do to provide exceptional service quality that creates a favorable outcome, and how does the salesperson fit into the process? First, in order for everyone in your company to become customer-oriented, they must think in terms of the whole process rather than just their own tasks. The goal is to develop a customer, and that's a process in which the salesperson is only one player. The process includes production people, finance and marketing people, as well as customer service reps. So it's not left to you to solve a customer's problem; the whole organization gets behind the effort. Building customer relationships is everybody's responsibility.[17]

THE 85/15 RULE

TQM is established today thanks to the pioneering work of W. Edwards Deming. One of Deming's most important lessons is his "85-15" rule.[18] When things go wrong in the field, there is an 85 percent chance the system is at fault. Only about 15 percent of the time can the individual salesperson be blamed. TQM means the organization's culture is defined by and supports the constant attainment of customer satisfaction, through an integrated system of tools, techniques, and training.

It is important to focus on how you relate to plant and office employees, because this can make a difference in the way they treat your customers. It pays to be liked and appreciated by staff people, especially those in sales support, credit, billing, and shipping. Take a moment from time to time to compliment and thank the support people in your company for the great job they are doing.

"I can live for two months on a good compliment."
Mark Twain

Prospects and customers notice and think about everyone they come in contact with during the sales encounter. The relationship between perceived effort and customer service is a powerful one. When you and the customer interact, the quality of the interaction itself is an important part of the relationship. If the customer feels that the salesperson is empathetic during their interaction, it translates more naturally to customer happiness.[19]

Most business success stories involve taking an old idea or product and doing a better job with it than the next company. Amazon.com didn't invent book selling; they just did it better, giving customers the ability to have convenience, speed, and a wide selection at their fingertips. Then there is Southwest Airlines! They aren't the oldest airline around, but no one before Southwest had figured out how to offer passengers a simple and consistent service without extra fees in a way that has kept it a profitable business while other airlines struggle to survive. The overall point is this:

You can get a lot out of a current product or service if you change the processes around it, or change the process by which it is delivered. The objective is to change those processes enough that you are delivering more value to your customers or, at the very least, hold on to those customers by offering a fair price.

The $332,000 Customer

Tom Peters, author of *A Passion for Excellence*, says, "A customer is not a transaction; a customer is a relationship."[20] The missing link in service often is intense awareness of the customer's point of view. The process of handling the problem is as important to customers as the solution of the problem itself. The logical inference is that every company better organize its service delivery system to answer every customer's implied question: "What are you going to do for me today?"

Peters uses the example of Dallas car dealer Carl Sewell, who has written a book called *The $332,000 Customer*, because a loyal lifetime Cadillac customer buys that much from him. Peters goes on to suggest that happy lifetime customers generate four or five other happy lifetime customers for you. So in fact, one Cadillac customer is roughly a $1,500,000 customer.

Two investments Sewell has made illustrate his understanding of the value he places on customer satisfaction. Number one, he bought a street sweeper to keep the front of his dealership extra clean. First impressions count for everything, and people judge his dealership by the cleanliness of everything including the road in front of it. Secondly, he convinced an upscale local restaurant to open a branch in his service bay. When it's a simple repair, a lot of his customers come in and enjoy a hot meal while the work is being done.

Some salespeople will read about TQM and say, "This is nothing new; it is simply common sense." They are right, of course, but it has taken many years for men such as W. Edwards Deming, Joseph Juran, and Genichi Taguchi to refine and teach this philosophy.[21]

SELLING IN A MULTICULTURAL WORLD

With all of the talk about the globalization of markets, it can be easy to forget to look within our own companies for examples of the increase in cultural diversification. The truth is that while other professions have seen jumps in their numbers of workers from diverse ethnic backgrounds, the sales profession has been slow to follow.[22] But according to the latest U.S. Census data, with the number of minority business owners now totaling 22.1 percent, you should expect to see advances in the numbers of multicultural sales professionals to follow.[23]

Today's Diverse Workforce

These changes are exciting! Think of the benefits your company has to gain from the knowledge and experience of salespeople from diverse cultures. The multicultural background of your own sales staff is the bridge to developing more meaningful relationships with customers from around the world.[24] Though it is important to remember that each customer is an individual who shouldn't be stereotyped, understanding the broad characteristics of the different cultures represented in the business world can lead to better relationships, both within your company and with all customers.[25]

> **Relationships remain at the heart of developing trust and partnerships in a multicultural sales setting.**

AN EMPHASIS ON DIVERSITY. Understanding the multicultural perspectives of your sales force and your customers does not come without effort. For this shift in understanding to take place, companies will need to focus on ways to make improved relationships with multicultural partners a priority. As with other aspects of communication coming from your company, this shift needs to happen in a way that reminds customers and employees alike that they are valued as individuals. No one likes to feel that they are simply being used. One such company that has made a successful commitment to ethnic diversity is technology titan Apple Inc. They believe that:[26]

> "GREAT IDEAS PUSH THE WORLD FORWARD. AND THEY CAN COME FROM ANYWHERE. AT APPLE, WE RELY ON OUR EMPLOYEES' DIVERSE BACKGROUNDS AND PERSPECTIVES TO SPARK INNOVATION. SO WE'RE HIRING MORE INCLUSIVELY, CHOOSING PARTNERS WHO MAKE DIVERSITY A PRIORITY, AND CREATING OPPORTUNITIES FOR THE NEXT GENERATION."

Equipped for Understanding

Once companies have made multicultural relationships a priority, they must take active steps to make it happen. Employee education is essential! Depending on the level of interaction with people from varied backgrounds, the training may involve only a small component of new employee orientation. For others, it may mean the need for ongoing training. Nissan Motor Co. has been offering language training to its employees for years because the company recognizes the value of cross-cultural training and skill sets.[27]

A key principle behind TQM is that customer satisfaction begins inside your company with employee satisfaction. Only when you understand, respect, and support salespeople from all backgrounds can you understand and relate well to your customers.

The evidence of improved relationships is in the sales figures. A study published in *Personnel Psychology* shows that minority salespeople working in pro-diversity companies increase their annual sales by $21,000 to $27,000 per individual. Patrick F. McKay of the *School of Management and Labor Relations* at Rutgers University, says, "A pro-diversity climate is important to mitigate discrimination among African-American and Hispanic employees because they are most likely to experience discrimination." The employees' confidence in their company is seen in their confidence as salespeople, which in turn is reflected in their increased sales.[28]

SUMMARY

- The traditional role of selling has evolved from the art of persuasion to the psychology of relationship selling.
- The relationship cycle of selling begins with approaching the prospect, discovering needs, presenting your product or service as the solution, overcoming objections, and gaining commitment. Service after the sale completes the cycle.
- The purpose of the relationship approach to selling is to discover the needs or

problems of the prospect. You become a solutions provider! It is customer-oriented and requires extensive knowledge of the prospect.

- Build relationships through customer-oriented continuous quality improvement. This is an outside–in approach, encouraging the mindset that every one inside and outside the company is a customer.
- Understanding the perspectives and needs of your multicultural sales personnel leads to improved relationships with all types of customers.

REVIEW QUESTIONS

1. Compare and contrast the stereotype of traditional selling and professional relationship selling.

2. What questions must a salesperson answer 'yes' to before it is possible to make a recommendation to buy?

3. What is the difference between the features of the product and its benefits? Which is most useful in the selling situation? Why? Should the other, then, be mentioned at all? How?

4. Name at least three reasons why a prospect may resist making a buying decision. For each reason, tell how the salesperson could have prevented this particular type of resistance.

5. If sales resistance is encountered, how can the salesperson close the sale in spite of the resistance? Is this always synonymous with what is regarded as "hard sell"?

6. What is the purpose of service after the sale? What does it include? Whose responsibility is such service?

7. Who needs to be acquainted with the organization's basic philosophy of business? If that philosophy is not understood by all members of the organization, what types of problems might result? Why?

8. To what extent must a sales rep agree with the company's commitment to continuous quality improvement?

9. Why is multicultural diversity within companies important for businesses today? What impact does increased diversity have on the customer?

IN-CLASS EXERCISES

The following in-class exercises help build teams, improve communication, and emphasize the real-world side of selling. They are meant to be challenging, to help you learn how to deal with problems that have no single right answer, and to use a variety of skills beyond those employed in a typical review question. Read and complete each activity. Then in the next class, discuss and compare answers with other classmates.

EXERCISE 2.1 – CAN YOU SPOT "RELATIONSHIP SELLING?"

Divide into 4-person teams for this exercise. Working individually, conduct an online search to find 2 sales training videos that reflect traditional selling techniques and 2 sales training videos that present relationship selling techniques. Exchange your results with your other team members (this can be done online as well). Discuss everyone's results and, as a team, decide which single example of each approach is best or most obvious, and why.

Be careful that your team's final selection includes 2 videos that focus on the same part of the sales cycle (e.g., closing vs. closing, approach vs. approach, presentation vs. presentation). Otherwise, when you present your videos to the rest of the class, they would have no logically compelling reason to decide between them; they would be comparing apples with oranges, as it were.

In class (utilizing available technology), present your team's two selections and invite discussion of each by the class. Prod the class to consider each example in light of the two approaches to selling described in Chapter 2. Without presuming that one approach is superior to the other, ask the class which approach they find most effective, and why. No matter which video a majority of the class seems to prefer, see if you can convince them otherwise!

EXERCISE 2.2 – ENJOYABLE SELLING

For this exercise, pair up with another student whom you do not already know. Agree between you that for this exercise one of you will adopt the role of traditional seller, and the other the role of relationship seller. Outside of class, develop a complete sales script from approach through closing for selling your counterpart a new home entertainment system. Your script should be developed according to traditional sales methods or relationship sales methods as outlined in Chapter 2.

In class, alternate making your respective sales pitches to one another. Regardless of whether a sale was closed successfully in either case, jot down a brief response to each of the following questions. Think about the reasons for your responses, and be prepared to discuss them in class or online.

- What difficulties arose as you employed your script to sell the home entertainment system to your counterpart?
- Can you attribute any of these difficulties to the method of selling—traditional or relationship— that you used?
- As a customer, what did you find annoying, if anything, about your partner's approach to selling?
- As a seller, what did you find most annoying about your approach to selling?
- Given your total experience in this exercise, which approach to selling do you prefer, and why?

CASE STUDIES

The following case studies present you with selling scenarios that require you to apply the critical skills discussed in the chapter and give you training through practical learning situations. They are meant to be both engaging and challenging, and like the exercises, don't have one right answer.

CASE 2.1 – THE NERVOUS VP FOR SALES

As vice president for marketing & sales for Netwerx, Inc., a firm specializing in videoconferencing equipment and software systems, Tom Nelson was nervous. He had just left a meeting with the company's chief financial officer, Brad Poindexter, that had not gone well. Tom had passed along the news from one of his sales managers that a major account was on the verge of going sour. The sales manager had reported that Secure Title, a title search and insurance company with offices in 50 major metropolitan areas, had not responded to communications regarding renewal of their annual contract. The account was worth $450,000 per year to Netwerx; and in the current business climate, they could not afford to lose it. Worse, word on the street was that Secure Title was aggressively shopping for a lower price, since its own business had fallen off due to the commercial real estate collapse. Brad, the CFO, had pushed Tom hard: "What in blazes is the matter with your people? Tell 'em to get on the horn and find out what's going on. If we lose this account, heads will roll, starting with yours, Tom!"

Tom had been worried for quite a while before this crisis. From a friend in R&D, he knew that Netwerx was about to roll out an improved, more efficient software package that would run on their existing videoconferencing hardware, but no meetings with marketing and sales had been held. Moreover, other vendors with inferior products were touting their lower price with some success. Netwerx had already seen a 17% decline in annual revenues. With no Christmas bonus last year, some of his salespeople were getting restless.

Ever since the annual meeting of the National Marketing and Sales Association last fall, Tom had been mulling over the desirability of shifting strategies for Netwerx. At the meeting, he had been exposed to a series of presentations on "relationship selling" and TQM. Netwerx had never entertained such an approach. Up to this point, the company had focused on touting the superior features of their system, giving their clients tickets to sporting events and golf outings, and aggressively closing sales. But Tom feared that such a traditional approach might not be effective in a sluggish economy. A meeting of Netwerx's executive committee was scheduled for next week. The CFO had made it clear that he expected a positive report from Tom.

What should Tom say to the executive committee? Which factors should Tom consider as he decides what to do?

CASE 2.2 – 4-LEAF-CLOVER'S TRANSITION

The "boiler room" at 4-Leaf-Clover, a 66-year-old financial planning firm, was aptly named. Hour by hour, day in and day out, the phones never stopped. Using automatic dialers connected to a high-end CRM (customer relationship management) system, the sales force continually called random prospects to elicit new business. Typically, after a few perfunctory questions, attention would turn quickly to a presentation of the features and advantages of new financial instruments structured for wealthy individuals who were not averse to risk. The psychological temperature of the stress-filled room was high. Most staff members quit after less than a year; those who stayed more than 2 years were called "veterans." What worked in the past, however, was no longer as effective, especially in a volatile economy plagued by recent financial scandals.

Jasper Harrington, vice president for sales at 4-Leaf, has just convinced his superiors that something different, called "relationship selling," should be tried. Harrington wants to begin with a select group of 6 high-producing salespersons to see if they can outperform their colleagues regarding total revenue acquired over a period of 6 months. If the project is successful, the new program will be rolled out company-wide. The only catch? Harrington must train his trial group himself.

How should Harrington structure his training? What points should be emphasized for the sales group? Where do you think Harrington will encounter the strongest resistance from this group? What can Harrington say that might convince the trial group to make the switch to becoming consultants, rather than just salespersons, for their clients?

As the project goes forward, how should Harrington measure the performance of the trial group in terms somewhat more meaningful than total revenue produced? What other criteria of performance are important for assessing the success of relationship selling?

Chapter 2 Footnotes

1. Dusto, Amy. "60% of U.S. retail sales will involve the web by 2017." *Internet Retailer*, Oct 30, 2013. Web.
2. Smith, Ned. "Will Technology Advances Mark the Death of a Salesman?" *Business News Daily*, June 15, 2014. Web.
3. Hunter, Mark. "Is a Salesperson Nothing More than a Website that Breathes?" *The Sales Hunter.* Sales Motivation Blog, 2013. Web
4. Christian Grönroos, *Service Management and Marketing: A Customer Relationship Management Approach*, 3rd Ed. (Chichester: John Wiley & Sons, 2007).
5. Debbie Howell, "Selling trust, expertise hits home with customers," *DSN Retailing Today*, March 27, 2006.
6. Dasteel, Jeb. "Award-Winning Companies Put Customers First." *Forbes*. Forbes, Jan 15, 2014. Web.
7. Barbara Geraghty, *Visionary Selling* (New York: Simon and Schuster, 2007), 240.
8. Robert McGarvey and Babs S. Harrison, "How Tech Hip are You?" *Selling Power* (March 2013), 77.
9. Richard Lee, "Expert touts importance of using social media," *Advocate*, Stamford, Conn: (Mar 20, 2011), C1.
10. Bill Brooks, "The Power of Active Listening," *The American Salesman*, Vol 51, Is. 6, (Jun. 2006), 12.
11. Rhonda Abrams, "Strategies: Make customer retention priority No. 1," *USA Today*.com.

Posted May 29, 2009, accessed April 7, 2015.

12. Hanzo Ng, "After sales service secrets!" *Malaysian Business*, Kuala Lumpur: (April 1, 2009), 54.
13. Manus Rungtusanatham, Jeffrey A Ogden, Bin Wu, "Advancing theory
14. development in total quality management: A 'Deming management method' perspective," *International Journal of Operations & Production Management,* Bradford: (2003), Vol. 23, Is. 7/8, 918.
15. Quint Studer. "How to achieve and sustain excellence: there are seven ways to hardwire excellent outcomes. Do you know what they are?" *Healthcare Financial Management*; (June, 2007).
16. Jude P. Morte. "Special Feature: Best Employers in the Philippines," *BusinessWorld*, Manila: (May 29, 2003), 1.
17. Rose Knotts. "Rambo Doesn't Work Here Anymore," *Business Horizons*, (January February 1992), 44-46.
18. Mark Godson, *Relationship Marketing* (Oxford: Oxford University Press, 2009), 18.
19. W. Edwards Deming, *Out of the Crisis* (Cambridge, MA: MIT, 2000).
20. Margery Weinstein, "How May I Train You? Customer service training programs put the focus on buyer bliss," *Training* (Aug 2006), 29.
21. Tom Peters, "Meeting the Dangers and Opportunities of Chaos," *Personal Selling Power*, Vol. 10, No. 6, (September 1990), 49.
22. Anonymous, "TQM: A snapshot of the experts," *Measuring Business Excellence*, Bradford: (2002), Vol. 6, Is. 3, 54-57.
23. Craig A. Martin, "Racial diversity in professional selling: an empirical investigation of the differences in the perceptions and performance of African-American and Caucasian salespeople," *The Journal of Business & Industrial Marketing*, Santa Barbara: (2005), Vol. 20, Is. 6, 285.
24. "USA Quick Facts," *U.S. Census Bureau*, accessed August 4, 2015.
25. Barbara J. Bowes, "The business case for workplace diversity," *CMA Management*, Hamilton: (Dec 2007/Jan 2008), Vol. 81, Is. 8, 14.
26. John Hooker, "Cultural Differences in Business Communication," Tepper School of Business, Carnegie Mellon University, December 2008, accessed Feb 12, 2015.
27. See more at http://www.apple.com/diversity/Gale, Sarah Fister. "Corporate Foreign Language Training on the Rise." *Workforce*, May 16, 2013.
28. Clif Boutelle, "Minority Sales Personnel Have Better Results in Workplaces With Supportive Diversity Climates," *Society for Industrial & Organizational Psychology, Inc.*, accessed June 9, 2015, Web.

PART II

CULTIVATING AN ETHICS CLIMATE AND DEVELOPING COMMUNICATION SKILLS

Few professions give you more opportunities for rejection on a daily basis than does the field of sales. Because of the often-cutthroat nature of selling, some salespeople do whatever it takes to stay ahead and edge out the competition. ***CHAPTER 3*** discusses the need for a strong ethical and moral character to sustain a sales career. Honest and caring service brings customers back and assures success. Success in professional selling also depends upon your ability to have a productive exchange of information with prospects and customers.

The more you understand about prospects and their decision-making process, the more readily you can discover what they need and want, and this is covered in more detail in ***CHAPTER 4***. Because success in relationship selling depends on accurately getting your message across to prospects, chapter 4 also describes how to break through communication barriers.

An especially useful tool for gaining insight into how the prospect is thinking is knowledge of the social styles model, which is discussed in ***CHAPTER 5***. A social style is the way a person sends and receives information. It is a method for finding the best way to approach a prospect and to set up a working relationship with that person.

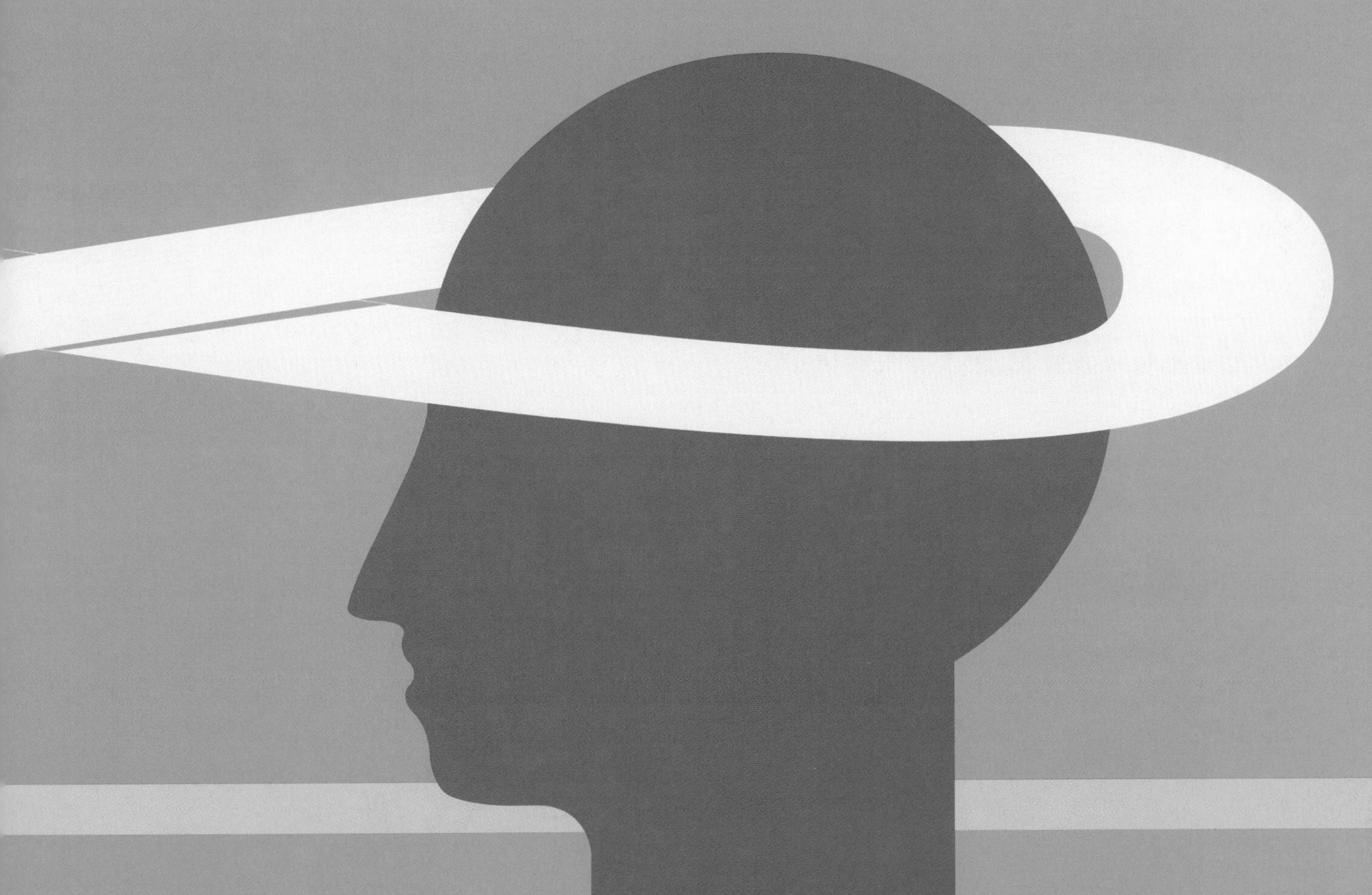

CHAPTER 3 ETHICAL AND LEGAL ISSUES IN SELLING

OVERVIEW

Few professions give you more opportunities for rejection on a daily basis than does the field of sales. Because of the often-cutthroat nature of selling, some salespeople do whatever it takes to stay ahead and edge out the competition. This chapter discusses the need for a strong ethical and moral character to sustain a sales career. Honest and caring service brings customers back and assures success. Success in professional selling also depends upon your ability to have a productive exchange of information with prospects and customers.

OBJECTIVES

- Develop principles upon which to base ethical behavior.
- Identify the sources of influence on ethics and ethical behavior.
- Understand your role in maintaining the ethical position of the organization and simultaneously behaving in an ethical manner toward customers.
- Discover what loyalty to the company requires in the event that your employers may be involved in questionable ethical behavior.
- Recognize the implications of federal and local laws regarding ethical standards.

WHICH RACE ARE YOU RUNNING?

One of most the significant books published in the area of business ethics is *The Power of Ethical Management*. Written by Dr. Kenneth Blanchard and Dr. Norman Vincent Peale, this book is of special significance for salespeople who are on the firing line between their customers and their employers.

Kenneth Blanchard is the co-author of *The One Minute Manager* and *The One Minute Manager Library.* Dr. Blanchard is the founder of a management consulting firm, Blanchard Training and Development Inc., in Escondido, California. Dr. Norman Vincent Peale was the author of thirty-four books. *The Power of Positive Thinking* is one of the most widely circulated books ever published.

The basic message of *The Power of Ethical Management* is simple: You don't have to cheat to win! Blanchard and Peale tell us that many people demand immediate tangible evidence that ethical conduct works, but such evidence is often not available. In fact, you may actually get farther in the short run by cheating. But in the long run, where it really counts, you never gain by unethical conduct.

The authors remind us that "nice guys may appear to finish last, but usually they're running in a different race."

When salespeople focus on their purpose—solving the problems of clients and helping customers be more successful and more profitable—they understand the need for ethical behavior. Cheating, lying, and short-changing the customer on service may bring a satisfactory profit today, but is a sure way to court failure for the future.

ETHICS IN MODERN SOCIETY

Erin Hood feels as though she is being torn apart. The pharmaceutical company she works for is pressuring her to meet a sales quota twenty percent higher than last year's. She is a single parent with two children, and she sees an opportunity to meet her sales quota if she can beat out a competitor for a large order from a drugstore chain. She is tempted to plant some carefully worded negative comments about the competitor in the ear of the store chain's purchasing agent. What should she do? What would you do?

Erin is facing a situation that falls in the category of ethical considerations. Because salespeople are relatively free and independent operators, they may encounter more ethical dilemmas than many other business people. For this reason, you must be clear on your own ethical standards before getting caught up in something that escalates beyond your control.

Ethics is an old subject, but it is certainly not worn out. Greek philosophers suggested that, "A merchant does better to take a loss than to make a dishonest profit." Ethics is a long-debated subject for salespeople in particular thanks to some of the earliest salespeople tarnishing the profession. In the early 1900s con men would try to sell parts of the Brooklyn Bridge to immigrants. This is what coined the phrase, "If you believe that, I've got a bridge to sell you!"[1] The image of salespeople, maybe even dating back to before the bridge scammers, is usually filled with less than positive words like – deceiving, pushy, fast talking, exaggerating, and at least a dozen more.

People have longed questioned how businesses can even have and act in accordance with ethical standards—and for good reason. Given the myriad of scandals in investment banking, subprime mortgages and insider trading, it's widely assumed that corruption is common within the global marketplace.[2] Today, America seems to be constantly reeling from the shocking, unethical, and immoral activities of a variety of business and government leaders and other public figures. It is not companies, institutions and political organizations, however, that are unethical; individual people are unethical. Ethics is a personal matter—the ethics of a business, government, or other organizations is merely a reflection of the combined value systems of its members.

Business ethics is an aspect of *societal ethics*. Traditional values seem to have given way to a widespread sense of anything goes; and "Sell at any Cost!" seemed the mantra the early salesperson learned.[3] Look at what we parade in front of people, implying approval, in the media and society: Illicit content, constant violence, conspicuous consumption, and an overarching motto of, "Do *what* you want, *when* you want." As a result, many Americans want immediate personal gratification and will act in whatever manner seems to promise it.

Some say that business ethics is an *oxymoron*, a contradiction in terms. They suggest that business and ethics are incompatible because "ethics is values-ridden and grounded in philosophy and religion" while businesses need to be ruthless and dishonest in order to finish first.[4] This thinking is ludicrous! The notion that honest businesses and salespeople finish last is poisonous, and it is untrue. You CAN be an ethical salesperson who works for an ethical, upstanding organization. And in fact, if you are among the ethical ones in business, you will enjoy a longer, more satisfying career.

Unethical behavior is self-destructive; it generates more unethical conduct until a business or person hits rock bottom financially, spiritually, and morally.

THE ORIGIN OF ETHICS

A legal standard is enforced by laws and statutes, but an ethical standard is an outgrowth of the customs and attitudes of a society. Most of us have a shared idea of what we mean by ethics, but defining it in a way that everyone would accept is hard. Essentially, ethics is a systematic effort to judge human behavior as right or wrong in terms of two major criteria: ***Truth*** and ***Justice***.

The root of the word *ethics* derives from the Greek word *ethos*, which means the character or sentiment of the community. A society cannot exist unless people agree fundamentally on what is right and wrong, just and unjust. Without shared norms of behavior, we would have anarchy in our political system and chaos in our daily lives. The three most important value-forming institutions in America are family, church, and school. Many people believe that the decreasing strength and changing roles of these three institutions have produced a society with lower ethical standards than those of its earlier history.

The Bases for Ethical Systems

Philosophers and ethicists point to two systems to describe ethical thinking. The first of these is the *deontological* base, the use of specifically stated rules, for example, the Ten Commandments or the Golden Rule. Some believe these rules come from a higher power, some think the rules are intuitive, and still others hold that the rules are discovered by using reason.

The second system of describing ethical systems is the *teleological* approach. This system defines right and wrong in terms of end results. Though research suggests that organizational follow-through and individual moral approaches to ethical problems also influence decision making at the management level, a foundational study reported by Dr. Thomas Wotruba found that executives' response to ethical problems is predominantly utilitarian.[5,6] The utilitarian model falls under this approach and is illustrated by the idea proposed in the nineteenth century by Jeremy Benthem that society's goal is to produce "the greatest good for the greatest number."[7]

This approach says that in trying to determine a course of action in an ethical dilemma, the individual should assess what good or harm would come to the parties involved and follow the course of action that would have the most positive results for the most people. In fact, several studies have found that if employees perform actions that violate their company's stated rules—their managers would react more harshly if the outcome of the acts were negative rather than positive. In other words, punishment was less severe if management saw the outcome as "good."[8]

With these two bases consciously or unconsciously affecting us, we can expect to experience ambivalent attitudes when faced with making ethical decisions.

Guidelines for Ethical Behavior

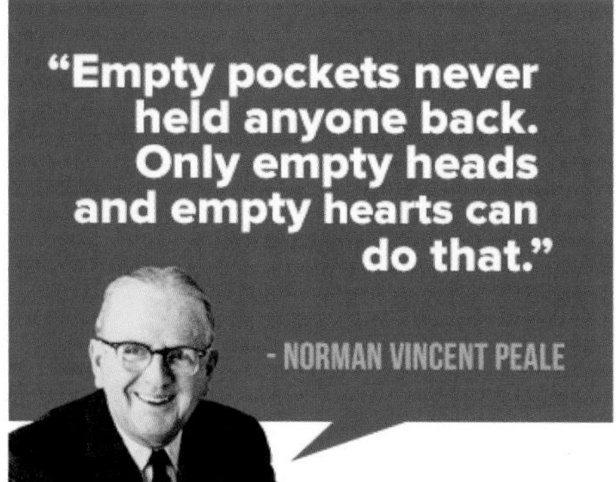

Today, no matter which specific method of ethical decision-making is followed, most Americans embrace three basic guidelines: *Universal nature, truth telling, and responsibility for one's actions.* Without them, the free enterprise system itself would be threatened and any kind of business exchange would be difficult. Our society would disintegrate into a dog-eat-dog environment.

UNIVERSAL NATURE. The universal nature guideline is a derivation of the Golden Rule. We want others to play by the same basic rules by which we would play in a similar situation. This guideline sets up a basic level of trust between people and makes life predictable.

TRUTH TELLING. Prospects and customers need to believe that what others say is true. The idea of honesty may originate in a set of rules we have been taught, but truth telling makes sense on purely logical grounds as well. Trust facilitates cooperation, buyer commitment, and the development and maintenance of long-term, client-salesperson relationships.[9]

It's not always simple to be truthful with prospects. At times, it is easier to tell a white lie if it means setting up the all-important face-to-face interview or getting a commitment over the phone. For that reason, some salespeople's cold calling techniques have become entrenched in lies. Would you trust someone who lies in his or her first conversation with you? Of course not—and neither will your prospects.

RESPONSIBILITY FOR YOUR ACTIONS. President Harry S. Truman kept a sign on his desk stating, "The buck stops here." He reminded himself that he had no one to blame when things went wrong. Individuals may choose to live by this attitude and accept personal responsibility for their actions, or they may attempt to follow the impulse of the moment and blame someone else for the consequences. If society and we demonstrated a higher level of trust and credibility based on a willingness to accept responsibility for personal actions, our system would work more efficiently and in a less suspicious atmosphere.

INFLUENCES ON A SALESPERSON'S ETHICS

Although individual salespeople each have a basic value system and may know what is right and wrong, they encounter many new influences and experience many new pressures on the job. Nothing creates more direction for employee's decision-making or a better balance for judgment than do ethical guidelines.[10] Knowing in advance what can be expected and having a feel for how to balance and integrate them into a personal code of ethics make handling ethical decisions easier for any individual.

> Unethical behavior occurs in sales because people forget the real purpose of professional selling—to satisfy the needs of others.

Company Code of Ethics

Many companies have codes of ethics; some companies adhere strictly to the code as part of corporate culture and may have ethics training for new employees and an ethics committee to rule on ethical dilemmas. A recent study examined the relationships among ethics code awareness, perceived corporate ethical values, and organizational commitment. Two key findings emerged: First, those aware of the existence of an ethics code in their organizations viewed their organizations as having more ethical values than those not aware of an ethics code. Second, respondents showed higher levels of commitment when they were aware of an ethics code in their companies.[11]

The *United Professional Sales Association* (UPSA) is an organization of member-based sales professionals whose overall mission is "advancing the profession of sales." They have designed an entire Ethics Selling Framework upon which its members must abide; it reflects best practices and points out what is not permissible in today's business climate. Various portions of their members' ethical code of conduct include:[12]

- I will maintain high standards of integrity and professional conduct.
- I will accept responsibility for my actions.
- I will continually seek to enhance my professional capabilities.
- I will sell with fairness and honesty.
- I will encourage others in the profession to act in an ethical and professional manner.

Exhibit 3.1 discusses a new day of national observance that the UPSA put into effect to emphasize the extreme importance of ethics in selling.[13]

EXHIBIT 3.1 A NEW HOLIDAY?

The UPSA has declared May 24th "International Stop Selling Day" to address the critical professional shortcomings of salespeople due to a lack of customer focus, a standardized ethical code, and global adoption of a buyer's bill of rights.

"We encourage all salespeople to pause and reflect on their professional responsibilities on *International Stop Selling Day*. We encourage our members, and implore non-members who consider themselves a sales professional, to participate in this important event. Professionalism requires a proactive approach to increasing professional competence. There is a difference between being a ***salesperson*** and being a ***sales professional***. We also believe that many salespeople do not receive adequate sales training that focuses on critical competencies required to be productive—and we're doing something about it by providing real-time access to top-notch sales trainers and thought leaders in a global forum to advance the profession" says Brian Lambert, UPSA Founder and Chairman.

Think your sales organization will get behind International Stop Selling Day? Tell your manager about it and see if your company wants to join in on a new holiday!

Driven by recent government actions and fear of retribution and by the competitive advantage clear ethical standards may gain, companies are paying more attention than ever to the behavior of their employees. Ethics is a monetary issue as well! For example, a study conducted by researchers at the University of Central Missouri found that ethical behavior in business to business selling had positive economic impacts; when salespeople acted with strong moral judgment, they helped build better, customer-oriented relationships that resulted in long term sales.[14]

Some companies are thorough and exacting in implementing a code of ethics, but others keep their codes buried in filing cabinets; still others have no formal code of any kind. Implementing a code of conduct statement communicates to salespeople—and their customers—that companies have high moral standards. In addition, organizations can gain several benefits when they adhere to a core set of ethical values embodied in a code of conduct:

- **GREATER MOTIVATION AMONG CO-WORKERS.** Although many employers have yet to fully recognize the significance of staff morale, in a recent U.S. survey, 94 percent of responding employees declared company ethics to be an important, if not critical, aspect to their working lives.[15]
- **A DEMONSTRATED RESPECT FOR THE LAW.** When top management makes a formal commitment to endorse an ethical company culture, the subject becomes of greater significance and, consequently, the company's personnel pay more attention to compliance with the laws and regulations affecting the organization.
- **IMPROVED BUSINESS RELATIONSHIPS.** Due to pressures exerted by investors, consumers, and human rights groups, advertising campaigns have been launched to boycott the products of certain companies that were accused of not adopting ethical standards. From this perspective, a clearly defined ethical culture is a useful way to choose business partners with which long-term ties are desired.

AS A SALESPERSON, YOU NEED TO KNOW WHERE THE COMPANY STANDS AND WHETHER ITS STAND IS CONSISTENT WITH YOUR OWN.
AND THE TIME TO DO THIS IS BEFORE YOU'RE HIRED, NOT AFTER.

Corporate Social Responsibility

Ethics codes fit into the larger, increasingly more popular framework "Corporate Social Responsibility" (CSR). CSR focuses not only on the managerial processes needed to monitor, meet, and even exceed ethical norms within the company, but also on the development of products and policies that reflect good corporate citizenship to the client or consumer. Though this can mean sponsoring a fundraising event like a major run, a local team, or a charity, it can also mean choosing products or developing procedures that reflect the company's environmental good will. This is often called "going green." A growing number of companies are making CSR a major component of their product pitches. Because products must have key benefits to the consumer, companies are hoping to tap into the consumer's personal concern for the environment. In other words, especially in green marketing, "doing well by doing good is the new mantra of the socially responsible bottom line."[16]

Starbucks, for instance, strives to combine consumer driven demands with environmentally and socially responsible production methods. Starbucks CEO Howard Shultz writes to the heart of this method in his book *Onward: How Starbucks Fought for Its Life without Losing Its Soul:*[17]

> ***"Valuing personal connections at a time when so many people sit alone in front of screens; aspiring to build human relationships in an age when so many issues polarize so many; and acting ethically, even if it costs more, when corners are routinely cut—these are honorable pursuits, at the core of what we set out to be."***

Executives as Role Models

The likelihood that unacceptable selling practices will occur has much to do with how executives behave. If a sales manager gives the impression that you must do anything possible to make more sales, salespeople infer that dealing unethically is acceptable in order to succeed. More than anything, an organization's culture influences sales reps' behavior with clients. That is why sales managers must emphasize ethical selling behavior in words and actions.

"Boss, I admire you because you never ask me to do anything you wouldn't do yourself."

The company's top executives must keep in check the pressure the managers put on their salespeople. If the CEO comes around once a year with a pep talk on moral behavior but proceeds the rest of the year to use underhanded methods of doing business, salespeople get a mixed message. Ethical conflict may also arise when salespeople's ethical values differ from those perceived to be held by their immediate supervisors or top management. Here are some ideas to consider that may foster ethical behavior within an organization:[18]

- Codes of ethics that are effectively communicated are likely to result in greater ethical behavior.
- The presence and enforcement of codes of ethics have been found to be associated with higher levels of ethical behavior.
- Corporate goals and stated policies strongly influence managers' decisions on whether to act ethically or unethically.
- When a climate is created where ethical values and behaviors are fostered, supported, and rewarded, more ethical behavior will exist.

> "As a manager the important thing is not what happens when you are there, but what happens when you are not there."
>
> **Dr. Kenneth Blanchard**

Examples Set by Colleagues and Competitors

A salesperson sometimes discovers that colleagues and/or competitors are acting unethically. Imagine that you are riding in a cab, and a colleague asks the driver to provide a receipt for expense account purposes and to indicate a figure higher than the actual fare. Do you join in the activity, rebuke the colleague, report the colleague—commonly called *blowing the whistle*—or ignore it? A customer reports that a competitor has said you have an alcohol problem and are therefore undependable. Do you simply deny the charge, or do you retaliate by making detrimental remarks about your competitor? These are tough questions, so decide now where you stand on such issues to avoid making a decision in the moment based on peer pressure or other social pressures.

The Bottom Line

A company's survival will surely be compromised if common values are not established and acted upon and if salespeople take casual views of the legal and ethical implications of their behavior. Short-term profits may be maximized by unethical behavior, but the company's very existence could be threatened if it were hit with huge fines or an unwanted exposure in the media. Although short-term profits are important for both the company and its salespeople, the long-term success and good name of the company must always be the first priority.

Groupthink and Gamesmanship

Groupthink refers to the pressure exerted on salespeople to be part of the group and not to buck the system—to be team players, no matter what. Being a team player is good if the team has ethical goals and plays by ethical rules, but if the group's thinking runs afoul of your own personal code of ethics, you must weigh your options carefully. Psychologist Irving L. Janis warns against "groupthink," which he suggests can cause flawed judgment.[19]

There are examples of groupthink in every profession, and the pharmaceutical industry has not been spared its share of such activity. Two salespeople and three pharmacists pleaded guilty to their roles in a scheme involving the illegal sales of drug samples to pharmacies in New Jersey and New York. The operation generated more than a $1 million in illicit profits for all the parties involved. The salespeople, former *Procter & Gamble* reps, stole samples from doctors' offices and sold them to the pharmacists.[20] They also paid doctors and office personnel to obtain supplies. Here, a number of people conspired to cheat others and somehow convinced themselves that what they were doing was all right.

Gamesmanship is becoming totally caught up in winning simply for the sheer joy of victory and a dislike of losing. Much of our culture nurtures this type of competitive spirit—from winning the high school football game to beating a friend at chess or golf. The typical gamesman in selling looks for shortcuts and is willing to use any technique to sell a product or service. To the gamesman, winning means doing whatever is necessary to make the sale.

One case study demonstrated that, in numerous circumstances, salespeople and staff in a hostile workplace full of a gamesmanship mentality simply used their feelings in order to survive. The study showed irrational emotions being used as strategic tools of defense against a vindictive, aggressive, and hostile work place.[21] The dangers of gamesmanship are quite clear—the temptation to cross over the line into unethical or illegal behavior.

DEVELOPING A PERSONAL CODE OF ETHICS

Clearly many competing forces that influence a salesperson's decisions have an ethical dimension. Situations often arise in which a clear right or wrong is not easily apparent and discretion in behavior is up to the individual. Because the influences that come to bear upon a salesperson do not always agree and because conflicting demands are numerous, each salesperson must develop a personal code of ethics that supersedes all other claims.

Responsibility to Self

In the final analysis, the small voice of conscience is the arbiter of conflicting ethical claims. It provides the ability to say that you have made the best decision under the circumstances and take full responsibility for it.

Responsibility to the Company

Salespeople sometimes rationalize that cheating here or there in dealing with the company would not hurt. After all, the company makes lots of money and what you do would never be noticed. Several areas particularly lend themselves to temptations to be less than ethical:

ACCURACY IN EXPENSE ACCOUNTS. Often padding expense accounts is relatively easy. A salesperson can add extra mileage, submit charges for a meal that was actually eaten at a friend's house, or take friends out to dinner and report the charge as entertaining customers. Abuse of expense accounts is prevalent in both government and business circles. Falsification of expense accounts is not only unethical, but it can also lead to dismissal if it is detected. As a practical matter, it unnecessarily increases the costs of the company and may put it at a competitive disadvantage.

HONESTY IN USING TIME AND RESOURCES. The temptation to do some shopping between sales calls, to linger over a third cup of coffee in a restaurant, and to sleep late in a hotel room are examples of ways a salesperson may misuse time. This ultimately hurts both the salesperson and the company because fewer sales calls are made. Dishonesty in expense accounts and in time and resources can be considered as theft. As one business journal reports, "according to the FBI, internal theft is the fastest growing business crime" and is responsible for the failure of one third of businesses.[22]

Responsibility to Competitors

Being honest and refraining from taking unfair advantage are the basic guidelines when dealing with competitors. Making untrue, derogatory comments about competitors or their products is poor business. At the very least, the legal implications of this behavior simply make the risks too great. In the same sense, pumping a competitor's salesperson for information at a trade show in order to steal their customers is not ethical. Some salespeople go so far as to use sabotage, espionage, and dirty tricks to gain unfair advantage over a competitor. These tactics include planting spies in a business to hear their sales presentation or persuading a customer to put out a fake request for bids to see what bids competitors would submit. The basic theme in this area is to gain customers fairly and squarely by providing quality products and superior service.

Responsibility to Customers

Behaving honestly and providing quality information and services are the primary ingredients for establishing mutually satisfying relationships with customers. Fortunately, the stereotype of the silver-tongued, flattering, deceptive, door-to-door salesperson of the past is disappearing. Still, many opportunities for unethical tactics exist.

OVERSELLING OR MISREPRESENTING PRODUCTS. Some salespeople persuade customers to buy more than they need because the salesperson needs to meet a quota or wants to win a trip to the Caribbean. Overselling eventually catches up with the salesperson because customers realize that they have more than they need. In addition, repeat sales probably won't be possible for a very long time. Lying about the capabilities of a product, the date the company can make delivery, or the nature of the warranty are all unethical ways to win a quick sale while running the risk of legal action or a permanent loss of the customer in the long run.

GIFT GIVING. Although giving a customer a token gift as a thank-you or as a reminder of the salesperson and the company is customary, the intent with which a gift is given usually reveals its ethical or unethical nature. If a gift is a way to get business or a bribe, then it is unethical and may well be illegal. Sometimes a salesperson may even give an "under-the-table" gift in order to secure an order.[23] The value of the gift in comparison to the sale is also something to consider. In America, it is generally understood that no gift should exceed a monetary value of between $25-50. That being said, one study has suggested that in the pharmaceutical industry even small gifts like pens can influence the recipient's decision making processes without the person being aware of this influence.[24] It may be wise for the salesperson to explore the ethics behind giving even small gifts.

ENTERTAINING CLIENTS. Policies regarding entertainment are similar to those that cover gift giving. In some industries, entertaining a client with a meal, an excursion, or tickets to the theater or a football game is customary. If the intent is as a means of saying thank-you to a customer or of developing a more personal relationship, entertainment may be acceptable and even expected. Finding out the rules of behavior in a particular industry and within an individual company is important.

Operating in a Global Environment

Salespeople today may operate not only in the United States but also in a foreign country where norms of behavior may be different. Which morality should salespeople follow, their own or that of the country in which they find themselves? In some countries, "grease" or "speed" money makes the wheels of a government agency or a company move faster. In Japan, there is much gift giving in business relationships, and it is viewed as a time-honored tradition rather than a bribe. A company usually has guidelines for an employee to follow in a foreign country, but bribery is universally condemned and is in fact illegal whether it is practiced at home or abroad.

Exhibit 3.2 displays a brief excerpt from global computer and technology giant *Hewlett Packard's* global gift and entertainment policy. While customs and practices can vary among cultures, sharing modest gifts and entertainment is often an important way of creating goodwill and establishing trust in business relationships. All of us have a responsibility to make sure that our business gifts and entertainment practices are reasonable and consistent with guidelines such as the ones Hewlett Packard (HP) formed for its sales force.[25]

EXHIBIT 3.2 HEWLETT PACKARD GIFT & ENTERTAINMENT POLICY

SUBJECT TO THE SPECIFIC RULES OUTLINED FURTHER IN THIS POLICY, THE FOLLOWING BUSINESS AMENITIES ARE GENERALLY PERMITTED:

- Pens, calendars, mugs, t-shirts, and memo pads.
- A local sporting event or entertainment valued at less than $50 USD
- Gift cards or coupons for HP products and services valued at less than $50 USD
- Gift cards for products and services that do not compete with HP's products or services valued at less than $25 USD
- Any travel, meals and entertainment must be reasonable and directly related to the promotion, demonstration or explanation of HP's products or services.

THE FOLLOWING BUSINESS AMENITIES ARE NEVER PERMITTED:

- Cash, loans, stock, stock options, and cash gift-cards.
- Any gift or entertainment provided in direct exchange for a reciprocal action.
- Any item or entertainment that is illegal or sexually explicit, involves gambling, or would otherwise violate our values or our Standards of Business Conduct.
- HP employees may never accept cash (or cash equivalent) in return for advocating or selling products from a partner/supplier, except commissions and customer loyalty programs as allowed under HP's Conflicts of Interest Policy.
- You may not accept any combination of gifts/travel/meals/entertainment totaling more than $500 USD per person from the same non-HP source more than once per quarter.

ETHICS AND JOB TENURE

When is it time to look for a new job? Of course, you want to be affiliated with a company of which you as a salesperson can be proud. Disagreements or issues of unethical behavior on the part of the company may, however, emerge during your employment. Deciding how to handle conflicts involving ethics can be stressful because your decision may mean either your termination or resignation. Weigh the options carefully and determine who is being helped and who is being hurt. Are there any alternative, creative options that minimize risk and allow career and conscience to be reconciled?

Whistle Blowing

According to Nancy Hauserman, "In the pursuit of the goals of productivity and consumption, we have failed to preserve individual and community values. The individual has been reduced to a cog in the corporate wheel, a capital investment, a corporate property."[26] This attitude can make salespeople feel unimportant and fear that their ideas, suggestions, or revelations are not valid. This type of reaction is particularly relevant if someone attempts to pass on valuable information to superiors and is rebuffed.

CONSIDER THE FOLLOWING SITUATION:

Sandra Baker landed a job as a software company sales rep. She is required to go on frequent business trips with her manager across the country. On the second trip, her manager books a dinner with a potential client at a posh restaurant. She does a quick tally of the meal, appetizers, desserts, and drinks in her mind—the potential client's meal adds up to over $150. She's just familiarized herself with the company code of conduct policy, which states client meals should be under $50. She decides this must be an exception, but also decides to watch her manager more carefully. On her next trip, the manager engages in the same kind of behavior. This time, Sandra questions him; he responds by saying he'll just report there were more people at the meal. He also implies, as a junior, she should be careful with her own reputation and job security. What should someone like Sandra do?

In Sandra's situation, a number of options could be considered:

- Make discreet inquiries into how common this type of expense is in the company and then decide how to proceed.
- Talk to her manager about the gift giving and see if they can implement a more ethical way of entertaining clients.
- *Blow the whistle* on the manager by reporting him to his superior.
- Ignore the whole situation and continue selling.
- Look for another job.

As careful as a salesperson may be when joining a company, an ethical dilemma such as this may arise eventually. In the best of all possible worlds, the violation should be exposed and those responsible punished, but what if pointing a finger at someone would cause the whistle-blower to be fired and put self and family in financial difficulties?

On the surface, the wiser course appears to be to keep quiet and let the problem resolve itself. Sometimes the best policy is to keep quiet until solid evidence can be accumulated or until the co-conspirators are identified—but silence as a long-term strategy is indefensible. The violation is likely to be exposed at some point, and being part of a cover-up is not a desirable position.

In some cases, inaction can even be grounds for legal action.

How the Company Treats the Salesperson

The company may treat its salespeople as partners joined with it in a common mission or simply regard them as cannon fodder out in the field. Salespeople are an extremely valuable resource to a company and deserve to be treated fairly, informed of decisions affecting them, and protected from situations in which they might be under pressure to make unethical decisions. Glenn Wilson discusses what companies can do to prevent unethical behavior among salespeople:[27]

- Avoid setting up management-incentive systems in a way that makes fudging the data tempting.
- Be accessible to salespeople in order to get early warnings on troublesome developments.
- Set up appropriate controls not only on financial accounts but also in customer complaints, salesperson dissatisfaction, and expense accounts.
- Set sales goals that are motivating but not impossible to achieve.

If salespeople know their ideas are important and their judgment valued, they feel ownership in the organization and want to do a better job overall. According to *Forbes*, *Google* is ranked as the world's number one employer in terms of employee satisfaction. "Google stepped up their game in support of work-life balance and families," said *Glassdoor* CEO Robert Hohman. "Increased maternity leave, increased paternity leave, reworked on-site daycare—they've really made an effort to allow people to have strong families as well as give their best to Google. That came through loud and clear and seems to be what pushed them over the edge this year."[28]

Companies like *Google* and *In-N-Out Burger* (who came in at #8 on the list this year) have adapted to this new reality that workers need to feel valuable, so they are treating their employees not as forces to be controlled but as individuals to be empowered, in order to unshackle their skills, talents and potential.

Managing the Sales Territory

One of the most excruciating decisions that salespeople face is that concerning territories. A salesperson may have spent years cultivating customers in a territory only to have it divided by management or even taken away. The most important thing is to involve your sales reps in the decision and treat them in a straightforward manner.

Fortunately, today's data-rich environment provides access to all kinds of information for helping sales managers address the problem of assigning fair and balanced territories. A first step is creating a database that captures profitable account workload. Then, by analyzing that data by salesperson, it's possible to identify territories with gaps in customer coverage, as well as territories where sales talent is underutilized. Using a structured territory design process and mapping software, local sales managers can make informed account reassignment decisions that close coverage gaps and better utilize sales talent.[29] In the end, more customers get the attention they deserve, salespeople all get a fair challenge, and it becomes easier to identify and reward the true top performers.

WORKPLACE HARASSMENT

Another part of building and participating in an ethical business is the development and adherence to workplace harassment and discrimination guidelines. The *United States Government's Equal Employment Opportunity Commission* defines ***workplace discrimination*** as engaging in acts that prevent people from being hired, from keeping a job, or from receiving an equitable wage based on their age, gender, disability, national origin, pregnancy, race/color, or religion. ***Workplace harassment*** can be defined as any act, including offensive remarks, unfavorable treatment, or creating a hostile work environment, that may also eventually lead to the employee leaving or being fired from the job. The EEOC further defines sexual harassment, which violates Title VII of the Civil Rights Act of 1964, even more extensively:

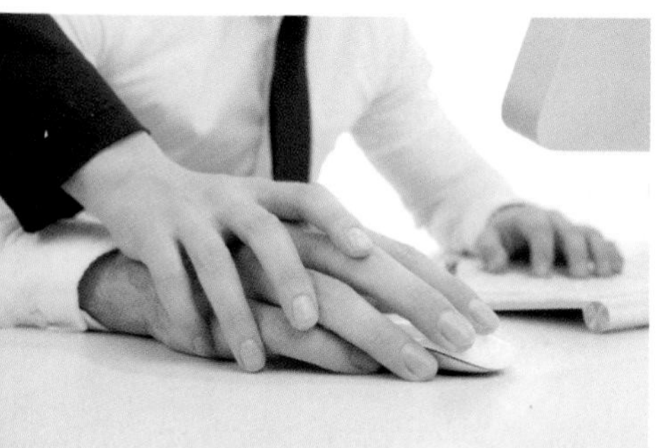

"Sexual harassment can include unwelcome sexual advances, requests for sexual favors, and other verbal or physical harassment of a sexual nature. Harassment does not have to be of a sexual nature, however, and can include offensive remarks about a person's sex. Both victim and the harasser can be either a woman or a man, and the victim and harasser can be the same sex.

Although the law doesn't prohibit simple teasing, offhand comments, or isolated incidents that are not very serious, harassment is illegal when it is so frequent or severe that it creates a hostile or offensive work environment or when it results in an adverse employment decision (such as the victim being fired or demoted).

The harasser can be the victim's supervisor, a supervisor in another area, a co-worker, or someone who is not an employee of the employer, such as a client or customer."

Sexual Harassment in Action

In today's legal environment, any institution's failure to recognize the consequences of workplace sexual harassment can be a capital blunder. For employees in organizations lacking sound policy practices, the negative impact from sexual harassment—including liability, embarrassment and lost productivity—can be extensive. Here are three real world examples of what harassment looks like in the workplace:

- Joanna Garcia, a bank teller, reported that a female supervisor was allegedly talking nonstop about male and female genitalia and graphically describing sexual encounters. "It didn't feel like a bank," says Garcia. "It felt almost like a nightclub."
- Another woman reported that her boss announced, "Come to dinner with me." It wasn't a request. When she asked, "In what context?" he replied, "You know what context."
- A married male sales manager reported that a sales rep came into his office one day and started to rub his shoulders. On another occasion, she said she wanted a hug and proceeded to place her arms around him. On a few other occasions she would come up behind him and jab her fingers into his side to tickle him.

"With the advent of social media, there is a much more casual relationship between co-workers and supervisors, and that absolutely creates more opportunity for people to cross the line between professional and unprofessional conduct," says David Lowe, a San Francisco employment lawyer.[30]

ETHICS AS GOOD BUSINESS

Ethical behavior may sometimes appear to be an unattractive alternative. After all, for every inside trader, fraudulent salesperson, or immoral politician who gets caught, perhaps hundreds get away with unethical behaviors. However, the recent bumper crop of ethical scandals in corporate America has brought with it a renewed concern for ethics. Some of the newfound conscience in corporations has filtered down to business people and individuals in every walk of life.

Gary Edwards of the nonprofit *Ethics Resource Center* in Washington, D.C., says that ethics is receiving more attention partially because of awareness on the part of businesses of "the enormous costs of unethical activity, in fines and penalties, in increased government regulation, and in damage to their public image."[31] In short, companies are paying attention to ethics because it happens to be good business strategy.

THE SOCIAL MEDIA CONNECTION

Using Social Media to Promote Ethical Practices

It's been said that it takes a lifetime to build a good reputation and only one second to destroy it. This has never been truer than it is today, in an age where everything we say and do has the potential to be almost immediately shared through social networking. If you want to maintain—and even build on—your ethical reputation (both yours and your company's), then be aware of what you are posting on social media sites, even on your personal, non-work-related profiles. You just never know who's watching.

NAVEX Global and PwC recently sponsored a groundbreaking study from the Ethics Resource Center around Social Networking in the workplace. The study concluded that both having a policy and conducting training on social media change employee online behaviors. For this reason, it seems that more organizations need to teach their employees what is acceptable and, more importantly, what is NOT acceptable to post on both professional and personal social media pages. Here are just a few ways to use social media to promote yourself and your organization, rather than detract from both:

- Use social media tools (such as Facebook and YouTube) to publically share your organization's good deeds and commitment to ethics and compliance.
- Start a company blog dedicated to ethics and compliance.
- Host a moderated conversation group (like you see on LinkedIn) and allow compliance professionals to post content, ethical questions, and stories—and then employees can respond.
- Ask employees to submit nominations for people they work with whose behaviors/actions demonstrate high levels of integrity. Share the submissions on YouTube after they have been approved.

Checkpoints in Ethical Decision Making

Professional salespeople who are honest and aboveboard in relationships with employers, customers, and competitors alike become trusted and valued individuals. The key to making repeat sales is to build up these kinds of relationships and maintain them. A well-defined personal code of ethics as part of one's character and as a basis for behavior is an invaluable asset. When faced with an ethical conflict, a standard set of questions to ask yourself is helpful. Use the five questions suggested below to guide your thinking.

A FIVE-QUESTION ETHICS CHECKLIST:

1. Is it legal? Look at the law and other standards.
2. Is it fair to all concerned?
3. Would I want someone else to act this way toward me?
4. How would I explain my actions to someone else?
5. How will it make me feel about myself?

These questions first require careful evaluation regarding existing standards and personal liability. Next, the questions are designed to activate your sense of fairness and rationality. Last, realize that your personal feelings are important because negative feelings adversely affect positive performance. Ultimately, if your truthful answer to any one of these questions damages your self-image or causes you to be troubled by your conscience, then you should probably avoid the action in question. The ethics checklist can also be applied to the actions of a salesperson's company. An issue many sales professionals face today is how to sell products and services for a company that condones unethical practices.

LEGAL ISSUES FACING THE SALESPERSON

A serious problem faced by company sales forces today is a combination of antitrust law complexity and inadequate preventive legal guidance. Companies must properly train salespeople about required legal compliance to keep violations to a minimum. We would have practically no need for laws if all businesses played by the same ethical rules of the game. However, too many firms and individuals find the temptation to violate rules irresistible. Their violations, basically, fall into two broad categories:

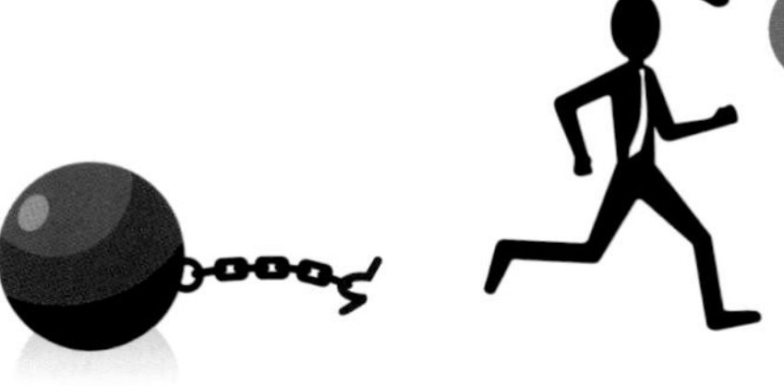

1. Monopolistic actions, such as price-fixing or the acquisition of competitors.
2. Deceptive actions, such as false claims about products or services; or disparaging remarks about competitors.

A number of laws have been passed to preserve fair competition such as the Sherman Antitrust Act, the Federal Trade Commission Act, and the Clayton Act. You might consider these government regulations to be your rules of the game. They serve to protect two groups: The consumer by preventing monopolies and eliminating practices that tend to be deceptive; and business competitors by establishing rules that prevent powerful rivals from depriving smaller firms free access to the market and by protecting competitors from those who would engage in deceptive practices.

Whenever you aggressively pursue an account, you can face temptations. In the heat of the battle, you may exaggerate or perhaps actually think you have said something clearly to the prospect. For example:

When in Doubt, Spell it Out

A sales representative must completely and in the clearest language possible warn the prospect of any potential hazard connected with use of the product. Saying, "*Use of this equipment at improper voltage levels will result in damage to the product and concomitant operator hazard*" may not be good enough. A better statement would be, **"Equipment must be plugged into 115 volts only. If used at a higher voltage, it can fly apart and injure or kill you."** The courts may rule that the vague wording in the first statement is analogous to a sign in your yard that reads, "Please keep off the grass," which is a horribly insufficient warning if you know that the grass conceals poisonous rattlesnakes.

In view of all the laws affecting business, obviously sales representatives can say or do many things to get themselves, as well as their companies, into quite a bit of trouble. Since jail time for those who break antitrust laws has doubled, and the fines they face are much higher, it's safe to say crime doesn't pay. Exhibit 3.3 points out six tactics for salespeople to consider following as protection for themselves and for their companies when out in the field selling.[32]

EXHIBIT 3.3 PROTECT YOURSELF AGAINST VIOLATING ANTI-TRUST LAWS

1. Know the difference between "sales puffery" and specific statements of fact made during the sales presentation and avoid using unwarranted exaggeration to make your story sound good.
2. Thoroughly educate each customer on all aspects of the product before completing the sale.
3. Know the technical specifications, capabilities, design peculiarities, and special characteristics of the products you sell.
4. Read carefully any and all promotional literature published by your company on the products being sold. Challenge what you consider to be untrue or exaggerated claims.
5. Study the company's terms of sale policies. Overstating your authority to establish prices can legally bind the company.
6. Stay current on all federal as well as state laws which affect warranties and guarantees.

THE UNIFORM COMMERCIAL CODE (UCC)

In addition to the federal antitrust laws, many other laws deal directly or indirectly with personal selling. Because of the diversity of these state laws, an attempt to cover them here is impractical. However, one set of regulations is consistent among the forty-nine states that have adopted it (Louisiana is the lone exception). The *Uniform Commercial Code* is a set of guidelines that spell out in some detail the conditions under which a sale may be consummated. It is a law that covers virtually all business transactions. The following aspects are governed by the UCC:

1. An offer to sell may be legally binding if it is made in writing, conveyed electronically or simply stated orally by the salesperson. A distinction is made between a legitimate offer to sell and an invitation to negotiate or deal.
2. The financing of the product or service must be explained clearly and completely. Salespeople must know the legal ramifications of any credit arrangements made with customers. Truth in lending also requires full disclosure of finance charges prior to closing the sale.
3. The salesperson must know the legal responsibilities if either party fails to live up to respective contractual obligations.
4. Warranties and guarantees offered by the seller are basically the same and are governed by the UCC. The code defines both express warranties and implied warranties. *Express warranties* are statements and promises found in the advertising, sales literature, and labeling and in oral statements made by the salesperson. *Implied warranties* are a result of state law and the assumption that the product complies with those laws. Implied warranties are also in effect unless a disclaimer is made. To be on the safe side, the salesperson should state what is promised as well as what is not promised. The warranty statement should also set time or use limits and clearly specify who is providing the warranty.[33]

THERE IS NO PILLOW AS SOFT AS A CLEAR CONSCIENCE.

Despite any short terms gains you may make by behaving unethically in dealing with companies or individuals, doing the right thing is the only way to conduct yourself in the long run. Unethical behavior is selfish behavior, but when you abide by honest practices, you can rest easy knowing that you have other's best interests at heart and not simply your own.

"Explain it to me one more time. What's the difference between ethical behavior and being an annoying goody-two-shoes nerd?"

SUMMARY

- It is essential that you develop your own personal code of ethics, but you should also be aware of the ethical obligations your company sets forth.
- Salespeople who find themselves in situations in which company violations are evident must make difficult choices about whether to blow the whistle on the company or settle on another strategy that could include finding another job.
- Ethics is a smart business decision because salespeople who are honest in relationships with employers, customers, and competitors become trusted and respected business professionals.
- Sexual harassment is a serious issue in the workplace. Report any harassment immediately, and avoid getting too close with co-workers (especially those of the opposite gender).
- When faced with an ethical conflict, use a standard checklist of principled questions to guide your thinking.
- Forty-nine states have adopted the Uniform Commercial Code, which defines in some detail the conditions under which a sale may be consummated. It defines exactly what is meant by a sale, sets out required information for financing and truth in lending, and states a salesperson's legal responsibilities.

REVIEW QUESTIONS

1. We have heard much about questionable corporate activities, insider trading scandals, defense contract fraud, health risk cover-ups, and so on. Does this mean that corporations are not interested in ethics—that the bottom line is that corporate greed takes precedence over moral responsibility?

2. What kinds of management tactics make salespeople more likely to exhibit unethical behavior?

3. Should there be any focus on morality in institutions? After all, you cannot have institutional integrity without first having individual integrity, and isn't that the domain of home, church, and school?

4. Does having a corporate code of ethics for salespeople really do any good? Out in the real world where salespeople compete for sales, is a code of ethics practical? Do salespeople need channels of communication and support structures along with an ethics code?

5. Some years ago a Fordham University priest attended the Friday luncheon meeting of the Sales Executives Club of New York where he talked much about honesty in day-to-day business dealings. Asked why he did this, he replied, "What sales executives have to do puts them, among all business people, at the greatest risk of losing their souls." Do you agree with his statement?

6. A half century ago the medical department at Johns Manville Corporation began to receive information implicating asbestos inhalation as a cause of asbestosis.

Manville's managers suppressed the research and concealed the information from employees. The entire company was eventually brought to its knees by questions of corporate ethics. How can we explain this behavior? Were more than fifty years' worth of Manville executives immoral?

7. When some specific safety precautions are needed in connection with using a product, what are the responsibilities of the salesperson in giving this information to the customer?

8. For your personal reflection: Do you believe you would ever be at risk of succumbing to groupthink or gamesmanship and participating in unethical or illegal activities? Have you ever been persuaded by peer pressure to do something for which you were later sorry? What can you do to lessen the possibility of compromising your own personal ethics?

IN-CLASS EXERCISES

The following exercises help build teams, improve communication, and emphasize the real-world side of selling. They are meant to be challenging, to help you learn how to deal with problems that have no single right answer, and to use a variety of skills beyond those employed in a typical review question. Read and complete each activity. Then in the next class, discuss and compare answers.

EXERCISE 3.1 – WHAT IS THE EFFECT OF COMPANY CODES OF ETHICS?

Pair off with another student with whom you have worked previously in this class. After briefly conducting online research to locate some major companies in your area that have codes of ethics (you might have to contact their human resources office to obtain a copy), identify one company for further scrutiny. Interview a sales manager at that company and ask the following questions:

1. Does your company have a code of ethics for employees in sales? Do you have a copy?
2. Is the content of the code included in sales training for new employees? Are they tested on their understanding of it? Are they required to indicate their acceptance of the code?
3. Do you use or refer to the code when deciding whether a particular sales practice should be adopted or followed? If so, does the code actually influence your decision? If you don't use or refer to the code, why not?
4. In your opinion, does the code of ethics actually help or impede the company's ability to succeed?

After the above interview, proceed to interview a salesperson for the same company, but without the knowledge of the sales manager. Ask the same four questions and later jot down a record of the responses. In class, for each question, role-play the response of the sales manager and of the salesperson. See if the class can account for any differences between them.

EXERCISE 3.2 – CROSSING THE LINE?

You will work independently on this exercise. As a class, in groups, or independently, view the film Disclosure (1994), starring Michael Douglas and Demi Moore. Take notes, and be prepared to discuss the following questions:

1. Was Tom Sanders (Michael Douglas's character) a victim of sexual harassment according to law, or was Meredith Johnson (Demi Moore's character) merely aggressive in pursuing what was otherwise a consensual relationship?
2. At what point might Meredith have crossed an ethical or legal line?
3. What actions might Tom have taken to prevent any inappropriate behavior, and when?
4. Given Tom and Meredith's previous relationship and their current positions, was there anything that Tom could have done to preserve his dignity while still retaining his job?
5. To what extent was the company liable for protecting Tom against Meredith's predatory behavior?
6. By reversing stereotypical gender roles, has this film created a distorted picture of sexual harassment that amounts to an injustice against female employees?
7. If you were in Tom's shoes, what would you do?

EXERCISE 3.3 – ASK AN ATTORNEY

Invite an attorney to class that works with sales contracts and a sales representative he or she is acquainted with. Ask the attorney and sales rep to present several real-life mini scenarios of borderline sales activities from their personal experiences. Let the students decide (in writing and orally) if those involved acted ethically and legally and explain why.

CASE STUDIES

The following case studies present you with selling scenarios that require you to apply the critical skills discussed in the chapter and give you training through practical learning situations. They are meant to be both engaging and challenging, and like the exercises, don't have one right answer.

CASE 3.1 – SELLING OFF-LABEL

In the pharmacy industry, off-label marketing involves selling prescription drugs for purposes and conditions that are not identified on the FDA-approved label and accompanying specifications. This means that a drug that has been approved and tested for efficacy and safety for very specific uses is marketed and prescribed by physicians for uses for which such testing has not been performed or concluded. Accordingly, selling drugs off-label violates important ethical codes for the industry and is considered a criminal offense.

Over the past several decades, pharmaceutical companies have been found in violation of such laws and codes. In recent years, several major companies—*Johnson & Johnson, AstraZeneca, Eli Lilly & Co.*, and *Pfizer*—have paid enormous fines and been subjected to other penalties for such violations.[34] Since 2004, *Lilly, Bristol-Meyers Squibb*, and 4 other companies have paid $7 billion in fines and penalties. Most spectacularly, Pfizer alone paid $2.9 billion in fines and settlements in 2009 for this practice.[35] Despite the fines, billions more were retained as revenue from off-label sales. With such sums at stake, the pressures on company representatives are immense.

Gwen Olsen was a sales representative selling Haldol (Haloperidol) for ***McNeil Laboratories***. Haloperidol is an antipsychotic drug that is also used to treat verbal and motor tics as in Tourette's disorder as well as explosive behavior in children. When Gwen found that her sales quota for this drug was going to fall short, thereby disqualifying her for an important bonus, she asked her manager what to do. He recommended marketing the drug to nursing homes and physicians who cared for their patients. The suggestion worked, and Gwen increased her sales by 25%. Nevertheless, she noticed that the drug was being used for off-label reasons, mainly to control the behavior of elderly patients who were difficult to manage. The extreme decline of one patient whom Gwen had befriended caused Gwen to undergo a crisis of conscience for her role in the unapproved use of the drug. For the full account, watch Gwen's description of the situation that she faced by following the link: http://www.youtube.com/watch?v=v5jYU20dH4A&feature=player_embedded.

After watching the video, come to class prepared to discuss the following questions:

1. Was what Gwen did unethical or illegal? Citing principles discussed in Chapter 3, explain your answer.
2. Should Gwen really be upset at her own behavior? Doesn't most of the responsibility fall on her manager and the company?
3. Knowing how difficult it is to find high-paying sales positions, do you think Gwen did the right thing by leaving pharmaceutical sales? Would you? Explain.
4. Leaving questions of legality aside for a moment, should selling drugs off-label really be considered unethical? If a society's ethics is simply the sum-total of individual decisions, and if selling off-label continues to be widespread in the pharmaceutical industry, how can anyone say that a strategy that is routinely adopted by so many is unethical?

CASE 3.2 – BOXED IN

As the smoke curled up from the small fire in his boss's ashtray, Nick Roberts realized that he was in a tough spot. Having just graduated from college, he had recently moved to Dallas, Texas, with his wife and infant son. He had majored in economics and history as an undergraduate and, through connections provided by his wealthy father-in-law, had landed a lucrative position as corporate salesperson with ***Southwestern Container Corporation.*** The company manufactured and sold corrugated containers to businesses throughout the southwest. He and his wife were thrilled about his new job and their prospects for the future. But now, Nick wasn't so sure.

You see, the fire in the ashtray served a very real purpose and was no accident. Nick's boss had just concluded a phone call in his office with his counterparts at two other companies. As the 20-minute conversation among the three competitors proceeded, Nick and the other sales staff were allowed to listen via speakerphone. The sole topic discussed was the price structure for various grades and sizes of corrugated containers for the region.

The three companies thrived on competing for business accounts based on service, but they had come to realize over time that competing on price or price plus quality reduced their profits. If they could agree on price, they could sell boxes more cheaply to larger customers and more expensively to smaller customers. And overall, they could keep prices elevated without having to worry about being undercut by a competitor. Life was easier, simpler, and more lucrative that way. At the conclusion of the conference call, Nick's boss touched a match to his notes and dropped the burning paper into his ashtray.

As the meeting broke up, Nick was sweating. What should he do? If he sold containers according to the agreed price structure, was he acting unethically? Could he even go to jail? After all his father-in-law had done to get him this job, how could he just walk away? How would his young family survive? Should he blow the whistle on the entire company? Nick's mind was swirling. What would you advise him to do, and why?

Chapter 3 Footnotes

1. Weber, Patricia. "Salespeople Take Note: Let Me Sell You a Bridge or Sell Ethically!" Patricia-Weber.com. Accessed September 12, 2015. Web.
2. Cragg, A.W. "Business, globalization, and the logic and ethics of corruption." *Business Communication Quarterly* 69, no. 2 (2006): 158.
3. "Say it with pride: I am a salesman!" *Business Line*, April 2004: 1.
4. McQueeny, Edward. "Making Ethics Come Alive." *Business Communication Quarterly* 69, no. 2 (2006): 158.
5. McClaren, Nicholas. "Ethics in Personal Selling and Sales Management: A Reivew of the Literature Focusing on Empirical Findings and Conceptual Foundations." *Journal of Business Ethics* 27 (2000): 286.
6. Wortruba, Thomas. "A Framework for Teaching Ethical Decision-Making in Marketing." *Marketing Education Review* 3, no. 2 (1994): 4.
7. Christians, Clifford G. "A Framework for Teaching Ethical Decision- Making in Marketing." *Journal of Mass Media Ethics* 22, no. 2-3 (Summer 2007): 114.
8. McClaren, Nicholas. "Ethics in Personal Selling and Sales Management: A Reivew of the Literature Focusing on Empirical Findings and Conceptual Foundations." *Journal of Business Ethics* 27 (2000): 286.
9. Galper, Ari. *Sales Ethics: When Did It Become Okay to Lie?* Unlockthegame.com, August 23, 2015. Web.
10. Barnett, Tim and Valentine, Sean "Ethics Code Awareness, Perceived Ethical Values and Organizational Commitment." *The Journal of Personal Selling* 23, no. 4 (Fall 2003): 359.
11. Ingram, Thomas and Schwepker, Charles. "Improving Sales Performance Through Ethics: The Relationship Between Salesperson Moral Judgment and Job Performance." *Journal of Business Ethics*, November 1996: 3.
12. Rogers, Beth. *Rethinking Sales Management*. Wiley: New York, 2007. Print.
13. "International Stop-Selling Day Declared by the United Professional Sales Association for May 24th." *PR Newswire*. May 4, 2015. Web.
14. Schewpker, Charles H., Good, David J. "Moral Judgement and Its Impact on Business Sales." *Journal of Business Ethics* 98 (2011): 619.
15. Bragg, Arthur. "Ethics in Selling, Honest." *Sales and Marketing Management* 138, no. 7 (May

1987): 44.

16. Smith, J. Walker. "Selling Doing Good." *Marketing Management*, January/February 2008: 56.
17. Schultz, Howard. *Onward: How Starbucks Fought for Its Life without Losing Its Soul*. Rodale: New York 2012. Print.
18. Ferrell, O.C., Ingram, Thomas, Schewepker, Charles. "The Influence of Ethical Climate and Ethical Conflict on Role Stress in the Sales Force." *Academy of Marketing Science Journal*, Spring 1997: 13.
19. Trent, Karen. "The Dangers of Groupthink." *Teamwork*, June 1990: 1.
20. Strout, Erin. "Doctoring Sales." *Sales & Marketing Management*, May 2001: 59.
21. Perrone, Jasmin and Vickers, Margaret H. "Emotions as Strategic Game in a Hostile Workplace: An Exemplar Case." *Employee Responsibilities and Rights Journal* 16, no 3 (September 2004): 167.
22. Holsworth, Jeanette. "4 Ways to Curb Employee Theft." *Gainesville Biz Report,* Accessed December 10, 2014. Web.
23. Hockenull, Terence A. "Weekender Marketing." *BusinessWorld*, August 2004: 1.
24. Katz, D. "All gifts large and small: towards an understanding of the ethics of pharmaceutical gift giving." *American Journal of Bioethics* 3, no. 3 (2003): 39.
25. Global Business Gifts, Travel and Entertainment Policy. Policy# HP011-02. Revised Nov 1, 2014. Accessed October 2, 2015. Web.
26. Hauserman, Nancy R. "Whistle- Blowing: Individual Morality in a Society." *Business Horizons* 29 (March/April 1986): 4.
27. Wilson, Glenn T. "Ethics, Your Company or Your Conscience." *Working Woman*, 1984: 67.
28. Dill, Kathryn. "The Best Places To Work In 2015." *Forbes*. Forbes, Dec 10, 2014. Web.
29. Andris A. Zoltners, PK Sinha, and Sally E. Lorimer. "Why Sales Teams Should Reexamine Territory Design." Harvard Business Review, August 7, 2015. Web.
30. Ruiz, Michelle. "What Sexual Harassment at Work Really Looks Like." *Cosmopolitan*, Feb 16, 2015. Web
31. Lill, David J. "Issue of Ethics Often Faces Professional Salespeople." *Nashville Business Journal*, April 22- 26, 1991: 5.
32. Stack, Steven M. "The High Risk of Dirty Tricks." *Sales and Marketing Magazine* 135, no 7 (November 1985): 58
33. *Uniform Commercial Code*, Accessed April 11, 2015.
34. "Drugmakers Continue Off-Label Marketing Despite Large Fines," *NJ.com*, June 6, 2010.
35. "Pfizer Broke the Law by Promoting Drugs for Unapproved Uses," *Bloomberg.com*, November 9, 2009. Web.

“Communication
—**THE HUMAN CONNECTION**—
is the **key** to personal and career success.”

– ***Paul J. Meyer***

CHAPTER 4 PURCHASE BEHAVIOR AND COMMUNICATION

OVERVIEW

This chapter is all about understanding why people buy and communicating with them in a way that forms meaningful, lasting relationships. The more you understand about buyers and their decision-making process, the more readily you can discover what they need and want. Because success in relationship selling depends on accurately getting your message across to prospects, this chapter also describes how to break through communication barriers. Good communication is the cornerstone of a sound relationship, and when it comes to professional selling, it's not an optional skill.

OBJECTIVES

- Comprehend the Purchase Decision Process
- Determine the differences between individual and organizational buyers.
- Learn the environmental influences on the purchase decision process.
- Find out what goes into the successful sending and receiving of a message.
- Examine methods for overcoming communication barriers.
- Understand the importance of using the voice as a communication tool.
- Explore the effects of body language and proxemics in selling.

"Four score and seven years ago our fathers brought forth on this continent, a new nation, conceived in Liberty, and dedicated to the proposition that all men are created equal.

Now we are engaged in a great civil war, testing whether that nation, or any nation so conceived and so dedicated, can long endure. We are met on a great battlefield of that war. We have come to dedicate a portion of that field, as a final resting place for those who here gave their lives that that nation might live. It is altogether fitting and proper that we should do this.

But, in a larger sense, we cannot dedicate—we cannot consecrate—we cannot hallow—this ground. The brave men, living and dead, who struggled here, have consecrated it, far above our poor power to add or detract. The world will little note, nor long remember what we say here, but it can never forget what they did here. It is for us the living, rather, to be dedicated here to the unfinished work which they who fought here have thus far so nobly advanced. It is rather for us to be here dedicated to the great task remaining before us—that from these honored dead we take increased devotion to that cause for which they gave the last full measure of devotion—that we here highly resolve that these dead shall not have died in vain—that this nation, under God, shall have a new birth of freedom—and that government of the people, by the people, for the people, shall not perish from the earth."

You just read the famous *Gettysburg Address* given by President Abraham Lincoln at the dedication of the Gettysburg National Cemetery on November 19, 1863. The entire speech lasted about two minutes with a total of 268 words: 198 are one-syllable words, 50 are two-syllable words, and only 20 are words of more than two syllables. Despite the lack of eloquent or complicated verbiage, the Gettysburg Address is recognized as a classic model of great oratory.

When asked to explain Britain's wartime policy to Parliament, Prime Minister Winston Churchill said, "It is to wage war, by sea, land and air, with all our might and with all the strength that God can give us." As Neil Armstrong first set foot on the moon he said simply, "That's one small step for man, one giant leap for mankind." These leaders demonstrate that you don't have to use big words to make a big impact.

Not only are small words more understandable and exact than large words, they also add elegance to your speaking and writing. Realize and appreciate the persuasive power of a well-written sales proposal. Just think how much more you could sell if you could talk and write equally well. If you must choose between a large word and a small word, pick the small word every time. Take a lesson from your local highway department. Place a sign at the boundaries of your speech that reads: *Caution—Small Words at Work.*

WHY PEOPLE BUY

Consumer behavior is the set of actions that make up an individual's consideration, purchase, and use of products and services.[1] The term consumer behavior includes both the purchase and the consumption of products or services. Your role is vital in this process of matching the organization's offerings to the needs of the prospective buyer. The three situations below involve consumer behavior and illustrate some diverse aspects of the purchase decision process:

1. A retail salesperson working at an Apple store in Las Cruces, New Mexico convinces a middle-aged couple to purchase a MacBook Air by emphasizing his parent's own enjoyment of and success with the product.
2. A nonprofit fundraiser representing the ***San Diego Zoo*** visits a prominent philanthropist and presents a new program that, once launched, will give public school students 24/7 access to live video feeds—along with teaching from the animals' doctors and caregivers—of the most popular zoo exhibits for educational purposes in the classroom. He convinces the philanthropist to give $1 million to fund the program, focusing on the wealthy man's known love of and support of children's causes.
3. ***Yum! Brands***, the restaurant company who owns the brands ***Kentucky Fried Chicken, Taco Bell,*** and ***Pizza Hut***, has decided to upgrade their registers in a test market of 13 states. If the new registers—with all the high-tech bells and whistles—are a success, they will implement the new systems nationwide, and possibly in several of their international markets. This major capital investment requires consideration by top executives, tax specialists, production personnel, and marketing personnel. Three competing salespeople will have direct, frequent contact with all of these ***Yum! Brands*** personnel and will call in technical experts to assist. The purchase decision will take many months to complete.

Countless factors determine whether or not a prospect will make a decision to spend personal or company funds on a purchase. For physical products, one major determinant of a brand's competitiveness is how a product's package is perceived. For organizations that sell a service without tangible packaging, much is then determined by how the company has branded itself and marketed its list of services. The difficulty lies in measuring or projecting the marketplace impact of a particular design or branding system for your product or service.

For years, it has been accepted that consumer research should take place to test potential packaging changes for well-established brands. Certainly, fundamental changes to the appearance of household names like Cheerios, Tide, or Kraft products would not happen without consumer research to assess new design systems. However, relatively few companies take a disciplined approach to evaluating the performance of their current packaging and presentation of their products or services. As a result, major decisions to change a brand's appearance are often made on the basis of intuition or in response to competitive activity. In other cases, unnecessary redesigns may waste resources and risk confusing or alienating its users. Brand usage and familiarity are powerful forces, and it is vital that your product or brand image appeal to the senses of your prospect, especially for higher priced items.[2]

However, the process does not end with the sale of a product or service neatly presented in a well-designed package. Salespeople must be equally concerned with consumer satisfaction after the sale. This chapter introduces a model of the consumer's decision-making process, considers a number of environmental factors that influence this process, and then examines both the verbal and nonverbal elements of the communication process, with special emphasis on *body language* and *proxemics*.

The Purchase Decision Process

Consumers make multiple decisions every day, and each decision they make depends on how they process information.[3] The model shown in Exhibit 4.1 provides a useful tool for examining the buying process. It presents a view of the buyer as someone observed not in a single act, but in a complex problem-solving process. Obviously, this model cannot provide all the answers for salespeople, but it does provide knowledge that can be used in individual sales situations as a guide for understanding what the prospect faces and deciding how you can best assist in the decision-making process.[4]

EXHIBIT 4.1 MODEL OF THE PURCHASE DECISION PROCESS

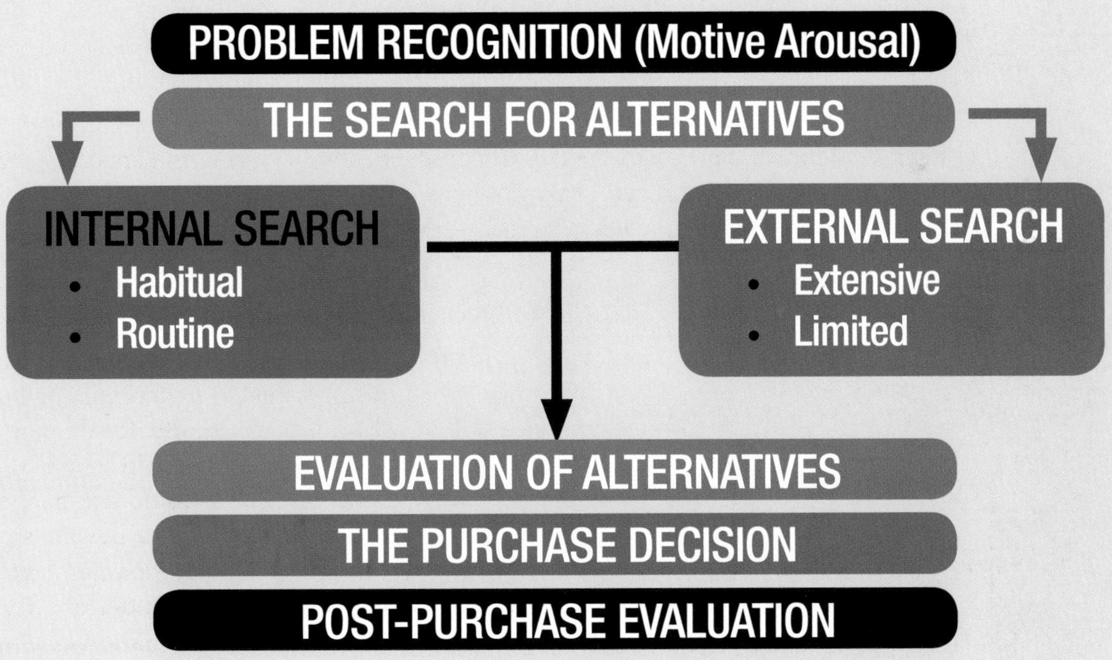

To understand why an individual makes a certain purchase decision, you must look at events leading up to and then following the purchase act itself. A buyer passes through five stages:

1. **Problem recognition**
2. **Search for alternatives**
3. **Evaluation of alternatives**
4. **The purchase decision**
5. **Post-purchase evaluation**

PROBLEM RECOGNITION. The purchase process begins with conscious recognition that a problem or need exists and must be satisfied. A need may be something regarded as necessary, or something that the individual wants or desires and therefore perceives as a need. No one takes action until motivated to do so, and this motivation arises from the awareness of a need. Therefore, salespeople must recognize needs that are already active or to find a way to create or stimulate recognition of a need of which the prospective buyer has not yet become aware. All kinds of needs affect buying decisions. In his Hierarchy of Needs, which is often portrayed in the shape of a pyramid with the largest, most fundamental levels of needs at the bottom and the need for self-actualization at the top, Abraham Maslow defined the five levels of needs as physiological, safety, social, esteem, and self-actualization. Regardless of the kind of need, some buyers will not be aware of the nature of their needs until a salesperson brings them out into the open.

SEARCH FOR ALTERNATIVES. After recognizing an unsatisfied need, the buyer begins to search for information concerning the available alternatives. The search may involve both internal and external sources. The internal search makes use of the buyer's previous experiences, learning, and attitudes, and often occurs without conscious effort. Even in the organizational markets, much purchasing is routine. A great deal of it can be done through catalogs or simply a phone call to a regular supplier. However, the external search process adds dynamics. It may require an extensive information search or a more limited search for alternatives.

The Internet provides consumers with faster, more advanced ways to search for alternatives. To successfully compete in the online marketplace, companies are looking for ways to implement social media in their marketing campaigns in order to reach online customers.[5] Online buying provides more options because customers can research and compare competing products.

EVALUATION OF ALTERNATIVES. The search process provides the buyer with knowledge of several alternative products. All individual consumers have specific criteria they use for making a decision—*personal mental rules for matching alternatives with motives*. These criteria are learned by actual experience with the product or derived from information obtained from commercial or social sources.

If you can determine the buyer's decision-making criteria, you can tailor the presentation to focus on specific product or service benefits that differentiate your product from those of the competition. Once you have matched the prospect's buying motives with what you have to offer, the determinant attributes come into play: *Price, reputation, service capabilities, and design components.* Identifying the dominant buying motives that determine a particular buyer's behavior in the actual decision-making process is vital to closing the sale.

PURCHASE DECISION. After evaluating all the alternatives discovered during the search process, the buyer is ready to make the purchase decision—actually, a whole set of decisions. Buyers want to minimize their risk and simplify the decision-making process as much as possible. The professional salesperson knows this and assists the buyer in making decisions. Find out how the product or service fits into the buyer's system by asking questions: *Who else will use it? How is it to be used? Where? When? With what other products will it be used?*

Your role in assisting prospects to reach a satisfactory purchasing decision is what makes relationship selling such a rewarding and fulfilling career.

POST-PURCHASE EVALUATION. The purchase decision process continues after the product or service choice has been made. The buyer evaluates the purchase in terms of pre-purchase expectations and decides whether it has been satisfactory. Sometimes the buyer experiences post-purchase anxiety or *cognitive dissonance*, also commonly known as buyer's remorse. The magnitude of the anxiety or tension depends on the importance of the decision and the attractiveness of the rejected alternatives. You can help lessen this feeling by providing exceptional customer service and follow-up after the sale (as discussed in Chapter 14).

THE SOCIAL MEDIA CONNECTION

Social Networking Can Help You Influence the Decision Making Process

Complex decisions are filled with risk, whether they are made for personal or business reasons. To increase trust and confidence in making high-stakes company purchase decisions, B2B (business-to-business) buyers are now leveraging their professional networks—all made easier by social media. New global research conducted by IDC finds that "online social networks play a vital role in the purchase process of 84 percent of the most senior B2B buyers." In the final stage of the purchasing process, when stakes are highest, online professional networks like LinkedIn are the number one information preference of buyers. IDC expects the "practice of online social buying to increase as the use of online social networks, particularly professional networks, expands."

This is especially important to salespeople, since some say that the rise of digital communications has already eroded many of the face-to-face opportunities in sales. For example, IDC's "2012 IT Buyer Experience" study reported that an average of nearly 50 percent of the purchasing process for technology solutions is complete before a salesperson ever becomes involved. Fewer face-to-face encounters may not be the only change to be aware of now. The processes of relationship building, gaining referrals, and getting recommendations are also shifting online. To succeed today, sales professionals must answer their "social phones."[6]

INFLUENCES ON THE PURCHASE DECISION PROCESS

Buying motives cannot be observed directly, but can be inferred from observed behavior. Exhibit 4.2 illustrates some of the many psychological and sociocultural factors that influence a buyer's purchase decision process. You must understand the significance and impact of these factors at the various stages of the decision-making process:

1. **Behavioral factors,** can greatly affect problem recognition and decision making. For the most part, people display three types of behavior that affect their decisions: 1) *Innate* behaviors (instinctual), 2) *Learned* behaviors (acquired), and 3) *Adaptive* behaviors (evolved).

2. **Sociocultural factors,** such as culture, physical environment, and social class, all influence the nature and scope of the information search.

3. **Psychological factors,** such as the mood of the moment, attitudes, and perception of oneself, combine with sociocultural factors to influence purchase decisions.

You can make positive use of these factors by becoming proficient in the art of communication—the sending and receiving of messages in a manner that results in understanding, productive discussion, and fulfillment of a want or a need.

EXHIBIT 4.2 INFLUENCES ON THE BUYER'S DECISION PROCESS

Psychological Influences: It's All in Your Head

Several psychological factors affect a prospect's buying decision. You must be aware of these factors and understand the role they play in the process. Once you learn how these factors influence the sales process, you can use them to your advantage in future selling situations as they enable you to more accurately read the prospect's overall disposition.

PERCEPTION. Individual behavior is an organized and meaningful response to the world as that particular person sees it. We perceive situations according to our own personal needs, values, expectations, past experience, and training. Exhibit 4.3 illustrates the difference in individual perceptions. How many squares do you see? Check the answer given in the chapter endnotes at the end of this chapter.[7] If you didn't see that many, you may be exercising *selective perception*. What prospects perceive as important to them is often not what you think is most important. Clients, as well as prospective customers, now have significantly higher service expectations today than ever before.

EXHIBIT 4.3

HOW MANY SQUARES DO YOU SEE?

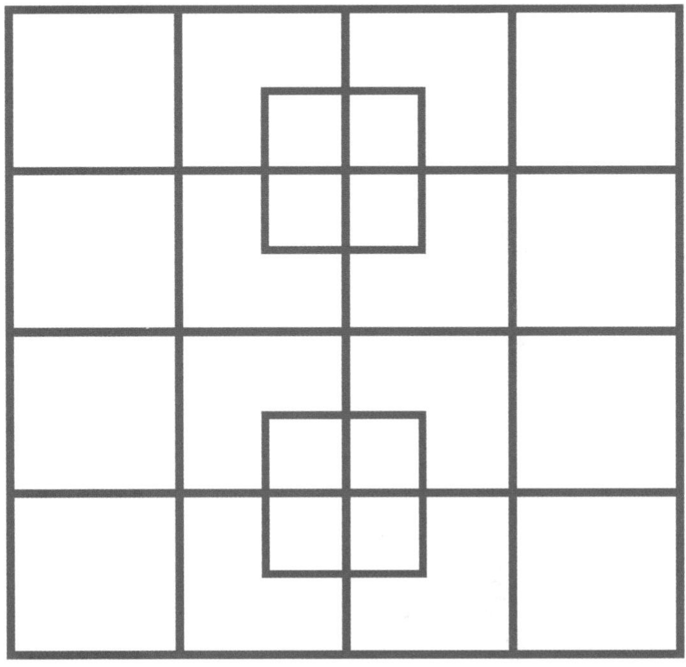

MOOD OF THE MOMENT. Decisions are also influenced by an individual's psychological state or the mood of the moment. On some days a minor mishap may be laughed off, but if nothing has gone right all day, the same situation may make your blood boil.

ATTITUDE. Attitudes are merely habits of thought and habitual patterns of response to stimuli and experiences. Because they have been used so often, they have become automatic and are used to save the time that would be required to think about a situation and make a decision. For example, some prospects operate from the concept that what has been done in the past is the best way to do things in the future. In other words, their attitude is that change is bad. Any attitude that makes the purchase decision more difficult creates a barrier that must be overcome before a sale can be made.

Negative attitudes are a problem because they are often unconscious. Because they are often habitual responses based on past experience, the individual involved no longer thinks about them and is unaware that they exist. In contrast, prospects who adopt attitudes of open-mindedness, enthusiasm, innovativeness, and willingness to explore new ideas are a joy for the relationship salesperson to find.

SELF-IMAGE. Self-image is an individual's unique and personal self-appraisal at a given moment in time. It affects what is perceived as reality and, as a result, how communication proceeds. In choosing how to communicate, even more important than what is true is what the person believes is true.[8] Self-image often has a great deal of influence on a prospect's tendency to be a conspicuous consumer. *Conspicuous consumption* is a relatively new trend in which consumers spend money on unnecessary and unproductive leisure expenditures and big-ticket items that are considered more "flashy" than practical. Perhaps it is a way purchasers can compensate for a less than positive self-image, or perhaps they practice conspicuous consumption for other reasons. Regardless of the motive, be aware of the power of this buying motive.[9]

Sociocultural Influences

In addition to psychological influences, it is essential to understand how sociocultural influences operate to determine people's communication.

CULTURE. Culture is a way of looking at life that is handed down from one generation to another. Arguably, it is almost completely learned. The effects of culture can be observed in what people do, see, and use, and in how they reach judgments about people, events, and experiences. Individuals' values develop as a result of their reactions to the environment in which they live. Our cultural environment exerts a powerful influence on how messages are both sent and received. A large percentage of Americans attach a positive connotation to concepts such as success, competition, efficiency, freedom, and material wealth. However, the positive reception to these words is not universal.

Even more pronounced are cultural differences that affect communication among people from different parts of the world, a fact that has broad implications for salespeople in the modern marketplace.[10] Exhibit 4.4 illustrates that selling to and dealing with prospects from overseas demands cultural sensitivity. For example, in Japan that means showing a business card the same respect you would show a person.[11]

EXHIBIT 4.4 TREAT A BUSINESS CARD WITH RESPECT

Jane Seigel faced the moment she had been waiting for. Her firm had been courting a big Tokyo meeting planning company for the past six months. At a National Speakers Association convention, Seigel had the good fortune (or so it seemed) to meet with the firm's representative to discuss services her company might buy. "She handed her business card to me in the traditional Japanese way," Seigal recalls—extending the card while holding onto both corners. "I took the card and scribbled a note on the back of it." Much to her dismay, Seigel looked up to find the woman appalled at what Seigel had just done. "I quickly put it away and then apologized profusely, but the damage was already done." Jane lost a sale worth $100,000 to her company!

A GLOBAL PERSPECTIVE. Foreign cultures adhere to business customs, protocols, and body language used in basic communication that differs greatly from what is used in America. If you want to sell to international customers, whether here or overseas, you must first establish rapport. Insensitivity to other people's customs and ways of communicating may derail your best selling efforts. With major companies moving large portions of their operations overseas, American business people, and specifically those in sales, must be aware of the differences they will encounter when dealing with others outside the U.S. and learn how to best use those differences to their advantage.[12]

Those who sell to international customers may get by with a wink and a "see ya later," but only if they know how their language and gestures will be interpreted; body talk does not have a universal language. According to Diane Ackerman's book, *A Natural History of the Senses*, "Members of a tribe in New Guinea say good-bye by putting a hand in each other's armpit, withdrawing it, and stroking it over themselves, thus becoming coated with the friend's scent." Thank goodness that when we say goodbye to a client, we can just shake hands—or can we?

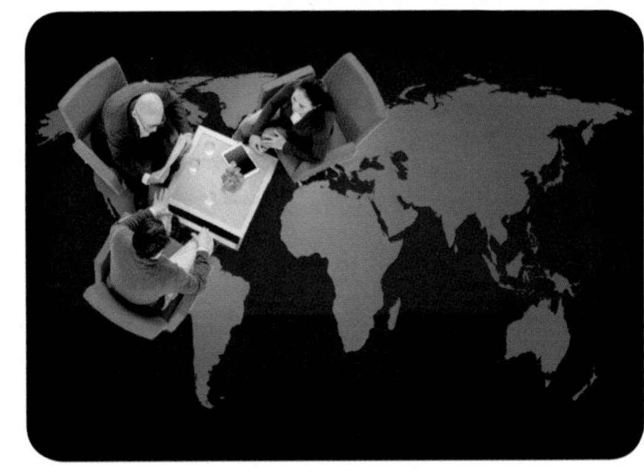

In France, the traditional American handshake is considered much too rough; a quick handshake with slight pressure is preferred. Throughout Latin America, however, the greeting is often more exuberant. A hearty embrace is common among both men and women. They often follow it with a slap on the back. In Ecuador, greeting a person without shaking hands is a sign of special respect. Throughout India, it is considered rude to touch women, so never offer to shake their hands. Exhibit 4.5 provides you with a few more interesting and important business differences among various cultures.

EXHIBIT 4.5 INTERESTING CULTURAL BUSINESS DIFFERENCES

1. Avoid slang or sports metaphors such as, "That proposal is way out in left field!" or "Are we in the ballpark on price?" They may mean nothing to other cultures.
2. Always use your last name when answering the telephone in Germany such as, "Schultz speaking." When you call a customer say your last name first: "This is Schultz, Thomas Schultz."

3. In France, Italy, Switzerland, and Japan, the business card is an extension of the person who gives it so cards need to be treated with much respect.
4. In Latin America and China business can only proceed with business after a relationship has been built.
5. In Japan, you can never be too polite, too humble, or too apologetic. Make apologizing routine. This is one of the greatest areas of cultural difference between our two countries.
6. Always appear to be less informed and less skilled in the negotiation process than you really are. To the Japanese there is no such thing as a quick deal.
7. The British and Russians are masters at using the pressure of silence. Don't speak until your prospect has responded to your last comment.

ORGANIZATIONAL VS. CONSUMER BUYING

Business-to-business (B2B) buyers include all organizations—both profit and nonprofit—that buy products or services for their own use, resell to other organizations, or sell to the ultimate consumer. The five-stage purchase decision process fits the ultimate consumer buyer adequately, and the two processes are generally similar, but the organizational buyer follows a more complex purchase decision process. The following are the four main areas where fundamental differences exist between consumer purchasing and organizational buying:

Decision Maker. The ultimate consumer is the decision maker in a purchase. In an organizational setting, decisions are often made by a team, commonly referred to as a buying center. The *buying center* is an ad hoc, cross-departmental, decision-making unit consisting of all individuals who play a role in formulating the purchasing recommendation.

Buying Criteria. Individual consumers have a limited set of factors to weigh in making a buying decision, whereas business markets often require products that are complex, expensive, and purchased in larger quantities.

Length Of Relationship. Organizational buyers desire to stay with suppliers longer, to reduce the need for frequent negotiation. This interdependence underlies the need to build a long-term relationship. As a result, many business buyers and sellers have formed what are referred to as strategic business alliances.

Buying Motives. Every buying decision made—consumer or organizational—is based on a dominant motive. Buying motives may be either rational or emotional. Your selling skills are not nearly as important as the customer's reasons for buying. In fact, your reasons for selling are useless if they don't match the customer's reasons for buying.[13] Individual consumers often buy based on emotion and later attempt to rationalize their decisions. For organizational buyers, however, rational motives are usually dominant, though they often take emotional motives into account as well. The two lists below provide the basic motives that lead to both consumer and organizational purchases.

CONSUMER BUYING MOTIVES

- Alleviate fear
- Secure social approval
- Satisfy bodily needs
- Experience happiness or pleasure
- Gain an advantage
- Imitate
- Dominate others
- Enjoy recreation
- Improve health

ORGANIZATIONAL BUYING MOTIVES

- Economy
- Flexibility
- Uniformity of output
- Salability
- Protection
- Utility
- Guarantees
- Delivery
- Quality

Multiple Buying Influences

The responsibility for organizational buying decisions may lie with more than a single individual. Organizations often set dollar limits beyond which purchase decisions must involve additional executives, more red tape, and more paperwork. Buying committees or teams drawn from the various departments become involved in decision making. The members of this team, called a *buying center*, share common goals and knowledge relevant to the purchase decision. A major reason for working with the buying center is to discover the key person or persons who actually make or strongly influence the final decision. Researchers have identified five specific roles played by the people who constitute a buying center:[14]

1. **Users.** These individuals are those who will actually use the product or service purchased; for example, a telemarketing sales force whose members will be the primary users of a proposed new telephone system.
2. **Buyers.** Buyers have formal authority to make the purchase, such as the purchasing agent.
3. **Influencers.** Influencers are the individuals who provide information, directly or indirectly, throughout the buying process to members of the buying center. For example, the supervisor for the telemarketing division may suggest certain features needed in a telephone system to make the calling process more efficient.
4. **Deciders.** This role is played by those who have the power and authority to choose from among the various suppliers. They make the final decision.
5. **Gatekeepers.** Within any typical organization, the information needed in the decision making process is influenced by the gatekeepers—those who control the flow of information into the buying center. Gatekeepers are invaluable to the group's decision-making process.

THE COMMUNICATION AGENDA

Relationship selling thrives on good communication. *Communication* can be viewed as the verbal and nonverbal passing of information between you, the sender, and your prospect, the receiver. However, for effective communication to take place, each person must understand the intended message. Thus, the goal of communication is a mutual understanding.

Exhibit 4.6 shows the channel through which communication must flow in a selling situation. At each intersection the potential exists for both roadblocks and opportunities. Although the model considers communication from the salesperson's perspective, in any successful relationship both parties participate meaningfully in an active two-way process.[15]

EXHIBIT 4.6 THE COMMUNICATION MODEL FOR VERBAL AND NONVERBAL MESSAGES

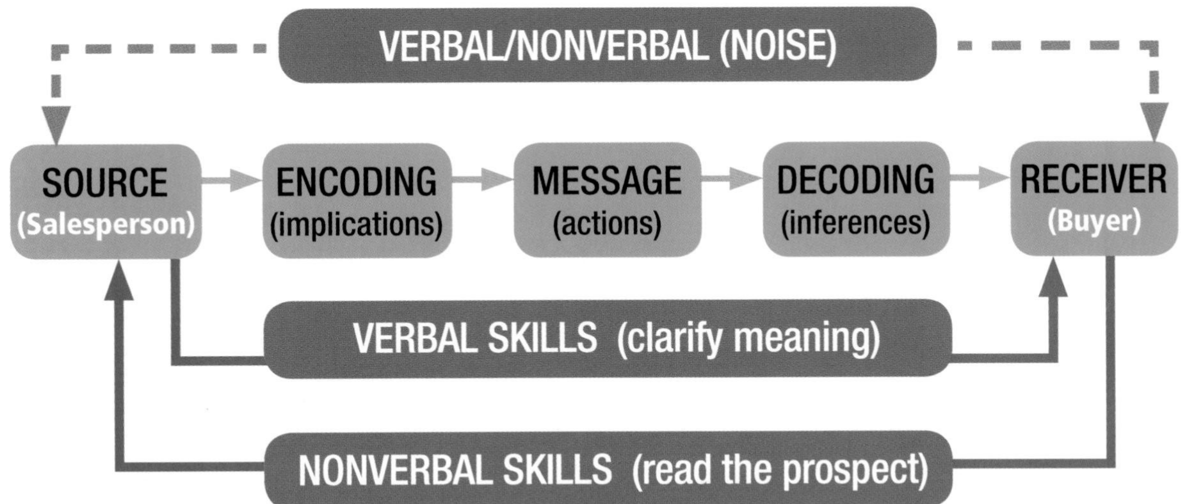

Encoding the Message

Encoding is the process in which the salesperson converts an idea or concept into symbols the buyer can clearly understand. You know what you are trying to say; the real challenge is getting your point across. This requires the proper mix of symbols to express your meaning correctly. The most common symbols used in delivering a message are words, pictures, numbers, sounds, physical touch, smell, body movement, and taste. You must encode the message, organize it, and put it into a presentation format the prospect will understand, accept, and believe.

> Effective encoding of your message is based on a thorough knowledge of the prospect's needs.

Communication is successful if the symbols chosen make it possible for the prospect to understand. The ultimate challenge in communication is to transfer your thoughts, ideas, and intentions without distortion or omission. Because communication is affected by the assumptions and needs of both parties—as well as by outside factors such as time constraints, interruptions, and the environment—communication is often far from perfect.

THERE ARE THREE BASIC PURPOSES FOR ENCODING YOUR MESSAGE:

1. To influence the attitudes and behavior of the prospect.
2. To move the buyer through a sequence of mind changes until a buying decision is made.
3. To obtain affirmative action upon the five fundamental buying decisions: need, product, source, price, and time.

The Message Itself: More Than Words

The actual message is a blend of symbols that are used to influence a change in a prospect's attitude or behavior, and it involves both verbal and nonverbal elements. In his book, *Silent Messages*, Albert Mehrabian points out that words convey only 7 percent of feelings and emotions, tone of voice conveys 38 percent, and visual communication conveys the remaining 55 percent.[16] Nonverbal elements in the presentation make up the majority of the total impact. *In essence, it's not what you say, but how you say it.*

If verbal and nonverbal messages conflict, the listener generally relies on the nonverbal message. Exhibit 4.7 illustrates the contribution of various factors to the messages we deliver to others and the amount of control we maintain over each one. The factors most easily controlled are those that have the least effect, and those with the biggest impact are the most difficult to control because they happen automatically.

EXHIBIT 4.7 THE ABILITY TO MANAGE COMMUNICATION DIMENSIONS

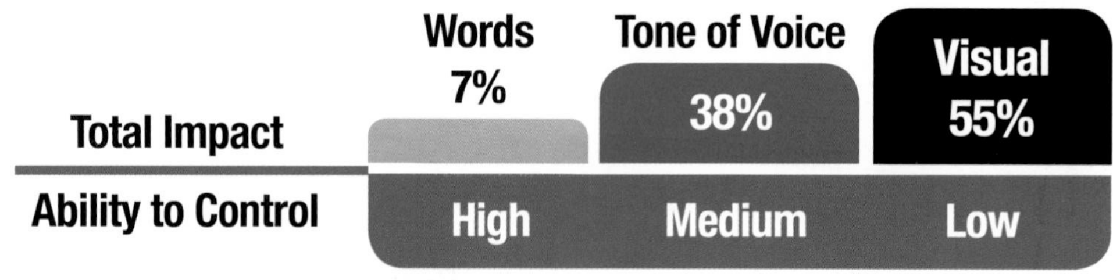

The process of delivering the message begins with visual impressions because they happen first. Read this scenario of a salesperson walking into a prospect's office for the first time:

> *Ron, a technical salesperson, walks hesitantly into Sally's office wearing a listless, slightly worried expression. Ron was up all night with his sick toddler, but Sally doesn't know that. All she knows is that Ron's expression doesn't convey confidence or trust, and so she is immediately wary—and that provides an instantly unappealing visual message. Ron then extends a clammy palm with a "dead-fish" handshake, and an unpleasant touch is added. He tries to force a smile, but his rather unenthusiastic message is delivered in a monotone, and the sound itself drowns out the words.*

In this scenario, the cluster of negative nonverbal cues completely masks the real message. Sally will never really even know or compute what Ron is saying, even if she really does need what he is selling. Research suggests that if the first thirty seconds of a communication result in a negative impression, you must spend the next four minutes just to overcome that impression before any communication can truly begin.[17] Unfortunately, the prospect may decide not to buy before the situation can be reversed.

Decoding the Message

Decoding is the mental process by which prospects figure out the meaning of a message. It is the way in which your prospect attempts to translate the symbols used in your presentation into something that relates to their needs. If the message was obviously both understood as intended and also accepted, there is no problem. At this step in the process, either real communication or misunderstanding will occur. Your prospects listen to your message, and then make their own inferences or conclusions. If the prospect fails to understand the message, *the result is called noise, which means that a breakdown in communication has occurred.* This happens when there are barriers to effective communication, as discussed in the following section.

Common Communication Barriers

Seldom does the buyer interpret exactly the same meaning that you intended, and when the result of decoding is different from what you encoded, noise exists. Anything that interferes with or distorts understanding of the intended message is called noise, and it can take many forms that may affect any or all parts of the communication process. There are logical reasons why your sales message may not be understood or accepted. Here are some reasons for such miscommunication:

WORDS. All language is a code. Even if you and your prospect use the same words, you are likely putting out different meanings. This is especially true when it comes to electronic forms of communication where it is difficult for the reader to interpret the true meaning of the words.[18] Noise is created when words are inappropriate or are written in a confusing manner. For example, casual profanity that may offend the listener, language implying that the listener is poorly informed, language that assumes too much knowledge on the listener's part, language that obscures the real meaning, or formatting of written words that may seem offensive to the reader.

DISTRACTIONS. Any element or interruption that may focus the prospect's attention on something other than the message is a distraction. The effectiveness of marketing programs is tied to the level of distraction of the consumer.[19] Some typical distractions are inappropriate dress, uncomfortable room temperature, loud noise that makes concentration difficult, confusing language in marketing materials, or a nagging personal problem occupying the prospect's mind. Telephone calls, people walking in to you ask questions, and emergencies represent the kinds of interruptions that reduce or distort the impact of the message.

TIMING. If a prospect has some reason for not wanting to listen, no amount of communication skill on your part is enough. The prospect may be feeling under the weather, may be preoccupied with an unpleasant disciplinary task, or may be facing a pressing deadline. Some prospects need time to warm up before getting down to business; others want to get right to your proposal and skip the small talk.

TECHNICAL ERUDITION. Information overload often complicates a message. Prospects need time to process information from different sources. An unconscious desire to appear personally knowledgeable often results in the salesperson talking too much, poorly organizing the presentation of features and benefits, or wrongly assuming that the prospect has adequate knowledge. As a result, the prospect fails to see a need for the product or service. Avoid using technical terms or jargon without clarification.[20]

LISTENING HABITS. If the prospect is a poor listener, the salesperson is faced with a monumental challenge in designing a message and delivering it in an effective and successful manner. The other end of the spectrum is the salesperson who is a poor listener, who never picks up the prospect's cues that are the keys to wording the message for quick acceptance.

The buyer will draw conclusions from the messages received and react accordingly. Recognizing this *feedback* is crucial to a salesperson's success. During face-to-face communication, verbal and nonverbal feedback is immediate and very revealing. Become skilled in receiving feedback so that you can adapt your sales presentation to fit each individual buyer's requirements. Use the feedback loop from the prospect to you to bring you closer to an exact understanding of what is being said by each participant. This filters out the noise and results in clear communication.[21]

USING YOUR VOICE AS A SALES TOOL

The first impression you make is often based on your voice. When you call for an appointment, your voice is all you have for communicating. A voice that is pleasing and confident is a great asset. Your voice and how you use it play an important part in your success in selling. Several basic components of verbal communication deserve your attention.[22]

ARTICULATION. If you have ever seen the classic movie *My Fair Lady*, do you recall the device Professor Higgins used to help Eliza Doolittle improve her speech? He had her talk with marbles in her mouth. To be understood at all, she was forced to form her words with extreme care. As a result, her articulation improved. When you speak, do people hear separate words and syllables, or *doyourwordsallruntogether*? A salesperson with poor articulation leaves prospects confused and bewildered.

VOLUME. The normal volume of the speaking voice varies during conversation. The same is true of a sales presentation. Stressing a benefit may call for increased volume. Lowering your voice, sometimes almost to a whisper, may produce quite a dramatic effect; it causes the prospect to lean forward (a body position that signals agreement or approval) to avoid missing your words. Variation in volume enhances the message if it is not overdone.

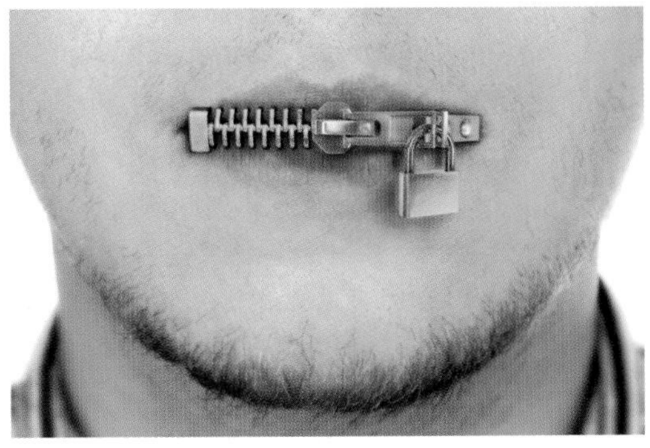

SILENCE. Silence is a powerful selling tool. Use it to give the prospect time to absorb the full impact of what you have said. Slight pauses between major points in the presentation suggest that you are thoughtful, intelligent, and analytical. Pauses also give the prospect an opportunity to comment, ask a question, or think about how the idea you have presented can be applied to an existing need or problem. Avoid becoming so enamored with the sound of your own voice that you talk all the time.

RHYTHM. The rhythmic pattern of your speech comes from your basic personality style and your emotions of the moment. Some voices seem to flow in long, continuous sentences, whereas others come in short, choppy chunks. Just as the rhythm in music changes to indicate that something new is happening, the same thing happens in speech patterns. Be alert to any changes in your own or the prospect's speech patterns. Changes are even more revealing than initial patterns. If the prospect suddenly shifts to a more drawn-out rhythm, for example, the message may be "Let me think more about that" or "I don't believe what you're saying."

RATE. The tempo of your delivery should be comfortable for you as a speaker and for your listener. Speaking too rapidly may cause you to lose a prospect who customarily speaks more slowly and feels that your fast pace is pushing for a decision without allowing time for thought. Speaking too slowly may make the prospect want to push your fast-forward button. A moderate pace allows you to enunciate clearly, establish natural rhythmic patterns, and speed up or slow down for proper emphasis of some point.

SELLING WITHOUT WORDS

Although people have the option not to speak, they are, nevertheless, always communicating. Nonverbal signals are a rich source of information, and one's own nonverbal behavior can be useful in responding to others, making stronger connections with clients and colleagues, and conveying certain impressions about oneself.[23] Different people have different levels of competence in nonverbal communication skills, and some professions require more skill than others. The success of a professional gambler depends on the ability to exercise strict control over nonverbal messages to disguise a bluff. A mime depends exclusively on nonverbal skills to deliver a message.

However, to achieve excellence in the sales profession, you must be skilled in both verbal and nonverbal communication. Two particularly important components of nonverbal communication are body language and proxemics.

Body Language

Body language can be conceived of as messages sent without using words. The essential elements of body language include shifts in posture or stance, facial expressions, eye movements, and arm, hand, and leg movements. It includes every movement and gesture, from the subtle raising of an eyebrow to the obvious leaning forward of an interested listener. Through body language, prospects express their emotions, desires, and attitudes. As a result, body language is a valuable tool for discovering what the prospect is really saying.

When you can read the prospect's body language and, in addition, control your own body signals to add impact to your words, you are likely to be understood.

THE LANGUAGE OF GESTURES. Important signals involve body angle; position of hands, arms, legs, and the face—especially the eyes and lips.[24] All of these should be observed as a cluster of gestures that together state a message. A prospect sitting with arms crossed may be communicating doubt or rejection or may simply be sitting comfortably. In this case, you must also observe whether the legs are crossed, the body withdrawn, the eyes glancing sideways, and an eyebrow raised. All these signs, taken together, surely suggest doubt or rejection, but one of them in isolation is inconclusive.

BODY SIGNALS. A hunched figure, rigid posture, restless stance, or nervous pacing may contradict what a person says verbally. Prospects allow you to sit closer if they feel comfortable and lean toward you if they like what you are saying and are intent on listening. John Molloy, author of bestselling book, *Dress for Success*, used videotape to study the behavior of successful and unsuccessful salespeople. One mannerism difference noted was the relative calmness of professional salespeople in comparison to those who were less successful. Their body movements were smooth and unhurried; there were no jerky motions, particularly when handing a contract or a pen across the table. Every movement was gradual. Less successful salespeople exhibited jumpy, nervous movements that were picked up—perhaps unconsciously—by prospects.

Look for changes in the prospect's body posture and gestures. For example, one who is ready to buy shows signs of relaxation: Nodding in agreement, mirroring your movements, moving to the front of the chair, extending the palm of the hand outward toward you, and uncrossing legs. Your posture and gestures also communicate your feelings to the prospect. If you sit in an open, relaxed position, you are likely to be more persuasive and better accepted than if you sit in a tight, closed posture.

HAND MOVEMENTS. Rubbing the back of the neck may indicate frustration, but it can also indicate that the prospect has a sore or stiff neck from painting the bathroom ceiling over the weekend. Next time you are speaking with a client, notice his hand movements and read his hands as indicators of what he is really feeling. People can say so much with simple, unthinking hand motions. Evaluate the following hand gestures in the context of other nonverbal clues.

1. **Hand and head gestures.** Tugging at the ear suggests the desire to interrupt. Pinching the bridge of the nose and closing the eyes says that a matter is being given serious thought.
2. **Posture.** Leaning back in the chair with both hands behind the head communicates a sense of superiority.
3. **Involuntary gestures.** Involuntary hand gestures that contradict a facial expression are likely to reveal the true feelings. Tightly clasped hands or fists indicate tenseness.
4. **Steepling of the hands.** Fingertips together, forming what looks like a church steeple, often indicate smugness, self-confidence, or feelings of superiority.

FACIAL EXPRESSIONS. Eyebrows, eyelids, eyes, lips, jaw, mouth, and facial muscles all work together to communicate feelings and emotions. Research attributes as much as 70 percent of nonverbal message sending to the muscles of the face.[25]

The face is a highly reliable indicator of attitude. A person may avoid eye contact when trying to cover up true feelings. Increased eye contact signals honesty and interest. Be sure to maintain eye contact at critical moments of the presentation. For example, when describing technical characteristics of the product, direct the prospect's eyes to the product itself, the brochure, or the specification sheet. In contrast, when stressing the benefits of using the product, maintain direct eye contact.

Lack of eye contact sends a negative message that neutralizes the impact of the intended benefit. Proper eye contact makes a positive statement that words alone cannot.[26] In a survey conducted by Incomm Research, 80 percent of trade show attendees said they were more likely to perceive a company or product positively if its sales reps were smiling.

Suspicion and anger are shown by tightness around the cheeks or along the jaw line. Muscle movement at the back of the jaw line just below the ears indicates an angry gritting of the teeth. A sudden flush of facial redness may warn that the situation has taken a bad turn; embarrassment or hostility may be radiating under an apparently calm exterior.

An isolated gesture or posture is seldom a reliable indicator of attitude or feelings. Obviously, you have to take a look at the buyer in the context of the whole situation. The buyer may fold her arms just to be more comfortable. Generally, if there is an objection, the whole body will become more rigid. When a cluster of gestures is consistent with the verbal messages, it is relatively safe to accept their validity.

Proxemics

Proxemics is the distance individuals prefer to maintain between themselves and others. Most people seem to consider the observation of desired distance a matter of courtesy. Violations of distance comfort risk closing down the communication process. Highly successful salespeople tend to move closer to clients when closing a sale. The difference between how successful and unsuccessful salespeople use physical closeness can be observed in the prospect's reaction. Carefully test for the existence of comfort barriers; then place yourself just outside those barriers.

Exhibit 4.8 shows the four basic zones or ranges that apply in the typical sales situation. Generally speaking, the intimate zone is about two feet (hence the expression, "Keeping someone at arm's length"). Enter this range only if invited. Moving inside the intimate zone, except for a handshake, is not a good idea. Beyond that, we all have a personal zone, which is an envelope around us extending from two to four feet. Move into the buyer's personal zone only after invitation, which typically occurs after you establish a satisfying professional relationship. The outer shell is the social zone, which extends up to 12 feet.[27]

EXHIBIT 4.8 HOW TO USE SPACE

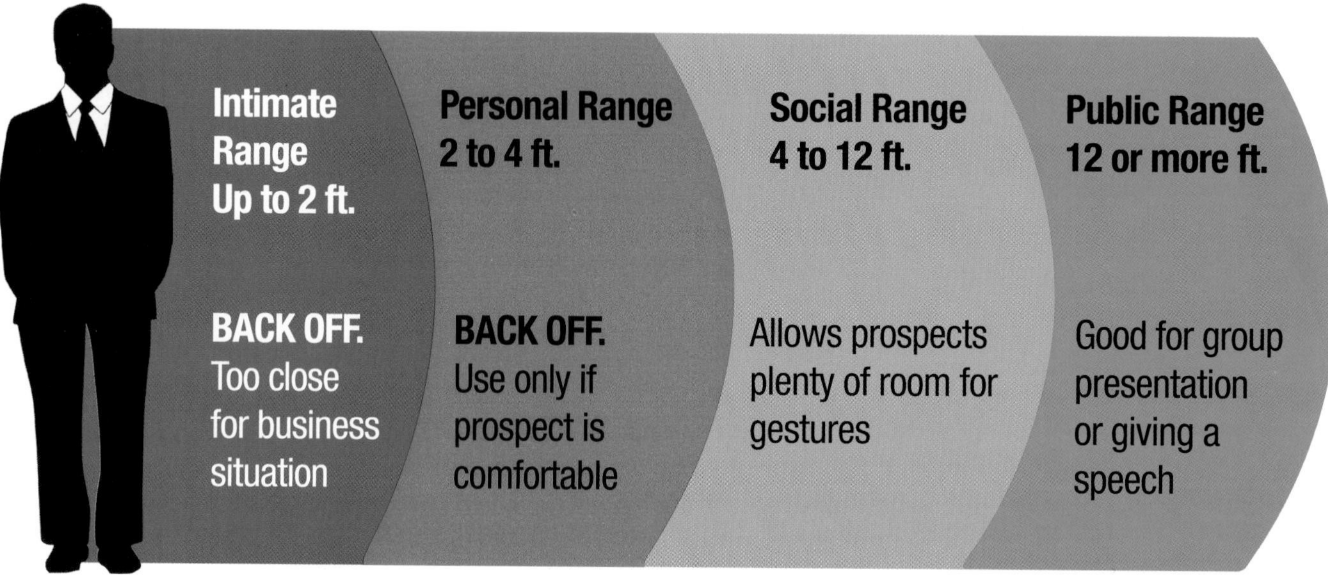

A number of factors enter into the amount of space various individuals need. Cultural differences, age, gender, and personality are important, as is the type of relationship that exists between salesperson and client. Peers tolerate a closer range of contact than people with a wide gap in age or status. Conversations between two women occur at closer range that those between two men or between a man and a woman. People with outgoing, open personalities are willing to be closer than those who are shy or withdrawn. Salespeople can move closer to long-term clients than to new prospects.

SUMMARY

- The consumer's purchase decision process involves five stages:
    1. Problem recognition
    2. Search for alternatives
    3. Evaluation of alternatives
    4. The purchase decision
    5. Post-purchase evaluation

- Organizational buyers must abide by specific restrictions and buying procedures, often consult with other executives, and must deal with budget constraints. Purchases of this nature often involve a purchasing team, sometimes referred to as a buying center.
- Salespeople are successful in closing sales when they discover the buying motives of the prospect, present benefits of the product that relate to those motives, and are sensitive to both psychological and sociocultural influences.
- Communication is the vehicle for delivering your message in a manner that the buyer comprehends, accepts, and believes.
- Understanding body language and how prospects use their space adds to your ability to communicate with the prospect.
- We send the majority of our messages in daily communication through nonverbal means. We are always communicating!

REVIEW QUESTIONS

1. Formulate a brief definition of consumer behavior.
2. Why must salespeople understand consumer behavior?
3. What are the five stages of the buying-decision process? What is a salesperson's function in each of these stages?
4. What is cognitive dissonance? How can a salesperson prevent it?
5. What differences exist between individual and organizational buyers?
6. What is a buying center?
7. What are the three main purposes a salesperson may have in encoding a message to be presented to a prospect?
8. How can you be sure someone has received, understood, and accepted your message?
9. What is the role of perception in the buying-decision process?
10. What are some of the psychological influences on the purchase decision process?

IN-CLASS EXERCISES

The following exercises help build teams, improve communication, and emphasize the real-world side of selling. They are meant to be challenging, to help you learn how to deal with problems that have no single right answer, and to use a variety of skills beyond those employed in a typical review question. Read and complete each activity. Then in the next class, discuss and compare answers.

EXERCISE 4.1 – LEARNING FROM ADVERTISING

For this role-play, divide into teams of 4 persons each. Outside of class, conduct an online search for two videos of TV advertisements, one of which reflects having considered the psychological, behavioral, and socio-cultural influences on customers' purchase decisions as outlined in Chapter 4, and the other of which does not. As a team, discuss and analyze the two videos that your team has selected in terms of why each ad is or is not effective vis-à-vis the purchase decision process. Be prepared to show and discuss your videos in class, pointing out precisely those features of each video that your team found to be effective or ineffective, and why.

EXERCISE 4.2 – BRIEF SELLING SITUATIONS

Appoint 3 students to participate in an active role-play in front of the class. Divide the class into teams and give each group a brief selling situation. Give each group fifteen minutes to prepare a presentation and invite the 3 students in the role play to present their situation to the class. Allow each team to critique the presentation in terms of their own ideas and the following:

- The model of the purchase decision process
- The ultimate consumer or organizational buying motives
- Any psychological or sociocultural influences present
- The communication process in general
- Barriers to effective communication

EXERCISE 4.3 – CHOOSE YOUR WORDS

Does word choice affect understanding? What common saying has been reworded in each of the statements below?

- A single in-and-out movement of a small cylindrical object with an oblong opening in one end through which an elongated fiber is passed produces the fortuitous circumstance of precluding the necessity of performing nine such procedures at some future date.
- A wildly gyrating fragment of consolidated solid mineral matter is never encapsulated in a cutaneous layer of bryophytic living organisms that do not possess locomotive qualities in themselves.
- You may succeed in conducting a large, solid hoofed herbivorous mammal of the family Equidae to the brink of a reservoir of liquid oxide of hydrogen, but there is no surety that you will succeed in coercing said mammal to imbibe a potation.
- Members of the populace who sojourn in habitations of an amorphous inorganic transparent material made largely of silicates are well advised to eschew propelling concretions of earthy or mineral matter.

CASE STUDIES

The following case studies present you with selling scenarios that require you to apply the critical skills discussed in the chapter and give you training through "real world" practical learning situations. They are meant to be both engaging and challenging, and like the exercises, don't have one right answer.

CASE 4.1 – THE RETURN

Ben's manager was not happy. "Do you realize what you just cost this company?" he growled at Ben. "We just took back a $1,600 home entertainment system from some guy named John Stafford. He was hot. Said that Ben Walker had just pressured his wife into buying this piece of crap and that he'd never do business here again. What happened, Ben?"

"I don't know," Ben replied. "Mrs. Stafford seemed very content with the purchase. Said her husband had been wanting something like this and that she wanted to surprise him. She signed the contract and paid with her credit card. No problem as far as I could tell."

"Well, there was a problem all right!" Ben's manager hissed. "Mr. Stafford didn't like the features on this system, especially the audio. It wasn't like anything he'd been looking for. So now we have to eat the restocking costs, and you're out the commission. This had better not happen again. I want you to go think about it and tell me what went wrong and how you're going to avoid this kind of mess in the future." With that, the manager stormed back into his office.

Ben was perplexed. For the eleven months that he'd worked at Ocean Front Appliances, he had come to enjoy selling the three major product lines they carried. Sure, there was pressure, but the commission structure was high enough to make it worth enduring. In the case of Mrs. Stafford, he thought he'd done his job, at least well enough to get the sale. Over lunch, he confided in Marcia, another salesperson who was very successful, that he didn't understand what had happened.

"I remember her," Marcia replied. "I was just on the other side of the display while you were working with her, and I thought at the time that this one could go sour."

"What do you mean?" Ben asked.

"Well, Mrs. Stafford was obviously nervous. She kept saying, 'I just don't know.' And then, you'd explain some other feature, and she would respond, "Do you think my husband will like this?"

"I remember. I kept having to reassure her," Ben said. "So I thought I'd just move on and show her how terrific this system really is."

"I know, Ben, but when she kept backing up, you should have recognized the clue that she really wasn't ready. You closed her, but I think she appeased you to get out of the store."

That stung. Ben was going to have to really think about this some more.

Given the above scene, what do you think, in light of what you've read in Chapter 4, that Ben should consider? Specifically, where did Ben go wrong with regard to the customer's decision process, the customer's motivation for buying, and communication?

CASE 4.2 – X-RAY VISION

Carla was furious. As a representative of MediTech, she had just spent the better part of 3 months cultivating the purchasing agent for a regional medical firm in her territory to buy the latest upgrade of MediTech's fMRI (functional MRI) machine, only to be told when she tried to close the sale that he would have to "consult others." Todd, the purchasing agent, had never mentioned consulting anyone before now. For him to brush her off like that, Carla fumed, was insulting. When she stormed into her sales manager's office with her tale of rejection, however, he remained unperturbed.

"What do you mean, 'I should have known better?'" Carla exclaimed. "How could I have known that Todd would resort to such a transparently cheap dodge?"

"Look. I know you just came over to us recently from pharmaceutical sales," replied her manager, "but that experience should have taught you something."

"What?"

"Well, for starters, think about what you're selling. It's expensive, and the time before it becomes obsolete isn't all that long."

"But Todd knew all that some time ago. I never hid anything from him. He didn't bat an eye when I told him what their 5-year projected cost would be," said Carla.

"Maybe not. But he's not the one who is most impacted by increased cost. Think about who will use the new fMRI. Physicians, that's who. And you know even better than I how much physicians like to be in control," the sales manager pointed out.

He continued, "Unless they're convinced directly that there's a huge medical benefit that will justify the higher fees they must charge, they'll revolt. Those issues are outside Todd's responsibility."

Even though Carla's manager was accurate in pointing out the details that he mentioned, what was Carla missing in her general approach to Todd? What should she have done differently? Why should the points that her manager raised with her have caused her to change her approach? What can she do not to remedy the situation and get the sale?

Chapter 4 Footnotes

1. Wayne d. Hoyer, Deborah J. MacInnis, *Consumer Behavior 5th Edition.* Mason, OH: Southwestern College Pub., 2009, 3.
2. Scott Young, "Measuring Success: Using Consumer Research to Document the Value of Package Design," *Design Management Review*, Spring 2006.
3. George M Zinkhan, Karin Braunsberger. "The complexity of consumers' cognitive structures and its relevance to consumer behavior." *Journal of Business Research.* New York: (June 2004). Vol.57, Is. 6, 575.
4. For an expanded description of the model, see James F. Engel, Roger D. Blackwell, and Paul W. Miniard, *Consumer Behavior* (Hinsdale, IL: Dryden Press, 1990).
5. *Alex Jefferies, "Sales 2.0: Social Media for Knowledge Management and Sales Collaboration," Aberdeen Group (September 30, 2008).*
6. *There are 40 squares in the figure.*
7. Aron O'Cass. "Fashion clothing consumption: Antecedents and consequences of fashion clothing involvement." *European Journal of Marketing.* Bradford: (2004). Vol.38, Is. 7, *869.*
8. Ben Steverman, "Conspicuous Consumption is Back: Subdued fashions of the recession years are fading as wealthy Americans again flaunt luxury purchases," *Bloomberg Businessweek* (January 27, 2011), Accessed October 8, 2015. Web.
9. Schaub, Kathleen. *Social Buying Meets Social Selling: How Trusted Networks Improve the Purchase*

Experience. International Data Corporation. April 2014. White Paper.

10. Yinlong Zhang, Karen Page Winterich, Vikas Mittal, "Power Distance Belief and Impulsive Buying," Journal of Marketing Research (October 1, 2010).
11. Betsy Cummings, "Selling Around the World," *Sales & Marketing Management* (May 2001), 70.
12. Julien Cayla, Eric J. Arnould, "A Cultural Approach to Branding in the Global Marketplace," *Journal of International Marketing*, (December 1, 2008).
13. Jeffrey Gitomer. "Where's the Sales Beef? It's Client's Buying Motive." *Boulder County Business Report*. Boulder: (July 23-August 5, 2004). Vol. 23, Is. 16, 6A.
14. James P. Morgan, "Cross-Functional Buying: Why Teams are Hot," Purchasing (April 5, 2001).
15. V. Emre Ozdemir, Kelly Hewett, "The Effect of Collectivism on the Importance of Relationship Quality and Service Quality for Behavioral Intentions: A Cross-National and Cross-Contextual Analysis," *Journal of International Marketing* (March 1, 2010).
16. Albert Mehrabian, *Silent Messages* (Belmont, CA: Wadsworth Publishing Company 1971).
17. Deb Varallo, *A Dress for Success Seminar*, Belmont University, Nashville, TN, (November, 2006).
18. Yubo Chen, Qi Wang, Jinhong Xie, "Online Social Interactions: A Natural Experiment on Word of Mouth Versus Observational Learning," *Journal of Marketing Research* (April 1, 2011).
19. Stephen M. Nowlis, Baba Shiv, "The Influence of Consumer Distractions on the Effectiveness of Food Sampling Programs," *Journal of Marketing Research* (May 1, 2005).
20. Derek Dean, Caroline Webb, "Recovering from Information Overload," *The McKinsey Quarterly* (January 31, 2011).
21. "INSIGHTations: Bits and Bytes from Around the Blogosphere," Accessed April 12, 2014), MarkketingPower.com, Accessed July 19, 2015. Web.
22. This section on the voice was adapted from: Jeffrey Jacobi, "Voice Power," *Selling Power* (October 2000), 66; Robert A. Peterson, Michael P. Cannito and Steven P. Brown, "An Exploratory Investigation of Voice Characteristics," *The Journal of Personal Selling & Sales Management* (Winter 1995), 1-16; John H. Melchinger, "Communication-One Key to Unlock Your Sales, " *Personal Selling Power*, Vol. 10, No. 3 (April 1990), 51.
23. Carol Kinsey Goman, Ph.D, *The Nonverbal Advantage: Secrets and Science of Body Language at Work* (San Francisco, CA: Berrett-Kockler Publishers, Inc., 2008) 159. 29. This section was inspired by Alessandra and Wexler, *Non-Manipulative Selling*, 95-113; Gerhard Gschwandtner, *Non Verbal Selling Power* (Englewood Cliffs, NJ: Prentice-Hall, 1985), 3-80; and John T. Molloy, *Live for Success* (New York: Perigord Press, 1981).
24. James Borg, *Body Language: 7 Easy Lessons to Master the Silent Language* (United Kingdom: Prentice Hall Life, 2008), 37.
25. David Lambert, *Body Language 101: The Ulitimate Guide to Knowing When People Are Lying, How They Are Feeling, What They Are Thinking, And More* (New York, NY: Skyhorse Publishing, Inc., 2008), 59-60.
26. www.kevinhogan.net Accessed May 11, 2015.
27. Yun Chu, William F. Strong, Jianyu Ma, Walter E. Greene "Silent messages in negotiations: the role of nonverbal communication in cross-cultural business negotiations," *Journal of Organizational Culture, Communications and Conflict* (July 1, 2005).

CHAPTER 5

FINDING YOUR SELLING STYLE

OVERVIEW

To be the most effective salesperson you can be, you must learn more about what really influences the driving force of your business—your customers. An especially useful tool for gaining insight into how the customer is thinking is the ***social styles model.*** In this chapter, we will dig into each of the four dominant ***social styles***, which are the ways a person sends and receives information. The social style model is a method for finding the best way to approach a prospect and to set up a working relationship with that person, and ultimately, close more sales while forming more lasting relationships.

OBJECTIVES

- Recognize the different behavioral styles.
- Identify your own dominant social style.
- Learn how to deal with people who operate from each of the various styles.
- Understand the concept of versatility and how it affects your ability to relate to all social styles.
- Become familiar with gender issues in selling.
- Discover how neurolinguistic programming (NLP) can be useful to salespeople.

Several weeks into her job as a fundraiser for a non-profit organization that provides care for special needs children, Sue Wagner realized that something was wrong. The problem was not with the work itself. Sue loved launching public awareness campaigns, helping plan special events, and writing appeals. The issue started once she was one-on-one with donors.

Sue went into every meeting with a new prospective donor ready to wow them with her organized, thorough, and detailed presentation, complete with charts and graphs to back up all points. Sometimes in the middle of her presentations, prospects would actually interrupt her with what she considered to be thoughts or questions that were irrelevant to the points she was trying to make, which would complicate the carefully laid out plans made by Sue.

She tried not to appear irritated with them, but most prospects just didn't seem interested in what she had to say. Sue often found herself scratching her head as she left empty handed from yet another prospect meeting. "People just aren't giving like they used to," she'd sigh as she headed back to the office.

Some might call such incidents a few cases of some bad luck. Others would say that perhaps those prospects were never going to say yes in the first place. Maybe Sue is not doing a good enough job of explaining her cause, or perhaps she is over explaining it. Let's call Sue's problem what it really is—the inability to connect to different social styles. Sue, as you will learn in this chapter, has an *analytical* social style. And unknowingly, she had communicated disrespect to some of her prospects that had entirely different styles of communicating.

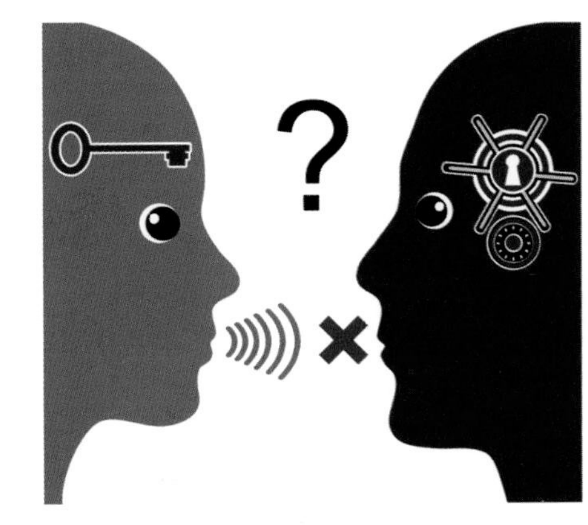

This lack of understanding and knowledge concerning behavioral styles can cause lost sales and damaged or ruined relationships. Does Sue need to change who she is in order to fix this problem? Absolutely not. She does, however, need to learn the art of *Social Style Flexing*, which amounts to being versatile enough to adjust your own personal pace and priorities to facilitate interaction with a person of another style. This "flex" can only be accomplished through a good understanding of the four styles we will discuss in this chapter.

TODAY'S SOCIAL STYLES MODEL

Because of the importance of communication in the selling process, successful salespeople constantly search for new ways to make their communication more effective. They are eager to learn how they may better anticipate and avoid conflict situations. Gauging your client's personality will help you close the sale and succeed in business.[1] A selling transaction, whether it involves products, services, or ideas, is a communication exchange in which two individuals develop a mutually desirable solution to a problem about which both are concerned. The best sales relationships are long-term ones based on mutual trust and credibility. The pertinent question then becomes:

> **"How can I sell so that I demonstrate respect for the customer, build credibility for myself and my product and company, and set up a mutually beneficial situation for both of us?"**

The concept of behavioral styles is of tremendous importance for salespeople; and it is an idea developed by the Swiss psychologist Carl Jung.[2] Jung built upon and extended the knowledge of the adult ego state developed by Sigmund Freud, who first introduced the idea. Jung's work on behavioral functions resulted in a theory of personality that included four functions: *Intuition, thinking, feeling, and sensing.*

Several behavioral style models of special interest to salespeople have been developed and introduced by various authors. David Merrill and Roger Reid began the development of their Social Styles Model in the early 1960s. Dr. Paul Mok, working independently of Merrill and Reid, developed what he referred to as the *Communicating Styles Technology Model. The Wilson Learning Corporation* and *Dr. Tony Alessandra and Associates Inc.* expanded and added their own research to these original models. The material presented in this chapter has been gleaned from these four related approaches.[3]

Everyone learns as a child that family members and friends have different personalities. In your family, you had time to learn the ways you can best persuade or get along with various relatives. In a business or social situation, you have less time to evaluate and adjust your persuasive skills. The prospect's manner and social style are often deceptive and you may miss what is happening. The most common mistake is not understanding how prospects think and make decisions.[4] The social styles model provides a useful tool for making such an evaluation in the shortest possible time.

The better you understand personality types, the more successful you will be in communicating with the various people you meet.

Each person has a primary communicating style that is blended or fine-tuned by a secondary style. These primary and secondary styles shape others' perceptions of you and filter your perceptions of other people. A second dimension to this model comes into play when you are under stress. At such times, you may shift to a different style of behavior. You may be aware of the shift yet feel unable to prevent it. People use four basic styles to deal with the world. Each is based upon one of four basic functions of human personality:

1. The **driver** or **sensing** function of taking in here-and-now sensory information and reacting to it.
2. The **expressive** or **intuitive** function of imagination and abstract thought.
3. The **amiable** or **feeling** function of personal and emotional reactions to experience.
4. The **analytical** or **thinking** function of organizing and analyzing information in a logical fashion.

DRIVERS

EXPRESSIVES

AMIABLES

ANALYTICALS

Everyone uses each of the four functions, but the frequency of use differs among individuals.[5] These styles can even be observed in young children. Behavioral patterns, Jung claimed, are genetically determined and are seen in infants during their first days of life. Like adults, young children process experience according to their own individual styles. It is important to recognize that on occasion, people will have the tendency to switch from one pattern to another as their mood, nature or purpose of the purchase changes.[6]

Behavioral Styles in Selling

Four basic concepts underlie the behavioral styles communication model presented in this chapter. They are meant to guide you toward success in selling by allowing you to improve your communication with prospects and clients. Here are the concepts:

1. A style is an overall approach used to receive and send messages. It consists of verbal, nonverbal, and behavioral elements. Everyone uses a blend of the driver, expressive, amiable, and analytical styles, although each person has a favorite style that is used more often than others.
2. Every person operates the majority of the time from a favorite style. This is the primary style. Everyone also has a secondary or backup style that may replace or modify the primary style.
3. Because style is reflected in behavior, you can identify someone else's primary style by observing behavioral clues. These clues include use of time, manner of speech, typical reaction to others, and approach to job performance.
4. People respond favorably to a style that is similar or complementary to their own primary and backup styles. When a salesperson's style is too different from that of the prospect, the resulting style conflict can be disastrous to the outcome of the transaction. What is said is often much less important than how it is said.[7]

In selling, most of us tend to use one or two predominant styles, and your choice of style affects what you do and say. It also affects what prospects hear and believe during your presentation. Understanding the strengths and liabilities of your primary communicating style and learning to be versatile in your style can help you sell to more prospects more often.[8] The objective of this chapter then is to help you learn how to manage your daily interactions with customers and prospects more productively.

Exhibit 5.1 illustrates that your most damaging weaknesses (-) are merely exaggerations or over-extensions of your strengths (+). Your behavior responds to circumstances like the volume dial of a radio. When the volume is just right, the music is pleasing.

EXHIBIT 5.1 SOCIAL STYLE STRENGTHS AND WEAKNESSES

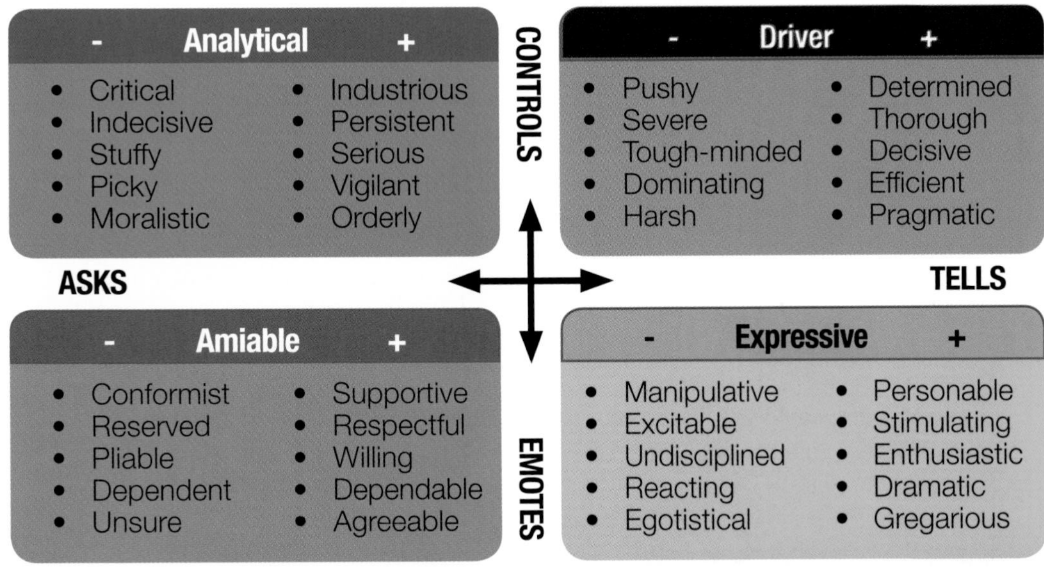

Similarly, when a behavioral style is used in moderation it is a *strength*; when overused (that is, when the volume is too high), it becomes a *weakness* and leads to ineffective communication. Professional selling is all about managing relationships. Most people don't even think about working on relationships in their daily lives. On the other hand, relationship salespeople take time to think about and understand the people around them. The relationship selling approach will strengthen and enhance your selling style by turning you into a relationship-oriented helper. The relationship style of selling is the 21st-century approach to helping clients and prospects buy.

Remember that a customer is not a transaction—a customer is a relationship!

When you go for your next job interview, you will likely be asked to take a personality test. The use of personality inventories in personnel selection has grown in popularity over the past decade. A recent study that summarized the results of fifteen prior studies that investigated the relationship between personality traits and job performance has found convincing evidence of the effectiveness of the use of personality inventories in applicant selection.[9] Although your personality style is not a true predictor of overall work performance, it can predict success in specific occupations or relate to specific criteria.

The emphasis in studying behavioral style characteristics is on surface behavior, not on an in-depth personality analysis. Human behavior is predictable because ninety percent of our actions are controlled by habits and attitudes.[10] The social styles model does not describe a person's complete personality because it omits reference to the individual's beliefs, ethics, abilities, and intelligence. What it does is describe the basic attributes or characteristics of behavior: *assertiveness* and *responsiveness.*

ATTRIBUTES OF BEHAVIOR

When you meet someone for the first time, your mind subconsciously reacts to two main characteristics: assertiveness and responsiveness. *Assertiveness* represents the effort a person makes to influence or control the thoughts and actions of others. *Responsiveness* is the willingness with which a person outwardly shares feelings or emotions and develops relationships.[11]

Assertiveness and responsiveness levels vary from one individual to another, and anyone may be high or low in either dimension or in both dimensions or anywhere in between. Several basic terms provide a thumbnail sketch of the characteristics of each dimension:

LOW IN RESPONSIVENESS

- Formal and proper
- Fact-orientated
- Guarded, cool, and aloof
- Disciplined about time
- Seldom makes gestures
- Controlled body language

HIGH IN RESPONSIVENESS

- Relaxed and warm
- Open and approachable
- Dramatic and animated
- Flexible about time
- Orientated toward relationships and feelings

LOW IN ASSERTIVENESS

- Introverted
- Supportive, a team player
- Easygoing
- Avoids taking risks
- Good listener
- Reserved in their opinions

HIGH IN ASSERTIVENESS

- Risk-taker
- Swift in decision-making
- Willing to confront others
- Very competitive
- Take-charge attitude
- Expresses opinions

Recognizing Social Styles

Combining the assertiveness and responsiveness characteristics makes it possible to develop a map of what others are doing or saying. Exhibit 5.2 shows the relationships among the four social styles. The horizontal axis is the range from the least to most assertive. Assertive people take a stand and make their position clear to others. Because they are ambitious, competitive, and quick to take action and express strong opinions, they are located on the telling end of the social style axis. Nonassertive individuals are seen as cooperative, silent, and slow to act, and they are located at the asking end of the axis. The least assertive individuals are in quartile D, and the most assertive in quartile A, with quartiles B and C representing intermediate levels of assertiveness.

EXHIBIT 5.2 THE SOCIAL STYLES PROFILE

NONRESPONSIVE (CONTROLLED)

Wants facts and figures; precise about time; task-orientated; objective and reserved

NONASSERTIVE (ASKING)

Inquisitive; slow-acting; low risk taker; non-verbal; cooperative

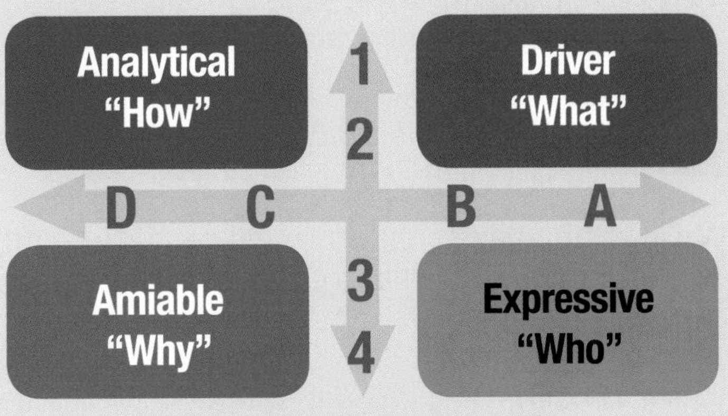

ASSERTIVE (TELLING)

Fast; active; high risk taker; verbal; directive; competitive

RESPONSIVE (EMOTIONAL)

Expressive about feelings; wants feelings and emotions; imprecise about time; people-orientated; subjective

The vertical axis indicates the range from least to most responsive. Non-responsive individuals, those in quartile 1, are largely indifferent to the feelings of others, reserved, and no-nonsense in attitude. The responsive individuals found in quartile 4 are strongly people-oriented, concerned about relationships, and subjective. Those in quartiles 2 and 3 display intermediate levels of responsiveness.

Identifying the Four Behavioral Styles

Identifying the levels of assertiveness and responsiveness a person demonstrates is not a precise method of complete personality evaluation. With study and practice, however, Dr. Mok suggests that you can become 70 to 80 percent effective in using your observations to predict habitual behavioral patterns and be prepared to use your knowledge to improve the communication environment. Each possible combination of the two traits suggests one of the basic social styles. The four styles are linked to distinctive and unique habits of interactive behavior. The name given to each style reflects general characteristics rather than full, specific details. Keep in mind that no one style is preferred over another. Each has its own strengths and weaknesses, and successful people as well as failures are found in each style group, as are people of both sexes and all ethnic groups, ages, and other segments of the population.[12]

Drivers tell and control, are high in assertiveness, and low in responsiveness. They control others by telling them what to do and control themselves by remaining objective. They are task-oriented and combine personal power and emotional control in relationships with others. They are *control specialists.*

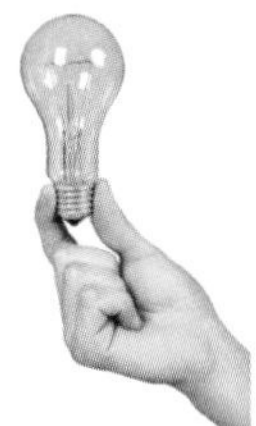

Expressives tell and emote. Like drivers, they are highly assertive, but they are also high in emotional responsiveness. They attempt to tell people what to do, but place more emphasis on their relationships with people than they do on the task itself. They are *social specialists.*

Amiables ask and emote, are low in assertiveness, and high in responsiveness. They rely on a personal feeling approach to get things done. They are *support specialists*, combining personal reserve and emotional expression.

Analyticals ask and control, and they are low in assertiveness and responsiveness. They are highly task-oriented but soften that style with low assertiveness. They ask rather than direct. They are *technical specialists*, combining personal reserve and emotional control.

EARNING YOUR Ph.B. - BECOMING A PROFESSOR OF HUMAN BEHAVIOR

We are all in the people business, no matter the industry. As a salesperson, you observe and verify behavior and have a constant need to become an expert at interpreting what you see. In any personal relationship, everybody has his or her own particular point of view. When you understand behavioral styles and what motivates each of the styles, you can adapt your own style to meet the needs of others. Just exercise a bit of applied psychology. All of us have a way we like to be treated.

To earn your Ph.B., you must start using Psychological Reciprocity in your communication with prospects and clients. ***You make the initial attempt to adapt to the prospect's social style. The prospect is then motivated to move toward you—to reciprocate.*** Real communication and understanding occur much quicker than if each person stays firmly rooted in his or her own particular style.

Becoming more knowledgeable in behavioral styles helps you present your product or service in the most meaningful way. Most experts believe that styles are fixed early in life—it's what you do with your style that makes a difference. Using ***style flexing*** is a great way to complement the other person's style and create a mutually beneficial environment.

VERSATILITY AS A COMMUNICATION TOOL

When people of different styles meet and behave strictly according to the characteristics of their own personal styles, conflict often results. A salesperson who is an amiable and a prospect who is a driver can quickly arrive at cross-purposes. A driver client wants to get facts and to accomplish the task at hand; the amiable salesperson wants to cultivate a personal relationship.

When such a situation occurs, the only way to avoid an escalation in miscommunication or a conflict is for one of the two people involved to engage in some style flexibility. In an ideal situation, both are willing to move part way, but the salesperson must be capable of making most of any necessary temporary adjustments.

The willingness to try behaviors not necessarily characteristic of your style is called *behavioral flexibility* or *versatility*.[13]

Versatility is a person's willingness to control personal behavior patterns and adapt to other people as a means of reducing the possibility of ineffective communication. The salesperson's own personal style does not change, but rather techniques are applied that work in that particular situation.[14] For example, when meeting with an analytical, the expressive salesperson can incorporate versatility by talking less, listening more, and focusing on facts. Versatility should never be equated with either insincerity or mere imitation of the prospect's style. Versatile salespeople seek a reasonable compromise. They do not become so highly changeable that their pace and priority needs are constantly set aside for those of clients.

The more versatility you have, the better your chances are for success. If you understand that each individual has a unique behavioral style you will be better able to adapt your approach to match. This means that you will need to learn how to 'read' the behavior patterns of each prospect. By doing so, you will be able to respond to your prospect's style in a way that makes it easy for you to communicate, exchange information, and close a sale.[15]

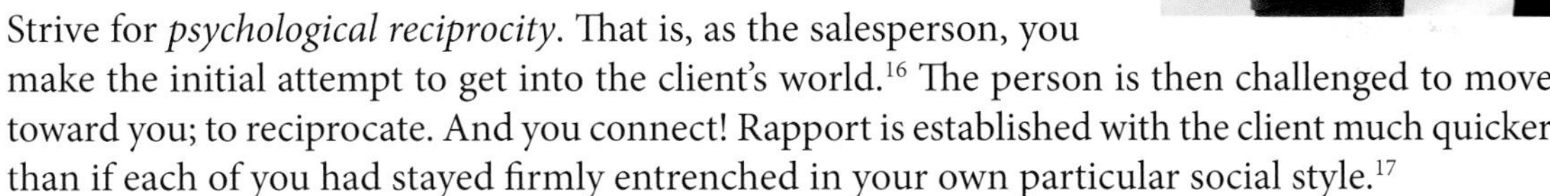

Strive for *psychological reciprocity*. That is, as the salesperson, you make the initial attempt to get into the client's world.[16] The person is then challenged to move toward you; to reciprocate. And you connect! Rapport is established with the client much quicker than if each of you had stayed firmly entrenched in your own particular social style.[17]

Be aware of the multitude of areas in a sales situation that make versatility one of the greatest tools you have to get a yes from your prospects. The following aspects of a face-to-face interview often require the need for you to stay versatile, responsive, and ultimately, willing to adapt and change to fit each situation:[18]

Comfort. Does the prospect seem nervous or edgy?

Tension. Is there an air of tension or general discomfort?

Prospect assertiveness in asking questions. Does the prospect provide you with more sales ammo by asking questions that may reveal a way to sell them?

Prospect responsiveness to your presentation. Is the prospect with you, or do they seem to be preoccupied?

Level of openness. Is the prospect sharing pertinent information that will help you better discover how to serve his needs?

The Interaction of Styles

The dimensions of assertiveness and responsiveness operate in people's pace and their priorities. *Pace* is the speed at which a person prefers to move. Those who are low in assertiveness (analyticals and amiables) prefer a slow pace; those high in assertiveness (drivers and expressives) prefer a fast pace in conversation, deliberation, and problem solving.[19]

Priorities concern what a person considers important and tend to be related to the dimension of responsiveness. Those who are low in responsiveness put tasks at the top of their priority list, and those who are high in responsiveness put relationships in first place. Conflicts that involve only priorities or only pace can be handled with relative ease; real trouble results when the styles of two people conflict in both pace and priorities.

Fortunately, few people are locked into a single style. Between the extremes of each dimension are many degrees of responsiveness and assertiveness. The descriptions of the four styles, then, do not represent absolutes. If you deal with every customer in the same way, you will close a small percentage of all your contacts, because you will only close one personality style. But if you learn how to effectively work with all four of the personality styles, you can significantly increase your closing ratio.[20]

Salespeople who do not adjust their behavior to meet the needs of clients face deteriorating situations. For example, an expressive salesperson's questions may be interpreted as a personal challenge or attack by an analytical prospect. If the analytical prospect responds to the questions merely to save face, the expressive salesperson then tends to talk more, move faster, and push the analytical into still greater conflict.

> "Personality is to a man what perfume is to a flower."
> **Charles M. Schwab**

In any situation, conflict is finally relieved in a manner typical of the individual style. The expressive usually attacks verbally. The driver tends to become overbearing, pushy, and dictatorial. The amiable generally submits in order to avoid conflict at all costs but experiences resentment and distrust. The analytical withdraws—flight rather than fight. In a conflict situation, most people tend to move to the extreme dimensions of their favorite style.

To avoid distrust and ultimately a breakdown in communication, you must meet the needs of your prospects, especially their behavioral style needs. Treat them as they want to be treated, and move according to the pace and priority they desire. The most successful salespeople are be able to help customers verbalize problems, and to create a solution that customers would not have developed alone by letting them set the pace.[21]

Identifying Pace and Priority

How do you go about determining someone's pace and priorities? Ask yourself these three questions and observe the answers:

1. How fast does the person make decisions and get things done?
2. How competitive is the person? Not primarily in sports, but:
    - Is the person competitive in a conversation?
    - Does the person fight for air time in a meeting?
3. How much feeling is displayed in a verbal and nonverbal communication?
    - How often does the person smile?
    - Do they gesture broadly?

Your goal is to identify pace and priorities accurately and respond in an appropriate manner. How can you find out your prospect's information preferences? Use one of these statements to assist you:[22]

1. "Ordinarily I have an organized presentation and get right to it, but today maybe I should get to know you better. What would you like me to do?"
2. "I am prepared to get right into my presentation or if you prefer we can chat a bit so that I can learn about you and your organization. Which do you prefer?"
3. "There are a lot of ways I can start explaining exactly how this process would work based on the concerns you were kind enough to share with me at our meeting last week. Would you prefer I start with the end in mind and then work backwards, or would you like to hear the step-by-step details first?"

The expressive and amiable styles would respond to these statements indicating a desire to chat and get to know one another. The driver and analytical styles would want you to begin your presentation.

GENDER STYLE DIFFERENCES

While it is essential to recognize and adjust to different social styles, it is also necessary to recognize the contribution that gender makes to our communication in the business world. The issue of *proxemics*, the distance that individuals prefer to keep between themselves and others, also becomes more recognizable when speaking to someone of the opposite sex.[23] That is why we must be sensitive to gender issues and adjust to them just as we do for social style differences. If not handled correctly, these seemingly insignificant differences can break down communication lines and damage relationships, and this ultimately hurts your company and your income!

There is no proven significant differences between men and women in how smart they work, in how hard they work or in how well they perform.[24] Although there have been numerous studies conducted over the past several years regarding sex-related differences, the results are often contradictory. The plethora of research does, however, provide some new perspectives to consider concerning the growing role of women in corporate America. In various studies, women demonstrated higher levels of contingent reward, or behaviors in which a leader rewards followers for the completion of tasks. Contingent reward behavior has been identified as a predictor of effectiveness, which would suggest that women possess a leadership advantage in some cases.[25]

Relating to the Opposite Sex

Whether or not you have experienced how gender differences hinder relationships in selling when handled improperly, it is clear that the unequal treatment of employees by management hinders the success of any business. A research study by *Russ & McNeilly* concluded that managers who treat male and female sales reps the same miss the potential benefits that different gender styles provide.[26]

A key question to ask is whether or not gender differences, in and of themselves, create diverse ways of thinking or different behavioral relationships. If so, what are some things to be aware of when you're selling to someone of the opposite sex? Research by *Siguaw & Honeycutt* found that women were engaged more frequently in customer-oriented selling than were their male counterparts.[27]

Despite significant advances in gender relations, inequalities still exist in the business world that sometimes make it difficult for men and women to fully relate to each other. In a recent study on gender inequalities conducted through a survey of successful women professionals, the researchers examined two possible ideologies that could explain gender inequalities:[28]

1. The first asserts that the inequalities are a result of differences in training, experience, and personal motivation, and suggests that women who fall behind have only themselves to blame.
2. The second ideology states that the inequalities are a result of various structural factors such as discrimination, stereotyping, and exclusion from social groups and networks.

Which ideology is more accurate—or a combination of both—remains to be seen. Either way, we must work to overcome ingrained stereotypical ideas of gender roles and recognize the importance of both sexes at the negotiation table.

When men and women find themselves sitting across from one another at the bargaining table, they must learn to adjust their styles. During the sales interview they should use the strengths unique to their gender.

Just because something is written about the differences between men and women, it does not mean that it has value in every selling encounter between men and women. For example, when a woman nods her head, that doesn't necessarily mean she agrees with what a man is saying. When a woman crosses her arms, she is not automatically indicating she is closed to the idea being presented. She just may be tired or cold. Likewise, if a man doesn't look you in the eye when he is speaking, that does not necessarily mean he's hiding something—it may be his style. Acting on generalities, regardless of gender, can kill a sale more quickly than anything else.[29]

While there are some fundamental differences in how men and women interact, there are no absolute truths and, in sales, we must be careful about making assumptions based on gender alone. So rather than focus on your prospect's gender, you should cater to your prospect's character and personality first and foremost.

Exhibit 5.3 provides some suggestions for dealing with gender differences. You must be prepared to communicate effectively with your male and female sales managers, fellow sales reps, as well as the men and women decision-makers you call on. No one can make a sweeping statement about how all women or all men like to sell or be sold. In any selling situation it's vital to communicate in a way that substantiates what's meaningful to that individual, and gender may help determine what a client feels is important. Subtle, gender-based changes may give you the edge you're looking for to boost sales.[30]

EXHIBIT 5.3 GENDER FLEXING TO MAKE THE MOST OUT OF MEETINGS

FOR FEMALE SALESPEOPLE SPEAKING WITH MALE PROSPECTS:

- Speak confidently and clearly. It has been established that men will interrupt women, especially if they sound tentative or unsure.
- Feed them data. Men love facts. Let them know you have done your homework. Remain enthusiastic; just rein it in a bit.
- Practice your humor. Women tend to use humor less than men. Being funny at the right moment is very important.
- Watch your language. Consider steering clear of overtly feminine vocabulary when presenting to men. Words like "lovely," "charming," or "adorable" might not resonate with a male audience. At the same time, don't try to sound like a man by speaking more abruptly than you normally do or using foul language.

FOR MALE SALESPEOPLE SPEAKING WITH FEMALE PROSPECTS:

- Report talk vs. rapport talk. Male bonding through storytelling and anecdotes is fine; in general, when talking to women, make sure you ask about their work, their families, and their passions so that you can connect over a shared topic of interest.
- Stop interrupting. Men interrupt women more often than other men. This is a good way to lose a sale. Learn to listen.
- Feel the sale. There is more to selling than numbers. Women are often more interested in emotional satisfaction, so in the same way that you do with all personality types, make sure you mix in the right amount of facts with emotion to find the perfect combination.
- Control your language. Regardless of where you live, never use the words "honey," "dear," or "sweetie." Even though these words are fairly common in some areas, such language might be offensive to some people.

Culture Style Differences

To succeed in the global market, sales managers and teams need to understand how cultural differences affect behavior and business. According to author Sinan Caykoylu, sales managers and sales teams cannot adopt a "one size fits all" approach to their leadership style. They need to be able to diversify their approach in a way that allows them to understand how different cultures and genders react to certain behaviors.[31] For example; in many Arab countries it is critical to follow the customs of the area to avoid offending those with whom you are dealing. A salesperson should not inquire about a man's wife or any other female relationships. It is important to learn the customs and personal cultural background of your prospect before your presentation or even your first introduction. Without this knowledge, your words, actions, and body language may inadvertently offend your prospect, costing you the sale.

READING THE PROSPECT'S ENVIRONMENT

Important clues to a client's style are in the environment as well as in verbal and nonverbal actions. Observe how the office is decorated and arranged, how objects are displayed, and what seating arrangements are available. Suppose that upon entering a prospect's office, you notice family pictures on the desk, nature posters, a round desk, and a separate seating area with four comfortable chairs. What would be your first impression of that client's behavioral style? Did you say *amiable*? If so, you are right. Next, you can confirm or adjust your initial impression by observing the prospect's actions and speech. If the prospect rises to greet you personally and sits in an easy chair your impression of amiable would tend to be confirmed.

Let's try another example. You enter the prospect's office and notice a diploma, an achievement plaque, and a poster on the wall that says "Why not?" The desk presents several jumbled stacks of paper and a generally chaotic appearance. Two overstuffed chairs by the open side of the desk provide seating. A bookcase with stacks of books and folders intermixed and a plant on the file cabinet, complete the furnishings. The disorganization, the wall decorations emphasizing achievement, and the comfortable and accessible seating suggest that this office houses an *expressive*.[32]

Verbal, Nonverbal, and Behavioral Characteristics

You can use knowledge of the four social styles to read prospects' environments for clues as to their style, and you can also characterize them by their observable behavior (i.e. what they say, what their body language says, and how they act). Although we all possess traits from each of the styles, one style ordinarily dominates. Of course, identifying a social style does not provide a crystal ball that unerringly predicts a person's future actions and decisions, but it does provide a basis for forming reasonably accurate expectations about recurring behavior and for being prepared to respond appropriately. Both verbal and nonverbal clues are useful in identifying social style.[33]

THE SOCIAL MEDIA CONNECTION

Can Your Prospects' Social Media Pages Reveal Their Social Style?

Social media has changed the way businesses operate. It can also change the way you prepare for your next meeting with a prospect. You may be able to use your prospects' social media pages to determine their social styles before you even meet them. Here are some interesting findings from a recent study conducted by CPP, the official publisher of the Myers-Briggs Type Indicator:[34]

In general, individuals with a preference for feeling (amiables) reported spending more time engaging in certain activities on Facebook in their personal time than did individuals with a preference for thinking (analyticals).

When it comes to LinkedIn usage, those with a preference for intuition (expressives) and thinking (analyticals) reported using LinkedIn more often than individuals with a preference for sensing (drivers) and feeling (amiables).

The study also showed that 29 percent of amiables and expressives reported interacting at least once a week on social media, and 17 percent of them reported that they shared information about their professional life online at least once per week. This is in contrast to drivers and analyticals, only 16 percent of who reported interacting at least once per week on social media—and only 8 percent of them reported sharing information about their professional life at least once a week online.

As for Twitter, more individuals with a preference for intuition (expressives) reported being active users of Twitter than individuals with a preference for sensing (drivers).

What does this all mean? Well, it could indicate that, although not the case in every situation, a person's proclivity toward posting, liking, tweeting, commenting, and recommending may tell you what personality type he or she favors. What does your social media presence say about you and your personality?

ALL ABOUT DRIVERS

Drivers exhibit minimum concern for the feelings of others. A vice-president of marketing for a major theme park in Ohio was heard to say, "My secretary used to drive me to distraction. I'd ask her how her weekend went and she'd actually tell me. In detail! All I wanted to hear was fine or not so hot." Now those are the words of a true driver. If you say something harsh, they don't even seem to notice. They consider yes-people to be weak. Stand up to drivers. Sell to them by showing them what your product can do. Drivers' feelings are not easily hurt because they do not take things personally.

Drivers tend to be intense, competitive, fast-paced, and goal-oriented. They pride themselves on the ability to get things done. They like to make things happen. They are willing to accept risks and want to know the estimated outcome of each option. Convince them that your proposed action works and that it will provide all the benefits you promise. They are more impressed by what they see and hear than by what others say about you or your offering.

Drivers are action driven, resourceful, organized, and pragmatic. They also tend to impose high standards on themselves and others. As a result, they may be seen as impatient or tireless. They push to perfect their own skills but also invest time and effort in coaching other people in skill development. At their worst, they appear to give inadequate consideration to the long-range consequences of their actions. They draw criticism for seeking to impose on others their expectations for drive, speed and zeal. Under stress, drivers can seem anti-intellectual and may defensively overreact to any opinions differing from their own, especially to those that seem to resist action. Drivers are likely to feel that any failure is evidence that others were not loyal enough or willing to work hard enough to make the project a success.

Presentation Strategies for Drivers

Drivers do not care as much about developing a personal relationship with salespeople. Therefore:

1. Spend less time attempting to relate to them on a personal level.
2. Move fast and isolate the most dollar-related product benefits that can be verified by producing concrete evidence.
3. Do not make a lengthy presentation citing all the benefits. Be brief and stress the bottom line.
4. Any visuals you choose to show must be absolutely relevant to the major points.
5. Ask questions to involve them, get them to talk, and allow them to lead.
6. They will test you to see what you are made of; so be willing to joust with them. If you challenge them, challenge the concepts rather than the person.
7. Answer objections immediately, and never try to bluff.
8. Present several alternatives from which they may select their own solution.
9. A close that highlights an immediate opportunity works well.

ALL ABOUT EXPRESSIVES

Expressives temper assertiveness with concern for the feelings of others. They are motivated by recognition, approval, and success. You must compliment them. They desire success, but are recognition motivated. Show them how to win. Let them talk and they often sell themselves. Tell them who else uses your product. Testimonials from well-known people or people they respect are important.

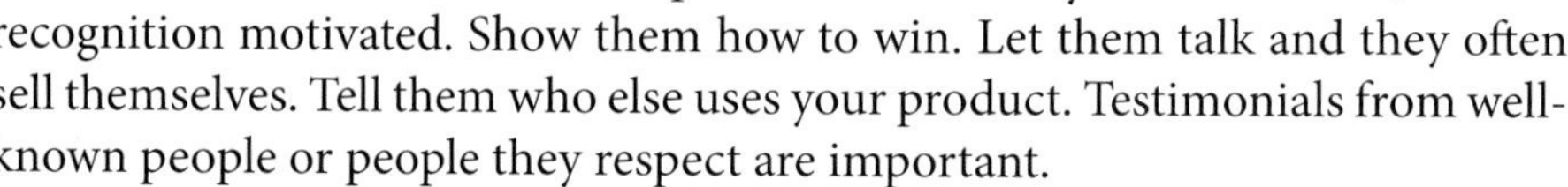

Expressives pride themselves on originality, foresight, and the ability to see the big picture. Reinforce their self-image as visionaries and idea people, and they will be receptive to your ideas. At their best, expressives often see new possibilities and present fresh ideas and approaches to problems. At their worst, they seem to base decisions on opinions, hunches, or intuition rather than on facts. They want to delegate the details to someone who has time for it while they are free to dream. They may be impatient when others demand some documentation before accepting the vision or ideas they offer. Under stress, expressives run the risk of seeming detached. They appear indifferent to problems and seem to be living in an ivory tower. They may spend time defending their ideas instead of trying to make them work in practical manner.

Expressives thrive on spontaneity. The expressive's love of risk-taking makes it easier for them to take a chance on your product. Refer to the product as a "sure bet" or guarantee that you will "make this risk pay off big." To reach them, you must emphasize the importance of risk-taking to making progress and meeting goals, and show the expressive your product's payoff potential by sharing exactly what it can do and what that means to them. When you have a qualified expressive whose needs match your product's benefits, you should not have to do much persuading. Remember, expressives are intuition-driven.[35]

Presentation Strategies For Expressives

Expressives are visionaries and dreamers. Therefore:

1. Show them how they can personally win and how their company benefits.
2. Open with innovative ideas for them to grow through your offering.
3. Ask open-end questions that allow them to talk at length about "their" plans for growth. Then relate your product's benefits to their plans.
4. Present proposals and seek feedback, using them as sounding boards. Convey respect for their intelligence, foresight, and prominence. Be careful, however, to avoid patronizing them.
5. Use some showmanship. They like to see the product binder, but are not necessarily interested in the details of what it contains.
6. Never argue or back them into a corner.
7. Ask if they want you to respond to their stated concerns. Often they respond, "No, I just wanted you to know how I am thinking."
8. Use testimonials, especially from well-known people because they identify with who else uses the product.
9. Allow them to carry out their own game plan, not yours.

ALL ABOUT AMIABLES

Amiables are submissive, people-oriented, and willing to go along with the crowd. They need time to get to know you personally, so allow plenty of warm up time. They are undisciplined in the use of time. Agreeable in nature, they are also easily hurt. They want to be liked.

Amiables tend to be perceptive and observant individuals who are concerned with whether they like you, trust you, and can picture a positive long-term relationship with you. They are highly people-oriented in their management style and resent doing business with anyone who makes them uncomfortable or is unresponsive to their feelings. Their business decisions are markedly influenced by how their various options might impact the people in the organization. Before they accept your proposal or idea, they must be convinced that you personally believe in it. They must also know what risks are involved—especially risks to personal relationships.

Amiables at their best are truly perceptive and aware, skilled in communication, and empathetic listeners. Their insight enables them to assess organizational politics accurately. At their worst, they seem more concerned with the process of interaction than with the content of the matter at hand. They appear to be flying by the seat of their pants instead of relying in any measure on logic and thought. They seem to regard their own emotions as facts and act on the basis of their feelings. They may be criticized for being defensive, over-reactive, and too subjective.

Belonging to a group is important to amiables. To sell effectively to them, you have to show them that you are a team player. Position yourself as their newest team member by first building rapport, then work side-by-side with them to accomplish the goals they've set. To minimize the amiable's insecurities, talk about the problems your product can solve and how solving them will help improve control and performance in the workplace, which will enhance management's image of them. It is the amiable's job to nurture the team, so don't forget to outline what your product will do for the people in the company.

Presentation Strategies For Amiables

Amiables must be convinced that you are authentic and have their best interests at heart. They have a difficult time saying yes. Therefore:

1. Plan to approach with as much personal information as possible.
2. Avoid a rigid or canned approach and presentation.
3. Make an informal presentation with visuals and testimonial information integrated.
4. Show that you understand and accept their feelings.
5. Spend some time relating. Move to a first-name basis quickly.
6. Be open and candid. Develop a personal relationship with them.
7. Offer them money-back guarantees and personal assurances.
8. Avoid asking directly for their business. Instead, suggest an easy next step.
9. Be prepared to use third-party references and case histories that link them to others.

ALL ABOUT ANALYTICALS

Analyticals are thinkers. They need time to assess and assimilate what they hear and see. They want to know just how things work and often say they want time to think things over. Product information is crucial. Know everything possible about your product, and don't expect to hear them say much.

Analyticals tend to be highly logical, organized, and unsentimental. They tend to be fact-oriented and value accuracy. Their contribution to the management team is their ability to solve difficult problems and make sound, rational business decisions based on evidence and intelligent inferences rather than on imagination or gut feelings. They take a logical approach to responsibilities. The more supporting data you can provide for your ideas, the more likely you are to sell to them. They have little interest in your opinions and more in your ability to assemble and organize supportive data for use in weighing options and arriving at a systematic, well-thought-out solution to problems.

At their best, analyticals appear to be a consistent force for progress. They are top-flight planners and doers. They can cut through untested ideas and emotional fervor to find the core truth. They are effective organizers for research and planning. They are valuable in executing logical, painstaking, and profitable projects. At their worst, they are overly cautious and conservative.

They emphasize deliberation over action. They may become so involved in evaluating all the various details of a situation that others may regard them as indecisive stumbling blocks to innovative action. Under stress, analyticals can become rigid and insecure. They may fear taking risks. They seem more concerned with being right than with seizing opportunities.

Presentation Strategies for Analyticals

Analyticals are data-oriented and slow to make decisions. They read and study everything. Therefore:

1. Know their business thoroughly. Go in with facts and the evidence to back them up.
2. Use a logic-based, low-key style of relating.
3. Be sure prospects understand the structure of how you will present the information and solicit feedback.
4. Emphasize tested, proven, well-documented aspects of your product's benefits.
5. Make use of visual aids—charts, graphs, written "leave-behind" documents— in the presentation.
6. Present information in a controlled, professional, highly organized fashion.
7. Point out the pros and cons of your offering. They will be thinking about them.
8. Present a detailed summary of major points and use the summary as a close.
9. Avoid saying, "Well, in my opinion. . ." They don't care about your opinions, just facts that you can document.

NEUROLINGUISTIC PROGRAMMING

An entirely different approach to communicating effectively and understanding more about prospects is offered by neurolinguistic programming (NLP). It looks at how people create the results they want. In your career, this understanding can be the difference between success and a lost sale.[36] ***The primary focus of NLP is to pinpoint styles by eye-movement exercises designed to ascertain whether one is visual, auditory, or kinesthetic.***[37] When it first began to attract attention, many people considered NLP to be just another pop-psychology craze similar to the various communication approaches that have been offered as the ultimate answer for managers who wanted increased personal power and influence, for lawyers who wanted to sway judges and juries, and for salespeople who wanted to sell anything to anyone.

Instead, however, NLP offers one more way to observe people and understand their needs. It is entirely different from the behavioral styles theory, but in no way contradicts it. Neurolinguistic programming is the brainchild of linguist John Grinder and psychotherapist Richard Bandler.

Identifying Modes of Perception

NLP is based on recognizing and then appealing to the dominant modes of perception used by another person. We all use these modes to map reality and build a model of what the world is like that can guide us through our environment. NLP is the science of how the brain learns. All of us have a basic learning mode: *visual, auditory* or *kinesthetic*. Each is used in various situations, yet most of us will favor one mode.[38]

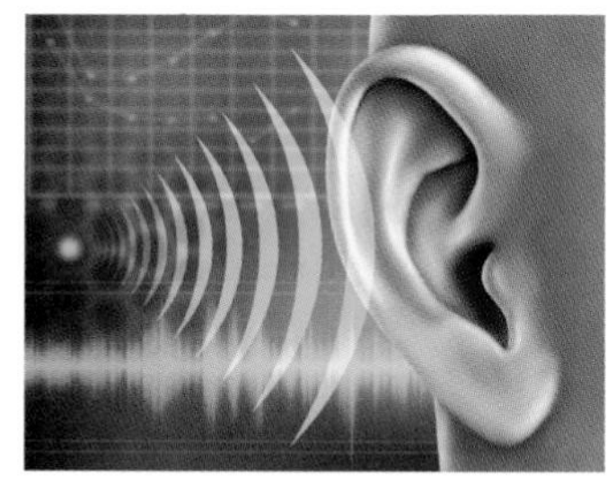

AUDITORY. Some people perceive the world largely by *hearing*. They learn more quickly by listening than by reading or seeing. Experiences presented through other senses are mentally translated into an auditory mode. These are the people who test ideas by how they sound. They often use responses like, "I hear what you're saying," "It sounds good to me," and "I'm hearing a lot of complaints about that situation." Ways to reach this style of learner are to use webcasts, podcasts, and discussion groups.

VISUAL. Other people perceive the world largely through *sight*. They learn and form opinions from what they see. They are the ones who originated the saying, "Seeing is believing." They form mental pictures of their experiences as a means of interpretation. They frequently use sentences like, "I see what you mean," "I'm in a fog about the whole concept," and "Do you get the picture?" This visual style responds best through videos, graphs, pictures, diagrams, and illustrations. Other ways to reach this style of learner is through the use of video webcasts or in-person demonstrations where they can see facial expressions and body language.

KINESTHETIC. A smaller number of people perceive the world through the sense of *touch*. They feel life. Everything has a texture that either attracts or repels them. Subsets of the kinesthetic mode are the gustatory (taste) and the olfactory (smell) modes that sometimes come into play for kinesthetic people. Those operating in the kinesthetic mode say things like, "This deal just feels right (or wrong)," "That was a smooth presentation," "That transaction left a bad taste in my mouth," and "I smell something rotten about this deal." Tactile or kinesthetic learners respond best when they can interact with the information being presented. Some ways to do this is to have interactive surveys, demonstrations, websites, or games.

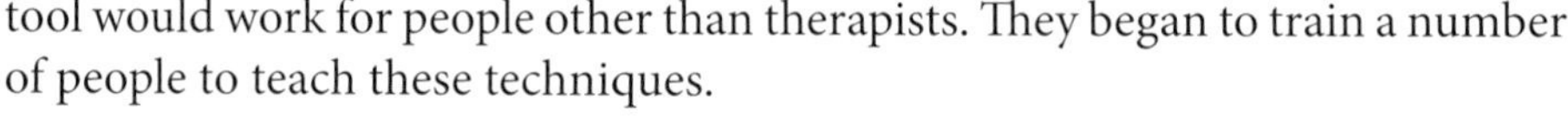

Bandler and Grinder first used this information to teach therapists how to recognize these representational modes and use them to build rapport with their patients, to establish a climate of trust, and to improve communication. They soon realized that this powerful communication tool would work for people other than therapists. They began to train a number of people to teach these techniques.

NLP has been used by people who have turned it into a powerful manipulative tool for their own benefit to the detriment of others. When used ethically, however, it is a helpful method for cutting down the time needed to build trust and rapport—a necessary process in relationship selling.[39] Its misuse does not discount its effectiveness; many kinds of knowledge can be twisted into tools for satisfying personal greed by those whose value systems allow such unethical action. If you look at NLP as an additional tool for interpreting the behavior, needs, and motivation of people, you can use it just as ethically and helpfully as you can use the information about behavioral styles and body language.

Some salespeople seem to have a natural or intuitive ability to identify a prospect's behavior and personality traits and to adapt to them. They seem to possess an automatic radar system that instantly and unobtrusively sends out test signals, interprets the feedback, and then chooses the best tactics for establishing rapport. Developing such skills is one of the most difficult parts of sales training. NLP is one technique you can use to develop this ability.

Learning Eye Cues

Our eyes are seldom still. The direction they move during a conversation reveals the system of perception that is active at the moment. Exhibit 5.4 illustrates the various eye cues that help to identify the operative system. Eye movements in most people are similar and can usually be expected to show the processes shown in the exhibit.[40] It's important to note that some left-handed people reverse the normal right and left eye cues; therefore, eye cues can be used only as clues to be confirmed by further observation.

EXHIBIT 5.4 EYE CUES INDICATING THOUGHT PROCESSES

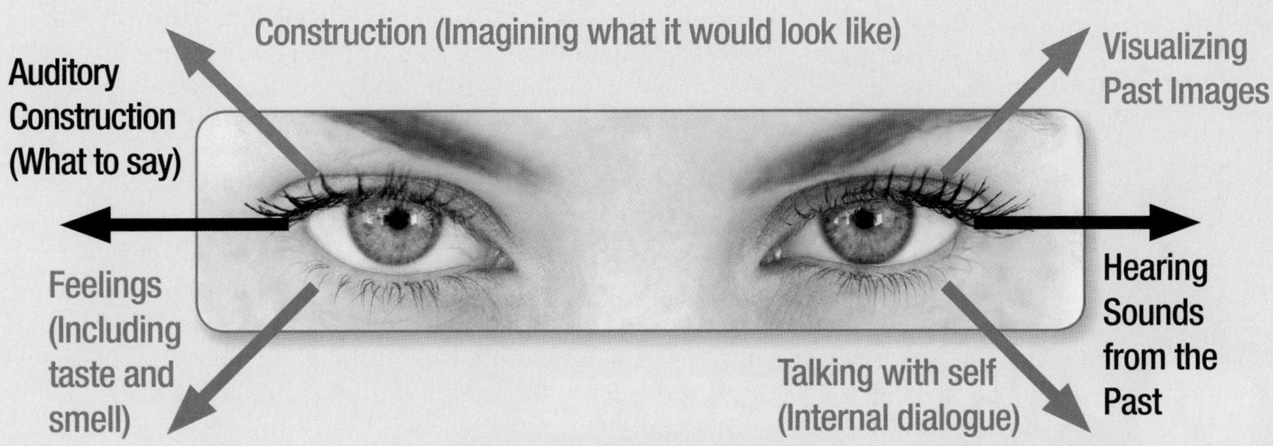

VISUAL PERCEPTION

Looking up and left—Visualizing (remembering) from the past; picturing the past mentally

Looking up and right—Visually constructing an image to see what it would look like

KINESTHETIC PERCEPTION

Looking down and right—Remembering past feelings

AUDITORY PERCEPTION

Looking sideways to left—Hearing sounds or voices from the past (remembering)

Looking sideways to right—Constructing a future conversation; thinking of the right words to use

Looking down to left—Holding an internal dialogue with oneself; how something sounds

Salespeople are only as good as their reflex actions allow them to be. Rather than a Ph.D., perhaps a salesperson should have a Ph.B.—and become a *Professor of Human Behavior*. There's an old saying—if you want to get better at something, learn more about it. Learn about social styles and NLP; study people and their wide variety of reactions, and soon enough, your understanding of social styles will become a powerful sales tool.

SUMMARY

- Knowledge of behavioral styles is a useful tool for gaining insight into the thinking of buyers. The model uses the assertiveness and responsiveness dimensions of behavior to assess an individual's social style.
- Versatility is your ability to adjust your own personal pace and priorities to facilitate interaction with a person of another style.
- Recognizing typical behavioral cues makes it possible to classify people quickly into one of four basic personality styles: Driver, expressive, amiable, or analytical.
- Gender differences require diverse ways of thinking and using our behavioral relationships. Adjust to different gender styles to enhance communication.
- A related tool for communication is neurolinguistic programming (NLP), which uses observation of eye cues and typical predicate words to discover the particular perceptual field a person is using at a given time.
- Never attempt to adopt a style that is an insincere imitation of the prospect. Take the lead in finding common ground with the prospect. Practice and use psychological reciprocity.
- A related tool for communication is neurolinguistic programming (NLP), which uses observation of eye cues and typical predicate words to discover the particular perceptual field a person is using at a given time.

REVIEW QUESTIONS

1. What is meant by assertiveness and responsiveness as dimensions of behavioral style?
2. Which style is characterized by each of these pairs of dimensions?
3. Low assertiveness and high responsiveness
4. Low assertiveness and low responsiveness
5. High assertiveness and high responsiveness
6. High assertiveness and low responsiveness
7. What is a backup style and what is its importance to the salesperson?
8. Explain this statement: The strengths of a particular behavioral style are the source of that style's typical weaknesses.
9. Point out some strengths of each of the four behavioral styles and show how they can be used as assets in selling. Identify some of the weaknesses of each and tell how they can damage sales effectiveness.
10. Are there any "absolute truths" in the ways that women and men will always behave in a business situation?
11. What social style is associated with excellent planning skills and a tendency to be risk-averse?
12. What social style is known to free delegate tasks and are recognition motivated?

IN-CLASS EXERCISES

The following exercises help build teams, improve communication, and emphasize the real-world side of fundraising. They are meant to be challenging, to help you learn how to deal with problems that have no single right answer, and to use a variety of skills beyond those employed in a typical review question. Read and complete each activity. Then in the next class, discuss and compare answers.

EXERCISE 5.1 – READING YOUR SALES STAFF

Because of this course and what you have learned from this book, many of you will eventually become sales managers or leaders in your organization. How well you succeed will largely depend on how well you are able to "read" other people, to determine their basic personality orientation and to respond appropriately. You might as well begin to practice that skill now when there is relatively little risk.

Using the chart in Exhibit 5.2, write down where your dominant social style falls on the chart. Briefly describe why you characterize yourself in the way that you do.

Next, pair up with another class member whom you do not know. It is essential for this exercise that you not know the other person in any significant way. As your instructor directs, in class or before, the two of you should chat for 10 minutes about any topic(s) whatever. At the conclusion of the chat, jot down where your conversation partner falls on the chart in terms of social style. Briefly add the most important reasons for your decision.

Do gender differences play any role in your analysis? Your partner should do the same for you.

Finally, based on what you've learned from Chapter 5, each of you should describe what you think the greatest challenge will be for the other person in relating to other people. Why? What suggestions would you offer to help your conversation partner in becoming more versatile in relating to others? Be insightful and constructive in your comments.

EXERCISE 5.2 – LEARNING STYLES VS. PRESENTATION STYLES

For this exercise, the class should be divided into teams of 4 people each. Each team should break out for a 20-minute discussion of the learning styles of each team member. Do some team members respond better to auditory means of communication rather than visual? Are there primarily visual learners represented on the team? What about kinesthetic aspects of communication and learning? During the discussion, team members should share anecdotes about the most memorable presentations they have witnessed, and why.

Following the initial discussion, the team should then spend 10 minutes critiquing modes of communication in this course. Do the class presentations in this course favor auditory learners, visual learners, kinesthetic learners? Based on the principles of neurolinguistic programming (NLP), briefly list constructive suggestions for improving communication and learning in this course. Finally, for the remainder of the class, the teams should come together to discuss their findings, especially their suggestions for improving communication in the course.

CASE STUDIES

The following case studies present you with fundraising scenarios that require you to apply the critical skills discussed in the chapter and give you training through practical learning situations. They are meant to be both engaging and challenging, and like the exercises, don't have one right answer.

CASE 5.1 – THE CLIENT WHO WOULDN'T SAY ANYTHING

Jimmie Caldwell was frustrated. He had just returned to his office after meeting with Marjorie Styles, owner of a local jewelry store. After visiting his company's website, Marjorie had phoned to request an appointment at her office to discuss creating a new website for her store. Jimmie was a web designer and one of the founding partners, along with Alice Stallings, of the firm that had now grown to bill over $750,000 per year. Clearly, they knew what they were doing.

As Jimmie barged into Alice's office, slamming the door behind him, Alice looked up. "I take it that the meeting didn't go well," she said calmly.

"Boy, that's an understatement!" Jimmie declared. "Marjorie Styles is really exasperating. I don't know whether we can work with her."

"Why? What happened?"

"Well, when I walked into her office, I noticed that she had pictures of her family—you know, husband, kids, the family dog—on her desk. So I remarked, as I usually do, on how nice her family looked and asked about where they like to go on vacation. Marjorie said, 'Oh, anywhere,' and sat down. I tried a little more informal chit-chat, but she sort of stared over my shoulder. The entire meeting went downhill from there."

"What do you mean?" Alice asked.

"What I mean is that the woman wouldn't say anything! At least not anything helpful. For instance, when I asked her why she wanted to change her website, she said, 'Because the one I have now stinks.' I followed up and asked if she could be more specific, and she said, 'No, this website just doesn't work for me anymore.' 'What, exactly, don't you like about it?' I asked. 'Everything,' came the response. What am I supposed to do with that?"

"Well," Alice prodded, "what did you do with that?"

"I couldn't think of anything else. So I launched into a description of what we could do. You know, that we could change the color palette, insert some video on the home page, make the navigation more intuitive, improve email management, yada, yada, yada. I then handed her a copy of our fee schedule."

"And her response to all that was what?"

"Virtually no response. All she said was that she would have to think it over and that she would get back to me. I asked if she minded if I followed up in a few days, and she said, 'No, that would be ok.' And that was it."

Based on what you have read in Chapter 5, where did Jimmie go wrong? Specifically, what cues did Jimmie pick up on with Marjorie, and why do you think he misread them? Based on the admittedly sketchy information in Jimmie's report to Alice, how would you characterize Marjorie's basic social style? What is Jimmie's style? Why might their respective differences in style have resulted in miscommunication?

What should Alice do in response to this situation? Should she try to help Jimmie understand why Marjorie might have responded to him as she did? Should she have Jimmie contact Marjorie to meet with her again in a few days in order to try a different approach? If so, what should that approach be, and why? Or should Alice contact Marjorie herself, taking Jimmie out of the loop, and try to repair the situation. How might Alice's approach differ from Jimmie's. What could Alice do to obtain Marjorie's business?

CASE 5.2 – ANOTHER BORING MEETING

Human beings have probably been complaining about boring meetings ever since sitting around the fire in front of their cave. Today's sales meetings are no exception. Derek Johnson's last sales meeting turned out to be a model for inducing lassitude among his sales force. The meeting lasted for 90 minutes, and despite the assistance of a steaming vat of coffee, a couple of people in the front row were actually dozing by the time the meeting ended. On the way down the hall back to his office, Derek overheard comments such as, "Boy, that sure was a waste of time!" and "I hate meetings when we're told to be enthusiastic while the meeting itself is dead." Rather than endure more disrespect, Derek was tempted to cancel sales meetings altogether and just let everybody sink or swim on their own.

Nevertheless, as a mere sales manager, Derek knew that his vice president would never tolerate his running a sales team without meetings. Besides, the office supply company for which Derek worked was taking delivery on Blackberry's PlayBook, Research in Motion's answer to Apple's iPad. Since Derek's company didn't carry the iPad because of licensing restrictions, he knew that PlayBook sales would be crucial to this year's success. To make sure that his team understood the PlayBook's features and would promote it vigorously, Derek concluded that he needed to have yet another sales meeting.

This time, however, he determined that things would be different. In the first place, he invited a regional representative from Research in Motion to help explain the PlayBook's features. In fact, the RIM rep promised to bring a 30-minute video that would thoroughly present the PlayBook in the most favorable light. Derek had previewed the video online and knew that the music and visuals were terrific. No one would be sleeping through that! He also had a stack of promotional literature to hand out to everyone. This meeting would indeed be different!

From what you have learned from Chapter 5, would you say that Derek is on the right track? What theoretical principles underlie Derek's new approach to the PlayBook sales meeting? If you were attending the meeting, what more should Derek do to keep you from falling asleep? What could Derek do to make the meeting even more effective in generating enthusiasm and improving learning?

Chapter 5 Footnotes

1. David Newton. "Sell to the Psyche" Kitchen & Bath Business. New York: (April 2004), Vol.51, Is. 4,
2. Carl G. Jung, *Psychological Types* (New York: Harcourt Brace and Co., 1924).
3. I am indebted to these individuals and their companies for sharing this valuable information with me. For more detail, see David W. Merrill and Roger H. Reid, *Personal Styles and Effective Performance*, (Radnor, PA: Chilton Book Company, 1981); Paul Mok, *Communicating Styles Technology* (Dallas, TX: Training Associates Press, 1982); Larry Wilson, *Social Styles Sales Strategies* (Eden Prairie, MN: Wilson Learning Corporation, 2000); Tony Alessandra, Phil Wexler, and Rick Barrera, *Non- Manipulative Selling* (Englewood Cliffs, NJ: Prentice-Hall, 1987).
4. John R. Graham, "Four Basic Categories of Prospects," *Personal Selling Power, Vol. 13, No. 8* (November/ December 1993), 56.
5. John L. Bledsoe, "How to Improve Your Relationships with Clients- and Your Staff, Too," *The Practical Accountant* (Institute for Continuing Professional Development, 1984).
6. Michael E Rega, Lisa M Clayton. "Recognizing behavioral buying patterns," *Agency Sales. Irvine*: (November 2003). Vol.33, Is. 11, 34.
7. Interpretation Manual for Communicating Styles Technology developed by Dr. Paul Mok, President of Training Associates Press of Richardson, Texas (Dallas: T A Press 1975), 5.
8. Robert F. Kantin and Mark W. Hardwick, *Quality Selling Through Quality Proposals* (Danvers, MA: Boyd and Fraser Publishing 1994), 28.
9. Chet Robie, "Effects of Perceived Selection Ratio on Personality Test Faking," *Social Behavior and Personality*, 2006.
10. Steven I. Miller, Jack Kavanagh, "Emperical Evidence," *4 J.L. & Educ.* (1975), 159.
11. Merrill and Reid, Personal Styles, 88-117.
12. Todd Duncan, "Your Sales Style," *Incentive* (December 1999), 64-66.
13. Hugh J. Ingrasci, "How to Reach Buyers in their Psychological 'Comfort Zones,'" *Industrial Marketing* (July 1981), 64; Merrill and Reid, Personal Styles, 88-117.
14. Seth Godin, "The Dating Game," *Sales & Marketing Management* (May 2001), 34.
15. Michael Leimbach, "Sales Versatility: Connecting with Customers Every Time," (Accessed April 22, 2011: www.salesopedia.com/relationships-relationships/2273-sales-versatility-connecting-with-customers-every-time).
16. David Newton. "Sell to the Psyche." *Kitchen & Bath Business*. New York: (April 2004), Vol.51, Is. 4, 41.
17. Tom Hoek, guest lecture at Belmont University, Nashville, TN, March 23, 2006. Mr. Hoek is president of Insurance Systems of Tennessee.
18. Wilson Learning Library, *Versatile Selling: Adapting Your Style so Customers Say Yes!* Nova Vista Publishing: Belgium, 2006.
19. Tony Alessandra, Phil Wexler, and Rick Barrera, *Non-Manipulative Selling* (New York: Prentice Hall, 1987), 112.
20. Rod Nichols, "How to Sell to Different Personality Types," *Personal Selling Power, Vol. 12, No. 8* (November/ December 1992), 46; and Malcolm Fleschner, "The Microsoft Way," *Selling Power* (January/February 1998),86.
21. Jeff Thull. "Recognition Smarts," *Incentive. New York*: (September 2004), Vol.178, Is. 9, 120.

22. Bruce Seidman, "The Psychology of the Sale, Part 1," *Salesdoctors.com* (February 14, 2000),2.
23. Patrick Schul and Brent Wren, "The Emerging Role of Women in Industrial Selling: A Decade of Change," *Journal of Marketing, 56* (July 1992), 38.
24. Henry Cole. "Marketing Real Estate Services: Smart Work versus Hard Work in Personal Selling." *Services Marketing Quarterly*. Binghamton: (2004). Vol. 25, Is. 2, 43.
25. John P Dugan, "Explorations Using the Social Change Model: Leadership Development among College Men and Women," *Journal of College Student Development*, (Mar/Apr 2006).
26. Fredrick A. Russ and Kevin A. McNeilly, "Links Among Satisfaction, Commitment, and Performance," *Journal of Business Research*, 34, 1 (September 1995), 57-61.
27. Judy A. Siguaw and Earl Honeycutt, Jr. "An Examination of Gender Differences in Selling Behaviors and Job Attitudes," *Industrial Marketing Management*, 24 (1995), 46; Robert Sharoff, "She Said, He Said," *Selling* (May 1994), 54-58.
28. Erin A. Cech, Mary Blair-Loy, "Perceiving Glass Ceilings? Meritocratic versus Structural Explanations of Gender Inequality among Women in Science and Technology," *Social Problems, Vol. 57, No.* 5 (August 2010), 371-397.
29. Paula Zmudzinski, "Gender Mutters," *Selling Power* (March 2000), 8.
30. Gary Bachelor, "Selling Beyond Gender," *Selling Power* (January/February 1996), 66-67.
31. Sinan Caykoylu, *Cross-Cultural and Gender Differences in Leadership Style Perspectives: a Comparative Study between Canada and Turkey,* (Saarbrücken, Germany: LAP Lambert Academic Publishing, January 7, 2010).
32. Personal Communication with Roger H. Reid (July 21, 2001).
33. Vincent Alonzo, "Role Call: Defining Your Reps' Personality Types Can Open a Window to Motivate," *Sales & Marketing Management* (June 2001), 34-35; Helen Berman,"Selling to Different Personalities," *Folio: The Magazine for Magazine Management* (June 1999), 34-35.
34. Smith, Craig. "How Do Myers-Briggs Personality Types Use Social Media?" DMR, Dec 22, 2013. Accessed October 7, 2015. Web.
35. Richard Jensen and Roy Spungin, "Analyze Your Prospects to a tee," *Selling Power* (July/August 1997), 80-81.
36. Zenith Training and Development, "The Psychology of Selling Excel¬lence," Accessed August 18, 2015.
37. Fran Abrams. "Learning? It's all in the mind." *The Times Educational Supplement. London:* (May 21, 2004), Is. 4584, F8.
38. Bruce Tuckman, David Monetti, *Educational Psychology* (Belmont, CA: Wadsworth Cengage Learning, 2011), 168.
39. Gareth Roderique-Davies, "Neuro- Linguistic Programming: Cargo Cult Psychology?," *Journal of Applied Research in Higher Education* (2009), 57-63.
40. Reg Connolly, "The NLP Eye Accessing Cues," *The Pegasus NLP Newsletter*, Accessed April 18, 2015. Web.

PART III

GAINING KNOWLEDGE, PREPARING, AND PLANNING FOR THE PRESENTATION

Part three is comprised of the all-important processes that must occur before the first sales call is ever made. ***CHAPTER 6*** prepares you for success in a sales career by focusing on gaining product knowledge, developing a specific plan for self-motivation and goal setting, and introducing the use of sales force technology.

Chapters 7 and 8 discuss the procedures for locating and qualifying prospects and identifying the information needed to prepare for an effective presentation. ***CHAPTER 7*** is a thorough look at prospecting. As the saying goes, "I'd rather be a master prospector than a wizard of speech and have no one to tell my story to." ***CHAPTER 8*** discusses the process of gathering preapproach information and presents a six-step telephone track for scheduling that critical first appointment with a prospect.

CHAPTER 6 PREPARING TO SUCCEED IN SALES

OVERVIEW

Before you ever call on a new prospect, there are a number of important steps to take to ensure your success. These steps are a part of the all-important processes that must occur before the first sales call is ever made. Chapter 6 prepares you for success in a sales career by focusing on gaining product knowledge, developing a specific plan for self-motivation and goal setting, and introducing the use of sales force technology. When you walk into a meeting prepared and armed with proven sales concepts, your chances of making the sale greatly increase.

OBJECTIVES

- Study what type of information makes up the product knowledge needed for success in selling.
- See how sales technology tools impact salespeople and how to use them to your advantage.
- Examine the various types of social media available and know which ones to focus on as a salesperson.
- Understand the concept of product positioning.
- Identify the three types of motivation and how they operate in affecting human behavior.
- Learn how to accept personal responsibility for maintaining self-motivation and exercising initiative in selling.
- Recognize the importance of setting and achieving goals for personal success.

SUCCESS IN SALES INVOLVES MORE THAN SIMPLY GETTING A PERSON TO SAY YES.

IF IT WERE THAT SIMPLE, EVERY SALESPERSON WOULD BE SUCCESSFUL.

DO YOU HAVE WHAT IT TAKES?

A lucrative, long term selling career involves a combination of the training provided by your company with your own active preparation in learning as well as personal commitment. Because the company's bottom line ultimately depends upon your efforts, your preparation is a significant mutual concern; and the more help your company gives, the easier your job becomes. Adequate preparation for success in selling involves at least three areas that are discussed in this chapter.

1. Product knowledge 2. Sales force automation 3. Motivation and goal setting

Certain elements in each of these three areas are the primary responsibility of the company; some are primarily your responsibility. No matter who bears the responsibility, both you and your company are active participants. Too much is at stake for either party to take a passive approach to preparation.

THE RIGHT KNOWLEDGE

Newly hired salespeople may have some general knowledge of the company's field or industry and may even have some knowledge of the specific product they will be marketing. However, salespeople are often hired with little or no knowledge of the company and its products, or even of the industry. *Obtaining product knowledge is one of the first prerequisites to success.* A study conducted among buyers about their perceptions and attitudes toward the salespeople they interact with indicated that buyers' greatest dislike is an unprepared salesperson.[1] Ultimately, two things must take place to achieve the preparedness buyers are looking for: First, your company must provide you with adequate product information to make you feel comfortable representing the product, and more importantly, it is up to you to study and learn about your product.

What do you need to know about the product? One answer to that question is everything! Nevertheless, you cannot delay beginning sales activity until you have learned everything. In fact, in most cases it is impossible to learn everything due to changes and advances in technology. And once you do begin making calls and closing sales, you can never cease to learn about the product or service.

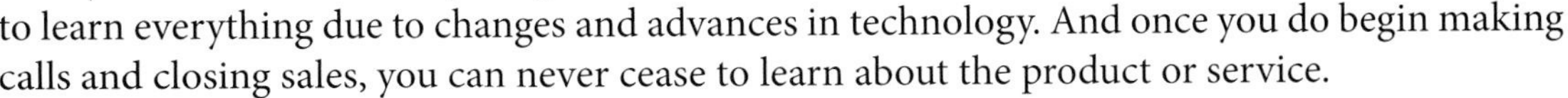

The Product or Service

Product knowledge begins with the product itself: Its specific features, its benefits, and its acceptance in the marketplace. Product knowledge includes knowing all available options—how it can be adapted to the particular customer's needs and how it performs under varying conditions. Detailed product knowledge prepares you to answer any question a customer might have and to offer whatever reassurance is necessary in the process that helps the customer reach a decision.

When you are thoroughly educated on the product, you can answer detailed, technical questions from expert buyers or explain it in simple terms to someone who is considering such a purchase for the first time. You seldom tell a prospect all the information you have, but having all the information gives you an entire library from which you can choose the best items for the current situation. Exhibit 6.1 shows how two salespeople used specific product knowledge with varying results.

EXHIBIT 6.1 A TALE OF TWO SALESPEOPLE

A software salesman called on the owner of a small business who was looking for a solution to the mountain of paperwork that was slowing up shipping of orders. The salesman had been well trained in product knowledge and was eager to demonstrate his expertise. He overwhelmed the prospect with computer jargon—co-processors, dual in-line circuit boards, gigabytes, and java archives—and he peppered his sales talk with terms like mbps, OS, and OEM software. He left without an order.

Later, another technical salesperson called. She told the prospect how quickly the product she represented would process orders so they could be shipped, and how time and paper handling could be reduced in preparing and sending invoices. She then explained that daily reports could be produced to summarize orders received and shipped, cash received, and other transactions that would provide solid information upon which good business decisions could be made in a timely manner. She got the order!

Performance

Performance information is another vital area of product knowledge. How long will your product last? What kind of wear and stress does your product tolerate? How easy is it to upgrade? How much training is necessary for an employee to operate or use? Can it be repaired? Who performs needed maintenance? Are spare parts readily available? These are all questions relating to specific performance issues, and if your customer doesn't voice them, rest assured that he is thinking them.

In the more technical industries, salespeople have access to company engineers and advisors who furnish engineering and technical information when it is required; sales knowledge in this case means knowing who to call on and when to ask for back up. If a product is too technical for a person to understand, be sure you can explain the benefits in a way that will be understood.

Manufacturing

Product knowledge also includes knowledge of the manufacturing methods and processes that affect the performance or durability of the product; and these vital ingredients of quality affect buying decisions. An understanding of the manufacturing process may help enable you to explain why a price that seems high to the prospect is actually quite reasonable, or why delivery takes longer than the buyer had expected.

Distribution

The company's distribution methods are another important area of product knowledge. What delivery channels are used? Are exclusive dealerships granted in certain areas? Is selective distribution used? Do discount houses and chains sell the product in competition with other types of retail outlets? Another important element of distribution concerns pricing policies. Such policies include dealers' costs, availability of quantity discounts, applicable credit terms, and whether the company will consider negotiating special deals.[2]

Company

Product knowledge also involves gaining as much information as possible about the company you represent. You need to know something about the history of the company: Who founded it and when, how the present product line evolved, the company's position in the marketplace, its past and present performance and growth, its primary customers or clients, and any other information that may be of interest to prospects are a few examples of the types of facts that help you sell more effectively.[3] It is important to be aware that your prospects may be almost as knowledgeable about your company and its products and performance as you are.

THE SOCIAL MEDIA CONNECTION

Prospects Can Tell A Lot About Your Company Through Social Media

Social media marketing, or SMM, is a form of Internet marketing that implements various social media networks in order to achieve marketing communication and branding goals—and every day, more and more companies are figuring out how to leverage their social media presence and their SMM to increase sales.

It makes sense, given the fact that so many prospects are going online before they buy to compare companies and learn more about the organizations that interest them. You and your company can leverage this fact by ensuring that what your company posts on social media sites:[4]

- **Is Planned.** Consider keyword research and brainstorm content ideas that will interest your target audience.
- **Has Great Content.** Content reigns king when it comes to social media marketing. Make sure you are offering valuable information that your ideal customers will find interesting.
- **Has a Consistent Brand Image.** Using social media for marketing enables your business to project your brand image and core identity across a variety of different social media platforms.
- **Features a Blog.** Blogging is a great social media marketing tool that lets you share a wide array of information and content with readers.
- **Contains Links.** While using social media for marketing relies primarily on your business sharing its own unique, original content, it's also great to link to outside articles as well. Linking to outside sources improves trust and reliability, and you may even get some links in return.
- **Gives You a Way to Measure Success with Analytics.** You can't determine the success of your social media marketing strategies without tracking data. Google Analytics can be used as a great social media marketing tool that will help you measure your social media marketing techniques.

Service

Once a product or service is sold, your responsibilities have just begun. It is outstanding after-sale service that will cement the relationship and ensure repeat orders—and repeat commissions! If you sell a product, you must know the company's service policy in regard to repairs, updates, and replacements. What charges are made for service? Who performs the service? What kind of consulting service is available to adapt or adjust the product to the customer's needs? Your customers will inevitably ask some or all of these questions, so it is imperative that you know the answers.

Competition

Another overlooked area of product knowledge is information about the competition. Learn about your major competitors' product lines; know their credit terms, their prices, their delivery schedules, and their reputations for service. Most buyers—either personal consumers or company purchasing agents—are not weighing the advantages of buying a product against those of not buying; rather, they are trying to decide which product to buy, yours or the competition's offerings. The following story is an example of how one salesperson used his knowledge of the competition's product to make the sale:

Ken Andrews was involved in a highly competitive bidding situation for his company, a manufacturer of GPS systems for automobiles. He was facing a representative of a Japanese competitor who Ken knew had a lesser-quality product but offered it at a lower price. Ken's product had superior attributes and was easier to use, therefore giving him the edge in technology and quality. The selling opportunity presented for him was to show how the prospect's company could save money over the next 3 to 5 years by buying a more expensive, but higher-quality product. The end result of his sale was that he won at a higher price through a better product offering.[5]

One of the advantages of studying your competition is that you are reminded of the good points of your own product and what makes it unique. This will help refresh your presentations, especially if you have been selling the same product or service for a long time. Once you are reminded of what makes your product different from the competition, you can stress those areas where your product excels and effectively gain a lasting advantage over your competition. Exhibit 6.2 provides an overview of the four areas of competitive advantage.

EXHIBIT 6.2 DIFFERENTIAL COMPETITIVE ADVANTAGE

PRODUCT SUPERIORITY	SERVICE SUPERIORITY	SOURCE SUPERIORITY	PEOPLE SUPERIORITY
Versatility	Delivery	Time Established	Personal Knowledge and Skill
Efficiency	Inventory	Competitive Standing	Skill of Support Personnel
Storage	Credit	Community Image	Integrity and Character
Handling Time	Training	Location	Standing in Community
Safety	Merchandising	Size	Flexibility of Call Schedule
Adaptability	Installation	Financial Soundness	Interpersonal Skills
Appearance	Maintenance	Policies and Practices	Mutual Friends
Design			Cooperation
Mobility			
Packaging			
Life Expectancy			

SALES FORCE AUTOMATION

Paper calendars and Rolodexes are long gone, and the electronic information age is here! Today's professional salespeople are not simply computer-savvy; they use every outlet available to them to do their jobs. Social media, webcasts, integrated marketing, email, and database marketing are just a few of the tools that salespeople use every day to communicate with their customers and companies. Laptops, smartphones, and tablets have become instrumental and indispensable tools to foster and build relationships with customers and to manage information and key accounts with greater efficiency.

With the automation of today's sales industry, salespeople can have clear direction and the right incentives, but if they don't have the right tools, their numbers will suffer despite their best intentions. Sales force and sales task automation is unavoidable, but there is one danger to such mechanization. It goes back to the old adage of "garbage in, garbage out." Technology doesn't solve problems by itself. In fact, if you automate a mess, you just have an *automated* mess.[6] Unfortunately, many companies simply don't take the time to understand the underlying processes before adding the technology. For example, your company could add an expense reporting system for salespeople to submit to accounting, but then forget to buy a license for the accounting department to allow them to use the system.

Proper steps must be taken to ensure that you and your company are ready to automate!

To keep up with the increasing demands of the continually changing, increasingly competitive marketplace, salespeople are expected to become more productive at everything they do. They must see more prospects, provide more value, and do a better job with each customer on which they call. The good news is that technology relieves salespeople of many administrative duties that would normally rob them of time that could be spent planning and selling. Through the use of technology, salespeople can quickly analyze facts and figures and transmit information efficiently to both their customers and companies.

Web-Based Sales Training

If you want to excel at something, the best way to improve is through practice. In the past, salespeople at most companies would have periodic "training bursts" in the form of a three-day training event here and there, but then they were sent back to their jobs, and there was no more practice. That's like a quarterback throwing passes for a few days and then deciding that's all the training he needs for the season—which would never happen. Thus, unlike athletes, salespeople haven't historically continued their training.

The problem continues today. In a recent study by *The Bridge Group*, a sales consulting firm based in Hudson, Massachusetts, they found that one out of seven companies never train their salespeople, and more than half of the companies train their employees one to four times a year.[7] Another study conducted by the *Association for Talent Development* found that more than one-third of third-year sales professionals average only three to six days of sales training annually, and 39 percent of tenth-year sales professionals average zero to four days of sales training.[8]

The answer to this problem is here, but it is still being underutilized—and it comes in the form of Web-based sales training, or *eLearning*. With the ease at which we can go online and access virtually anything at any time, web-based technology makes training easier and more affordable by maximizing flexibility and effectiveness for both the sales force and sales managers. The benefits of web-based training include:[9]

- 24-hour access to training programs—allows for fast and convenient training.
- Increased interactivity among large and spread out sales teams.
- Instant access to new product information and current product updates—allows sales force to have up-to-the-minute accuracy of information.
- Direct performance measurements with immediate feedback.
- Reduces costs of airfare, hotel stays, and convention expenses.
- Sales reps can focus their attention on the specific training they need.

THE IMPACT OF SALES TECHNOLOGY TOOLS

The companies that find ways to respond quickly to customer needs and make information readily available to their business partners will gain the all-important competitive edge. The implementation of an effective sales force automation program provides numerous company benefits which relate directly to improving the bottom-line—your company's profit.[10] Sales force automation can help increase your sales efficiency in two functional areas:

Improved Communication

LAPTOPS. Laptops provide you with desktop power wherever you go. With Wi-Fi connections now almost ubiquitous, laptops are indispensable for salespeople to maintain constant access to important contact information, sales scripts, and emails. They enable greater time management during flights or commutes, where the busy salesperson can type away at important documents or stay caught up on reading reports.

SMARTPHONES. Smartphones have it all. They are a computer, the Internet, your email, phone, address book, notepad, road map, and entertainment all in one. One popular smartphone on the market today is the *Apple* iPhone, but the *Samsung* Galaxy also has large contingents of loyal users.

TABLETS. Between a laptop and smartphone in size, tablet computers are popular for their ease of use and extreme mobility, both in the business and the personal entertainment landscape. With similar features to the iPhone, tablets such as *Apple* iPad, *Samsung* Galaxy Tab, and *Google* Nexus make working on the go easier than ever.

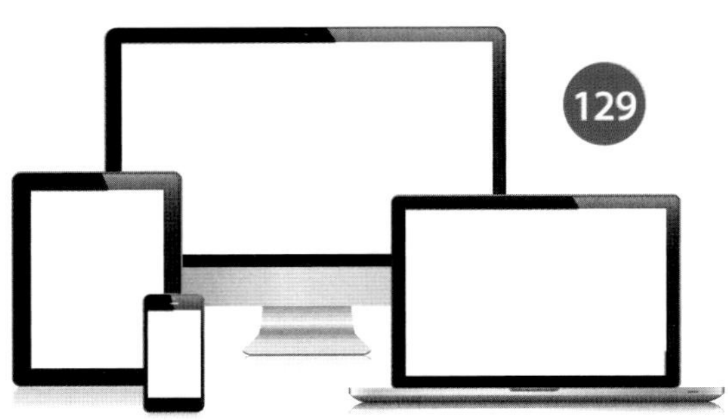

Never again will you miss an important email while on a sales call or at lunch. Face-to-face interaction with global clients without travel costs is a way of life for business today. Many salespeople are conducting the majority of their sales calls through videoconferencing with *Cisco* or *Skype*. Live-feed video conferencing is a great alternative for proposals and presentations.

Telecommuting—also known as remote work or telework—is a work arrangement in which employees do not commute to a central place of work. It is a practice that is more widespread today because of the advances in communication technology. Not only can you stay on top of your email, but you can also update databases, product information, and appointments from the comfort of your home or nearby coffee shop. Many companies still encourage their salespeople to conduct business from the office, but for more disciplined salespeople, this is an excellent option.

Increased Productivity and Production

CUSTOMER RELATIONSHIP MANAGEMENT (CRM) SOFTWARE. In the world of professional selling, *customer relationship management* (CRM) is a broad term that covers concepts used by companies to manage their relationships with customers, including the capture, storage, and analysis of customer information. CRM is more than just contact management software; it is a tool that can move companies to a higher level with customers. Well-integrated CRM systems are used daily as the central point of customer contact.[11] One of the leading products on the market is *salesforce.com*, who offers a cloud-based solution to organizing your business and reaching out to prospects and clients.

With the number of quality CRM programs available, the key is to find one with which you feel comfortable working and can easily understand. Websites such as *CompareCRM.com* have reviews and comparisons of the latest Contact Managers on the market to assist in making the best decision for your needs. CRM-related apps are also available for managing contacts on the go and for coordinating sales information among members of a team.

SALES APPS. Another way that salespeople can maximize the use of their smartphones and tablets is through the use of apps designed for mobile sales. Managing sales operations when the team is in the field was once a challenge, let alone the uphill battle faced by the in-the-field sales reps, who were often left to fend for themselves with last-minute scenarios they weren't quite prepared for. But all that's changed thanks to the mobile revolution and a slew of useful mobile sales applications that totally empower field reps to close deals from anywhere.

Today's sales apps put the portability in sales intelligence. The multitude of apps available can provide you with the data, evidence, and social proof you need to transition prospects through the buying process with ease. Whether you're looking for a mobile solution that makes CRM data easily accessible, a robust solution for delivering presentations on the road, or process orders with a whole host of third-party vendors on the fly—there's an app for that.[12]

MAPPING PROGRAMS AND GPS. With the level of sophisticated mapping technology available today, no salesperson should ever be lost or late to an appointment. Real-time location finders and interactive mapping systems are widely available on smartphones and come standard in most new car models. With the information clearly plotted on a map and a friendly voice guiding you, effectively navigating your territory has become immeasurably more accurate.

SOCIAL NETWORKING

Now more than ever, salespeople have increasing opportunities to relate to customers and prospects on a daily basis through social media. According to recent data, the average user logs almost 2 hours per day on social platforms, which represents about 28 percent of all online activity. Micro-blogging, which includes Twitter, is also up slightly to a little over three-quarters of an hour per day, and now accounts for about 13 percent of total time spent online.[13]

The field is wide open for savvy salespeople and innovative companies to use the social media phenomenon to their advantage. As with other technology tools, the question isn't, "Should I use social media to help me sell?" but *"How will I use it?"* What will be the impact of social media on sales forces in the next few years? We are certainly entering an exciting time in the life cycle of this phenomenon.

Social Media Sites

Every individual has preferences and styles that determine their personality and what makes them unique. Some people prefer quiet one-on-one conversation, while others are most comfortable in a rowdy group discussion. The same goes for social media preferences: Each customer has likes and dislikes about the various sites available today, and companies must be willing to meet the needs of their customers on this issue as on others. Salespeople, too, must pay attention to customers' communication preferences and work to communicate in the way that is most comfortable for the one who is most important in the sales relationship: The customer.[14]

The following is a list of the most commonly used social media sites that are beneficial for salespeople today and a few tips for using them to your advantage in professional sales:

FACEBOOK. When Facebook was created in 2004, its original purpose was to provide a way for students on college campuses to network with one another. As of today, however, there are over 1.45 billion active monthly users who log in to Facebook across the world.[15] Companies and salespeople utilize Facebook fan pages to build profiles of their products and services and to keep their brand prominent in the daily newsfeed of Facebook users. When it comes to Facebook, it pays to write regular, fresh posts and include interesting topics, not just pictures or personal thoughts. Here are a few tips for salespeople to get the most out of Facebook:[16]

USEFUL FACEBOOK TIPS FOR SALESPEOPLE

1. **Like your clients' Facebook pages.** This is a great way to stay on top of what those businesses are talking about in public, which can help you understand what they are trying to accomplish.

2. **Organize your Facebook friends into custom lists.** Create a list for current customers and clients that you are already connected to in Facebook. Create a second list of potential customers and clients. Creating these lists allows you to isolate the posts from the people you put on these lists and quickly add your voice to the conversations they are having on FB by commenting on posts or sharing their posts.

3. **Search for prospects using a Facebook graph.** Did you know its possible to find out which of your friends work at a certain company, or even if they have friends who work for that company? Go to your Facebook page and in the top left, next to the Facebook logo, type in "My friends who have friends that work at Company X" (where Company X is a fairly well known company in your field) and see what turns up.
4. **Post something related to your work.** As long as you keep 80 personal of your posts personal in nature on your personal page, you can do some posting about what's happening at your work. Of course, keep things positive and remember you're doing this with a business purpose in mind.

LINKEDIN. LinkedIn is the business side of social media. On LinkedIn, you won't find photos from your college roommate's recent vacation or status updates about what's for dinner. As the world's largest online professional network, LinkedIn currently has over 150 million users, including executives from all Fortune 500 companies. If you are ready to get serious about LinkedIn, take a long hard look at your contacts. *Contacts are the currency of LinkedIn.* If your contacts are predominantly family, friends, and old school pals, you've got some work to do.

Perhaps one of the most important things to remember about LinkedIn is that *connections breed connections*. Your "first level" contacts open up a route to a wide range of second and third level connections. This is how you scale your network. Strike while the iron's hot—whenever you meet anyone (online or off) always follow up quickly with a connection request while you are still fresh in his or her mind.[17]

WHEN IT COMES TO LINKEDIN, CONNECTIONS BREED CONNECTIONS.

TWITTER. For many people, LinkedIn comes to mind when we talk about social media for professionals. However, in a surprising new trend, according to a study by *Kitedesk* and *A Sales Guy*, Twitter has edged out LinkedIn—even if by a small margin—to become the most used social tool for salespeople. Twitter has always been associated with community building and quick, 140 character missives, but there's more to it than that. Twitter is a more natural and spontaneous way to strike up a conversation with people. LinkedIn, while it lets you connect with people, isn't so great when it comes to *engaging* with them. Twitter also allows you to get into a conversation with anyone you want. And since Twitter offers users the option to receive direct messages from non-followers (as long as that user has their settings adjusted accordingly), the opportunities for salespeople to communicate about their brands or businesses is broadened significantly.[18]

OTHER SITES. Aside from the powerhouse sites listed above, dozens of other social networking sites cater to almost any need. Google+ is rising in popularity, and YouTube has long been recognized as one of the most useful sites for business and personal use. Depending on the field, a salesperson may need to be involved in a niche site as well as the major ones. For example, people in the book-publishing world may want to relate to potential readers on Goodreads.com, while those in the music industry have found sites like Noisetrade.com to be an effective way of relating to listeners and potential music buyers. Whatever the product or service is that you sell, it is imperative to find out the latest ways to network with other salespeople and customers.

PRODUCT POSITIONING

The level of competition today is astounding. There are so many brands, and for every brand there are salespeople trying to get the sale before the next guy. It's a fast-paced, cutthroat race, and the competition is coming from all over the world. That makes *positioning*—the marketing strategy of differentiating a product or company in the mind of a prospect—more important than ever. Once a business identifies what makes it unique in the eyes of the consumer, that element should become the focus of its entire marketing and sales strategy. What makes your company and your product line different? Here are 5 key actions to take to find the best possible answer to the question you will almost surely hear from prospects:

"HOW IS YOUR COMPANY, PRODUCT, OR SERVICE BETTER THAN THE OTHERS?"

1. **FIND OUT** what qualities of your products and services are most important to your customers. Use that information to custom-design a unique niche for yourself.
2. **PUT TOGETHER** a marketing strategy built around several features that are important to your customers and will set you apart from the competition. And then develop an integrated marketing communication message that reinforces those attributes in the customer's mind.
3. **REMEMBER** the way you service your customers or sell to them can be a powerful difference. For example, if you are in an industry where the prevailing culture stresses face-to-face selling, the ability to buy directly online can be very attractive.
4. **RECOGNIZE** that focusing on the few attributes that really set you apart means you can't be all things to all people. ***When you shout, "Hey, everybody," you end up satisfying nobody.*** Focus on those customers that are a part of your specific target market.
5. **KEEP** an eye on how your competitors are positioning themselves. Be ready to respond to their claims and make sure you maintain a differential competitive advantage.

Positioning refers to developing a specific marketing mix to influence potential customers' overall perception of a brand, product line, or organization. The term was popularized by Jack Trout and Al Ries in their book, *Positioning: The Battle for Your Mind*. Positioning is the place a product occupies in potential customers' minds relative to competing offerings. Once a position is selected, product, price, place, and promotion strategies and tactics are designed to reinforce the sought-after position. These marketing mix components represent a bundle of individual dimensions that are designed to work together to create a competitive advantage.

Positioning on a company-wide scale does not typically fall under the responsibility of salespeople. Even so, it's important to know that the best companies have *integrated marketing campaigns* in which all elements—from the efforts of salespeople to brand messaging on social media—work together to form one comprehensive, consistent positioning strategy.

MOTIVATION AND GOAL SETTING

Salespeople often find that they have the needed product knowledge and sales and computer skills but have trouble getting around to using them, or else they work hard and long but find that what they accomplish fails to bring them lasting satisfaction. The missing ingredient is motivation.

Numerous definitions have been given for motivation. Perhaps the simplest is that *motivation is the reason for taking action*. This definition can be expanded slightly to say that motivation is the *impetus* to begin a task, the *incentive* to expend an amount of effort in accomplishing the task, and the *willingness* to sustain the effort until the task is completed.

The question most asked of business consultants is, "How can we motivate our sales force?" The answer most given by consultants is, "You can't." The reason for this answer is that the question typically implies that somewhere there are strategies, techniques, or gimmicks that, once discovered and implemented, will double or triple sales motivation and productivity. Consultants realize that genuine and lasting motivation is not something management does, but rather a process that management fosters and allows to happen.[19]

The primary responsibility for developing and sustaining motivation rests with you; the company's role is to provide a supportive climate in which the development and sustaining of motivation is encouraged. Bob Nelson, author of 1001 Ways to Reward Employees, says, "What motivates people the most takes just a little time and thoughtfulness." Recognize them as individuals and you're giving them what they most crave. Read *The Lighthouse Story* for an inspirational idea that cost just a few dollars but paid enormous dividends.[20]

THE LIGHTHOUSE STORY

Jonathan Berger, director of strategic accounts for Square D/Schneider Electric, had a salesperson on his team close a very important account that put a fairly large bonus in the sales rep's pocket. So Berger decided to take the extra step that made this sale a truly memorable triumph. He knew the sales rep's wife had a passion for photographing lighthouses, so he sent her a small crystal lighthouse with a note that recognized her husband's achievements and thanked her for her support and the time she had invested. The wife wrote Berger back and said, "Never has anyone in any company ever acknowledged my existence or the contribution I make to my husband's career." This story is good enough to pass on.

> "People often say that motivation doesn't last. Well, neither does bathing—that's why we recommend it daily."
>
> **Zig Ziglar**

Practical Motivation for Salespeople

All motivation theories agree that motivation arises as a response to either an external or internal stimulus. Recognizing those stimuli that operate in your own experience can help you discover ways to control either the stimuli or your responses to them in a way that produces a positive, sustained motivational power and the success you desire. *Motivation* may arise in *fear*—the fear of punishment or withholding of acceptance if behavior does not conform to expectations. It may come from *incentive*—the promise of reward for desired behavior. But the most effective type of motivation is that arising in *attitude*—behavior chosen because it fits the values and standards chosen by the individual as guiding principles for living and performing.[21]

FEAR MOTIVATION. Fear as a motivating force has some value. Fear is a natural emotion designed as protection from danger. Fear motivation has some advantages.

- It protects the individual from self-destruction or harm.
- It protects society from undesirable behavior.
- It is sometimes the quickest way to accomplish a desired reaction.
- In spite of these advantages, fear motivation has serious disadvantages that more than offset its benefits.

Fear is external. It is effective only as long as the enforcing power is stable. When the parent, teacher, or sales manager is out of sight, fear motivation is materially weakened.

Fear is temporary. Threats or punishment may control behavior for a time, but people tune out warnings if they discover that threats are not always carried out.

Fear is negative. It is directed largely toward not doing something or toward doing something unpleasant merely because it is an imposed duty rather than a chosen activity. A warning not to do something creates a void that may be filled by another equally undesirable behavior.

INCENTIVE MOTIVATION. The use of incentives for motivation is generally considered more enlightened than the use of fear. The attempt to produce motivated activity by offering incentives is common in sales organizations. Some common incentives used include the appeal to work harder to earn increased commissions; contests, certificates, and plaques for quotas reached; bonuses; the promise of an enlarged or better sales territory; and perks such as a reserved parking place, a private office, a personal secretary, or a company car. You have to understand what motivates each individual on your team and use that information.[22] Like fear motivation, incentive motivation has advantages.

- Incentive motivation calls for extra effort. When a promised reward is highly desirable, salespeople put forth almost superhuman effort to win it.
- Incentive motivation is positive and promises something desirable. Salespeople are not frozen into inaction by fear of being punished or deprived.

Like fear motivation, however, incentive motivation carries built-in disadvantages.

Incentive motivation is external. Behavior depends upon the initiative of the person who offers the reward rather than upon the salesperson who will earn it.

Incentive motivation is temporary. A salesperson may put forth a great deal of effort to win a sales contest or to earn some desired reward but not continue that level of activity or effort once the contest is over. A promised reward that is *not perceived as desirable* provides no motivation for action.

Incentive motivation can backfire. Incentives once earned often come to be *regarded as rights* instead of a special privilege for outstanding performance. For example, salespeople who qualify for a company car by high productivity and enjoy this reward for several years feel incensed if the requirements for having a company car are raised and they fail to meet the new quota, even though they improve their sales for the year.

ATTITUDE MOTIVATION. Attitude motivation operates on the concept that the only lasting and uniformly effective motivation is the personal motivation that comes from the internal structure of the individual. It is based on a strong self-image and a belief in the possibility of success. Attitude motivation is self-motivation. All great salespeople inherently possess this powerful, internal drive. Self-motivation can be shaped and molded, but it cannot be taught.[23]

Self-motivation is the result of the choices made by individuals in response to conditioning influences. Fear and self-doubt are the habitual attitudes of some people, but others choose, instead, to respond to life positively. For example, some salespeople who are told they're too inexperienced decide that they are and always will be. Then they wait for someone to tell them what to do.

However, others respond to the statement by choosing to believe that their condition is temporary. As a result, they are willing and eager to try different activities, stretch their imaginations, and attempt new goals. They do not wait for someone else to motivate them; they are always reaching out for new experiences. These salespeople are self-motivated. What you are, then, is not entirely a result of what happens to you. What you are is a result of how you react to what happens to you, and your reactions are a matter of choice.

The advantages of attitude motivation are the opposites of the disadvantages of fear and incentive motivation:

Attitude motivation is internal. Because attitudes come from within, you do not need to wait for an outside stimulus to make appropriate choices and take action.

Attitude motivation is permanent. An attitude, once thoroughly established, continues to operate on an automatic basis until you do something to alter it. Self-motivation is the only kind of motivation that can be sustained over a long period of time.

Attitude Motivation Through Goal Setting

The single most important tool for developing self-motivation is a program of personal goals. A personal goals program creates desire—one of the most powerful emotions operating in human experience. If you want to be able to choose where you will go with your sales effort, and how you will get there, you need clear goals and strategies. Only then will you have the power to direct your efforts.[24]

Exhibit 6.3 is the *Million Dollar Personal Success Plan* that Paul J. Meyer, founder and chairman of the board of *SMI International,* developed for his own use at the age of nineteen. It provides a workable plan for achieving success in selling.

EXHIBIT 6.3 THE MILLION DOLLAR PERSONAL SUCCESS PLAN

By Paul J. Meyer. Founder of SMI International Inc.

I. CRYSTALLIZE YOUR THINKING

Determine what specific goal you want to achieve. Then dedicate yourself to its attainment with unswerving singleness of purpose, the trenchant zeal of a crusader.

II. DEVELOP A PLAN FOR ACHIEVING YOUR GOAL, AND A DEADLINE FOR ITS ATTAINMENT

Plan your progress carefully: hour-by-hour, day-by-day, month-by-month. Organized activity and maintained enthusiasm are the wellsprings of your power.

III. DEVELOP A SINCERE DESIRE FOR THE THINGS YOU WANT IN LIFE

A burning desire is the greatest motivator of every human action. The desire for success implants "success consciousness" which, in turn, creates a vigorous and ever-increasing "habit of success."

IV. DEVELOP SUPREME CONFIDENCE IN YOURSELF AND YOUR OWN ABILITIES

Enter every activity without giving mental recognition to the possibility of defeat. Concentrate on your strengths, instead of your weaknesses… on your powers, instead of your problems.

V. DEVELOP A DOGGED DETERMINATION TO FOLLOW THROUGH ON YOUR PLAN, REGARDLESS OF OBSTACLES, CRITICISM OR CIRCUMSTANCES OR WHAT PEOPLE SAY, THINK OR DO

Construct your Determination with Sustained Effort, Controlled Attention, and Concentrated Energy. OPPORTUNITIES never comes to those who wait… they are captured by those who dare to ATTACK.

CRYSTALLIZED THINKING. You must know what you want to achieve. If your goals are hazy and poorly defined, you cannot plan concrete action steps for their achievement. You must write down and date your goals. Monitoring your status keeps you focused.[25] Without specific action plans, much of your time and effort is wasted. Chapter 15 will address action plans and effective time management techniques in much greater detail.

A PLAN OF ACTION WITH DEADLINES. A written plan of action keeps you on track and headed toward the achievement of your goals. You know exactly what to do next. A written plan also reveals conflicts between various goals so that you can plan ahead and make a reasonable schedule for the time and resources needed to reach all your goals. Deadlines provide you with the needed time frame for achieving your goals. They give you something to aim for.26 Because most of us now use such a small percentage of our real potential, target dates serve the purpose of drawing out more potential and using it to bring desired goals into being. Deadlines help you maintain a positive attitude of expectancy toward goals achievement. They eliminate distractions and help you to think creatively.

SINCERE DESIRE. A burning desire to achieve the goals you want often makes the difference between a wish and a goal. A *wish* is something you would like to have but are not willing to invest enough time or effort in order to achieve it; a *goal* is something you want so intensely that you will exert whatever effort is needed to reach it. The more goals you achieve, the more desire you develop. The greater your desire, the more you can achieve. Desire is an ascending spiral of success.

SUPREME CONFIDENCE. Success demands supreme confidence in yourself and your ability. Self-confidence enables you to undertake challenging goals and believe you can succeed. Self-confidence lets you see problems as opportunities and obstacles as stepping-stones to success. Self-confidence builds your credibility so that the buyer is open to considering the solutions suggested. Self-confidence makes it easy to ask for the order—not once, but again and again until the sale is closed successfully.

The secret to developing this kind of confidence is a growing list of goals accomplished. Each time you succeed in reaching a goal you have set and worked toward, you gain added belief in your own capability to achieve. Confidence in your own personal ability is the greatest source of security you can possess.

DOGGED DETERMINATION. Determination to stick to your plan of action until your goal is achieved is an outgrowth of desire and confidence. When you have a burning desire to achieve your goals, you are not easily swayed by others' thoughtless comments, by the disapproval of someone who does not understand your goals, or the active opposition of those who fear to be compared with you in either effort or results. Determination is the quality that enables you to continue calling on a difficult prospect until you close the sale. Determination gives you the creative freedom to discover new tactics for achieving your goal when your first effort fails and to think up more ideas until you discover a way that works.

All of these success elements are interdependent. Use of each increases your power to use the others. Success in any one intensifies your belief in the others. Self-motivation is the only real and lasting motivation. Its development is your responsibility. The company and sales manager can provide a climate in which self-motivation is easier, but even the most negative climate cannot de-motivate you without your permission.

SUCCESS AND THE TOTAL PERSON

Organizations emphasize that sales forces are essential to corporate success. However, organizations seldom pay much attention to what constitutes success for an individual. Too often success for salespeople is measured only in terms of the amount of sales generated. This narrow view of success has been responsible for destroying the self-confidence of untold numbers of salespeople. An understanding of what success really means frees you to become all that your potential allows.

"Success is the progressive realization of worthwhile, predetermined, personal goals."

This definition of success is especially applicable to salespeople, who can begin their careers with relatively little training compared to that required of other professionals. Because success is progressive, you can be successful immediately just by choosing to pursue goals that are personally fulfilling and then beginning to work toward them. Obviously, such a beginning is not made at the level expected of a master salesperson with long experience but at a level consistent with present reality. When you learn this truth, you have the patience to study, learn the art of selling, and practice your skills.

Too many people fall into the same erroneous thinking that organizations often follow in measuring success. Those "worthwhile, predetermined goals" must involve more than money and position or the success that is achieved is likely to be hollow. Mike Singletary, former head coach for the San Francisco 49ers and pro bowl linebacker for the Chicago Bears, has spoken to Christian youth groups all over the country. As a member of the NFL Hall of Fame and devoted father and husband to a wonderful wife and seven children, he is someone who should be heard. In his motivational and inspirational talks, Mike encourages his young audiences to develop their potential in all areas of life, not just their athletic skills. Likewise, salespeople who concentrate only on career success and neglect other areas of life find their lives less than happy.

Money and position aren't all that matters to most people. For this reason, goals must be set in every area of life: Physical and health, mental and educational, family and home, spiritual and ethical, social and cultural, financial and career. Total personal growth in these areas is effectively pictured in Exhibit 6.4 as spokes on a wheel. If some spokes are uneven, the wheel that represents total life achievement is not round. The ride is very rough, and the passenger feels dissatisfaction and a vague sense of uneasiness or unhappiness. Unmet needs prevent the enjoyment of achievements in other areas. Monetary success means little to the salesperson whose family life is shattered, health ruined, or the respect of friends lost. All areas of life must be included in a plan for becoming a "total person."

EXHIBIT 6.4 THE WHEEL OF LIFE

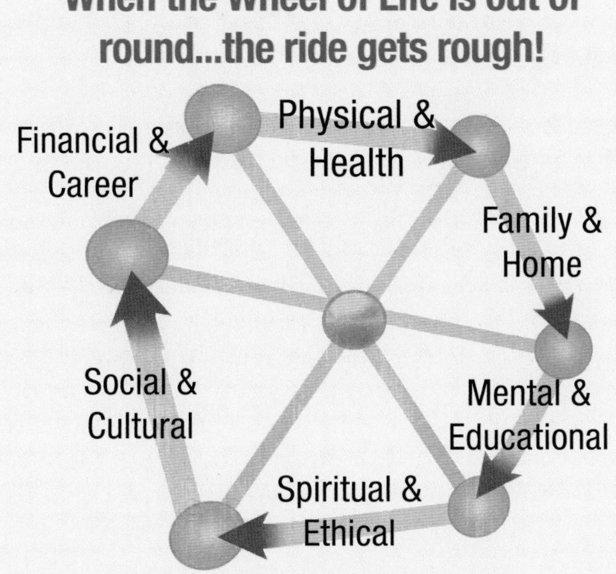

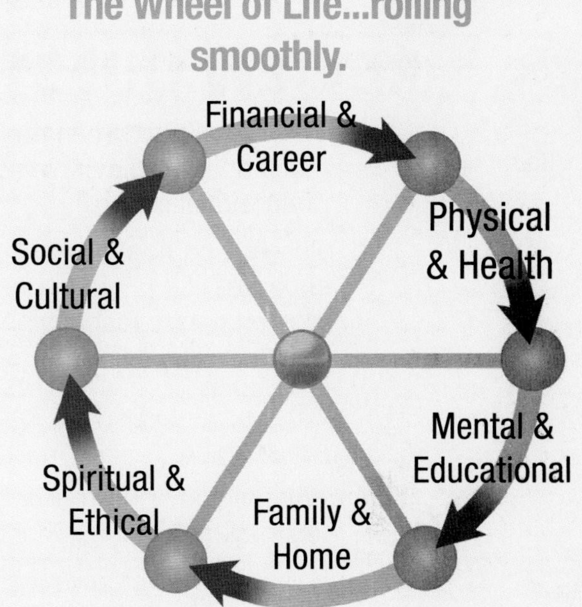

Success has different meanings for different people and that not every salesperson belongs in a particular organization selling a specific product or service. To succeed, salespeople must market a product or service in which they personally believe. Once salespeople know what they want from a selling career and dedicate themselves to achieving those goals, the responsibility for reaching success is largely in their own hands. *Too many people confuse action with progress and effort with results. Trying hard does not guarantee success.* Success comes as a result of determining the desired goals, finding out what activity is required to reach those goals, and then completing those actions based on a personal commitment to oneself.

SUMMARY

- Preparing for success in a sales career includes three areas of special importance: Product knowledge, sales force automation, and motivation and goal setting.
- Product knowledge includes knowledge of the entire industry or field and specific knowledge about your product or service.
- Sales force automation and technology tools increase your personal productivity, communications capabilities, and transaction-processing efficiency.
- Social media is a way for salespeople and companies to connect with others in their business, as well as customers and prospects. Relating through social media is another aspect of the overall sales relationship between salesperson and customer.
- Positioning refers to the place a product occupies in customers' minds relative to competing offerings.

- All motivation comes primarily from one of three sources: Fear, incentive, and attitude. Fear and incentives used as motivating forces are limited in effectiveness because they depend on someone else as the source. Attitude motivation is internal and permanent.
- Successful goal setting begins with crystallized thinking about what is important to you, then developing a plan of action with deadlines for achievement.

REVIEW QUESTIONS

1. What contribution can business school courses make to success in selling? How much academic work in sales or marketing is necessary to guarantee success in professional selling?
2. Does the company that hires you have any responsibility for preparing you for sales success? If so, what specific types of knowledge, information, or other input is the company's responsibility?
3. Name at least four areas of product knowledge that are important for salespeople.
4. What advantage does knowledge of the competition's offerings provide for the salesperson?
5. What would you do about product knowledge if you were hired to sell a highly technical product for which you have little background or understanding?
6. Sales force automation can help increase a salesperson's effectiveness in at least two distinct ways. Discuss each one and give an example to illustrate.
7. Name at least four social media sites that are popular today. What are the main uses of each site?
8. Explain how fear and incentives are used as sources of motivation. Can you give an example from your own experience of how both of these were used by someone else in an attempt to motivate you?
9. What limits the effectiveness of fear and incentives as motivating forces?
10. What are the advantages of using attitude as a basis of motivation?
11. Explain how goal setting affects self-motivation.
12. How does a personal goals program produce self-confidence? What is the value of self-confidence to salespeople?

IN-CLASS EXERCISES

The following in-class exercises help build teams, improve communication, and emphasize the real-world side of selling. They are meant to be challenging, to help you learn how to deal with problems that have no single right answer, and to use a variety of skills beyond those employed in a typical review question. Read and complete each activity. Then in the next class, discuss and compare answers.

EXERCISE 6.1 – POSITIONING YOUR COLLEGE

Every organization—businesses both small and large, not-for-profit organizations, professional societies, etc.—must differentiate itself from its peers and competitors. Your college or university is no exception. The competition for students among higher education institutions is keen. After all, without the revenue supplied by a sufficient number of students through tuition and financial aid programs, many colleges and universities would have to close their doors. To appeal successfully to enough students, colleges and universities must position themselves vis-à-vis their competitors, i.e., they must communicate to prospective students how they are different from and superior to other schools in meeting student needs. Salespersons (and, yes, admissions officers for colleges and universities are salespersons) often overlook the importance of positioning in their quest for product knowledge.

Imagine that you are the Director of Admissions at the college or university through whose good auspices you are taking this course. The Vice President for Enrollment Management has just asked for your professional estimate of the school's current positioning strategy and your recommendation for any changes that you think are warranted. What do you say in your one-page report?

Be sure that your report draws upon your analysis of your college's website and other marketing materials and that you have at least looked at the websites of some of your college's closest competitors. How is your college presenting itself as distinctive? Does it work? Is there anything that you think should be changed in your college's current strategy? Bring your findings to class and be prepared to discuss them.

EXERCISE 6.2 – HOW MUCH PRODUCT KNOWLEDGE IS ENOUGH?

For this exercise, you should pair up with another student in the class. Most people are aware that B2B sales, especially for highly technical products, require a great deal of product knowledge and knowledge of the business in general. But many assume that retail sales—where many salespersons get their start—is easy in that regard. After all, how much is there to learn about most retail products?

Select a retail product line and, with your partner, interview at least two salespersons who handle that line. Please try to conduct your interviews when the stores are not busy or outside regular business hours, since nearly all retail salespersons work on commission. When they are talking with you, they can't make any money. The products might be mobile phones, household appliances, furniture, upscale clothing, sports equipment—nearly anything at all. Keeping in mind the various types of product knowledge presented in Chapter 6, ask the salespersons what sort of training their company provided to acquaint them with their products. Ask them how long it took until they felt comfortable presenting features and answering customers' questions about their products. Find out how much they need to know about their company's procedures, methods of getting their products into customers' hands, their company's history, financing or payment policies, etc. And finally, ask how often they have to update their product knowledge in order to remain on top of their game.

Summarize your findings in one or two pages and be prepared to discuss what you learned in class or online.

CASE STUDIES

The following case studies present you with selling scenarios that require you to apply the critical skills discussed in the chapter and give you training through practical learning situations. They are meant to be both engaging and challenging, and like the exercises, don't have one right answer.

CASE 6.1 – MOTIVATION THROUGH COMPENSATION

Dwayne Connors, Regional Vice President for Sales at DirtCheap Corporation (an agricultural equipment manufacturer), didn't know where to turn next. Because of declining sales, his predecessor had been fired. The company had tried a policy of management by fear that was approved at the highest levels. During that three-year period, the company had reduced the base pay of all salespersons whenever they failed to meet the month's quota. The rationale was, "If they don't sell, why should we pay them [their full base pay]?" As the company president put it, "Confronted with the fear of disaster, they'll perform." Well, they didn't. Some salespersons resigned outright. Others failed to make quota month after month. As district sales manager, Dwayne noticed the plunging morale and declining sales figures. He had promised a different approach that, he thought, would get better results.

So, for the past nine months, Dwayne had instituted a system of positive incentives. First on the list was a compensation structure that awarded salespersons a higher percentage commission the more they sold. For example, if a salesperson made quota, a 10% commission on total sales would be added. If a salesperson sold 150% of quota, a 25% commission would be paid, and so forth. Increased productivity would therefore be rewarded directly and immediately; and some salespersons had the potential of earning large sums, even surpassing Dwayne's fixed salary. In addition, Dwayne initiated a series of sales contests for lines of equipment that were overstocked. For a period of 4 months, sales improved and morale began to improve. Dwayne thought he had licked the problem by using carrots rather than sticks.

But now, after the last five months of stagnating results, Dwayne was stymied. Sales had slumped once again, although not alarmingly. He was beginning to receive caustically worded emails from his superiors at headquarters wondering when his "new approach" would pay off. What to do?

Given what you have learned in Chapter 6 about attitude motivation or self-motivation, how would you advise Dwayne? What steps might he and his sales managers take to help the sales force to improve their motivation to succeed? If graduated commissions and sales contests didn't turn the tide permanently, what might?

CASE 6.2 – RESCUING GREYHOUNDS

After 35 years of a very successful career in technical sales, Walt decided to give something back to his community during his retirement. He and his wife had rescued a couple of retired racing greyhounds in recent years and found them to be adorable, loving companions. So it seemed natural as a result for Walt to volunteer his services to the local greyhound adoption organization. Little did Walt know what he had gotten himself into!

Because of his background in sales, the organization's executive director decided that Walt should become the group's chief fundraiser. The job called for Walt to write grant proposals, visit philanthropic foundations to solicit financial support, and to make presentations on the organization's behalf to various community groups. In short, his job was to "sell" the organization and its needs to those who could provide financial and other resources.

From his experience selling air quality monitoring systems, Walt appreciated the value of product knowledge. Without it, a sales representative could not respond to a client's questions and concerns, could not position the product vis-à-vis the competition's offerings, and could never gain sufficient confidence to convince a client to buy. In fact, Walt put so much emphasis upon product knowledge that he assembled a team to keep him abreast of new developments. But what was the "product" in the case of the greyhound rescue organization? What did Walt need to know in order to sell this product effectively?

Based on the principles and categories of product knowledge presented in Chapter 6, describe the "product" of Walt's greyhound adoption agency and outline in a page or two what Walt needs to know about it in order to represent the agency effectively. This might require some research regarding retired racing greyhounds and the agencies that try to help them.

Chapter 6 Footnotes

1. Anonymous, "Study Indicates Sales Professionals Spend Little Time Preparing for Calls; Preparation for Sales Calls Significantly Less than Managers and Buyers Desire," *Business Wire*. New York: (Nov 29, 2005), 1.
2. C.S.M. Currie, R.C.H. Cheng, and H.K. Smith, "Dynamic pricing of airline tickets with competition," *The Journal of the Operational Research Society*. Oxford: (Aug 2008), Vol. 59, Is. 8, 1026.
3. David G. Knott, Jeff Boschwitz, and Decio K. Mendes, "Know Your Company's 'DNA,'" *Best's Review*. Oldwick: (Jul 2004), Vol. 105, Is. 3, 46.
4. Wordstream. *Guide to Using Social Media for Marketing*. White Paper. Accessed September 1, 2015. Web.
5. Tate Williams. "The Age-Old Face-Off." *Sales and Marketing Management*. New York: (April 2004). Vol. 156, Is. 4, 64.
6. Marshall Lager, "The Alignment: CRM capabilities and business processes enable technology to shine," *CRM Magazine*, July 2007.
7. Markowitz, Eric. "New Tools for Sales Training." Inc.com, May 3, 2011. Accessed July 7, 2015. Web.
8. For more information, please visit, https://www.td.org/, Accessed October 20, 2015.
9. From a telephone interview with Paul Goldner on May 16, 2001; and adapted from Erika Rasmussan, "Training Goes Virtual," *Sales & Marketing Management* (September 2000), 108.
10. Denise Bedell, "Know Thy Customer's Behavior," *Global Finance*. New York: (Nove 2005), Vol. 19, Is. 10, 54.
11. Anne Stanton. "The "Why" Behind CRM Software." *Infotech Update*. New York: (March /April 2004), Vol.13, Is. 2, 5.
12. Phillipson, Cobhan. "43 mobile sales apps: tools to streamline your sales enablement

processes & operations." Docurated.com, August 17, 2015. Web.

13. *Bennett, Shea. "28% of Time Spent Online is Social Networking." Social Times. January 27, 2015. Web.*
14. Barbara Giamanco, "6 Tips for Driving Social Sales Success," *Salesandmarketing.com*. Posted March 10, 2011, accessed April 27, 2015, Web.
15. "By the Numbers: 200+ Amazing Facebook User Statistics." *DMR*. Last Updated September 23, 2015. Web.
16. Myerhoff, Alice. "5 Steps to Maximizing Facebook for Salespeople." *Salesforce.com*, March 18, 2014. Web.
17. Bratton, Anna. "Ten Tips for using LinkedIn for sales prospecting." *Salesforce.com*, Accessed November 1, 2015. Web.
18. Newman, Daniel. "Is Twitter Really The Favorite Social Network For Sales Professionals?" *Forbes*. July 7, 2015, Web.
19. Anonymous, "Author Presents Six Strategies for Motivating Employees," *Healthcare Financial Management*. Westchester: (Nov 2010), Vol. 64, Is. 11, 26.
20. Robert McGarvey and Babs S. Harrison,"Easy as Pie," *Selling Power* (March 2000), 116.
21. The sections of this chapter dealing with motivation and goal setting were taken largely from Paul J. Meyer's *Dynamics of Personal Goal Setting, Dynamics of Personal Leadership*, and *Dynamics of Personal Motivation* (Waco, TX: Success Motivation, 1991, 1992, and 1993, respectively).
22. James Wilkins, "The 'why' is what drives positivity," *Conference andIncentive Travel*. London: (Mar 2011), 16.
23. Paul Werlin, "Seven Keys to Self- Motivation," *Bank Investment Consultant*. New York: (Aug 2010), Vol. 18, Is. 8, 25.
24. Rajen Devadason, "Thermometer or thermostat?" *Malaysian Business*. Kuala Lumpur: (Jan 1, 2011), 58.
25. Donna L. Cohen, "Plan Your Way to Success and Increase Sales," *Agency Sales*. Irvine: (Oct 2006), Vol. 36, Is. 10, 36.
26. Valentino Sabuco, "What's Really Important to You?" *The Saturday Evening Post*. Indianapolis: (Jul/Aug 2007), Vol. 279, Is. 4, 46.

Qualities of High Sales Performers

1. **Exchange information** rather than present products. They tend to ask a variety of questions that help the customer to analyze, evaluate, speculate, or express feelings.
2. **Know when to close.** They advocate their products only after they have identified or created an important need and involved the customer in developing the solution.
3. **Sell to people, not organizations,** and demonstrate a strong commitment to meeting customer needs.
4. **Are perceived by prospects as genuine advocates** of prospects' needs, even while actively promoting the company and its products or services.
5. **Provide added value** to the customer. They act as a resource able to directly provide expertise to prospects and clients.
6. **Regularly establish trust** within their own organizations by sharing information, encouraging participation in decisions, and recognizing the contributions of the internal staff to their success.
7. **Engage in positive behavior** such as maintaining eye contact, showing enthusiasm, asking questions about customers' needs, restating those needs accurately, and being prepared with effective responses to objections

CHAPTER 7

BECOMING A MASTER PROSPECTOR

OVERVIEW

Prospects are the lifeblood of professional sales. Without a regular stream of new prospects, organizations would not survive. Every salesperson needs new prospects in order to excel—and this chapter discusses the procedures for locating and qualifying those prospects. As the saying goes, "I'd rather be a master prospector than a wizard of speech and have no one to tell my story to."

OBJECTIVES

- Understand the importance of prospecting.
- Find out who your prospects are.
- Learn the characteristics of a qualified prospect.
- Become familiar with a variety of prospecting methods including referrals, centers of influence, and social media prospecting.
- Understand how to manage prospect information accurately and consistently.
- Get a quick and concise glimpse at the power and influence of analytics on your bottom line.

THE CONCEPT OF PROSPECTING

A salesperson without prospects is as useful as a doctor without patients. Great salespeople ask smart questions, know how to close a deal, and have excellent follow-up techniques; the one trait they demonstrate more consistently than any other is constant prospecting, enhanced by creative approaches that build value and lasting relationships. They see opportunities everywhere and they know it's not just the numbers—but the numbers are what count.[1] After all, you have to see more to sell more.

If your closing ratio is lower than you'd like, the problem may be that you don't have enough qualified prospects. If you see enough people, sooner or later you will sell to someone. To succeed in selling, locate qualified prospects in advance—before you need them. Develop multiple sources from which names of prospects flow constantly.

> "Dig the well before you thirst."
>
> ***Confucius***

Both the marketing and sales departments need access to a central storehouse of all prospects and customers where employees can track responses to marketing campaigns and look at the history of sales efforts. As the company interacts with that prospect or customer, every piece of communication and history needs to be in one spot. Call it a CRM system or a sales force automation (SFA) system, but the key is to get marketing, sales and, if possible, other departments to work from the same contact record.[2] Here are three other basic principles to help you hold onto leads in a highly competitive market:

1. **Qualify Leads.** Pay attention to lead qualification. Have a process in place and the resources and skills to qualify those leads. Generating leads is akin to building the Alaskan pipeline. Figure out how to build the pipeline and get the oil flowing.
2. **Nurture Leads.** There will likely be some leads that aren't ready for sales. A nurturing process that includes phone calls, email, social media contact, and direct mail is necessary to keep in touch with those prospects until they're ready to see a salesperson.
3. **Add Value.** The worst thing you can say is something like, "I'm just calling to find out if you've gotten that budget yet." Email case studies or relevant and insightful articles based on your research about them and their company. That way, you are not only checking in, you are contributing to their productivity.

The last principle may, in fact, be the most critical part of prospecting, and here is why: All human behavior, at its root, is driven by the need to avoid pain and the desire to gain pleasure. Even when we do something that appears to be painful, we do it because we associate pleasure with the action. *But what does this have to do with prospecting?* Everything! All human beings essentially have the same mental triggers that drive actions.[3] In order to influence and understand your customers, you need to know what those triggers are and how to utilize them during the prospecting phase of the sales cycle.

> You have to convey to leads, as quickly and effectively as possible, that you have an answer to one of their "pain points."

Why is this so critical? Because our minds decide what to buy. So, if you know how minds function, you have the power to influence the decisions they make. Of course, in order to influence someone, you need to know what already influences him or her. You find this out by getting clear on whom your audience is. This chapter will reveal how to get to the bottom of that important question by walking you through the process of turning "just another lead" into a qualified—and even eager—prospect.

> I would rather be a master prospector than a wizard of speech and have no one to tell my story to.
>
> ***Paul J. Meyer***

QUALIFYING THE PROSPECT

Establish a pattern for prospecting to avoid wasting a monumental amount of time calling on leads that are not prospects. When all you have is a name and email address, you have only the *possibility* of developing a prospect. Exhibit 7.1 illustrates the process of moving a name from the status of lead to that of a qualified prospect.

EXHIBIT 7.1 ACTION OF THE SALESPERSON IN DEVELOPING LEADS INTO QUALIFIED PROSPECTS

SALES LEAD

Research needs, history, ability to pay, authority to buy, etc.

PROSPECT

Evaluate information gained, add personal informaton.

Truly qualified prospects are those who are a fit for you because they possess the necessary characteristics that make them logical buyers for your offering. Apply a detailed screening process to each lead to increase your chances of successfully completing a sale.[4] The best prospect can be defined this way:

A Class "A" qualified prospect is one to whom you have been referred by a person the prospect respects, one who has the ability to make a buying decision and to pay for the product or service, and one about whom you have all the personal information you need to make a good presentation.[5]

There are few things as disheartening as going through the entire sales process only to discover that the person with whom you are speaking was never a real prospect to begin with. So, in order to avoid this, you must ensure that you have found a class "A," qualified prospect before you spend your valuable time trying to sell something to someone who cannot or would not ever buy from you.

One of the best ways to determine if you have a qualified Class "A" prospect is to use the MADDEN Test. When you use The MADDEN Test to qualify prospects, it will help you ensure that they have **MONEY**, are **APPROACHABLE**, have **DESIRE**, have **DECISION-MAKING** ability, are **ELIGIBLE**, and have a **NEED** you can satisfy. So, the next time you think you might have a Class "A" prospect, use the MADDEN Test, which is detailed as follows:

MONEY

Separate the talkers from those who actually have the means to buy. You will save yourself and your organization a great deal of disappointment by determining a prospect's ability to pay before spending your time and energy gaining a client who may quickly become more of a liability than an asset. It's not always easy to determine purchase capacity. However, there are ways to determine potential based on: Whether an individual has made similar-sized purchases in the past, is a past customer, the individual's profession, and his or her known friends, colleagues, and social circles.

APPROACHABLE

Can you get an appointment? The president or CEO of a large company may grant an initial interview only to a senior level executive in your company. Do not hesitate to ask for such help when there is real possibility of gaining an important client. Some individual prospects are often approachable only if you are willing to fit your time schedule into their unique time needs, so make sure you discover what works best for *them*, and then adjust your schedule accordingly.

> "Don't judge each day by the harvest you reap, but by the seeds you plant."
>
> ***Robert Louis Stevenson***

DESIRE

Prospects may have no real interest in your company or what you have to offer. They may be happy with their current vendor or supplier. Is there anything you can discover about them or their company that would lead you to believe they will want what you have to offer? You can successfully reach prospects only if you create or discover a desire to satisfy a *pain point* in their business or personal lives, and how your offering is the solution. In other words, you have to help them find their WHY!

Be sure the person you call on is the decision maker. If you are unsure, then start with the head of the company. If you reach the CEO or COO, conducting business may be easier than you think. They earned the top spot by making tough calls and appreciate the tough call you've just made. A survey of business-to-business (B2B) sales companies revealed that 63 percent of respondents found reaching the right decision maker was the key to improved sales.[6] Salespeople spend a great deal of time talking to people who are not in a position to make a buying decision. After you have developed a level of comfort with the prospect, ask who else will be involved in making the decision and set up an appointment with all individuals at one time if possible.

ELIGIBLE

Determine whether the prospect is eligible to buy from you. Some prospects are already committed to a competitor and cannot buy. Others need a product with greater or smaller capacity than you can offer, or are in need of a service that is more or less extensive than yours. There is no sense in spending your valuable time calling on a prospect who is locked into a brand new five-year contract with a competitor.

NEED

Determine the need level for your product or service. To accomplish this you must seek out the most up-to-date information about an individual's company and ask questions and listen carefully to determine what the prospect's buying motives are in order to uncover any specific needs. Then decide if your company has the products that effectively satisfy those needs. Ask yourself— is the business your company may gain worth the amount of time you must invest to get it? This part of the qualifying process is meant to ensure that you have discovered a potential prospect's WHY—and whether your product or service is the answer.

THE SOCIAL MEDIA CONNECTION

Social Media Provides a New and Improved Way to Qualify Prospects

In the past, it wasn't always easy to pass a lead successfully through the MADDEN Test. After all, how can you know things like a person's interest, ability to pay, or authority to make the decision before you even meet with the individual? Luckily for salespeople, social media has made qualifying prospects a little bit easier. Here are some helpful secrets for how to use social media to seek out and discover qualified prospects:[7]

1. **Start at the top.** Get connected to company executives first. Start by tailoring your pitch to the company you are targeting, and then search for the CEO or top management on the social networks. You will soon find the social network where they are the most active, and then you can make your move.
2. **Know more than your competition.** Start by choosing a target company and research it. Search their posts for information on promotions, purchases, acquisitions and contracts. Take note when the company announces that they will be speaking at a certain conference and then search for a video from that conference. Once you have a clear idea of what they need, it is far easier to position yourself as the best solution—and then you can present the perfect information at the perfect time.
3. **Make prospects come to you.** Perhaps the best social media tool for making your prospects come to you is a blog. Use Google's Keyword Planner to find out what people really want to know about your industry and offer relevant content in a series of blogs and e-books. Promote this content on social media and ask your employees and friends to share away.
4. **Rotate your lesser-known social networks.** When it comes to how many social media networks you join, just signing up isn't going to do you much good unless you stay active on it. In order to cast a wide net that's effective, you have to be systematic in covering as many as you can. Pick a single social network that is lesser known or niche, like Pinterest or MySpace (yes, it still exists) and for the next month, focus a portion of your prospecting efforts there. Go where everyone else isn't and start capturing all the underserved revenue sources.

Using social media networks for prospecting can be a profitable endeavor, if you know what you are doing and do it well. Following these secrets to social media prospecting can get you on the right track toward generating a list of leads that can successfully pass the MADDEN Test.

METHODS OF PROSPECTING

While it may be true that practice makes perfect, this is only applicable to prospecting when you practice the correct methods. Incorrect practice on a musical instrument only produces an increased ability to make errors. This idea applies to prospecting—aimless, hit-or-miss prospecting, no matter how much of it is done, generally leads to failure. To streamline the job of prospecting and produce better results, master a number of different methods and use the ones that work best. A few companies still provide leads to their sales forces. For the most part, however, the job of find leads and qualifying them as prospects rests squarely on your shoulders. The following is a list of ten prospecting techniques discussed in this chapter.

1. **Referrals—**The use of referrals is one of the most powerful prospecting techniques available to sales professionals.
2. **Center of Influence—**A person who believes in what you are selling, influences others, and is willing to give you names and help to qualify them.
3. **Social Media—**Prospecting through social media to find and qualify prospects in a cost effective and time effective way.
4. **Group Prospecting—**Bringing a number of people together at the same time and place and capturing their names and other information about them.
5. **Strategic Calling—**Calling on a lead without first making an appointment and knowing little about the person.
6. **Email and Direct Mail—**Choosing or creating a mailing list of individuals, businesses, or professional people who appear to be at least partially qualified and sending them a communication that requests a reply.
7. **Current Customers—**Your company's existing customer database can be a goldmine of new business.
8. **Business and Civic Groups—**Membership in various civic groups such as the Chamber of Commerce gives you opportunities to meet people who can become prospects for a product or service.
9. **Networking—**In networking groups, salespeople from different businesses share information about the sales climate and exchange prospect information. At networking events, a number of businesses may come together to target specific prospect demographic groups.
10. **Websites—**A company can market its services and find customers utilizing the power of the Internet.

1. Referrals

A *referral* is a name given to you as a lead by a customer, a friend, or even a prospect who did not buy, but felt good about you and your product. According to global information and measurement company *Nielsen*, people trust recommendations from business colleagues, friends, and family 92 percent of the time—and more than all other forms of marketing.[8] Thus, the factor that makes this prospecting method valuable is its *leverage*. Until the proper time to use that leverage arrives, a referral is just a lead like any other.

Once you qualify a referred lead by securing all the information needed to show that this person fits the pattern of prospects upon which you call, you are then ready to use the valuable leverage that is yours by reason of the referral. Those who provide referrals should be willing either to make an initial contact for you or to allow you to use their names. Referrals work because people are naturally fearful or skeptical of strangers, especially those who try to persuade them to make some kind of decision. People accept you and your product more readily if someone they know and respect has sent you.

GAIN MORE REFERRED LEADS. Salespeople do not have more referrals because they don't ask, or perhaps because they don't know how to ask. There are two reasons why people do not immediately provide referrals. The first is that they find it difficult to think of names. Basically, they simply do not want to exert the mental effort to decide who might be interested. The second reason is they consider themselves to be *conscientious objectors*—they claim they just do not give referrals. Sales professionals estimate that 20 percent of clients won't give referrals no matter how you ask. Another 20 percent of clients will always give referrals. It's the other 60 percent where a plan of action is essential.[9]

Exhibit 7.2 illustrates a step-by-step approach to use when you ask for referrals. Practice and rehearse it with your favorite clients or those who have given you referrals in the past. Customers think of themselves as professionals, and they like to buy from professionals. Asking for referrals should become an automatic part of every presentation you make.

EXHIBIT 7.2 YOU CAN GAIN MORE REFERRED LEADS

1. **Ask for referrals with respect.** Open the dialogue with something like this, "I have an important question I want to ask you." This will capture your prospect's attention and indicate to them just how significant this is to you.
2. **Ask for their help.** Soften them up by saying, "I'm trying to build my business, and I would value and appreciate your help."
3. **Explain the course of action you propose.** Tell them what will happen if they give you a referral, and also let them know that you will remain professional and report back to them.
4. **Gain their permission to explore.** You might give them another softening statement: "I understand how you feel." Then you can go on to say, "I was wondering if we could agree on who you know who might also benefit from the products I have to offer. Are you comfortable with that?"
5. **Narrow their focus by describing your ideal prospects.** Once you have been given names, make a first step toward qualifying them. Ask your client, "If you were in my place, who would you see first?" Ask why. Then find out which one to contact next.
6. **Report back to them.** Whenever you receive referrals, be sure to report back to them the result of your interviews with leads.
7. **Thank them.** Always offer thanks for giving you referrals regardless of whether they bought from you.

WHAT TO ASK. The principal thing you ask for in a referral is for your client to make it easy for you to contact a new prospect. The variable in each situation is how this contact should be made. What to ask for depends upon your client's need for control of the situation:

- Some customers want to handle the communication themselves.
- Others want minimal involvement. They prefer that you initiate the contact for them.
- Still others may have very specific instructions on what they want you to do or say with their referrals.

The best way to find out how much control your client wishes to have is to simply ask by using an alternate of choice type question: "Would you prefer that I call Mr. Evans, or would you want to personally call and talk to him on my behalf?" Here is a sample statement that can be used to make the client feel comfortable about giving you names:

"I'm not asking you to recommend me or my product. All I really need is an introduction to some people you know. It can even be through LinkedIn if that's easier for you! I will talk to them, as I have with you, in a professional manner and give them an opportunity to learn about me and my company."

WHEN TO ASK. Make asking for referrals a part of the selling cycle. A logical time to ask for referrals is right after the close. A customer who buys is sold on you and likely to feel good about giving you names. Sometimes, however, a customer wants to use the product or service before giving referrals. Often, salespeople go after referrals at the wrong time. They start asking for referrals before the ink on the contract is dry. You can't ask for referrals; *you must earn them.* The best referrals come from satisfaction, not a signature.

THE MILLION-DOLLAR REFERRAL

Michael Twining, sales rep for a large distributor of agricultural products, has a clever way to secure more referrals. Whenever he gets a referral by an existing customer he quickly mails a handwritten thank-you note and includes a lottery ticket with the message: ***"Thanks a million for the referral. I hope you win a million!"*** It costs very little and always creates a lot of good will and laughs on his next visit with that customer. Michael says, "It almost always gets me at least one more referral."[10]

2. Centers of Influence

This method of prospecting is a specific application of the referral method. In both methods, you begin with a satisfied customer or with a person whose interest in you or your product has developed to the point of desiring to help you. The important distinction between the two is that a *center of influence* can give you far more prospects and is both willing and able to provide new names on a continuing basis.

The best sales tool you have is a person who believes in what you are selling, is influential with a number of people who are potential customers, and is willing to give you the names of these people and help you qualify them—that is the essence of a center of influence. When you have several centers of influence, you always have plenty of prospects. People respect the center of influence to the extent that an introduction from this source virtually assures you of an audience. Cultivate their friendship, sell yourself, and ask centers of influence to help. Getting that person on your team can open doors that would otherwise remain closed. Think how you would react if such a person called you and said:

I had lunch this past week with Curtis McDonald, a business associate of mine. I think he is a person you would like to meet, and I told him about you. He will be calling you this week; I hope you will meet him.

Centers of influence are one of the most valuable assets you can have as a salesperson. Follow up every lead they provide, and then report your results to them and thank them. Find a way to show your gratitude by being of service to them. After all, a mutually beneficial relationship is rewarding to both parties.

3. Social Media

As you read in the *Social Media Connection* earlier in the chapter, social media can be a powerful and useful prospecting method. Keep in mind, however, that being on social media and actually putting it to good use are two vastly different things. Prospects are not going to seek you out—you've still got to work for them! Here are some tips for finding prospects on your favorite social media sites quickly:

TWITTER. Twitter is a gold mine for prospecting, ready for you to shake your pan and let the leads fall out.[11] It is both simple and easy to use Twitter's "search" function to attach industry-specific keywords to Twitter users who may be interested in what you're offering. It doesn't matter what you sell or what industry you are in—anyone can use the search function and see quality results. You can even take your Twitter-mining one step further with *HubSpot's Social Inbox*. Social Inbox helps you track who is who in your Twitter list and searches by showing your contacts database of leads, opportunities, and customers, and merging it with your social media activity. Utilizing this tool means moving the most enticing prospects on Twitter right up to the top.

FACEBOOK. Facebook may seem pretty consumer-focused on the surface. So, for salespeople unsure of how to engage businesses and potential prospects via Facebook, it can be easy to identify the right prospects thanks to one of Facebook's more recent tools search tools called *Graph Search*. What's unique about Graph Search is that it gives you search results based on very specific search queries. Here is a good example of how specific your search can be: "Marketers in Boston looking for inbound marketing software." Because Graph Search pulls information from Facebook users' profiles, it's a premier way to discover prospects who don't already live in your news feed.[12]

LINKEDIN. LinkedIn is the most business-friendly social media channel, but it's also universally understood that many of its users are more wary about strangers connecting with them—that is, unless, you've got the secret ingredient for finding leads and prospects on LinkedIn: Groups. Over half (53 percent) of LinkedIn users join 10 or more groups.[13] That makes it the best place to insert yourself into relevant conversations and provide useful advice, tips, and content to get you noticed and attract potential prospects to you and your business.

PINTEREST. According to recent surveys, Pinterest is now the third-most popular social networking site behind Facebook and Twitter.[14] One feature that Pinterest has in common with Twitter and Facebook that can help you find and sort prospects is *hashtags*. When Twitter exploded in popularity, hashtags became a way to connect the millions of posts from around the world into groups and categories. Today, hashtags on visual Pins are like clues into the mind of the Pinterest user due to the visual nature of the post. For regular users, hashtags are a way to connect with other Pinterest users on their favorite topics. For you, they make it easy to pull out pins that users have deemed related to the keywords you use in your prospecting efforts.

Social media prospecting is about *creating context* with people so that your social interactions might eventually lead to a sale. Of course, social media can be quite noisy, busy, and filled with a lot of fluff—and sometimes, prospective customers can be buried in a sea of look-alikes. But with a little effort and some strategizing, more prospects will appear.

4. Group Prospecting

Many companies use group prospecting with great success. The idea is to bring together a number of people, from eight to twenty or more. The group may meet in a home, a conference room in a hotel, or in an office. Your purpose is to inform prospects about your product or service.

Many reps in the financial services industry use group information sessions to gathering people together for the purpose of offering free information about retirement, financial planning, their finances, or investing strategies. During that session, the professional has the opportunity (in the form of a captive audience) to find and hone in on people's *pain points*. After such a session, it is always imperative to follow up with attendees and strike while the iron is hot.

A variation of this method is to attend or set up an exhibit at a networking meeting that targets a specific demographic. Yet another variation is to look for groups of potential prospects and offer to be a guest speaker. Members of civic clubs may be ideal prospects for you, and they are always looking for speakers who have beneficial information for their members. If you establish your credibility, you may be able to close your speech with a brief presentation. Meet as many members of the audience as possible before and after the meeting, ask for business cards, and give them yours. If they were impressed enough to want you to call, you know you have a qualified prospect.

5. Strategic Calling

In the world of professional selling, cold calling has long been a dreaded part of a salesperson's day. But, if you dread it, you may not be doing it right. Calling on prospects without first gaining an appointment can be an enjoyable part of your day if you accept the reality of the situation. Call it *cold calling* or *warm calling*; it doesn't really matter. All that really matters is your state of mind. For most salespeople, it is not meant to be your only source of leads. However, strategic calling on potential prospects who were not expecting your call can serve as an excellent supplement to other prospecting efforts—if it is carefully planned.

The real issue with this prospecting technique rests in the message itself and how you communicate it. You must be able to communicate with a prospect so that they understand and resonate with what you have to say. *In short, planned prospecting is a communication skill*—and like any communication skill, it can be learned and it can be improved upon.[15] You have a brief amount of time on the telephone or at a person's door to catch and engage your prospect. If you are not able to do that, the call ends without achieving your desired result. If you have the proper skills,

however, it is possible to have extremely productive conversations with prospects no matter how you choose to categorize them, "warm" or "cold." Here are some other tips for calling:

USE AS A SUPPLEMENT. Because this method of prospecting is designed to supplement your current prospect list, be careful that phone calls and in-person cold calling never take so much of your time that you neglect calling on qualified prospects and existing clients. Set aside a specific amount of time each week for making calls, but never at the expense of more profitable activity.

ALWAYS PREPLAN. Develop several effective icebreakers and interest capturing statements and experiment until you find which ones work best for you. Your statement should be something relevant to them and their situation that causes prospects to remember you when you later call for an appointment to make your presentation.

STAY ENTHUSIASTIC. When you make these calls, the person you want to talk to is almost certainly too busy to speak with you. If you remain enthusiastic in spite of such responses, you make a positive impression on the executive assistant or receptionist. You may even get enough information to qualify prospects without meeting them. Impress them with your professionalism and you will find those doors to the buyers open more easily.

GOLDEN OPPORTUNITIES

Most salespeople would agree that calling without an appointment is the toughest part of selling. But, at the same time, the rewards can be great. So, change your mindset about such calls by referring to them as opportunity calls—because that's what they really are. Viewing calls as golden opportunities gives you even greater incentive for selling to clients and prospects. Now go out and create some golden opportunities for yourself![16]

6. Email and Direct Mail

The ultimate success of email and direct mail prospecting depends upon the management of your mailing list. Some lists are better than others, and the best investment of your time and budget demands careful planning and analysis. The product or service you sell has a great deal to do with what kind of list you use. The goal is a list of people or businesses that are already at least partially qualified prospects.

Don't overlook directories for developing your email and direct mail lists as a source of prospects. Some directories are useful in identifying possible prospects; others are helpful in learning more about prospects to determine whether they have the potential to become customers. Exhibit 7.3 provides some suggestions for sources of email and direct mail lists. Keep in mind that much of the time, the best lists are not readily available to the general public.

The best lists are those that you have created over time through past prospecting and networking efforts. Be patient—and the list will come.

EXHIBIT 7.3 SUGGESTED SOURCES FOR BUILDING DIRECT-MAIL LISTS

MEMBERSHIP ROSTERS

- Professional societies and trade associations
- College Alumni lists
- Civic clubs (Kiwanis, Lions, Civitan, Optimist)
- Special-interest groups
- Community business groups (Chamber of Commerce, etc.)

DIRECTORIES AND DATABASES

- People you have networked with in person and through Social Media
- Professional online directories or purchased database lists
- People you have done business with in the past
- E-newsletter subscription field from your own website

Develop a coding system to show which types of lists produce the highest percentage of responses—and then code the names of people who actually respond. This can be done fairly easily through email, since you can track and record open rates to see how effective your messages are at getting through. An *open rate* is a measure of how many people on an email list open (or view) a particular email campaign and is normally expressed as a percentage.

7. Current Customers

It would be a mistake not to mention one of salesperson's most powerful and ever-present sources of business—and that is the existing customer base. Every business needs new customers, but don't ever forget that your easiest and most predictable source of new revenue is right under your nose:

It comes from the loyal customers who already know your company.

Acquiring new customers is expensive—five to ten times the cost of retaining an existing one—and the average spending of a repeat customer is a whopping 67 percent more than that of a new one.[17] So, sure, put some energy into new prospecting methods and business development, but make sure you know that coming up with creative ways to sell more to your current customers is just as important.

8. Business and Civic Groups

Membership in civic groups can give you opportunities to meet people who are prospects for your product or service. Meetings provide you with regular times to meet more people and build relationships. Exhibit 7.4 lists tips for using membership in civic clubs as prospecting opportunities.

In selecting groups to join, consider the kinds of prospects you need to meet. It is also beneficial to choose organizations to which decision makers belong. Set goals to meet a certain number of new people at each meeting and to reconnect, or establish stronger relationships, with a certain number of others. Keep an updated file of the organization's members as you meet and learn about them. Avoid actively selling at the meetings, but you may ask someone to tell you the best time to call to set up an appointment. Building relationships through these contacts lays the groundwork for active selling in the future.

EXHIBIT 7.4 TIPS FOR USING MEMBERSHIPS FOR PROSPECTING

- Carefully select the groups you join.
- Assume leadership responsibilities to work for positive visibility.
- Set contact goals for each organization meeting.
- Follow up with contacts.
- Maintain an information file on the contacts made in each organization.
- Use "re-meet" goals to help you develop closer relationships with people.
- Reach out to new members.

9. Networking

Networking refers to the active cooperation between business people to share information about the business climate, specific happenings in the business community, and prospects. It involves the 3 C's:

1. **Connecting**
2. **Communicating**
3. **Cooperating**

Sharing information and names of prospects just makes sense. So, go ahead and mingle! As effective and handy as some of the newer, digital approaches to finding prospects are, good old networking should still be an essential part of your weekly routine. Engage with people face-to-face, tell them about yourself, your business and your product, and ask about them. Exchange contact details, add them to your database and keep in touch. There is another prospect waiting behind your next conversation if you enter into each conversation wanting to discover not just what that person can do for you, but also how you can serve him or her.

10. Websites

In today's age, there is no excuse for not having a well designed, user-friendly website, especially as consumers continue the shift to online tools as their primary means of contact. A website acts as the company's representative, so you want it to reflect your professionalism in terms of design and content quality. Exhibit 7.5 outlines the reasons you need a website working for you.[18]

EXHIBIT 7.5 WHAT A GOOD WEBSITE CAN DO FOR YOU

1. **Your site can effectively prospect for new clients.** A search engine-optimized site can attract customers who may not have otherwise called or even known about your business or products.
2. **Your site can offer 24/7 support.** Even when your business is closed, your website stays open, offering product and service information to your potential clients.
3. **Your site can cater to all personalities.** Introverts are quiet by design; they aren't likely to pick up the phone or walk in to talk with you until they have done as much online fact-finding as possible. For these people, the Internet is a very valuable tool. And don't forget the extroverts; they too will appreciate the information you share on your site.
4. **Your site can be professional and knowledgeable.** Your website can be appealing, charismatic, equipped with in-depth product knowledge and up-to-date information—and can make a great pitch. You have complete control over the information, and you can change and rework that information until you get it just right.
5. **Your site can convince customers to return—**Your website can convince people to come back. Keep your site content dynamic and fresh, giving visitors a reason to return and see what's new.
6. **Your site can gather information—**A carefully designed site can gather visitor information. Your site might offer newsletter subscription, product sales, friend referrals or marketing surveys. A visitor who interacts with your site can give you a name and contact details. In other words, a visitor who interacts with your site becomes a lead.
7. **Your site can help you close—**Your site design should mimic your company's real life strategy when it comes to closing a sale. If you are selling products, an online shopping cart might be in order. If you are selling services, you might need an online signup or contact form.
8. **Your site can make follow up easier—**The actual sale should not be the end of the sales process. Design your site so that feedback is encouraged. Customer satisfaction surveys or short post-sales polls (built into your site) can give great feedback and can help you to improve your sales strategy.

ESSENTIAL WEBSITE COMPONENTS. An endless array of sales websites and blogs exists on the Internet today, so yours or your company's site really needs to stand out from the crowd. The most professional looking sites remain relatively clean and simply designed; in other words, they know who they are marketing to and design the site for that audience. The best sites are also user friendly, with easily navigable pages and links to key content. According to some experts, the sites with the most value, however, are often linked to blogs with more user interaction and high-quality content that is not a recycled product pitch; continuous updates and marketing efforts here are key.[19]

USE AFFILIATE PROGRAM MARKETING. You may want to offer ad space on your website, or even place ads on other affiliated sites. *Google AdSense* is the most well known affiliate marketing program and can even earn your website some revenue. Google AdSense targets and customizes ads based on your website's content. You can choose how you would like your site to be paid for these ads, whether through user visits, earnings by user location, browser type, and referring source or by AdSense impressions, clicks and revenue.[20] Alternately, if you are the advertiser, you can bid on premium ad space available on other websites. Of course, you should research other affiliate marketing programs, decide if you want to broker your own ads, or opt for a no-ad website based on your ideal prospect's profile.

On their own, each of these prospecting techniques are only mildly effective. However, when combined, they create a powerful prospecting arsenal. No matter what methods of prospecting you elect to use, your own powers of observation provide many of your best prospects. The only way to get better at something is to practice, right? Then it stands to reason that if you want to become more skilled at recognizing qualified prospects among a sea of leads, you must practice and learn what to look for.

Social media tools make observation more powerful and accessible than ever. By following Facebook pages and Twitter users, you'll be able to keep connected to your current clients at the same time that you can track prospects who follow them. Keep an eye on feeds for event notifications, announcements, birthday notices and even changes in relationship status. Send a congratulatory note to a client on a new marriage or baby; send a personal message to a prospect who is launching a new store. If you are connected in LinkedIn, join a relevant group and follow conversations on hot topics. Explore the public profiles of connected groups and individuals—you never know how or when a valuable connection could present itself.

MANAGING PROSPECT INFORMATION

Diligent prospecting is useless if you do not have a system for managing and using the information you find. Many contact management systems on the market today will help you organize your contacts and priorities, but be aware of how to classify and prioritize contacts so you can make the most of your prospecting time.

Initial Recording of Leads

The initial information you need about prospects depends a great deal upon the product or service you sell, but it will, in all likelihood, include these items:

1. Prospect's full name and nickname (if you know it)
2. Email address and business or home address
3. Direct phone number (cell phone is best)
4. Name of company he or she works for
5. Position in company
6. Family information (spouse, number of children, etc.)
7. Personal information (club memberships, college attended, hobbies)

8. Approximate income (if your product or service is to be sold to the individual rather than to the company)
9. Source of prospect (Did you get his or her name from a referral or otherwise?)

Prospect Classification

When you first find the name of an individual or company prospect, assign a classification to the name. One classification system uses the letters A, B, and C.

Class A prospects are those about whom you have adequate information to make a presentation. You know they have the money to buy and the authority to make a decision. Ideally, you also have a referral from someone they respect.

Class B prospects are those about whom you have inadequate information to make the best possible presentation. You may not know enough to be sure they need your product or service. You may not know whether they have the authority to make a decision or whether they can afford to buy. You may not have a referral to help open the door. When one or more of these items is missing, the proper action is research rather than approach.

Class C prospects are people whose names you have found in some way, but about whom you have little or no information other than a name. They are leads, not prospects.

Prospecting activity involves not only finding new leads but also qualifying existing leads by adding information that allows you to move them up to Class A status.

Scheduling Contacts

When you have classified a prospect as Class A, determine when you will initiate contact, either by telephone, email, social media, personal visit, or direct mail, according to the method of approach you choose. Set up your smartphone calendar or contact management system to send reminders to ensure you take the proper action on the date assigned. Once a prospect's name enters your file, it stays there permanently until you close a sale or determine that the person is not a prospect for your product or service. If you make a presentation and do not close, choose a time for a new attempt and schedule an appropriate time for contacting the prospect again.

When you discover that a person is not a viable prospect for you and will probably not become one in the foreseeable future, then that person can still be an important contact. The impression you have given by your professionalism may cause that person to recommend you to someone who will prove to be an excellent prospect.

THE POWER OF ANALYTICS

The world of business analytics is a vast land of possibility, especially in the area of prospecting. With companies, data "experts," and consultants all approaching analytics differently, it can also be overwhelming. Put simply, there are two main areas in analytics:

1. Data and statistics-driven predictive modeling that enables prospect and client segmentation and opportunity identification.
2. Reporting and the software that allows you to retrieve information from a client or prospect database.

Setting aside the complicated terminology and the latest buzzwords—such as big data, data mining, and donor intelligence—it really boils down to performing and then utilizing *data analysis*, all driven by the need to sell in a more targeted and precise manner. In short:

It's about harnessing the power of information in a way that leads to more sales.

What does the term *data analysis* mean? It can be summed up as this: *Data analysis* is "the process of extracting, compiling, and modeling raw data for the purpose of obtaining constructive information."[21] The key word in that definition is *constructive*. Data analysis is only valuable if it serves a purpose. Data analysis for its own sake is neither useful nor particularly insightful, and it is by no means a magic wand. But it can go a long way toward providing solutions if you:

- Have a question that needs answering.
- Need to choose between different options.
- Believe that showing information in a quantitative fashion would increase clarity or motivate audiences to act.

So, how can you take a bunch of numbers and turn them into something that is useful—or in other words, something that allows you to segment leads and potential prospects in a way that helps you become more laser focused in your marketing and approach methods? You have to have three things: 1) Accurate data (i.e. information) that can be quantified, 2) Tools to extract and compile the information, and 3) Ways to model the data so that it provides useful information. When you use it right, data analysis can provide useful, intuitive information. In fact, proper use of analytics can answer questions like:

"Are my phone calls to potential prospects any more effective in the **morning** or after **lunch**?"

"What is our company's **second biggest** selling **month**?"

"How well are we doing in increasing **year**-over-**year** sales?"

With the right data, there really is no limit to what you can discover through analytics because the answer to such questions will allow you to focus your time, energy, and resources where they will glean the biggest payoff. There is one important thing to note about the questions above: Note the words in bold. Those words highlight the fact that there need to be different variables to study—two factors that can be measured or investigated to test whether (and how) they are related—in order for data analysis to yield valuable results.

Using all the web tools available to you—whether through social media, e-newsletter campaigns, researching company websites, or purchasing data sets from data mining companies—there is simply no excuse for making a truly *cold* call anymore. Being as thorough as possible in your approach to prospecting goes a long way in securing new accounts and allows you to achieve the treasured personalized approach to selling. Put yourself in your clients' shoes and you can offer your clients a real solution. This accomplishes more than merely establishing a solid rapport with prospects; it builds a relationship that will inevitably yield more success in the future.

If you fail to plan, you plan to fail.

SUMMARY

- Prospecting is the skill that keeps salespeople in business. Once you have leads, qualify them to determine whether they are true prospects that have a need for your product and are in a position to make a buying decision.
- Make sure prospects pass the MADDEN test.
- Two of the most effective prospecting methods are referrals and centers of influence. When someone they respect makes the introduction, you have a built-in sales assistant— the influence of the person who provided the lead and the initial contact.
- Social media provides a powerful new way to seek out, discover, and attract new qualified prospects.
- Group prospecting is securing names of possible prospects at trade shows, through speaking engagements, or in any situation where you have the opportunity to meet a number of people. Planned "opportunity" calling also provides a supplemental source of new prospects.
- Networking is a valuable source of new prospects for salespeople who are willing to share information about their customers or clients. It's all about connecting, communicating and cooperating.
- A classification system will help you methodically catalog your prospects as Class A, B, or C prospects. Such a system will save you time and frustration.
- Use the power of analytics to analyze your sales results in order to improve and possibly even determine where to spend more of your prospecting efforts.

REVIEW QUESTIONS

1. How does your skill in prospecting exert a direct effect on your ability to close a sale?
2. What characteristics make a qualified prospect?
3. What are the ten prospecting techniques listed in this chapter and which ones should you use most often?
4. What is a referral? How do you get referrals?
5. What is the advantage of having referrals from your clients?
6. What is a center of influence?
7. What is one way to use Twitter to find new prospects?
8. How does networking work for salespeople?
9. How long should a prospect's name remain in your prospecting system?
10. What three things are required in order to have data analysis provide you with useful, intuitive information?

IN-CLASS EXERCISES

The following exercises help build teams, improve communication, and emphasize the real-world side of selling. They are meant to be challenging, to help you learn how to deal with problems that have no single right answer, and to use a variety of skills beyond those employed in a typical review question. Read and complete each activity. Then in the next class, discuss and compare answers.

EXERCISE 7.1 – FINDING THE RIGHT CMP

For this assignment, you will work individually. Imagine that your company's vice president for sales and marketing has concluded that the company is dropping too many good sales leads because there is no good way to track contacts or continuing developments. At a major sales meeting, the vice president asks the entire sales force to recommend a good contact management program (CMP) that will allow anyone in the company to access contact information. The vice president emphasizes that the program should be robust, well tested, and relatively inexpensive. The salesperson who compiles the most complete and persuasive recommendation and whose choice is actually adopted by the company will receive a nice bonus and a chance for promotion. You want the bonus and the promotion.

After conducting research online, select three acceptable CMPs and recommend one as superior. Which criteria do you use in making your final recommendation? How do you respond to the recommendations of others in your class?

EXERCISE 7.2 – QUALIFYING THE PROSPECT

For this exercise, the class should be divided into teams of four persons each. One of the most important, yet most difficult, tasks of any salesperson is to qualify the prospect. Chapter 7 recommends the MADDEN approach to qualifying prospects. This approach identifies the information that salespersons need in order to consider a prospect or lead "qualified."

Nevertheless, asking for the necessary information (or finding it by other means) is often difficult. For example, it would be tactless and counterproductive to ask, "Do you have the money or authorized budget to pay for this product?" Or again, imagine the response to the direct question, "Do you have the required authority to purchase this product?"

The MADDEN approach specifies what you need to know. The task for your team in this exercise is to think of how to obtain this information, to devise clever, inoffensive ways of soliciting needed information from prospects. In the first instance, confine your methods to what you might say or ask in a personal interview. If you have time, develop other research methods that might help you obtain the needed information.

Jot down your recommendations and the reasons for them, and be prepared to present and discuss them in class or online.

CASE STUDIES

The following case studies present you with selling scenarios that require you to apply the critical skills discussed in the chapter and give you training through practical learning situations. They are meant to be both engaging and challenging, and like the exercises, don't have one right answer.

CASE 7.1 – THE TRADE SHOW

Judy had just accepted a position as sales representative with *NewLine Papers*, a manufacturer of high-quality specialty papers for businesses that use direct mail to promote their products and services. Typically, such businesses must use papers that are attractive to look at and hold, that absorb inks quickly because of high-speed printing, and that can stand up to the rigors of automatic folding equipment. In order for Judy to learn more about the business and to acquire good leads, her sales manager has sent her to the U.S. Postal Forum (USPF) annual meeting in Las Vegas.

Judy decided that for this trip to pay off in terms of generating solid leads she needed to engage in careful planning. A quick check of USPF's website allowed her to compile a short list of attendees who might be interested in *NewLine's* latest product. About a week before the trade show, she phoned a couple of them to arrange an appointment. They willingly agreed; so she flew to Las Vegas in the hope that she could snag an order, not just a couple of good leads. This would surely impress her manager!

After checking in at the convention hotel, Judy called Ned Harris, her first appointment for the next morning. Ned wasn't in, but she left a message indicating that she could meet him just off the lobby at 10:00 a.m. Her second appointment, Anita Scoby, answered on the second ring. She and Judy agreed to meet tomorrow afternoon at 2:30 following a major speech by the head of the U.S. Environmental Protection Agency. So everything was all set.

Ned arrived for their meeting the next morning a couple of minutes late, explaining that he was not a morning person and needed a second cup of coffee. They moved to the hotel's coffee bar and settled at a small table. Judy brightened when Ned reported that his company had actually done business with *NewLine* some years before. Immediately, Judy pulled out a couple of samples from her briefcase and launched into her presentation of the outstanding features of the new product. Ned listened attentively, sipping his coffee and sitting with arms folded. When Judy finished her spiel, she asked if he had any questions. He didn't. She then asked whether Ned's company would be interested in placing a trial order. He replied, rather curtly, that he didn't know, that he would have to get back to her on that, and that he was late for another meeting. With that, he picked up his newspaper and left, leaving Judy reflecting on what had happened.

Her meeting that afternoon with Anita Scoby was even more brief. Before Judy could begin to describe the samples that she had placed before Anita, Anita cut her off, explaining that she had no authority to engage in any such discussion, that while she was interested in Judy's product, her own role was in sales for her company, and that she was attending the trade show merely to network with other clients. She wished Judy luck and promised to pass along Judy's information to more appropriate people at her firm.

As Judy flew home the next morning, she wondered what she had done wrong. She had researched attendees of the trade show and had obtained appointments, but she was returning home with no orders and, worse, no real leads.

Where do you think Judy went wrong? What would she need to do in order to become a "master prospector?"

If you were sent to the trade show by your manager, what would you have done? What would have been your objectives? Which tactics would you have employed to fulfill those objectives?

CASE 7.2 – THE OVER-EAGER REALTOR

Sherry Huffman had just moved with her husband to San Diego from upstate New York where she had lived for her entire life. At age 30 and having worked in real estate for seven years, Sherry had no intention of giving up her career. She therefore joined a real estate company in San Diego and began searching for prospects. She realized that being a realtor in San Diego was going to be more challenging than in small-town New York where she was already known by nearly everyone in the area. In her new, larger city, she would have to cultivate a new sphere of influence in order to build up a web of former, satisfied clients who could subsequently help generate new business. In other words, Sherry realized, she would have to network aggressively (among other tactics) in order to succeed.

There was only one problem: networking, in the sense of meeting and cultivating new acquaintances, was new to Sherry. In New York, she was already networked; she didn't have to work at it or meet new people. Now, however, she would have to get to know new people to the point where they could begin to trust her.

Sherry's first foray into networking was to join the local Chamber of Commerce. What better source of new prospects, she thought, than successful, established businesspersons from a variety of fields? In typical fashion, she approached the task enthusiastically.

At the first meeting of the Chamber that Sherry attended, she introduced herself to the president and proceeded to work the room. As small groups of people carried on sometimes animated conversation during the cocktail hour, Sherry went from one group to another, introducing herself, distributing her business cards to all, and saying something like, "Hi! I'm Sherry Huffman. I just joined ***Golden Bear Real Estate***. Here's my card. If any of you are in the market to buy or sell real estate, please give me a call." Generally, people looked at her a little quizzically, politely took her card, and returned to their conversation. Sherry began to get the feeling that something was wrong. This wasn't going to be easy.

After dinner, the Chamber president approached Sherry. "I couldn't help noticing how you managed to introduce yourself to everyone before dinner. Very impressive! But I think it would be wise for you to slow down a little. This isn't a real estate open house, you know."

The president's words stung. On the way home, Sherry's eyes welled up and she pounded the steering wheel in frustration. What had she done wrong? How could she rectify the situation? What changes would you recommend to Sherry to turn her into a master prospector through networking?

Chapter 7 Footnotes

1. Farber, Barry. "Get On Track." Entrepreneur (February 2003): 138.
2. N.A. "Why Sales Leads Fall Through The Cracks, And How SFA Can Make The Difference." Customer Interaction Solutions (July 2006).

3. Nanavati, Akshay. "15 Psychological Triggers to Convert Leads into Customers." Kissmetrics.com, accessed October 4, 2015. Web.

4. Beveridge, Dirk. "Qualifying Your Prospects." The American Salesman 36, no 6 (June 1991): 6-9.

5. Meyer, Paul J. Sales Training Material for Distributors of SMI International, Inc. (Waco, TX).

6. Prashad, Sharda. "Tailored Sales Pitches Work Best." Toronto Star (October 20, 2005).

7. Gergaghty, Shauna. "7 Secrets to Prospecting Using Social Networks." TalkDesk.com. February 19, 2014. Web.

8. *Neilson. "Global Trust in Advertising and Brand Messages." Nielsen's Global Trust in Advertising Survey, April 10, 2012.*

9. Cates, Bill. "Referrals 101." Selling Power (October 2000): 56.

10. Twining, Michael. "Million To Win." Selling Power (March 2000): 50.

11. *Vaynerchuk, Gary. "How Will Twitter Monetize?" GaryVaynerchuk.com, Accessed November 1, 2015. Web.*

12. *Hibma, Maggie. "Got 5 Minutes? Use It to Find a New Prospect on Social Media." Posted on Hubspot Blogs, September 24, 2013. Web.*

13. *Bretbarth, Wayne. "LinkedIn Infographic: Want To Know What Others Are Doing?" Infographic posted on PowerFormula.com, March 4, 2012. Web.*

14. *The 2015 Digital Marketer: An Experian Marketing Services Benchmark and Trend Report. Experian Marketing Services. Published 2015.*

15. *Weiss, Wendy. "A "Warm Calling vs. Cold Calling" Rant." BusinessKnow-How.com, Accessed July 24, 2015. Web.*

16. Stewart, Irby F. "Golden Opportunities." Selling Power (March 2001): 62.

17. Fenn, Donna. "10 Ways to Get More Sales from Existing Customers." Inc.com, August 21, 2010.

18. Adedia.com staff. "A well designed website can be your personal sales assistant." www.adedia.com, accessed May 25, 2015.

19. Internet Marketing Strategy Diva. "Tips for creating successful sales websites." Internetmarketingstrategydiva.com, accessed April 27, 2015.

20. www.google.com/adsense, accessed June 14, 2015.

21. *Seminar from Sanford Institute of Philanthropy, "Basic Data Analysis and Data Gathering for Fundraisers," January 2015.*

CHAPTER 8

PREAPPROACH & TELEPHONE TECHNIQUES

OVERVIEW

The previous chapter introduced you to some of the best prospecting methods available to you in the world of professional selling. This chapter has been designed to build on that material, and then take it a step further to help you get the most out of your prospecting efforts. In this chapter, we will discuss the process of gathering preapproach information and present telephone techniques that will help you have more success in scheduling that critical first appointment with a prospect.

OBJECTIVES

- Learn the goals of the preapproach and the planning needed to make it effective.
- Study how to prepare for an effective preapproach.
- Understand how the preapproach fits into the sales cycle as an extension of prospecting, including the power of social media in the preapproach phase.
- Discover effective methods for making telephone calls that are successful in leading to presentations.
- Understand the six-step telephone track and how to use it to make appointments.
- Learn some of the best ways to follow up with prospects after the call.

FINDING THE RIGHT PROSPECTS

See enough people. See the *right* people. See them at the *right* time.

That course of action sounds logical enough—but the pivotal part of this advice is the "right people." How can you be sure that you are investing your time in calling on qualified prospects? The answer lies in your diligence in collecting information about the leads you record in your prospecting system.

Collecting the right information takes time and effort, but with practice, it will become a regular part of your daily life as a salesperson. For example, when someone gives you a referral, ask questions to learn what you need to know about that prospect. Research the prospect's business or industry and the company itself. Find that person on the social media sites and see what his or her profiles reveal about the individual's personality, tastes, and tendencies. Discover personal information that will help you know what kind of personality to expect. The various activities that provide this necessary personal and business information are called presale planning or the *preapproach*.

The preapproach is the planning and preparation done prior to actual contact with the prospect. In gathering such information, you learn who to call, why, when, and where. Seemingly insignificant details might be the key to the approach that spells the difference between a sale and a no-sale. Leave nothing to chance.

The sales cycle is a continuous process with no clear break between one phase and the next. In practice, you cannot separate the prospecting, preapproach, approach, and need discovery elements into different segments; rather, they blend together and become one. They are discussed separately for convenience, but the exact point where one phase ends and the next begins will likely never be the same. Exhibit 8.1 illustrates the absence of clear dividing lines between these steps in the relationship selling process, and it also shows that it is possible to discover that your lead is a qualified prospect at any point in time during the process.

EXHIBIT 8.1 FOUR PHASES OF THE SALES PROCESS

The numerous types of selling vary so widely that few broad generalizations can be made about the amount of preapproach information to gather. Depending on the type of selling in which you engage and the product or services being sold, the preapproach differs considerably. *At times, qualifying prospects can only be accomplished during the approach and need discovery process by asking questions, observing, listening, and interpreting verbal and nonverbal signals.*

PREPARING TO WIN

Before engaging in the actual presentation, you must analyze all the information you have available to you about a prospect to understand as much about him or her as possible. Then, during the preapproach phase, try to understand the prospect's current needs, current use of brands, and feelings about the competition.

In addition, you must identify decision makers, review account histories, assess product needs, plan a sales presentation to address the identified concerns of the prospect, and set call objectives. Salespeople also develop a preliminary strategy for the sales process during this phase, keeping in mind that the strategy may have to be refined as they learn more about each prospect.[1]

The type and quality of information uncovered during the preapproach is vital. Just as students dislike doing homework after school, many adults have a similar aversion to the groundwork and prefer to skip ahead to the "real work." However, the preliminary steps are a must. Successful sales professionals rarely even make a cold call without some sort of preparation.[2] When they are ready for a formal sales call, professional salespeople have studied and analyzed the prospect's personality, company, operations, needs, and financial position.

One of the most thorough ways to prepare is to develop a checklist of questions to answer before you make a sales call. Exhibit 8.2 presents a checklist designed to help gather the essential sales information you need before you are face-to-face with a prospect.

EXHIBIT 8.2 PREAPPROACH INFORMATION CHECKLIST

- √ What business is the company in? What are its products and markets? Who are its primary customers?
- √ How big is the company? Where does it rank within its industry? Can this company give me enough business to make this call worthwhile?
- √ Who is the ultimate decision maker in buying my product?
- √ Who else influences the buying decision?
- √ How often does this company buy my type of product or service?
- √ How well is the company satisfied with its present supplier of similar products?
- √ What plans does the company have that could affect its future need for my product?
- √ What are the background and personal interests of each person concerned in the buying decision?
- √ Is the company's staff technically informed? Can I help them develop greater expertise?
- √ Do we (or can we) use their products or services in our company?
- √ Do any of our top executives know any of their executives personally?

Prepare for the Presentation

Do your research to find out about the prospect and develop a purpose for the call, linked to a potential client benefit. Set a goal for each contact with a prospect, know what you want to accomplish, and how you plan to do it. There is much more to preparation than simply gathering and reviewing information. Rehearsal eliminates the stammering, nervous speech habits, and repetition that can result from lack of preparation.

Allow time in your daily schedule to prepare the sales approach and presentation you will use in each call. Decide how you can make the best possible use of sales literature and other tools provided by your company in this specific call. Review company websites and the personal profiles of your contacts on LinkedIn or other social media sites. Plan how to incorporate visual aids into your approach and presentation for maximum effectiveness.

When preparing for a presentation, making a video of your sales talk allows you to see how you really look. Webcams and smartphones make self-video easier than ever. Video also allows you to hear your use of "non-words" such as um, uh, and you know. Here are some rehearsal tips:[3]

- Practice your presentation with specific customers in mind.
- Video presentations to show sales reps their strengths and weaknesses.
- Make large, exaggerated motions until you feel comfortable making more natural-looking gestures.

Visualize Successful Selling

Salespeople can learn a great deal from the training habits of world-class athletes. Many track stars use visualization techniques to help them focus on a specific event. An integral part of their training consists of what are called "mental toughening sessions." They run the race over and over in their minds. Over a ten-year period, Edwin Moses won 122 consecutive races in the 400-meter hurdles. His power of visualization became so acute that when he mentally visualized hitting a hurdle, he actually felt the pain in his leg.

To further illustrate how powerful visualization can be, consider this amazing example. After the Vietnam War, a reporter interviewed an Air Force captain who had been a prisoner of war for over seven years. The former POW had just played a superb game in a golf tournament. When the reporter mentioned his surprise at the captain's skill after so long an absence, the captain said, "I've played this course perfectly for the last seven years." The reporter replied, "I thought you hadn't played golf in the last eight years." The captain said, "Well, actually I haven't physically played the game in the last eight years. However, for the last seven years in my cell as a POW I have been playing this course mentally."[4]

You can practice this same type of mental exercise. Positively affirm the feeling you want to create and visualize the outcomes you want to obtain. Think about what you will say and anticipate the prospect's responses. Create a mental image of the desired results, and then live it over and over in your mind. Practice out loud; your mind believes the sound of your own voice. *Remember that your mind cannot separate a real experience from an imagined one.*

SOURCES OF PREAPPROACH INFORMATION

When you know what information you need, you can identify a number of valuable sources for obtaining it. The information you gather will help you get in to make a presentation as well as guide you in preparing a strategy for the interview itself. For example, you can ask colleagues on your company's sales team for information they have on particular prospects. Current customers are also excellent sources of information, and they may be happy to share what they know. The quickest way to gain information these days is to consult online search engines, industry websites, and social media profiles. In most cases, there is nothing wrong with calling on prospects without an appointment. At the very least, a cold call gives you the opportunity to learn something that validates them as, at least, partially qualified prospects. You cannot predict the most beneficial sources of information, so keep your eyes and ears open so you won't miss a great opportunity![5]

Here's a useful tip—read magazines and newsletters that are related to your customer's industry. You likely read publications that are pertinent in your field, so your clients probably also read publications relevant to their fields. You can also subscribe to email newsletters and updates from companies and organizations in your client's industry. This is a great way to uncover ideas to serve their needs better. However, just researching and reading are not enough. You must know what to look for.[6] Here are six items to consider that may give you valuable information:

1. **Mergers.** Will new alliances give you better opportunities to see companies that have denied you access in the past?
2. **Personnel Changes.** Watch for new appointments by your customers, prospects, and competitors.
3. **Changing Product Lines.** Firms that drop or add products may be suggesting a new emphasis that gives you a reason to call.
4. **Advertising Plans.** Have your competitors or customers changed advertising agencies? Are they creating a new approach or pushing certain products? New advertising campaigns or revamped websites may signal a change in the company that elicits the use of your product.
5. **Online, TV, and Magazine Ads.** Online ads, television commercials, and print ads are a source of invaluable clues. Look at the features being stressed and the image being portrayed.
6. **Sales Training.** The news media highlights new sales training endeavors. Is your customer or prospect developing a sales training program of which you can make use?

Excellence in selling requires a keen awareness that the hardest work takes place during the preapproach, but all that hard work leads to the desired end result—a yes. You must be prepared to answer the questions that are in the minds of prospects when you first contact them. Exhibit 8.3 lists ten questions that buyers have, although they don't often volunteer to ask you these questions.

EXHIBIT 8.3 TEN QUESTIONS YOUR PROSPECTS ARE WONDERING

1. What are you really selling?
2. Why do I need it?
3. Who is your company and are they reputable?
4. How much will it cost?
5. Who else is using it, and are they satisfied?
6. What kind of a person are you?
7. Is your price truly competitive?
8. How does your solution compare to the alternatives?
9. Why do I need it now?
10. What is your record for support and service?

Building Self-Confidence

A beneficial feature of preapproach planning is that it builds personal self-confidence. Knowing that you are prepared gives you an added measure of self-confidence that is transmitted to the prospect. The opposite of this confidence is fear, and fear comes primarily from the unknown.

A definite plan for each prospect means you are more likely to be accepted. A purchasing agent for a large, international food processing plant who sees many salespeople described his reactions like this:

> *I turn away salesman after salesman because they come in like lost sheep. They hope that somehow they'll stumble into an order. I get the impression that they figure I'll do the selling for them. I haven't got time for people like that.*

Salespeople call on professional buyers whose job is to make sound purchasing decisions for their companies. These professionals expect to interact with another professional, not an unprepared amateur. If you walk confidently into the buyer's office and get down to business immediately without wasting the prospect's time with unnecessary questions, you increase the likelihood of a successful close. And by emitting an air of self-confidence, you add to your perceived value.[7]

SETTING UP THE SALES INTERVIEW

Preapproach involves doing research, studying a company's website, and discovering other companies with whom they currently do business. It also encompasses the methods used to set up the face-to-face interview itself. There is more to consider than simply picking a day and time. Below are some factors that must be addressed and thoroughly planned to ensure you walk into the most ideal situation when you meet with a prospect.

Timing

With a little research, you can determine the best time to call a prospect you have not previously met. For example, Powell Kenney, former vice-president of *Clampitt Paper Company* in Fort Worth, would see salespeople only between 5:30 and 8:30 a.m. each weekday morning. He did not want his regular work routine disrupted by listening to sales presentations.

Ordinarily, sales calls can be scheduled for almost any time during the business day. Like Mr. Kenney, however, most prospects have a time when they are more receptive to your presentation. Some like to see salespeople the first thing in the morning. Others prefer to handle routine matters first. Fortunately, prospects have different preferences to the extent that salespeople can fill the workday with appointments.

If every buyer insisted on appointments before 8:30 a.m., salespeople would be in serious trouble. If a particular prospect does not seem to have a preference for a time of day to see salespeople, try to discover when most salespeople call on this prospect. If most call in the morning, schedule your call for late in the afternoon. Many executives work past 5:00 p.m. and will see you. In fact, they may well appreciate your diligent work ethic.

Gaining Entry

Before you can arrange a face-to-face meeting, you must choose a way to contact the prospect and set up the interview. Appointments can be set up in several basic ways. You may send an email requesting an appointment, make contact through the appropriate social media, call on the company in person, or telephone the prospect and schedule a specific time and date for the interview. Writing an email for an appointment may not produce an answer or may require several contacts to set a mutually convenient time. Unscheduled visits have a low probability of finding the prospect available for an interview.[8] Often times, it requires a combination of several methods to get an agreement to meet.

With email, texting, and social media replacing phones now more than ever, it's getting tougher to set up a meeting in the first place.[9] But the telephone still works with a little diligence. Often times, you will have to wade through a complex automated system, but eventually, you will get through to someone. After you make contact, in many cases, a few minutes are all that are required to make an appointment. Using the telephone successfully requires the same basic selling skills as a face-to-face call, plus some additional skills to meet the special challenges of telephone use. Finding a prospect in a bad mood or under a time constraint, the surprise element of a call, and the lack of visual contact are some of the elements that may prevent you from feeling as comfortable with the telephone as you do in a personal contact.

Before you see the king, you have to get across the moat.

GATEKEEPERS. In an ideal world, you could just pick up the phone or drop by a prospect's office and reach the decision maker right away. But that's not how it works. There is often something standing in your way—or more like *someone*. You find yourself talking to a gatekeeper, someone who is trained to screen out unwanted sales calls or anything else that would waste the boss' precious time.

You've probably heard that to get past gatekeepers, you have to "soften them up." But a friendly smile and a little charm will only get you so far. And for many gatekeepers, engaging them in small talk is the kiss of death. It tells them you're attempting to distract them, and they quickly shut you down.

You've got to give gatekeepers the credit they deserve. Statistics show that the majority of them have significant influence over the purchase of certain products and services. *That is why it is a mistake to view them as barriers to overcome.* In reality, they could just be your greatest allies. Exhibit 8.4 outlines six ways to build rapport with gatekeepers.[10]

EXHIBIT 8.4 BUILDING RAPPORT WITH GATEKEEPERS

1. **Adjust Your Attitude.** Gatekeepers appreciate respect, and they can recognize insincerity.
2. **Honesty Is the Best Policy.** Don't lie to increase your chances of seeing their boss. Gatekeepers will inevitably discover your falsehoods, and once this happens the possible sale has ended before it has begun.
3. **Sell to the Gatekeeper.** Gatekeepers have influence over buying decisions. So if you show them how their company can benefit by using your product or service, the chances of you making the final sale increase.
4. **Question Gatekeepers.** Ask them what are the needs and goals of their company, and they just might be willing to tell you.
5. **Be Thoughtful.** Remember to thank gatekeepers for their help, but also remember special occasions such as birthdays and holidays. Don't go overboard, and don't use these gifts as payoffs. Gatekeepers are intelligent and know what's going on.
6. **Be Patient.** It may take longer than you expect to get through the door, but if you keep your patience and persistence, a positive outcome is the result.

Being charming and friendly with gatekeepers isn't enough. **What you need is *substance.*** Don't assume that a gatekeeper doesn't want to hear or wouldn't be able to understand what you have to say. ***Be ready to interact on the same level with gatekeepers.*** Treat them as equals and send the message that you respect them. Who knows? They may even do some of the work for you and make your case in front of their boss.

PREAPPROACH AND SOCIAL NETWORKING

The extent to which social media plays a powerful role in business today is astounding—but increasing your social media presence by no means guarantees results. In order to be able to use your social networking accounts as viable sources of preapproach information, it means that potentially qualified prospects have to be among your friends, networks, and followers. Use the following tips for maximizing the reach of effectiveness of LinkedIn, Twitter, Facebook, and other sites to boost your preapproach efforts.

Get Selectively LinkedIn

LinkedIn is the largest *professional* network in the world, and there is great benefit to be had if it is used correctly. To get the full benefit of LinkedIn for reaching prospects, salespeople need to be able to count on *all* of the people in their network. In other words, the people in your network actually matter (as opposed to the people who "like" your Facebook Fan page). Sometimes, that means turning down invitations to connect on LinkedIn, which is an unappealing thought to many people. It may be tough, but quality over quantity matters, especially on LinkedIn. When it comes to deciding whom to include in your LinkedIn network, here's a good rule of thumb:

If you would never pick up the phone and call a person, do not add that person to your LinkedIn network.

LinkedIn has a wealth of information for conducting research on potential clients. It's like a giant qualified prospect database just waiting to be utilized. The information on prospects' profiles (and the people in their own networks) can provide you with valuable clues on how best to appeal to them. You can also use this social network to determine who in your company's sphere of influence can introduce you to a prospect.[11] So, know who you are connecting with rather than blindly accepting all requests, and steer clear of the automated requests that send a generic invitation like: "Mrs. X would like to connect with you on LinkedIn." It's much more effective to send a personal note along with the invitation.

Get to the Point on Twitter

Twitter can do some great things for salespeople who take the time to understand what it can do and what it cannot do. Twitter was created as a way to share short messages as a "micro-blog," a mini-posting of useful information that is limited to 140 characters. The platform is so popular because it gives people a way to keep in touch with important ideas and people, and companies without having to read overwhelming amounts of text.

But to measure success by your number of Twitter followers would be a mistake. So much of the advice available today is all about increasing your followers. But again, it's important to consider quality, not just quantity. Do you have the *right* followers? Services like *Klout.com* try to measure influence not just by how many followers you have, but whether those followers actually interact with you.[12] Do they re-tweet your messages? Or are they just following you in the hopes you'll follow them so their numbers look big to *their* audiences? Look for followers who talk about things that are relevant to your business or some other connection, and those are the connections really worth having and learning more about.

Inspire Through Your Facebook Page

Most people are familiar with the power of Facebook, but what some don't realize is that one of the most common barriers to getting the most out of Facebook is setting up the wrong type of account. If you don't get it right the first time, you'll find yourself making a mass post later down the line asking all your hard-earned followers to switch accounts. If you join Facebook for the first time, you will initially be setting up an *individual* account. Once you're registered, you can then set up a group or page. *Groups* are largely old news, although they do have some extremely useful features such as allowing you to email all members and make the group private. *Pages* are the way forward for most organizations. It's a lot simpler than a group, anyone can 'like' a page to show their support, and anyone can read what you're posting, with or without being a fan or liking your page.[13]

Work the characteristics of each of these sites to your advantage by approaching new contacts on LinkedIn, for example, via previously established professional connections in your industry and by interacting on a more informal basis with prospects through Twitter and Facebook. Once rapport has been built, interaction can be carried over from one site to another.

The door is wide open for social media to become a powerful tool for approaching new clients. As with approaching potential customers in person, on the telephone, or through email, advance research and self-confidence can go a long way toward showing people that you understand their needs and that you are offering a product or service they would benefit from.

TELEPHONE TECHNIQUES

Direct marketing expert Bob Stone defines telemarketing in this manner:

Telemarketing utilizes sophisticated telecommunications and information systems combined with personal selling and servicing skills to help companies keep in close contact with present and potential customers, increase sales, and enhance business productivity.

It is a marketing discipline that uses telecommunications technology as part of a well planned, organized, and managed marketing program that prominently features the use of personal selling, using non-face-to-face contacts.

Proper telephone usage helps you qualify prospects, budget time, and save money. In addition, good telephone techniques enhance your image and precondition the prospect to receive you favorably. Phoning for an appointment implies that you are courteous and considerate of the prospect's time. The initial phone call helps to create a selling situation because, just by agreeing to see you, the prospect tacitly indicates interest in your product or service.

Getting the Appointment: A Mini Sale

You must regard the use of the telephone to set up appointments as a true sales activity and not just a necessary evil. You must also remember what you are selling. The mini-sale is selling the prospect on the idea of giving you an appointment; your purpose is not to sell your product or service on the telephone.

You can make a large number of inquiries in a fraction of the time it takes to make personal visits. You will likely find that personal visits made with an appointment not only reduce waiting time, but prospects will be more receptive because those who are not really interested do not schedule appointments.

Making First Impressions

The quality of your voice, the hesitation in your voice, the volume, and the strength of your speaking style all convey an image to another person. Do you come across as being sincere, honest, confident, strong, knowledgeable and likable? If you sound weak and tentative or use words like *well*, *sort-of*, *maybe*, or *perhaps*, that says to the prospect, "I'm not sure that this is going to a good investment of time for you." Some people even include phrases like, "*Well, to be honest with you*," which says to the prospect that you aren't always honest.

THE #1 MISTAKE. Even more common than using weak words is another mistake. In fact, it's the most common mistake salespeople make over the phone (and in person): *Making it all about you (and not the prospect).* Consider how you would react to this type of telephone call:

Hi, I'm Leonard, and I was born and raised on Long Island. I've been working here for almost ten years, and these guys are like my second family. Before I worked here, I lived abroad for a few years, which, as you can imagine was amazing! But I knew I couldn't start a family over there, so I came back here and started my own company before I...

We are hard wired to seek out people who are interested in us. Your prospects are no exception to this. So, when you start off the call with who you are and what you do, it triggers their *flight response*, and they will be scheming for ways to end the call as soon as possible.

THE #2 MISTAKE. Cold calling is *not* totally a numbers game. And when you "smile and dial" up someone about whom you know absolutely nothing, you've probably just blown a potential sale. If possible, don't make a phone call to someone you know nothing about. Use all of the preapproach tools available to you: Websites, press releases, social media, anything!

THE #3 MISTAKE. Don't ad lib your calls. YOU NEED A SCRIPT. It takes skill to disarm someone in fifteen seconds or less, so you have to prepare and then practice so it doesn't sound scripted.

People buy from the people they like. Remember you're projecting your personality over the phone.[14] How you say something can be as important as what you say. Put a smile in your voice and the prospect can literally hear it. The most successful salespeople project positive voice qualities such as sincerity, courtesy, and confidence.

Evaluate Your Telephone Voice

Your voice makes an immediate impression that can portray you as friendly or distant, confident or timid, spontaneous or mechanical, and relaxed or nervous. So, how do you come across over the phone? Make a recording of yourself while on the phone and evaluate the following attributes:

PITCH. In normal speech, pitch varies. These variations are known as *inflection*. The more inflection you use, the more interesting your tone of voice becomes. Keep in mind that when you are under emotional stress, the pitch of your voice will tend to rise and become shrill or strained. Watch it! The pitch of your voice is a gauge of confidence and poise.

VOLUME. Check the volume or loudness of your voice. You may even get a friend to help you determine this. Is it too soft or too loud? Often when people are tired or upset, their voices fade, and they will be asked to speak up. Be sure to speak loud enough to be heard, but not so loud that you sound overly forceful.

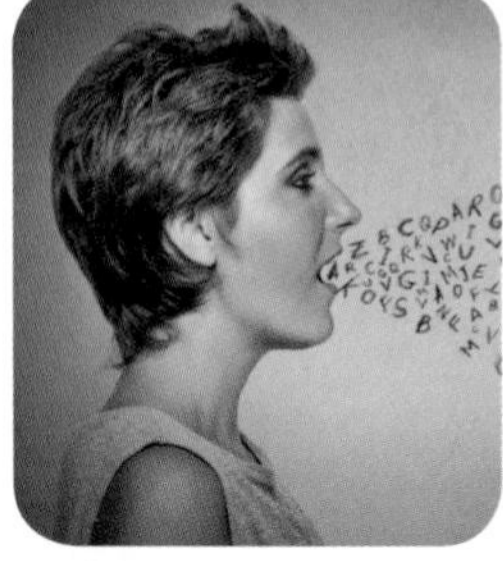

RATE. If you speak too slowly you'll likely lose the attention of the listener. Conversely, your listener won't be able to follow you if you speak too rapidly. In either case, your message won't get through.

QUALITY. The quality of your voice is its most distinctive and individual characteristic. This is where the essence of warmth, understanding and "likeability" come into play. Smiling as you speak enhances your vocal quality. Being angry, upset, or in a hurry negatively affects your vocal quality.

ARTICULATION. The price of poor articulation is high, particularly in business. You must enunciate your words very clearly or your listeners will misunderstand you. Faulty articulation and incorrect word pronunciation give your listener the impression that you are sloppy, careless, and lack knowledge.

The telephone is one of the most powerful, efficient, and cost-effective business tools you have at your disposal. Telephone manners and etiquette are critical components of a professional image. Through experience, you'll develop your own telephone style.

Organizing the Call

Inadequate preparation reduces the effectiveness of your delivery. Ask yourself these four questions to help you stay on track:[15]

1. **Why am I calling?** Do you want to make an appointment, check on a customer's need to reorder, or follow up an inquiry?
2. **What is my proposal?** Your plan should have two parts: 1.What do you want from the person you call, and 2. What commitment you will make. Jot down some notes and be specific!
3. **What would make this person want to grant my request?** Before calling, determine why the person you are calling will do what you request.
4. **How does my telephone script sound?** Identify those key words or phrases in your telephone sales call that you can emphasize to make your message more convincing and sincere.

Before you ever pick up the phone, go through a mental checklist to ensure that you are fully prepared. Exhibit 8.5 presents ten strategic checkpoints to consider when you are preparing to use the telephone to set up appointments.

EXHIBIT 8.5 SECRETS TO BECOMING A TELEPHONE SUPERSTAR

1. Arrange a specific time each day to telephone. Determine a specific number of calls to make during that time period.
2. Arrange for privacy to avoid interruptions. Make as many calls as you can in the allotted time.
3. Develop a well-written, structured script. Know exactly what to say before you call. However, never make your call sound like a canned spiel. You can avoid sounding canned by doing one thing—practice, practice, practice!
4. Verify that you are actually talking to the person that you intended to call. Be sure you have the correct pronunciation of the name. Use the name several times during the call.
5. Tell the prospect just enough to get the appointment. You know a lot more than you need to tell at this time. Just peak his interest so that he agrees to a meeting.
6. Show excitement and enthusiasm in your voice. Give your voice the emotional feel of shaking hands over the telephone. Put a smile in your voice. You can even try placing a mirror by the phone to watch your expression.
7. Never argue; be sure to ask for the appointment. Always offer a choice of times so prospects can choose a time that is convenient for them.
8. Sell your own name. Ask the prospect to write it down so you are remembered when you arrive for the appointment.
9. Be courteous. Say thank you and begin sentences with phrases like, "May I ask ..." and "If I may...."
10. Watch your language. Choose your words carefully for greater impact. Repetition of nonfunctional expressions like, "I see," "uh huh," "you know," and "fantastic" are irritating and unprofessional.

Dealing with Voicemail

Voicemail is a part of sales. Maybe prospects are away from their desk and not able to answer the phone. If you do get voicemail, make sure you're prepared to leave a message. When you leave a message, don't give too much information that will allow prospects to make up their mind about your product or service. Have a call to action in your message and give them a specific reason to call back that will interest them. Here are a few other voicemail tips:[16]

1. Give your phone number twice. This way if the listener doesn't write it down the first time, he or she gets a second chance without having to repeat the message.
2. Try to avoid leaving messages on a Friday afternoon because messages left at this time are the least likely to be returned.
3. Monday mornings can also be a bad idea for voicemail as higher priorities demand attention, and your call may not be one of them.
4. Some of the best times to leave a voicemail are 7 AM to 8 AM and 4:30 PM to 6:30 PM.

THE SIX-STEP TELEPHONE TRACK

The key to using the telephone effectively is to engineer conversations that sound like normal talk. They have to be two-sided, but simultaneously get people to sell themselves on seeing you. When you try to set an appointment by phone, you don't have the advantage of being able to show your prospect what a great product you offer. Instead, you need a careful strategy that allows the prospect to take an interest in what you're saying and agree to meet with you face-to-face. Use the six-step outline in Exhibit 8.6 to plan your appointment-setting calls so that the next time you talk to prospects, you're sitting face-to-face with them.

EXHIBIT 8.6 THE SIX-STEP TELEPHONE TRACK

STEP 1	STEP 2	STEP 3	STEP 4	STEP 5	STEP 6
Introduce Yourself and Your Company	Provide a Tangible Benefit	Personalize the Call	Take the Pressure off the Call	Overcome Resistance	Request an Appointment

1

Step 1: Introduce Yourself and Your Company

Most sales relationships depend heavily on initial impressions. When you place a call, the prospect will most likely make a judgment about you before your first twelve words are said.[17] How you introduce yourself, therefore, and what you say immediately thereafter are of vital importance. A weak or tentative opening puts you at a severe disadvantage throughout the rest of the call. Your opening words should be simple and to the point. They should simply tell who you are, who you represent, and confirm that you are speaking to the correct person:

Good morning, I'm Monica Johnson with Bandito Plastics. Am I speaking with Mr. Eric Stone? Good!

Smile as you speak so that you transmit a warm, friendly personality. Watch the rate at which you speak. Prospects instinctively pay more attention to someone who speaks at a moderate and energetic rate.

2 Step 2: Provide a Tangible Benefit

A phone call is an interruption of your prospect's work. To sell people on the idea of granting you an appointment, you must detach their attention from what they were doing or thinking when the phone rang and attract it to what you propose. That's why you've got to give them a *REAL* reason to stop and listen. Follow your introduction with a brief but hard-hitting benefit for listening to you. Give just enough to capture the prospect's attention, but short of describing full details of any benefit(s) you will present later in person:

...I'm calling because we've recently helped a number of shipping companies like Titan Transport decrease their packing costs by as much as twenty percent...

Notice in the above example that Monica mentioned another client—and a competitor—*Titan Transport*. The mention of one of their competitors (or anyone in their field) will help bring the prospect into the conversation by introducing the thought, *"Oh, xyz company is working with this person..."* Just make sure you know that the prospect is familiar with the person or company you mention.

If you were calling someone because of a referral, this would also be a good time to mention the person who referred you to this prospect. A respected referral source is often enough to get the prospect to hear you out during this initial telephone call. Then you must generate enough interest to motivate the prospect to agree to give you an appointment. Here is an example of how to use a referral in this step:

We recently started working with Reynolds International, and we were able to reduce their outbound freight costs by 22 percent last month. The CEO, Murphy Reynolds, was so thrilled with the results that she asked me to get in touch with you and see whether we might also be helpful to you.

3 Step 3: Personalize the Call

The next step is where all of that preapproach you have done up to this point comes to good use! You must now personalize the call by using information from your preapproach research. In this example, Monica learned about the company's recent margin pressures from an article in an industry-specific magazine. According to the article, strong air cargo volume on Asia-U.S. routes in the last quarter has placed significant pressure on international shipping businesses like the prospect's company, forcing them to drastically increase volumes at lower profitability rates just to keep their heads above water. Now, she needs to present that information in a way that converts attention into interest and lets the prospect know that she is actually aware of his company's situation (indicating this isn't "just another cold call"):

...Now, I know that at your company and others, there is tremendous pressure on margins these days, especially in the last quarter...

The inclusion of this impactful, concise fact answers the all-important and unspoken question in the mind of every single one of your prospects: *"WHAT'S IN IT FOR ME?*[18] After you have established a legitimate purpose for the call, you are ready to move to the next step.

Step 4: Take the Pressure off the Call

Monica has done a good job of making interesting and personalized statements, but the work is not over yet. Now it's time to take the pressure off the call and get permission to continue. Never assume that it's okay to forge ahead. Make it simple and to the point:

...May I ask you a few questions to see if there's any chance we could help your company as well?

Ultimately, the key point that Monica successfully conveyed is that she is looking for a problem she **MIGHT** be able to solve. She disarmed her prospect by letting him know that she only wanted to ***"see if there's any chance"*** that what she had to say could help his business.

5

Step 5: Overcome Resistance

Using the telephone to set up appointments gives rise to two types of objections: *An objection to receiving the telephone call and an objection to granting an interview.* A prospect who was engaged in an activity of interest or importance may feel irritated by an interruption and prefer to resume that activity. This prospect's goal is to get you off the phone by refusing to become interested in what you have to say.

If a prospect offers an objection at this point, remind them that there is no pressure to make any kind of decision, and that what you have to say may not even interest them—but it doesn't hurt to check! Here are two examples of how to word such a statement:

Not every company is right for our product. But my clients always tell me they're glad I checked! Do you have a quick minute for us to figure out whether or not it's worth our time to meet in person?

This may or may not be right for your company. When it is a fit, it saves most of my customers close to 20% on their shipping costs and increases their margins. May I ask you a couple of questions to see if this is worth looking into further?

Prospects who do not want to grant an interview often fear that they cannot successfully defend their own ideas or decisions when faced by an experienced salesperson. *They are afraid that they will buy.* Admitting that your product or service really is not right for everyone can overcome this obstacle. *Convey to your prospect that you want to find out together whether or not you can help him or her (and if you can't, then the conversation is over).*

6 Step 6: Request an Appointment

Remember that your goal at this point is to secure an appointment with the prospect so that you can make a complete presentation. If you launch into a full presentation, the prospect can easily say, "I'm not interested" over the phone—and then you have nowhere to go. The conclusion could be much different when you give an excellent presentation in person. So, try the "KISS" approach to setting the appointment: *Keep It Simple, Salesperson!* The telephone itself encourages brevity, so just ask for the appointment confidently and directly.

After you ask another question or two to ensure that the prospect has some interest and saw value in your benefit statement, add this:

Most of my clients agree that it's best to go over the details in person. I know you are busy. To make it easier for you, I can stop by next Monday or Tuesday in the morning for a few minutes. How do those days look on your calendar?

If those days don't work, but the prospect genuinely wants to meet with you, he or she will offer you an alternative. If those days "don't work" because the prospect really does not want to meet with you, then you can circle briefly back around to any *pain points* you learned about the prospect from your preapproach efforts—such as the profit margin pinch that Monica's prospect is currently experiencing—or what you know about his or her industry. If that attempt is also unsuccessful to secure the appointment… well, then you are on to the next call!

"Everything should be made as simple as possible but not simpler."

Albert Eistein

When you combine the six-step telephone approach with confidence and friendliness, you are likely to find yourself getting face-to-face with more responsive and receptive prospects. At the most, this script will take three to four minutes, and that's only if the prospect offers multiple objections, or in a better scenario, shows interest! With the proper preapproach, each call can take its own unique twist and keep you from sounding canned.

You will hear no's, but you will also hear, "Yes, I'd like to meet with you." Persistence is the key—so keep smiling and dialing.

AFTER THE CALL

One of two things will happen on a phone call: *You either got an appointment or you didn't.* Either way, immediate action is required once you hang up the phone. Whether or not prospects agreed to meet with you, reach out within 48 hours telling them it was nice to speak with them, asking more about their business needs, and finding out how you can refer business to each other and help each other's businesses grow.

If the prospect agreed to the meeting, confirm the date and time and send an invitation from your calendar to confirm the meeting. You can also slip something in the mail—a brochure and a thank you note (handwritten of course) are good items to send to prospects who agreed to meet with you. If the appointment is a week or more out on the calendar, there's a greater chance the prospect will cancel on you as the conversation's details and reasons for meeting with you fade from their minds. Keep your ears and eyes out for opportunities to drop in the mail or attach by email a document, resource, or article you found that would be of interest or pertinent to them.

If a prospect did not agree to meet with you, you can still send something to entice them to get on your online mailing list or a flyer about a special promotion. If the conversation was pleasant enough, that "no" may become a "yes" some day with the right follow-up. Here are some other great ways to turn a refusal on the phone into a customer down the road:

TO DO LIST

Follow Up
Follow Up
Follow Up . . .

1. **Add Them to your Database.** Add anyone you speak with to your email database (if appropriate) and make sure they get an email notice within a week or so. Do NOT add them to a mass email newsletter unless they verbally agree to receive it or opt themselves in online.
2. **Make a Creative Impression.** If you're really trying to get their business and you're not getting anywhere, drop by promotional products with your card and brochure or send it in the mail. Make sure your promotional products stand out from your competition and are unique or memorable. However, this can be time-consuming, so reserve this type of activity for the really big prospects.
3. **Plan Year-Round Mailings.** Send out holiday cards not only for Christmas, but also for Easter, the 4th of July, or whichever holidays you prefer—and even on their birthdays. There are many companies who provide card-sending services and will do this for you (for a fee).

Sometimes the best thing you can do is just drop a handwritten note in the mail from time to time. Whether or not a prospect has agreed to meet with you, this simple follow-up can add class and a personal touch.[19] Notes are often more likely to get through to the person than an email or even a phone call.

THE SOCIAL MEDIA CONNECTION

Can You Use Social Media to Follow Up After the Call?

After you connect with a new prospect on the phone, it's important to start deepening that relationship as quickly as possible. Social media is the perfect venue to accomplish this. After a successful (or even unsuccessful) call, it's helpful for your prospects to be able to put a face with the voice they just spoke with on the phone.

Engaging with social media after an initial connection with a new prospect is a fine balance. Come on too strong with your sales pitch and a hard sell and your prospects will go running. Engage too little by only following or visiting their profiles and they'll feel like you are just doing reconnaissance. The easiest way to find this balance is to focus on delivering value. Social media is not the appropriate medium to close a sale, but it is certainly the right place to start or continue one. By providing advice and helpful content, you can open a dialogue and establish yourself as a trusted resource.[20]

SUMMARY

- Planning and preparation are essential to securing an appointment for a personal sales interview.
- Your preapproach planning may utilize cold calls designed to meet the prospect and request an appointment, an email to introduce yourself and your company, contact through social media, or a telephone call to request an appointment.
- The attempt to set up a sales interview is a mini sale in which the product is a live sales interview, and the purpose of the phone call is to sell the prospect on the idea of granting that interview.
- The six-step telephone track for making appointments includes: Introduce yourself and your company, provide a tangible benefit, personalize the call, take the pressure off the call, overcome resistance, and request an appointment.
- Save the detailed description of your product and its benefits for the actual face-to-face meeting. Keep the telephone discussion focused solely on getting the appointment.
- After the call, follow up with prospect who agreed to an appointment and with those who did not.

REVIEW QUESTIONS

1. What are the steps to follow in preapproach planning?
2. What information do you need about a prospect before you call to request an appointment for a sales interview?
3. What are the important sources for obtaining information about a prospect?
4. In what way may a telephone call to request an appointment serve to qualify the prospect?
5. What advantages and disadvantages does calling for an appointment present in regard to the first impression you make on the prospect?
6. What is the six-step framework for making a telephone presentation?
7. If the prospect asks you to describe your proposition over the telephone, how would you handle the situation?
8. Who should be in control of the flow of the preapproach telephone call? How do you make sure control is in the proper hands?
9. What ways can social media be used in the preapproach with potential customers?
10. Suppose that you telephone to make an appointment with a prospect. When the assistant answers, you say, "Mr. Steele, please, Joan Gray calling." If the secretary responds, "May I ask the nature of your call?" What answer would you give? If you give your answer and are then told that Mr. Steele is too busy to see you, what do you say then?

IN-CLASS EXERCISES

The following exercises help build teams, improve communication, and emphasize the real-world side of selling. They are meant to be challenging, to help you learn how to deal with problems that have no single right answer, and to use a variety of skills beyond those employed in a typical review question. Read and complete each activity. Then in the next class, discuss and compare answers.

EXERCISE 8.1 – PHONE SCRIPT

The class should be divided into teams of 4 persons each. The primary objective is for each team to write a telephone script for a salesperson who aims to secure an appointment. At the conclusion of the exercise, each team should share their script with the rest of the class either during a regular class session or online in order to receive constructive criticism. Each script should include the following features:

- Description of the caller's business and product or service offered.
- Preapproach analysis of target's business, need for product/service, and person to whom call is directed.
- Use of the 7-step Telephone Track to structure the script.
- Use of the ten buyer questions (Exhibit 8.3) to structure anticipated objections.

Each team's script should be directed toward one of the following situations:

1. Arrange appointment to meet with a new prospect for the first time.
2. Arrange appointment to meet with an existing, dissatisfied customer.
3. Arrange appointment to meet with an existing customer whose order for the product/service is due for renewal.

The first class session, or portion thereof, should be devoted to team discussion of their project and how they want to address it. The actual production of the script should be done outside of class and in a way that team members can consult with one another. A subsequent class session, or portion thereof, should be devoted to critiquing selected scripts.

EXERCISE 8.2 – SCREENING PROSPECTS

For this exercise, pair up with another student in the class. Often, the degree and nature of preapproach planning varies by the general business field. Your task in this role play is for you and your partner to interview a salesperson in financial services (financial planning, insurance, brokerage firm, bank, etc.). Your objective is to learn how this salesperson goes about gathering and using information about prospects prior to approaching them. What information is sought? How? How is the information used to prepare for an initial approach?

If, perchance, no information is sought or no preapproach planning occurs, that, too, is significant information for you! Your next question should be, "Why not?" Jot down the results of your interview and be prepared to report and discuss in class or online.

CASE STUDIES

The following case studies present you with selling scenarios that require you to apply the critical skills discussed in the chapter and give you training through practical learning situations. They are meant to be both engaging and challenging, and like the exercises, don't have one right answer.

CASE 8.1 – CROSSING THE MOAT

Rich Cohen sells paint. Although his job might not sound glamorous to some, he enjoys the challenge since it involves his skills as a chemical engineer as well as a marketer. The problem is that Rich isn't selling as much paint as he used to. And the company's owner is becoming disturbed by the falloff in business. As he recently remarked to Rich, "We need more new business. We can't subsist merely on our existing base, since many of them have cut back because of the recession."

From his extensive preparatory research about prospective clients, Rich knows that many could use his company's product, especially the recently developed exterior paints that stand up to northeastern winters much better. But over the past several months, Rich has developed a rather long list of potential clients with whom he has been unable to arrange an appointment. Once he gets an appointment, Rich is effective, but getting the appointment is another matter.

Recently, over drinks after a tough week, Rich confided in one of his buddies at the company, Millard, who seems to have an easier time generating new business in his territory.

"I don't get it, Millard. Why won't these guys see me? If I get 20 minutes, I can show 'em how to cut down on their do-overs and save themselves a ton of money."

"Well, Rich. I've always said, 'Before you can see the king, you have to get across the moat.'"

"What in the world does that mean?"

"It means that you have to deal with the person who controls the drawbridge. If that person doesn't lower the bridge, you never get to speak to the king."

"And how do I do that? Whenever I call, I can hear the grumpiness on the other end of the phone. And they always bluntly tell me that their boss isn't accepting any calls, is busy, is out of the office, blah, blah, blah."

"Then sell the bridge-keeper, Rich. Once you help that person with their problem, they'll escort you across that bridge and right into the throne room!"

As he drove home, Rich began to develop a plan of action that depended on asking gatekeepers ("bridge keepers") about their problems. Rich figured that if he could make their life a little easier, a little more pleasant, his chances of seeing their boss would improve.

What do you think Rich should include in his plan? What sort of questions should he ask the next administrative assistant to answer his call? How much and what kind of information should Rich provide the assistant? How can Rich demonstrate genuine empathy without offending the all-important bridge-keeper?

CASE 8.2 – GOSSIP OR USEFUL INFORMATION?

"Hey! Guess what I heard?" Running to catch up with Nancy, Hank was out of breath.

"What?" Nancy replied, wishing that Hank would dial it back a little.

"*LongMeadow* is merging with ***LD Mobile Homes***! Do you know what that means?" Hank exclaimed.

"Well, it means that one of our clients is disappearing," Nancy answered. "What else?"

"No, no! You don't get it!" yelled Hank. He was becoming annoying. "We'll now have a shot at LD's business. We've never been able to even get an appointment before."

"What makes you think they'll see us now?" Nancy asked evenly. But her mind was turning. Her insurance company was, perhaps, about to lose a client; instead, she saw an opportunity to gain an even larger account. She wasn't sure how Hank knew about the merger, and she didn't want to know. Now, however, presuming that Hank's outburst was reliable, she needed a plan to turn his gossip into solid information that would elicit an appointment.

What information does Nancy need to gather? Presuming that the merger is still a secret, how should she go about obtaining the information needed to approach LD Mobile Homes? What strategies should she employ? And when should she make her initial approach?

Chapter 8 Footnotes

1. Kenneth L. Fields, "There's no substitute for telephone prospecting," American Agent & Broker. St. Louis: (Mar 2010), Vol. 82, Is. 3, 26.
2. Michael Crom, "How to improve on sales calls," Gannett News Service. McLean: (Sep 28, 2006), 1.
3. Chad Kaydo, "Lights! Camera! Sales!," Sales & Marketing Management (February 1998), 111.
4. Rich Wilkins, "Visualize Your Success," Professional Selling Power, Vol. 13, No. 1 (January/February 1993), 69.
5. Jhan R. Dolphin, "Early Birds: Preparation is key to sales success," Light Truck and SUV Accessory Business & Product News. Fort Atkinson: (Mar 2008), Vol. 21, Is. 2, 14.
6. Kate Maddox, "Lead management takes cooperation," B to B. Chicago: (Dec. 11, 2006), Vol. 91, Is. 17, 3.
7. Jennifer Keim, "Eric Kline: Be a confident sales rep," HME News. Yarmouth: (Oct 2007), Vol. 13, Is. 10, 82.
8. Adapted from John J. Franco, "Ring Up More Telephone Sales with Well- Trained Personnel," Business Marketing, Vol. 71, No. 8 (August 1986), 84; and "Telephone Closes Are Up," Personal Selling Power, Vol. 14, No. 4 (May/June 1994), 20.
9. Susan Greco, "The Need for Speed," Inc., April, 2007.

10. "Getting Past the Gatekeeper," Selling Power (July/August 2000), 56; Jan Gelman, "Gatekeeper," Selling, Vol. 2, No. 1 (July/August 1994), 54-56; and Nanci McCann, "Protocol," Selling, Vol. 1, No. 9 (May 1994), 79; Jack Foster, "Maximizing FACE TIME with Customers," Agency Sales. Irvine: (Jul 2010), Vol. 40, Is. 7, 40.
11. Wallace, Nicole. "How Fundraisers Can Get More Out of LinkedIn." *The Chronicle of Philanthropy*, April 18, 2013.
12. Boland, Steve. "Twitter for Nonprofits: It's Who (Not Just How Many) You Know." *Nonprofit Quarterly*, September 25, 2012.
13. Mansfield, Heather. *Social Media for Social Good: A How-to Guide for Nonprofits*. New York: McGraw-Hill, 2012. Print.
14. Susan McGinnis, "Smart Talk: Make an impression," HME News. Yarmouth: (Feb 2011), Vol. 17, Is. 2, 19.
15. Jeffrey Jacobi, "Voice Power," Selling Power (October 2000), 66.
16. Kamo, Mike. "The Secret To Following Up On Leads Without Annoying Prospects." *Stride*. May 22, 2014.
17. Barry Z. Masser and William M. Leeds, Power-Selling by Telephone (West Nyack, NY: Parker Publishing Company, 1982), 56.
18. John Boe, "Selling is a Contact Sport: Keys to Effective Phone Calling," The American Salesman. Burlington: (Nov. 2010), Vol. 55, Is. 11, 12.
19. Sawa, Katrina. "10 Simple Ways to Follow Up with Prospects." Forbes.com, Accessed October 4, 2015. Web.
20. Salesforce. *The Smart Guide to Successful Social Selling*. Ebook.

PART IV

THE FACE-TO-FACE RELATIONSHIP MODEL OF SELLING

Consider this the "how to" portion of the textbook, the face-to-face segment of the sales cycle. The following chapters are the very heart of professional selling. It is the valuable time spent in the actual sales interview; and it is the time when a commitment is obtained and kept.

What happens in the opening minutes of a meeting is crucial to the overall success of the sales interview, and ***CHAPTER 9*** focuses on those opening moments—the approach. ***CHAPTER 10*** is devoted to the art of asking questions and listening effectively. You will learn critical questioning and listening skills to help carry you through the entire sales interview. The SPIN® Selling technique is explained and dramatized using a practical example. ***CHAPTER 11*** then details techniques to use in the presentation itself. Units of conviction are the building blocks on which to build a meaningful sales presentation, and the five elements that comprise a unit of conviction are both explained and illustrated.

Chapters 12 and 13 present the psychology behind handling objections and closing the sale. You will be introduced to a plan to handle objections, and a portion of ***CHAPTER 12*** explains several ways to deal with the price objection. ***CHAPTER 13*** stresses that closing the sale is the natural conclusion to a successful sales interview.

CHAPTER 9

APPROACHING THE PROSPECT

OVERVIEW

This chapter focuses on the most critical elements of your face-to-face time with prospects, which is the first few minutes—and often the first few seconds—of your encounter. You will learn how to present yourself in a way that builds trust and credibility as we continue to focus on building your reputation as an expert in your field. As the saying goes: ***You've only got one chance to make a great first impression.*** And the approach is your chance to solidify that you and your product or service are the right choice.

OBJECTIVES

- Discover the purpose of the approach.
- Learn the importance of first impressions and ways to control them as a means of improving your performance.
- Understand how nonverbal language affects your ability to establish rapport with a prospect.
- Examine the elements of the greeting and how to control them.
- Discover ways to get the attention and capture the interest of the prospect.
- Explore different types of approaches and the best circumstances in which to use each one.

SETTING THE MOOD

You did your homework, and your prospecting and preapproach efforts uncovered potential clients. You successfully arranged a personal meeting with a prospect. So now what? What happens during the opening of the face-to-face encounter profoundly affects the success of the entire presentation and your ability to get a commitment to buy. The approach is the actual contact the salesperson has with the prospect. More importantly, it is your opportunity to set the mood of the presentation and perhaps even your future relationship with the customer.

This is the point of the selling process where the sales professional meets and greets the prospect, provides an introduction, establishes rapport that sets the foundation for the relationship, and asks open-ended questions to learn more about the prospect and his or her needs.[1] The approach is important because it determines the character of your relationship with a prospect, including how receptive the prospect will be to your presentation and whether the close will be difficult or easy.

Although the overall success of the interview depends on more than the approach, an effective approach creates a favorable buyer-seller environment. The approach is often overlooked or taken for granted. Although the approach is usually considered in the context of the first call on a prospect, every meeting with a new prospect or an established customer includes an approach.

Salespeople tend to use the same approach over and over, but prospects and situations are not the same; instead, salespeople should make a practice of using various types of approaches that fit the needs of a specific situation, whether calling on new prospects or on established customers. An effective approach achieves four key objectives:

1. To make a favorable or positive impression on the prospect.
2. To gain the prospect's undivided attention.
3. To develop positive interest in your proposition.
4. To lead smoothly into the need discovery phase of the interview.

FIRST IMPRESSIONS

In his book, *Contact: The First Four Minutes,* Leonard Zunin says that the first four minutes of initial contact with a prospect are crucial. He suggests that four minutes is the average time the prospect takes to decide whether to buy from you. Others say it takes even less time than that. However long this mental process actually takes, one thing is certain: Prospects start judging you from the moment you walk in the room.[2] Impress the prospect with a show of good manners, clear enunciation, good grooming, and appropriate dress; when you look and act like a professional, the prospect, consciously or subconsciously, begins to trust you. People make quick decisions based on feelings, emotions, or hunches. The more positive their feelings, the more they hear and accept what you say. The opening moments of the approach must be designed to create an atmosphere of trust. The first ten words you speak will reveal volumes about you.[3]

The initial impression you make on a new prospect is much like a homebuyer who looks at the potential home for the first time. Sellers and their realtors go to great lengths to present the home in the best light possible through a process called "staging." Staging things as seemingly insignificant as the optimal location of the furniture and other items in the seller's home can make a difference between a sale or no sale.[4] Remember that this is a business meeting, not a personal lunch with a close friend. You must put your best foot forward from the beginning in order to ensure that the prospect hasn't said "no" in his mind before he ever hears your presentation.

Successful salespeople know how to make other people feel important. It does not matter how knowledgeable they are about their product lines or how many closing techniques they have memorized. Unless they earn their prospect's trust and confidence, they are not going to make the sale—period.

A salesperson must be able to work effectively with a prospect even in the presence of a personality clash. You also have to temper the first impressions you make about a prospect; spend some time and look further before making an unalterable judgment.

There's something about a good initial person-to-person contact that instinctively leads to more sales.

Prospects watch and evaluate virtually every personal characteristic you have, so your approach must be impeccable.[5] Positive first impressions count. Here are some guidelines for making the first impression a favorable one. After all, you never get a second chance to make a good first impression.[6]

YOU GET ONE SHOT... SO MAKE IT COUNT!

Visual Factors

- Correct any detail that could become a visible distraction such as a tattered briefcase, a messy car, or inappropriate grooming.
- Nonverbal communication is powerful. Pay attention to what the prospect sees in your body language as well as in what you wear.
- Don't wear jewelry such as lapel pins, tiepins, or rings that advertise your membership in a specific organization that may not be admired.

Professional Habits

- Be prompt, or even early. Set your watch five minutes ahead if necessary.
- Present a clear agenda. State the purpose of your call right away. Make it clear that you are not going to waste the prospect's time.
- Be prepared with as much information as possible about the prospect (both the individual and company).

Building Rapport

- Pronounce the prospect's name correctly. A person's name is a personal identifier; mispronouncing it takes away some of the owner's status.
- If you pay the prospect a compliment, make it specific and sincere.
- Respect the prospect's personal space.
- Look for common ground like mutual friends, membership in the same religious or civic group, or similar hobbies.
- Be enthusiastic. Enthusiasm is infectious if it is sincere.

Physical Actions

- Shake hands, maintain eye contact, and greet the prospect warmly, but never say, "How are you?" as it may sound contrived and insincere. Instead, open with a more specific greeting, including the use of the prospect's name.
- Refrain from personal habits like smoking or chewing gum, or from using careless language that might be offensive to some people.

Although first impressions may be dependable signposts for the feelings you leave with a prospect, first impressions do have some weaknesses:

1. They are likely to be based on feelings and emotions.
2. All behavior traits do not show up simultaneously, and an initial short interview may not provide enough time for all traits (either favorable or unfavorable) to surface.
3. The prospect may deliberately control behavior and allow you to see only certain chosen personality traits.
4. Some event immediately preceding the interview may strongly influence the prospect's current behavior.

Be willing to wait before you conclude that you and a prospect are experiencing a personality conflict that cannot be overcome. Your job is to establish rapport, build confidence, and make the prospect feel comfortable. Do everything in your power to satisfy the needs of your prospects and refuse to allow first impressions to prevent a mutually beneficial sales experience.

NONVERBAL LANGUAGE

Nonverbal language—including grooming, clothing, accessories, posture, tone of voice, and time and space aspects—vitally affects first impressions, despite the fact that nonverbal factors actually provide limited or shallow insight into the true person. Salespeople must be sure the statements they make with their nonverbal language are favorable because the impressions formed during the first few minutes of an initial encounter between two people will last indefinitely. Successful salespeople increase the odds in their favor by taking advantage of the power of first impressions. *Visual impressions* almost always come first. Fortunately, you can do a lot to shape the visual impact you make when a prospect first sees you.

Projecting an Image

You want your clothes to command respect, inspire credibility and create trust—you must come across as the authority on the product or service that is offered.[7] Your clothes speak volumes about you, your company, your work, and how you relate to customers.

When you know that you are dressed appropriately, you feel good about yourself. When you are confident and at ease, you emanate an air of competence that the prospect unconsciously accepts and interprets as credibility.[8] Total appearance is important because the prospect's initial attention is focused on you and not on your proposition. *If you want to be successful, you must look successful.* A salesperson who wears an ill-fitting, un-ironed suit, for example, creates a negative impression and sets up this line of thinking in the mind of the prospect:

This salesperson is dressed sloppily. He must not be making many sales.

↓

Because he's not making many sales, he must be having difficulty selling his product.

↓

If the product is not selling, something must be wrong with it.

↓

I don't want an inferior product.

LOOK THE PART. We must look the part of a professional to be viewed as one. Lois Frankel, author of the bestselling *Nice Girls Don't Get the Corner Office*, says that research shows about 60 percent of our credibility comes from how we look.[9] Personal appearance and behavior are the easiest areas to address on the road to greater success, yet all too often sales professionals choose to ignore this aspect.

Unspoken rules for appropriate dress extend into every aspect of professional life. When we go to the doctor, we want the doctor to be dressed in a manner that projects his authority and knowledge. Would you trust a surgeon to operate on you who is dressed in shorts and a t-shirt? Of course not! So how can you expect a prospect to buy an expensive product or service if you don't, well, look the part? Dress in such a way that commands respect and credibility; but remember, everything in moderation.

Your objective is to focus the prospect's attention on the benefits of buying your product or service. Anything that detracts from that focus works against you. Whether you are meeting at the prospect's office, your office, a neutral location, or the prospect's home, always look professional. Pay attention to the crispness and cleanliness of your clothing and ensure that you do not look sloppy in any way. Here are two sets of guidelines for appropriate dress that fits many situations. The first is ***business casual***, which is a style of clothing that is less formal than traditional business wear, but is still intended to give a professional and businesslike impression.[10]

The second is ***dressy casual***, which is often confused with business casual. Dressy casual clothing is not all that different from what is typically described as business casual but has a bit more informality. For men, the look is very similar, although the clothing might be more conservative for a business casual event. Women's clothing tends to be a little more dressed up; a nice top and skirt might be worn instead of a suit, for example. A woman might also wear more jewelry than she would for business casual. The nature of the meeting or event should always be considered when choosing an outfit from the following guidelines:

Business Casual for Men:

- Sport coat or blazer with slacks or khakis, all professionally laundered
- Professionally laundered shirt, optional tie
- Polo or Golf shirt (professionally laundered)
- Loafers or loafer-style shoes with dress socks and matching belt

Dressy Casual for Men:

- Seasonal sport coat or blazer, and slacks
- Dress shirt, casual button-down shirt, open-collar or polo shirt
- Suit with or without tie

Business Casual for Women:

- Modest skirt, khakis or pants
- Modest top or sweater
- Conservative dress
- Dress shoes or heels (not flip flops)

Dressy Casual for Women:

- Dress
- Skirt and dressy top
- Dressy pants outfit
- Nice jeans and dressy top

Business casual style is not intended to convey a lack of professionalism, just a more comfortable, perhaps less boring way of projecting one's best. *Professional* is the key word to remember when dressing business casual. Always be aware that you do not dress too casually. Rather, make sure your clothes reflect your position and the message you wish to convey to your clients.

People feel comfortable dealing with those who seem to fit into their own lifestyle. If your clothes are too formal, you may cause the prospect to feel intimidated. On the other hand, if you dress too casually or carelessly, wear distracting jewelry, or have an unusual hairstyle, prospects may unconsciously feel that you do not consider them or this meeting important.

We all have a million things on our mind. For you, one of the big ones is this: "How can I grow my business and my customer base?" For your prospects, they want to know: ***"With all the products and services out there, why should I do business with you when there are ten salespeople in line right behind you?"*** Hopefully, you are ready to answer that question with passion and conviction. But also remember this:

> You are the ambassador of your company, and no matter how much you may think that your product or service sells itself, it is your visual appearance that speaks first.

The Handshake

"Leadership has less to do with position than it has with disposition."
John Maxwell

Your voice inflection and pronunciation and how you shake hands are as important as what you say. Make sure not to inflect your voice up at the end of each sentence; you must project yourself as a leader, not as insecure or apologetic. Confidence signals to the prospect that you believe in what you sell. Do you stand behind what you sell, or are you just trying to pay the rent?

When combined with your tone of voice and facial expression, your handshake reveals to a prospect your mood. The business handshake is an essential selling technique to make a positive lasting impression. When the first handshake with a prospect is a firm one, you'll have the beginning of a strong business relationship.[11] Here are some guidelines for an effective handshake:

SHAKING HANDS LIKE A PRO

"Of course I remember you. You're the salesman with the firm handshake."

- Maintain eye contact for the duration of the handshake.
- You may wait for the prospect to initiate the handshake. (Some people have germ phobias or prefer not to be touched.)
- If your palm tends to be moist, carry a small handkerchief with powder and pat your hand several times just before entering the meeting.
- Apply firm, consistent pressure on the hand and avoid limp-wristed, wet-fish, or bone-crusher handshakes.
- Hands should meet at an equal distance between you and the prospect in a vertical position. If your hand is over the prospect's, this implies dominant intentions. If your hand is on the bottom, you are signaling a submissive nature.

THE PROPER GREETING

In order to increase the odds of making a good impression during the meet-and-greet, use the business etiquette *Rule of Ten*. The first ten words you speak should include a form of thanks: "Good morning, Mrs. Robertson. Thank you for agreeing to see me," or "Good afternoon, Ernie. It's a pleasure to meet you."

Casual questions like *"How are you?"* or *"How ya' doing?"* have lost all semblance of meaning. How does the prospect respond? "Great" or "Just fine, thank you," but what if the prospect is not feeling great and what if business is not going great? If a prospect covers up real feelings with a conventional answer, a vague feeling of uneasiness results from the untruth. When a prospect asks you, "How are you doing," come up with your own unique response delivered with a smile on your face and enthusiasm in your voice. For example, instead of responding with the typical "Fine, Thanks," you can say, "Fantastic!" Your prospects will appreciate your positive attitude (and enthusiasm is a great catalyst for making sales).

A proper greeting isn't just about a friendly face or the proper words, but an appealing surrounding also helps. Sometimes this is out of your control, especially if you are meeting the prospect on his turf. However, if you have the opportunity to select the meeting location, find a spot that is warm and inviting, and one in which you will not have to shout in order to be heard. Salespeople often meet clients at coffee shops. These are great neutral locations and often have free Wi-Fi for presentations done on your laptop or tablet. You may want to avoid coffee shops around the busiest times of the day (early morning and lunch) or outside distractions could diminish any good impression you attempt to make.[12]

THE SOCIAL MEDIA CONNECTION

How Instagram and Facebook Can Make the First Meeting Better

People love posting pictures. It's definitely one of the favorite pastimes for those who are active on social media. There is no limit to the kinds of pictures of people post, from pictures of their family activities to pets, hobbies, favorite destinations, and more (much more). Luckily for a salesperson, these online pictures can be a great clue to how the prospect presents himself or herself. They afford you with a great opportunity to see how a person dresses and what type of attire is most comfortable for him or her. Keep in mind that casual pictures with family don't tell the whole story; instead, look for pictures of the prospect at work or at work functions.

People also love to tag their locations when they post on Facebook. This can be a great clue as to where a prospect likes to have coffee or lunch. If the initial meeting will be at a location outside of the prospect's office, it may be wise to pick a location that you know the prospect enjoys—and social media comments and photos may give you a clue as to some of the best places to meet.

Use of the Prospect's Name

People do not like to have their names forgotten, mispelled (oops, I meant misspelled), or mispronounced. Typically, when we meet someone, we hear our own name, but we may or may not hear the other person's name. If we forget a name or mispronounce it, we send out this message: "I care more about me and my name than I do about you and your name."

Imagine how a prospect feels when you say, *"So you see, Ms. . . . ah . . . uh . . . excuse me (shuffle for prospect card or appointment calendar) uh . . . Mr. Hill, I mean, Lill."* The prospect probably stiffens, the environment turns a bit frosty, and you may well walk out without an order.[13] Now recall how pleased you were when someone remembered your name after just a casual meeting several weeks previously. You would stand in line to do business with such a person.

Improving your memory for names is not as difficult as it may seem. Several books are available to help you devise a method to correct a careless memory for names. Exhibit 9.1 gives some suggestions for remembering names.

EXHIBIT 9.1 HOW TO REMEMBER CUSTOMERS' NAMES

"Remember that a person's name is to that person the sweetest and most important sound in any language."

Dale Carnegie

Pay attention
Ask to have the name repeated (even spelled). It will impress the person.

Concentrate
Look for characteristics that distinguish this person from others.

Associate
Relate a characteristic with some gimmick to help you recall the name.

Observe
Study people regularly to strengthen your ability to see characteristics and practice your imagination.

Repeat
Use the prospect's name several times during the interview.

Small Talk or Get Down to Business

In the initial face-to-face meeting, both parties may experience what might be called *relationship tension*. Prospects fear being sold something they do not want, and salespeople face the fear of being rejected. The opening few minutes of conversation are designed to find a comfort level for both parties so that rapport can be established. The purpose of small talk at the opening of the interview is to gain an advantageous, positive beginning that breaks the ice and eases the tension. Small talk may be a discussion of topics entirely unrelated to what you are selling, but it's not just idle conversation—it's ***chit-chat with a purpose.*** Here are some basic questions that are nonthreatening, easy to answer, and objective:

1. Are you a native of this area?
2. Where did you go to school?
3. What are your favorite weekend activities?

This type of socializing at the beginning of the interview eases tension and may give you some insight into your prospect's behavioral style. It warms up a cold environment and has the side benefit of providing additional information about the prospect. If the prospect seems withdrawn or even hostile, this warm-up conversation helps you determine whether that is the prospect's real personality or whether you have arrived on an especially bad day.

Speaker, trainer, and author James Malinchak teaches his clients this easy and simple rhyme when approaching a new prospect: *"When you meet someone new, they don't want to talk about you."* It's true! People love to tell you what they do in their spare time, talk about their accomplishments, or tell you about their families. So, remember this rhyme and it will remind you to let your prospects and customers talk about themselves or their interests. This non-selling conversation is important. An ideal topic for initial chit-chat is one that relaxes the prospect, is of personal interest, and relates, if possible, to your objective so that you can move easily into the attention getter and then into need discovery.[14]

People have no confidence in salespeople whose only interest is self-interest, who seek to use their clients instead of being of use to their clients.

GETTING THEIR ATTENTION

Getting a prospect's attention is more than a gimmick. Remember at this point prospects are still thinking, "What does this person want with me? Why should I allow my work to be interrupted?" Unless prospects want to listen, they won't—so give them a reason. Just as the newspaper uses a headline to make you take notice, you must also develop an attention getting opening that breaks through their preoccupation and focuses attention on the selling situation. You can use two basic methods of getting attention: *Appealing to the senses and through the introduction of a benefit.*

APPEAL TO THE SENSES. An appeal to the senses gets the prospect involved in the presentation. Be sure to use a little dramatization. Show something the prospect can see; hand the prospect something to hold.

INTRODUCTION OF A BENEFIT. Introduce a benefit by a statement that relates to the prospect's need for your product or service. Highlight the value of the product or service especially in terms of how it may save prospects their most valuable resources— time and money. If you can modify the product to suit your prospect's particular needs, also be sure to outline this option.

Suit the Approach to the Person

Most people today have more work than they can hope to complete during regular working hours. Individual consumers, purchasing agents, engineers—anyone a sales representative might contact—feel time pressure and quite naturally regard you as an intruder. Prospects may react with resentment toward anyone who appears intent upon "stealing" precious time to engage in "small talk." How much or how little time you give to small talk or chit-chat depends on the behavioral style of the prospect, the circumstances of the moment, and the nature of your visit. If you sense that the prospect wants to get on with the interview, move on.

An effective attention-getting statement requires preparation. If you have done your homework in gathering preapproach information, you already know enough to have some idea about both the needs and the behavioral style of the prospect. If you spend a few minutes in small talk you gain further clues to confirm or adjust your preapproach information. Use what you know to plan an effective attention-getting device to introduce the heart of your presentation. Exhibit 9.2 suggests ways to gain prospects' attention by appealing to their behavioral styles during your initial exchange.[15]

EXHIBIT 9.2 USING BEHAVIORAL STYLES TO CHOOSE THE RIGHT APPROACH

Expressive—Open in terms of long-range goals or implications.

Mr. Arnold, I would like to show you how our innovative service will help your department reach its long-term potential.

Analytical—Open in very specific terms.

Mr. Arnold, I would like to give you the background on our service and then list the ways in which I think it will reduce your overhead, increase your productivity, and improve your profit margin by ten percent. (Be prepared to do so.)

Amiable—Open in supportive, people-oriented terms.

Mr. Arnold, I am aware of some of the pressing concerns you must be facing at this time, and I believe our service will help you and your people overcome some of these problems.

Driver—Open in results-oriented terms.

Mr. Arnold, our service will help you increase your sales by fifteen percent in just six months. Are you interested? (Be prepared to prove your statement.)

Build a Foundation of Trust

As the business world grows more complex and information becomes more accessible and more overwhelming, buyers aren't looking for someone with fact-sheet-style knowledge. No one has time for salespeople like that anymore. They want someone who they can trust to lead them through unfamiliar territory.

You have the product and company knowledge you need, but when it comes to gaining attention, and more importantly, *earning trust* during the initial meeting or meetings, it can be a tricky situation. Buyers know that you're there to make a sale. So, how can you convey that you are there to serve *their* interests first instead of your own? To answer that question (and discover the secret ingredient for building trust), let's read about Annie:

> *Annie sells a complex line of cloud computing solutions to small- and medium-sized enterprises. At her first appointment of the day, her prospect Doug cuts to the chase. "Look Annie, I'll be the first to tell you that I don't know much about this technology. In fact, all this cloud stuff is kind of... over my head—pardon the pun."*
>
> *Annie gives a chuckle (it's not the first time she's heard that one) as Doug continues. "You're around the 6th or 7th tech salesperson I've had in here, and so far everyone seems to really good at telling me what their stuff can do. But what I really need to know is what I should do."*

Doug wants someone to tell him what he needs. He doesn't want another lesson on how to convert to cloud servers. How can Annie convince Doug that he can trust her to tell him what to do without him even fully understanding the product?

What is the primary thing standing in the way of Doug trusting Annie (and of your buyers trusting you)? Let's examine this in a different way: There is a personal stylist named Katrina who works in an upscale department store selling designer suits to men. Katrina has already made almost double what the other stylists have made so far this year. We are going to listen in during one of her sessions to find out how she's doing it:

> *Her new customer John just arrived and is contemplating which suit to try on first. As he picks out one of the most expensive suits and holds it up, Katrina touches his arm, slowly and deliberately looks around to make sure no one is listening, and then whispers to John, "My supervisor would fire me if he heard me telling you this, but the only advantage you'll be getting with that suit is the brand name. That designer recently changed manufacturers and the quality isn't what it used to be." Then she carefully checks for prying eyes again before suggesting a much less expensive alternative.*

What did she do? She gave a signal (albeit a manipulative one) to John that she's looking out for his best interests with no thought to her own now-diminished commissions.

All prospects are worried about being *taken*. Katrina used this fact to her advantage by suggesting something that appeared to contradict to her own desire for financial gain. And by doing this at the beginning, she has influenced how John will view every recommendation that she gives him from that point on. So, when she suggests the most expensive ties, the most expensive shoes, the most expensive belts, and the totally unnecessary wallet, he assumes she is still looking out for him.

Is Katrina really looking out for John? In Katrina's case, she sent a *false signal*. And if John comes back and sees Katrina go into her "I could get fired for this" act, the jig will be up. Maybe she won't care because she got her commission. But sooner or later clients will catch on to her game.

What's the difference between Katrina's tactics and sincerely putting the buyer's needs first? It's the secret ingredient for gaining trust: ***Integrity***. Integrity is not a short-term gimmick; it's a long-term commitment that builds your authority over the long haul. Let's see what happens when Annie puts Doug's interests first:

> *Annie has a wide range of cloud capabilities, and one of them is a starter package with the basic functionality that fits most of her clients' needs. She also has the "bells and whistles" package, complete with high price tag and high margins. Doug asks about that package first because they are expanding and he thinks they'll need the capabilities soon.*
>
> *But Annie shoots him straight. "That package requires a fully staffed IT department, and I remember you saying your IT department is a one-man team. Let's review your current IT capabilities—we may find that the starter package fits you better right now. And you can always upgrade later."*

Did Annie just talk herself out of a big commission? No. She knows the most expensive package won't work for him given his current situation. Doug could make it work, but it would mean incurring some unbudgeted IT costs. She tells Doug the truth and boosts her credibility—and proves the weight of her integrity.

Doug may go with the basic package after she goes through her presentation, or he may decide to ramp things up now. Whatever he decides, it will be a choice made with all the facts because his trusted ally Annie has his best interests at heart.

TYPES OF APPROACHES

Because every prospect and every selling situation is different, you must have several approach methods available in order to use the one that best fits the particular circumstance. Learn the principles of each of the different types of approaches so that you can use whichever one is appropriate for a particular situation. How many approach techniques are enough? The answer is simple—you cannot have too many. The personality style of prospects, the mood they're in as you greet them, and your own feelings and mood that particular day suggest the need to have an opening for every occasion and every situation. You may have to deviate 180 degrees from the opening and presentation you had planned.

Before launching into any approach prior to your presentation, make sure that sufficient rapport has been established. Here are 8 possible approaches for you to consider:

Relevant Benefit Approach

This approach is useful when you already know a need that the prospect has or a specific "pain point" based on his or her answers to your questions or your preapproach efforts. (*Pain* is a reminder that unless your prospect has a need to solve a problem, they are not going to buy a product or service.) The benefit statement should be unique and appeal to the prospect's dominant buying motive. It should be sincere and must never sound like a gimmick. Something new and different about your product or service that paves the way for the rest of the interview is a good choice.

Thank you again, Ms. Robinson, for agreeing to see me today. Based on what we've discussed so far, there's a new product we launched that I believe you will find particularly intriguing, as it provides the ideal solution for your needing to ramp up your IT capacities without adding any additional IT staffing.

Because salespeople want to offer tangible value to their customers, presenting this benefit statement may well cause the prospect to seek more information. Such a statement often sparks questions from the prospect that lead directly into the presentation. It also shows that you have been listening to what the prospect has been saying.

Curiosity Approach

The curiosity approach works best when you know something about the prospect's needs and why they agreed to meet with you in the first place. People with certain behavioral styles, particularly analyticals and drivers, may find this approach unappealing (they may think it sounds "gimmicky"). Used sensibly, however, this approach is an effective opener to your presentation. Suppose you are selling a telecommuting software package so a sales force can get up-to-date information on their laptops when they are out in the field selling. You might say something like this:

Mr. Sherrill, have you ever been in a meeting when a written report analyzing a new competitive product is brought to your attention for the first time, and you want to share parts of it with your salespeople immediately? Do you know how much time you are losing by having to edit the report manually?

Question Approach

The question approach quickly establishes two-way communication. It enables you to investigate the prospect's needs and apply the benefits of your product or service to those expressed needs. This type of approach suggests your interest in the prospect's problems and draws attention to the need to identify problems.

You may frame a leading question designed to obtain mental commitment from the prospect and at the same time show a major benefit. Here are two examples of how this might be done:

1. *Mr. Dyer, would you like to have distinctive-looking, quality-driven reports and the most up-to-date pricing information to share with your customers?*

2. *Do you feel you could get more accomplished in meetings if you had complete and current information at your fingertips? Wouldn't you also like the capability to easily edit that information, thus enabling you to provide your customers with the best support possible?*

4 Qualifying Question Approach

This variation of the question approach seeks a commitment from the prospect. This qualifying question approach asks the prospect to consider buying the product; it can help determine whether you have a prospect who is cold, lukewarm, or red hot toward your opportunity. Here are two illustrations of how this technique could be used:

1. *Mr. Spieth, if I can satisfactorily demonstrate to you that the service provided by our company will save you at least $5,000 within the next three months, would you be willing to do business with us?*

2. *Mr. Mickelson, I am looking for individuals who have the discretionary funds to invest in an opportunity that will produce a return on their investment of at least 15 percent. If I can show you the evidence to support this claim, would you be willing to invest with us?*

These may seem like bold questions, but if the prospect says yes, you have a sale—provided you can back up your statement with valid proof.

5 Compliment Approach

Opening with a compliment is like walking on eggshells, but this opening is highly effective if used properly. Follow the same guidelines you would use in any situation: *Offer compliments with empathy, warmth, and sincerity.* The purpose is to signal your sincere interest in the prospect. Sources of information for the compliment will vary. Information from a person who provided a referral or from an item you saw on social media, in a newspaper or trade journal about the prospect can tell you about significant accomplishments that you genuinely admire. You can also see hints in the company office as you arrive or see an item in the prospect's private office that suggests a potential basis for a compliment.

Camco Inc., with international headquarters in Houston, sells gas-lift equipment, well-completion systems, safety systems, and wire line tools and units to the oil industry. At a time when the oil industry is experiencing some instability, a Camco salesperson would be out of line to compliment a prospect on the company's prosperity. Instead, a compliment should center on some other commendable factor:

> *I have been impressed with your continuous emphasis on safety on your offshore drilling rigs. I noticed the recent announcement that your company ranked first in safety ratings last year. You must be proud of that achievement.*

This type of compliment not only builds rapport but also directs the prospect's train of thought toward safety and the related products that Camco has to sell. Whenever a compliment is used as an opening, it must be *specific*, of *genuine interest* to the prospect, and *sincere*.

Referral Approach

The referral approach is especially useful because it helps you establish leverage by borrowing the influence of someone the prospect trusts and respects. This approach enhances your credibility and increases the likelihood that the prospect will give you full attention. Here are two good examples:

1. *Miss Reid, your former partner Rob Hibray has recently completed one of our courses in personal leadership. He told me that you are also interested in growing as a person and in becoming a better leader, and suggested that you would like to hear about what our company has to offer.*
2. *Rita Dadosky, who recently purchased an inventory software package from us, suggested that I contact you, Mr. Parker. She thought you would like to have an opportunity to consider whether our technology solutions and cost-saving features could also be of benefit to you.*

Educational Approach

The educational approach reflects the trend towards relationship selling. Here, salespeople research the field so thoroughly, they are able to present new information to the prospect by becoming an authority not just on the product, but on the industry or market the product serves. The presentation becomes less of a sales pitch and more of an educational lesson for the prospect. This shifts the power dynamic in favor of the one doing the teaching, which could be especially effective in a virtual meeting, where you can't develop your credibility, at least initially, face-to-face. Here is how this approach could be implemented:[16]

Sarah, we've done some studies and found out that in your industry, there are five things that make companies fail and five things that make them succeed. I'm going to be sharing this information with [name their competitors here], and I wondered if you were interested in seeing this same data.

Hands-On Approach

This approach is useful when meeting with visual, outgoing, and overtly friendly prospects so that you can be assured they are open to active involvement in the discussion. This approach consists of actually handing the product or some physical representation of it to a prospect to produce a positive reaction. The product approach provides a visible image of the product or service. This approach should focus on the uniqueness of the product and, as far as possible, allow the product to tell its own story.

Remember, bringing the product to the prospect stirs interest, permits a demonstration, makes a multiple sense appeal, and usually creates in the prospect a feeling of commitment to listen and to participate actively in the presentation. For example, a smartphone sales representative might say:

Mr. Stone, chances are, your busy field reps rarely have time to sit down. So why give them a computer that needs a lap? Our new smartphone helps them work better anywhere. Here, catch.

Sometimes you cannot bring the actual product with you because of size or other constraints. You can use other devices to simulate the actual product. A piece of literature, a sample of the output of the machine, a small working model, a flash animation or model, a picture—any visual tool that the prospect can hold or look at helps to focus his attention. If you are selling a service, such as a time-management program, hand the prospect a letter from a satisfied client that identifies specific benefits of the program.

TRANSITION FROM THE APPROACH

Whatever approach you decide to use, it should be directly related to your plan for beginning the need discovery phase of the presentation. The exchange of conversation in the approach phase allows you to move smoothly into the questions you plan to ask to discover the needs of the prospect. If your opening has involved "chit-chat with a purpose," the transition is fairly simple.

Any *compliment* you offer should relate to the general area of your product or service so that the presentation grows naturally from the opening. A *relevant benefit* opening obviously leads directly into deeper need discovery. A *product approach* immediately gets the prospect involved in examining your offering. The *referral approach* focuses upon your product or service the approval of someone whom the prospect respects; it emphasizes the referring person's belief that the prospect will be interested.

Because the actual presentation of benefits cannot begin until the prospect agrees to having a need for what you have to offer, whatever you can do to make need discovery seem a natural process will be helpful. Chapter 10 deals with the critical task of discovering needs by asking questions and listening. The degree of rapport established between you and the prospect during the approach determines how willing the prospect will be to answer your questions and accept your buying recommendation.

SUMMARY

- What you do and say in the initial moments of the face-to-face or online interview has a profound effect on the success of the close. Plan those initial moments carefully. The first 10 words out of your mouth are crucial.
- Be aware of the power of first impressions. You never get a second chance to make a good one.
- Proper dress and grooming give the prospect the feeling that you are competent.
- Appropriate choices in dress and grooming let the prospect focus on your sales message instead of on your physical appearance.
- The greeting is important to create a favorable first impression. Use the prospect's name often and begin with some "chit-chat with a purpose" to feel out the mood and behavioral style of the prospect.
- Use a firm handshake, maintain eye contact, and make use of voice properties that reflect confidence.
- Confirm or modify your impressions of the prospect's behavioral style and adapt your plans for the presentation accordingly.

- A good approach forms a natural transition into the need discovery phase of the selling process. A number of different types of approaches are available.

REVIEW QUESTIONS

1. What are the four objectives of an effective approach?
2. What are components of Nonverbal Language? Why are these items called Nonverbal Language?
3. What would you consider appropriate dress for calling on an insurance executive? A manager of a health and fitness facility?
4. What is the purpose of small talk? How can you use it to best advantage? For what kind of situation is small talk a negative?
5. Name and explain the eight types of approaches discussed in the chapter. Why does a salesperson need to master several approaches?
6. What are the advantages of bringing a product to the prospect? What are alternatives if bringing the actual product is not feasible?
7. Should the greeting you use be planned ahead of time, or should you depend largely on the inspiration of the moment? Justify your choice.
8. Under what conditions would you change the approach you had planned when you arrive for an interview?
9. List some guidelines for making a good first impression.
10. What are some weaknesses of evaluating a prospect totally on your first impression?
11. What can you learn about a prospect from a handshake?

IN-CLASS EXERCISES

The following exercises help build teams, improve communication, and emphasize the real-world side of selling. They are meant to be challenging, to help you learn how to deal with problems that have no single right answer, and to use a variety of skills beyond those employed in a typical review question. Read and complete each activity. Then in the next class, discuss and compare answers.

EXERCISE 9.1 – DRESS FOR SUCCESS!

On a day selected by your instructor, come to class dressed for the role of salesperson to represent a company or organization in a field in which you would like to work. You should attend to the details of your attire and appearance as much as possible in order to make a good first impression. In addition, be prepared to role play greeting your prospective customer for the first time through the first words of your approach. Your instructor will invite other members of the class to critique your appearance and your initial greeting or exchange.

Alternatively, you can dress for a job interview with the company or organization for which you would like to work. You should prepare to role play your greeting and your approach through your response to a typical interview question, "So tell me about yourself." Again, your colleagues will be invited to critique your appearance and your initial greeting or exchange.

EXERCISE 9.2 – FIRST IMPRESSIONS

For this exercise, pair up with another student in the class. In this role play, one of you will play the part of a B2B customer, while your partner will play the part of the salesperson. You may select the product or service to be sold.

According to Chapter 9, every salesperson has approximately 4 minutes to make a successful first impression and approach. Much depends on how quickly the salesperson can evaluate the personality or social style of the prospect so that the approach can be adjusted to fit the prospect's basic traits.

For this role play, you should work together outside of class to develop two brief scripts. For the prospect, you should select one of the basic social styles (review these if necessary). For that social style, create a script for both the prospect and salesperson that is unlikely to work. Create another script that you think is likely to succeed. Rehearse both scripts and be prepared to role play them in class.

CASE STUDIES

The following case studies present you with selling scenarios that require you to apply the critical skills discussed in the chapter and give you training through practical learning situations. They are meant to be both engaging and challenging, and like the in-class exercises, don't have one right answer.

CASE 9.1 – A REFERRAL GONE AWRY

Rita Thurber represents a small publisher, Coastal Maine Publishing Co., that typically markets a small list of poets, travel magazines, children's books, and good, but relatively unknown, authors of fiction. Rita is opening up a new territory on Maryland's Eastern Shore, and is meeting the owner of an independent bookshop, Sam Wetherington, for the first time. Since the store is located in an upscale village to which the wealthy escape from Washington, D.C., and where tourists moor their sailboats, Rita surmises that the store's clientele would be a perfect match for her company's offerings.

Rita has prepared carefully for this interview. She is dressed stylishly in a navy blue blazer, grey slacks, a pink striped blouse, and low heels. She has researched Mr. Wetherington's online merchandise, and she comes armed with a referral from one of her own authors. The bell tinkles as she steps through the front door, and she immediately spots Mr. Wetherington sitting at a desk behind the counter.

"Hi. Mr. Wetherington? I'm Rita Thurber from Coastal Maine Publishing. It's nice to meet you," Rita says as she strides across the room, her hand extended in greeting. "Thanks for agreeing to meet with me."

"Welcome to my shop," replies Wetherington, shaking her hand. "Please call me Sam."

"You have a lovely store here. Just like Milton Stokes described it. In fact, Milton is the main reason I'm here. As you may recall, we feature his books of poetry."

"Oh, yes. Milton. We hosted a book signing for him once. Big mistake. He teaches at the local college part-time, and we thought it might get some new customers here from the college people and their families. But it never worked out. Milton's a terrible poet, and his stuff just doesn't sell. I took a large shipment of his latest volume, but had to return nearly all of it to your company. What a terrible experience."

"Oh, I'm sorry." Rita responded. Sam's negative criticism threw her for a loop. Using Milton's name clearly got things off on the wrong foot. What could she say to turn things around—and quickly?

CASE 9.2 – GRASPING THE RELAY BATON

Jamie couldn't believe her good luck. After accepting a sales position last month with OfficeDecor, Inc., a company that sells office furnishings to medium size companies and professional offices, she learned that she will be assigned to a different territory with sole responsibility for new and existing accounts. Sally, the salesperson previously responsible for that territory, left the company under something of a cloud (Jamie hasn't been told what the problem was); sales in the territory had declined during the past year as well. Still, Jamie was excited when Pete, her manager, called her in for a meeting. This was her big chance!

"Well, Jamie, I bet you're excited to be assigned to this territory," Pete said. "You know, however, that you're walking into a difficult situation. The territory has a lot of potential, but taking over from someone else under these circumstances can be challenging."

"I know, Pete," Jamie replied, sitting on the edge of her chair. "But I think I'm up to it. It's not like customers in this territory haven't heard of OfficeDecor. I know the product line, and most of the customers are already qualified."

"That's true," Pete agreed. "And I'm sure that you can break the ice with new prospects just fine. But Sally left some of her customers with a bad experience by overpromising delivery schedules. You're going to have some fence-mending to do, and I want you to think carefully about how you're going to approach these people."

"Well, I'm not going to make the same mistake that Sally did," promised Jamie. "But you're right: I've never had to deal with this sort of situation before. Introducing myself, getting their attention, reassuring them that I understand their needs and problems, and so forth will be a big challenge initially."

"Exactly," said Pete. "It's like running a close relay race when you're a couple of paces behind the leader. You can't afford to drop the baton. We're counting on you. Let me know what you come up with."

Recognizing that every situation is a little different, Jamie realized that she needed to develop a basic script that would launch her approach. She decided to consider basic sales approaches and to combine two or three that would help her to achieve her initial goals.

What should Jamie include in her script? Which approach(es) would offer the greatest promise in this situation? Why? Write out a one-paragraph script for Jamie and be prepared to explain your reasoning.

Chapter 9 Footnotes

1. Dolak, Dave."Sales and Personal Selling." http://www.davedolak.com, Accessed November 9, 2015).
2. Engleberg, Isa N. and Wynn, Dianna R. *Think Communication.* Toronto: Allyn & Bacon, 2011. 110; Morton, Brain. "Be prepared to make a good, quick first impression." *Ottawa Citizen* (May 23, 2007): 1.
3. Laidman, Jenni. "Make it Count." *The Tennessean* (June 21, 2001): section D, 1-2; Kahn, George N. Kahn. "The Impression You Make." *Smooth Selling* 62 (1967): 2.
4. Anonymous, "Home staging assists sellers." *USA Today* (in Collaboration with the Society for the Advancement of Education) (April, 2007).
5. L.R., Vithyaa. "Importance of customer service." *Business Times* (October 19, 2004): 1.
6. Isabel Lee. "Art of selling one's skills crucial in clinching job," South China Morning Post. Hong Kong: July 17, 2004. pg. 5.
7. Leotta, Joan. "Dressed to Sell." *Selling Power* (October 2000): 89.
8. Alessandra, Anthony J. and Wexler, Phillip. *Non-manipulative Selling.* Reston, VA: Reston Publishing, Inc 1979: 87-93.
9. Frankel, Lois. *The Thin Pink Line.* Feb 25, 2009 (accessed July 2, 2015).
10. "Attire Guide: Dress Codes from Casual to White Tie." EmilyPost.com, April 13, 2015.
11. Lydia, Ramsey. "Seal the Deal Sales Technique." (Accessed November 9, 2014).
12. Solnik, Claude. "Immaculate receptions: The art of greeting clients to your firm." *Long Island Business News* (Jul 21, 2006).
13. Adapted from "Here's an Easy Way to Remember Your Customers' Names." *Master Salesmanship*. Concordville, PA: Clement Communications, Inc.. (1979): 3; and McCann, Nanci. "When You Forget a Prospect's Name." *Selling* (March 1994): 101.
14. Porter, Henry. "Opening for Every Occasion." *Sales Management* 109, no 9 (October 30,1972). 6-8.
15. Mok, Paul P. "CST Influencing Model" from *CST: Communicating Styles Technology.* Dallas: T.A. Press, Inc. (1982): 13.
16. Holmes, Chet. "The Ultimate Sales Approach." Successmagazine. (Accessed May 3, 2015).

CHAPTER 10

IDENTIFYING NEEDS BY QUESTIONING AND LISTENING

OVERVIEW

This chapter is devoted to the art of asking the right questions and listening effectively. You will learn critical questioning and listening skills to help carry you through the entire sales interview, from need discovery to the close and beyond. This is a vital part of the process because the most successful salespeople don't ask their way into a sale; they listen their way into a sale. The SPIN® Selling technique is also explained and dramatized using a practical example.

OBJECTIVES

- Understand the purpose of asking questions.
- Learn how to select questioning tactics appropriate for the sales situation.
- Study specific questioning techniques.
- Examine SPIN® Selling and its applications.
- Understand the functions served by various types of questions.
- Appreciate the importance of listening in sales.
- Become acquainted with techniques for improving listening skills.

THE KEY TO WINNING IN SALES

What really lies at the heart of selling? Some may say selling is filling a need, while others say it's solving a problem. Some people say it's closing the deal as quickly as possible, and by any means necessary. The problem is, none of those definitions really work. Selling is ultimately asking people what they do, how they do it, when they do it, where they do it, who they do it with, why they do it that way; and then, and only then, helping them to do it better.[1]

Telling isn't selling—asking is!

The problem created by the misconception that talking equals selling lies in its assumption that every prospect uses the product or service for identical purposes and in the same manner. But in actuality, each prospect has unique needs. Of the many benefits you have to offer, only a few will be the key motivators for a particular prospect.[2] The challenge is to determine their buying criteria before beginning your presentation and then use only the specific benefits that address their particular situation.[3]

Salespeople should become *Doctors of Selling*. Physicians know they must clarify the patient's problem and conduct a pragmatic diagnostic process before they can prescribe any treatment. Doctors of selling follow an identical process: They diagnose potential buyers fully to uncover any needs they may have for the salesperson's product or service. If you went to your family doctor complaining of back pain, and the doctor—without asking any questions—wrote a prescription for a medicine, would you take it? Let's hope not! You would not believe the doctor could make an accurate diagnosis and prescribe the appropriate medicine without making a thorough examination and asking a number of probing questions about the problem. You would expect the doctor to understand your problem—not the problem of back pain in general—before prescribing treatment. Your prospect has the right to expect the same professional attention.

NEED DISCOVERY: THE CRITICAL STEP OF THE CYCLE

The evolution of relationship selling has reached the point where the need discovery step in the sales cycle is often more important than making the presentation, handling objections, or closing.[4] Exhibit 10.1 shows the relationship between need discovery and the other basic steps in the face-to-face sales process. At this point of need discovery—not in the close—the sale is most often lost. In reality, more time should be spent in the approach and in discovering needs than in any other steps of the process.

Need discovery is the foundation upon which a successful sale is built.

Telling prospects what they need is a mistake. Asking questions that allow prospects to discover their own needs and share them with you sets you up as a sounding board for the solutions they "discover" while considering your proposal. Prospects are more receptive when they feel that the solution is their own idea. Successful sales interviews contain more requests for opinions and suggestions by the salesperson and fewer statements of disagreement and tension. And in successful interviews, salespeople control the direction of the interview by the way they ask questions.[5]

EXHIBIT 10.1 NEED DISCOVERY'S ROLE IN THE SALES PROCESS

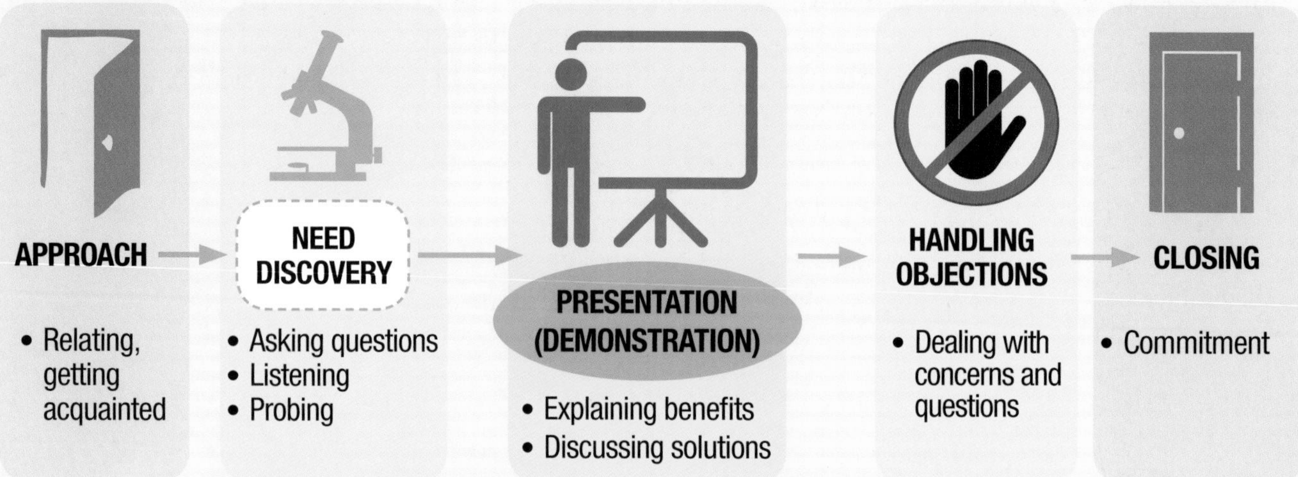

People are often unaware of a problem until they are questioned about it. Here is an example: An insurance agent sold a seemingly uninterested prospect a policy by asking one simple question followed by an observation. The agent asked, *"How much life insurance coverage do you have as protection for your family?"* When the prospect replied that he had $75,000, the insurance agent shrugged his shoulders and remarked, *"I guess you don't plan to be dead very long, then, do you!"* This statement could offend some people. However, for this prospect, it caused him to realize for the first time the substantial disparity between what he had and the actual amount needed that would enable his family to maintain their current lifestyle, should something unexpected happen to him.

> Salespeople don't convince prospects. They help prospects realize that they already have a need.

Specific Planning of Questions

Asking the right questions is a skill all too often neglected. The majority of the time in sales situations it isn't about asking just any questions. It is about asking the right questions that help us to understand the perspective of the prospect, clear any misunderstanding, strengthen or break our assumptions, lead to new discoveries, and even close the sale.[6]

The old standbys—*who, what, when, where, why, and how*—are a vital part of the sales interview. Decide in advance what you need to know, and then plan what types of questions will elicit that information in the quickest and most efficient manner consistent with the prospect's social style and situation.

Because the sale is made in the mind of the buyer and not in the mind of the salesperson, using the questioning process to gain agreement on key issues is paramount. Once you have gained agreement on key issues, you must assist the prospect in prioritizing those issues and agree that those are the problems or concerns that must be addressed before they make a decision to buy. Prospects are more likely to buy if you establish points of agreement early in the interview.

Some salespeople hesitate to ask questions because they are afraid the prospect will refuse to answer. However, prospects that refuse to cooperate during the need discovery phase are unlikely to cooperate at the end of the sale either. Communication is a two-way street that demands participation by both you and the prospect. If you are to involve prospects in the sales process, you must be prepared to ask the questions that maximize participation. The right questions never materialize out of thin air. Your questions should attempt to achieve four objectives:

1. To discover the prospect's "hot button" or dominant buying motive.
2. To establish the purchase criteria or specifications.
3. To agree on a time frame for completion of negotiations.
4. To gain prospect agreement on the problem(s) before making the presentation.

Strategic Questioning Suggestions

As you select specific questioning methods, keep these three tactics in mind:[7]

1 **AVOID CONFUSING LANGUAGE.** An account executive selling ad space in a business magazine to a small business owner should avoid terms such as *kerning*, *bodoni extra bold*, *mistral fonts*, or *bleed page* unless certain that the prospect is technically sophisticated and would expect to use such terms. In the same way, using company stock numbers, codes, or abbreviations may confuse the client. Your goal is to promote understanding and not to demonstrate how smart you are.

2 **ESTABLISH A CLEAR AGENDA.** Chapter nine presented four specific objectives of the approach: *To make a favorable first impression, to gain attention, to create interest, and to serve as a logical transition into need discovery.* This transition into need discovery requires that you tell the prospect exactly what you intend to accomplish during the interview session. You are to provide a clear agenda for the sales interview. Always let the prospect know what you want to accomplish. You can set up the desired atmosphere by requesting permission to ask questions. Here are two practical *permissive questions*:

1. I believe I can offer you a service that will be of considerable value to you, but in order for me to be sure, and to know a little more about your particular situation, would it be okay if I ask you a few questions?
2. The only way for us to know how my company can best serve your needs is for you to give me permission to ask a few personal questions. Will that be all right with you? Oh, and may I make some notes while we talk?

3 **GIVE EACH QUESTION A PURPOSE.** An ambiguous question or one with multiple meanings creates misunderstanding between you and the prospect. Proceed logically, one topic at a time. Murphy's Law operates here: Anything that can be misunderstood will be misunderstood. A corollary to this principle is equally important: Phrase each question to produce the maximum amount of information so that the number of questions needed to elicit the required information is as small as possible.[8]

KEY QUESTIONS THAT BUILD RELATIONSHIPS

If you listen more than you talk, you are taking a positive step in the right direction. But are you listening for the right information? In the world of professional selling, the questions you ask are just as important, if not more so, than the fact that you are taking the time to ask them. That means that you need to ask the questions that give you the answers you need to get the most out of your conversations. Asking the *right* questions, in the *right* way, changes the sales process in significant ways, to the benefit of both parties.

There is a series of specific questions that work wonders for salespeople who use them correctly. They are five questions that invite a dialog between prospect and salesperson that work to establish trust and create a clear channel of communication:

THE MOTIVATION QUESTION: "WHY ARE YOU PASSIONATE ABOUT THIS PRODUCT/SERVICE?"

This question focuses the discussion on the prospects' motivations. Their motivations might be personal, driven by their needs at home, or they may be business related. Their boss may be relying on them to increase margins, update software, or improve some other process within the organization, which means that they feel the pressure to deliver exactly what their superiors are expecting. Every prospect has his or her own source of motivation for buying, and if you aren't sure what that stimulus may be, then all you have to do is ask them!

THE SUCCESS QUESTION: "WHAT DO YOU WANT TO ACHIEVE?"

This question is known as the *Success Question* because it hones in on what constitutes *success* for your prospect. This short, simple question can keep your prospects talking for hours. The beauty is in its simplicity; there are so many directions your prospects can take with their answers. Here are some variations on this basic question:

- What inspired you to take this appointment today?
- What products or services are most likely to get your attention?
- What do you want this meeting to accomplish?
- If we left this meeting today with a plan for incorporating this product into your company, would that make you happy?

THE FRUSTRATION QUESTION: "WHAT DO YOU WANT TO AVOID?"

This question will give you an even more complete picture of the prospect when it is paired with the *Success Question*. It allows you to see both spectrums of prospect motivation, both the things that motivate them to seek out solutions to their problems, and the things they want to avoid when it comes to making buying decisions. Here are some variations of this basic question that may fit your needs:

- What is it about [issue, problem, need] that is affecting your business/life? How important is it that this be addressed?
- When you think of your current suppliers/vendors, what would you change about your interactions with them or their products/services?
- What do you dread might happen if [issue, problem, need] is not resolved? Why is that important to you?

THE RIGHT FIT QUESTION: "WHAT HELPS YOU DECIDE WHICH PRODUCTS TO BUY?"

This question can work wonders. It can reveal a prospect's expectations, or in other words, what they expect in return for buying what you are offering (i.e. the "what's in it for me" of relationship selling). Here are some variations:

- How do you choose what companies do to business with?
- What do you have to see or know about a product/company in order for you to make a yes decision?
- What would a company need to show you, after you've made a commitment, to convince you that you've made a wise investment?
- When you think about vendors you've done business with in the past that sell similar products/services, what did you like best about them? Why was that important to you?

You must be as diplomatic as possible when asking the "right fit" questions in order to engage the prospect's trust and not be disparaging of another company or a competitor.

THE COMMITMENT QUESTION: "HOW INVOLVED DO YOU WANT TO BE IN INCORPORATING THIS CHANGE IN YOUR BUSINESS/LIFE?"

Some prospects want to sign the contract and never think about the purchase again. Others want significantly more involvement and follow-up. Learning your prospects' perspectives can help you assess their desired level of engagement desired or follow up after the contract has been signed.

Asking these questions won't guarantee a sale, but they comprise the first critical step in building deep, authentic relationships over the long haul with your best potential customers. With the insight that these questions provide, you can quickly determine whether the prospect merits the significant investment of your time and attention. The questions don't just help you—they help the prospect convey to you, in the most direct way, how to add them to your growing client base. Not to mention, utilizing these questions toward the beginning of your meeting with a new prospect will reveal the best course of action to take for the remainder of your interactions and in the presentation itself.

THE SPIN® TECHNIQUE

Neil Rackham is president and founder of *Huthwaite Inc.* and the author of the book *Spin Selling.* His corporation's 12-year, $1 million research into effective sales performance resulted in the unique sales strategy, the SPIN® method: ***Situation, Problem, Implication, and Need-Payoff questions.*** Successful salespeople don't ask random questions. This model represents how relationship salespeople probe and is meant to serve as a guideline rather than a rigid formula.

There is a distinct pattern in a successful call. The answers you get will be used during the presentation to help underscore how the benefits you give support, reinforce, and provide answers to the questions you have asked during need discovery. The questions provide a road map for you, guiding the sales call through the steps of need development until explicit needs have been agreed upon. People don't like to think, and certainly don't want to admit, their problems are that obvious.[9] You want to allow prospects to discover for themselves the problems they have.

SPIN® Selling in Action

Let's take a specific example of a company and demonstrate the SPIN® method just as they might use it. A business with overdue accounts receivables has three options: 1) It can hire a conventional percentage-based agency, 2) It can hire a flat-fee agency, or 3) It can do the collecting internally. *Transworld Systems Inc.* (TSI) is a flat-fee agency, and it is also one of the largest collection agencies in the country. TSI works with over 60,000 clients helping them to recover their slow-paying and delinquent accounts without having to pay up to 50 percent of the collection as charged by a conventional agency.

Many clients with a wide range of account balances have found the TSI system to be the only economical method of obtaining professional third-party collection results. TSI pays the money they collect directly to the client, the client maintains control of their accounts, and they do not have to pay a percentage. TSI has a low flat fee that enables clients to assign their accounts in the early stages of delinquency, thus providing the best opportunity for successful recovery.[10] Here is the SPIN® technique in action:

SITUATION QUESTIONS. These questions are designed to find out about the customer's situation. These are data-gathering questions; they ask about the prospect's general state of affairs or circumstances as it relates to the services TSI has to offer. They help the TSI salespeople get to know prospects and obtain the initial information.

The ultimate purpose of situation questions is to look for a general understanding of the prospect's needs. The following questions have an important fact-finding role, are non-threatening, and help to build an atmosphere of trust and cooperation:

- About what percentage of your customers do not pay their bills on time?
- Do you currently use a collection agency?
- Are you responsible for making the purchasing decision?
- How many active accounts do you bill each month?
- Do you do all the collection of overdue accounts internally?
- Do you have out-of-state accounts?
- Is the billing and follow-up done in this office?

PROBLEM QUESTIONS. Once the TSI salespeople feel comfortable about the buyer's situation, they move on to a second type of questioning technique. These questions explore needs, any difficulties prospects may be having, and dissatisfactions in areas where TSI's service could be the solution. The goal in this step is to have the prospect realize and then acknowledge, "I really do have a problem with the collection of my accounts receivables."

TSI wants to determine explicit needs or uncover the prospect's *hot button* or *pain point*, that one thing that could drive them to say yes in order to relieve the pain or discomfort they feel in some aspect of their life or business. Remember: The sale is made in the mind of the buyer, not in the mind of the TSI salesperson. ***Customers don't want to be told they have a problem, and so allow them to discover it for themselves.*** Whatever they say is true—but when you say it, they doubt it! You're searching for areas where the services TSI offers can solve their specific problem. If you can uncover problems your service can solve, then you're providing the buyer with something useful. Ask these kinds of problem questions:

- Do you know how much it costs to do your collecting internally?
- Do you ever get mail back? Wrong address? No longer at the address?
- At what point do you consider an account to be a concern or problem?
- Do you ever get checks back NSF or ACCOUNT CLOSED?
- Do you have a service to help recover these checks? If yes, is it a guaranteed service?

IMPLICATION QUESTIONS. Implication questions build up the magnitude of the problem so that it's seen as serious in the mind of the prospect, and then the salesperson uses need-payoff questions to build up the value of the solution. *Implication questions are the language of decision-makers*, and if you can talk their language, you'll influence them. In larger sales, you need to ask this third type of question. The phrasing of implication questions is critical because you want the prospect to discuss the problem and how it might be improved.

Attach a bottom-line figure to the implication questions. The TSI salesperson wants the prospect to agree that the implications of the problem are causing such things as loss of revenue, ill-will with some of its customer base, prohibitive cost of time and money in trying to do the collection themselves, and expensive percentage-based collection agencies. The prospects must see that the problem is serious enough that it outweighs the cost of the solution, namely, using the services of TSI. The TSI salesperson might ask these questions:

- Would it help if the money were paid directly to you? In the last five years, we collected over $2.4 billion for our clients and the money was paid directly to them.
- Do you know most collection agencies deposit the money they collect into their own bank account and hold it up to 60 days?
- Would it be important to you to recover a larger share of delinquent accounts and bad checks faster than a conventional collection agency and put the money directly into your hands and let it work for you?
- Is it safe to say that you would like to collect delinquent accounts quickly, without disturbing ongoing relationships with those customers?

NEED-PAYOFF QUESTIONS. *How would that help? What benefits do you see? Why is it important to solve this problem? Is it useful to solve this problem?* These questions get the customer to tell you the benefits that your solution offers. Such questions actually get prospects to name benefits and tell you why they should buy. These questions help you build up the value of your proposed solution in the customer's mind. You want to focus the customer's attention on the solution rather than on the problem. This creates a positive problem-solving atmosphere.

In the words of an eight-year-old named Quincy, ***"Implication questions are always sad; need-payoff questions are always happy."*** That's because implication questions are problem-centered, while the following need-payoff questions are solution-centered:[11]

- Would it be useful to speed up the rate of collection, and at the same time be guaranteed that you will recover at least twice as much as you pay for our service?

- If you could create the perfect agency, what would you want them to do for you?
- We automatically send out a report detailing the status of each account assigned for collection. Does this sound like something that would interest you?
- Do you want the account handled diplomatically or intensively? We have another division that handles the hard-core collection problems. Would you like to have that option?
- Would you like us to send a "thank you" card to the debtor after the account has been paid?

COMMON QUESTIONING TECHNIQUES

Questions are generally classified by the type of answers required and by the purpose they are intended to serve. Begin the questioning process with closed-ended questions or fact-finding questions that are easy to answer and therefore not threatening to the prospect. If the first few questions are reasonable, the prospect begins to gain confidence and feel comfortable with the questioning process. The next questions then, although progressively more challenging, seem easier to handle. The major types of questioning techniques are summarized in Exhibit 10.2.

EXHIBIT 10.2 TYPES OF QUESTIONS AND TECHNIQUES

General Types of Questions

1. **Closed-ended questions.** Provide a series of responses from which the prospect selects one, are easy to answer, used to get feedback, and can be used to get prospect commitment.
2. **Open-ended questions.** Identify a topic but do not provide structured alternatives for responses, usually begin with "how" or "what", cannot be answered "yes" or "no", and are designed to stimulate the prospect's thinking.

Classification of Questioning Techniques

1. **Amplification questions.** Ask prospect to expand on an answer. Do not direct thoughts but encourage prospect to continue talking.
2. **Internal summary questions.** Assimilate information presented, put it in perspective, and ask if the interpretation is correct; may repeat all of prospect's last response in the form of a question.
3. **Getting agreement on the problem.** Restate the problem, get prospect to agree, and attempt to get commitment.

CLOSED-ENDED QUESTIONS. These questions are direct, fact-finding questions that are designed to reveal background information about the prospect's business and/or family. They ask an either-or question or request a choice from a series of suggested responses. Closed-ended questions are usually answered with a very brief response, often a single word. They often ask for a yes or no response or a choice between two alternatives. They are directive questions for which you want specific answers:

- How many employees do you have working the day shift?
- With what cloud-based accounting software companies are you familiar?
- Is crash-test safety reporting important to you?
- Does your company pay the full cost of employee health insurance, or do the employees pay part of the cost?

You may also phrase closed-ended questions to get feedback or to gain commitment:

- Would you like delivery Friday, or is Monday of next week better?
- Are you responsible for making the decision to purchase from us, or will there be others involved?
- Do you know what your customers do with your product after buying it?
- Do you prefer to pay up front, or would you like to arrange a monthly payment plan?

Closed-ended questions may be used as a substitute for telling the prospect something. A question can sometimes make a point in a more telling manner than a statement because the prospect must think to answer it, and thinking makes a stronger impression than hearing. Consider these two ways to impart the same message:

Our procedure will completely eliminate waste in your welding operations.

VERSUS

How much savings would you have if you used a procedure that completely eliminates waste from your welding operations?

The first method tells the prospect something. The salesperson hopes the prospect is impressed, but that may not be the case. Unless the prospect reacts strongly enough to the statement to break in with a comment, any skepticism is buried until some later point, where it emerges as a vague objection or stall like, "Well, we're not thinking of making any changes just now."

CHARLIE BECAME THE TOP SALEMAN IN HIS COMPANY ONCE HE LEARNED THE POWER OF EFFECTIVE QUESTIONS!

Using the question method, however, gains attention because the prospect has to think about an answer. Disbelief surfaces immediately where it can be dealt with instead of being postponed until later when the salesperson is trying to close. Here are the primary purposes served by asking closed-ended questions:

- Uncover specific facts.
- Reduce prospect tension because they are easy to answer.
- Check for understanding and receive feedback.
- Maintain control by directing the flow of conversation.
- Reinforce prospect commitment to a specific position.

OPEN-ENDED QUESTIONS. These broadly phrased questions allow prospects plenty of room to answer as they wish. They call for explanations. Open-ended questions encourage prospects to discuss their needs by explaining their preferences, expectations, or judgments. Open-ended questions tend to be general rather than specific. Use them when you want the prospect to talk freely. You can encourage the prospect to verbalize feelings by asking questions that begin with "What do you think?" or "How do you feel?" Talking out loud often helps people clarify and organize their thoughts. Real feelings are actually revealed when they are verbalized.[12]

Open-ended questions help you and the prospect sort out ideas and begin to make decisions. Here are some examples of questions that give prospects the freedom and responsibility to express their own thoughts and use their own information in the decision-making process:

- What options would you want on your new Mercedes?
- How do you think I might be able to help you?
- In a perfect world, what would you like to see us deliver?
- What are five unique characteristics of your business?
- What benefits would you expect from our ten-week, self-paced time-management program?

Open-ended questions reveal attitudes that a salesperson must be aware of if the sale is to be closed. You cannot easily ask a prospect, "Are you motivated by pride?" but you can ask open-ended questions designed to detect this emotion, and you then have the answer to the direct question you cannot ask. Open-ended questions often begin with "how" or "what." Here are the primary purposes served by asking open-ended questions:

- Allows the prospect to move in any direction.
- Cannot be answered with "yes" or "no".
- Designed to stimulate the prospect's thinking and increase dialogue.
- Help determine dominant buying motives (rational or emotional).
- Uncover the social or behavioral style of the prospect.

CLASSIFICATION OF QUESTIONING TECHNIQUES

The questions salespeople ask can be classified by the purpose they are intended to perform. Three basic classes of questions can be used: *Amplification, internal summary or reflective,* and *questions to gain agreement on the problem*. Either open-ended or closed-ended questions may be asked for any of these purposes, depending upon the situation. If one type of question does not provide all the information needed, another type can be used to get a more specific response or to elicit a better sense of the prospect's point of view.

Relationship selling is more than a process in which two people sit together in a room and take turns talking. As the salesperson, you must be certain that the prospect knows what you are talking about and understands it. You must also be sure that you understand the prospect, know that person's needs and desires, and be certain you can satisfy them.

You need feedback, and asking questions is the best method for receiving feedback.

Be careful how you phrase the questions you ask. Place the responsibility for not understanding on yourself rather than on the prospect. "Do you understand what I said?" or "Did you get that?" or "Are you with me?" seems to imply that the prospect may not be too bright. You must take responsibility for any possible misunderstanding by asking, "Have I explained this clearly enough? Is there some part I need to clarify or go over again?"

Amplification Questions

Amplification questioning techniques encourage prospects to continue to provide enlightening information and also encourage them to explain the meaning of a statement made. Amplification questions help both salespeople and prospects. At times prospects may not make themselves clear; they may wander off the subject or may stop talking before you can fully understand their position. In a subtle manner, these techniques ask the prospect to expand on or clarify the meaning of a statement and help identify the frame of reference used. There are four types of amplification questions:

DOUBLE-CHECK QUESTION. A double-check question is a means of giving feedback to the prospect. It involves taking the information the prospect has provided, rephrasing it, and handing it right back. A prospect might tell a motor freight salesperson, "Every Tuesday and Thursday the whole yard is backed up with trucks for the entire afternoon." The salesperson might offer feedback by saying, "Now as I understand it, you find that your loading platforms get badly jammed at peak hours." This statement is actually a question because it evokes an answer. It serves the dual purpose of clarifying the salesperson's impression of the situation and solidifying the prospect's opinion.

NONVERBAL GESTURES. Visual cues such as nodding the head or leaning forward show that you are listening, believe the prospect is on the right track, and understand what the prospect is saying. You may also inject appropriate words or phrases to encourage the prospect to continue: "You don't say?" "Is that right?" "That's interesting!" You may imply a question by the nonverbal choice of silence accompanied by a slightly raised eyebrow or furrowed brow.

SILENCE. Silence is a powerful sales tool. When prospects avoid telling you the whole truth, the knowledge that they are being less than honest makes them uncomfortable. Your silence convinces them to go ahead and tell you the whole story. Silence allows you to slow down and relax the pace of asking questions. Take their social style into account—some prospects want to think and contemplate longer than others before responding to your questions. Give people time to reply at their own pace. Silence also gives you valuable time to formulate your own next question or comment.

CONTINUATION QUESTIONS. Continuation questions encourage prospects to keep on talking by making a positive request for more information. Such questions do not push for a particular response or for agreement; they just encourage more communication from the prospect. Here are two examples:

1. What additional thoughts or questions do you have regarding our shipping policies?
2. Could you tell me in a bit more detail why you feel that way?

There are several advantages to using amplification questions:

- These techniques encourage the prospect to continue to provide revealing information.
- They also allow the salesperson to rephrase what the prospect appears to have intended.
- Amplification questions can Invite the prospect to expand or clarify any point of disagreement.
- They can serve to narrow down generalizations and clear ambiguities.

Internal Summary Questions

Probes designed to get prospects to think, see, and consider your interpretation of the situation may be called *internal summary* or *reflective* questions. Summarize what you understood the prospect to mean. You want to assimilate the information provided, place it in the perspective that suits your purpose, and ask if the interpretation is correct.

You achieve this by repeating all or part of the prospect's last response in the form of a question or by rephrasing the entire idea expressed by the prospect, feeding it back in a slightly different form, and asking for confirmation. Consider the following example in which a company president explains why the firm may not be able to sponsor an in-house blood drive. Note how the salesperson empathizes and rewords or echoes the president's remarks but suggests the process can be accomplished without disruption:

Prospect (company president): My company has always felt the need to support the charitable activities of organizations like yours. But where do we draw the line? I am constantly besieged with requests for my company's time. We have only so many hours a day.

Salesperson (fundraiser): I certainly understand how you feel. If I were in your position, I'd probably feel the same way. I sense that the blood donor program is something you wholeheartedly endorse. But with only so many hours in the working day, humanitarian concerns take a back seat to the realities of the business world. However, if you thought this could be accomplished with a minimum of time lost, and you felt your employees really wanted to do it, it could be done. May I tell you how we manage it?

These types of questions are useful throughout the interview. Every salesperson knows about summarizing the key benefits just before asking for the order: "Now, as I see it, we've agreed that a complete line, with these particular items featured, will move for you with the proper promotion. Am I right about that?" Such summary techniques help lead to a successful close.

The summary question may be used to underscore points on which you already agree. An occasional summary of the points to which the prospect has already agreed will fix them firmly in the mind of the prospect and demonstrate just how wide an area of agreement there is between the two of you.

Getting Agreement

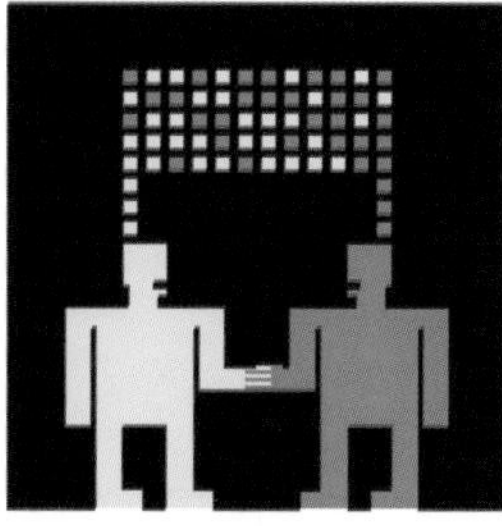

In *Open the Mind, Close the Sale*, John Wilson says that the salesperson's failure to confirm the problem is one of the biggest mistakes in selling. The underlying purpose of asking questions is to determine whether the prospect has a problem or need that you are capable of solving. State the problem in your own words and get the prospect to agree, "Yes, that's it." Never begin the actual presentation phase of the sales interview until the problem has been clearly established in the minds of both you and the prospect. Begin the formal statement of the problem by using such phrases as these:

- Let me attempt to summarize what we have been saying.
- As I understand it, here is (are) the problem(s) we must solve.
- Based on your answers to my questions, I see the problem as . . .

After you pinpoint the problem, you must seek confirmation. Get the prospect to agree by following your summary of the problem with questions like these:[13]

- If I show you some comparisons demonstrating that my company can save you money without sacrificing quality, would you commit to our program?
- Is that a fair statement of the way things stand?
- If I can satisfactorily demonstrate a solution to these concerns of yours, would it be enough to earn your business?

If the prospect agrees with the problem statement, you are ready to present the specific benefits of your product or service that can solve the problem. Even if the prospect disagrees with your summary of the problem, you have both learned by sharing information.

THE SOCIAL MEDIA CONNECTION

Asking the Right Questions on Social Media

Today, more than three out of five Internet users engage in social media—and its popularity grows every day. Perhaps more interestingly to salespeople, research reveals that one-quarter of social media and online discussion mentions a product, service or brand. The opportunity to engage with and listen to potential prospects via social media is clear, and more and more companies are finding it essential rather than optional.

Your sales efforts can be enhanced by combining listening and asking research. One success story demonstrates how social media was used to reshape a baby diaper campaign. Traditional survey results (not conducted on social media) showed that the majority of consumers believed that “environmentally friendly” was the most important product attribute. But in authentic, online conversations that were allowed to progress between users on social media, results indicated that “organic” and “avoiding diaper rash” were the most important product features. The social media analysis revealed a more accurate picture of consumer sentiment around product desires. This led to a new campaign theme centered on “Caring,” which produced phenomenal results for the brand.[14]

So how do you ask good questions on social media? First decide what kind of answer you want. Are you looking for short answers with no room for discussion, or are you trying to create dialogue? Closed-ended questions on social media assume answers that can be given in a few words or result in Yes or No choices. Open-ended questions usually require more deliberation and can easily lead to secondary questions and answers that flesh out a concept, opinion, or provide critical problem solving information. Social media can be a resourceful tool for your organization’s strategic and marketing plans if you ask the right questions—and then listen to the responses you get from prospects and customers alike!

LISTENING

Everybody wants the secret to closing more sales, but it's no secret. ***If you're not closing sales, you're not listening to the customer.*** Salespeople are so busy telling their prospects or customers all the wonderful things that their products or services will do for them instead of being quiet and letting the prospects tell them what they need.[15] Prospects are not patiently sitting at their desks waiting for you to call so they can buy your product. People are not easily sold, which is why you must do more than mechanically go through your script. Prospects can sense insincerity, and they will know if you are not really listening to them and giving only scripted generic responses.

Listen—your prospects will reveal their needs and show you how you can help them.

Eighty percent of waking hours is spent communicating, and about half of that is spent listening. Effective listening is not just hearing what the prospect is saying. Faulty listening results in misunderstanding and lost opportunities. Research indicates that 60 percent of misunderstandings in business are due to poor listening.[16] Fortunately, improved listening skills can be learned. Actively listening to prospects not only increases the effectiveness of the interaction, it also greatly increases the chance of making a sale.[17]

To succeed in professional selling, you must be able to offer a product or service that satisfies the buyer's needs. Presenting features and benefits is not always enough. How they are presented may be as important as what is presented. Listening is the key to finding ways to present benefits that enhance the possibility of a close. Effective listening helps sales professionals catch verbal and nonverbal signals indicating a prospect who is interested in buying their product or service. Unfortunately, good listening skills usually require a change in our behavior, which is why it can be so hard for salespeople to become good listeners.[18]

Psychologists claim that listening uses only about 25 percent of our brain. The other 75 percent either thinks about what to say next or stops listening if the conversation is boring or of no interest. To improve your listening skills, practice these five mental activities as you listen:

1. **AVOID PREJUDGMENT.** Not only should you allow the speaker to complete a message before you comment or respond, but you should also wait until you have heard the entire message before judging it. Making value judgments colors your thinking and creates emotional blind spots that can block your ability to make a solid buying recommendation. Jumping to conclusions is a common fault of poor listeners.

2. **BE PATIENT.** Listen more and give "verbal nods" of encouragement. This allows speakers plenty of time to answer questions and encourages them to express their ideas. Speak at the same speed as the other person: Matching speed is a rapport builder. In addition, find the person's mental rate of speed and then adjust or modify your thinking to that rate. Even

though the speaker is saying something exciting, wait until the message is complete and you are sure that you understand it all before you contribute your own thoughts.

3. **TAKE NOTES.** Remembering everything a person says is difficult. Open your tablet or phone and take notes (or utilize the old fashioned way of note taking and use pen and paper). Be sure to include what the prospect says as well as your thoughts on how to meet those expressions of needs, requirements, or desires. The mere physical action of writing down a few key words reinforces your memory and understanding. You can go back to the prospect's own words to help you show your product's applicability to the problem.[19]

4. **REINFORCE.** Anchor, in your mind and in the prospect's, the points made by the prospect. Use your own reinforcing responses to achieve this purpose. If the prospect says the mileage per gallon a car gets is important, respond, "Yes, that is very important." Later, tell what mileage the prospect could get with your car. If the prospect says, "Our secretaries spend too much time making copies," respond, "That has to be a problem." Then later emphasize how your copier cuts secretaries' time by copying on both sides of the paper in one operation and by running more copies per minute.

5. **CAPITALIZE ON SPEED OF THOUGHT.** We can process about 600 words a minute, but even a fast talker gets out only 100 to 150 words in that time.[20] Thus you can think about four times as fast as the average prospect talks. All that spare time is valuable. The poor listener uses it to fidget impatiently, to think about what happened earlier in the day or what will happen later, or to plan what to say as soon as the prospect takes a breath. Successful salespeople have a plan to follow for using this time profitably:

   - **Anticipate where the prospect is going.** If you guess right, your thinking is reinforced. If you are wrong, compare your thoughts with those of the prospect; look for the point the prospect is making.
   - **Mentally summarize the message.** Pinpoint problems, misconceptions, attitudes, objections, or misunderstandings. What you learn can be an excellent guide to the topics that should be stressed in the presentation and at the close.
   - **Formulate a response.** Be careful not to formulate one before you hear everything the prospect wants to say. Listen, understand, and then turn the prospect's words to your advantage.
   - **Listen between the lines.** Nonverbal messages are as important as verbal ones. Watch facial expressions, body movement, and position; listen to the tone of voice and volume changes.

SUMMARY

- Asking questions is the primary tool for identifying problems. Need discovery lays the groundwork for the presentation and close. When you ask the right questions, prospects clarify problems in their own minds as well as in yours.

- No standard set of questions is universally applicable. The product or service, your preapproach information, and the prospect's behavioral style help determine the questions you ask.
- Questions may be either closed-ended or open-ended. A closed-ended question asks for a yes-no response or a choice between alternatives. Open-ended questions ask for opinions, explanations, or judgments.
- Ask questions according to their structure: Amplification, internal summary, and questions designed to gain agreement.
- Listening is one of the most neglected skills in any type of training program. Taking notes focuses your attention on what the prospect is saying and avoids prejudgment of ideas. Reinforce what you hear by comparing the prospect's ideas with your own.
- People can think at a rate much faster than they talk. Use this spare thinking time to anticipate where the prospect is going, mentally summarize what you hear, form a response, and refine the message as your listening continues.

REVIEW QUESTIONS

1. What factors determine a salesperson's ability to formulate the right questions?
2. What is the difference between manipulation and consultation? Which is most useful to the successful salesperson? Why?
3. What kinds of questions allow the salesperson to discover the prospect's behavioral style? How does this information aid the salesperson?
4. What tactic is useful as a transition from the approach into need discovery?
5. Who should control the needs-assessment phase of the interview? How is control maintained?
6. What is the purpose of the open-ended question? Formulate an open-ended question that might be used to sell investment property.
7. Describe in detail all the instruction you have had in school, at home, or elsewhere in listening skills.
8. In what situations do you find it hardest to listen? Easiest? What makes the difference?
9. Is listening easier if a visual factor is added? For example, do you prefer to talk to someone in person or on the phone when you have something serious to discuss?
10. Educators say learning that involves more than one of the senses is more effective. Explain how this applies to listening and taking notes, to simultaneously listening and looking at visual aids, and to listening to music versus watching television.

IN-CLASS EXERCISES

The following exercises help build teams, improve communication, and emphasize the real-world side of selling. They are meant to be challenging, to help you learn how to deal with problems that have no single right answer, and to use a variety of skills beyond those employed in a typical review question. Read and complete each activity. Then in the next class, discuss and compare answers.

EXERCISE 10.1 – TEN QUESTIONS

Pair up in class with another student as directed by your instructor. Imagine that the two of you are seated next to one another on a flight from Hawaii to San Francisco. You represent a company that supplies electronics components for jet engine controls, while your seat mate is a procurement officer for a company that manufactures jet engines. Since your companies are well known to one another, you are aware that your flight companion's company is not a client of your company. This is a once-in-a-career chance: you are determined to gain an appointment with the other company to make a full-scale presentation.

On the spur of the moment, compile a list of no more than 10 questions along with anticipated responses that you can ask your seatmate that will secure the appointment.

Next, role-play your questions. Did they succeed? What type of questions did you ask (your partner can help categorize the questions)? Would other questions have been more successful? If you role-play your questions in front of other class members, what do they think of your effort?

EXERCISE 10.2 – A NEED FOR QUESTIONS?

For this exercise, the class should be divided into teams of 4 persons each. On each team, 2 persons will undertake the following role play: Select a technical device such as a smartphone. One person, acting as salesperson, will sell the phone to the other, but without asking the customer any questions. This process should take no more than 5 minutes. Whether the sale is closed successfully does not matter. The other 2 members of the team will simply observe.

Thereafter, the remaining 2 members of the team will undertake the same exercise, but this time the salesperson will conduct the sale by asking questions in order to determine the customer's need. The 2 nonparticipants will simply observe.

After both role plays have been concluded, the team will discuss and critique both. Which role play—without questions or with questions—seemed to go more smoothly? Which felt better or more natural to the participants? To the observers? Why? If you were employed to sell this product, which approach would you use, and why?

CASE STUDIES

The following case studies present you with selling scenarios that require you to apply the critical skills discussed in the chapter and give you training through practical learning situations. They are meant to be both engaging and challenging, and like the in-class exercises, don't have one right answer.

CASE 10.1 – CLANGING POTS AND PANS

Jack Lund couldn't figure out what had happened. As a representative for WearStrong Restaurant Supplies, he had been supplying equipment to Midwest Diners for the past 15 years. Midwest ran a string of 88 Greek diners in 10 major metro areas from Detroit through Indianapolis and Des Moines. They had been one of Jack's first major clients, and he counted the owner, Mark Antonopoulos, a friend. He and Mark had attended trade shows together and on many occasions had golfed together whenever Jack was in the Chicago area. From the time that Mark had opened his first diner, Jack had come through with a good deal as Mark expanded his business one location at a time. That's why the phone conversation just a few minutes ago was so disturbing.

Jack had just called Mark to let him know that it was time once again to begin his regular replacement rotation. Every five years, Mark's diners had to replace their aluminum cookware. Although sturdy and capable of being scrubbed to a mirror finish, WearStrong's top-of-the-line, heavy aluminum pots and pans could withstand only so much abuse. The replacement schedule called for replacing every pot and pan in each kitchen every 5 years, but stretching the process out over three years for all 88 stores. When Jack mentioned to Mark that another replacement round was due to commence, he was met with a long silence.

"Jack, I just don't think we're going to do that this time," Mark finally sighed. "You see, we've decided to go with a 3-ply line offered by one of your competitors. They have a durable, non-stick finish with a copper lining underneath. It can save us cleanup time and still provide an even heat."

"I don't get it, Mark. You know that WearStrong manufactures the same sort of item, but you never expressed any interest in it. You said that our aluminum pan had been a workhorse for you, and you saw no reason to change."

"I know. I know. But do you remember, Jack, when you met last with our operations people here in Chicago? They mentioned that they were interested in saving time in cleanup costs, among other things."

"I think I recall something along those lines, Mark, but since you didn't say anything, I figured everything was all right the way it was," replied Jack.

"Well, it wasn't. You really need to pay closer attention, Jack." Mark paused. "Tell you what. The deal isn't done yet. In light of our long-term association, I'll give you one more shot. You can meet with our people next Tuesday, but bring your 'A' game." With that, Mark clicked off.

What do you think had gone wrong? What can Jack do to save the situation? If you were advising Jack, how would you suggest that he prepare for next Tuesday's meeting? Precisely how should he approach Midwest Diner's operations executives? What sort of questions should Jack be prepared to ask next Tuesday?

CASE 10.2 – SMOTHERING THE SALE

Kurt Edwards had just landed on his feet. After working for fifteen years as regional manager for a major moving and storage company, he was laid off when the housing bubble burst. People couldn't afford to sell their homes for a loss in order to move, and Kurt's company had to downsize. Kurt's supervisory responsibilities had included maintaining the company's fleet of moving vans in good working order. Now, however, he had been hired in sales by a major truck parts distributor in the Northwest. Kurt was poised to make more money than he ever had in his previous management position. After all, he knew firsthand what his new clients would need.

As part of his training, Kurt accompanied his district manager in the field. Today, they were calling on the WashMont Hauling Co., a major carrier in Washington and Montana. As they got out of their car, Kurt's manager told him, "After I introduce you, you're on your own. You know the product line. I'm just going to sit back and watch. Go ahead as if I'm not there."

"Ok," Kurt replied, eager to show his manager that he knew his stuff.

Once inside, they proceeded to the office of Bruce Olds, fleet operations manager. After the usual pleasantries had been exchanged, Kurt turned the conversation to the purpose of their visit.

"As we get started, Bruce, I want to assure you that, with me, you will be dealing with someone who understands your situation. I managed a fleet of moving vans for 15 years; so you can be confident that I know what you're facing these days."

"Well, I'm glad to hear that," Bruce replied. "You see, . . ."

"I'll bet your chief problem is delivery of spare parts on time, especially those that wear out more quickly," Kurt interrupted. "That's always the way it was for me. But our company has solved that problem so that you'll never have to worry about having portions of your fleet stranded for lack of parts."

"That's wonderful," Bruce said, "but, you know, . . ."

"And for a large account like yours," Kurt continued, "we can warehouse the parts for you for daily delivery. The large volume allows us to absorb that cost for you. Would you like to solve your major problem today for the next six months?"

"Well, Kurt, I'm not sure that I'm ready to go there just yet. Perhaps you could call back once I've got a better handle on just what our needs are," Bruce said, standing and extending his hand.

Back in the car, Kurt's manager exploded, "What was that about? You don't know the first thing about sales! You smothered the guy!"

"What do you mean?" asked Kurt. "I solved his problem for him. He just wasn't ready."

Based on what you've learned from Chapter 10, what happened here? Why was Kurt's manager so angry? Why didn't Kurt's knowledge and connection with Bruce produce better results? What do you think Kurt's manager should recommend in terms of additional training for Kurt?

Chapter 10 Footnotes

1. Jim Scheer, "Asking Good Questions," *Office World News,* Jan/Feb 2006.
2. Ginger Trumfio, "Underlying Motivation," *Sales & Marketing Management* (June 1994), 71.
3. Kristen des Chatelets. "Asking the Right Questions." *Dealerscope. Philadelphia* (June 2004). Vol.46, Is. 6, 26.
4. Andrew Rudin, "Just the Facts! How Asking the Right Questions Will Yield the Right Answers," *SalesVantage.com,* Accessed October 4, 2015.
5. John O'Toole, "The Want Makes the Sale," *Selling* (June 1994), 43.
6. Camille P. Schuster and Jeffrey E. Davis, "Asking Questions: Some Characteristics of Successful Sales Encounters," *Journal of Personal Selling and Sales Management,* Vol. 6, No. 1 (May 1986), 17.
7. Anonymous, "Probing Skills Course Aims to Educate the Learner about the Role of Questions in Various Situations and the Importance of Asking the Right Question at the Right Time," *Business Wire,* Jan 17, 2006.
8. Ingram, Thomas N. *Sell.* Instructor ed. Mason, OH: South-Western Cengage Learning, 2012. Print.
9. Tim Connor, *The Soft Sell* (Crofton, MD: TR Training Associates Intl., 1981), 67.
10. Neil Rackham, *SPIN Selling* (New York: McGraw-Hill), 1988.
11. Information gathered from Transworld Systems, Inc. www.transworldsystems.com, Accessed May 2, 2015.
12. Rackham, Ibid, 89.
13. Todd Youngblood, "Let Customers Sell Themselves," *Selling Power.* March 2001, 52.
14. "Using Social Media to Ask the Right Questions." *Nielson.com.* September 8, 2011. Accessed October 20, 2015. Web.
15. Steve Atlas, "When and How to Use Your Favorite Close Effectively," *Selling Power.* September 2000, 48.
16. Warren Greshes, "Prospecting Skills III," *Warren Greshes Video, Brightcove.com;* Accessed July 30, 2015.
17. Jan Flynn, Tuula-Riitta Valikoski, Jennie Grau, "Listening in the business context: Reviewing the state of research," *International Journal of Listening,* Vol. 22, Issue 2 (2008), 141-151.
18. Joseph DeVito, *Human Communication* 10th Edition (New York, NY: Longman, 2008).
19. N. Nicholson, "Listening and Learning," *Communication World* (July 2007), 2.
20. Jonathan Steele, "Active Listening: Mastering This Skill and Master Communication," *Speechmastery.com* (posted April 1, 2011) Accessed August 4, 2015.

SUCCESS IS NOT FINAL
FAILURE IS NOT FINAL
IT IS THE COURAGE
TO CONTINUE THAT COUNTS

Winston Churchill

CHAPTER 11

MAKING A COMPELLING PRESENTATION

OVERVIEW

At this point in the selling cycle, you have studied your prospects and discovered more about what drives them to buy, and now you are ready to make your presentation so they can see the benefits of becoming customers. This chapter details techniques to use during the presentation to continue building on the connection and rapport you established during the questioning and listening process of the relationship. The key elements that comprise a unit of conviction—the building blocks on which to build a meaningful sales presentation—are both explained and illustrated.

OBJECTIVES

- Understand how to make a presentation.
- Learn how units of conviction help prospects reach a buying decision.
- Discover effective tactics for making a sales presentation.
- Study different methods for involving the prospect.
- Understand the significance of using a demonstration and effective virtual tools.
- Examine the different types of sales aids available.
- Recognize the value of using technology in making presentations.

Want to buy? There's an ***app*** for that.

Some may think that in a few years, that's all salespeople will have to say to their customers. With the proliferation of social media, smart phone apps, and websites in every facet of our lives—and the ease with which we can access endless mountains of information any time, anywhere—it's tempting to suppose that face-to-face selling is soon to be a relic on the road to extinction.

Nothing could be further from the truth.

In fact, over the next few years, salespeople will be able to leverage developments in technology to more accurately identify prospects in advance, and then use that data to drive face-to-face visits and stimulate sales. Granted, the future of person-to-person interactions with the younger generations will look and feel a little different from classic sales, ***but face-to-face prospect engagement will continue to be the driving force in professional selling.*** In fact, it is the technology tools themselves that will enable in-person selling to remain an affordable, rapid approach to build relationships effectively and increase sales and profits.

Relationship salespeople will continue to prosper in the future if they understand one simple concept: ***There is a big difference between presenting data versus information.*** It is easy to fall into the trap of creating a data-dense presentation, filled with facts and figures that can confuse or complicate a presentation if their significance is not explained. How data dense are most sales presentations? Here are some interesting and surprising facts:[1]

- The typical salesperson presents six to eight features or benefits during the sales presentation. Twenty-four hours later the average prospect remembers only one benefit.
- In 39 percent of those cases they remember the one benefit incorrectly.
- In 49 percent of the cases they remember something that wasn't mentioned at all.

These days, we're all so busy, and our brains are so bombarded with technology and interruptions, that we welcome any opportunity to slow down and really become engaged in an effective presentation. And in those moments, we don't want to hear facts; we want to hear tangible pieces of useful and targeted information that will remind us why we want and need to hear this presentation in the first place.

In short, data and numbers are important—but data is *not* what elicits sales. Customers buy when they see that what you have to offer will solve a problem or fill a pressing need, not when you impress their intellects. The future of professional relationship selling is going to be based on real-time value and how well sales professionals become trusted advisors in guiding clients to solutions to their problems. The future belongs to those sales pros that can present and share their knowledge, offer wisdom, and create value in a way that benefits the prospect in tangible ways.

STRIVE FOR PASSION, NOT PERFECTION. More often than not, customers buy because of the rapport building established over time. *Selling really is all about relationship building.* There are hundreds of competitors waiting in line for the same customers you are—which is why it all comes down to the way you present yourself and your product or service and the value you create for the customer. ***Sales presentations must be listener-centered.*** *People want to have their problems* *solved.* In his book *What They Don't Teach You at Harvard Business School,* Mark McCormack said there are three fundamental selling truths:

1. If you don't know your product, people will resent your efforts to sell it.
2. If you don't believe in your product, no amount of personality or technique will cover that fact.
3. If you can't sell your product with enthusiasm, the absence of it will be infectious.

Nobody buys from a dispassionate seller; if you don't believe in the product, no one else will. The more options a sales rep creates for the prospect, the greater the chance for a sale.[2] Don't worry about making the perfect presentation. It probably will not happen! Prospects are looking to you for knowledge of what you're selling and how it can help them solve a problem or become more successful. You must truly believe in what you're selling and show some passion when doing it—that is far more important than perfection.

CALLING ON REGULAR CUSTOMERS. If you are calling on the same person on a regular basis, you may tend to give the same old presentation over and over or even skip the presentation entirely and merely ask, "What do you need today?" If you are unwilling to put some real work into your selling and are content just to "take orders" all your life, your best opportunity to become rich is to win the lottery! Vary your presentation. Provide new ideas to help your customer make money, save time, or increase efficiency. Plan to use ideas like these:

- Give the customer a new advertising or merchandising idea.
- Help the customer develop an overall marketing plan for improving the business.
- Tell some new product fact that the customer needs to know.
- Share a piece of industry or trade news of personal interest to the customer.

BEGIN WITH PLANNING

Everything important begins with planning. Over the last few decades, sales professionals strived to find ways to quantify best planning practices and ways to target key prospects. The best salespeople learn to dutifully target, segment, and measure inputs, outputs, and performance. *The Nielsen Corporation* has built a multibillion-dollar business of gathering and distributing sales data to analyze and report with perceived expertise. Consumers and organizations eat it up; some even refer to this research and planning as a *science.*[3] This may seem like an overstatement, but effective planning based on statistics and research, in fact, has become highly methodological and even scientific in its approach. Random, haphazard action never leads to success in any worthwhile endeavor, and in this respect, selling is no different from any other undertaking.

How well you plan what takes place during the sales interview plays a major role in the success you achieve when closing time arrives.

When planning your presentation, here is a good rule of thumb to follow: *When you are developing a brand new sales talk, plan on spending one hour of preparation time for each minute of presentation time.* For example, if you are speaking for twenty minutes, you should invest twenty hours in research, development, organizing, outlining, fleshing out, and rehearsing your presentation. It sounds like a lot of time—and it is—but it's necessary if you want to deliver a dynamite presentation. If you invest the time to construct a superb, researched presentation, you'll be able to deliver the same or a similar version to other prospects. As Dr. Norman Vincent Peale once said to me, "I give the same mashed potatoes for each speech, I just change the gravy."

Call Objective

The most successful salespeople have specific objectives for each sales interview. In many instances, the call objective is to present your product or service and secure an order. In others, your objective is to discover the prospect's needs so that you may prepare a proposal for later consideration or to persuade the prospect to set up a presentation to a group of people who are jointly charged with the responsibility for a buying decision. In these latter instances, you will probably plan several interviews that, taken together, contain all the elements that may be considered parts of "the presentation." The difference is that you accomplish the various steps in successive interviews rather than in a single meeting with the prospect.

Whether you intend to complete the presentation and the close in a single call or in a series of calls depends upon the type of product or service you sell and the size of the expected order. The single-call close is appropriate for selling items that can be ordered upon the decision of one person; if a buying center is involved, multiple calls are usually necessary.

Tanis Cornell was a Global Enterprise Manager for *NetApp, Inc.*, a leader in the data storage industry. She once managed one of their Top Enterprise Accounts, AT&T. Tanis had a team of 25 people either partially or totally dedicated to selling and supporting this one account. Her approach to selling a major account involved a complex interview process. Here is the system she used:

1. **Initial call.** Develop rapport and establish a need. Judge how far to go by how quickly a relationship is established. Take notes all along to help build a trust level.
2. **Survey call.** Interview all key decision makers to get information. The decision is ultimately based on three factors: cost, quality, and service. Discover which one is most important to this client.
3. **Proposal call.** Present a buying recommendation. Recognize the fact that this is a joint or buying center decision, and give each person what that individual needs to reach a decision. Use trial closes.
4. **Closing call.** Get verbal and/or written commitment.
5. **Follow-up calls.** Continue meeting with executives, managers, and department heads until a solution is reached. Consider each meeting as a mini contract negotiation.

The sale may be closed on any one of the calls, but often it requires many more than four calls to reach the closing call. For larger sales with multiple calls involved, the complete sales cycle could take up to a year. That is why it's critical to have a system in place so that you know what to expect.

Sales Call Planning

Many companies, especially those whose product or service entails extensive research into customer needs, require salespeople to prepare a presentation plan in written form. The plan reveals the need for any additional information, makes it possible to check needs and goals against suggested solutions, and makes sure you have a clear picture of the entire situation before arriving for the personal interview. Planning for sales calls can be low tech—written on a sheet of paper—or done on a tablet, smartphone app, or a plug-in that is compatible with your CRM system.

Using the latest technology for call planning will produce added benefits. The Professional Selling Skills® Call Planner, for instance, plugs into Salesforce CRM and can track accelerated sales cycles, collaboration with sales teams, minimizing productivity losses, storing and sharing best practices in call planning, and gaining insights into sales strengths and weaknesses. Using a sophisticated call planning tool in combination with excellent online business resources can increase profit margin substantially.[4] Whichever sales call tool you choose to use, however, you should keep in mind the key questions your planning process should answer. Exhibit 11.1 is an example of the kind of information you need to gather to create the best sales call planning sheet possible.[5]

EXHIBIT 11.1 SALES CALL PLANNING INFORMATION

1. **Company Name**
2. **Type of Company**
3. **Address**
4. **Individual(s) to contact and their positions**
5. **Background and profile of buyers**
6. **Major competitors to be aware of and their sales reps**
7. **Objective for this particular call**
8. **Best time to see buyer**
9. **Expressed needs or problems**
10. **Strategies and tactics useful for the situation**
    a. **Best approach to use**
    b. **Specific fact-finding questions**
    c. **Features and benefits to stress**
    d. **Anticipated objections and techniques to answer them**
    e. **Closing techniques to be used**
11. **Sales tools to take**
12. **Results of the sales call**

PRODUCT-ANALYSIS WORKSHEET

Prospects don't know as much about your product or service or why they need it as you do. That's why you're here! You must not only know all the facts about your product but also be able to relate your knowledge directly to the specific needs of the prospect. If you can quote prices, catalog numbers, shipping dates, delivery schedules, and credit terms but have no solid, convincing evidence of the product's value to offer upon which the prospect can base a buying decision, you are afflicted with what has been called the salesman's curse: ***You know your product better than you know how your client's business can use it.***[6] A salesperson who suffers from the salesman's curse is in the same league as a math student who can recite all the formulas in the algebra book but never knows which one to use to solve the problem. Before you can expect a signed contract or purchase, you must figure out how to improve your customer's business and then find a way to persuade the prospect that the solution you offer is the best possible. You can do this by preparing units of conviction.

Units of Conviction

Units of conviction are concise, carefully prepared "mini-presentations" used as building blocks to construct the information you present. When the individual units of conviction are combined, they form what is referred to as a *product-analysis worksheet*. Preparing a product-analysis worksheet helps you evaluate the various characteristics of your product so that you are better able to present it to your prospects. When you prepare units of conviction and add them to your store of available options, they become a permanent part of your selling arsenal. A single unit of conviction consists of five elements:

1. A feature of your product or service
2. A transitional phrase
3. The benefits the feature provides
4. Evidence to support your claims
5. A tie-down question to gain the prospect's agreement

1 **FEATURES.** *Features* are the tangible and intangible qualities of the product or service you sell. They are facts that are the same no matter who uses the product or service. The tangible features of a product include observable factors such as color, size, capacity, speed of performance, material from which it is made—anything that can be detected through one of the five senses.[7] Intangible features are also important: The service given by the company, price, delivery, availability of service, and even the service and support that you promise.

2 **TRANSITIONAL PHRASE.** The ability to translate features into *benefits*—the value or worth that the user derives from the product or service—is one of the strengths of a relationship salesperson. Even if you know which feature can fulfill the buying motive, you cannot expect the prospect to make the connection automatically. You must make the verbal transition. The prospect does not know your product as well as you know it and has to have features and benefits connected by transitional phrases. Some salespeople call these *bridges*.[8] While the actual words may vary, they are all designed to accomplish the same purpose: To connect, in the prospect's thinking, the features to their benefits. These phrases all serve the purpose of answering the prospect's question, ***"What's in it for me?"*** Some common transitional phrases are:

- "This is beneficial to you because . . ."
- "This lets you . . ."
- "This heads off all the problems of . . ."
- "What this means to you . . ."

Begin preparation of units of conviction by listing in writing all the features of your product or service. If you sell more than one major product, make separate lists for each one. Then go back and list all the ways the first feature can benefit your prospect. If you neglect this preparatory step, you will find yourself confronting prospects who listen to the features you describe and ask, "So what?" and you will have no appealing answers. When you have prepared units of conviction in advance, finding the right one is just like reaching into your briefcase and pulling out a sample; you know what is there and all of it is at your fingertips for instant use when you need it.

BENEFITS. Every feature of your product has numerous benefits. Of the numerous benefits a product or service has to offer, only four or five will be key motivators to a prospect, and these will be different for each prospect.[9] Your task is to find out which ones are the key motivators. Here's an exercise to practice identifying the benefits of one feature: What are the benefits of a 270-horsepower engine in a luxury car? They could include a smoother ride, power to spare when passing a slower car, quick acceleration away from a hazard, the feeling of being in charge, less wear and tear, and higher resale value, among other things. The point is that one feature does not equal one benefit. List your product's top ten features, and then come up with at least five different benefits for each feature.

Remember, features only justify the price; benefits justify the purchase. This gives you multiple new ways to close more sales.

Exhibit 11.2 shows a features and benefits card prepared by *Hartmann Luggage Company* for their carry-on luggage and carry-on totes. These cards are distributed by the company's marketing managers to retail salespeople to help them sell the product.

EXHIBIT 11.2 FEATURES AND BENEFITS EXAMPLE: HARTMANN CARRY-ON TOTES

FEATURES	BENEFITS
1. Seven Pockets and Compartments	Lots of places for extra items. Allows for easy organization and the ability to find small items quickly.
2. Two-Way Carry Strap	Adjusts to hand or shoulder strap. You decide how to carry the bag most comfortably.
3. Full-Opening Front Pocket	Easy access to your most important items. Even has room for small laptop or tablet.
4. Sized to Fit in Airplane Carry-Ons	Contents arrive when you do. No waiting for baggage. All belongings with you during flight.
5. Easy-Access Large Center Compartment	Makes packing and unpacking easy and fast. No fumbling with hard-to-reach zippers or pockets.
6. Waterproof Pocket Inside Center Compartment	Great storage for smartphone, ear buds, and wallet. Can also be used as a cosmetic/toiletry compartment. Keeps insides dry and separates spillable items from the rest of the contents.
7. Large Outside Back Pocket plus Zipper Pocket	Large pocket allows you to put in last-minute items for easy access. Zipper pocket is an ideal place for phone, wallet, key, ID, and money.
8. Lightweight yet Strong	Lightweight permits you to add more clothing and electronics without making the bag too heavy. The strength and durability of the bag protects its contents.
9. Teflon-Coated Fabric	Stays attractive. Easy to clean.

4

EVIDENCE TO SUPPORT CLAIMS. Just as you present benefits to head off the prospect's question "So what?" you must also present evidence to support the claims you make to head off the questions, "Can you prove it?" and "Who says so?" Even if you have been successful in establishing a high degree of credibility and trust with the prospect, you are unlikely to be looked upon as an all-knowing sage with all the answers whose statements are to be accepted without question. You must be prepared to back up what you say with:

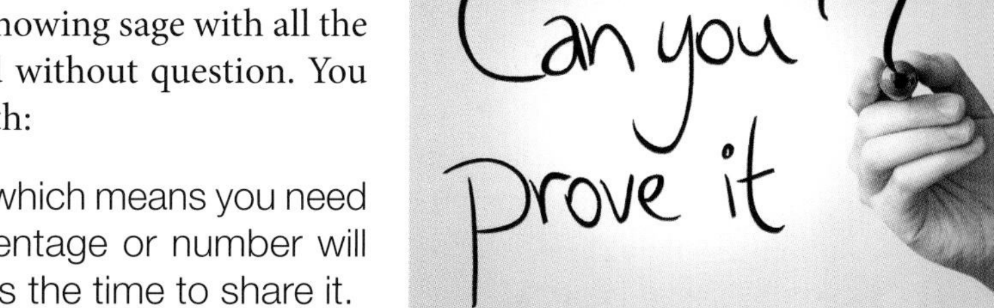

1. **Facts and Statistics.** Numbers matter, which means you need to utilize quantifiable results. If a percentage or number will help back up what you just said, now is the time to share it.

2. **Testimonials.** The best possible recommendation of your product or service is for one of your satisfied customers to provide a testimonial. This person can express his or her satisfaction with you and the product, which predisposes the prospect to accept what you say.

3. **Demonstrations.** Show your product in action. Demonstrations are obviously more useful if you have a tangible item that can be touched and seen by the prospect. You can also show a video demonstration if it's not possible to bring the actual demonstration with you.

4. **Samples.** Samples are intended to provide an appeal to one or more of the five senses. A salesperson for a company who supplies mosquito nets to Africa, for example, may bring one along.

5. **Case Histories.** The use of examples or case histories is another way to present the satisfaction of other clients and customers. You may tell the prospect about other people whose circumstances are similar and how you were able to solve their problems or how they are enjoying some benefit from using the product. Use these guidelines when planning this type of evidence:
   - **a.** The case history must be authentic.
   - **b.** Use details to indicate you are intimately familiar with the situation.
   - **c.** Back up the example with pictures, letters, articles, and other evidence.
   - **d.** Relate it directly to stated areas of need.

The evidence used to back up the features and benefits you present must be carefully tailored to the needs, problems, and personality of the prospect. For example, use cost-saving evidence for a prospect who is especially interested in economy; but use testimonials from prominent people for a prospect who is largely motivated by the desire for status. Use everything you know about the prospect's social style as input for every step in the sales process.

THE TIE-DOWN. The *tie-down* is an essential step in building units of conviction, although it usually consists of no more than a single question that asks for the prospect's agreement. Your goal is to translate *features* into *benefits* for the prospect, to provide the necessary *evidence* to prove your points, and to gain a *commitment* to act. Here are some examples of tie-down questions:

- Considering these facts, you agree with me that this is a safe tire, don't you, Ms. Cooper?
- I believe you will agree with me, Mr. Trybus, that this is a better way for handling this process than your present method, won't you?
- I think you can get an idea of the enormous advantage you will have with one tenth of a minute billing, can't you, Ms. Grimmett?

The tie-down is important throughout the presentation to check on understanding and agreement and to make sure the prospect is ready to proceed to the next point. One of the functions of the tie-down is to ask a series of questions, all of which the prospect can be expected to answer yes. Then when you attempt a close, the prospect more easily says yes again. Suppose, however, that you ask, "You agree with me about this, don't you?" and the prospect says, "No, I don't." Where are you now? You are in a better position than you were before you asked the question because you now know you have a problem. Had you not asked this question and found out about the lack of agreement, you would have pushed on to the close and to failure. Now you are warned about the existence of a problem and can go back to find its source and correct it, ask another tie-down question, and move forward again when agreement is reached.

Exhibit 11.3 is a complete unit of conviction for a wireless phone company. Notice the tie-down at the end—the question that leads the prospect into agreement.

EXHIBIT 11.3 UNIT OF CONVICTION: CELL PHONE PROVIDER

Feature	While many wireless providers still offer plans based on minutes and data used per month, we now offer unlimited talk, text, and 4G LTE data for as low as $60 per month.
Transitional Phrase	What this means is…
Benefit	You never have to worry about being charged for sending too many text messages again, and you can check your Twitter feed and watch as many movies as you want without worrying about overage charges.
Evidence (Facts/ Statistics)	Here's an illustration of the savings and value you will receive. Watching movies or TV shows on Netflix uses about 1 GB of data per hour for each stream of standard definition video, and up to 3 GB per hour for each stream of HD video. That means that after just a few movies or one weekend of binge watching without being connected to Wi-Fi, on other plans, you could already be over your data limit! With two of the other major wireless providers, daily Netflix, YouTube, and Amazon Prime Video usage could amount to hundreds of extra dollars in data charges per month.
Tie-Down	I think you can get an idea of the enormous advantage you will have with unlimited talk, text, and data, can't you, Jesse?

CRAFTING YOUR PERSONAL PRESENTATION STYLE

Once you have done your research to find out about the prospect, set goals for each additional contact with a prospect, and planned out multiple units of conviction, it's time to choose your intended presentation style. This includes choosing how well rehearsed you will be. There is much more to preparation than simply gathering and reviewing information. Rehearsal eliminates the stammering, nervous speech habits, and repetition that can result from lack of preparation.

When you rehearse and internalize your presentation, you allow the passion for your product to shine through.

But how much should salespeople really rehearse? As long as people have been attempting to analyze the selling process, a running controversy has raged over the use of "canned" presentations. Opponents point to presentations that are obviously memorized and delivered in a robotic manner likely to produce a disengaged bored listener in the shortest possible time. Supporters of memorized presentations point to the many advantages of knowing exactly what to say and when.

The question is not likely to be settled once and for all because the difference lies more with the person making the presentation than with the method of delivery itself. In deciding how you will deliver the message you want prospects to receive, consider the unique features of the three basic choices:

Memorized Presentation

Even though it is memorized, a presentation should never *sound* memorized. It should be internalized to the point that it is a personal message that can be conveyed in a conversational tone. The memorized presentation must be used as a guide to lead you and your prospect through the process and not merely be recited. Because every prospect has different needs, using a memorized word-for-word presentation for the entirety of a presentation would be a mistake. However, planning out portions of your presentation offers some advantages, especially to new salespeople. Using presentation points that have worked well for others in the past means that they are both reliable and proven to be effective. In addition, memorizing portions of your presentation can be a confidence builder for those who are new to the world of selling.

Memorizing your presentation as well as your answers to the most commonly asked questions or objections prevents you from committing pitfalls from which you may never recover. Salespeople are not expected to know every last detail about a product, but starting a response with, "Um, I think..." is not an option.[10] You have to be confident in your answer. By memorizing your presentation and learning the answers to common concerns, you can attain that much needed confidence and set yourself apart.

Outline Presentation

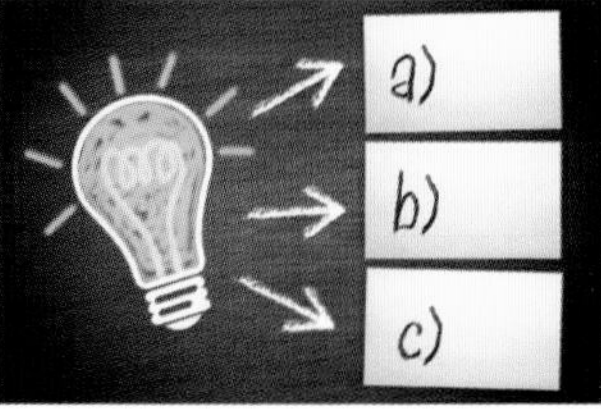

With this technique, exact words are not planned in full detail. You know what content will be presented but are confident enough of both knowledge and skill to believe that the right words will be available as needed. This is the same process that most experienced public speakers use. Using an outline presentation successfully depends upon the development of numerous units of conviction that are thoroughly internalized, and the outline is built by considering all the information available about the prospect. Most salespeople who use an outline method follow the same general outline for most presentations. They may, however, have several approaches or openings from which to choose, numerous units of conviction to present, and all sorts of evidence to present—all of which can be combined and recombined to meet the needs of the specific situation.

Procter & Gamble is one company that recommends its sales reps follow an outline plan for presentations. Exhibit 11.4 is an outline for a presentation written by one of its sales managers.

EXHIBIT 11.4 PROCTER & GAMBLE SALES PLAN

Purpose of the Sales Call—Sell 40 cases of Folger's one-pound bags for display.

Background of Account—Chain store with $100,000 weekly volume. Store is allowed to select displays in addition to headquarters' displays. Store's current need is to increase dollar volume per customer transaction. Manager has also expressed concern with labor cost. This particular store has a back stock of eight cases of canister creamers.

Summarize the Situation—The store manager said several weeks ago that they want to increase dollar volume 7 percent in the next three months by increasing the average amount of each customer transaction. I want to suggest a way to sell more Folger's coffee to help achieve this goal.

State the Idea—My idea is for the store to display 40 cases of one-pound Folger's coffee with eight cases of canister creamers from the store's back stock.

Explain How It Works—Last year's records show that the store displayed 30 cases of Folger's one-pound coffee during this time, and it sold out quickly at regular shelf price. Now in the cold months, coffee consumption is the number one dry grocery item. Capitalize on customer appeal of Folger's, and enhance it with an appealing display with the canister creamers. Store now moves 10 cases weekly, and a special display will move 40 cases easily. Offer to help build the display, which will save time and labor for the store.

Reinforce Key Benefits—Show calculations of contribution this display can make to help reach the 7 percent increase desired: $2,678 in sales on coffee. Add the quality image created by Folger's advertising. The related item display will increase movement on creamers that are now sitting in back stock. The result is an increase in the average per-customer sale, which is the goal.

Suggest an Easy Next Step—Ask for a decision on which truck to send the 40 cases of Folger's and suggest a specific day, say next Tuesday.

Impromptu Presentation

Some highly successful salespeople, particularly those who have many years of experience, may say that they "don't prepare" for their presentations. Actually, their preparation time is distributed

in a different way than that of the less experienced sales reps—but they do prepare. The impromptu presentation follows the same principles that any other presentation would, but those who use an adlibbed approach are master people watchers. They understand people; they ask questions and listen. They know their product so thoroughly that they can seize almost magically upon the one thing that will best appeal to a specific prospect. They possess such charisma that the air of trust and credibility they create makes objections nonexistent and painlessly turn prospects into customers. As a result, these master salespeople spend most of their "preparation time" in gathering additional information about the prospect rather than spending time in consciously matching features and benefits to individual prospects.

EFFECTIVE PRESENTATION TACTICS

You have the option of approaching the task of telling your story to the prospect using a variety of sales tactics. Which tactics you choose depend upon what you have learned about the prospect during preapproach qualification, what you observe in the opening minutes of the interview, what you personally want to do, and what kind of environment you find in the interview location. The only limit to the number of different presentation tactics is your own creative imagination. The most common tactics are presented here; you will use all of them at one point or another as they fit into your sales activity. You will probably find yourself developing your own personal mixture of tactics—a blend that fits your personality, your product, and the needs of your prospects.

Participation

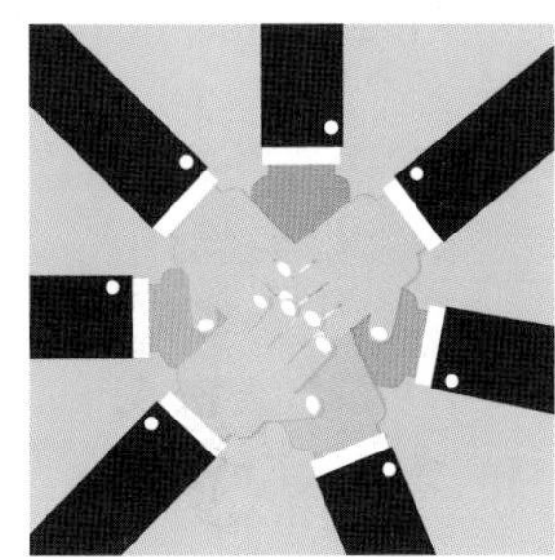

Every presentation—no matter how it is organized or what other method is used—must get the prospect involved. When prospects are shut out of the presentation process or choose to remain aloof, say nothing, and contribute nothing, they also buy nothing. The prime tactic for gaining the participation of the prospect is asking questions and then listening to the answers. Plan the questions to be asked during the presentation to gain maximum participation by the prospect.

Beyond asking questions, you should encourage prospects to ask questions about any benefit of the product you present or any factor involved in its application or use. Their questions prevent misunderstanding and give you the opportunity to direct your presentation to the problem or need that is most important to them.

Demonstration

Showmanship sells if it is more than mere carnival hoopla. There is a big difference between *showmanship* and *show-off-manship.* A well-timed dramatic touch seizes and holds the prospect's attention. A demonstration is an effective method of adding showmanship to the presentation while achieving the purpose of the presentation. A good demonstration provides you with these benefits:[11]

1. Catches the buyer's interest
2. Strengthens your selling points
3. Helps the prospect understand the proposition
4. Stimulates your own interest
5. Cuts down on the number of objections
6. Helps you close the sale

The value of a demonstration is that it involves more than one of the physical senses in the selling process. Remember these three points when determining how you will deliver your message to the prospect:

- If you rely solely on "telling" the prospect about your product, only the auditory sense is involved. If you add a demonstration, you include the visual sense.
- If you involve the prospect in the demonstration, you add the sense of touch. The more of the senses you can involve, the more quickly the prospect absorbs the information that leads to a sale.
- People remember 20 percent of what they hear and 20 percent of what they see, but they remember 50 percent of what they see and hear. By mapping your information out visually, you unquestionably increase how much your clients retain.[12]

Here are four principles to follow in using a demonstration as a part of your sales presentation:

1 **CONCENTRATE THEIR ATTENTION ON YOU.** The CEO of a large corporation once called a meeting of his associates in his office. When they came in, he was juggling several tennis balls. Finally, he tossed aside all but one and said: *"We all have many things on our minds—like these tennis balls. But we must put them aside and concentrate on one problem at a time or we'll waste time trying to juggle them all."* This demonstration illustrates the situation when you go to call on a prospect. You must focus the prospect's attention on one thing—what you are saying. A planned demonstration is an excellent tool for accomplishing this purpose.

"OK, I'm now going to read out loud every single slide to you, word for word, until you all wish you'd just die."

Agnihit, sequo que voluptas quae nimet moluptis qui nossim quaersp eriscil igentinullat.

When you fill your prospects in on the agenda and key points in your introduction, you send a signal as to what "files" your audience should open in their minds. When you cover the points in the body of your presentation, you place the data you wish them to comprehend and retain in those "files" they have opened. When you repeat the salient points at the end, you are essentially hitting the *save* button and reinforcing the data already presented. Remember that your prospect, unlike the reader of a written document, cannot re-read a passage they did not comprehend or look up a word not understood.

2 **GET PROSPECTS INTO THE ACT.** Invite the prospect to operate your device, taste your food, smell the fragrance, feel the depth of the tread on the tires, or listen to the quiet sound of your machine in operation. If you are selling an intangible, hand the prospect photos, charts, or a prospectus. Get as many senses as possible involved. The *Gulf Coast Regional Blood Center* in Houston asks a prospect to put a thirty-letter word puzzle together. The sales representative hands the prospect a small box full of letters that, when properly arranged, spell:

WILL YOU HAVE BLOOD WHEN YOU NEED IT?

This demonstration dramatically illustrates how crucial a company-sponsored blood drive is to the community and to individuals.

3 **KEEP PROSPECTS GLUED TO THE SCREEN.** As technology becomes more advanced, more salespeople are engaging in virtual meetings—often called *webinars*—through *Cisco*, *Skype* or any other web-based application. A webinar can be mutually beneficial for both parties because it dispenses

with the inconvenience of travel time and costs. Virtual conferencing also enables prospects and salespeople to form sales relationships over great distances. Virtual meetings do have some pitfalls. The average person has a 5 to 8 second attention span, which itself is decreasing as we integrate the Internet into our daily lives. Think of all the ways—social media, news sites, or email—your prospect could be distracted by what's on their screen! It's your job to ensure that your presentations are riveting.

PAINT A PICTURE WITH METAPHORS. Metaphors imply comparisons between otherwise dissimilar things without using the words "like" or "as," often creating a dramatic visual image. Remember, *"facts tell, stories sell."* Painting a mental picture is a hook that grabs prospects and reels them in. Here is a creative metaphor to use with prospects:

Picture yourself in a desert without a canteen. In the distance you see a water well. There's a bucket with a rope nearby. Now, would you jump into the well headfirst or would you use the bucket and rope? What my firm can do for you is supply you with the bucket and rope—the tools you need to succeed.

Metaphors, analogies and similes can bring special life to sales presentations. These are effective ways to reinforce concepts, while building rapport and winning people over to your way of thinking.[13]

THE SOCIAL MEDIA CONNECTION

Creating a Backchannel on Social Media to Enhance Your Presentations

More and more salespeople are using social media to engage their prospects and extend the reach of their product or service. Twitter, Facebook, and numerous custom online tools allow presenters to create a ***backchannel***—an online conversation about a presentation or the presenter—for their prospects' ideas and feedback. This two-way engagement can enrich understanding as well as the presentation's effectiveness. Here are some tips for improving your presentations with social media:[14]

1. **Engage With Your Audience Before the Presentation.** Before you meet a prospect, you can lay the groundwork for making your future presentation. Listen to your prospects' tweets and use them as trigger points for building your specific presentation to them. Look for trends in their tweets and posts. Are they launching new products? Buying new companies? Expanding to a new market? If any of those announcements could be a trigger for something you sell, mention that you saw the update or tweet during the course of the presentation, and ask them how that issue is affecting their business.
2. **Create a Separate Hashtag.** Make it easy for your prospects to talk about your company or your presentation on social media by creating a unique hashtag to isolate it. Because Twitter hashtag searches only go back 6 to 10 days, create an archive to ensure the Twitter backchannel will be available later.
3. **Welcome the Backchannel.** Make sure to make readily available your Twitter username, other social media handles, and the hashtags for your presentation. This provides a visual cue that you welcome the backchannel from the start, and it will give your presentation—whether it is to 1 or 100 people—a highly interactive and customized feel.

4. **Make Your Key Points Tweetable.** Make your presentation social media-friendly by expressing each of your main points as a ***tweetbite***, which is a soundbite (under 140 characters of course) that will get picked up and tweeted by your audience. Ensure your tweetbites are easily retweetable by allowing space for your username. If you're using slides, display your tweetbites. You can also program both *PowerPoint* and *Keynote*—two of the most common presentation mediums—to publish tweets when you click on a slide using add-ins like *Slide Tweet* for PowerPoint, and *Keynote Tweet* for Keynote.
5. **Learn From the Backchannel.** Enrich your future presentations by analyzing the blow-by-blow account of how your presentation was received. The feedback is likely to be more genuine and detailed than a typical evaluation form. In your next presentation, drop what fell flat, clarify areas of confusion, and capitalize on what resonated most with your prospects.

PRESENTATION SALES TOOLS

Sales aids fall mainly into the categories of *audio*, *visual*, or *audiovisual*. Many people are visually oriented. That's why exciting, illustrative slides, and computer-driven programs are effective presentation tools. Sales aids are used primarily to help the prospect visualize or otherwise experience the benefits of the product or service or to help you organize the presentation so that your prospect receives an ordered, logical message that is easily remembered. There are two things to remember when using sales tools to enhance your presentation: 1) Low tech items like flip charts can still be used as simple but effective ways to engage prospects, and 2) With today's technology, the sky is the limit when using presentation tools.

Tablet or Flip Chart

Companies may provide their salespeople with tablets or laptops for use during presentations. Some companies prefer small flip charts or binders. These low-tech tools are helpful if the meeting environment is not conducive to a computer or audio-visual based presentation. When such a tablet or organizer is provided, a planned or outlined presentation usually accompanies the visual and is coordinated with it. The presentation and visual help you cover all the features and benefits and overcome objections. Having an organized presentation that is ready at the click of a button not only provides additional input for the prospect, but also prompts your memory about what to cover next and keeps the interview on track. A well-designed visual presentation via a low-tech or tech-based device has these characteristics:

1. It is built around user benefits.
2. It fosters two-way communication because you can concentrate on listening attentively to the prospect rather than worry about what to say next.
3. It increases the closing rate by leading naturally to that point.
4. It helps you tell the complete story in less time.
5. It helps the interview get back on track after an interruption by reminding both you and prospect what was being discussed.

Although the company-prepared organizer is a good beginning tool, most successful salespeople develop additional visuals that are useful for their personal style and type of selling. You may choose to include letters from existing customers expressing satisfaction with the product, the company's responsiveness, and your personal service. You can also post pictures of clients actually using the product or service on your social media pages, and then show them during the presentation.

For presenting more complicated equipment or processes and for presenting to a group instead of a single prospect, visual aids are especially helpful. Exhibit 11.5 presents some useful guidelines to follow when preparing visuals.[15]

EXHIBIT 11.5 GUIDELINES FOR PREPARING VISUALS

- Keep your visuals simple.
- Text should be in short phrases, not complete sentences.
- Leave plenty of white space and follow a consistent format.
- Use colors that are functional, not decorative. Colors should be easy on the eyes (use red sparingly).
- Never put the whole presentation on a visual and simply read it to the prospect.
- Tables or charts with complex data must only be used for groups that need to study the information closely.
- Charts and graphs should present one idea at a time to ensure clear understanding.
- Line charts show how several variables change over time.
- Bar charts show relationships between two or more variables.
- Pie charts are used to show relationships among parts of a whole at a given point in time.

Audiovisual Presentations

"The world is but a canvas to the imagination."
Henry David Thoreau

With the capability of today's tech devices, there is no reason why any salesperson should not have an up-to-the-minute, creative and engaging presentation a click away. *PowerPoint* may not always be the answer anymore in terms of quality and professionalism. Instead, you and your company may want to invest in a professional, designer-quality presentation program. These are often compatible with your CRM system, so that dates of presentations, presenters, and other variables can be tracked. In addition, web or cloud-based presentations are now being widely used because they take the fear of system crashes out of the picture. If you've got a reliable Wi-Fi connection, you've got the capacity for a great presentation.

SITUATIONAL SELLING

Master salespeople have a specific plan for every sales interview, but they never feel slavishly bound by that plan. *Relationship selling requires flexibility.* No matter how much you learn about a prospect before you appear for the interview, you can never be absolutely sure what kind of situation to expect when you arrive. Instead of finding a calm, receptive prospect ready to listen and evaluate your product, you may find one who is angry, resentful, or emotional. If planning has been adequate, you can shift gears and make a different kind of presentation, switch to another purpose for the interview, or even delay the presentation until a better time.

Many salespeople find their tablets or smartphones ideal when making sales calls. With those tools in hand, you don't walk into a buyer's office lugging a briefcase or folder during the initial call. Instead, you can be prepared to take an order, calculate it, offer "what ifs," and make any changes right on the spot.[16] The ability to exercise this type of flexibility is called *situational selling*—fitting yourself to the situation and making each contact with the prospect beneficial to your ultimate purpose of closing a sale.

The Setting

Where the sales interview takes place is often a vital factor in determining its success. The prospect's office is often the best place if interruptions can be controlled. If the prospect has a private office, the door can be closed and calls can be held. The prospect feels at ease and in control in familiar surroundings and is not required to put forth effort or travel time to accommodate you. You are a guest and automatically a person to be treated politely and with respect.

If your information tells you that this prospect customarily tries to control every interview and every person, however, you might decide that meeting at a place where you are the host or even on neutral turf would give you more potency. Some salespeople make effective use of what is called a *power lunch*. Inviting the prospect to lunch at a carefully selected restaurant gives you an opportunity to present your product or service with several distinct advantages:

- You are away from an office where interruptions may occur.
- You are the host, and the prospect, as your guest, feels obligated to listen politely.
- The atmosphere is nonthreatening.
- Relaxing over the meal relieves some of the stress of making a decision.

Interruptions

No matter how carefully you schedule an interview, your best-laid plans often go astray. Asking the prospect at the beginning of the interview if the secretary could hold all routine calls until later can prevent many interruptions. This tells the prospect that you believe the interview is more important than routine matters, but that you know some important duties could take precedence over the interview.

When preapproach information indicates that a particular prospect's duties involve continuous supervision of a work group's activities or that the prospect does not have a private office, consider arranging the interview away from that environment. When an interruption does occur, your sense of timing will tell you whether the discussion can be resumed or whether scheduling a later interview would be better.

If you decide to continue, summarize what has been said up to the point of the interruption. If a problem or need has been identified, state it again and ask a question designed to gain the prospect's agreement. Review in more detail the last major point made in your presentation, and again check for agreement or commitment by asking a question. Be sure the prospect is back on track and is following your planned path of reasoning. If you decide to come back later, attempt to set up a time for the interview. If the interruption is caused by some real crisis that demands the prospect's immediate attention, say you will come again later and leave so that the prospect may give full attention to the urgent problem.

When you do come back, begin the presentation all over. You can safely assume that the interruption has probably completely erased the effect you had built. Preface points with phrases like these: "You will remember that we discussed," "As I told you the other day," or "I believe you told me that." Intersperse your remarks with questions that check on what the prospect remembers, and you can quickly discover what needs to be repeated in depth and what can be quickly reviewed.

"Creativity is thinking up new things. Innovation is doing new things."

Theodore Levitt

SUMMARY

- Despite advances in technology and the growth of online sales, face-to-face sales will continue to be the driving force in professional selling.
- How well you plan what takes place during the presentation plays a major role in the success you achieve when closing time arrives. Use a sales call planning sheet (either on your laptop or download a smartphone app) to get the most out of every meeting.
- One way to choose what you will present is to develop units of conviction. Each unit of conviction includes:
    1. A feature of your product or service
    2. A transitional phrase
    3. The benefits the feature provides
    4. Evidence to support your claims
    5. A tie-down to gain agreement
- You can memorize a presentation, use an outline that allows you to present each of your selling points in an orderly and systematic way, or opt for an impromptu presentation based on your years of experience and your level of preapproach.
- Personalize each presentation to the needs of the prospect. One of the most important tactics available is prospect participation – even in virtual presentations.
- Sales aids include all sorts of visuals and audiovisuals. The Internet and presentation software make anything possible. Many people are visually oriented, which is why exciting, illustrative graphics are effective presentation tools.
- Interruptions represent anything that distracts the prospect's attention from your

message. The setting of the sales interview requires that you be prepared to take advantage of any situation. You must learn to control these distractions and transform them into buying opportunities.

REVIEW QUESTIONS

1. Why must the prospect become involved in the selling process?
2. Define "salesman's curse." Why is it a problem?
3. How does a salesperson learn to personalize units of conviction? Why is this important?
4. Distinguish between a feature and a benefit. Why is it important to know both?
5. What is a tie-down and why is it an important part of the sales presentation?
6. Describe the types of evidence that may be used to back up a claim.
7. How can a novice salesperson prevent a memorized sales presentation from sounding memorized?
8. What are the pros and cons of using a well-designed organizer as an integral part of your sales presentation?
9. What self-prepared visuals could be used by a salesperson selling a landscaping service?
10. How can a salesperson get back on track after an interruption?

IN-CLASS EXERCISES

The following in-class exercises help build teams, improve communication, and emphasize the real-world side of selling. They are meant to be challenging, to help you learn how to deal with problems that have no single right answer, and to use a variety of skills beyond those employed in a typical review question. Read and complete each activity. Then in the next class, discuss and compare answers.

EXERCISE 11.1 – PRESENTATION PLANNING

The class should be divided into teams of 4 persons each. This role play requires your team to plan (not deliver) a presentation of MimioPad™, a product in the MimioClassroom™ family of products from DYMO™/Mimio® ITT. This major sales presentation is to be delivered to the buying center of a community college so that the product will be placed in the hands of every full-time faculty member. Each member of the sales team should produce a portion of the presentation plan in one of the following areas:

- Presentation style, including persuasive reasons for the recommended style.
- Product analysis, including features and benefits, proof of claims, and tie-down

question for each unit of conviction.

- Presentation tactics.
- Presentation sales tools.

The team should discuss and modify each section as necessary and present everything in a unified document. Each team's presentation plan should be shared with other teams online or in hard copy. In a subsequent class session, discussion will focus on differences among the plans, the reasons for such differences, and which planning features are optimal.

EXERCISE 11.2 – FEATURES AND BENEFITS

For this exercise, you will work independently. Select a product of your own choosing. After conducting appropriate research (online or otherwise), prepare a "features and benefits chart" for the product (see discussion in Chapter 11, including Exhibit 11.2). Make the chart as complete as possible, and for every feature, list at least one customer benefit (bear in mind that each feature can have more than one benefit).

Once the chart is complete, write out a one-page summary of a sales presentation approach in which you structure at least two units of conviction (see discussion in Chapter 11). Be prepared to share and discuss your chart and sales presentation approach in class or online.

CASE STUDIES

The following case studies present you with selling scenarios that require you to apply the critical skills discussed in the chapter and give you training through practical learning situations. They are meant to be both engaging and challenging, and like the in-class exercises, don't have one right answer.

CASE 11.1 – TEACHING IS SELLING!

Dave Casper's dean was not happy. From the moment that Dave walked into the dean's office, he knew that this would not be a convivial meeting. Peering over the top of his reading glasses as Dave sat on the edge of the sofa, the dean asked, "Have you had a chance to review your student evaluations from last semester? They're substandard once again."

"I know, Dean Farber. You'll notice, however, that I get high marks for knowing the material and for being prepared for class. I just don't know what to do about the rest," Dave replied.

"Well, you're going to have to figure it out," the dean retorted. "Too many students are withdrawing from this course. Since macroeconomics is required for business majors, we can't have that because it delays completion of their program. If you can't solve the problem, I'll have to find someone else who can get the job done."

Dave realized that defending his teaching approach and arguing with the dean was not the right strategy. "Do you have any suggestion? I'm not above trying something different."

"I'm not an economics professor. But your colleague, Martha Oakshott, has stellar reviews. Moreover, her average assigned grade is 'C+'; so she's not bribing the students with high grades. Go talk with her and see if you can learn something useful." With that, the meeting was over.

When Dave knocked on Martha's office door, she greeted him warmly. "Hi, Dave! What brings you here today?"

"Dean Farber suggested that I talk with you. My student evaluations are low again, and he thought you might have some suggestions for me."

"OK. Tell me what you're doing now," said Martha.

"As you know, I have a reputation for thoroughness and organization. I always get through the required material, and I'm extremely organized in class. For years, I have copied a detailed outline of my lecture on the board, and then I go over each point in order, embellishing whenever I can. I've refined my system so that I always finish on time. You know how students hate to be late getting out of class."

"Wow! You sure are organized," she said, struggling somewhat unsuccessfully not to wince.

"I can never stick to the material that well. But tell me, what exactly are you selling?"

"Selling? I don't know. I never thought of teaching as selling anything."

"Oh, but we're all selling something," said Martha with a twinkle. "Just for starters, aren't you trying to convince your students that macroeconomics is important for them as individuals, that what happens on a macroeconomic level will affect their careers directly, and that they should therefore pay attention to national and international economic developments?"

"I guess so. But how do you sell an idea like that? It's so abstract."

Martha then proceeded to explain in some detail what she meant by selling an idea. What do you think she told Dave? What sort of strategies did she advise him to try? How could Dave improve his classroom presentation in order to engage his students more effectively? Do or should selling techniques as outlined in Chapter 11 play any role at all in Dave's approach to teaching?

CASE 11.2 – DOROTHY'S DEBUT

The president of Dorothy Strong's company, SurgiMax, decided that it was time to make a splash. The company had just developed a new, high-intensity fiber-optic light and lens system, called a laparoscope, for surgical use. The new laparoscope was much smaller, but could generate a higher resolution image for viewing on a monitor. This would allow surgeons to perform noninvasive microsurgery in places that were impossible before. Since there were already hundreds of thousands of older laparoscopes already in use, surgeons would need to be convinced of the advantages of the new model before significant sales could be generated.

A convention of West Coast surgeons was coming up in San Francisco, and SurgiMax was on the program. The president himself usually made these presentations, but this time he thought he would call on Dorothy, his new vice president for sales and marketing, to do the honors. It would be an impressive way to introduce the new product: Dorothy was energetic, passionate about improving health care, and extremely successful as a salesperson in her own right. There was only one catch: there would be over 1,200 surgeons in the audience, and Dorothy had never addressed such a large group. While Dorothy was an expert at relationship selling, she had never had to anticipate the needs of so many people in a situation where no interaction was possible.

As Dorothy planned her presentation, she realized that she needed to accomplish three major objectives: (1) seize and hold the attention of 1,200 surgeons (who were typically skeptical and jaded) for at least 30 minutes, (2) present the features and benefits of the new laparoscope without appearing to be a medical authority, and (3) convince as many in the audience as possible to contact her or SurgiMax for more information.

How would you advise Dorothy regarding the following questions or issues pertaining to her big day?

Should she memorize her presentation, or should she use an outline approach?

What sort of visual or audio/visual aids should she use, and how much?

Should she use technical jargon and medical terms in describing the laparoscope's features?

What sort of evidence should she introduce to back up her claims that surgeons would find convincing?

As she moves through the presentation, what sort of tie-down questions should she introduce (even if no immediate responses are possible)? Or should she just forget about tie-down questions in this situation?

How should she end her presentation so that her audience desires more information?

Chapter 11 Footnotes

1. Brooks, Bill. "What is the Difference Between What Customers Need and What They Really Want." *The American Salesman* (January 2001): 3-5.
2. DiResta, Diane. *Knockout Presentations*. Chandler House Press (1998).
3. Engler, Bill. "Marketing Magic Inspired by P.T. Barnum." Marketingprofs.com, Accessed May 23, 2015.
4. Hoover's White Paper Series. "How to Convert Prospects to Sales Faster With Pre Call Planning." WhitePaperCompany.com, Accessed May 3, 2015.
5. Schultz, Mike and Doerr, John. "Sales Call Planning: What to Know Before Every Sales Call." Whillsgroup.com, Accessed May 3, 2015.
6. Hannan, Mack. "The Three C's of Selling: A Sure Cure for the Salesman's Curse." *Sales & Marketing Management* 10 no 7 (May 1976): 93.
7. Women's Business Center. "Features and Benefits." Onlinewbc.gov, Accessed November 23, 2014.
8. Taylor, Robert F. *Back to Basic Selling*. Englewood Cliffs, NJ: Prentice- Hall (1985): 75.
9. Trumfio, Ginger. "Underlying Motivatio." *Sales & Marketing Management*. (June 1994): 71.

10. Arbel, Tali. "Proceed with Caution: Presentation Roadblocks, Even the most seasoned salespeople know it: Presentations cause anxiety." *Sales and Marketing Management*, Accessed August 4, 2015, Web.

11. Kahn, George N. "You're on Stage." *Smooth Selling* (1975): 2.

12. National Sales Development Institute. *10 Steps to Greatness in Selling.* Waterford, CT: The National Sales Development Institute (1980): 10-12.

13. Marks, Ronald B. "Dramatize Your Presentation or Lose the Sale." advancedselling.com, Accessed November 20, 2014.

14. Mitchell, Olivia. "9 Tips for Enriching Your Presentations With Social Media." *Mashable.com*, December 4, 2009. Accessed October 7, 2015. Web.

15. Holcombe, Martha W. and. Stein, Judith K. "How to Deliver Dynamic Presentations: Use Visuals for Impact." *Business Marketing* 71, no 6 (June 1986): 163-164; Kern, Richard. "Making Visual Aids Work for You." *Sales & Marketing Management* (February 1989): 46-49.

16. Rosenthal, Bill. "How To Power Up Your Sales Force with Tablets." *Sales and Marketing Management,* March 3, 2014, Web.

"OBSTACLES ARE NECESSARY FOR SUCCESS BECAUSE IN SELLING, AS IN ALL CAREERS OF IMPORTANCE, **VICTORY COMES ONLY AFTER MANY STRUGGLES AND COUNTLESS DEFEATS."**

– OG MANDINO

CHAPTER 12
WELCOMING OBJECTIONS

OVERVIEW

Chapter twelve invites you to take a different approach to objections from soon-to-be customers by welcoming resistance into the sales process. In this chapter, you will learn how prospect objections are often signs of interest. You will also discover the various types of objections you will encounter, and finally, the best ways to overcome them.

OBJECTIVES

- Develop a positive attitude toward objections.
- Understand why prospects have sales resistance.
- Learn how to uncover hidden concerns or questions.
- Know the basic strategies for overcoming sales resistance.
- Become familiar with the six-step plan for dealing with sales resistance.
- Learn specific techniques to overcome objections.
- Discover tactics to handle price concerns.

REDEFINING OBJECTIONS

It's time for an attitude shift regarding the word "objection." Why? Well, if it weren't for objections, you'd be out of a job! Look at it this way: If it was *so* obvious to *every* prospect why they should buy your product or service that they do so freely and without hesitation, there would literally be no need for the work of salespeople. So, as we move into a discussion of how to handle objections from prospects, let's redefine them as a *positive* event.

Of course, that is easier said than done. Simply mentioning the word may send some salespeople into a state of panic. The problem with the word *objection* is that it brings to mind some sort of clash between salesperson and prospect—in which case, someone wins and someone loses. However, what many fail to understand is hearing the word "*no*" and hearing an *objection* are two vastly different things. Objections move prospects nearer to the close and reveal what they are concerned about. In fact, an objection often reveals the key to successfully closing the sale.

Sales trainers often refer to objections as the real beginning of the sales process. In short, objections often signal that you are on the right track! Zig Ziglar, one of the most well-known and respected sales experts of all time, always said that we should welcome objections and start viewing them as encouraging rather than disheartening.[1]

"Always bear in mind that your own resolution to succeed is more important than any one thing."

Abraham Lincoln

If the prospect has been properly qualified, objections are really buying signals. Offering an objection is another way for the prospect to say, "Here are my conditions for buying," or "I want to buy as soon as you answer a few more questions or reassure me that buying is the smart thing to do." Welcome objections! They are the verbal and nonverbal signs of sales resistance that give you the chance to discover what the prospect is thinking. These objections later become leverage for closing the sale. Successful sales presentations—those that end in a sale—often have twice as many objections as those presentations that are unsuccessful.[2] Qualified prospects will not raise objections to a proposal in which they have no interest. They simply wait—and then say no.

An *objection* is anything the prospect says or does that presents an obstacle to the smooth completion of the sale.

That definition sounds simple enough, right? It's not quite that easily defined due to the fact that sales resistance, or an objection, contains elements of both logic and emotion. When people really want something, logic can take a back seat to emotion. Of course, this is not always the case—especially when it comes to complex business transactions. Regardless of how much emotion is involved in the process, objections are a normal and natural part of almost every conversation—not just in sale situations, but whenever people discuss any current topic.[3] People want their opinions and concerns to be heard.

A purchasing decision usually involves risk. People face the risk of actually having to make a decision, the risk of trying something new, or perhaps worse, the risk of buying something that does not work for them or the situation. To ease the fear of risk, people object, raise concerns, or ask questions in hopes of getting answers that will convince them that the buying decision is in their best interests. Objections are so common that research indicates a prospect will say "no" at least five times before they actually buy.[4]

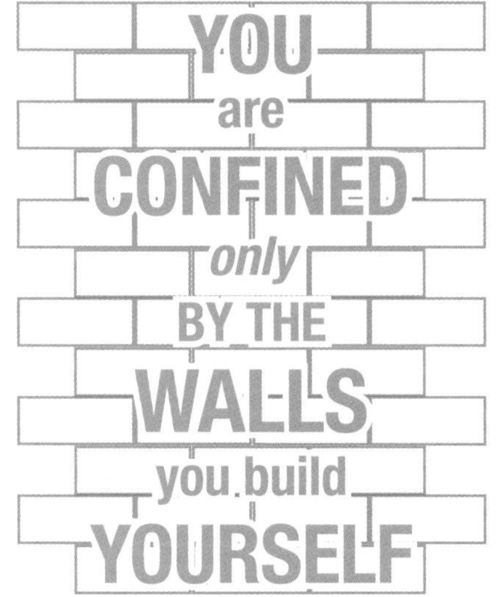

The first task in answering an objection is to calm the prospect's emotions by proving that you are open to reason. Pause before responding; then acknowledge that you respect the prospect's opinion and find the views expressed worthy of consideration. People are open to changing their opinions and attitudes when they are convinced that others value their opinions, understand how they can feel that way, and grant them the right to those opinions. Show a measure of empathy; thus, the key to maintaining a positive sales environment is to *disagree without being disagreeable.*[5]

Arguing with a prospect, particularly in response to objections, is one of the easiest and most disastrous mistakes you can make. The negotiation process is not a battle that you win and the prospect loses; rather, it is a situation of mutual cooperation and mutual benefit. People who are forced to agree seldom actually change their minds. Never force a prospect into making a decision; prospects are more likely to stay sold and come back to you for repeat business if the decision to buy was their idea.

TYPES OF OBJECTIONS

The difficulty with objections is that they have the tendency to sound like *obstacles* that will stop the sale. When the prospect objects, you must understand what type of sales resistance is being offered before you can handle it effectively. Sales resistance may be separated into four general categories: *The stall or put-off, the searcher, the hidden objection,* and *the stopper.*

1 The Stall or Put-Off

When prospects offer a *stall* or *put-off objection,* look for the true meaning behind their words. Oftentimes, the prospect is simply trying to avoid making a decision; the stall is a way of saying, "I really don't want to think about your proposition right now because I would then be forced to make a decision."[6] Other times, the prospect is "not convinced that your offering will help his bottom line."[7] However, you should rarely experience this kind of stall if you have properly qualified a prospect at the beginning. The stall could mean that you have not presented a compelling enough reason to buy, or, in other words, that "you don't yet have a clear understanding about the problem your product or service will solve."[8] A stall is a classic sales killer unless you can build on the sense of rapport you've established with the prospect. If you hear a stall, ask a relevant question, and truly care about the response. You are much more likely to gain a sale if you ask questions, uncover the prospect's genuine concerns, and focus on the relationship, not the sale. Here are some examples of how stalls are phrased by prospects and some suggestions for responding to each stall:[9]

1. I have to leave in fifteen minutes; I have an important meeting.
I understand—we are both busy people, and I don't want to keep you from your work. I will call you again in a few weeks. Then, I will only need a few minutes to get your opinion on the specific issues that are most important to you and your business right now, and how our organization might help find the solution.

2. Just leave your literature with my assistant. I will look it over in the next week or so and then call you.
I'd love to leave some material. I think you'll find we've covered a lot of it already. I must have not made myself clear at some point along the way, and for that, I apologize. Would you tell me which areas require a better explanation?

3. I must talk this over with my partner.
I certainly understand wanting to involve your partner in a decision like this. Can we ask him to join us now, or set up a meeting that works for everyone's schedule?

How you handle a stall is really a test of your *attitude*. If you believe you have a qualified prospect whose needs will be satisfied by your product, then you do not allow a put-off to put you off. You should try to uncover the real reason behind the stall.

2 The Searcher

The second type of objection is called a *searcher*, which is a hidden request for additional information.[10] Some prospects object simply to get more information even though they have already mentally decided they want to buy. The customer just wants to be convinced that buying your product or service is the right thing to do. Here are some suggested responses for handling the four most common searcher objections with finesse:

1. I'm not interested.
I understand. There is no reason why you should be interested until I explain how our company is allowing people like you to pay their bills and medical expenses even if they are unable to work. Are you aware of how much a three-day stay in the hospital costs, even with major medical insurance?

2. I don't have the money for this.
If you did have the money, would you want it? Good! What is it about the product that is so appealing to you?

3. We are satisfied with what we have now.
I can certainly respect that. It's nice to talk to someone who is happy with what they have! Tell you what—I'd still like to make sure I understand what you like and maybe even what you'd change about your current equipment, so that next year, perhaps you'll remember us as you assess your needs for upgrades. Now, if you could change one thing about your current process, what would it be?

4. I really like the competitor's product.
I am not surprised to hear you say that. Their product does have some interesting features. Allow me to show you how what we are doing this year is actually quite cutting edge and can't really be directly compared to their efforts…

3 The Hidden Objection

The third type of sales resistance is called the *hidden objection*. This kind of resistance is often more difficult to overcome. The prospect refuses to let you know the real concern. Many times the reason is actually quite personal, so the prospect prefers not to reveal it or has a vague feeling that cannot be articulated easily. Exhibit 12.1 pictures the hidden objection as an iceberg lurking below the surface. Just the tip of the iceberg is revealed. You know the prospect has a hidden objection when the answers fail to make sense.

Based on the presentation up to that point, the reasons for not buying are not logical. That means the prospect likely has other reasons for objecting that are not directly related to something specific in your presentation or your product. For example, a prospect may simply not feel comfortable revealing these four real concerns:

1. "Circumstances have changed since you first spoke with me. Recent family problems have caused severe financial hardships, and I do not have the ability to pay for your product."
2. "I find this whole situation distasteful, and I don't want to deal with you. I don't like you, but social convention prevents my being blunt enough to tell you so."
3. "I really don't know what my objection is. It just doesn't feel right. Quite frankly, the product looks like a cheap imitation to me."
4. "I really wasn't in the market for your product. I just wanted to hear what you had to say for future reference."

EXHIBIT 12.1 THE HIDDEN OBJECTION

4 The Stopper

Prospects often have legitimate reasons why they feel unable to buy. This fourth type of objection is what can be called a stopper.[11] The *stopper* is an objection to which no satisfactory solution can be found. For instance, if you can promise delivery no sooner than six months from now and the prospect absolutely must have the product in three months, you cannot—or at least, you should not—make that sale. Not every prospect is a fit for your product or service. This is inevitable, and if you encounter such a situation, simply recognize this and move on to a more qualified prospect with a real need for what you sell and the ability to buy.

THE HEART OF SALES RESISTANCE

The relationship salesperson must get to the heart of the prospect's objection before it can be negotiated successfully. Before you can assemble the appropriate facts, logic, and evidence to resolve a vaguely stated objection, you must know the basis for the prospect's point of view.[12] To make intelligent responses to customer resistance, you must know the underlying circumstances.

Most objections that an experienced salesperson hears are not original. If you have been selling for any length of time, your chance of encountering an objection you have not heard before is remote. Eighty percent of buyers will give you the same five or six objections. You should therefore be ready to handle each one in advance and have practiced handling them in a training course or sales meeting first.[13]

To deal effectively with the objections you hear, develop a worksheet to categorize them and the responses you use to answer them effectively. Write out your responses word for word, commit them to memory, and practice delivering each one so that it becomes a responsive, intrinsic action. Polish and refine your responses; keep a record of how they are received. You will soon be able to choose the best possible response from your prepared list for each situation you encounter. Exhibit 12.2 lists six basic categories of buyer resistance with examples of what the prospect might say or, in the case of hidden objections, might think.

EXHIBIT 12.2 CATEGORIES OF BUYER OBJECTIONS

Product Objections

- The materials are not up to industry standards; the product is poor quality.
- I'm not sure the products won't hold up over time.
- This has the same features as your competitor but is priced higher.

Company Objections

- Your company is not well known. I prefer to deal with large, established companies.
- I've never heard of your company or know anyone who has done business with you.
- Didn't your company get some bad press recently?

Aversion to Decision-Making

- We are happy with what we have.
- See me on your next trip.
- I want to think it over.
- We don't have room for your product line.

Service Objections

- Your delivery schedule doesn't work for us.
- We need same-day response on all service calls.
- Your maintenance contract doesn't meet our needs.

Objections to Salesperson (Possibly Hidden)

- You are not very well prepared.
- You're not really listening to my concerns.
- You're trying to sell me too aggressively.
- I don't like you.

Price Objections (Possibly Hiding Real Objection)

- I can't afford it.
- Your pricing structure is out of line.
- I'm going to wait until prices come down.

WHEN TO ANSWER OBJECTIONS

A lot more has been said about how to overcome objections than about when to answer them, but choosing the proper time to answer them is just as crucial as the answer itself.[14] In determining when to answer an objection, you must consider the type, why it has been raised, the mood of the prospect, and in what phase of the interview it is raised. Timing is important in any negotiation. Prospects introduce an objection at a time that favors their position. Why shouldn't you choose to handle it when the timing favors your position? Normally, there are four logical times for responding to the buyer's concerns that we will discuss:

1. Answer it immediately when it is raised.
2. Anticipate and forestall objections.
3. Postpone the answer until later in the presentation.
4. Do not answer an excuse.

1. Answer Immediately

Most valid objections should be answered when they are raised unless you have a logical reason to wait. If you feel the objection is valid and postponing an answer could cause problems, then obviously it should be handled immediately. Answering an objection right away prevents it from festering in your prospect's mind and blocking out the more important information you are presenting. Never answer until you are sure of the real concern, and once it is discovered, answer in thirty seconds or less. Answer questions briefly and honestly; be congenial and intelligent.[15] A sincere and immediate response conveys professionalism, respect for the prospect's point of view, empathy, and listening skills. The right answer removes the resistance and promotes the sale.

2. Anticipate and Forestall Objections

Every product or service has both strengths and weaknesses. Because no product is perfect, a prospect may well identify a negative feature or shortcoming in what you sell. Hoping that the prospect will fail to notice a negative feature is futile. Instead of waiting for the prospect to raise a specific objection, anticipate the objection and forestall or answer it in the presentation before the prospect can ask. Just as companies want to stay ahead of the curve in technology and product advancements, you must strive to stay ahead of the "objection curve."[16]

Weave into your presentation factual answers to anticipated objections, so they are answered before the prospect verbalizes them. Anticipating objections requires a well-thought-out, planned presentation delivered from the prospect's point of view and focusing on value. Don't just identify potential roadblocks; spell out how to overcome them as well. The more obstacles you remove in advance, the easier it is for others to welcome your suggestions.[17]

A good strategy for anticipating and overcoming objections is to do your homework first: Before you meet, make sure that your prospect is indeed a viable prospect—that the prospect matches your ideal customer profile. When you call on a prospect who is not a good match for your offering, you make things harder for yourself. Such prospects don't even need or want what you have to offer— so naturally they have objections![18]

Of course, dealing with an objection early in the presentation does not guarantee that it will not be raised again. However, you are at an advantage in such a situation for two reasons:

- The objection has much less impact the second time.
- You may recall the original answer, expand upon it, and then move on into a close or back into the presentation if necessary.

3. Postpone the Answer

Some answers to objections are better postponed. This tactic is logical when you are planning to cover that very point further along and the prospect has simply jumped ahead. To answer early might disrupt the flow of the presentation and make the answer less effective. For example, the prospect may be wondering about price and ask, "How much is this going to cost me?" This often occurs before you have had the chance to establish the value of your product. If you answer immediately, the price may seem too high because the prospect has not yet learned enough about the product to make a value judgment. The price may depend upon options selected; in that case, you cannot quote an accurate price. You may need to build a better foundation before risking a confrontation with the prospect.[19] You can postpone answering an objection by saying something like this:

1. I can appreciate that you would be interested in that, and I assure you we will discuss it completely, but before we even consider that issue, I want to be sure that my service can satisfy your needs. Will that be all right?
2. Mr. McCreary, your concern for price is quite understandable. The actual amount paid for the product, however, will depend upon the options you ultimately select. Let's consider the price for the system after we establish the specific features you will require. Is that fair enough?

The price question should be answered near the end of the presentation, after need, value, and benefits have been discussed. For the most part, however, postponing an answer to a prospect's question should be done as infrequently as possible.

4. Do Not Answer an Excuse

A final alternative is to simply not answer an excuse. After all, some issues don't have a worthwhile answer. On some sales calls, prospects raise concerns that have nothing to do with your discussion. They say things that have no relevance to the point you are trying to make. In reality, they are offering excuses for not buying rather than valid resistance. By acknowledging excuses, you may actually turn them into real objections in the prospect's mind. If you must reply to excuses, suggest to the prospect that you will answer them at the end of the presentation. If the question is a serious objection, the prospect will repeat it later. Exhibit 12.3 summarizes the factors to consider in choosing the best time to deal with objections.

EXHIBIT 12.3 TIMING CONSIDERATIONS FOR OBJECTIONS

1. Answer the Objection Immediately

- Answer immediately so the prospect can concentrate on the rest of the sales story.
- Answering the prospect immediately shows them your sincerity.
- An immediate answer prevents prospects from inferring that you are unable to answer.

2. Anticipate the Objection and Answer It Before It Arises

- This option should be considered only when you are fairly certain that the prospect will bring up the objection.
- Anticipating the objection prevents a future confrontation and shows your objectivity.

3. Postpone an Answer Until Later

- Postponing an answer allows you to present many more benefits that have the effect of reducing the significance of the objection.
- Postponing an answer allows you to maintain control of the interview by keeping to your agenda rather than to that of the prospect.
- Postponing an answer gives you time to think about how you will answer it.

4. Do Not Answer an Excuse

- Not acknowledging an objection is one way to separate it from an excuse. The serious prospect will repeat it.
- By not answering, you suggest that the excuse is not relevant and imply that bringing it up again is not necessary.

A SIX-STEP PLAN FOR IDENTIFYING OBJECTIONS

Why do salespeople need specific plans to handle objections? The answer rests in maintaining control. If you allow a prospect to derail you from your presentation with every question or comment, you lose control of the flow of the conversation; when this happens, your perceived value decreases—and so do your chances for making the sale.[20]

You can best handle prospects' objections successfully by first identifying them, and then placing them in the proper perspective—then the well-handled objections become powerful aids. To handle them skillfully, you need a definite negotiation strategy so that you react naturally to buyers' concerns. Knowing that you have a strategy gives you confidence; then you can welcome objections instead of shuddering at the very thought that the prospect may not go along with your proposition. The following steps are part of the six-step plan that, once internalized, you can use instinctively and automatically to welcome and overcome objections:

STEP 1: Hear the Prospect Out

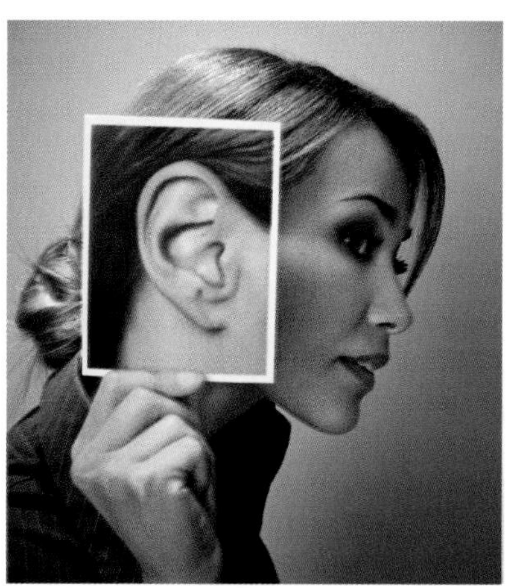

Be happy when the prospect raises an objection, because it provides the information needed to complete the negotiation. Never interrupt a prospect who is expressing an opinion; rather, listen carefully to what the prospect says. Observe the prospect's verbal and nonverbal behavior, and listen to what is not being said. Recognize the prospect's right to express opinions and concerns. The prospect is really telling you what to do, and their objection is saying to you:

- "Give me more information."
- "Go over that service agreement again—it wasn't clear."
- "Reassure me one more time that this is a good decision."

Simply paying attention is the first step in becoming more responsive to your prospect's objections. Active listening will help you to better respond to what your prospect is saying. If you really listen, then you can pinpoint what the source of the objection is. This process will help you to better explain the ways your product or service can serve your prospect's needs and be of value to them in the long term.

STEP 2: Confirm Your Understanding of the Objection

Restate the prospect's objection to make sure you understand just what it is; this is a critical negotiation tactic. Use your own words and repeat what the prospect was saying to clarify and classify the real objection and to indicate to the prospect that you understood what was said. In addition, you give yourself time to formulate an answer. Say, "Now as I understand it, your position is... ," and then explain the prospect's position in your own words. When you prove you understand, the prospect is ready to listen to you.

> **Restating the objection in a sympathetic manner dissolves the prospect's defensiveness and helps you avoid the temptation to argue.**

Your purpose in this phase is to evaluate and isolate the stated concern. Determine whether the reason given for not buying is the real reason, simply an excuse, or a statement hiding the actual objection. You may decide to answer immediately, not answer an excuse, or seek more information. If you need more information before you can answer, ask questions until you have the information you need. There are a number of questions you might ask the prospect that can help you isolate the real issue and confirm your understanding.[21] These questions include:

1. Other than that, is there any other reason that would prevent you from purchasing?
2. I am glad you brought that out into the open. Is this your only concern?
3. If we can work together to find a solution to this important concern, would that help you make a purchase decision?

It may help to ask the prospect to explain the objection. At times, the prospect may not know fully what they are objecting to, and explaining it will help clarify the issue for both you and the prospect.

STEP 3: Acknowledge the Prospect's Point of View

All successful negotiations find points of agreement before you begin to answer an objection. Agree as far as possible before answering, and take responsibility for any misunderstanding. If the prospect indicates a bad experience with your company or your predecessor, believe it. Find a way to cushion your response so that it has a chance of convincing the prospect. After all, prospects believe they have good reasons for not buying and give you those reasons. Instead of arguing directly, soften your answer and say something like this:

1. I can certainly understand how you feel, Mr. Keenan. Others have had much the same feeling when I first presented the concept to them. (Then provide a plausible explanation.)
2. I appreciate your concern, and you do have a relevant point, Mr. Rogers. Thank you for bringing it to my attention. (And you really should appreciate it.)

STEP 4: Select a Specific Technique

In the next section of this chapter, six techniques are detailed for use in formulating answers to the types of sales resistance you may encounter. Not all of them work all the time. In deciding which of the techniques to use, take these factors into consideration:

- The prospect's behavioral style
- The stage of the negotiation process in which the objection is raised
- The mood (argumentative or receptive) of the prospect
- How many times the objection has come up
- The type of objection (searcher, excuse, stall, product or service)

You must decide quickly on the technique you will use and avoid showing that an objection has upset you. Keep in mind that far too many variables operate in a given selling situation to guarantee that every objection can be answered satisfactorily.

STEP 5: Answer the Objection

Negotiation is persuasion, not manipulation. Avoid explanations that merely cloud the issue and cause prospects to feel that you are trying to pressure them. The answer, however, must be conclusive; don't close off your answer with the question still up in the air. Present only as much information as required to gain the prospect's cooperation and commitment. Minimize the objection by not dwelling on it. Say just enough to dispose of it to the prospect's satisfaction. Be honest and factual, and do not promise anything that you, your company, or your product or service cannot deliver.

Prospects have their own needs, viewpoints, and ways of looking at things. Be sure to consider the prospect's ego and help the prospect win. Your answer should include a benefit and should be shaped to fit the behavioral style of that prospect. Finally, confirm that your answer satisfied the prospect. Gain agreement by suggesting, "Am I correct in assuming that I have completely satisfied you regarding...?"

STEP 6: Attempt to Close

Closing opportunities exist at various times throughout the entire negotiation process. Recognizing those times and capitalizing upon them is up to you. When you have successfully answered a major objection, you have created an opportunity to close, especially if you are near the end of the presentation. Attempt a trial close before continuing with the presentation. The trial close gets a prospect's reaction without exerting any pressure for making a definite decision. It may be used at any point in the sales presentation to test the water to see whether you have presented enough information for the prospect to make a decision. Typical trial closes start with "If you were to buy," "In your opinion," or "How do you feel about..."

If you receive positive buying signals from the prospect at this point, you can attempt to close. If the close proves unsuccessful, get back on track and continue the presentation until another opportunity presents itself.

SIX TECHNIQUES FOR NAVIGATING OBJECTIONS

Keep in mind that with any technique you must produce evidence to prove the validity of what you say. Techniques do not establish belief and credibility; that is your job. Techniques are merely vehicles for organizing your answer and your support for it. After an objection has been clarified and classified, you are in an excellent position to respond by using one or more of the following techniques.

1. Feel, Felt, Found

This practical technique overcomes a stall or a very personal concern. It can offset prospect hostility, pacify an unhappy customer, or inform someone who does not yet clearly understand the value of the product or service. Answer the prospect with this language:

> *I can understand how you feel.... I have had other customers who felt the same way until they found out....*

This approach serves several purposes. It shows prospects that you understand their concerns, and it reassures the prospect that having this kind of objection is normal. Now the stage is set to introduce information that can change the prospect's way of thinking. This technique says that other people who are now customers had similar misgivings but changed their minds after they found out some new information. These new facts allow the prospect to reevaluate your proposition. The following example illustrates how a financial executive in a sales role might use this negotiation technique with an unhappy client:

Financial Consultant: *Good afternoon, Mr. Reznor. I am Porter Andrews with Green Leaf Financial. I have been assigned to your account and would like to ... (suddenly interrupted!)*

Client: *So your company is playing musical chairs with its reps again. It took Lily Allen six months just to learn about my business needs and now I have to train someone new. Why can't you people give me someone who will stay with me?*

Financial Consultant: *I certainly understand how you might feel that way. Some of Lily's other clients have indicated that they felt the same way. However, the Green Leaf has found that someone with Lily's experience is an invaluable asset to our Problem Loan Division. I have previously worked with firms in your line of business (mention them and provide testimonial letters) and from my review of your account, I feel I have a pretty good understanding of your operation. (By the way, here are my credentials.)*

The *feel, felt, found* technique is commonly used in a vast number of industries, and if you are dealing with a seasoned professional, he or she may likely recognize that you are using this "technique" and get annoyed if they are aware of what you are doing. Then again, such a prospect might be impressed and even have a good laugh with you, not at you, because they will know what you are trying to accomplish.[22] Here is an example of how to rearrange your words slightly in these situations:

"Mrs. Akers, I do understand how you must feel. Frankly, lots of my customers have felt the same way when they first heard about our program, but what they discovered after further discussion was the benefits heavily outweighed the limitations."

2. Compensation or Counterbalance Method

At times, a prospect may buy in spite of certain valid objections. The prospect may be partly right or may have misunderstood a portion of what you said. Accept and admit any truth in the objection. Admit that your product does have the disadvantage that the prospect has noticed and then immediately point out how the objection is overshadowed by other specific benefits of the product. Your job is to convince the prospect that the compensating benefits provide enough value that the disadvantage should not prevent the prospect from buying. By admitting the objection, you impress the prospect with your sincerity and sense of fair dealing. Then you can select the real strengths of your offering to offset the prospect's negative feelings.

A good way to deal with this situation is to provide documentation such as *statistical evidence, a third-party endorsement,* or the *case history* of someone who faced a similar situation. This method works because the prospect is approached positively with an acknowledgment of expressed concerns, and then given a series of logical, compensating benefits to counterbalance the stated objection.

3. Ask "Why?" or a Specific Question

This method is helpful not only for separating excuses from real objections but also for overcoming objections. You can use questions to narrow a major, generalized objection to specific points that are easier to handle. If the prospect says, "I don't like to do business with your company," ask, "What is it that you don't like about our firm?" The answer may show a past misunderstanding that can be cleared up. If the prospect complains, "I don't like the looks of your product," ask, "Why do you object to its appearance?" The objection may be based on a relatively minor aspect that can be changed or is not true of all models.

4. Remove a Misconception

One way to answer buyer resistance is simply to assert that the prospect is mistaken. The denial technique is useful when the prospect clearly has the wrong information. Either a portion of the presentation was misunderstood or someone else has supplied incorrect information. This technique must be used with caution or it will antagonize prospects. You can sometimes tell prospects they have been misinformed, but you have to be careful how you do it. You could win the discussion but lose the sale.

Point out that the prospect's information is incorrect, but not by means of a direct, frontal assault. Present the denial thoughtfully and with dignity. Listen attentively to the buyer's concern, and then begin by saying:

> *Would you mind explaining the issue to me so that I can more fully understand? I want to make sure I can fully resolve this for you.*

This response allows the buyer time to cool down emotionally and perhaps to soften the statement. It also gives you the opportunity to regain your composure. After the prospect repeats the incorrect information, respond in this manner:

> *If I gave you that impression, I certainly do apologize. I really must have stated my position poorly; please let me correct it for you...*

Your attitude is critical when using this technique. Your goal is to earn the prospect's respect and avoid an angry reaction. However, you do want the prospect to know that you will not be intimidated—and sometimes a direct denial is your only recourse. A direct denial is a high-risk method of dealing with any objection, but it is necessary at times if someone has heard something about you, your company, or your products that could unfairly damage your reputation.

5. Boomerang Method

The boomerang method allows you to agree with prospects yet show them that their objections need not prevent a purchase. This method is often used in a situation where the point to which the prospect is objecting is actually a sales point in favor of buying the particular product or service. The boomerang method involves agreeing with the objection and then making another statement that translates the objection into a reason for buying. For example, a sales representative for Blue Bell Inc., might hear this type of objection:

"Blue Bell Ice Cream is too new to this area. My customers will not buy something they have never heard of before."

Then turn the objection into a sales point:

"There is no question that our ice cream is new to your area; that's why we are eager to build consumer awareness for the product. We intend to spend over $100,000 to tell your potential customers about our ice cream. Blue Bell uses its advertising messages to presell the product for you. If you agree to carry the product, we will generate a great deal of customer demand (and increase store traffic) for you."

The boomerang method works well when the prospect lacks complete information or perceives a drawback that actually may not exist. Be careful of the image you project when using this technique. If prospects feel that you are directly challenging them or perhaps patronizing them, then you could be in for a real battle. In that case, you might as well pull out your boxing gloves because you will have more use for them than you will for your order book.

The tongue-in-cheek method is an adaptation of the boomerang method. It uses a bit of humor that may soften up the prospects and turn away their anger. A salesperson for Strickfaden's Nursery in Sandusky, Ohio, used the technique this way:

Prospect: *"I'm not going to buy any more shade trees from you; every time I plant one I have too much dirt left over!"*

Salesperson: *"Yes, that is a concern. But the way to solve your problem is to dig your holes a little deeper."*

6. Curiosity Method

By now, you already know that prospects and salespeople work best together when prospects believe their specific needs are being addressed. The curiosity method works inside this relationship-driven approach. In other words, you should already be asking your prospects questions, so if they raise an objection, it will be natural for you to answer that objection with a question of your own. Take a look at the following scenario in which a web-based invoicing software system salesperson is trying to close on a sale:

Prospect: *"I don't think my clients will easily accept such a complex electronic billing system.*

Salesperson: *I wonder why that is?*

Notice the salesperson did not simply ask "why," which could seem aggressive and does not reflect an active listen attitude. Instead, the salesperson demonstrated a genuine curiosity about the s objection. This curiosity allows for an exploration and identification of specific needs. The salesperson can then more meaningfully explain the value of the product features.

FOLLOWING UP YOUR RESPONSE WITH VISUALS. Each of the six methods above have a time and place where they are most effective, depending on many factors such as the type of objection, the personality of the prospect, and the level of knowledge you have about the prospect and his situation. Because most people are visual learners, answering an objection with an *infographic* (graphic visual representations of information, data or knowledge intended to present information quickly and clearly) or a picture of your company's products in action or letters from satisfied customers are great ways to take the focus off the resistance and put it back onto the product and the prospect's needs. This idea works well with any prospect who is visually oriented, and it works especially well with the younger generation. In fact, although Facebook, Twitter, YouTube, and LinkedIn are the most widely used social networks for business, Instagram is growing in popularity in the business world. Owned by Facebook, Instagram is a social media site where the predominant age group of users is currently eighteen to twenty-nine years old. The site allows you to quickly share photos and short videos with your followers. This chapter's Social Media Connection provides you with five ways to make the most of visual sharing on Instagram for your sales career.

THE SOCIAL MEDIA CONNECTION

Getting the Most Out of Instagram

1. **USE INSTAGRAM TO REPORT LIVE.** On the field or at product launches, use Instagram to capture moments in real-time through photos and video. Always be sure to include a short caption.
2. **SHARE SCREENSHOTS OF PHOTOS (A.K.A. REGRAM).** Using the screenshot function on your smartphone, you can add images to your smartphone's photo library that can then be shared on Instagram. Create screenshots of your own photos or of branded images that you have posted on other social networks and then share them on Instagram.
3. **ADD HASHTAGS TO CAPTIONS.** Users that consistently use hashtags on Instagram have twice as many followers as those that don't. Instagram users regularly monitor hashtags, thus enabling you to gain more exposure to potential new followers. In addition to your own product or company-specific hashtags, you should also monitor and use the hashtags that are most popular on Instagram.
4. **USE THIRD-PARTY INSTAGRAM APPS.** There are a number of third-party Instagram apps worth experimenting with. In addition to Slidagram and Flipagram, explore Statigram for tracking your Instagram analytics and Copygram, which allows you to print your Instagram photos.
5. **SHARE DAILY.** To gain followers on Instagram, you must be active. If possible, post once in the morning and once in the afternoon or evening. Instagram images and videos have peak activity during the first four hours after sharing, so to be consistently active, strive to post twice daily.

DEMYSTIFYING PRICE OBJECTIONS

One type of objection surfaces so frequently that it requires additional examination: *The Price Objection.* Your prospects and customers want as much for their money as they can get. While that's not unexpected, you can't provide value-added service at reasonable prices if you give up too much at the negotiating table. How many times each week do you suppose a salesperson hears, "I just think your price is too high." To succeed in selling, you must see this type of sales resistance for what it is and overcome it.

The price objection is more difficult to pin down because it can mean many different things. The final price paid for a product or service depends upon the type of discounts available, advertising and promotional allowances paid by the seller, service after the sale, free trial periods, warranties or money-back guarantees, sales support service and training, delivery charges, and myriad other price-related variables. Then, too, the prospect may not really be objecting to the price but may just be hiding the real reason for not buying. When prospects says, "I can't afford it" or "Your prices are just too high," they may just be saying, "You have not convinced me that the value I will receive is worth the price I have to pay to get it." Often the buyer's concerns or questions about price represent an incomplete sales job!

Never be afraid to ask the full value for your offering, but be prepared with solid evidence to support the price you are asking. Do not be defensive or apologetic; you must believe that the price you are quoting is actually much less than the value your product will give the prospect. If your product has exclusive features that are not readily apparent, convert them to benefits and sell those benefits.

> People have a perceived price-quality relationship. They do not mind spending money when the quality and value of the purchase have been successfully established.

Four Methods for Conquering the Price Question

A product often has hidden qualities, and the prospect cannot see these qualities and does not fully appreciate them until they are pointed out. You must face the fact that you will not always have the lowest-priced product or service to sell. Competitors may be able to undersell you because they have the same basic costs but are cutting corners somewhere with lower standards of product quality, service, or delivery. A bargain price can turn out to be quite expensive—and you usually get what you pay for.

Be prepared to justify your asking price and show that it is fair. Understand and be able to apply the *differential competitive advantages* you have in product, source, people, or service superiority.[23] There are a number of negotiation tactics that can help you overcome the price obstacle. You may respond to the question of price by using one or a combination of the following methods.

1

DO A PRICE BREAKDOWN. The price that sounds intimidating in its entirety often sounds much smaller when you break it down into weekly or monthly payments and compare it to how the customer normally spends extra money. If the prospect is really objecting to the absolute magnitude of the price, then a logical response is to break the total cost down over a period of time. Here is an example of how you might use this technique to convince a physician:

> *I am glad you mentioned price, and I can certainly appreciate your concern. The upfront cost of the software system does seem like quite a bit of money. But you know how essential a professional graphics suite is for your practice. Adobe recognizes this and has just implemented a monthly payment plan. Just*

imagine, for the price of a yearly subscription to a magazine for your waiting room, your office staff will have access to the best software on the market.

Compare the one-time price of your product to the amount of money the prospect will save after years of using it. The clearer you make the distinction between what your prospects pay and what they get, the easier it will be for them to recognize your product's great value. That's your job—to establish value, not price.[24] Talk about the initial and ultimate costs. Look at the price-cost-value comparison from two perspectives: *Price* represents the initial amount paid for the product; *cost* is the amount the buyer pays as the product is used over time.

2 **EMPLOY THE PRESUMPTION OF EXCLUSIVITY.** What can you do when the price for your company's product is higher than that being asked by a competitor? Stress those features that are exclusively yours, identify extras that only come from you and sell quality, exclusivity—aka your product's uniqueness—and differential features. What does your product have that the competition cannot offer? No two products are exactly alike. Analyze your competitor's offering to see why the same product has a lower price. If your analysis indicates that you are offering more, then drive home those exclusive features. You may have to show more interest in the prospect than the competition that concentrates only on price. Go out of your way to isolate other needs of the prospect for which you can provide assistance.

If your company has a higher price, then it must be because you offer more to your customers. Identify your advantages and convince the prospect that the extras can be obtained only from you. In other words, justify the price with facts. Determine what the prospect wants more than anything else from your product, and then identify the features that satisfy those wants. This is called the *presumption of exclusivity.* Concentrate on those features until the prospects feel that only you can satisfy their needs. Consider this example of how one salesperson's lack of product knowledge prevented a sale:

A prospect was not convinced that the newest arrival in the company's product line was offering him a better deal and was reluctant to change suppliers. With every question that the prospect posed to Ron, the sales rep, it became evident that the prospect knew more about the various options and offers in the industry than Ron did. "Really?" Ron would say, "That's their new scheme?" For every answer, he went into a huddle with his boss, who appeared equally clueless. The prospect thanked him for his time and left without purchasing.

The prospect had the upper hand because Ron did not understand the concept of the *presumption of exclusivity.* A visionary salesperson will be able to not just anticipate knowledgeable prospects, but be so educated about his own industry and product line that he can show his product's unique features in such a way that prevents this objection from even surfacing.[25]

If a prospect gives you a hard time about price, stop selling price. Instead, show what the price buys. Make the cost seem unimportant in comparison to the value received. You may try something like these:

Mr. Dykes, allow me to share some information with you. The lower price of our competitor may not be the best buy for you. Let's look at the quality of our product and why we are more expensive on the front end. We pay our employees a fair wage, purchase superior-grade raw materials, and have a warranty period that exceeds our closest competitor by five years.

I can understand your concern about price. The good news is, our price includes training for your people; our staff is skilled at maintaining and upgrading the product over time. You will have easy availability of parts and a 100% money-back guarantee. We stand behind our product. We don't fight your complaints; we settle them promptly and equitably. The price paid for a solution to your problem should be based on what gives you the best solution. Don't you agree?

Draw the picture clearly and convincingly. Sell quality and exclusivity when the prospect argues price. If you sell the exclusive features properly, the prospect is not even thinking about price by the end of the presentation. Most buyers are fair-minded if you show why your company must get the price it does.

3 **PERFORM A COMPARISON.** Be prepared to present logical reasons for the price you are asking. One way you can do this is to compare the quality of your product to that of the prospect's company. For example, you could stress that both are selling superior products:

Mr. Givens, your own company makes a high-grade product that commands an exceptionally high price—and deservedly so. Your tool-and-die products warrant their outstanding reputation because of the top-quality materials used to make them. Our high-viscosity, high-grade motor oil is naturally suited for your machines. While it's true you can buy less expensive brands than ours, you would not be satisfied with their performance.

Acknowledging the superior nature of your prospect's product and suggesting that the prospect's company and your company are two of a kind makes considerable sense. This approach elevates your product to the same level of pride the prospect's company has in its products.

If you choose to make comparisons, be sure you have facts to substantiate your claims. Case histories and testimonials are useful for this purpose. For example, Curtis Randolph sells X-ray equipment to hospitals and clinics by focusing on company performance and referrals to build trust. "My customers are more concerned about what happens after they sign a purchase order than the actual price," says Randolph. He provides prospects with current customers and a referral list encouraging them to contact any or all of them. Randolph uses his company's reputation to build trust and justify the higher price.[26]

4 **SELL DOWN.** All prospects have a buying range, and because you've done the research on the prospect, you should have a good idea of what that range is before you make a presentation. It's a good idea to have a variety of options or benefits available for your product or service. Present the best, most comprehensive product or service first. This will accomplish two things. First, your prospect will know the quality of features available to them should they choose that option.

Second, it gives you the opportunity to reduce the price by removing features or presenting different levels of options. As an added benefit, it gives prospects a sense of control over the buying process without placing you in a position of devaluing the product or service offered. Here is how you can present the sell-down should a prospect present a price objection:

> *Although I believe our premium package is still the best for your company, we can certainly address your need to have a lower-priced option that will still meet your requirements.*

Always remember when dealing with price objections that your prospects know it is unwise to pay too much, but it is sometimes even worse to pay too little. Your customer may pay too much and lose a little money, but when they pay too little, they could lose everything, because the thing that was bought was incapable of doing what it was bought to do. The common law of business balance prohibits paying a little and getting a lot—it can't be done. So be patient with your prospects and focus on the benefits if they still seem fixated on price.

SUMMARY

- Success in handling objections depends on your attitude. If you assume that the sale is over when you hear an objection, it will be. If you regard an objection as an invitation to continue negotiating, you are likely to enjoy a successful close.
- Buyers offer objections for a number of reasons, many of which are psychological. Objecting to something enables them to avoid the risk of making a decision that has potentially unpleasant consequences.
- Some objections are valid and indicate either a logical reason for not buying or a need for you to present additional information before the prospect makes a buying decision.
- Classify and clarify the objections according to their type and apply the appropriate plan to overcome them.
- The six-step strategic negotiating plan for identifying objections gives you the opportunity to handle whatever objection you encounter.
- Experts in overcoming objections record the ones they hear, study them to determine which ones they hear most often, and develop logical answers to use whenever these objections come up.
- You will not always have the lowest-priced offering. Apply the competitive advantages you have in product, source, people, or service superiority and respond to the question of price by breaking the price down, employing the presumption of exclusivity, use comparison, or sell down.

REVIEW QUESTIONS

1. How does a salesperson sometimes cause a specific objection to be raised? What can be done to prevent this?

2. Who is responsible if prospects misunderstand part of the presentation or are not convinced that the product is applicable to their needs? Give examples of how objections reflecting these conditions are likely to be stated.
3. If you were selling homes in the price range of $400,000 to $450,000, how would you anticipate and forestall price objections?
4. In deciding when to answer objections, what factors would lead you to choose to answer them before they arise, postpone the answer until later in the presentation, answer them immediately, or ignore answering at all?
5. List the six steps in the strategic plan for handling objections.
6. List and discuss several strategies for coping with price objections.
7. How can an objection be considered a buying signal?
8. What are some underlying causes for psychological sales resistance?
9. Why might a prospect raise objections even when that prospect has already mentally decided to buy?
10. In what phases of the relationship sales cycle does negotiation play a part? Describe its purpose in each.

IN-CLASS EXERCISES

The following in-class exercises help build teams, improve communication, and emphasize the real-world side of selling. They are meant to be challenging, to help you learn how to deal with problems that have no single right answer, and to use a variety of skills beyond those employed in a typical review question. Read and complete each activity. Then in the next class, discuss and compare answers.

EXERCISE 12.1 – ANTICIPATING OBJECTIONS

Working with the same team of which you were a member for Role Play 11.1, review your presentation plan, but this time try to anticipate objections that your buying center counterparts might raise to various points in your presentation. For each objection that you identify, be sure to classify it according to category of objection (see Exhibit 12.2). Next, decide on when you intend to answer each objection and why. And finally, describe the technique or approach you would take toward answering each objection. In the case of price objections, be especially careful to describe how you would handle them. Be prepared to discuss the results in class.

EXERCISE 12.2 – WHICH OBJECTIONS ARE TRULY "STOPPERS?"

For this exercise, the class should be divided into as many teams as possible of 2 persons each. In categorizing objections, Chapter 12 mentions that there is one type, the "stopper," that actually calls a halt to the selling process because it cannot be answered successfully. One example of a "stopper" objection was provided.

In class, Team A (a 2-person team) identifies a product or service and begins to present its features and benefits to Team B. During the presentation, Team B interrupts with an objection. Team A then consults briefly and responds appropriately to the objection. The presentation continues, and Team B poses another objection to which Team A has an opportunity to respond. Whenever a "stopper" objection is posed—that is, an objection to which no appropriate response is possible—the presentation is stopped. Then the teams reverse roles so that Team B presents a product to Team A, and Team A poses objections. The team that responds appropriately or successfully to the largest number of objections wins.

CASE STUDIES

The following case studies present you with selling scenarios that require you to apply the critical skills discussed in the chapter and give you training through practical learning situations. They are meant to be both engaging and challenging, and like the in-class exercises, don't have one right answer.

CASE 12.1 – DON'T LET THE BEDBUGS BITE!

Research shows that people hate purchasing mattresses more than any other item for the home. There are good reasons for that. A mattress showroom is intimidating: all of the mattresses are laid out in rows, and they all seem to look alike. Moreover, there are thousands of brands, types, models, and price points, making it almost impossible to compare one store's mattress directly with another store's product. And, finally, there is no way for an ordinary customer to "look under the hood" in order to check independently the features built into each mattress. All the customer can do is lie down on the mattresses to test their comfort; and even that doesn't work well, because all mattresses begin to feel the same after about 5 tries. No wonder people hate the process, and no wonder bedding salespersons encounter so many objections!

Bob Driscoll's store, ***Mattress Mavens,*** carries only mattresses on the medium to high end of the pricing scale—$2,300 to $6,000—on the theory that customer satisfaction will be better. This not only cuts down on complaints and returns, but it also improves word-of-mouth marketing. Still, Mattress Mavens faces stiff competition from Doug's Discounts. Doug's produces a lot of TV ads that blare, "Why pay more for just a name? Come on down to Doug's for a quality night's sleep at a fraction of the cost!"

The ads drive Bob nuts because prospects who come into his store don't know what they are looking at or for. They don't have a clue about the shoddy materials that go into Doug's no-name bedding or, worse, about what a $500 mattress will do to their spine over time. Professional ethics prevent Bob from trashing the competition, but he has become frustrated at dealing with pricing objections day in and day out.

When Bob approaches his manager about the problem, he receives some really good support (pun intended!). The manager says that he has just requested some cut-away displays from StarCrest, the store's high-end vendor, so that customers can see and feel just how these fine mattresses are constructed. These will be displayed on the showroom floor along with a few cut-aways of disgustingly cheap mattresses for comparison. In addition, the company is sending videos that show the entire construction process, including the harvesting of wood for the frames, the production of the memory steel coils, the production of foam and cotton layers, and the stitching and packaging. Mattress Maven will play the videos in an endless loop on 6 monitors at various locations in the store. "But," says the manager, "when it comes to handling pricing objections directly, Bob, you're on your own!"

With all of the above support, what should Bob be prepared to do? How can he handle the pricing objections creatively and effectively? What strategies should he employ?

CASE 12.2 – "I MUST CHECK WITH MY SPOUSE"

Charlie Brandon had been selling home furnishings for 8 years. He had worked for high-end companies and discount outlets. And throughout his career, he had encountered more objections than even he had thought possible. Some people wouldn't buy leather furniture because they thought it felt hot; others thought it felt cold. (The truth was that leather always conforms to room temperature.) Charlie had worked out responses to most objections. It didn't mean that all customers actually bought, but Charlie never blamed himself for being unable to help most customers make a buying decision in their own interest. But there was one objection that stumped Charlie nearly every time, and that was some variant on, "I must check with my husband/wife."

There were, in Charlie's experience, two problems with this objection. In the first place, it could often be used to mask a more important, yet hidden, objection. And second, by invoking the privacy of the marital bond, a customer could thwart probing questions that might be considered offensive. Moreover, whenever this objection surfaced, Charlie knew that a customer rarely returned with spouse in tow. Even if they did return together, the second spouse was often grumpy and usually found some pretext to veto a purchase: the merchandise was always "the wrong color," "the wrong size," or "too expensive." It just never worked.

Now that Charlie had accepted a new position with a mid-level retailer, he thought he would attempt to address the problem again. Perhaps Tanya, his new manager, could shed some light on how to handle the spousal objection.

Having explained his previous difficulty with this objection, Charlie complained, "I just don't know what to do, Tanya. Now, every time a customer raises this objection, I just freeze."

"Well, Charlie, I have two suggestions for you," Tanya replied. "First, you need to qualify your customer more carefully and earlier in the process. When a man or woman comes in alone, find some way to ask who the merchandise is for, who is involved in the selection process. If another person must be consulted for whatever reason, then make just enough of a presentation to keep the customer in front of you interested and press for a definite appointment so they can be assured of your full attention."

"What's the second suggestion?" asked Charlie.

"The second suggestion applies later in the process, when your attempting to close after having made a presentation. Perhaps you couldn't qualify the customer for some reason. But now, you need to probe whether this is a real objection on its face or whether it masks some other concern," answered Tanya. "You need to come up with a list of gently probing, inoffensive questions."

"Ok, I'll try," Charlie responded, somewhat apprehensively.

Knowing what you've learned from Chapter 12, what sort of questions should Charlie ask? When should he stop, and why?

Chapter 12 Footnotes

1. Ziglar, Zig. *Zig Ziglar's Secrets of Closing the Sale.* New York: Berkley (Penguin Imprint), 1985.
2. Pell, Roger. "The Road to Success is Paved with Objections." *Bank Marketing* 22 (1990): 16.
3. Feiertag, Howard. "Finding out reasons for objections is key to overcoming them." *Hotel and Motel Management* 217, no 18 (October 2012): 14.
4. Boe, John. "Overcome objections and close the sale." *Agency Sales* 33, no. 9 (September 2003): 27.
5. Pollock, Ted. "How good a closer are you?" *The American Salesman* 48, no 6 (June 2006): 18.
6. Huisken, Brad. "Busting the sales busters, Part II," *JCK* 174, no 3 (March 2003): 66-67.
7. Lake, Michael. "Overcoming objections is the key to sales," *Hudson Valley Business Journal* (March 2008): 26.
8. Huisken, Brad. "Busting the sales busters, Part II," *JCK* 174, no 3 (March 2003): 66-67.
9. Gitomer, Jeffrey. "Make Objections obsolete to pave your way to sales." *The Central New York Business Journal* (December 2006): 21
10. N.A. "How do you address Objections? Here's a few ideas." *Life Association News* (November 1996): 16-18.
11. N.A. "Customer Objections: Do You Have the Answers?" *Professional Selling* 22, no 5 (March 1994): 3.
12. Anderson, Wilma G. "Nine mistakes to avoid when marketing to seniors." *National Underwriter* 107, no 20 (May 2003): 22.
13. Roberts-Phelps, Graham. "Objections Are Opportunities to Sell." *Personal Selling Power* 12, no 8 (November/December 2002): 34.
14. 14. Brooks, Bill. "Are you responsive enough for your prospects and customers?" *The American Salesman* 48, no 2 (February 2003): 21-23.
15. Ramsey, Robert D. "How to pitch a new idea." *SuperVision* 65, no 3 (March 2014): 8-9.
16. Kasper, Jim. "Objections: Questions in Disguise." http://www.salesvantage.com, Accessed September 10, 2015.
17. Brooks, Bill. "Time, budgets and excuses...how do you overcome them?" *The American Salesman* 47 no, 1 (January 2002): 13-15.
18. Weiss, Wendy. "Eliminate Objections: And close more sales this year." *Sales and Service Excellence* (January 2010): 4.

19. Graham, John R. "How to sell more when others are selling less." *The American Salesman* 48, no 2 (February 2003): 15-20.
20. N.A, "How To Control Your Sales Appointment, How salespeople can get and keep the power all throughout their selling interaction." 5min.com, Accessed July 17, 2015.
21. Farneti, David. "Opening Doors And Establishing Winning Sales Relationships." *Agency Sales* 34, no 2 (February 2004): 28-30.
22. Natenberg, Todd. "Overcoming Objections." *Self Growth*, Accessed September 1, 2015. Web.
23. Gross, T. Scott. "The Service Factor." *Selling Power* (October 2000): 45.
24. Weiss, Wendy. "The Price Is Right? How to handle a customer's objections to price of an item." *American Salesman* 46, no 1 (January 2001): 6.
25. Chadha, Rhadika. "Sellers of stuff: Salespeople should be trained to meet the demands of the ever-changing marketplace to stay abreast of competition. How do you distinguish your brand from the competition?" *Businessline* (January 22, 2004): 1.
26. Kendy, William F. "Handling the Price Objection." *Selling Power* (September 2000): 41.

SUCCESS IN THE END IS WHAT COUNTS, NOT FAILURE IN THE BEGINNING

ABRAHAM LINCOLN'S FAILURES FAR EXCEEDED HIS SUCCESSES

1831 - Lost his job

1832 - Defeated in run for Illinois State Legislature

1833 - Failed in business

1834 - Elected to Illinois State Legislature

1835 - Sweetheart died

1836 - Had nervous breakdown

1838 - Defeated in run for Illinois House Speaker

1843 - Defeated in run for nomination for U.S. Congress

1846 - Elected to Congress

1848 - Lost re-nomination

1849 - Rejected for land officer position

1854 - Defeated in run for U.S. Senate

1856 - Defeated in run for nomination for Vice President

1858 - Again defeated in run for U.S. Senate

1860 - ELECTED PRESIDENT

CHAPTER 13
CLOSING THE SALE

OVERVIEW

Despite the fact that many salespeople dread this phase of the sales cycle, closing the sale is merely the natural conclusion to a successful interview with a prospective donor. In this chapter, we will discuss how to face the close with confidence by detailing proper attitudes about closing, how to recognize signals that reveal a prospect's readiness to buy, and finally, specific techniques to use during the close. After all, the only way to get more sales… is to ask for more sales!

OBJECTIVES

- Develop productive attitudes and a professional perspective toward the close.
- Discover the importance of reassuring the prospect.
- Appreciate the value of persistence.
- Gain knowledge of how to deal with rejection.
- Develop a sense of timing in knowing when to close.
- Recognize buying signals.
- Study the different types of closes.

A CLOSING FRAME OF MIND

Finding new prospects, successfully making appointments through referrals and other prospecting techniques, establishing trust, and effectively explaining features and benefits can be difficult enough. But when it comes time to close, the results can be crushing, especially to inexperienced salespeople. After all, even seasoned professionals can have trouble wrapping up the sale. A close can be defined as:[1]

THE CLOSE:

A question asked or an action taken by a salesperson designed to elicit a favorable buying decision from the prospect.

Closing the sale is not really difficult for the salesperson who is conducting a professional sales interview with a qualified prospect and with favorable conditions. Although closing a sale is actually quite natural, far too many salespeople have adopted such a distorted view of the close that they dread trying, even though the close is their only reason for being there. ***In fact, in sixty-two percent of all sales interviews, salespeople fail to ask for the prospect's business.***[2] The usual scenario goes like this:

> *Well, Dr. Tompkins, that's about all I have to tell you. Is there anything else you would like to ask me? No? Okay, I guess I'll call you again in a few weeks. Have a good day. I enjoyed talking with you.*

Then the salesperson is standing outside the prospect's office wondering, *"What happened? I thought sure I had that order. What did I do wrong?"* The usual answer is that the salesperson did not do anything wrong. The salesperson just did not do anything.

Closing is not a separate event tacked onto the end of a sales interview—it is something that happens all along during the course of the presentation. Closing might be easier to understand if someone had devised a better name for it. The word *close* suggests something that occurs at the end of a process, so salespeople seem to feel that it is an isolated segment of the selling process that must be approached in some exact manner to produce success; but the opportunity to close may occur at any time during the sales interview. The wise professional watches for and takes advantage of every closing opportunity. By meeting the prospect's expectations and desires from the start, the close will occur naturally.

"Many of life's failures are people who did not realize how close they were to success when they gave up."
Thomas Edison

Always Be Closing

Closing begins the moment you speak the first word to the prospect and continues throughout the whole process until the order is signed, sealed, and delivered. You close on many points: the prospect's agreement to grant an interview, confirming the existence of a need, permission to make a survey or an on-site visit, permission for a trial installation, and acceptance of your explanation of product benefits.

The sale has actually been made or lost long before the time arrives to sign the agreement. The final step should be just a formality—a necessary step, but not one that requires making weighty decisions. Unless you complete the selling process by asking for the order, the only title you deserve is *conversationalist*. Ultimately, it's a simple concept; you must close from the beginning. Don't confuse this idea with the *hard sell*. A cutthroat approach alienates many potential customers. Instead, explain your agenda. Tell the prospective customer exactly what you're selling and how it can benefit their business. Being up front about your intentions promotes an honest, mutually respectful and rewarding discussion, paving the way for a smooth close.[3]

Failure at the close is the result of inadequate completion of the prior steps in the sales process: Inadequate prospecting, incomplete qualifying of the prospect, or too little probing to determine the prospect's needs. As a result, the presentation has focused on the wrong features and benefits, or the wrong evidence has been supplied to support claims for the product. A prospect's failure to buy, then, does not automatically brand you as a poor closer. Focusing only on closing as an indicator of sales skill is like expecting to hear Phil Mickelson say that putting is all that matters in golf. Of course, that final putt that wins the championship is the most obvious success moment, but obtain agreement throughout the sales process and the final step is the easiest one.

FUNCTIONS OF THE CLOSE

Even when all the steps leading to the close have gone well, the prospect may still hesitate. Logically, the prospect would gladly sign the agreement when a salesperson has a good product or service, has presented meaningful benefits, has a strategy for servicing the prospect's account, makes an impressive sales presentation, and successfully answers all of the buyer's concerns. However, the moment of decision is difficult for most people. Buyers take many risks:

- They must live with the purchase and pay for it.
- They may have to justify the buying decision to someone else.
- They may be responsible for an important impact on the company's productivity or profitability as a result of the purchase.

Risks are threatening to most people. Of course, you may also feel some strain at the moment of decision. You may be asking yourself, "Have I told the prospect enough? Did I find the real need? Did I read the verbal and nonverbal clues correctly? Is this the best moment to close? What if the answer is no?"

The *salesperson-prospect* relationship is much like the doctor-patient relationship. Just as a doctor urges his patient to follow the treatment closely, a salesperson must make wise decisions about the prospect's needs.[4] If you believe that the decisions you recommend are in your prospects' best interests, then you must support buyers and help them make the decisions that will solve their problems.

BE THEIR REASSURANCE. Consider how the prospective buyer is probably feeling and thinking. Do you remember the first time you jumped off a diving board? You thought, "The board is too high; I can't swim in the deep end; I'll choke on water." You thought about all the possible bad consequences. Perhaps a friend in the water encouraged you to try. When you finally jumped, you discovered that the water was fine, just as your friend had said. In the sales situation, you are the friend in the water, you know how the prospect feels and you offer the needed reassurance: "Come on in; you'll be glad you took that first dive; I'm here to help if you need me." Your attitude must be that you respect prospects and their decisions, whether or not they decide to jump in. You continue to reassure them until they finally make a decision. The next time you advise them to make a buying decision, they will trust your recommendation more readily.

Once prospects agree that they can benefit from using your product or service, your responsibility is to guide them to a close. You must never be discouraged by a no. If you honestly believe that a sale is an exchange of mutual benefits, then a no should set up this train of reasoning: The prospect is asking me to explain once more that this decision will work, so I will continue to reassure and close. Do not be discouraged when the buyer hesitates. People do not like to make decisions; without assistance and reassurance, some simply cannot make decisions at all.

A CLOSING CONSCIOUSNESS

The most important factor in successfully closing a sale is not having the lowest price or the best product. Your attitude is the crucial factor. You must have an absolute belief in what you are selling, and you must expect to be successful. If you assume that you will successfully close the sale, the prospect interprets your confidence as reassurance that the product will provide the needed benefits. Your positive attitude makes the difficult decision, "Yes, I'll buy" much easier. All they have to do is say, "Yes, you're right" when you recommend that they buy. *Confidence is contagious*; it infects prospects and draws them to your side. Confidence at the close allows you to ask for the order in a straightforward manner.

> Mr. Eastwood, we have agreed on the capacity of the printer, its speed capabilities, and the cost of supplying paper, and we have clarified your questions regarding the service contract. We could significantly speed up the process if we could settle now on a delivery date. Is Friday okay with you?

Closing is only frustrating if you have not identified customer needs, shown the right mental attitude, made a memorable presentation, and were perceived as a genuine advocate.[5] If you and the prospect have together defined the problem and worked out a solution, then the final question—the close—is nothing more than the last step in a sequence.

Self-Confidence

When you maintain a positive mental attitude, a high level of self-confidence, and belief in your product, you create an atmosphere within which you can handle the day-to-day rejections that are inevitable in the world of selling. Steve Simms, noted author and speaker, reveals how to shake off the shackles of rejection. Simms says that when prospects fail to follow your buying advice, you know that the rejection is seldom directed toward you personally but is instead a reflection of their own differing opinion about what will best fill their needs or a

result of their personal hesitancy to make a decision that they perceive as a risk. In other words, you have lost nothing except a little of your time, but the prospects who say no have lost the opportunity to benefit from using your product or service and of being your personal customer. The bigger loss is theirs.

Persistence

When it comes to the appropriate level of persistence in sales, Jim Duerr, a sales rep for *Chris-More, Inc.,* says, "You should push, but never be pushy." Duerr calls on Nashville commercial builders to convince them to use his company's line of plumbing supplies in their construction projects. Focused persistence involves asking whether doing *this* today will get you *that* tomorrow.[6] Jim suggests that, "Making repeat, meaningful calls demonstrates to prospects that you are not going to give up. *The idea is to be graciously tenacious—without being obnoxious.*"[7] Successful salespeople like Jim never take no for an answer unless it is in *everyone's* interest to do so. If the business is worth having, it is worth going after repeatedly—with repeated calls or repeated attempts to close during a single call. The extra effort often makes the difference between success and failure. Jim was able to secure a substantial amount of the plumbing needs at the *Gaylord Opryland* after the terrible floods that hit Nashville several years ago.

Gerhard Gschwandtner, founder and publisher of *Selling Power* magazine says that, "When you are at the point where you think it's not worth it, that's when you need to redouble your efforts. Customers are looking for someone who is dependable, who is persistent and who will do what it takes to get the best solution implemented within the customer's organization." When sales are slow and you feel like every step is an uphill battle, that's when you shouldn't quit. Salespeople who redouble their efforts will be rewarded handsomely by the payoff. "The pain goes away the minute you are victorious," says Gschwandtner, "but if you give up, the pain will persist for the rest of your life."[8]

How often do you ask prospects for their business? The answer often given is "one more time." Studies have shown that only about 2 percent of sales will close on the first meeting. That's an incredibly low percentage.[9] If only 2 percent of sales are closed in a one-time meeting, then the only way to make your time worthwhile is to follow up with prospects. You have not yet built a relationship, or a measure of trust. Selling should be a side-by-side, step-by-step process, involving both prospect and salesperson, in which the salesperson earns the right to close. There could be any number of issues that would keep someone from saying yes at the first meeting.

There are numerous studies that show that the average number of contacts it takes to close a big sale is around five.[10] Giving up after one or two meetings means that you have not even reached the 50 percent mark for the average number of calls it takes to make the sale. Being persistent results in success—determination and resolve will win sales.

When you understand the problems faced by prospects, guide them through the problem-solving process, watch for buying signals, and time the close to fit the prospect's behavioral style, your chances of a successful close skyrocket. Opportunities to close occur a number of times during the sales process; recognize them, persist, and ask for the order. Exhibit 13.1 describes the kind of persistence needed for success in sales.

EXHIBIT 13.1 PERSISTENCE... DR. SEUSS STYLE

One of the best examples of persistence is a story you probably loved as a child—*Green Eggs and Ham*. This Dr. Seuss classic describes the attempt of the "salesman," Sam I Am, to induce a wary "prospect" to try a meal of green eggs and ham. When his first straightforward offer is rejected, Sam I Am tries one assumptive close after another: "Do you want them here or there? Would you like them in a box or with a fox? Do you want them in a house or with a mouse?" Finally, the prospect tries green eggs and ham and is surprised to find them quite delicious. His no's seemingly never registered with the persistent Sam I Am. If you have not read *Green Eggs and Ham* lately, visit the children's section of the library and learn the story's important lesson about persistence.[11]

Dealing With Rejection

Many would-be salespeople leave the profession because of their inability to cope with the day-to-day sense of rejection they experience. They interpret a prospect's refusal to buy as a message that says, "You are personally worthless." Eleanor Roosevelt once said that, "No one can make you feel inferior without your permission." This concept is especially important for all sales reps to internalize.

> "My great concern is not whether you have failed, but whether you are content with your failure."
>
> ***Abraham Lincoln***

Sales professionals must learn to deal with rejection by keeping a positive attitude about themselves and how they make their living. True, they feel disappointment if they fail to close, but successful salespeople focus in on the sense of accomplishment they feel when they do close a sale.[12] To keep from being overwhelmed, accept the fact that rejection exists, see it for what it really is, and never make the mistake of allowing it to serve as a measure of your own self-worth.

What is a good batting average in selling? Professional baseball players who average .300 (three hits for every ten times at bat) or more for a full season are a small minority of players in the major leagues. Imagine failing to get a base hit seventy percent of the time. Consider some of the great names in baseball history:

- Babe Ruth hit 714 career home runs, but struck out 1,330 times.
- Cy Young won 515 games, but lost 313.
- Ty Cobb stole 96 bases one year but was caught stealing 38 times.

Baseball fans ignore the failures and instead concentrate on the successes of their favorite players. The attitude of all true professionals is: ***"I may have failed, but that does not mean I am a failure."***

A salesperson who never hears a 'no' is not a salesperson, but merely an order taker. Rejection is as much a part of sales as getting dressed in the morning, and salespeople who can't or won't deal with it had better find another career. The first thing to remember when handling rejection is that you just can't take it personally.[13] Refuse to permit anyone else to make you feel bad about yourself. Exhibit 13.2 describes nine specific tactics for coping with rejection.[14]

EXHIBIT 13.2 NINE TACTICS FOR DEALING WITH REJECTION

1. **Remind yourself that you are not alone.** How many rejections have exceptional salespeople faced on their journey to success? You see, you are not alone!
2. **Forgive yourself.** Mistakes are great learning experiences, but to benefit from them you have to keep moving forward. Continue to generate, gather and harvest prospects.
3. **Give yourself a pep talk.** Replace negative thoughts with positive ones such as, "I'm a great salesperson, and after they hear what I have to say, they'll want to buy from me."
4. **Refuse to give up.** Remind yourself constantly that persistence is key to success, and that rejection may not be pleasant but you won't let it stop you.
5. **You are not defined by your business card.** Remember you are important because of who you are, not what you do. Remind yourself of the difference between self-worth and performance.
6. **Engage in positive self-talk.** Separate your ego from the sale. The prospect is not attacking you personally. Say to yourself, "This prospect doesn't even know me; the refusal to buy is about the product, not me."
7. **Positively anticipate rejection.** Expect it, but don't create it. Think in advance what your response to rejection will be.
8. **Broaden your definition of success.** Instead of looking at outcomes, look at success as getting out there in the first place.
9. **Keep your pipeline full.** Commit to routinely attracting more customers than you need. "No, thanks" is much easier to handle when you have a steady flow of qualified prospects streaming in.

WHEN TO CLOSE

Most of the sales you make will not close themselves. Many factors go into the successful closing of a sale, from timing to presentation style.[15] The closing curve shown in Exhibit 13.3 illustrates how the closing process works. The sales made to the left of the will-buy line (WBL) shows that some sales will be closed almost at once, others are easy sales, and that most can be closed with an interest-building presentation. A few can never be closed. The key is recognizing the spots at which a close can be made—when the buyer gives a *buying signal*. The appearance of a buying signal is the critical moment during the presentation when a successful close is more likely.

EXHIBIT 13.3 THE CLOSING CURVE

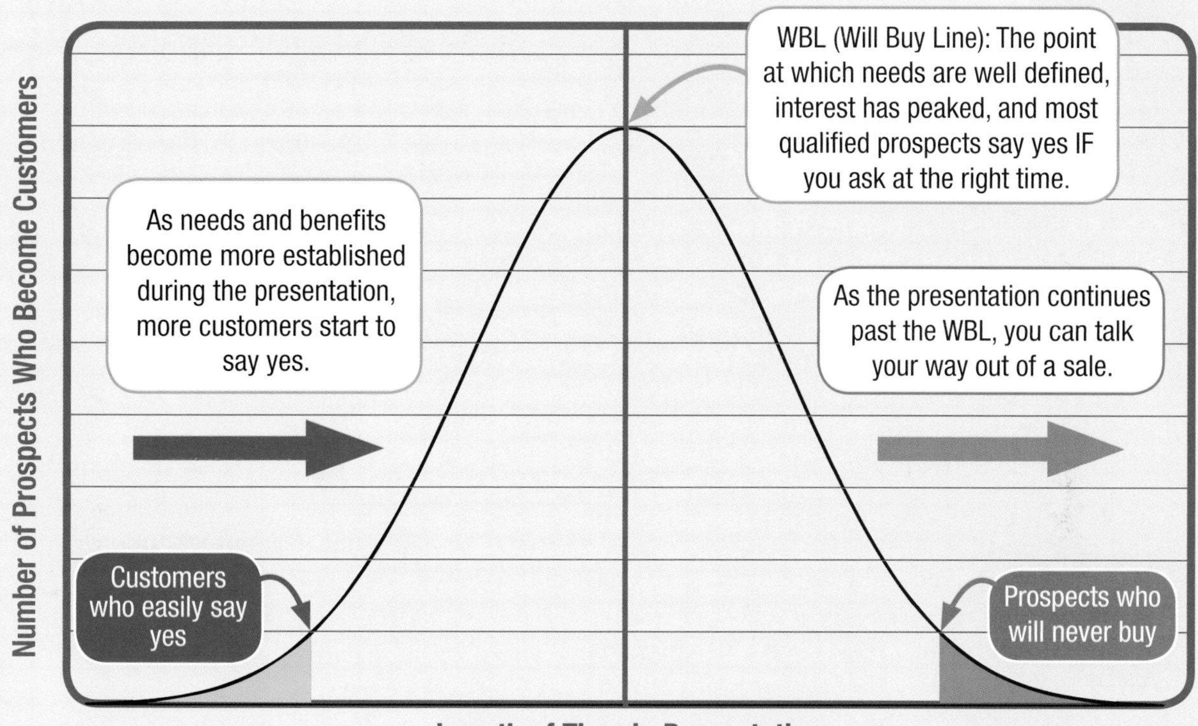

When you sense the psychological moment to close, do so immediately.[16] If you fail to recognize these critical moments at which the prospect is most nearly ready to make a buying decision and continue to talk past them, the close becomes steadily more difficult. After a critical point is passed, you must buy back the prospect's readiness to decide. In other words, you must once again convince the prospect that buying is the proper decision. Talking too much and *overselling* is a much greater danger than *underselling*. Your attempts to close early and often eliminate the possibility of going past the point at which the prospect is ready to buy.

The best psychological moment for closing may occur at any time during the presentation. When it does come, prospects signal in some way that you have convinced them and they are ready to buy.[17] You never have only one possible moment to close. You may be in the early stages of the presentation, you may have completely exhausted all the selling points you planned to present, or you may be somewhere in between.

RECOGNIZING BUYING SIGNALS

As you reach the point where the final decision is to be made, it's just as important for you to know *when* to ask for the order as it is for you to know how to ask.[18] *A buying signal* is anything the prospect does or says that indicates readiness to buy. Buying signals are all around us if we learn to recognize them.[19] Unfortunately, it's all too easy to become focused on your presentation that you overlook these signals even if they are obvious. Buying signals occur quickly and may be verbal, nonverbal, or both. Genuine buying signals show that the prospect has moved from evaluating your proposal to an appraisal of it.

A buying signal may come in the form of a question. A prospect may ask you to repeat some point or benefit previously discussed or stop you right in the middle of the presentation to ask how long delivery will take. However a buying signal comes, take advantage of it and close immediately. Always remember that when the prospect is ready to buy, you will receive a signal. Here are three of the most common nonverbal buying signals:[20]

1. **FREQUENT NODDING.** In conversation, people nod so often that it might come as a surprise that frequent nodding is a nonverbal buying signal. If you see your prospect nodding frequently, it is a sign that he or she is listening and engaged. However, it can also be a sign that he or she might already be familiar with the ground that you're covering. Be sure to stop occasionally and ask the prospect questions to keep him or her engaged and included when he or she is sending out this nonverbal buying signal.
2. **HANDLING DOCUMENTS, PRODUCTS, OR OTHER MATERIALS.** Handling the product, or if that is not possible, the documentation or accessories to a product, is a clear nonverbal buying signal. This type of handling is a person's subconscious way of imagining owning the product or receiving the service being sold. This is why many top salespeople encourage prospects to touch, handle, and examine things prior to a sale. Once a prospect is exhibiting this nonverbal buying signal, a sale could be imminent, especially if he or she has suddenly focused on one offering to the exclusion of others.
3. **CONSISTENT EYE CONTACT.** A prospect making consistent eye contact is exhibiting a classic nonverbal buying signal. He or she is engaged in the conversation, interested in what you have to say, and looking to see what you really think or feel about the product or service you're selling. The prospect also likely feels comfortable with you on a personal level, which a top salesperson knows has to happen before a deal can close. To understand how important eye contact is as a nonverbal buying signal, think about past deals that you've closed. Chances are that in every instance, consistent eye contact was one of the top nonverbal buying signals your clients were sending.

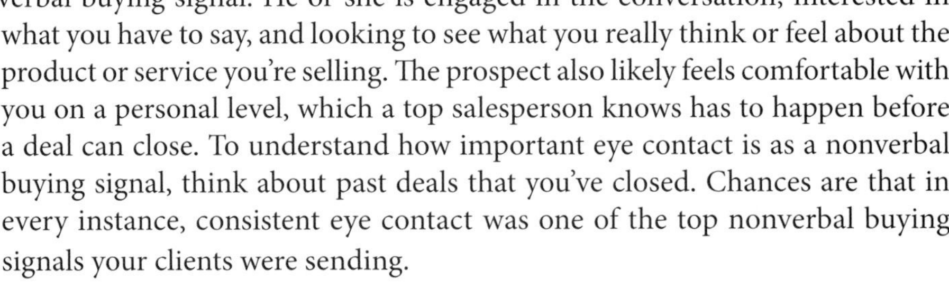

To know when to close, look for at least two nonverbal buying signals before you move to the next step. Other nonverbal buying signals include smiling, changes in posture, and rubbing chins or noses, which indicates rational thinking. Just by being aware of nonverbal buying signals, which sometimes contradict verbal buying signals that might be sent out at the same time, you can improve your closing ratio and become a top salesperson. Avoid the temptation to oversell and let nonverbal buying signals lead your pitch.

With the traditional method of selling, salespeople were taught to close, close, close. They were told to spend most of their time closing the deal. Trainers taught salespeople fancy closes to handle and overcome objections. Over the years, a new school of thought has evolved: *The school of possibility.* Imagine what would be possible if all the objections you typically hear at the 'closing table' were prevented and defused throughout the course of your presentation.[21]

Perhaps the most important reason for becoming experts at relationship selling is to create an atmosphere within which an act of trust can take place. People like to buy from people who truly understand them and take the time to get to know their unique situation.

The Trial Close

Instead of just watching passively for signs of interest, you must create situations in which interest can be generated and revealed. One way to create such a situation is through the use of a trial close. A *trial close* asks for an opinion; a *closing question* asks for a decision. A trial close, by asking for an opinion, serves as a thermometer that tells you whether the prospect is warm, hot, or cold to your proposition. It is designed to help you read the prospect's feelings and predict probable reactions.

In Chapter eleven, the *tie-down question* was discussed as one element in a unit of conviction. The tie-down and the trial close are used for basically the same purpose. When you get the prospects agreeing with you throughout the presentation they are much more likely to agree with you when you ask the closing question, that is, when you make the formal request for their business. You want to be careful not to talk past the sale.

During every sales call there will be a number of opportunities to close the sale. How do you know the proper time? When in doubt, test the prospect with trial closes such as:[22]

1. How do you feel about what we have discussed so far?
2. What do you think about the solution I've shared with you?
3. How does what we've talked about sound to you?
4. Based on what you've heard so far, what are your questions?
5. If you had your way, what changes would you make to the proposal?

Notice these are all open-ended questions. You need to ask a trial closing question that will get the prospect talking so you can learn about where you are in the sales process and when is the right time to ask for the sale.

The trial close is used to probe and to reveal how far along the prospect has gone in the decision-making process. The time to ask for the order is when the prospect is fully ready to buy. You can, however, ask for an *opinion* at any time.

A CLOSING QUESTION. A *closing question*, in contrast to the trial close, is designed to produce an answer that confirms the fact that the prospect has bought. Look at these two examples:

1. Would it be better for you to receive shipment of a full month's supply right away, or would you prefer to receive half at the end of this week and the other half in about ten days?
2. We can have the product delivered to your warehouse next week. Is Monday a convenient delivery day for you?

Silence: Your Most Powerful Closing Tool

What is the most powerful thing you bring to the table when it comes to the close? Salespeople are often taught to provide a *reason* when they ask for something. The idea is that people are more likely to agree to a request if it's accompanied by a reason. But is this really true in all cases—and especially in cases involving price?

We often hear that we have to *give something to get something*. For example, if you want to get a referral, you have to offer your customers some reason or justification for giving it to you, right? There's a study that allegedly proves this: A group of experimenters went around a college campus asking to cut in line to make copies. When they gave no reason for wanting to cut ahead, 60 percent agreed to the cut. When they gave a reason, 93 percent agreed. The "reason" the experimenters gave was, "Because I have to make a copy." So, they concluded that saying "because…" after a request is what made people more agreeable, not the reason itself. But interestingly, once they told people they wanted to jump ahead because they needed to make *multiple* copies, only 24 percent agreed, reason or no reason.[23]

The ultimate point that the study proved is that *justifications only work when stakes are low*—and when money is not involved. Justifications can help you get agreement on issues in the beginning or during the presentation. But when you are involved in a price negotiation, adding an explanation can actually work against you. In your mind, you may think you are reinforcing value, but as you list all that value after the price, your prospects won't hear any of those justifications. They will simply be thinking of reasons to object to that price.

What should you say after you ask a closing question or present the price? *The most powerful thing to say after the closing question or after presenting price is* ***nothing***. For example, let's say you close with a question like:

> *Would it be better for you to receive shipment of a full month's supply right away, or would you prefer to receive half at the end of this week and the other half in ten days?*

Then after you ask, say nothing until the prospect gives an answer. The pressure of silence is enormous. Silence is golden because of what it brings you. If you can remain silent after asking the closing question, only two outcomes are possible: 1) The prospect says yes or 2) the prospect gives you a reason for not wanting to buy.[24] In either instance, you are better off than you were before you asked the question. If the answer is yes, you have a sale. If the prospect gives you a reason for not buying, a concern has surfaced that you can convert into another opportunity to close.

Never miss the opportunity <u>not</u> to say something.

ELEVEN USEFUL CLOSING STRATEGIES

There is a multitude of closing techniques, and your best strategy is to have numerous techniques for different occasions and for prospects of all social styles. If you attempt to use the same close for every prospect, you will walk away from much of the business that should be yours. Your sales call plan should provide the preferred closing routine to fit with the presentation you expect to deliver. However, just as circumstances often dictate some changes in your presentation, they also point up the need for shifts in your closing plans.

For example, an insurance agent had prepared a comprehensive insurance program to present to a client. Upon arrival, the agent finds an excited prospect who shares information that he and his wife are actually expecting triplets. This prospect's needs have changed dramatically in just twenty-four hours. The presentation now becomes a work session to devise a new program, and the close the agent anticipated may not be appropriate. A salesperson with a full repertoire of closing techniques merely chooses one that fits the revised situation and moves on as though nothing unusual is occurring. The various closing methods described here are subject to combination with other methods to fit your unique personality, your product, and your prospect. Learn the principles upon which these techniques rest and adapt them to your needs:

1. Be Assumptive

In a sense, every close is *assumptive*. When you enter every sales interview with a positive expectation of success, you are assuming that the prospect will buy at the close. Your attitude throughout the interview is assumptive. Say, "*When* you use this product" and "*As* your program progresses." Avoid words like *if* and *should* because they are conditional and block closing action. Throughout the presentation, assuming that the prospect will buy allows the prospect to make the decision more easily by presenting opportunities to make smaller or easier choices.

To further promote an assumptive environment you can act as if they already purchased what is being sold. Talk about your product and what they are going to do with it. Discuss how it already fits into their lives. Do not talk about whether they are ready to buy or have already bought it. Just act as if it has always been theirs.[25] Here are some examples:

- *Now where will you put your new furniture?*
- *What will your boss say about your state-of-the-art upgrade?*
- *What do you like most about your new software?*
- *How will you use the cash payment from your accident policy?*

An assumptive approach to closing establishes a positive environment in which the prospect can more easily say yes. This works well with indecisive buyers who tend to be nervous about making a final decision. Present them with minor decisions that give them the opportunity to appear decisive in a small matter while they are actually painlessly making the big decision at the same time.

2. Make "Yes" the Natural Response (Continuous Yes)

By asking a series of questions with *yes* answers, it becomes more difficult for buyers to say *no* when they have said *yes* a number of times. That is why you must get agreement on minor points before you ask for the order. These questions begin in the need discovery phase. For example: "I'd like to ask you a few questions that help me understand your particular needs. Would that be okay with you?" *Yes.*

Then continue these questions during the presentation: "Do you like the idea of our same-day, free repair service?" *Yes*. During the closing phase you may ask: "Are you satisfied with the comprehensive guarantee that we offer?" *Yes*. "Do the financing terms seem fair to you?" *Yes*. "Then it seems we can go ahead with our plans to begin the installation process?" *Yes*. These are all closed-ended questions, so you must be confident that you will receive an affirmative response before you ask them. And, when the final closing question is asked, the prospect is inclined to keep on agreeing with you.

3. Let Your Actions Do the Talking (Physical Action)

Without directly asking for the order, begin taking some action that assumes the sale is completed. For example, begin filling out paperwork and ask the prospect for a signature when you finish. Begin to ask the prospect a series of questions and write the answers on the contract or agreement form. You might ask, "Do you use your complete middle name or just an initial?" Continue to fill out the information and then ask for a signature:

> *Now that we have reached agreement, I know you will want to expedite delivery. Just indicate your approval by placing your name right here.*

If the prospect does not object or stop your action, you just made a sale. This certainly won't do all of the work for you, but it nonverbally signals to the buyer that the deal is moving forward.

4. Come Out and Ask

Once you have covered all the necessary features and benefits of your product and matched them with the buyer's dominant buying motives, you can ask with confidence, "May I have your business?" This type of close is quite common when selling to industrial buyers. Many buyers appreciate a no-nonsense approach. Of course, be mindful of the buyer's behavioral style. Amiables, for example, could find this approach threatening.

Be sure to keep the direct close positive. Avoid the word *don't*. "Why don't we begin next week?" and "Why don't you try the product for a while and see what happens?" are open invitations to additional objections. Insertion of a negative into the close may implant doubt where none existed, and the prospect may try to tell you why not. Use positive statements like these:

1. *So, I will schedule delivery for next Tuesday?*
2. *Each workstation will come with laptops that have either 2GB, 4GB, or 8GB of memory. I suggest you select laptops with 4GB to begin.*
3. *Let's run your first ad beginning Friday of this week. Sound good?*

When you use this type of closing statement, then you and your customer can make positive plans together.

5. Give Them Choices (Alternative Choice)

In general, people like to exercise their freedom of choice, and salespeople like to lead their buyers toward an easy agreement. So, give the prospect a choice between two positive alternatives. Here are some suggestions:

1. *Would delivery be convenient on Thursday, or would you prefer Friday?*

2. *Do you prefer to pay up front, or is our monthly payment plan a better fit for you?*
3. *Where would you like the order sent—directly to your warehouse or to the main office?*

The idea is to offer the prospect a choice between buying A and buying B instead of a choice between *buying* and *not buying*. The question is not "Will you buy?" but "Which one?" *or "How much?"*

6. Summarize (Summary Close)

A summary gives both you and the prospect an opportunity to reconsider what was covered throughout the sales interview. Summarizing the major selling points is especially good when the prospect must defend a purchase to someone else. Give the prospect an opportunity to agree that the summary is correct.

Concentrate on those items that were of most interest to the prospect and that related directly to the dominant buying motives.[26] For example, a sales rep selling advertising space in an industrial magazine might use the summary close like this:

> *Mr. Bickley, let's review the major points on which we have agreed:*
>
> - *An ad in our magazine will give you maximum effective circulation coverage.*
> - *Your ads will enjoy high readership.*
> - *Businesses similar to yours have had a great deal of success advertising with us (refer to testimonials or case histories used during presentation).*
> - *Our marketing staff will help you develop ads for all the media you use, not just our magazine.*
> - *You'll receive free artwork and layout help included in our basic price.*

Bring up additional points only if the summary fails and you need additional ammunition to answer new objections. Once agreement has been expressed, the prospect is in a positive frame of mind, and the time is ripe to close. You can then combine the summary with a question like:

> *With all of these major benefits, you can see that advertising with us is a sound investment. Do you want to run your first ad on October fifteenth, or would November first be better?*

7. Give Them a Reason to Act Now (Impending Event)

This tactic uses a sense of urgency that is suggested by some event that will affect the terms or the effectiveness of the buying decision. This close must be based on truth and must not seem manipulative. The most common inducements are concerns that prices are going up or that resources will be in short supply:

> *My company has announced that prices on this product will go up five percent next month because of an increase in supplier costs. If I can call your order in now, you can stock up before the price increase becomes effective.*

Whatever the upcoming change or event is, it must be real and in the prospect's best interests to take advantage of an order placed now. When you have good information to work with, you can prevent a customer from running short of inventory or from facing an unexpected price increase, and this gains the appreciation and the loyalty of the customer.

8. Offer a Trial (Trial Order Close)

This technique involves asking the prospect for a trial order with no obligation. Prospects like it because their risk is low. Sometimes salespeople call this the *puppy dog close*. How could you ever return a puppy to the pet store and get your money back after the children have played with it for a week? By then, everyone is in love with it.

Suppose you are selling Dave Ramsey's *Financial Peace University™* program to financial planners, and one prospect says something like this: "I have never used material like this in my teaching or consulting activities. Let me think about it before I decide." Respond with:

> *I can certainly appreciate that. One thing that might be helpful to you is try the program for two weeks, risk free. This gives you plenty of time to work with the material firsthand and see if it is something that would be useful in your career consulting and training classes. We encourage you to listen to some of the audio, view the introductory DVD, go through the manual, and try it out in some actual financial counseling sessions.*
>
> *After two weeks, if you find that you can benefit from using it, just hang on to it and we will bill you the following month. But if you find that you can't use the material or that it's not suitable for your situation, all we ask is that you return it to us. Is that fair enough?*

9. Make a Balance Sheet (Balance Sheet Close)

This practical, decision-making format is familiar to most prospects, and they will feel comfortable as you use it. This tactic involves either using an old-fashioned tool known as a *sheet of paper*, or you can also use a tablet or laptop with a stylus pen. Draw a line down the center to form two columns. In the first column, list all the reasons for saying yes (the assets). Then list all the questions or concerns about a buying decision (the liabilities). Make sure the prospect can see as you write. The closing process is an analysis of the two columns to show the prospect that the reasons for buying heavily outweigh the reasons for not buying. You can begin like this:

> *The decision you are about to make is important. I know you want to be sure you are making a sensible choice. So that we will be sure to make the decision that is best for you, let's look at all the reasons in favor of buying this product and any questions or concerns about it. We can then determine which side weighs more and make your decision accordingly. Let's begin with the ideas that favor a positive decision today. Is that fair enough?*

Begin to list the reasons for buying, and be sure to avoid the word *objection*. Instead of talking about the prospect's objections to buying, state them as concerns or questions to be answered: "You expressed concern about delivery schedules." When you use the word objection out loud, you are setting up the prospect and yourself as adversaries—and if you are adversaries, one of you must win and the other must lose.

10. Do a Comparison (Cost of Ownership Close)

Rather than talking about price, in certain situations, you may want to focus on the total cost of ownership. Then total these costs and compare them to the prices offered by your competition. This works by comparing costs over time rather than only up-front payments. Here is an example of this technique:

> *Competing services may seem less expensive, but when you take into account installation, maintenance, and the lifetime of the product, our service is actually about half the price.*

Because people often focus on the immediate price, they miss the long-term cost that may be incurred. This comparison works by revealing costs over time rather than up-front payments alone. Lower service costs mean that you should be offering a more reliable product, and it helps to have evidence of your product's superior quality.

11. When the Answer Is "Not Today" (Call-Back Close)

Many sales opportunities are lost every day because salespeople take the prospect's decision not to buy as *permanent*. Studies show that many accounts are won by salespeople who call five or more times on the same prospect. Each time you return, you must present new information or ideas that will stimulate the prospect to buy. If you walk into the prospect's office and say, "Well, have you thought it over?" the prospect's natural tendency is to restate the original objection: "Yes, and I still feel it is not a good time to spend that much money." In other words: "No deal." Here is an effective plan for a call-back situation:

1. **Approach**. Begin by giving a reason for calling back: "Trina, after I left the other day, I realized that there is some information I did not give you that has a real bearing on your situation." Be sure you do have something different to present—new data, additional evidence in the form of testimonials, or whatever. Be sure it is pertinent and logical.
2. **Review**. Next, review the whole presentation. Begin with, "Let me review briefly the items we talked about last time." The last meeting may be fresh in your mind, but the prospect will not remember ten percent of what you presented. Throughout the review, use phrases like as you remember, you will recall, and we said that to suggest points of agreement from the previous meeting.

This second (third, fourth, or fifth) approach may not always work, but you know that you cannot sell to someone without face-to-face contact. Being there gives you the only opportunity you will ever have to sell this prospect.

AFTER THE CLOSE

We've talked a lot about learning to read the sales situation and selling when the time is right! Let's say you've done just that, and a *prospect* just turned into a *customer*. That is certainly an exciting time in any salesperson's career—but it may not be time for the champagne just yet. Some customers may still have unfinished business, and if you ignore it, you could find that your sale wasn't really complete just yet. Here's an example of what that might look like:

Jordan worked hard to close this deal with Rita. And after months of meetings, presentations, negotiations, and follow up, he finally got the yes he was after. Rita tells him to come by the next day to complete the paperwork. They are both elated as he leaves. In fact, Jordan is so happy, he takes his wife out for a night on the town to celebrate. The next morning he goes to see Rita and happily hands her the papers. But her look puzzles him as she takes the contract and sets it aside. She draws in a deep breath and says, "Okay, Jordan, here's the thing…"

Jordan thought it was a done deal—so what could have happened overnight? It turns out that Jordan had stopped selling just a little too soon. Rita had felt good about her decision because her current vendor's quality had been suspect for months. When she'd call to complain about it, things would get better for a while, but then the quality would start slipping again. That's why, when Jordan initially contacted her, she was open to hearing what he had to offer.

"Sorry, but pinky swear doesn't cut it anymore. My attorney has a few documents for you to sign."

But when it came time for the "break up call" to her current vendor after Jordan left, the vendor wasn't going down without a fight. He reminded Rita of how long they'd been working together. He also made her doubt Jordan's company by pointing out the fact that he knows her better than Jordan does due to their longstanding relationship, and "who knows" if Jordan will be able to keep his promises. Finally, he promised her that the problems were fixed and asked her to give them thirty days, free of charge, to prove it.

Jordan hadn't won the sale—and now he's about to take on an entrenched competitor who has the upper hand again. He could have avoided all of this by using the "*after the close*" *close*. Here's how it works—when a customer tells you that she is ready to sign, rather than celebrate, seal the deal by saying:

Rita, I'm excited about working with you, and thanks for the opportunity. Now, I'm sure that your current vendor will not want to lose your account. What are you planning to say to him?

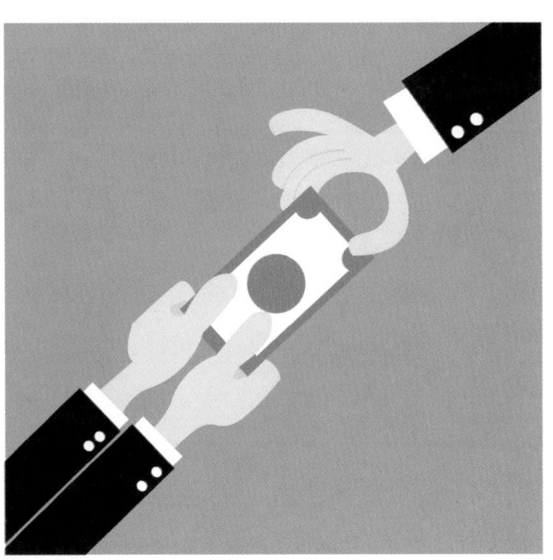

This statement allows your customer to consider the possibility that a phone call to the current vendor or supplier may not be an easy one. If a customer has never thought about that next step of the process before now, this gives you the chance to lock in the commitment. You will effectively reinforce in the buyer's mind the reasons for switching in the first place.

You may not use this technique every time, but it could prove to be an invaluable reinforcement in those instances when you are not sure whether a sale is really in the bag. As an added bonus, this technique is ideal for *Amiables* and *Expressives* who may have a harder time letting a current vendor go, so make sure you've done a good job of reading your prospect.

THE SOCIAL MEDIA CONNECTION

Using Social Media to Maintain Top of Mind Awareness

TOMA—*top of mind awareness*—is an important acronym in today's business world. Your customers are making buying decisions every day based on one factor: Who comes to mind. And when it comes to TOMA, brands will qualify under one of three conditions: **1) A Perennial Favorite:** The only way to increase your chances of getting in under this condition is to consistently provide great products and customer service to all your customers, **2) A Lingering Bad Taste:** You've heard the phrase, "I don't know what I want, but I know what I don't want." If the thing they don't want is your product, this is top of mind, but not in a good way, and **3) The Right Exposure:** This is your chance for top of mind awareness, and it is within your control.[27]

Let's say a prospect was qualified, but for reasons beyond your control, they were unable to make a commitment. But now, they are finally ready to make a purchase six months later. Will they remember you and buy from you? Or will they forget about you entirely and buy from one of your competitors?

Take steps today to ensure they remember you. Social media can help you do this, especially in conjunction with blogging and other forms of content marketing, including ***content curation***—which is the process of sorting through the vast amounts of content on the web and presenting it in a meaningful and organized way around a specific theme.[28]

It's rare to make an actual sale through social media, but what you can do is drive traffic from your social media pages to your other marketing channels. For example, when you post a new entry on your blog, announce it through your social media outlets. (Include a link to your blog article, of course.)

If you do video marketing, post links to your *YouTube* videos on social media. Have a compelling bit of content that arouses curiosity and makes people eager to check out the video. On your *YouTube* page, include your website's URL. On your Facebook fan page or LinkedIn business page, include a signup form for your email list.

Those are just a few of the ways to retain top of mind awareness among your prospects. And who knows? When the time is right to buy, they may just think of you!

SUMMARY

- Closing the sale is a natural conclusion to a carefully prepared and well-conducted presentation to a qualified prospect. Successful closing is often a matter of attitude.
- Learn to recognize buying signals. These enable you to close at the earliest possible point in the presentation.
- The most threatening element in the sale for many salespeople is the fear of rejection. Develop a plan for dealing with rejection.
- Both verbal and nonverbal clues point to the prospect's readiness to buy. The buying signals often suggest the type of close that would be appropriate.
- Close when the prospect is ready to buy.
- One effective tactic is a trial close that asks for an opinion rather than a commitment; this allows the salesperson to determine just how ready the prospect is to say yes!

- Use words like when or as during the close. Avoid words such as if and should because they are conditional and block closing action.
- Use a summary during the close to restate the major selling points made during the presentation. This repetition of benefits overcomes the prospect's tendency to forget or neglect main points.
- It may be helpful to present a balance sheet during the close in a pro and con format. This technique is often well received by analytical and amiable social styles.

REVIEW QUESTIONS

1. Discuss some strategies for handling the feeling of rejection that salespeople tend to experience from missing a sale.
2. Why do many prospects naturally say no when a close is attempted?
3. Why do many salesperson dread the close? Why is this fear unfounded?
4. When should the salesperson decide how to close? Why?
5. Should the planned close ever be changed in the course of the interview? Why or why not?
6. Timing is crucial in closing. Is attempting a close before the prospect is ready more harmful than trying to close past the critical point? Why or why not?
7. Distinguish between a trial close and a closing question. When is each appropriate?
8. What is the purpose of reassurance in connection with the close?
9. How many times in one interview should a salesperson ask for the order? How many times should you call on the same prospect to ask for an order?
10. What is the difference between persistence and pushiness?
11. Describe some typical verbal and nonverbal buying signals.

IN-CLASS EXERCISES

The following exercises help build teams, improve communication, and emphasize the real-world side of selling. They are meant to be challenging, to help you learn how to deal with problems that have no single right answer, and to use a variety of skills beyond those employed in a typical review question. Read and complete each activity. Then in the next class, discuss and compare answers.

EXERCISE 13.1 – PLANNING CLOSES

This is the final planning exercise for your team; therefore, you should use the same team that worked on role plays 11.1 and 12.1. Review your presentation plan as amended by your approach to handling objections. Now you need to insert appropriate closing attempts.

Although you are dealing with more than one person in the buying center, your experience as the chief decision maker should allow you to identify his/her personality type (driver, expressive, amiable, analytical). With all of the other information about the buying center's needs and concerns that you have developed, insert closing opportunities into your plan. Specifically, note the following points:

- When will you introduce trial closes (calls for opinion) and why? Which type of trial closes will you use?
- What sorts of nonverbal buying signals will you look for throughout your presentation?
- What type of final close (call for decision) will you attempt? Why? When?
- What will be the objective of your final close, your call to action (sale, trial order, call back, etc.), and why?

EXERCISE 13.2 – A SIGN OF TRUE LOVE?

For this exercise, the class should be divided into teams of 4 people each. Beginning salespersons often have difficulty remembering and noticing verbal and nonverbal buying signals. But put them in a social situation in which they are trying to attract the romantic attention of someone they admire, and they notice every little twitch and nuance!

As a team, you should brainstorm about various verbal and nonverbal cues (excluding overt verbal expressions of love or affection, or nonverbal expressions such as touching, hugging, or kissing) that indicate personal attraction of one individual for another. As you create your list, think also in each case of a corresponding or analogous buying signal, verbal or nonverbal, based on what you know about body language. The team with the greatest number of legitimate pairings (as determined by your instructor) wins.

CASE STUDIES

The following case studies present you with selling scenarios that require you to apply the critical skills discussed in the chapter and give you training through practical learning situations. They are meant to be both engaging and challenging, and like the in-class exercises, don't have one right answer.

CASE 13.1 – "DON'T TELL ME NO LIES!"

Harold was not feeling good about his last sales presentation. A customer who was somewhat interested in purchasing an entire season's worth of lawn care and landscape maintenance service had proved in the end to be indecisive. Harold had gone through all of the benefits of his company's service for the customer—how it would save him time and effort, how his lawn and shrubs would recover faster after the harsh winter, how his plantings would withstand the summer drought better—but the customer wouldn't pull the trigger.

Because getting new customers was so difficult for McPhee's Landscaping Service due to increased competition, especially from two large home improvement centers that had just opened, the company sent Harold to Atlanta for sales training. In light of the nature of the business, the trainers emphasized hard, aggressive selling that was designed to close the deal in one visit. Giving a customer an opportunity to think things over, they said, was the same as handing your business to your competitors. Needless to say, this meant that the trainers emphasized closing techniques as the heart of the entire sales process. When Harold returned to home to Cleveland, he told his boss that he was ready to try the new techniques.

The Atlanta trainers had emphasized using physical action (like filling out an order form before an actual yes is uttered) as particularly effective when dealing with amiable or analytical types who were otherwise indecisive. Harold's latest customer fit that mold perfectly, but didn't respond to this technique at all. So Harold turned to his last trick and told the customer that if he didn't purchase the contract today, the price would go up by 25%. He explained that the lower price was only available for those who signed on the dotted line in advance of needing the service. The customer signed and wrote out a check for the full, discounted amount. Harold thought to himself that this is like shooting fish in a barrel. It would be a good year.

Two weeks later, Harold's boss angrily reported that the customer had called to cancel the contract and demand a full refund. Apparently, the customer had learned from friends who had purchased later, after the lawn-mowing season had begun, that no price increase had occurred. At least one person had waited 10 days before signing a contract for the same price that Harold's customer was offered! The customer canceled because Harold had lied to him. Should Harold have been surprised by this turn of events? What was the matter with Harold's attitude toward selling? Which closing techniques should he have used that would have been more effective and that would not have involved deception?

CASE 13.2 – ALWAYS BE CLOSING MEANS . . . WHAT?

James Arnold sells airplanes, big ones. He heads a large team of salespersons, financial experts, contract attorneys, and aviation engineers that sells fleets of planes to major airlines around the world. In the current global economy and in light of increasing caution on the part of financially pressed airlines, his team has had to become more aggressive and focused on closing business. When James broke into sales at his father's auto dealership, the mantra, "Always Be Closing," was drummed into his head. Now, thirty years later, he realizes that something like this must be imparted to his team. But what can "always" mean for a sales cycle that can take as long as 7 to 12 months? In order to get a handle on what this might mean for the entire team, James calls a meeting of the primary team leaders.

"How can we keep ourselves and our clients directed toward completing the final transaction?" he asked. "What might 'Always Be Closing' mean for our respective roles?"

"Well, I know one thing," said Sherm Atkins, the chief engineer on the team. "If we are in a position of having to persuade anyone to buy our planes, we've already lost the sale. As we work out answers to problems and questions, some of which come from our clients, it must be one seamless process, in fact, a process of ceaseless assent."

"Very well put, Sherm," James answered. "But how do we make sure that happens?"

"I think the answer to that is really rather simple," interjected Marian, lead attorney. "We all work in very disparate areas and on long-term, complicated negotiations. But toward the end of every meeting with our counterparts from the airlines, we need to confirm agreement on what the next step is— whether that is merely to keep working on the same problem or to move on to something new—and get a commitment to keep moving forward. Every time. Without fail. If we do that, signing the final contracts will be a mere formality."

"I think your onto something, Marian," said Jim. "Let's try to unpack that a little."

What do you think? Given what you've learned from Chapter 13 about different types of and strategies for closing successfully, have Sherm and Marian captured what their team should be doing? Do you have any additional suggestions to refine or correct their approach?

Chapter 13 Footnotes

1. Brian Tracy, *The Art of Closing the Sale*. Thomas Nelson, 2007.
2. "Do Your Salespeople Ask for the Business Every Time?" *Sales Impact Group*, April 23, 2008. Accessed October 20, 2015.
3. Anonymous, "Closing the sale can be tough, but guidelines can ease the way," *San Fransisco Chronicle*, Wednesday, December 28, 2005; Page C-4.
4. Paul H. Green, "Closing A Sale," www.multiplex.com/Greensheet, July 9, 2001.
5. Jeffrey Gitomer, "A funny thing happened to me on the way to closing a sale," www.insiderbiz.com, July 15, 2001.
6. Anonymous, "The Truth About Getting Prompt Buying Decisions," *The American Salesman*. Burlington: (Jul 2010), Vol. 55, Is. 7, 21.
7. Jim Duerr, Personal Interview, September 26, 2012.
8. Selling Power Editors, "Persistence Leads to Success: Just Ask Gerhard Gschwandtner and Joe Sugarman," *Selling Power*, sellingpower.com, (January 5, 2004).
9. Cook, Matthew. "Three Reasons Why Persistence Matters in Sales." *Sales Force Research*, January 7, 2014. Web.
10. Clay, Robert. "Why 8% of sales people get 80% of the sales." *The Marketing Donut*. Accessed October 20, 2015.
11. Dr. Seuss, *Green Eggs and Ham* (New York: Random House, 1960).
12. Dave Kahle, "Closing the Sales," *The American Salesman*. Burlington: (Feb 2010), Vol 55, Is 2, 3.
13. John Boe, "Some Will, Some Won't, So What!" *The American Salesman*. Burlington: (Jan 2011), Vol 56, Is 1, 22.
14. Adapted and modified from "Sometimes I Say No," SellingPower.com (November 24, 2004), Pam Lontos, "Rejection Conditioning," *Selling Power* (June 1997), 78; and Tom Reilly, "Salespeople: Develop the Means to Handle Rejection," *Personal Selling Power*, Vol. 7, No. 5 (July/ August 1987), 15.
15. Ted Pollock, "How Good of a Closer Are You?" *The American Salesman*. Burlington: (Apr 2010), Vol 55, Is 4, 22.
16. Steve Beagelman, "The Art of Closing the Sale in 10 Easy Steps," *Franchising World*. Washington: (Feb 2008), Vol 40, Is 2, 52.

17. Anonymous, "Sales Technique Non-verbal communication: Body language matters," *Travel Trade Gazette*. Tonbridge: (Nov 30, 2007), 38.
18. Phil Sasso, "Listening in for more sales," *Professional Distributor*. Fort Atkinson: (Dec 2007), Vol 15, Is 9, 18.
19. Steve Atlas, "Listening For Buying Signals," *Selling Power* (March 2000), 38.
20. Cook, Matt. "3 Nonverbal Buying Signals Every Top Sales Person Looks For." *Sales Force Search*. December 12, 2012.
21. Keith Rosen, "How to Avoid a Prolonged Close," www.allbusiness.com, Accessed July 23, 2015.
22. Lappe, Neil. "Trial Closings: The Key to a 100% Closing Rate." *Web Strategies*, November 15, 2014. Web.
23. Allon, Gad and Eran Hanany. *Cutting in Line: Social Norms in Queues*. The Kellogg School of Management, July 25, 2011.
24. Iain Macfarlane, "Techniques to Improve Sales Success Rate," *Wisconsin State Journal*. Madison: (Aug 1, 2005), 8.
25. http://changingminds.org/disciplines/sales/closing/ownership_ close.htm. Accessed June 24, 2015.
26. Andy Cohen, "Are Your Reps Afraid to Close?" *Sales & Marketing Management* (March 2006), 43.
27. Wheeler, Brandy. "Four Marketing Tricks to Achieve Top of Mind Awareness." *Marketing DIY*, January 24, 2015. Web.
28. Florez, Fernando. "How to use Social Media to Close More Sales." *B2C*, August 25, 2014, Web.

"If people like you, they'll listen to you, but if they TRUST you, they'll do business with you."

– Zig Ziglar

PART V

MANAGEMENT ASPECTS: PERSONAL AND ORGANIZATIONAL

The service you give the customer after the sale has been completed can be as important, or even more important, than the sale itself. Building a loyal contingency of customers is the focus of ***CHAPTER 14.*** The customer absolutely defines quality in every transaction. Great salespeople don't talk customer service—*they live perfect service*.

CHAPTER 15 shows you how to get better control of your time and your activities. The chapter really is all about personal organization and self-management. You cannot manage time, but you can manage yourself and your personal activities. Administrative ability on the part of the salesperson is fundamental to success. Statistics indicate that only about 20 percent of a salesperson's time during a typical day is spent in face-to-face interviews with prospects.

Finally, ***CHAPTER 16*** details job responsibilities of today's winning sales managers who are responsible for being a coach, mentor, friend, cheerleader, and more to their salespeople. The chapter provides a useful introduction for classes in sales management.

CHAPTER 14

BUILDING CUSTOMER LOYALTY

OVERVIEW

The way you follow up with customers and clients after the sale has been completed can be as important, or even more important, than the sale itself. Keeping current customers happy and regaining lost clients is the focus of this chapter. The customer absolutely defines quality in every transaction, and they ultimately define the success of your organization, so you must learn how to make them feel every bit as important as they are. Great salespeople don't talk customer service—they live perfect service.

OBJECTIVES

- Examine the purpose of walking the walk when it comes to customer service.
- Determine what constitutes adding value.
- Know when and how to service.
- Understand your role in servicing.
- Appreciate how to upgrade and cross-sell current customers.
- Develop a systematic plan for follow-up activities.

DO YOU TALK SERVICE OR LIVE SERVICE?

At some point in your life, there's no doubt you had a horrible customer service experience that made you wish you'd never given that company a single dime of your money. But hopefully you've also had that magical customer service experience that not only solved your problem, but also restored your faith in humanity. The right kind of customer service can move mountains. Here are some customer service statistics that prove this point:[1]

1. A customer is 4x more likely to defect to a competitor if the problem is service-related rather than price or product-related.
2. The probability of selling to a new prospect is 5-20 percent. The probability of selling to an existing customer is 60-70 percent.
3. For every customer complaint, there are 26 unhappy customers who have remained silent (and are probably looking for a better solution).
4. 96 percent of unhappy customers don't complain, however 91 percent of them will simply leave and never come back.
5. 70 percent of buying experiences are based on how customers feel they are being treated, not on price or actual product.
6. 55 percent of customers would pay extra to guarantee better service.

Facts are facts—great customer service is essential for your clients and for you. While it's true that most companies say that their customers are their #1 priority, how many of them really walk the walk? You can have the greatest products and salespeople around, but if you're leaking customers through poor customer service, the company's bottom line and your compensation will suffer.

Every salesperson and every company should realize that their ultimate sustainability depends on their ability to generate consistent excellent service that keeps customers coming back and singing their praises. The cost of acquiring new customers usually far outweighs that of keeping existing customers. And no salesperson would consciously choose cold calling over reaching out to a satisfied customer for an additional sale, right? Surely, it's much more preferable to keep more of those customers you already have.

And yet, salespeople get so caught up in chasing the next lead or thinking that all their customers are after is the lowest price, despite the fact that studies prove that the majority of customers are willing to pay more for a better customer experience.[2] Your clients want you to follow-through, to do what you say, and to prove that all that time building a "relationship" wasn't just for your own selfish gain. As Benjamin Franklin once put it:

"Well done is better than well said."

Customers have an increasing rate of expectation for services and a decreasing tolerance for poor service, and as a result are more likely to migrate to the vendors who provide the highest-quality service. Your company's job is to create and keep a customer, and your job is exactly the same. Remember, no matter what your official title, you are a salesperson for yourself *and* your company. And the best way to increase your value as a salesperson is to build a loyal customer base through first-rate service. The customer absolutely defines quality in every transaction. Don't talk customer service—live perfect service.

"A lot of people have fancy things to say about customer service, but it's just a day-in, day-out, ongoing, never-ending, unremitting, persevering, compassionate type of activity."

Leon Gorman, L.L. Bean

STANDING OUT FROM THE CROWD

With competition growing at staggering rates, it's often difficult to differentiate one product from another, which means that the real differentiators are going to be the buying experience and customer service throughout. Start the process of standing out by making sure you're practicing the very best internal customer service with your own co-workers; do you treat your fellow salespeople how you'd like to be treated? Here are some other important questions from the *National Association of Sales Professionals* (NASP) that you and your sales team can ask to determine how you can stand out from the crowd:[3]

1. **Where do you want to be?** What do you want your customers to be saying about you, your team, your brand, and your company? Come up with some potential statements you'd want them to say if you asked them.
2. **What needs to happen?** Looking closely at the statements about what you want others to say about you, think about what sort of changes you'd need to make to ensure these statements come true. If you can't get there right away, prioritize one new activity at a time.
3. **Where am I now?** Assess where you are now with where you've just established you need to be. Do my team and I have the skills to fill the gap? Am I capable of taking on the changes required?
4. **How can you get there?** What do you need to do first? What do you need to do next? Work out a way to measure your customer service. This could be simple (like tracking your sales after implementing a new plan) or sophisticated (through the use of analytics), but do something.

Adding Value

Many companies can attribute their sales success to the ability of their salespeople to engage in value-added thinking. This type of thinking occurs when companies become less focused on promoting their own agenda and instead become more customer-centric. One such company is leading grocery retailer *Kroger*, whose "Kroger Plus" rewards program recognizes the value that lies within their loyal customers and rewards customers with offers relevant to their own shopping preferences. Kroger believes in targeting their existing customer base because of the opportunity they see—that even in their very best customers, there are still a lot of purchases they may make outside of Kroger.[4] When you are in the position of the customer, you recognize added value when you receive it—and you remember it! Here are two additional examples of value-added service:

- Salespeople from *Caterpillar Tractor* promise that their customers will receive ordered parts within forty-eight hours anywhere in the world. This after-sale service is both appealing and highly successful. The promise is not an idle one; if the delivery is not made within the forty-eight hours, the part is free.
- The air conditioner in your car goes out, and you take it in to the service department of a *Nissan* dealership to be repaired. They find they must order a part that will not arrive for two days. You mention to the service manager that you really need to get the car fixed before the weekend because you are planning a trip. Two days later when you take the car in to have the new part installed, the mechanic finds that the wrong part was shipped and they will have to reorder. The service manager asks you to wait for a minute and returns with a set of keys and says, "Here, we want you to use one of our demo cars for the weekend. The new part will be here early Monday morning, and you can pick up your car by noon."

When an automobile service department repairs your car's air conditioner, that isn't service; it's what you paid them to do. When you are provided with a car while they wait for a replacement part, that is service—and you remember it. The delay in getting the part was not their fault, but they knew the delay was not your fault either. Their concern was helping you have a comfortable trip. One weekend's use of a demo car was a small price for the dealership to pay for the kind of goodwill that will bring you back to purchase a new car the next time you are in the market. Some companies are recognizing that customers appreciate having their time and effort respected as valuable.[5]

The automobile industry estimates that a brand-loyal customer represents a lifetime average revenue of $300,000 to the dealer. If they refer two other customers and the revenue for service is added to these amounts, over $1 million of sales is gained by one satisfied customer.[6] The professional salesperson has numerous opportunities for follow-up activities that determine whether particular customers will reorder as well as whether they will tell others of their satisfaction or provide referrals. The relationship sales professional is sincerely and unselfishly helpful to clients and prospects alike. Sometimes value-added service costs nothing except thoughtfulness and a few minutes of time.

Herb Kelleher founded *Southwest Airlines* to set itself apart from other airlines. Since inception the company has been known for its low fares and attention to customer service. Southwest has maintained a high level of customer satisfaction not just because of its flights, but also because of its value-added service. Exhibit 14.1 shows how Southwest Airlines adds value, heart, and soul to its service and develops a fiercely loyal customer base.[7]

EXHIBIT 14.1 MAKING A DIFFERENCE WHEN IT WAS NEEDED MOST

A man was en route from a business trip in L.A. to his daughter's home in Denver to see his three-year-old grandson for the last time. The boy was being taken off of life support at 9 p.m. that evening so his organs could be used to save other lives. The man's wife called Southwest to arrange the last-minute flight and explained the emergency situation. Unfortunately, the man was held up by L.A. traffic and long lines at LAX and didn't make it to the gate on time. When he finally made it there 12 minutes after the plane was scheduled to leave, he was shocked to find the pilot waiting for him. He thanked the pilot profusely, and the pilot said, "They can't go anywhere without me, and I wasn't going anywhere without you. Now relax. We'll get you there. And again, I'm so sorry."

FOUR KEYS TO CUSTOMER RETENTION

The best way to increase your value as a salesperson is to build a loyal customer base through first-rate service and follow up. However, keep in mind there is a fine—but distinct—line between *badgering* and *fostering* a mutually beneficial relationship with frequent contact. And the real difference comes not from *when* you follow up, but *how*. Four keys to customer retention will help you learn how to follow up and connect with your customer base. By learning the keys to retention, you will enable your customers to feel as important and valued as they are to you and your organization.

Key #1: Think Like a Customer

People buy from people they like—and this is great news for several reasons. First, it allows you to consider your ultimate task to be a matter of finding and connecting with like-minded people. Second, it encourages you to communicate with passion and be genuine with others in an effort to establish honest and lasting connections. So, how can you effectively think like a customer? Here are some suggestions:

GET TO KNOW THEM. The best way to think like your customers is to get to know them better—and not just through an obligatory follow-up call or by following them on Twitter. The best way to get to know your customers is to ask questions (yes, even after the sale is complete). What made them say yes a few months ago may not be their motivating factors today. The only way to know that is to ASK. The important thing here though is to ask "why" as much as "how." Asking "how" helps you know what a customer wants to build, while the "why" question leads you to what they want to accomplish.[8]

LEARN MORE ABOUT THEIR CUSTOMERS. Your customers' customers are what matters most to them, right? So, take the time to find out more about their business and how they grow their own customer base. One of the first questions you should ask a new client is, "Who is your customer?" and, "Why would an individual or company spend money for your service?" This can help you identify places where you can trim or add to your existing offering to help their business (and not just your own).

COMMUNICATE COMPETITIVE ADVANTAGE. Your customers know there are virtually countless companies they could choose to do business with. So, expect for them to question their decision. You know your product or service is superior, but you can't assume that even your most loyal customers will continue to think this without occasional reminders. You also have no way of knowing who else has approached your customers since you last spoke with them. So, focus on how you communicate the ways in which you are different from other companies. Monitor both your traditional and emerging competition. Resolve all customer inquiries quickly, especially questions about pricing and quality.

SEND FEEDBACK REQUESTS. One of the best ways to gain insights into your customers is to conduct short surveys asking them what they love (or don't love) about working with you and your company. A lot of companies send out surveys, but the key is to reach back out to customers and tell them how you've implemented their suggestions! There is no better way to communicate with a customer than to show them you were listening. Let the conversation also be an opportunity for more feedback. You want customers to feel like they have an open line of communication to you at all times—whether that's for praise, complaints, or requests.

Key #2: Go the Extra Mile

Be willing to give your customers more than they demand and far more than they expect. ***Act from the desire to serve—not the desire to gain.*** When you make this your policy, you will do whatever you must to be of use and service to your client. Paul J. Meyer, founder of *SMI International,* once had a client who made a hobby of collecting rocks containing fossils. When Meyer was on a vacation trip one year, he found a rock with a particularly interesting fossil on it. He packed the rock carefully and mailed it to his client. That kind of extra service, when given from sincere interest, pays rich dividends.

Going the second mile may often involve a service for the customer that is unrelated to the business. Atlanta-based fast-food chain *Chick-fil-A* has adopted a policy of "second-mile service" for all of its 1,900 nationwide locations. A manager of a *Chick-fil-A* in Alabama took the policy to heart when he changed a customer's flat tire in the restaurant's parking lot while she ate, saving her the headache and expense of calling a towing company. Though this act is only one example, *Chick-fil-A* prides itself on being a company known for going the extra mile. When that same Alabama branch saw a 13 percent sales growth over one year without any menu or aesthetic changes, they couldn't help but believe the growth was due to *Chick-fil-A's* exceptional service philosophy.[9]

Determining your client's most basic level of satisfaction and keeping a constant flow of feedback is the best way to know if you and your company are consistently going the extra mile. *Benchmarking*—in which organizations evaluate various aspects of their processes in relation to best practices—is an excellent method of performing "preventative maintenance" in your processes and interactions with customers and prospects.

It pays to go the extra mile. Here are a few additional ideas that could be seen as going out of the way to follow up with the customer if there is a problem after the sale:[10]

- Offer to personally pick up or deliver goods to be replaced or repaired.
- Give a gift of merchandise to repay for the inconvenience. The gift may be small, but the thought will be appreciated.
- Reimburse for costs of returning merchandise such as parking fees or gas.
- Provide discounts on office supplies, car rentals, or express shipping.
- Acknowledge the customer's inconvenience with a small token of appreciation, and thank him for giving you the opportunity to make it right. Make the wording of the apology sincere and personal.
- Follow up to see that the problem was taken care of. Don't assume the problem has been fixed unless you handled it yourself.

Key #3: Say 'Thank You' Like You Mean It

How are you thanking your customers? For many salespeople, their idea of acknowledging the sale is emailing customers a copy of the receipt or contract. That's not follow-up—that's just part of the transaction! Some salespeople think they are doing really well when they tweet a thank you to a current customer. Saying thanks via social media is nice, but in most cases, it is simply not enough.

Even when salespeople do reach out and thank customers—well, let's just say that not all thank you's are created equal. Recent statistics suggest that only 38 percent of salespeople send any kind of thank-you note to customers after a meeting, and many who do receive them are getting form letters.[11]

Thanking your customers for their business seems like a no-brainer since we all want to be thanked for our business and for choosing one company when we could have chosen another. But saying thank you is not only the right thing to do, it's also a financially advantageous thing to do. In fact, customers who feel their salespeople are exceptional are 10 to 15 times more likely to remain loyal, which means more sales—and more commissions down the road.[12]

Most salespeople can answer the "who, what, when, where and how" of a business relationship. The missing element is "why." Why do your customers do business with you? Is it because they feel valued, protected or informed? These "why" factors have a definitive impact on customer loyalty. Your customers are not expecting to see their names written in the sky above their homes. They just want some warm, personalized follow-up thanking them for their patronage. If your resources are limited, consider enlisting the help of technology. The use of management software or a CRM program can help generate automatic, personalized email confirmations and thank you messages.

GET PERSONAL. The personal touch goes a long way when it comes to follow-up. Make sure that the salutation itself doesn't offend your customers. With all that technology offers today, there is simply no excuse for sending generic form letters anymore. Remember, they need to be personalized, as in "Dear [first name]." Always proof your letters and ensure your information is correct. And don't attempt to do any other selling or ask for referrals on the initial follow-up (that comes later). Creating personalized messages to customers doesn't have to take a lot of time or be a costly endeavor. But to have a powerful impact, your thank you letters should follow the 4 P's listed below. Thank you letters should be:

1. **Prompt.** Send the letter as soon as you have secured their business, preferably within forty-eight hours.
2. **Personalized.** Ensure that you are writing directly to the customer you dealt with (including their first name) and reference their specific purchase.
3. **Precise.** Convey (in a warm tone) gratitude and explain how any next steps or implementation will proceed.
4. **Positive.** Make your customers smile, feel glad they bought, and feel a sense of confirmation that they chose the right person to do business with. Let them know that because of their choice to say yes, they are now entering into a long-term relationship with someone who has their best interests at heart.

CUSTOMIZATION VS. PERSONALIZATION. Personalization is a must, but an important distinction needs to be made. To explain, here is a true story:[13] An alumnus of a university was asked about his reaction to a fundraising video he'd received from his alma mater. It was innovative, it was different, and it was customized. The email he'd received had a subject line with his name in it, and the body of the email had his name in it. The video itself also had his name in it!

Do you know what he said? *He said he didn't like it.* He felt that all that video told him was that his alma mater paid a lot of money to a video company to stick his name in there in a few places. It was *customized,* but it wasn't *personalized.*

Thirty-eight percent of customers attribute a good customer experience to personalization.[14] Using technology to insert someone's first name into something is no longer *innovative*, nor is it *personal*. Taking the time to write a personal note, acknowledge something specific to a customer, hand-address an envelope—now those are the actions that say something. It's not necessarily innovative; in fact it's pretty old fashioned, and that's why it will stand out.

Key #4: Treat Everyone Like a Big Customer

Thank you letters and follow up calls are important, and they should always be a part of your regular and ongoing activities as a salesperson. But keeping customers happy, engaged, and loyal takes more than that. When it comes to your customers, they want to feel special. After all, their purchase matters the same to them no matter what dollar amount they spent, from your smallest customer to your largest account.

The extent to which salespeople go to thank customers traditionally involves segmenting them, often based on their account size. In other words, only following up with really big clients is a common practice in the sales world. This is a mistake, because *every* customer wants to be treated like an important customer. Here is an example from the world of charitable giving: If you've ever made a small donation to an organization and received no recognition or acknowledgement for your contribution, no matter the size, it's safe to say that you didn't rush to donate to them a second time. There are also some people like to "test out" charities with small donations to see if they really want to get involved. But over time, nonprofits know that a small donor can become a large donor. Of course, it takes work on the part of the fundraiser to get them there. Similarly, a small customer can become a large customer with the right care and follow up. Just because a customer placed a small order the first time doesn't mean it will stay that way!

Never underestimate the power of customer loyalty, regardless of the size of the account.

You might want to consider circulating the names of smaller customers around the office where other team members can see them. Ask others, "Does anyone know this person?" Keep track of the contacts you have with your small customers. If you find out something, be sure to record the information. Did you find out something that indicates it might be worth your time to reach out to them? Making a personal connection is often the key to larger sales down the road. Large organizations can more easily ignore small sales simply because they have so many. But for smaller companies, every sale counts.

Thank you letters and emails are not the only ways to express your gratitude. Inexpensive gifts and tokens of appreciation can be a great way to make customers of all sizes feel appreciated. Consider giving away branded t-shirts, mugs, pens, or totes with your company's logo printed on the side to customers, or some other token that will both remind your customers of your company and make them feel appreciated. If you have the budget for it, a gift card can go a long way. Even a $10 *Starbucks* card can make a big impression.

Think of your customers as your portfolio of assets! Find out who they are, what potential they have, and the "why" behind their decision to buy from you. With the right amount of caring for those customers, you will eventually have more big customers than you ever imagined. We all want to feel special and needed; your smaller customers are no different. The most important thing to remember when it comes to customers of all sizes can be best summed up through the words of Henry James:

"Three things in human life are important: the first is to be kind; the second is to be kind; and the third is to be kind."

MAXIMIZING CURRENT CUSTOMERS

When so much time is invested in finding new customers, attempting to save time by neglecting post-sale follow-up is a costly mistake. A negative buying experience can be a bitter and enduring memory. There is no substitute for salespeople thanking their buyers and asking their customer base what else they can do to help them. All the efforts to retain your customers are certainly not without advantages. It really does pay to go the extra mile with customers. In fact, the payoff of exceptional, consistent customer follow-up can be summed up through the *four R's*:[15]

1. **Referrals.** Loyal customers encourage others to support your company over another, saving you some of the substantial cost of acquiring new customers. Where yesterday's "word of mouth" could influence a dozen individuals, today's "word-of-mouse" (via email, blogs, and social media) can influence thousands.
2. **Retention.** Customers who continue to buy from you provide a solid base for success.
3. **Reputation.** Loyal customers speak well of you to others. They increase public support and positive interest from future customers and even the media.
4. **Revenue.** Loyal customers give you more of what you and your company need—the revenue required to continue growing and prospering.

In addition to providing great service as a part of your daily routine, there are three specific ways you can maximize your current customer base:

1. SELL THEM MORE. This is such a simple but overlooked action—call on current customers and sell them more of what you're already selling to them. Other departments may have a need; sell them upgrades, enhancements, or additional products. Needs change over time. Sell your current clients something new. Keep them up-to-date on new products. Sell customers on you, strive to become a trusted member of their team, and opportunities will present themselves.[16]

2. UP-SELL THEM. *Upgrading*, also known as *up-selling*, is the process of persuading the customer to purchase a better-quality product or, perhaps, a newer product. Upgrading is largely a matter of selling your company and promoting the quality factors of your product and customer image. You ask for the upgrade because the newer or higher-quality product will serve the needs of the client better than the less expensive version of the same product. Most firms have products that vary in quality and price. And most buyers like to have choices when making a purchase. The only way you can succeed in upgrading is to believe one hundred percent in what you're doing, think ahead, service your clients, and create win-win relationships.

The cornerstone of selling—especially when trying to upgrade a client—relies on continuously qualifying the prospect throughout the buying process. It's ultimately the customer's choice and you don't want to oversell, but giving them options is just logical, especially given the statistics that up-selling leads to more purchases by the customer 58 to 72 percent of the time.[17] You want to sell to the real needs of the prospect. Salespeople need to remember they don't sell products—they sell results.

3. ENGAGE IN CROSS-SELLING. *Cross-selling* is the process of selling products that are not directly connected to the primary products being sold to new and/or established clients. For example, cross-selling occurs when in a conversation with your bank's loan officer about a loan for expanding your business, you casually mention how expensive it is to keep your two elementary school children in a private school. Several days later, you receive a note in the mail from that same loan officer with materials describing how a limited trust fund could be used to help pay college expenses and offering the bank's services to help set it up.

Cross-selling and upgrading have become increasingly important to many companies in the information age. Customers have to be convinced that what you have available is going to solve a problem or save them money before they're even willing to talk. To be truly customer-focused you have to make as many channels available as your customers are demanding. To do the best job of fostering lifetime loyalty, you need to know exactly what your customers are thinking. The ideal scenario goes like this: When a customer contacts the customer service hotline via email or telephone, the agents in the call center can pull up a comprehensive record of every interaction, no matter how, why, or when it took place. The most profitable callers are identified and then directed to the most knowledgeable agents right away. Agents get a view of customers that is so comprehensive, they can cross-sell and up-sell products to their customer base with ease.[18]

THE SOCIAL MEDIA CONNECTION

Using Social Media to Create Lifelong Customers

Can social media help you create loyalty among your client base? Absolutely! Here is a perfect example:

A writer named Christina McMenemy was in Nashville for a blogging conference a few years ago and adored the clock radio at the hotel where she always stayed when she came to Nashville—the ***Gaylord Opryland.*** During each stay, Christina found herself entranced by one of the features of the alarm clock that played light music; as in, the kind that you'd hear in a high-end spa.

Wanting to experience the same serenity at home, the blogger took to Twitter to ask the folks at the hotel where she could purchase one. Their response, essentially, was, "Sorry, it's made just for us, but here's a similar one at the Sharper Image." Unfortunately, the one they recommended lacked the spa music feature that Christina loved so much. She thanked them for the effort anyway as she resigned herself to the fact that she'd never be able to duplicate the sleep experience she got at Opryland. When she returned to her room later that day, she found a second clock radio sitting next to the permanent one, along with a handwritten note that said: "Christina, thank you for following us on *Twitter*. We hope you enjoy these spa sounds at home. If you need anything, please let us know."[19]

Opryland recognized an opportunity on social media to make sure a long-time customer had one of the best experiences ever. And they didn't just win a customer for life; they also bought plenty of goodwill with folks at the conference (and beyond) who subsequently heard about the story, as well as anyone who followed Opryland or Christina on Twitter. Christina posted on her social media pages, "You reaffirmed that there are still companies out there focused on great service, and you've made a lifelong fan out of me."

You never know when an opportunity might present itself on social media to turn a regular (or even on-the-fence) customer into a loyal, lifelong partner. So, make sure you read as many posted comments as possible and follow up on any questions that someone asks you, whether it's in a tweet, a Facebook post, or even in a picture caption on Instagram.

WINNING BACK LOST CUSTOMERS

In the world of car sales, there's a saying that goes, "Never try to sell someone a car; try to sell them five cars over twenty years." The best automobile salespeople don't look at a customer as a single transaction. They recognize that if they make the experience memorable, painless, and pleasant—and most importantly, if they make the customer feel truly special—the purchase will not be a one-time event. It is exactly the same no matter what you are selling. And in fact, if a customer buys one time and then never buys again, something has likely gone wrong. Someone or some process within the company has failed that buyer. Repeat customers should be a key component of your financial strategy.

Customers rely on their emotional experiences with salespeople more than any of the traditional factors, according to research by the Peppers & Rogers Group, which showed that:[20]

- 60 percent of all customers stop dealing with a company because of what they perceive as indifference on the part of salespeople.
- 70 percent of customers leave a company because of poor service, which is usually attributed to a salesperson.
- 80 percent of defecting customers describe themselves as "satisfied" or "very satisfied" just before they leave, which means that there wasn't really anything wrong—but there certainly wasn't much in their transactions with a salesperson or a company that encouraged any sense of loyalty.

Even so, a certain amount of customer attrition is to be expected, and there are a number of reasons why someone will stop buying. Some of those reasons (a change in their financial circumstances or no longer having the need for what you sell) are beyond your control. Others (loss of interest, increased demands on their time, or simply forgetting) can be overcome with a little creativity and personal attention—and those are the customers who will make your efforts worthwhile. So, what do you do when one of your clients stops buying? Here are three strategies for re-energizing your client base:

1 Concentrate Your Efforts

Winning back customers may require a significant investment of your time and resources, so you must make sure you plan your efforts to re-engage lapsed accounts before you leap into action. Begin by identifying your best prospects that have gone elsewhere. In terms of maximizing your efforts, consider limiting your attention to those who have stopped purchasing in the last two to three years.

Once you have a list of past customers targeted for recommitment, begin by doing research into their purchase history. Looking for patterns in the way they have purchased in the past can provide key insights that will help you win them back. Consider when they first started doing business with you. What was your company doing at that time that could have induced them to buy? Consider the time of year they bought. Certain customers may make seasonal purchases; if this is the case, a simple note with an email subject line that says something like, "We missed you this year!" may be all it takes to re-engage them by reminding them that you are still around.

Remind Them of Their "Why"

Remember that every single one of your customers was once inspired to say yes to what you have to offer. So, try to get them thinking about what first drew them to you. If your company has an important anniversary coming up, hold a party to celebrate it, and invite former customers to get involved in the fun.

Also, consider calling lapsed customers to ask about how they first heard about your company. The idea of calling up a customer to ask them why they *used to buy* may make you uncomfortable, but if there were no significant reasons for their leaving, it will remind them of why they bought and may encourage them to buy again. On the other hand, if you learn that something went wrong—the customer was offended in some way—take the concern seriously, try to remedy the problem, let them know they are valued, and ask for another chance to win their confidence.

Shake Up Your Email List

There is a term in the world of mass email known as *unemotionally subscribed*. These are people in your email database who have not opened or clicked an email message from you or your company in an extended (several months or more) period of time. They have not unsubscribed, nor have they marked your message as spam. They either ignore the messages or take the time to delete one every time a message lands in their inbox.

The percentage of your list that is considered *unemotionally subscribed* can be as high as thirty percent, according to some sources.[21] So, that means that nearly one out of every three people on your email list are not interacting with your emails at all. Once you figure out who fits this "inactive" criteria, you have a few options. You can: 1) Unsubscribe them, 2) Move them to a new list where they receive fewer messages, 3) Send a "we miss you" type email, or 4) Set up a re-engagement email series in which you actively pursue former customers through a series of messages with various *requests for action*.

No one method is better than the other. But if you want to give your "unemotionally subscribed" followers another chance (and for them to do the same for you), consider getting creative with a "We Miss You" email campaign that provides them with several calls to action, such as sending them to a funny video on your website when they "click here to stay on our list" or sending them to a picture of a sad kitten if they choose "click here if you'd like to be removed from our system."

In the end, no one relishes the prospect of reaching out to former customers with the hope of renewing their commitment. It is a frustrating process in which a considerable amount of effort and work often yields frustratingly few results. But with more organizations vying for the attention of an over-messaged and overwhelmed public, the ability to effectively re-energize your existing customer base is becoming an increasingly important component of selling.

Dealing with Angry Customers

It's no fun to lose a customer, but winning back a customer who has turned to a competitor helps your feelings as well as your bank account. The first step in regaining a customer is to discover why you lost the account. If customers leave because they feel they've been badly treated, it is your responsibility—not the customer's—to mend this relationship. Exhibit 14.2 gives some of the most common excuses given by salespeople for losing accounts.

EXHIBIT 14.2 EXCUSES SALESPEOPLE GIVE FOR LOSING ACCOUNTS

- If it isn't price, then it's because the competition uses unfair or unethical tactics.
- My company fails to back me up; delivery is late, or quality deteriorates.
- That customer is just too difficult for anyone to get along with.
- The customer never cared about anything but price, so I was helpless.
- I just don't have time to make all the service calls I'd like to make.
- There can't be anything wrong with my sales techniques. I'm doing exactly what I've been doing for years.

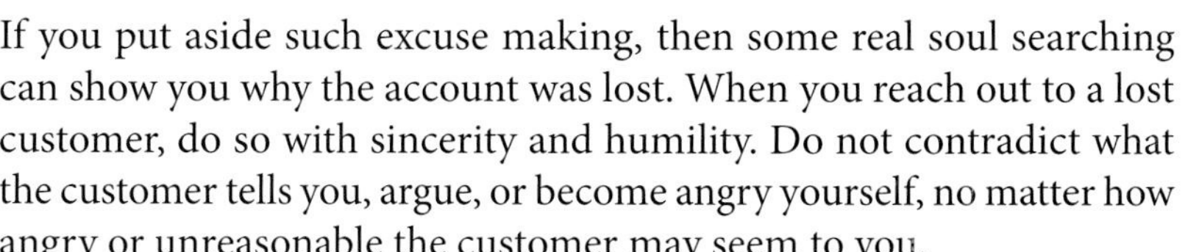

If you put aside such excuse making, then some real soul searching can show you why the account was lost. When you reach out to a lost customer, do so with sincerity and humility. Do not contradict what the customer tells you, argue, or become angry yourself, no matter how angry or unreasonable the customer may seem to you.

"We'd like to hire you for our Customer Service Department. It's practically impossible to look at a penguin and feel angry."

When faced with an angry customer, you have two choices. One, you can walk away and consider the account lost; or two, you can resolve the conflict and further reinforce the relationship.[22] If you listen politely, ask additional questions, and probe for hidden feelings, the mere act of telling you what is wrong often defuses the negative feelings of the customer. The former satisfaction that was experienced in doing business with you or your company surfaces and the customer may be quite happy to consider reestablishing your relationship.

Do your best to glean every bit of current information you can regarding this angry customer, along with what you know of your relationship with the customer in the past, in order to decide what went wrong.

Take some time for problem solving. Until you discover and acknowledge the real problem, you cannot solve it. Sometimes the answer is unpleasant. If the problem lies in your actions or attitudes, you must accept responsibility so that you are free to solve the problem and regain the account. If you deny your obvious responsibility, you escape into excuse making and are blinded to the options available for regaining the customer's goodwill. When you know what the problem is, you can plan strategies for rebuilding the account.

A PLAN FOR TRACKING FOLLOW-UP

With the vital role that customer service and follow up plays in the success and longevity of your career, you can't afford to take follow-up planning lightly. Your system for tracking follow-up should be as well organized as your prospecting system. Use a contact software program to set up files listing the customer's name, the date of each contact, and the form it took (telephone call, meeting, email, social media). Whatever organizing system you choose, be sure to have a specific, written plan for reaching out to your existing client base.

Every level of customer truly is important to your career, but when it comes to major clients, having a specific plan in place to follow up with them is essential. Here is a simple but powerful eight-step plan you can use to retain your most valued customers (Note: This plan is also a highly effective way to target your most important prospects):[23]

1. **Start a Short "Best Client" List.** Select a manageable number (perhaps less than 30) of your best customers and create a separate database with their names only.
2. **Create Files for Each.** Open and work from a file you create for each individual client.
3. **Identify Partners.** Find centers of influence that you have in common or who know the customer in some way. Be sure to write these names down in the appropriate file.
4. **Talk to Influencers.** Consult with influencers about this individual or company and record any and all findings. You never know what piece of information will prove to be useful down the road.
5. **Pick a Contact.** Select a primary player within your organization to deal with the customer. For the largest major client, the more experienced that contact is, the better.
6. **Develop a Targeted Strategy.** Develop a strategy for individual customers based on what you know about them, their needs, and their purchase history with your organization.
7. **Plan a Year Ahead (Month by Month).** Plan your moves for the next year with each customer and establish objectives for the year. As a general rule, plan one move per month for your best clients. That "move" could be as simple as sending an email with some relevant and timely info for their business.
8. **Review and Revise.** Record and review your results and refine your strategy as needed.

The process never ends with the sale—unless you intend for that purchase to be the only possible one you will ever receive from a customer or with anyone that customer can influence. The sale is not complete until the customer is satisfied and feels appreciated by both you and the company. You carry the responsibility for their satisfaction a long time after the deal is done. It is not enough to "pass the buck" and assume the customer will stay engaged through mass emails, your Twitter feed, or annual mailings. It takes days, weeks, or even months to get a customer. Regaining a lost customer after poor follow up will be much more expensive and time-consuming than keeping a current customer satisfied.[24]

GAINING A NEW CUSTOMER COSTS 5X MORE THAN KEEPING A CURRENT ONE.

CONTACT FREQUENCY AND MEDIUM. Decide how often you will contact each client based on what has worked well for you or other salespeople in the past and based on your experience with each client. Some customers require far more work than others. If you come across high-maintenance customers, note that in their file and respond accordingly. Consider the personality and needs of your major clients and determine what care is needed to maintain a solid relationship with your highest priority clients. Decide also whether contact will be by email, social media, telephone, in person, or a combination. Personalized contact in the social media age means knowing which social media platforms your customers prefer. It's important to reinforce that you should not seek to upsell or ask for something (like a referral) every time you follow up. Keep your name before the customer with direct-mail items like these:

- Information about new products that might interest them.
- Your in-house newsletter that could include interesting stories.
- A letter with a self-addressed reply card on which the customer can send in comments or ideas for your company.

Give close attention to the effectiveness of each type of contact you make. Discard methods that do not work, and repeat methods that do. Keep your follow-up records as meticulously as you do your data on prospecting. Know what you have done for each customer, what you plan to do next, and when.

SUMMARY

- Service after the sale adds value to what you sell by showing the customer that you are willing to take care of any problems. Service after the sale can be more important to your client than the actual sale itself.
- The right kind of customer service brings you repeat business over time. A buying decision is a one-time action unless you turn it into a habit with effective follow-up and follow through procedures.
- Service is an ongoing activity. It is never too soon or too long after the sale to provide service.
- Sell current customers more of what you are already selling to them. You do this by cross-selling or up-selling to your customer base.
- Service is the key to winning back lost accounts. No matter what causes the loss of an account, that loss is a signal for renewed service activity. Contact the former client with sincere concern and interest.
- Plan, execute, and track any personal visits, telephone calls and mailings to your customers and measure how effective they were.

REVIEW QUESTIONS

1. List the 4 keys to customer loyalty.
2. What is meant by "adding value" in connection with selling? Can you give an example of a time when you experienced extra value as a customer?
3. Think of a situation in which failing to keep up with personnel changes could cause loss of sales for a salesperson.
4. List some types of problems a customer might have that you, as a salesperson, could solve before they become serious by following a regular servicing program.
5. What is the salesperson's responsibility if a piece of machinery or equipment is installed and then is found to be defective or has some part missing?
6. Discuss the importance of service as an ongoing activity.
7. Explain how you would go about setting up a systematic plan for follow-up activities.

8. Describe some of the particular services that are beneficial to buyers for a retail business.
9. Is prospecting for new customers or servicing existing ones more important? Justify your answer.
10. Describe some specific servicing activities that could be used to win back a lost client.

IN-CLASS EXERCISES

The following in-class exercises help build teams, improve communication, and emphasize the real-world side of selling. They are meant to be challenging, to help you learn how to deal with problems that have no single right answer, and to use a variety of skills beyond those employed in a typical review question. Read and complete each activity. Then in the next class, discuss and compare answers.

EXERCISE 14.1 – MAINTAINING THE LOOP

You will work independently on this exercise in class. Imagine that you own a website development, marketing, and hosting company that employs 8 people. Five of your staff work in sales and marketing, while three manage the technical backend. There is no separate customer service department. All 5 of your sales staff, yourself included, do it all: prospect for new customers, sell your services, respond to requests for assistance, and follow up with customer requests and needs. You don't sleep.

As you acquire more customers, you realize that you need to systematize serving their ongoing needs and problems. In other words, you need to develop a customer follow-up and service plan. For the next 15 minutes, jot down as many items as you can think of that you will include in your service plan for this business. Be prepared to explain or justify the items on your list.

EXERCISE 14.2 – HOW FAR SHOULD ONE GO?

For this exercise, you should work independently. Chapter 14 offers several examples of salespersons who "go the extra mile" for their customers. As you think about the responsibilities of yourself as a salesperson, jot down brief answers to the following questions:

1. Should there be limits on what a salesperson is expected to do by way of customer service?
2. If so, what are those limits, theoretically speaking?
3. What limits, if any, would you personally adhere to?
4. Provide some concrete examples of actions that you would refuse to take in the interest of customer service.
5. Provide some concrete examples of actions that you would consider taking that would be considered extraordinary ("going the extra mile") by most people.
6. Should salespersons be rewarded or compensated for customer service actions that exceed company requirements?

CASE STUDIES

The following case studies present you with selling scenarios that require you to apply the critical skills discussed in the chapter and give you training through practical learning situations. They are meant to be both engaging and challenging, and like the in-class exercises, don't have one right answer.

CASE 14.1 – TO TWEET OR NOT TO TWEET

Nutmeg Appliances operates 35 stores throughout the State of Connecticut and southwestern Massachusetts. They offer complete lines of kitchen appliances, TVs, and home entertainment centers. Competition in this business is fierce. Customers are always shopping for bargains for such products and are often complaining about missed deliveries and malfunctioning equipment. The pace on the sales floor, in operations (delivery and installation), and customer service is, to say the least, brisk. In this environment, however, Nutmeg executives take the enlightened and financially prudent view that increasing customer loyalty must be a top priority. Living off new customers who walk in the door is not a viable option, especially in a stressed economy. Customer retention is vital.

Therefore, Nutmeg routinely holds meetings involving representatives from sales, operations, and customer service to see how they can improve service to their existing customers. This morning's meeting addresses a controversial matter: how to position the company vis-à-vis the burgeoning social media, especially Facebook and Twitter. Questions for discussion and decision include the following:

1. Should Nutmeg establish corporate accounts on Facebook? On Twitter?
2. How can these accounts be utilized to the best advantage of the company?
3. Should Nutmeg assign someone to monitor these accounts to filter out negative or critical comments? Why should negative comments be filtered out? Why should they be permitted?
4. Should these accounts be monitored in such a way that individual employees from sales, operations, or customer service are alerted whenever there appears to be a comment posted by a customer with whom an employee has had contact?
5. Should all employees be encouraged to participate through these accounts, or should Nutmeg restrict participation to designated company spokespersons?

As a representative of sales, you immediately recognize that the decisions taken in response to these questions will affect the company's bottom line and your livelihood. What do you recommend for each of these questions, and why?

CASE 14.2 – THE NORDSTROM™ WAY

Sandra was so frustrated that she was ready to quit on the spot. She loved selling, and she loved selling computers and related equipment. It was her company's lack of commitment to customer service that she hated. She was convinced that the company's refusal to take customer complaints seriously was hurting sales and depriving her of a chance to develop long-term relationships with her customers. And that, in turn, deprived her of commissions.

She took her complaints directly to her regional vice president, Ernest.

"Ok, Ernie," Sandra declared upon taking a seat in front of Ernest's desk. "I'm here to renew my demand that this company begin to change its policies and devote some resources to customer service."

Clasping his hands behind his head, Ernest (Ernie) replied, "Well Sandy(!), you and I have had this conversation before, and the company hasn't changed its mind. Why do you keep pressing?"

"I'm on your case because I know that customer service works," said Sandra. "When I started out in sales, I worked for Nordstrom™, a company that has won awards for the highest quality customer service since they were founded in 1901. Not only am I convinced that I made money because of their policies, but it's a fair bet that customer service helped them expand to 115 department stores in 28 states today. This company is missing out. I'm missing out."

"Well, how do you expect a computer company to adopt Nordstrom's policies and survive?" asked Ernie. "From what you tell me, we'd go bankrupt in a matter of months."

"I know that Nordstrom's policies are counterintuitive," responded Sandra. "As you may know, Nordstrom instructs all of their sales associates to use their own judgment in accepting returns of merchandise for any reason or no reason; and in case of any doubt, to err on the side of the customer. In practice, that means virtually unlimited returns are allowed."

"We can't begin to do that. Our merchandise costs hundreds, sometimes thousands, of dollars per unit," Ernie replied, leaning forward in his chair.

"Well, you should know that at Nordstrom, I regularly accepted $3,000-coats and $800-shoes as returns, even when they showed signs of wear and couldn't be resold," Sandra answered. "But over the long term, these same customers bought more than they returned. The company made money and I made money."

"Sandy, this isn't Nordstrom, and we don't sell shoes." Ernie stood, indicating that this meeting was over. "It appears that you have an important decision to make. Call me to let me know what it is."

So, based on your understanding of Chapter 14, who is correct? Should Sandra's computer company adopt Nordstrom's customer service policies? Does the difference in product matter in deciding this issue, as Ernie claims? Would a Nordstrom-like policy of customer service mean more sales for the computer company in the long run? What sort of changes in customer service might the computer company make short of adopting Nordstrom's unlimited return practice? What should Sandra do? Should she quit, or not?

Chapter 14 Footnotes

1. Brookes, Nicola. "The multibillion dollar cost of poor customer service." *New Voice Media*, January 8, 2104. Web.
2. 2011 Customer Experience Impact Report. *RightNow Technology*, Jan 10, 2012.
3. Ashton, Leigh. "Customer Service: Your Most Important Sales Tool?" *National Association of Sales Professionals*. Accessed September 19, 2015. Web.
4. Matt Nitzberg, "Putting the Shopper in Your Shopper Marketing Strategy," *Shopper*

Marketing, posted June 17, 2009, Accessed April 14, 2015.

5. Helen Edwards, "Slavery doesn't pay," *Marketing*. London: (May 26, 2010), 18.
6. Brett Stevenson, "Million Dollar Customers – they're all around you!" *Dealer Marketing Magazine*, posted June 3, 2010, Accessed April 14, 2015.
7. Conradt, Stacy. "11 of the Best Customer Service Stories Ever." *Mental Floss*, October 9, 2015. Web.
8. Grubbs, JC. "5 Ways to Get to Know Your Customers Better." *Business Collective*. Web. Accessed October 4, 2015.
9. Andrea V. Hernandez, "Not settling for 'good': Phenix City Chick-fil-A crew embraces 'second-mile service' policy," *Knight Ridder Tribune Business News*, Washington: (Sep 26, 2006), 1.
10. Wilkins, Rich. "Go the Extra Mile by Giving Extra Service." *Selling Power*, Accessed October 17, 2015. Web.
11. "66 Crazy Sales Figures." *White Paper*. IKO System. Accessed September 26, 2015.
12. Dooley, Ken. "The No. 1 reason why customers stay or leave." *Customer Experience Insigh*t. June 10, 2013.
13. Strathy, Maeve. "Customization Versus Personalization." *What Gives Philanthropy*, January 2, 2015
14. Genesys Global Survey, 2009.
15. Todd Beck and Anne Smith, "Four Keys to Customer Loyalty," *The Catalyst*, Accessed July 7, 2015. Web.
16. "Get More From Current Customers," in the Selling Ideas section of *Selling Power* (October 2000), 62.
17. Susan Spielberg, "You want fries with that?" *Nation's Restaurant News*. New York: (Oct 4, 2004), Vol. 38, Is. 40, 86.
18. Kathleen Cholewka, "CRM: Calling All Customers," *Sales & Marketing Management* (May 2001), 25-26.
19. Stansberry, Glen. "10 Examples of Shockingly Excellent Customer Service." *Open Forum*, May 4, 2010. Web.
20. Dooley, Ken. "The No. 1 reason why customers stay or leave." *Customer Experience Insight*. June 10, 2013.
21. Waldow, DJ. "We Miss You! A Creative Re-Engagement Email Campaign," *Brand Driven Digital*. September 19, 2013.
22. "Turn Conflict with a Customer Into a Selling Opportunity," *Personal Selling Power*, Vol. 12, No. 8 (September 1992), 73.
23. Kathy Lievense, CFRE, "Donor Centered Fundraising." Report Published by The Summit Group, 2012.
24. D. Geoffrey Brewer, "How to Stay in Touch," *Sales & Marketing Management*. (February 2008), 109.

CHAPTER 15

PERSONAL, TIME, AND TERRITORY MANAGEMENT

OVERVIEW

You cannot manage time, but you can manage yourself and the actions that comprise your day. This chapter shows you how to get better control of both your time and your activities, and it's ultimately about personal organization and self-management. Administrative ability on the part of the salesperson is fundamental to success. Many times, salespeople have more work than one person can handle, so it's up to you to make the most of the time you have to work on the highest priority items—in other words, actions and conversations that will increase sales.

OBJECTIVES

- Discover how to develop an effective time management attitude.
- Recognize the need for organizing your activities and surroundings as a means of controlling your time.
- Develop a procedure for getting organized.
- Establish an effective organizing system for all activities.
- Learn how contact management and mapping programs increase productivity.
- Examine the need and the process for managing travel time in your sales territory.

TIME CONTROL AND SELF-MANAGEMENT

The term *time management* is a contradiction. Because every minute has sixty seconds and every hour has sixty minutes, time itself cannot be managed—it can only be used. What *can* be managed, however, are you and your activities. So in actuality, time management is really personal organization as well as self-management; and it involves three areas:

1. **Self-management (also known as self-discipline)**
2. **Planning and organizing**
3. **Systems and techniques to form routines**

Time itself is a precious commodity. Although a continuous supply of time is available, it cannot be stored for future use, and it cannot be reclaimed if it is wasted. When you realize that life itself consists of time, the value of time becomes clear. We loudly denounce attitudes or practices that show a lack of respect for human life, but we don't seem to notice when we throw away priceless hours in useless activity or idleness.

The key to time management is strict and disciplined adherence to a rigid schedule, while remaining flexible enough to let anything happen at any time.

Time is made up of a series of events. The key to managing time is controlling these events to your advantage.[1] Time control and self-management can be learned; you have the ability to control your present thoughts and actions and to decide how to use your time. Here are some symptoms of time mismanagement. See if any of these sound familiar to you:[2]

- Letting paperwork pile up on your desk and emails pile up in your inbox.
- Delaying decisions, thus frustrating both your superiors and your co-workers.
- Getting farther behind every day.
- Working late and having to work weekends.

Most of us can relate to some or all of those symptoms; so, here is an easy visualization exercise that may help you get a better grip on time's worth:

Pretend that the president of your bank informs you that you have been chosen to receive a special prize: Every day for the rest of your life, $86,400 will be deposited into your account. The only stipulation is that it must all be spent every day. Anything left at the end of the business day goes back to the bank. You can't hold anything over from one day to the next.

Those first weeks are exhilarating. By the end of the first month, you have received over $2 million. After a while, however, you begin to have trouble spending that much every day. Think how you would feel the first time $20,000 slipped away from you and went back to the bank because you failed to spend it all. You would quickly realize that using this much money every day calls for some serious planning.

This imaginary scenario is not entirely fantasy. The old adage is true: Time is money. Every day, 86,400 seconds are deposited in your account and into the accounts of everyone else. You cannot save any unused time for another day. How many of your 86,400 seconds go back to the "bank" unused depends on your skill in planning and managing your time. The important questions are these:

1. How will you spend your time?
2. How will you invest your time?
3. How much time will go to business, to service for others, to family, to leisure?
4. How much time will be reserved just for you, for the things you want to do?

A TIME MANAGEMENT ATTITUDE

Your most important asset is time, and how you use it is crucial to your success. Renowned speaker Ira Hayes once said:

> *"The inability or lack of desire to become organized is responsible for the vast majority of failures. It is why otherwise bright people turn out to be only mediocre performers and achieve only a small degree of the success that they rightfully could achieve. A disorganized desk, car, or way of life leads to rushing around and confusion and generally results in a poor attitude which makes people around you question the advisability of doing business with you."*

Everybody has the ability to manage his or her time. The *desire* is the variable that makes the difference, and taking charge of your life depends on your personal choices. Like most success factors in selling, time management depends on attitude. The first line of defense to protect your time is to identify precisely how it can be eroded, and then learn effective means for managing it.[3]

"Dost thou love life? Then do not squander time, for that's the stuff life is made of."
Ben Franklin

Nearly everything that we think, say, or do is governed by patterns of behavior that we develop over the years. We develop most of them early in life and rarely change them. The only way to lose a habit is to stop practicing it. ***Stop practicing negative habits and start practicing positive ones, and your life will improve automatically.***[4] If you want to achieve high-quality results in professional sales, establish healthy habits and patterns. The people who most efficiently control their time have the best idea of what they want to accomplish.[5]

Here's an idea to try:

Get to work by five o'clock in the morning three times a week, and you'll gain an extra day. You will realize a great feeling of satisfaction at eight o'clock when you have already finished what would have taken you at least six hours to do during normal working hours because of the interruptions.

In sales—more than in many other professions—the management of time is a matter of personal choice and responsibility. Mental preparation is necessary to win the race against time. Developing a time management attitude helps to overcome life's obstacles. Just as Olympic champions practice diligently and relentlessly to perfect their athletic techniques, you can practice time management techniques and maximize the benefits to be enjoyed from both professional and personal pursuits.[6]

You can let the whole subject of time management assume such proportions that the mere thought of attempting to master it becomes frustrating. It is estimated that the typical salesperson spends an average of only two hours a day in productive selling. However, just increasing the time spent with a customer doesn't do very much for you, it's what you do with the time that's important. That why one of the greatest weapons salespeople have at their disposal is **focus**. You probably can't get to every last thing on your to-do list every day, and if you tried to, you'd be working around the clock. So what you must do is *focus* your time so that it matches opportunity.

Keep a positive perspective toward time and your use of it. Here are some suggestions for establishing the kind of time attitudes that will bring you success:

1. Make a list of the activities you want to complete during the next week to achieve the results you desire.
2. For an entire week, keep an hour-by-hour record of exactly what you do with your time. Summarize your record and compare what you actually do to the list you made of what you want to do to achieve your goals. (Exhibit 15.1 illustrates the type of form you can use for this purpose.)
3. At the end of each day and at the end of each week, take a personal accounting of what you have accomplished compared to what you set out to do.
4. List the five habits or attitudes that were the biggest obstacles to the achievement of the results you wanted. Write out a plan for changing these habits or attitudes. Conduct another time analysis study three months from now and compare the two. Determine whether you are making progress in replacing these habits or attitudes with new ones.

Conducting a detailed personal time-analysis study at least twice a year is a good habit to establish. Just as you schedule a regular medical checkup (or at least you should), plan for a time management checkup to keep you aware of how well you are using your time resources.

EXHIBIT 15.1 DAILY TIME SURVEY

	Prospecting	Calling for Appts.	1-on-1s with Prospects	Travel	Paperwork	Meetings	Sales Training	Preparing for Presentations	Preapproach Work
6AM									
7AM									
8AM									
9AM									
10AM									
11AM									
12PM									
1PM									
2PM									
3PM									
4PM									
5PM									
6PM									
7PM									
8PM									

GETTING ORGANIZED

Many professionals have the skills to be successful, but they are often held back by their bad habits. If you are disorganized or inefficient, the first step towards organization is to determine what type of "time abuser" you are. There are three types:[7]

1. **Procrastinators**—Do you leave assignments until the eleventh hour and then throw yourself into a panic, working round-the-clock in a vain attempt to meet a deadline?
2. **People Pleasers**—Do you chronically take on more and more responsibility out of a fear of confronting authority and eventually commit too much time to unproductive projects?
3. **Perfectionists**—Do you take more time than is allotted to satisfy extremely unrealistic but deeply internalized standards of excellence?

Once you identify what type or types you may be, and before you can gain any measure of control over your time, you must lay the groundwork for effectively handling the onslaught of information you encounter every day. The following techniques can help you handle the information in the most efficient way possible.

I. Remove the Clutter

You can think more clearly and more creatively if you remove as much clutter as possible from your life and your living space. Remove unnecessary papers from your work area—your desk, your attaché case, and your car. Even if the stacks of paper are neat and appear to be well organized, they promote a subconscious psychological tendency to review and think through the items in sight. According to a national Harris Interactive survey by Cambridge Home & Office Accessories in Stamford, Connecticut, more than 84 percent of salespeople polled are pilers—they regularly stack up their paperwork instead of filing it.[8]

In a few seconds you can think through all of the tasks that are represented by a sizable stack of paper. For all practical purposes, however, your mind does not differentiate between doing a task physically and doing it mentally. If you mentally review a big stack of paper a dozen times a day in the process of deciding which one to tackle next, or which one to avoid, you are exhausted long before the day is over. Once you decide to dispense with clutter, tackle the job at once. Follow this plan to eliminate the disorder from your surroundings and your life:

1. **Collect the Clutter.** Gather up all the clutter that affects you and take it to one convenient work area. Empty your car, bedside table, pockets, and any other cubbyhole where you stick things that are waiting to be done. Dump all the clutter into one container.
2. **Sort the Clutter.** Divide the clutter into two categories: Time-critical material (that is, items with a specific due date) and "someday" material (that is, items that need to be addressed but have no specific due date). Removing clutter allows you to think more clearly and creatively.

3. **Deal With Priorities.** Deal first with the time-critical items. Provide a series of thirty-one folders to represent the days of the month. (This is commonly called a 1-31 file.) A computer master calendar is just as handy and can quickly retrieve each day's notes or retrieve items by subject. You may still need the 1-31 file to collect reports, memos, and other written items. Examine each of the items you have identified as time critical. If it involves a meeting or a specific hour of the day, write it on your calendar. Then put each item in the folder for the day that the first action must be taken to meet the due date. Each day check the appropriate folder as you make your daily to do list. Then each item will be accomplished on time.
4. **Set Up Categories for the Rest.** Now begin to organize the someday material. Set up two convenient files—the stacked in-out file boxes are helpful. Label these files reading and projects. Go through your someday items and sort them in the two files according to their nature. Pull out a reading item to take along when you are going somewhere that might involve a wait, and then use waiting time to catch up on reading. The material in the projects box may then be sorted into folders for each separate project.

II. Handle Interruptions

To handle interruptions properly, you must first determine whether an occurrence is truly an interruption or part of your job. Only when you understand this difference are you able to control your attitude toward the people and the circumstances that threaten to get in your way as you are doing your job. Once you determine that an interruption is part of your job, decide whether it is more important than what you are currently doing or whether it should be postponed. This will help you keep your priorities straight and reduces procrastination.[9]

Interruptions typically fall into three categories, each of which you can handle with the right attitude. Exhibit 15.2 lists the three types of interruptions and examples of the most common ways that people experience them.

EXHIBIT 15.2 TYPES OF INTERRUPTIONS

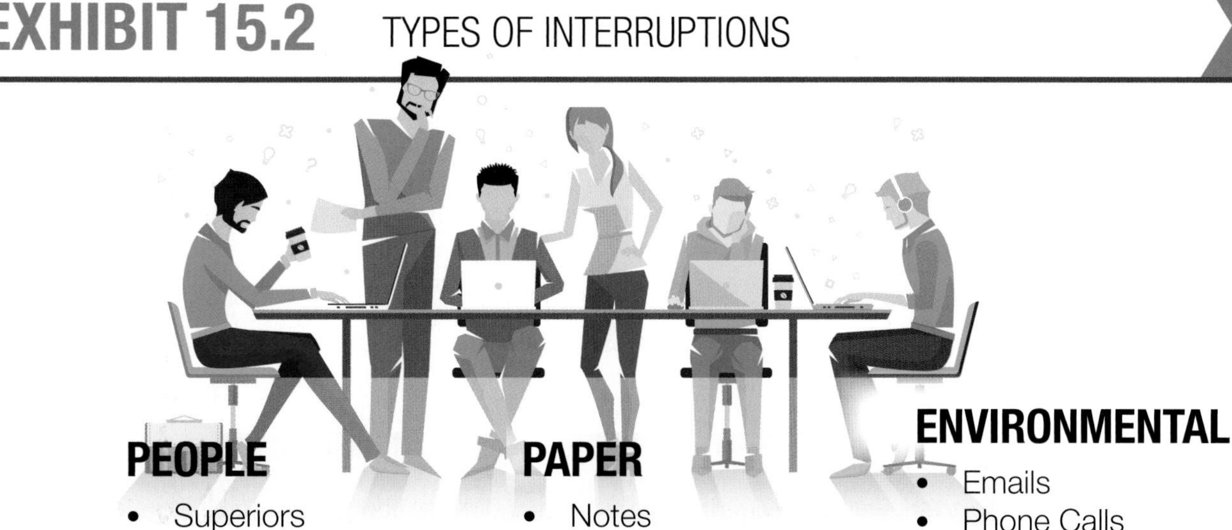

PEOPLE INTERRUPTIONS. People interruptions are the most frustrating because they are the most difficult to solve, and who the person is makes a difference in the way you respond. If your superior interrupts you, remember that that person probably has the right to interrupt you. If you are working on an item of extreme importance with a tight deadline or are due to leave for an appointment with a prospect, however, you can properly ask respectfully whether your superior might wait until your project or call is completed. It's okay to say "no" to your superiors.[10] Because your work is important to the success of the organization, and therefore to your superior as well, most bosses consider such a request to be a mark of both effectiveness and self-confidence on your part.

"The average American worker has fifty interruptions a day, of which seventy percent have nothing to do with work."

W. Edwards Deming

When a client interrupts you either by phone or in person, adopt the attitude that this contact is not an interruption. You do not automatically put your full day at the disposal of a client's whim, but you do give full attention while the client is talking and then do whatever is necessary to take care of the situation.

Your superiors, co-workers, and customers are not the only ones who can disrupt your day and pause or even stop the flow of work you are doing. Family members and friends have been known to wreak havoc on productivity. When choosing to answer calls, texts, or emails from people outside work, consider how much that interruption may set you back or delay your progress, and when possible, give yourself a certain window of time each day (perhaps during lunch) to connect with friends and family members.

PAPER INTERRUPTIONS. Sales forces are increasing their use of technology and moving more toward a paperless environment where much of the data gathering, correspondence, and presentations are handled on their tablets, smartphones, and laptops. However, no matter how "virtual" things become, physical paperwork will always be a work of your life as a salesperson. Just as you do with any other kind of interruptions, prioritize paper interruptions. If you need to fill out paperwork, do so as the first or last activity on your agenda so that it doesn't interfere with the flow of your workday. If someone needs you to review a hard copy of some report or other paperwork, ask right away when your edits need to be done. If it's not urgent, make a note to yourself to handle the edits AFTER you've completed the task at hand.

ENVIRONMENTAL INTERRUPTIONS. Distractions in your work space can wreak havoc on productivity if not properly addressed and controlled. Instead of feeling overwhelmed by environmental distractions such as frequent phone calls, schedule a specific telephone time each day to set up appointments for sales presentations and to take care of other sales related business.

Email and social networking (for personal reasons) are notorious time zappers. Some organizations have tried to impose 'no email' days to cut down on interruptions and have banned the use of social networking sites such as Facebook and Twitter for non-business related communications. The starting point is to ban any casual use of email. Next, take the time to audit incoming mail and don't be afraid to be selective. Try to set aside specific periods to deal with it. Turn the sound off on the computer, so you are not alerted every time a message arrives.[11] Then the remainder of the day is free for those vital selling contacts. When you have a particularly important piece of work to complete, take everything you need to do the job and go to a place where you can work without any kind of interruption.

THE SOCIAL MEDIA CONNECTION

How to Use Your Time Wisely on Social Media

A study found that the average social network user spends 3.6 hours on social media every day! Considering you may only be awake for 16 hours each day, this means nearly 25 percent of our waking time is spent on Facebook, Twitter, and the rest. It's not reasonable for most people to cut social media out of their workday—especially considering what an important role it can play in finding leads, planning preapproach, and staying connected. What that means, then, is you must give yourself strict time limits on how much time to devote to social media during working hours. So, what if you only had thirty minutes? Here are some ideas for making the most out of a half-hour on social media:[12]

5 Minutes to Check your Mentions. For your first five minutes, dive into Mention to see all the times your name or your brand's name has appeared on social media, in blogposts, and across the Internet. ***Mention*** is an app that provides real time media monitoring for you and your product or company. Mention will track everything, and you can respond and reply right from your Mention dashboard.

5 Minutes to Check your Notifications. For the next five minutes, hop into the notifications section inside Facebook, Twitter, Google+, LinkedIn, and your other social media channels. For everything that slipped through the cracks with Mention (direct messages or being added to Twitter lists, for instance), here's your chance to follow up.

15 Minutes To Respond To Questions and Seek Out Influencers. Next, the 15 minutes to respond and react can include a bit of carryover from the first two items. If you happen to have a sea of notifications or mentions, definitely spend the time addressing each one. Then, hop onto your account and start engaging:

- Respond to the comments on your posts
- Respond to any direct mentions and @-mentions
- Answer any questions that involve your product
- Answer questions about your niche and industry (tip: use a saved hashtag search to track these)
- Engage with your VIPs, be it customers or influencers (tip: create a Twitter list for these)

5 Minutes to Roam. The last five minutes can be spent being free. If you've worked efficiently during the previous 25 minutes, it's nice to pop in and out every so often and experience social media in real-time, responding and engaging with whatever catches your eye at the moment. Just keep your eye on the clock!

AN ESTABLISHED ORGANIZING SYSTEM

The challenge for salespeople is to discover the methods that work for them, and typically this will be different for everyone. What's important is that you take the guesswork out of the sales process and replace it with a defined business process. Recognize that success is a percentage game; sales is a profession in which there can never be 100 percent success. Just because you have a clean desk and an organized filing system won't guarantee you will make more sales; but it certainly won't hurt. If you find a certain system that works for you, just keep doing it—in other words, repeat successful behaviors.[13] This is a secret of success at any level of competition.

Selling is not a game that requires perfection. You only need to figure out ways to stay ahead of the competition. Identify the behaviors that will consistently improve your performance and you will be well on your way to creating a powerful sales discipline. In order to be on your way to staying ahead of the competition, you must first remove the unnecessary disorder from your environment. Once you remove the clutter and the incompletions from your work area and get a firm grip on controlling interruptions, two simple tools will help you organize your activities:

1. The Master Calendar

Your master calendar should list only specific time commitments such as appointments with clients and meetings to attend. When using a computerized calendar, you can link your master calendar with your cell phone or smartphone so that you can access the information no matter where you are. There are numerous calendar software applications that can be downloaded onto your cell phone, smartphone, tablet PC, or laptop. All of your information can be stored in these calendars and can be accessed easily for your review. Most of these programs also have a notes feature where you can enter additional information about the appointment.

2. Daily To-Do List

The second time-organizational tool you will need is a daily to-do list. Be sure to prioritize each item on your list. Highlight those activities completed, and carry forward the uncompleted items.[14] These lists can either be generated on paper or electronically.

A story about Charles Schwab, former president of Bethlehem Steel, shows the impact of this simple tool. Schwab called in consultant Ivy Lee and proposed a challenge, "Show me a way to get more done with my time, and I'll pay you any fee within reason."

"Fine," said Lee, "I'll give you something in twenty minutes that will increase your output at least fifty percent."

Lee then handed Schwab a blank sheet of paper and said, "Write down the six most important tasks that you have to do tomorrow and number them in order of their importance. Now put this paper in your pocket, and the first thing tomorrow morning look at item one. Work on it until you finish it. Then do item two, and so on. Do this until quitting time. Don't be concerned if you have finished only one or two. You'll be working on the most important items. If you can't finish them all by this method, you couldn't have finished them by any other method either; and without some system, you'd probably not even decide which was the most important."

Lee continued, "Use this system every working day. After you've convinced yourself of the value of the system, have your men try it. Try it as long as you wish and then send me a check for what you think it's worth." Several weeks later, Lee received Schwab's check for $10,000—an impressive sum of money some 80 years ago.

As much as we may want to, no one can alter time. The trick to managing your time is to manage not your time, but your activities. Keep a daily to-do list of what needs to be accomplished and use the list to make sure you are moving the sale forward.[15] The value of a to-do list is apparent, but it becomes even more valuable when you use it not only to identify needed tasks but to establish priorities for them. Putting top priorities first is the only way to be sure that your activities are making a direct impact on your goals. Sales success depends on establishing and steadfastly pursuing a series of goals. When you develop specific and measurable growth goals, you gain the determination and drive it takes to succeed.[16]

Charles A. Coonradt, president of *Western Leadership Group*, says, "In the absence of clearly defined goals, we are forced to concentrate on activity and ultimately become enslaved by it." Using a to-do list helps you develop the automatic habit of attaching a *when* to every thought, idea, commitment, or promise. When it comes to using a do-list and prioritizing your day, remember that the method itself is not nearly as important as the practice!

The Integrated System

Your notes, master calendar, and to-do list can be merged into one file that is capable of being synchronized with all of your technological devices so that you can access the information whenever you need reminders. You can safely forget about incomplete tasks until they surface in your system. Together these organizing tools form a system that makes organization of your daily activities an automatic process. At the close of each day's work, transfer any leftover items from today's to-do list to the new list for tomorrow. Then consult your notes and your master calendar to find all the items you have scheduled for tomorrow. Check any specific times associated with those items, such as the time for an appointment or meeting. Now you are ready to begin work tomorrow without even thinking about what to do first. You are ready to begin your day with the task of highest importance.[17]

POSITIVE ATTITUDES TOWARD TIME

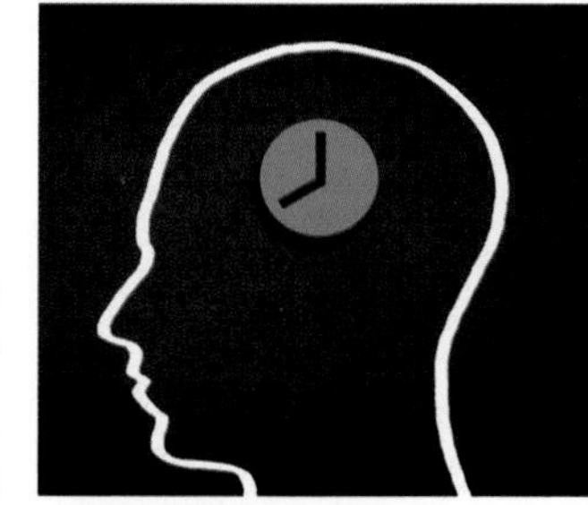

An important concept for good time managers to understand is the *Pareto Principle*. It states that 80 percent of the value (or the frustration) of any group of related items is generally concentrated in only twenty percent of them. In other words, "a minority of the input produces a majority of the results." The principle, named for the Italian economist who proposed it, holds true for many areas of today's experience. For example:

In Measuring Value, You Receive...	
80% of:	**From 20% of:**
Sales	Customers
Productivity	Activity
Profit	Products
Referrals	Clients
Commission/Income	Orders

In Measuring Frustration, You Experience...	
80% of:	**From 20% of:**
Absenteeism	Employees
Errors	Workers
Complaints	Customers

Likewise, 80 percent of your success comes through the achievement of the top 20 percent of your goals. In managing your time effectively, you must recognize that which items you complete, not how many items you complete, determine your success. To identify the special 20 percent of your activities that have the potential for producing the greatest success, practice establishing different categories of priorities.

"A" priority items are the most pressing. They include the items that must be done by a specific date if you are to reach one of your major goals and items that would damage the reputation of your company or your personal credibility if you failed to accomplish them.

"B" priority items are any items that can be done at any time within the next week or month without causing any repercussions.

"C" priority items would be nice to do at some time when you have nothing else pressing to do, but you would suffer no real loss if you never got around to them.

Obviously, you want to give first attention to your "A" priorities and carefully number them in the order of their importance. Your goal is to complete as many "A" priorities as you possibly can each day and then supplement them with any "B" items you can.[18]

Time Goals

Once you have established the habit of using a to-do list, begin to record next to each item your estimate of the amount of time you will need to complete it. Estimating the required time lets you judge whether you can complete everything. If you can't, you have the possibility of getting someone else to help before you fail to complete some vital item. Time studies have shown that even people who know which items are most important and set priorities still waste an average of fifteen minutes between items of work in simple procrastination or in trying to decide what to do next.

A second benefit of estimating completion times is to help in avoiding procrastination. A deadline—even an informal estimate of the time required—pushes you to complete the work in the allotted time. Northcote Parkinson, a British naval historian and author of *Parkinson's Law,* is noted for his observation that *work expands to fill the time allowed for its completion.* Something about a stated time allotment seems to establish a mental set that causes you to use just that amount of time. If the time is short, you work efficiently and push for completion. If the time allowance is too generous, you procrastinate, spend extra time getting ready to work, and find a dozen small interruptions to make sure you don't finish too early. By estimating times for completion, you eliminate the tendency to procrastinate.

Anyone who expects sales success should also expect hard work and long hours. If you always seem to have more work than working hours, though, you may be due for a refresher course in time management. The following eight techniques can't give you more time, but they can help you make the most of what you've got. Follow them to help you get—and keep—time on your side.

1 **PLACE A TIME LIMIT ON MEETINGS.** If you or your salespeople tend to dread meetings, maybe it's because they drag on too much and accomplish too little. Knowing your meeting lasts only an hour should help keep things moving. Before each meeting, decide on a limited number of topics to discuss and a limited time period for discussing them. Exhibit 15.3 looks at six powerful tips for getting the most out of your next sales meeting.[19]

EXHIBIT 15.3 HOW TO RUN A DYNAMIC SALES MEETING

Sales teams have a lot of meetings—and for many of us, we've come to view meetings as interruptions. It doesn't have to be that way. Below are six keys to make your next meeting a place where decisions get made and you leave feeling energized and motivated:

1. **Give People a Reason to Be on Time.** Begin meetings on time and start with some fun. Reward those who are punctual to help eliminate the lateness factor. Start the meeting off with a short trivia game for which the winner gets a gift card. That will give people a reason to get there on time!
2. **Add Value.** Add value by providing the team with quick sales tips, and help the team better execute on a key sales skill that will help them close business.
3. **Have Rules for Individual Updates.** To ensure individual updates don't take up too much of the sales meeting, follow these three rules: 1) Set time limits, 2) Highlight key learning points from their successes or setbacks, and 3) Know when to take individual issues offline.
4. **Motivate and Reward.** Build motivation into every team meeting. This isn't about big gifts or exceptional moments -- the simplest "thank you" can have great meaning.
5. **Do a Capability Activity.** Every sales meeting must stretch and challenge team members' skills to keep them at the top of their game. Capability activities can focus on prospecting, networking, lead generation, client meetings, presenting solutions or closing. The capability activity is all about ongoing skill development and is the key to creating value at the meeting.
6. **Follow a Standard Agenda.** Follow a format for each meeting around these principles so that you'll have a standard, consistent and easy-to-follow agenda that will keep you focused and on track. This will help reduce meeting preparation time dramatically.

2 SET DEADLINES AND BEAT THEM. When you've got a lot to do and not a lot of time to do it in, deadlines can help you to stay on schedule. Prioritize your tasks, and then draw up a schedule for completing them. Don't make the mistake of waiting to start on a task just because the deadline seems far away. Chances are, something will come up to fill the extra time you think you have.

3 TAKE ADVANTAGE OF YOUR PEAK TIME. To be most efficient at the jobs you like least, tackle them at the time of day when you feel most productive. Pay attention to your moods and work output throughout the day to find out when you're most productive, and save your worst jobs for when you're at your best.

4 DON'T OVERLOAD ON OVERTIME. If your workweek consistently exceeds a reasonable number of hours, ask yourself why. Identify the tasks that take up the most time and look for ways to complete them more efficiently. Also, compare the number of hours you're working to what you're actually getting done. A too-small return on your time investment indicates a problem.

5 **DO SOME DELEGATING.** Don't feel guilty about delegating responsibility—if you take on a job that someone else could handle more effectively, you're not making the best use of your company's resources.

6 **IT'S OKAY TO SAY NO.** When it comes to time management, many of us are our own worst enemy. You'll never have enough time to finish your work if you're always biting off more than you can chew. When people ask you to take on extra projects, they are putting a monkey on your back. If you agree to take on too many jobs for others, you are soon carrying an impossible load of monkeys and accomplish nothing.

7 **PUT IT IN WRITING.** To remember phone numbers, important dates or anything else, write them down. Freeing your mind of clutter helps you think more clearly, and concentration is key to productivity.

8 **CULTIVATE HELPFUL RELATIONSHIPS.** Create and keep lasting relationships that result in people gladly working to assist you, and this can be one of your most powerful time-management strategies.

Managing Travel Time

One of the most important considerations for field salespeople is protecting their time for making those vital sales presentations. Travel through a territory is, in a sense, nonproductive although necessary time. The key to making the most out of your travel time is to weigh the amount of time spent on the road with your other daily activities to ensure that you are spending enough time doing the things that really matter. The way to begin to do that is to keep track of your time. Keep a log that creates a snapshot of how you spend your time. It's vital to include on this log the amount of time you spend traveling, and then try to keep that time to a minimum.

As you learned earlier, the *Pareto Principle* says that 80 percent of your business will come from twenty percent of your customers. Thus, you must determine how much time and energy each account receives. It may be helpful to divide all accounts into A, B, C and D accounts and spend a fixed amount of time with each level of account.[20] Here is a graphical representation of this prioritizing system:

	Description	Amount of Time to Spend
A	High-volume, repeat customers	40%
B	Moderate sales volume, but reliable customers	30%
C	Lower volume accounts	20%
D	Accounts that cost you more time and energy to service than you receive in profits.	10%

Outside salespeople travel through time and space, so it will help if they set themselves in motion on the most efficient route between customers and prospects. Sales professionals pay close attention to the routing and scheduling of their calls. They take into consideration the proper mix of accounts on each trip. Prioritizing is useful for determining a profitable mix of account visitation and servicing. A common mistake is to call on "D" accounts simply because they are located near "A" accounts, and require little travel. These customers do not need to be called on with the same regularity as the "A" accounts. Instead use your time to prospect for new high volume, repeat customers.[21]

> **Ordinary people think merely of spending time.**
> **Great people think of using it.**

Ultimately, it's all about balance. If you are going to be an effective time manager, you need to balance the driving forces with the limiting forces in your life. Live within the zone between these two pressures so that you can be your most effective all the time.[22] You need self-discipline from the time you wake up in the morning until you go to bed that night. Spending your time more wisely starts with paying attention to how you spend it. Once you decide to take control of your time, you'll have the power to stop squandering it. Time is like talent—you can't create more of it, you just have to make the most of what you've got.

SUMMARY

- The ability to manage time efficiently and effectively is fundamentally a matter of attitude. Time is money. If you seek advancement and a comfortable income, managing time properly is one of the best skills you can develop.
- Interruptions are ultimately just time wasters, so handle them with planning and control. Interruptions come from everywhere—including people, paper, and environmental factors.
- A workable system for time management includes at least three elements:
- A master calendar for scheduling commitments.
- A daily to-do list to record activities to be done each day to reach your goals.
- A reminder file to hold items that will become important at a specific later date.
- Follow a list of time goals that will help you master your most precious commodity.
- Delegate tasks that someone else could do so that you can get back to the highest priority activities such as prospecting, reaching out to centers of influence, and making sales calls.

REVIEW QUESTIONS

1. Write a hundred-word statement giving your opinion about the importance of effective time management and its possible impact on your future in professional selling.
2. What three activities must your mind perform that affect how you use time? How does a system for time management make each of these tasks easier?
3. Describe an effective method for handling incomplete tasks.
4. How does a cluttered desk or briefcase affect time use? What kind of impression do you think a cluttered office or briefcase gives your prospects?
5. How does the appearance of a salesperson's car and briefcase affect professional credibility?

6. Describe the necessary elements of an effective organizing system.
7. What three main sources of interruptions cause time problems? Give some strategies for handling each type.
8. What can be done to limit the time needed for telephone calls?
9. How can the time needed for travel in the sales territory be kept to a minimum?

IN-CLASS EXERCISES

The following exercises help build teams, improve communication, and emphasize the real-world side of selling. They are meant to be challenging, to help you learn how to deal with problems that have no single right answer, and to use a variety of skills beyond those employed in a typical review question. Read and complete each activity. Then in the next class, discuss and compare answers.

EXERCISE 15.1 – DOING A, B, C

You will work individually on this exercise in class. Whether you are a full-time or part-time student, whether you are working or have family responsibilities (or both!), you are busy. Chapter 15 offers several suggestions for managing your activities more efficiently. During the next 20 minutes, you will construct and think about one of them: the To-Do List.

On a blank sheet of paper draw a grid with three columns: "A – Imperative," "B – High Priority," "C – Priority." Add three rows, one row for each of the next 3 days.

- "Imperative" means that an activity must be completed by a certain date/time within the 3-day period and that if it is not, dire consequences ensue.
- "High Priority" means that an activity must be completed anytime during the next week.
- "Priority" means that an activity can be completed at your discretion as you have time.

Next, enter activities in each cell of the grid and note an estimate of how long it will take to complete each activity. (You can allow time for daily activities such as eating and sleeping, but don't enter them into the grid.) During the next 3 days, keep an accurate record of which activities in each column were completed. Examine which activities were not completed and the reasons why. What challenges regarding management of your activities did your analysis of this brief to-do list reveal?

CASE STUDIES

The following case studies present you with selling scenarios that require you to apply the critical skills discussed in the chapter and give you training through practical learning situations. They are meant to be both engaging and challenging, and like the exercises, don't have one right answer.

CASE 15.1 – THE PESKY CLIENT

While she was busy working on her computer at 3:30 p.m., trying to complete two spreadsheets that she had to forward to her sales manager in a couple of hours, Janice's phone rang. With a groan, she reached for it, "Yes, Alice? What is it?"

"I'm sorry, Janice," replied Alice, "but it's Mr. Caruthers again. He called earlier around noon, but you were out."

"Do you know what he wants?" asked Janice.

"Something about those bearings that he talked about with you last week. I tried to refer him to Ed, but he said that he would only deal with you."

"Ok, Alice. I'll take care of it." Janice was perturbed. She had to submit her bi-weekly sales report and expense report by 5:30; otherwise, she wouldn't get paid and the numbers wouldn't make it into the company's monthly totals. Caruthers was one of her largest accounts, but he could be a blowhard and take up too much time.

Janice looked at her reflection in the small mirror that she kept next to the phone, put on a big smile, and pushed the lighted button. "Hello, Mr. Caruthers. It's nice to hear from you again. I'm sorry that I was out when you phoned earlier. What can I do for you?"

"Hi, Miss Stokes. I'm calling about those bearings that you promised me last week. I told you that if I don't get them by next Tuesday I'll have to shut down the line. Here it is, Friday, and I haven't heard anything from you." Caruthers was upset and worried.

"I'm sorry, Mr. Caruthers. I do know how important delivery of the bearings is to your operation. Let me check with our people, and I'll get right back to you," Janice replied in her most reassuring tone.

"All right. But I can't wait much longer." With that, the line went dead.

What should I do? Janice thought. If I discover that there's a problem with meeting Caruthers's deadline, there's really nothing I can do about it today. But if I call him back with that news, he'll never get off the phone. I might as well trash my reports. On the other hand, if there is no problem, I'm certain that Caruthers will be so relieved that he'll talk forever. He knows he's a good customer, and he expects me to give him a lot of attention. Either way, I'll miss my deadline.

What would you advise Janice to do? Should she take care of her reports before dealing with her best customer's problem? Or should she handle the Caruthers matter and explain the circumstances to her manager, hoping that he'll understand? What would you do, and why?

CASE 15.2 – "I'M LATE, I'M LATE . . . FOR A VERY IMPORTANT DATE"

The White Rabbit's song in *Alice in Wonderland* had become the mantra for Roberta's current existence. No matter how hard she tried, she just couldn't get her act together.

It seems she was always late getting to the office, late for appointments with clients, and late meeting her boyfriend for dinner. And this morning was no exception: at 9:20 a.m., she was just pulling into the parking lot. Greg, her manager, was sure to be on her case.

And he was. "Nice of you to work us into your busy schedule, Roberta," Greg growled.

"I know. I know. No matter how early I leave, I always get stuck in traffic." Even as she said it, Roberta realized how lame that sounded.

"Well, I can't let it slide. My boss has been reviewing time sheets, and you know what that means." Greg softened his demeanor a bit. "Come on in, and let's chat about it."

After they both settled in with their lattes, Greg asked, "So tell me, why do you think you have such a problem being on time?"

"I don't sleep well, Greg. I go to bed at a reasonable hour, but then I wake up around 1:00 or 2:00 in the morning, worrying about what I didn't get done and what needs to be done for the next day. I sometimes watch the clock tick over to 4:30 before falling back to sleep."

"Not good. Not good at all. You must be exhausted," Greg responded with some sympathy.

"And I know that telling an insomniac to get more sleep doesn't help."

"I know," said Roberta. "I've tried prescription and over-the-counter sleep aids, but nothing gets me through the night. I really don't know what to do. When the alarm goes off, I can barely drag myself out of bed, let alone to work."

"Maybe your problem is stress. And it sounds to me like your stress might be occurring from lack of organization," remarked Greg. "What do you think? Shall we try to work on that a little?"

"Ok. I've tried everything else," Roberta admitted plaintively.

In light of the discussion of activity management in Chapter 15, what do you think Greg suggested to Roberta in order to relieve her stress? What suggestions would you make to someone in similar circumstances? How do you manage stress so that you can get sufficient rest in order to function at a high level? If lack of organization is a problem, what can you change to better manage your affairs?

Chapter 15 Footnotes

1. Michael Jackel, Sabine Wollscheid, "Time is Money and Money Needs Time? A Secondary Analysis of Time-Budget Data in Germany," *Journal of Leisure Research* Vol. 39 Issue 1(2007), 77.
2. David Morrison, "Setting Boundaries on Commitments," *Public Management*, Vol. 92, Issue 3 (April, 2010), 20.
3. Laura Vanderkam, *168 Hours: You Have More Time Than You Think,* (New York, NY: Penguin Group, May 2010).
4. Laura Vanderkam, *168 Hours: You Have MoreTime Than You Think.*
5. "Time Management Tips for Busy College Students," *Daily Herald (Arlington Heights, IL)*

July 18, 2010: 4, *Questia*, Web, April 29, 2011.

6. John Adair, Melanie Allen, *Time Management and Personal Development* (London, England: Thorgood, 2003), 26.
7. Steven Berglas," Chronic Time Abuse," *Harvard Business Review*, Boston: (June 2004), Vol. 82, Is. 6, 90.
8. Anonymous, "Will the Piles Ever Go Away?" *USA Today*, New York: (March 2004) Vol. 132, Is. 2706, 8
9. Tom Cox, "7 Rules of Extreme Time Management," *Oregon Business Journal* (April 20, 2011).
10. Anonymous, "Get on Top of Your Time Management," *Pulse*, Tonbridge: (April 5, 2004), 38.
11. Sue Shellenbarger, "Managing Workplace Distractions," *The Wall Street Journal* (February 23, 2011).
12. Lee, Kevan. "What's the Best Way to Spend 30 Minutes of Your Time on Social Media Marketing?" buffersocial.com, October 30, 2014. Web.
13. Rick Davis, "All systems go: a systemized approach to selling can lead to organizational success". *Prosales*. Jan 2006. Accessed May 16, 2015.
14. Jane Collingwood, "Organization Strategies for ADHD," *Psych Central* (April 29, 2011) Accessed April 29, 2015.
15. Jane Collingwood, "Organization Strategies for ADHD.
16. William F. Kumuyi, "Setting and Scoring Your Goals: Goals are Stated Ambitions; and All Leaders Know They Must Set Them and Follow Them Up till They Are Accomplished. For, Failure to Set Goals Reduces Leadership to Management by Chance and Hunches-A Sure Recipe for Corporate Disaster," *New African* July 2008, *Questia*, Web, April 29, 2011.
17. Collingwood, "Organization Strategies." Accessed September 7, 2015.
18. Peter Taylor, "The Art of Productive Laziness," *Industrial Management*, Vol. 51, Issue 4 (July/August 2009), 18+.
19. Higgins, Kevin. "Six Secrets to a Successful Sales Meeting." *Entrepreneur*, January 9, 2014. Web.
20. Steve Atlas, "When the Customer Isn't Right," *Selling Power* (January/February 2001), 32.
21. For a more thorough discussion on "How to Run Your Territory Like a Business," See the booklet Territory Management, Bureau of Business Practice, Inc. (1989), 6-16.
22. Anonymous, "The Secrets of Time Management," *Agency Sales*, Irvine: (May 2004), Vol. 34, Is. 5, 40-41.

CHAPTER 16
MODERN SALES MANAGEMENT

OVERVIEW

Chapter 16 details the traits of today's top sales managers. This chapter is an excellent and thorough introduction to classes in sales management. It is based on real world, applicable material that future sales leaders can use in their role as a manager one day, as well as use to learn what the best sales managers are looking for in top recruits.

OBJECTIVES

- Examine the function of sales management in a company.
- Understand what is required of a sales manager.
- Discuss the recruitment and selection process of salespeople.
- Learn the differences in qualifications between sales managers and salespeople.
- Determine the specific responsibilities of the sales manager.
- Examine the distinctions of various compensation plans.
- Study orientation, training, and motivation practices used by managers.

MANAGING IN TODAY'S BUSINESS CLIMATE

Marketing and sales companies historically used the 4P's—*Product*, *Price*, *Place*, and *Promotion* to formulate strategy. Now a fifth P is needed: *People*. A sales manager's job is no longer to rule over the sales force using the traditional authoritative or micromanagement style. Individuals entering the sales world today have a different set of values. They have more education and sophistication, desiring managers who listen, encourage, teach, coach, and give them a voice in how they are managed. If the sales environment does not meet these requirements, they will search for one that does.

According to Dr. Ken Blanchard, co-author of the *One-Minute Manager*, young sales professionals are foregoing other aspects of the job, including financial considerations, to work in a caring, supportive environment. In a study by the *Families and Work Institute*, 3400 randomly selected men and women ranked their three most important job considerations, which were:[1]

1. **Open Communication.** Information is power; do not withhold information as a way to abuse your management position. Tell your sales force everything you know that is pertinent to their job. Involve them in the decisions that affect them.
2. **Effect on Personal and Family Life.** The explosion of two-wage-earner families and the growing number of families with single parents makes it more stressful to juggle all the demands of work and home life. Problems that did not impact the work place a generation ago, such as sick children or scheduling a day-care provider, means managers must find new ways to allow for greater flexibility and autonomy in individual jobs.

3. **Nature of the Work.** Workers want to feel their job is important to the success of the company. A wise sales manager takes every opportunity to let the sales force know how critical their efforts are in meeting company goals. Saying "thank you" frequently is easy, and best of all, it's free.

The sales manager's challenge is to walk the fine line between pleasing top management and keeping the sales force motivated. Sales managers must be coaches, facilitators, and cheerleaders for their people. Their main concerns must be how to shape a more supportive work environment and to find ways to help each salesperson be more productive.

Managers as the Vital Link

The sales manager is the link between individual salespeople and their customers and the organization's upper management. In a smaller firm, the sales management function may be assigned to the marketing manager. A larger, more diversified company may have several sales managers classified by geographic area, customer type, or product line, and each may report to a district or regional manager who, in turn, reports to the chief sales executive of the company. Increasingly, sales managers in companies of any size interact with marketing personnel to develop and carry out marketing campaigns using email and social media, both with existing customers and with prospects.

Both sales ability and management ability are required regardless of how broad or how limited the sales manager's job may be. The management ability required of a field salesperson is primarily applied in the area of personal time and activity management. The sales manager needs excellent management ability in addition to the basic sales abilities that everyone in sales needs. The amount of time spent in actual *sales activity* versus *administrative activity* changes at each level of management. The manager who directly supervises field salespeople spends more time in selling activities than in administrative duties, but a chief sales executive who is separated from field salespeople by several levels of sales management may be almost completely involved in administrative activity. In any case, today's sales managers and executives need a firm grasp of the available technologies to maximize their effectiveness on the job.

Sales force management plays a vital part in the overall success of any company. If salespeople do not sell the company's products or services, no amount of effort in sales or marketing planning will produce success. Although the failure of an individual salesperson to sell may occasionally be attributed to lack of ability or unwillingness to work, the failure of an overall sales force is more likely to result from a basic sales management problem: *The salespeople were improperly recruited, selected, trained, compensated, or motivated.* The costs associated with managing a sales force are often the largest single operating expense item for a company.

An Expensive Lesson

Most companies would agree that a good salesperson—someone who represents his company well, sells above expectations, and treats his position like a career and not just a stopping point between jobs—is invaluable. But most sales managers also know that those types of salespeople are often hard to find. So, the real question then becomes, how much does it cost to hire the *wrong* salesperson?

> Let's say you hire a new salesperson named Steven. After one month, it doesn't look good. After 90 days, it's worse. Finally, at the six-month mark, you decide to let him go. It's easy to believe that all you lost was six months of salary and benefits. Nothing could be further from the truth. In addition to salary and benefits you lost six full months of sales opportunities, management time, administrative costs and training costs. (See Exhibit 16.1 for a detailed list of those costs.) And these are just the obvious costs. Some of the hidden costs you may not have considered are vacancy costs, replacement costs, customer costs and employee morale costs. The final cost is loss of competitive edge. (Think of all the deals you got outsold in!)[2]

The cost of hiring the wrong salesperson can really add up, but when it comes to team leaders, the costs can escalate even more rapidly. In addition, the time invested in training a new salesperson ranges from eight weeks to two years. You start to get a clear picture of just how truly critical are the recruitment, selection, and training processes. And when you add in the *turnover factor*, you begin to fully understand that companies must have a process in place that provides them with salespeople who are committed and loyal for the long run.

EXHIBIT 16.1 THE REAL COST OF HIRING THE WRONG SALESPERSON

Hard Costs

- Salary and Benefits for six months = $27,000 (based on an annual base salary of $40,000)
- Recruiting costs = $5,000
- Training classes and materials = $3,000

Soft Costs

- Lost Opportunity Cost: If Steven had been successful, how much revenue would he have generated? Based on Steven's annual quota of $500,000, add 50% of annual quota to the total for lost opportunity = $250,000
- Lost Time Cost: His sales manager would have been more productive using his time working with someone who was generating revenue. Estimated cost is 15% of the manager's annual compensation of around $110,00 = $17,000

Immeasurable Costs

- Employee Morale Cost: Good team members resent having a non-performer on the staff.
- Customer Cost: Customers had to deal with a sub-par person, which can sour the relationship, and there is no way to calculate how much that cost the company.

TOTAL COST OF ONE HIRING MISTAKE: $302,000 (without counting the cost of low employee morale or lost customers)

HIRING THE RIGHT TALENT

If you want to be the best, you have to hire the best—and that isn't easy. Because of the intense level of competition in the world of sales (and due in part to the fact that sales positions are so plentiful), it can be hard to attract top talent to your team. Regardless of how hard the task may be, it must be done, because hiring right the first time around saves loads of time and money on training, while protecting yourself from failure six months down the road. It costs more up front to input a process correctly, but it definitely pays off over time.

The Power of a Proven Process

When you have a team full of the right people, all the time and energy you used to spend worrying about your salespeople can be spent on more useful activities, like growing a team of superstars and posting impressive numbers. When you can trust your team to work anywhere, any time, it's a liberating feeling. It's also exhilarating to discover this truth:

> **If you hire the right people,
> you shouldn't have to wonder if they're working.**

Having a consistent, powerful interviewing process is what represents the difference between being an average team and a top sales team. The wrong candidate may say the right things in the interview or look good on paper, but soon after he or she starts, it becomes obvious that this person is not a good fit for the position. Once you *onboard* (hire, initiate, and train) the wrong hire, it can potentially be a long, arduous, and expensive journey before the person leaves, so it pays to stay faithful to a consistent hiring process.

Why do some organizations have such high turnover? Is it because all sales positions intrinsically have excessive resignation rates? That seems to be the case on the surface, but that's not the whole story. The real reasons why high turnover plagues the sales profession are far more likely to be the following:[3]

- Too many sales managers simply hire the wrong people for the job.
- Many leaders are pressured to hire quickly. This can cause costly and irreparable errors. It's worth waiting for the right candidate, not just any candidate.
- A large percentage of leaders are inexperienced with the hiring and interviewing process, and they are never given any formal training on how to run the recruiting side of their business.
- Compensation confusion is a common culprit that causes turnover. If candidates are improperly informed about pay or find out the pay potential was verbally inflated when they interviewed, they will move elsewhere.
- High turnover is also due to broken or inadequate internal processes that exist in areas such as customer service, tech support, billing, and other departments.
- Even top performers will look elsewhere when there is a lack of connection between a leader and a salesperson, such as in the case of a personality clash.

Learning how to hire correctly is a *process*, not an easily implemented change. But with time and a solid, regimented plan in place, you'll never hire another person who "will do." You'll expect excellence and raise the bar on your own hiring standards.

Motivation Versus Experience

Because of historically high turnover and the fact that many of the best salespeople have come from other professions, it's increasingly difficult for managers to hire people based solely on their level of experience. Instead, the net must be widened to include other key factors. ***Some sales managers even say that in many cases, internal drive overrides experience.***

You can always *teach* the necessary skill set, but internal drive and motivation can't be taught. People either have it or they don't. You must look for this in every candidate you interview. It doesn't matter how desperate a manager is to hit their numbers; in most cases, hiring "just anyone" will backfire. It could take months or years to move an incorrect hire out of the organization. If you're having challenges attracting high quality candidates, your issue may be compensation, the company, the product, the leader, a personality clash, or just bad timing. However, if you do have a competitive compensation structure and work for a good company, there is no acceptable excuse for closing your eyes and hiring the first person who walks through the door in order to meet your minimums.

Winning leaders hire long-term team members, not temporary solutions.

Each sales manager learns through experience the best sources for finding recruits for specific types of sales jobs. Exhibit 16.2 provides you with a list of the most commonly used and recognized sources of recruiting for sales positions, from entry level positions to top executive positions.[4]

EXHIBIT 16.2 COMMON SOURCES FOR RECRUITING

1. **Within The Organization.** Occasionally an employee in the production or service portion of the business qualifies for a sales job. Students often take part-time jobs on the maintenance crew or in the office and are eager to enter sales when their education is complete.
2. **Network/Word Of Mouth.** Reach out to anyone and everyone who may be or know a qualified candidate. Consistently strive to put out feelers to existing contact lists, friends, family, neighbors, clients, centers of influence, and anyone else you know or do business with.
3. **Job Websites.** Post ads on pages like craigslist.com, gethired.com, careerbuilder.com, ziprecruiter.com and other online job-hunting sites. Take advantage of all that the web has to offer, but online postings should not be your only means of recruiting.
4. **Social Media.** All forms of social media are an option. Post messages on your Facebook business fan page about career opportunities, LinkedIn, and take advantage of your Twitter following to spread the word about your organization and the possibilities it offers.
5. **Outsourcing.** Headhunters or employment services are an option, but such outsourcing will require a sometimes-significant financial investment. However, it may be worthwhile since excellent team members can be worth their weight in gold.
6. **Targeted Lists.** There are countless ways to procure names and contact information. With the right purchased list, you can start a targeted direct mail campaign to a database of targeted prospective employees.
7. **Your Own Files.** Never throw away a resume; categorize them and keep them. You just never know when you may uncover a hidden gem that could have been easily discarded. Keep every resume that comes across your desk.

Do Top Salespeople Make Top Leaders?

It can be tempting for many sales leaders to promote top performers to become sales managers rather than go for an outside hire. It can be argued that top salespeople always make top leaders. It's a sound idea in theory—they excelled as salespeople, so now they can teach others the secrets to their success. Strangely enough, however, while some end up doing incredible jobs, many end up struggling intensely in their new role as leader and coach.

Why? It's because managing is not the same as selling—not even close. Many of the top performers are shocked and grossly overwhelmed when they move into a management role. They must learn to gain a new level of respect from their peers. This is not always an easy task, and often times the newly promoted salesperson is met with several challenges. They jump in headfirst only to be met with much resistance and aloofness from their newly inherited team. Here are a few key things to bear in mind when considering promoting a salesperson to a leadership position:[5]

- They will now need to depend on others to make their compensation unless they are an ***active*** selling manager.

- They must resolve the issues of an entire team, not just their own.
- They will be required to perform managerial tasks such as doing reports, creating effective meeting agendas, participating in leader calls, inviting guest speakers to calls and meetings, training new recruits, brainstorming new ideas for prospecting, and creating contests, shadowing reps on sales calls, and much more.
- They will also be required to resolve internal company or employee issues as well as external prospect and client issues.

Some people are not meant to be leaders or coaches, and that's perfectly fine. The good news is that there are many different elements to a winning sales team, and there is always room for more top performers. Every person has an important role to fulfill, and as the leader, you can ensure that there are no square pegs put in round holes.

THE INTERVIEW PROCESS

You will spend more time with your team during the workweek than you will with your family; so don't take the hiring process lightly. A large selection pool will give you best odds of finding the best performers, so ask for as many quality referrals and recommendations from employees and partners as possible. The operative word here is *quality*. It's better to have five great salespeople than ten average producers.

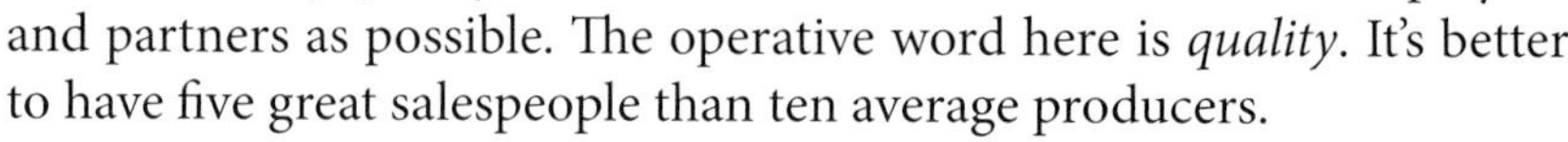

After you have gathered all quality leads and referrals, look for consistent top performance and the presence of any *job-hopping,* which is a possible sign of lack of loyalty and/or performance. After reviewing qualified resumes and determining the pool of candidates you'd like to interview, move to the preliminary phone interview.

The Phone Interview

Before meeting any candidate face-to-face, schedule an initial sixty-minute phone interview, even though you may not need all sixty minutes. This allows you to use your time wisely so you can efficiently weed out the low to average performers. You'll also be able to assess a candidate's phone skills. Are candidates energetic and well spoken? Do they have a good personality, directly answer your questions, take the time to ask thoughtful questions, and ask for an in-person interview? Examples of bad phone skills are interrupting, being unprepared, sounding unprofessional, speaking inappropriately, or being inarticulate. Ask the same questions to every candidate using a standardized interview sheet. Develop your own list of interview questions, and then make those questions available for your staff to use for phone and in-person interviewing.

In-Person Interviews

After the phone interview comes the in-person interview(s). Once you are face-to-face, probe and ask questions about past performance. Many hiring managers take résumés and answers at face value without digging deeper. Résumés and canned responses will not tell you the whole story; you have to search for the answers you need. Here are some great questions to ask about performance:[6]

QUESTIONS ABOUT PAST EXPERIENCE IN SALES

- How did you achieve the performance listed here on your résumé [ask about specific numbers if they are given]?
- How long is your typical sales cycle? At what point do you ask for the close?
- What was the average size of the deals you close? [Note if it is larger, smaller, or typical for your company/industry.]
- What was your monthly or quarterly quota? How often did you exceed it?
- Tell me about your largest sale. Who was involved, and how long did it take to close?

It's easy to throw some percentages on a resume; it's hard to back them up with proof. These questions are excellent ways to break through the fluff and the inflated numbers. If candidates flounder or find it difficult to back their results it's usually obvious in the interview, so it's best you are finding that out now.

QUESTIONS FOR CANDIDATES WHO ARE NEW TO SALES

- If I called your current manager or supervisor, what would he or she say about you?
- What things would your manager say are your strengths and what areas need work?
- What do you personally feel are your greatest strengths and what areas need work?
- What kind of goals motivate you the best?
- Tell me about an experience that demonstrates your work ethic.
- How do you expect to close sales? How will you know when a buyer is ready to buy?

The Next Steps

Tell candidates what the next steps of the interviewing process are going to be during the initial call. That way there are no surprises, and they don't have to sit by the phone wondering if or when they'll ever hear from you again. Exhibit 16.3 provides a summary of all steps of the interview and hiring process.

Take your time during the entire process. There is no set number of interviews that work in every situation. Meet with candidates again and ask different questions. Learning how to staff the right candidates takes time and practice. You have to ask the tough questions and consistently follow the same standardized hiring process to locate the ones who have got the "right stuff."

EXHIBIT 16.3 BASIC STEPS IN THE HIRING PROCESS

PHONE INTERVIEW	**Your chance to weed out low performers and those people who are not viable candidates for the position.**
IN-PERSON INTERVIEW	**The face-to-face meeting where you can determine candidates' ability to "sell" themselves.**

NARROW IT DOWN	**Select your top candidates. Each will have an interview with whomever makes the decision.**

FINAL INTERVIEWS	**Top candidates should also interview with two to three key executives, plus one to two sales reps.**

SELECT WINNING CANDIDATES	**Select your new team member(s), and advise them of their expected start date.**

THE SALES MANAGER AS A LEADER

Pushing yourself to greater heights of leadership is not just a good suggestion—it's crucial for your company's survival. It's not enough to just say, "Keep up the good work." Managers must create a motivational culture that challenges and inspires positive change in their salespeople.[7] The pressure is on everyone in this economy, so managers must be ready to step forward and lead a sales force toward success. One of the keys of leadership is motivating people. Sustained motivation comes from day-to-day motivation—and that has to come from sales managers who are leaders themselves.

THE SOCIAL MEDIA CONNECTION

Using Social Media to Recruit Top Talent

According to a recent survey, 73 percent of recruiters have hired a candidate they initially found through social media. LinkedIn is the favorite platform among recruiters, with 79 percent of talent departments using the site as a resource, while one third of recruiters have hired through Facebook and about 15 percent through Twitter.[8] Here are two companies that have nailed social media for recruiting—and what you can do to imitate their success:

UPS. Delivery giant UPS uses Twitter and Facebook to highlight the company's ***unique value proposition (UVP)***—a clear statement that describes the benefit of your offer, how you solve your customer's needs and what distinguishes you from the competition—for potential employees. For example, the UPS Facebook page highlights volunteer efforts and a diverse employee base. The company's pages also keep users and potential employees engaged by asking frequent questions and answering queries in real time.

To hone in on your ***UVP***, figure out how to apply your value proposition to a diverse group of candidates. Is it that you're a community of like-minded people, or that you invest in your employees' individual growth? Whatever your unique employer value, be sure to remind candidates of it on social media.

Marriott. The popular hotel chain is doing a lot of things right with its careers page on Facebook, which has 1.2 million likes. People come to the site to scan current openings and apply for positions, but they leave with a sense of what it would be like to work for the company. Candidates' questions are answered in real time by actual Marriott employees. The employees answering the questions use their first names to humanize the process.

In your social recruiting efforts, encourage your employees to become part of the conversation in their own individual way. When individual employees answer questions, they're often more creative, genuine, and present a fresh face to which candidates can relate.

Sales may be the lifeblood of a company, but some smaller companies don't have a formal sales manager position—and others delegate that responsibility to an already overworked producer, one who may be great at acquiring business but lacks the skill and will to lead others. "Our agency was profitable, but growth was not meeting my expectations," says Ralph Hartwell, founder of the *Hartwell Corporation* (THC) in Idaho. THC shuffled the sales manager job among various executives, so no one was consistently responsible for setting sales goals, monitoring progress, or achieving results.[9] Hartwell finally recognized the importance of having a solid leader in order to break through to the next level of success. Bob Nelson, author of *1001 Ways to Energize Your Employees*, says, "For today's employees, you can't light a fire under them. You have to light a fire in them."[10] Exhibit 16.4 gives sales managers powerful tips on how to motivate employees and then keep them motivated.[11]

EXHIBIT 16.4 TIPS ON MOTIVATION

Motivation is Caring not Scaring. Fear should never be used as a motivation strategy. It may get managers what they want now, but it will set them up for what they don't want in the future in the form of employee anger, resentment, and lack of enthusiasm and commitment.

Motivation Blossoms in the Right Atmosphere. When employees feel nurtured, appreciated, acknowledged, and respected, they'll give 100 percent of their time, effort, and commitment in return. The job of the manager is to create a work environment that provides employees with the opportunity to attain their goals and experience what they value most in their professional lives.

Walk the Talk. Modeling the behavior leaders want from their salespeople is the most effective way to change any behavior. If they want motivated employees, they need to become a role model for motivation.

The Law of Attraction. The law of attraction states that whatever we focus on we bring to ourselves. If sales managers focus on the lack of motivation in employees, they will find more and more examples of it. When they seek to learn more about motivation and create an atmosphere that fosters it, they will find more examples of motivation in the workplace.

Ongoing Commitment. Motivating employees is an ongoing process because people are continually growing and changing. As they achieve something they want or value, they then seek to achieve more of the same. If motivation is not kept on the managerial front burner, sales managers see the fires in their employees slowly fade and die out.

TQM and Sales Management

Despite the widespread use of Total Quality Management techniques in many of today's corporations, a high failure rate of TQM improvement programs exists—60 to 67 percent—according to research studies.[12] These failures occurred not because of basic flaws in the principles of TQM, but more so because of ineffective implementation systems. So, what can a sales manager do to ensure his techniques are successful? Here are five leadership skills that a sales manager can use to more effectively put TQM fundamentals into practice.[13]

1. Provide employees with a sense of mission.
2. Create a work environment where salespeople feel free to stretch their talents.
3. Give immediate feedback on what salespeople need to improve on so they don't have to guess.
4. Offer praise and reward in an appropriate way so that individual salespeople are recognized as well as the team as a whole.
5. Help and support employees in developing their talents and careers.

These skills are the basis for the sales manager's approach to the task of sales management. You must remember that *leadership* isn't an event; it is a process. Sales managers must be able to diagnose what their people need and remain flexible enough to provide for those needs.

Based on the leadership skills outlined above, Exhibit 16.5 recommends a new management style. To maximize a team's performance, sales managers must break away from the traditional management style and develop the winning style of management that will help their companies gain a competitive advantage. The idea is to lead, not to simply tell people exactly what to do. You develop people and ask how they think a task should be handled. The winning manager takes the sales force to the next level—after all, they can't accomplish that without the help and support of their salespeople.

EXHIBIT 16.5 TRADITIONAL MANAGERS VERSUS WINNING MANAGERS

TRADITIONAL MANAGERS

- Stick to their old ways and resist change.
- See themselves as cops or bosses.
- Make all the decisions on their own.
- Are reluctant to share information.
- Demand action, effort, and long hours.
- Neglect career-planning discussions and assume company will do that for them.

WINNING MANAGERS

- Thrive on, and relish, change.
- Think like a coach or team leader.
- Believe in group decision making.
- Are eager to share news and information.
- Expect progress and results to occur.
- Take initiative for planning own career and assist sales staff in planning theirs.

Adapted from: Dr. Wolf Rinke's book, *Winning Management: Six Fail-Safe Strategies for Building High-Performance Organizations*

Ask yourself: *Why do America's corporate giants invest many hours annually in supervisory and management development?* It's because they recognize that competent and consistent staff supervision is the principal ingredient of an effective and efficient organization; but in order to achieve this, supervisors and managers need to be skilled in communications, planning, scheduling, evaluating job performance, coaching, counseling, team building, handling employee problems and problem employees, resource allocation, and conflict management.[14]

"The key to management lies in always providing value to the people who work under you." This is the definition of strong leadership according to Edward Berube, president of *Conseco Insurance Group*.[15] Sales managers serve as champions to the people who report to them.

The qualifications that produce success for an individual salesperson are not necessarily the same as those needed for success as a sales manager. On one hand, a salesperson must possess a strong sense of self-discipline coupled with a fondness of independence. A sales manager, on the other hand, is continuously involved in interaction with a diverse clientele both inside and outside the organization. The freedom enjoyed by salespeople to arrange and manage their own time and activities is not as likely to be available to the sales manager who is held accountable for the overall effectiveness of a number of salespeople. Managing yourself and your own time is not the same as directing and managing other people's time and energies. Choosing the best salesperson for promotion to sales manager does not always work. A manager's job is to do whatever is necessary to achieve consistent production and growth, both personally and in all members of the sales force, and to build top-performing producers while maintaining a profitable business.

DETERMINING COMPENSATION

There aren't many other topics that a professional salesperson or a sales manager is more eager to talk to someone about than sales compensation. With all of the requirements and devices used, compensation plans can be quite complex. Compensation plans vary greatly depending on the company and the industry. In general there are three basic commission structures:

Straight Commission

A commission is usually figured as a percentage of sales volume. The plan might call for a simple percentage of total gross sales, or it could be based on a percentage of the sales less variable costs. The benefit of the latter plan is that it offers the salesperson concrete incentives for helping to keep selling costs low and therefore emphasizes profit instead of mere volume. The main benefit of a commission plan is the motivation it offers to salespeople for productivity. The disadvantage is that some salespeople are tempted to neglect activities that do not bring in short-term dollars, including service after the sale, helping with installation, and completing needed reports and related paperwork. The straight-commission plan is the plan of choice when aggressive selling is desired.

Straight Salary

At the other extreme is a plan based on a fixed amount regardless of volume. Once more common, today only about 4.5 percent of companies use straight salary as their sole means of compensation.[16] A straight-salary plan gives management the greatest ability to control the activities of salespeople. If the company has an unusual need for post-sale activities, developing new territories, or continuing technical training, salespeople do not feel that they are cutting their own income by giving time to that work. However, a salary plan offers less motivation for intense sales effort than the commission plan. Therefore, a salary plan is the plan of choice when management needs to control salespeople's activities and when aggressive sales activity is not necessary.

Combination Plans

One method to exercise control over sales activities yet retain the incentive value of a commission is a combination of a base salary and a commission or bonus paid on sales above a set level. Another type of combination plan makes use of a commission plus a draw against future commissions earned. This plan protects salespeople in slow seasons or when some outside circumstance lowers productivity temporarily. The company sets a base amount that the salesperson is guaranteed to receive. If commissions earned fall below that figure, a draw is paid to bring income up to the base level. If the salesperson earns commissions above the base next month, the excess is used to repay the draw. Exhibit 16.6 shows how the draw operates.

HIGH PRICE TO PAY FOR INADEQUATE PLANS. Although under compensating salespeople may seem like an attractive cost-cutting strategy for companies in the short run, over time businesses pay the price for underpaying employees in the form of turnover and a general lack of loyalty. In a *CSO Insights* survey on sales compensation performance, 63 percent of companies said that the compensation plan generally drives the selling behavior of sales representatives, and 11 percent said it consistently drives selling behavior.[17] It is obvious that compensation plans greatly impact the performance of salespeople, so companies must work to ensure that the impact is positive. Executives at *FedEx* realized they needed a new compensation plan for their sales organization because of the volume of complaints coming from field salespeople and sales managers about how confusing and unpredictable the pay program was. In a little more than a year with a new clearly laid-out incentive pay program, there was a dramatic shift in the sales force at FedEx and consequently, much happier salespeople.[18]

EXHIBIT 16.6 SAMPLE COMBINATION COMPENSATION PLAN

Month	Commissions Earned	Commissions Paid	Draw* Paid (Repaid)	Total Income
January	$1500	$1500	$0	$1500
February	$900	$900	$300	$1200
March	$1400	$1400	($200)	$1200
April	$1500	$1500	($100)	$1400
May	$1700	$1700	$0	$1700
June	$1200	$1200	$0	$1200
Total	**$8200**	**$8200**	**$0**	**$8200**

**Assumes company guarantees a base amount of $1200 per month. Some companies do not require an actual payback as shown in the example. They use the draw as a yardstick for performance.*

OTHER KEY ROLES OF A MANAGER

Sales mangers certainly have to wear many hats. Not only are they responsible for picking the right people, hiring the correct number of salespeople, determining how best to pay them, and leading them through a proven sales process, but they are also responsible for the following:

Sales Training

Every authority agrees that ongoing sales training is necessary, but measuring the benefits of sales training is a difficult process. In addition, what sales training should accomplish is also not clear, although almost everyone agrees that training is needed in product knowledge and in selling skills. Companies are interested in sales training because they want to increase sales productivity. The emphasis is largely on results. The chairman and chief executive officer of U.S. Steel expressed it this way:[19]

> *We support training and development activities to get results.... We're interested in the specific things that provide greater rewards to the employee, increased return to the stockholder, and enable reinvestment of sales revenue to meet the growing needs of the business. In other words, [we're interested in] those things, which affect the "bottom line."*

Sales managers agree that company training programs should address the purpose of developing in salespeople the characteristics of success. These characteristics usually include the following traits:

- Listening skills
- Enthusiasm
- Empathy
- Planning skills
- Personal organization
- Problem-solving ability
- Time and territory management

Designing and implementing the sales training program is the sales manager's responsibility. An effective program includes these basic elements:

1 **FIELD TRAINING AND OBSERVATION.** It is a good idea to have both an experienced salesperson and a manager assist in training new sales reps. Traveling with a senior sales rep to observe selling skills, personality traits, and work habits reveals much about

novice sales reps. New reps can also accompany different sales managers to pick out the strengths and weaknesses of each manager and eventually create their own style. Both managers and senior sales reps can impart more wisdom to a newcomer than many training courses might offer.

2 **GROUP SESSIONS.** Sales training sessions that focus on a single topic (such as prospecting, closing, or product knowledge) are valuable in sharpening skills for all members of the sales team. The group training session provides valuable interaction between salespeople and allows individuals to learn from one another. The *Cisco WebEx Training Center* is a great solution for online training of large groups spread over a wide geographic location.

A common form of training within group sessions is *role-playing*: One trainee assumes the role of salesperson and another trainee or the sales manager plays the role of a prospect. A third person may act as observer to critique the performance. They go through the various steps of the sales process to gain experience in using the sales aids, giving the presentation, asking questions, and handling objections. A session may cover the entire selling process or concentrate on one specific step in the process. The audio or video of role-playing sessions can be recorded for later review.

3 **ONE-ON-ONE SESSIONS.** The sales manager must be willing to spend time with individual salespeople to give specific feedback and encourage continuing development. One-on-one time can be used to pinpoint individual problems and help the salesperson to develop a program of personal growth to correct any problems discovered.

4 **INTERACTIVE TRAINING.** Interactive training is a type of learning model where trainees are given audio or video presentations, slide shows, self-tests, and the capability to determine what they want to learn, when they want to learn it. Salespeople using an interactive format will have higher rates of retention, take less time to train, have easier access to information, and have a higher comfort level. Sales managers now have the opportunity to work with one, or one hundred, salespeople in front of a computer to watch and learn new techniques or practice what they do best.[20]

5 **FEEDBACK**. The sales training program must provide for feedback on performance. When a skill is practiced in a training session, a method for tracking field improvement shows whether the training has been effective. When salespeople see that the training has made a direct impact on their performance and their incomes, they are eager to receive more training and give their best efforts to learning.

The amount of time spent in sales training for recruits and for experienced salespeople varies from industry to industry and also from company to company. Time for training is affected by the complexity of the industry, the commitment of the company to training, and the company's experience with past training programs. The exact procedure also varies as a result of the same factors. Some companies conduct concentrated training for new recruits before they are allowed to go into the field. Others use a mix of training and field experience to help recruits learn by doing. A few still hand the recruit a sales kit and follow the *sink-or-swim* method. The training period for recruits tends to be shorter for manufacturers of consumer products than for manufacturers of industrial products.

Supervision and Motivation

A sales manager must see that salespeople call on their accounts with sufficient frequency, prospect for new business, keep up to date on new developments in the general market, and receive continuous training in new product technology or advanced sales techniques. Guiding salespeople in setting realistic goals, offering appropriate incentives to trigger achievement of those goals, and rewarding them for success are the sales manager's responsibility. All of these areas are easy to track with the CRM software available today, as well as the ease of communication provided by smartphones and Wi-Fi access.

> "The key to successful leadership today is influence, not authority."
> **Ken Blanchard**

Motivation is at the heart of supervision. The sales manager's involvement in motivation is designed to provide an environment within which salespeople can develop the ability to motivate themselves. A sales manager is much like a professional sports coach. John Madden, legendary NFL coach, explained to a reporter his philosophy about motivating football players like this: "*I don't motivate them. I find motivated men and teach them how to play football.*"

The principle is clear: If the basic functions of recruiting and selection are successfully performed, training and motivation of the sales force become less of a problem and more of a solution to making more sales—and in turn, profit.

SUMMARY

- The functions of the sales manager differ considerably from those of salespeople although organizations often promote leading salespeople to positions in sales management.
- Sales managers are responsible for hiring right the first time to ensure that the costs of hiring the wrong salespeople are minimized.
- The sales manager must be both a skillful salesperson and an efficient manager. The sales manager stands between field salespeople and company management.
- The sales manager performs the usual managerial functions of translating the goals of the company into strategies and tactics that the members of the sales department can address through daily activities and seeing that those activities result in the achievement of the department's responsibilities to the company.
- In addition, the sales manager is concerned with helping salespeople develop personally and professionally so that they can make the greatest possible contribution to achievement of the organization's goals.
- Specific tasks of the sales manager include:
  1. Organizing the sales force
  2. Determining personnel needs
  3. Recruiting and selecting salespeople
  4. Designing a compensation plan that motivates salespeople and assures that sales activities will achieve desired goals
  5. Training salespeople to sell the company's product or service effectively
  6. Supervising and motivating salespeople.

REVIEW QUESTIONS

1. Are top salespeople automatically likely to be good sales managers? Why or why not?
2. What are the key functions of a sales manager?
3. What are the most common components of sales training?
4. What does the sales manager need to learn through interviewing a prospective salesperson?
5. What do you consider the most important incentives for salesperson productivity that a sales manager could provide?
6. If a company wants to exercise a great deal of control over the time and activities of its salespeople and does not especially need aggressive selling, what kind of compensation package is most appropriate?
7. If the organization's goal is high-volume sales and management is willing to have salespeople structure their own time and activities, what type of compensation plan is most likely to result in achievement of that goal?
8. What are some of the most easily accessible sources of recruits for positions as salespeople?

IN-CLASS EXERCISES

The following exercises help build teams, improve communication, and emphasize the real-world side of selling. They are meant to be challenging, to help you learn how to deal with problems that have no single right answer, and to use a variety of skills beyond those employed in a typical review question. Read and complete each activity. Then in the next class, discuss and compare answers.

EXERCISE 16.1 – ANALYZING JOB DESCRIPTIONS

You should work independently on this exercise. Job descriptions for sales positions are routinely posted on the websites of individual companies and recruiting companies, and on websites like Monster.com on LinkedIn. These descriptions are typically written by management and might include very specific requirements expressed in the jargon typical of the type of product or service that is to be sold.

Select a field or industry category in which you are interested. Search for sales positions in that field or category, analyze at least 3 job descriptions, and record what you find.

How much prior sales or marketing experience is required? Is the experience specific to the field or industry category?

What is the educational level required or preferred? Must relevant education be focused on a specific field?

What sort of general characteristics (e.g., excellent communications skills, team-building skills, ease of relating to diverse populations) are required?

What sort of specialized knowledge (e.g., experience with specific software applications, project management certification, technical or scientific knowledge) is required?

Since these job descriptions pertain to a field or area in which you are personally interested, which requirements as stated in the descriptions surprised you most? How do you plan to fulfill these and the other requirements listed for the positions that you researched?

EXERCISE 16.2 – THE PERFECT SALES MANAGER

For this exercise, the class should be divided into teams of 4 people each. On the basis of all the knowledge and experience you have gained in this course, you are about to find yourself working among colleagues in your first sales position. You will probably be a member of a small sales team that reports to a sales manager. As you get to know your colleagues, discussion turns to what makes a really good sales manager. On a periodic visit to your office, the regional director of sales announces to your group that a new sales manager is about to be appointed, and the regional director wants your collective opinion about the qualifications and characteristics that you think should be primary. Now is your big chance: What makes a perfect sales manager?

As a team, discuss the role of a sales manager and decide which characteristics, qualifications, and personality traits you would most like to see in your new manager. Bear in mind the needs of the company, not just the desires of those who must report to the manager. Rank your recommendations in order of importance for the regional director and provide reasons for your selections.

CASE STUDIES

The following case studies present you with selling scenarios that require you to apply the critical skills discussed in the chapter and give you training through practical learning situations. They are meant to be both engaging and challenging, and like the exercises, don't have one right answer.

CASE 16.1 – MUSICAL CHAIRS

As Vice President for Sales for a major auto supply chain, Leonard Wirt was under a great deal of pressure. After six months on the job, he was due to report to the owners of this privately held company what he thought should be done to improve sales and profitability. Since his recommendations were radical, he knew that this would probably be the toughest sales call of his career.

For the past 55 years, the company had been managed in a very traditional fashion, chiefly by fear. Salespeople, working on strict commission, who failed to meet annual quotas were routinely fired and replaced. Store managers who failed to meet profitability targets were transferred or fired. Because the business required extensive product knowledge about a wide variety of products, district and regional sales managers were traditionally recruited from the top sales performers. But when their districts or regions fell short, heads rolled. Despite all of these changes in personnel, profits continued to sag, and the owners continued to be unhappy.

Based upon his experience and knowledge of more successful approaches to management, Leonard was prepared to recommend sweeping changes. What changes do you think Leonard should recommend? Which changes should be made first, and why? Which changes would have the most immediate, positive impact on the company's profitability? Which changes recommended by Leonard do you think would be most risky? What sort of quantitative measures, other than overall profitability, should Leonard monitor in order to gauge the success or failure of his initiatives?

CASE 16.2 – THE NEW SALES TRAINER

Sam has been one of the top salespeople in his medium-size insurance company for about 6 years. He holds a college degree and had previous experience as a high school teacher before getting into insurance sales. Because of his sales achievements and his background in teaching, his vice president has asked him to take over as the new sales trainer for the company. As the vice president put it, "We're not getting enough production out of our sales force, and adherence to company policy has been lax. We need someone who can teach us how to whip our training program into shape." Not especially elegant, Sam thought, but clear.

The typical training program, not including studying for and passing licensing exams, for salespeople at Sam's company is 3 weeks—3 short weeks. To revamp the training program, Sam must develop a curriculum and structure the way in which that curriculum should be presented.

Based on what you have learned in Chapter 16 and the rest of this course, how should Sam address the following issues?

Which topics should be included in the training curriculum, and why?

Which topics should be given higher priority and, hence, more time, and why?

How can Sam hold the attention of new recruits for 3 weeks? What sort of presentation techniques should he employ for more effective retention and learning?

How can Sam monitor individual progress so that he can address individual trainees' problems before they get out of hand?

Chapter 16 Footnotes

1. Sara Calabro, "Meaningful Rewards," *Sales and Marketing Management*. New York: (Mar 2005), Vol. 157, Is. 3, 26.

2. Shamis, Barry. "*Have You Ever Thought About The Cost Of Hiring The Wrong Salesperson?*" *SalesRepHire.com, Accessed October 20, 2015. Web.*

3. Giang, Vivian. "A New Report Ranks America's Biggest Companies Based On How Quickly Employees Jump Ship." *Business Insider*, July 25, 2013.

4. Stromsoe, Mike. *The Unstoppable Profit Producer Program*. Agent Profit Mastery, 2015. Print.

5. Riddleburger, Barrett. "5 Compelling Reasons NOT to Promote Your Best Sales Rep to Manager, Inc.com." August 26, 2014.

6. Snider, Emma. "25 Sales Interview Questions to Recruit the Best Reps."HubSpot Blogs, July 9, 2015. Web.

7. Kathleen Cholewka, "Seven Signs You're Failing as a Manager and How to Avoid Them," *Sales & Marketing Management* (March 2012), 42.

8. Wood, Katherine. "5 Companies that have Nailed Social Media for Recruiting." *Social Studies*. December 2, 2014. Web.

9. Boone, Elisabeth, "Sales Management: Choices and Challenges," *Rough Notes*. Dec 2006, Accessed July 3, 2015.

10. Audrey Bottjen and Eduardo Canto, "Pep Talks That Inspire Reps," *Sales & Marketing Management* (June 2011), 66.

11. Widener, Chris. "Six Tips to Stay Motivated." *Sales Gravy*, Accessed October 21, 2015. Web.

12. Quint Studer, "How to achieve and sustain excellence: there are seven ways to hardwire excellent outcomes. Do you know what they are?" *Healthcare Financial Management.* June 2007.

13. Melissa Campbell, "'What Price Sales Force Satisfaction?,' *Sales & Marketing Management* (July 2004), 37.

14. John E. Baer, "The cost of inadequate leadership: ineffective management carries a hefty price tag for the typical 120-bed nursing home." Entrepreneur.com. Posted Sept 2006, accessed May 3, 2015.

15. Julie Strugeon, "Wanted: Successful Sales Manager," *Selling Power* (September 2000), 114.

16. Anonymous, "2010 Sales Compensation & Performance Management: Summary of Metrics," accessed May 3, 2015. Web.

17. Anonymous, "2010 Sales Compensation & Performance Management: Summary of Metrics," accessed May 3, 2015.

18. Andy Cohen, Jennifer Gilbert, Melinda Ligos."Extreme Makeovers." *Sales and Marketing Management*. New York: (May 2004), Vol.156, Is. 9, 36.

19. Edgar Speer, "The Role of Training at United States Steel," *Training and Development Journal*, Vol. 30, No. 6 (June 1996), 18-21.

20. See Cisco WebEx Training Center for an example of interactive training.

A

B

C

M

N

O

P

Q

R

S

T

U

V

W

Y

Z